1 MONTH OF
FREE
READING

at

www.ForgottenBooks.com

By purchasing this book you are eligible for one month membership to ForgottenBooks.com, giving you unlimited access to our entire collection of over 1,000,000 titles via our web site and mobile apps.

To claim your free month visit:
www.forgottenbooks.com/free902087

ISBN 978-0-266-86938-2
PIBN 10902087

CHESTER COUNTY

AND

ITS PEOPLE

Of all the things which man can do or make here below, by far the most momentous,
wonderful and worthy are the things we call books—THOMAS CARLYLE

EDITED BY

W. W. THOMSON

ILLUSTRATED

CHICAGO AND NEW YORK:
THE UNION HISTORY COMPANY
1898

PREFACE.

THE Publishers herewith present to their friends in Chester County this fine volume of local history. Upon examination it will be found full of interesting matter concerning the county, and will be accepted as a standard contribution to the history of the State. The Publishers have drawn freely from every available source, giving due credit therefor, and gratefully acknowledge their indebtedness to the press throughout the county and to the owners of private libraries and rare and valuable documents. In a work of this character, more or less hurriedly prepared, it has been found impracticable to avoid mistakes; but the Publishers, as is their custom, stand ready to correct, after notification, all errors by special errata sheet to be sent to every subscriber to be pasted in the book. We cordially thank our friends and patrons for their encouragement and support.

THE PUBLISHERS.

ILLUSTRATIONS.

TABLE OF CONTENTS.

CHAPTER I.

TABLE OF CONTENTS.

CHAPTER IV.

CHAPTER VI.

CHAPTER VII.

CHAPTER VIII.

CHAPTER IX.

CHAPTER X.

CHAPTER XI.

CHAPTER XII.

CHAPTER XIII.

CHAPTER XIV.

CHAPTER XV.

CHAPTER XVI.

CHAPTER XVII.

CHAPTER XVIII.

CHAPTER XIX.

CHAPTER XX.

THE BRANDYWINE.

By Hon. James B. Everhart.

How beautifully glides the Brandywine!
On and forever from dawn to decline—
Under the bridges and arches of trees.
Gilding the landscape and cooling the breeze,
Parting the pastures and swelling their stores,
Flowering, perfuming the sinuous shores,
Glossing the squirrel disporting above,
Sweetening the tanager's carol of love.

How beautifully flows the Brandywine!
Laving the limbs of the indolent kine.
Kissing the sedges and smoothing the stones,
Charming the air with its murmuring tones,
Bord'ring the cottage ensconced in the vale,
Whitening the wheat for the garner and flail,
Shaking the mill with its slumberous sounds,
And feeding the forge as it smokes and pounds.

How beautifully streams the Brandywine!
Slowly or swift with its silvery shine,
Under the cliffs* where traditional fame
Pictures the plunge of the desperate dame,
Rounding the hollow† where sunbeams illume
With changeable gleams the arboreous gloom,
Nearing the lodge of the Indian Maid,‡
Lingering alone where her fathers strayed.

How solemnly surges the Brandywine!
Armies of nations contesting its line,
Foreigners fording its turbulent flood,
Signal guns distantly pealing their thud—
Column on column, heroic with zeal,
Waving their pennants and flashing their steel,
Trampling the rushes and climbing the bank,
Startling their foemen, assailing their flank.

How solemnly surges the Bradywine!
Marking with crimson its course serpentine—
Forces reserved closing in from afar,
Scaling with fury the ridges of war,
Cannon exploding with terrible roar.
Dark'ning the heavens and rocking the shore,
Squadrons of troopers o'ersweeping the plain,
Regiments recoiling, retreating or slain.

How solemnly surges the Brandywine!
Teeming with many a sorrowful sign—
Heroes and horses, distorted and torn,
Bloated and dead, on its surface upborne.
Wounded ones writhing and wailing for aid,
Fragments and missiles o'er hillock and glade,
Havoc and horror, disaster and night
Palling the scenery and quenching the fight.

How exultingly leaps the Brandywine!
Welcoming Peace with her features divine,
Bearing the olive, and pouring her horn
Over the region so smitten and shorn,
Causing the barrens to bloom as the rose,
Soothing the passions of rage to repose,
Blessing the labors of genius and art,
Rearing the altar and crowding the mart.

How complacently pours the Brandywine!
Voicing its sounds in songs crystalline—
Orders abolished and merit secure,
Fortune unfolding her gates to the poor,
Science displaying the secrets of time,
Yoking the forces of nature sublime,
Progress and weal with the country allied,
And Glory adorning her banner of pride.

How beautifully rolls the Brandywine!
Hast'ning to mingle itself in the brine,
Water fowls dipping their wings in its crest,
Swimmers fomenting its waves into yest,
Holiday barks sailing gaily along,
Freighted with frolic and graces and song,
Fishermen watching the tremulous line,
And dreamers in quest of the Muses' shrine,
In the haunted dells of the Brandywine.

*Deborah's Rock is so called, says the story, from a disappointed girl of that name, who destroyed herself by leaping from it.

†Dungeon Hollow is the name of á picturesque turn of the stream near Painter's Bridge.

‡Indian Hannah was the last of the Lenape tribe. She lived in a hut near the Brandywine long after her people had disappeared.

CHAPTER I.

PHYSICAL FEATURES.

CHESTER COUNTY AND ITS PEOPLE.

CHAPTER I.

LOCATION AND AREA—TIMBER AND DRAINAGE—THE ROYAL CHARTERS—
EXPLORATIONS AND DISCOVERIES—THE FIRST SETTLERS—COLONI-
ZATION COMPANIES—LAND CONTROVERSIES—COUNTIES OR-
GANIZED—ORIGINAL EXTENT OF THE COUNTY—
COUNTY SEAT—THE SWEDES, WELSH AND
QUAKERS—THE BOUNDARY
CONTROVERSY.

CHESTER COUNTY, Pennsylvania, is situated in the south-eastern part of the State. It is in the form of an irregular oblong, with its greatest length, from northeast to southwest, and with no boundary corresponding to the cardinal directions, except the southern, which runs nearly east and west, separating it from Maryland and being the famous Mason and Dixon's line. A portion of the southeast boundary is the section of a circle, separating the county from the State of Delaware, and the other portion of the southeast boundary is Delaware County, Pennsylvania, which was once a part of Chester County. Montgomery County bounds it on the northeast, the two counties being separated from each other by the Schuylkill River. On the northwest it is bounded by Berks County and Lancaster County, the latter extending from Berks County down to the State of Maryland.

The county lies between 39 degrees 42 minutes and 40 degrees 30 minutes north latitude, and between 75 degrees 15 minutes and 76 degrees 15 minutes west longitude from Greenwich, Eng-

land, and between 55 minutes and 1 degree 40 minutes east longitude from the Capitol building at Washington, District of Columbia. In Maryland the counties which border it are Newcastle,
Delaware and Cecil. The line of the Pennsylvania Railroad passing through the county from east to west is thirty miles long.
The extreme length of the county from north to south is thirty-
six miles; its northern boundary is fifteen miles long; its northeastern twenty-one miles long; its southeastern, eighteen miles;
its southern, thirty miles, and its western-border line twenty-
eight miles, so that its entire periphery is 112 miles in length.
The area of the county is equal to 763 square miles, or 488,320
acres. It has a gently rolling surface, there being within its limits
no considerable elevations, the highest point on any railroad passing through it being 750 feet above the level of the sea, and its
greatest depression 200 feet above the same level.

Originally this county was covered with timber, the principal
varieties being the oak, hickory, walnut, sycamore and poplar.
The condition of the forests when first visited by white men can
hardly be conceived. The woods were quite free from underbrush
and the ground was covered with a short, thick, nutritious grass.
The trees were some distance apart, the lower limbs were high
above the ground, and it was a comparatively easy matter to ride
on horseback anywhere through the woods. The forests were
simply magnificent, and many men would no doubt ride to-day
a hundred miles on horseback to see such a sight. This condition
of things would probably have lasted many years had not the
Englishman come in to occupy the land; for the Swedes, who took
the country as they found it, occupied the meadow and open lands
along the rivers, never attempting to clear the woods of trees.
Sidney George Fisher says:

"In nothing is the difference in nationality so distinctly shown.
The Dutchman builds trading posts and lies in his ship to collect
the furs. The gentle Swede settles on the soft, rich meadow
lands; his cattle wax fat and his barns are full of hay. The

French enter the forests, sympathize with their inhabitants, and turn half savage to please them. All alike bow before the wilderness and accept it as a fixed fact. But the Englishman destroys it. There is even something significant in the way his old charters gave him the land straight across America from sea to sea. He grasped at the continent from the beginning, and but for him the oak and the pine would have triumphed and the prairies still been in possession of the Indian and the buffalo."

The various kinds of trees that grew here in the early day, when the forest was in its primeval state, are mentioned by William Penn, in a letter dated January 9, 1683, to the Duke of Ormond, then Viceroy of Ireland. Penn said:

"The land is generally good, well watered and not so thick of wood as I imagined. There are also many open places that have been old Indian fields. The trees that grow here are the mulberry (white and red), walnut (black and gray), hickory, poplar, cedar, cypress, chestnut, ash, sassafras, gum, pine, spruce, oak (black, white, red, Spanish, chestnut and swamp), which latter has a leaf like a willow and is most lasting."

That some of these trees grew to great size is shown by the fact that previous to December 31, 1897, on which day it was blown down in a storm, there was an ash tree growing on the farm of John B. Ralston in West Vincent Township which was one of the largest in its section of the county. It was twelve feet in circumference at the base, was clear of limbs for fifty-nine feet, and just below the first fork was seven feet in circumference. To the next limb above this it was thirty-five feet, making a straight shaft of ninety-three feet with but one limb. In 1895 this tree was photographed by Charles S. Bradford, of West Chester, for the Pennsylvania Forestry Association, and was then thought to be the finest tree in the county.

Early events in the settlement of the Atlantic coast are here briefly related for the purpose of comparison of dates, in order that the reader may properly place the first settlement of what later became Chester County among other movements of the kind. The first settlement in Virginia was made at Jamestown in 1607, and in 1609 the famous navigator, Henry Hudson, an Englishman in the service of the Dutch East India Company, discovered the great river which has, for most of the time since then, borne his name, and which at other times has been, or rather was called, the North River, the present Delaware River being called, to distinguish it, the "South River." The bay into which the Delaware River flows was discovered by Henry Hudson on August 28, 1609, when he was in latitude 39 degrees 5 minutes north. This bay was in 1610 visited by Lord De la Ware, and named Delaware Bay in honor of that nobleman.

Inasmuch as Henry Hudson was in the service of the Dutch, that nation laid claim to the territory on either side of the Hudson River and to that on either side of both Delaware Bay and Delaware River, thus claiming an extensive territory along the Atlantic coast for a considerable distance north and south. The Delaware River, one of the noblest of those flowing directly into the Atlantic Ocean, was known in the early history of the country by various names, particularly among the Indians, who called it "Pautaxat," "Mariskitton," "Makerish-kisken," and "Lenape-Whittuck." By the Dutch it was named the "Zuyt," or South River, Nassau River, Prince Hendrick River and Charles River. By the Swedes it was known as New Swedeland stream; by Heylin, in his "Cosmography," it was called "Arastapha," and finally by the English it was named the Delaware River; and as the English finally triumphed over their enemies or rivals in the settlement of the Atlantic coast, the name given by them to this fine stream has been retained.

Delaware Bay had at least two names applied to it before its present name became the permanent one, these two names being Newport Mey and Godyn's Bay.

The States General of Holland, on March 27, 1614, granted a

general charter securing "the exclusive privileges of trade during four voyages to the discoverers of any new courses, havens, countries or places, under which charter the merchants of Amsterdam fitted out five vessels, one of which was named the "Fortune." It belonged to the city of Hoorn, was commanded by Captain Cornelis Jacobson Mey, and arrived at the mouth of Delaware Bay. Its capes were named after himself, Cornelis and Mey. Another vessel commanded by Captain Adrian Block was burned at the mouth of "Manhattan River," and immediately afterward Captain Block built a small vessel, sometimes called a yacht, which was $44\frac{1}{2}$ feet long and $11\frac{1}{2}$ feet wide, which he named the "Unrest," or Restless, this being the first vessel built by Europeans in North America. In this small vessel Captain Cornelis Hendrickson made further explorations and expeditions up the Delaware River, and even went as far up it, it has been said, as the mouth of the Schuylkill. But whether this statement is correct or not, the extent and value of the discoveries made by Captain Hendrickson may be judged to some degree by the report he made to the States General, which report will be found of special interest, as it throws a great deal of light upon the condition of the country in this immediate vicinity at the time of his visit. This report is as follows:

"Report of Captain Cornelis Hendrickson of Mennickendam to the High and Mighty Lords States General of the free United Netherland Provinces, made the XVIIIth August, Ad. 1616, of the country, bay and three rivers, situated in latitude from 38 to 40 degrees, by him discovered and found for and to the behoof of his owners and directors of New Netherlands, by name, Gerrit Jacob Witzen, burgomaster at Aurit, Jonas Witzen, Lambreht Van Tweenhuysen, Palas Pelgrom and others of their company.

"First, he hath discovered for his aforesaid Masters and Directors, certain lands, a bay and three rivers, situated between 38 and 40 degrees.

"And did there trade with the inhabitants: that trade consisting of sables, furs, robes and other skins.

"He hath found the said country full of trees, to wit.: oaks, hickory and pines, which trees were in some places covered with vines.

"He hath seen in said country bucks and does, turkeys and partridges.

"He hath found the climate of said country very temperate, judging it to be as temperate as this country (Holland).

"He also traded for and bought from the Inhabitants, the Minguas, three persons, being people belonging to this company, which three persons were employed in the service of the Mohawks and Machicans, giving for them kettles, beads and merchandise.

"Read, August 19, 1616."

Dr. Smith, in his History of Delaware County, observes that it cannot be inferred from this report that Captain Hendrickson had discovered the Schuylkill, but he does not attempt to determine what three rivers were discovered by the Captain. He adds that if any knowledge of the Schuylkill River, or even of the Delaware River, was obtained it was probably from the three Indians purchased, or from the Indian tribes in general, which supposition appears to be strengthened by the fact that the States General refused to grant, or at least did not grant, the trading privileges to these applicants; and the trade to New Netherland, which was regarded by the Dutch as extending beyond the Delaware, was thrown open in a measure to individual competition.

There are writers, however, who do not agree with Dr. Smith on this point. Sydney George Fisher, in his "Making of Pennsylvania," says: "The first person who conquered the shoals and really explored the river was a Dutchman, Captain Hendrickson. In the year 1616 he penetrated as far as the Schuylkill, just below the present site of Philadelphia. He had a small yacht, the 'Unrest,' or 'Restless,' only forty-five feet long, which had been built at

New York after the loss of his larger ship. In using this boat
he may have been influenced by Juet's* warning that it would
require a vessel of light draft to explore thoroughly that great
bay."

Up to this time it would appear that discoveries for the purposes of colonization had not been thought of by the Dutch, and
that their attention was engrossed wholly by the extension of
trade. But now a proposition was made which, in its execution,
changed the current of history. This proposition was made by
the Directors of the New Netherland Trading Company, for the
emigration to America of a certain English preacher versed in the
language of the Dutch, then residing at Leyden, together with
more than four hundred families from both Holland and England,
whom he had assured the petitioners he could induce to accompany
him. These petitioners also asked that two ships of war might
be dispatched "for the preservation of the country's rights, and
that the aforesaid minister and the four hundred families might
be taken under the protection of the government; alleging that
His Majesty of Great Britain would be disposed to people the aforesaid lands with the English nation."

This petition did not meet with a favorable reception. But
the preacher referred to, the Rev. Mr. Robinson, and a portion of the
four hundred families, did embark for America—started from Delft
in the Mayflower and Speedwell, July 16, 1620, and as is well
known, though they were destined for the Hudson River, yet they
landed at Plymouth, Mass., and became the pioneers of the
renowned Pilgrim Fathers.

The Dutch West India Company, though incorporated in 1621,
did not go into operation until 1623. Then, having taken posses-

---

* This was Robert Juet, Henry Hudson's mate, who was with him in his
explorations of the Hudson and Delaware Rivers, and also Hudson's Bay, and
was also one of the mutineers, who put Hudson and his son on a boat, leaving
them to their fate.

sion of the Hudson and Delaware Rivers, they sent out a vessel under the command of Captain Cornelis Jacobson Mey and Captain Adriaen Joris Trenpont, the former of whom, passing up the Delaware River, erected Fort Nassau, near, as has since been ascertaind, the mouth of Little Timber Creek, the date of its erection having been 1624. The seat of government of New Netherlands was fixed upon Manhattan Island, and Peter Minuit made governor, or director, as he was more properly called. This settlement on the Delaware, however, was of short duration, being vacated in 1625, for the purpose of strengthening the colony on Manhattan Island. But later, in order to maintain their possessions on the Delaware, the Dutch sent out two of the directors of the West India Company, Samuel Godyn and Samuel Blomaert, to purchase a large tract of land at the mouth of the bay, which purchase was confirmed July 16, 1630. A small colony on Lewes Creek was cut off by Indians, and a colony of English from Connecticut attempted in 1635 to settle on the Delaware, but were taken prisoners by the Dutch and sent to Manhattan.

A Swedish West India Company was organized as early as 1630, for the purpose of colonization and commerce; but owing to the death, in 1632, of Gustavus Adolphus, nothing was accomplished until 1637, when a settlement was made, or rather projected, on the Delaware River. Two ships, named the "Kalmar Nyckel" and the "Gripen," or, in other words, the "Key to Kalmar" and the "Griffin," were placed under the command of Peter Minuit, who will be remembered as a former director, or governor, of Manhattan Island, in the service of the Dutch, and with these two vessels he sailed from Gottenburg late in the year 1637. Some time during the following March Minuit purchased land on the west side of the Delaware River from the Indians, these lands lying on what these Indians called the Minquas River, to which river Minuit gave the name Christina, in honor of the Queen of Sweden, and upon these lands he erected a fort, which he named Fort Christina, about two and a half miles above the mouth of the river of the same name. While these proceedings of the Swedes were not pleas. ing to the Dutch, they did no more than to protest against them, and, according to Acrelius, the Swedes purchased lands of the Indians along the western bank of the Delaware, as far up as the present site of the city of Trenton.

Upon the Delaware Minuit left twenty-three men under the command of Mans Kling and Henrick Huychens, the former being the military and the latter the civil governor of the colony.

The "Kalmar Nyckel," in 1640, brought out reinforcements for the colony, and in 1641 the same vessel brought out a third expedition, being this time accompanied by the "Charitas." Many of the colonists coming at this time were Finns. By permission of the Swedish government a colony of Hollanders was established below Christina. In 1642 a further expedition sailed from the old country in two vessels, the "Stoork" and the "Renown," under command of John Printz, who, thinking that Fort Christina did not sufficiently command the river, erected a new fortress on the island of Tenneconk, or as it has been known for many years, Tinicum, this island at present being within the limits of Delaware County, but being a part of Chester County when this county was first established. It is separated from the mainland by Darby Creek.

This fortress on Tenneconk Island was named New Gotten- burg, and in addition to the fort, Governor Printz erected a fine mansion for himself and his family, which he named "Printz Hall," a very handsome and convenient home, which, after standing for about one hundred and sixty years, was accidentally destroyed by fire within the limits of the present century. Within eight months from the time of his arrival Governor Printz erected another fort, which he named Fort Elsinborg, upon which he mounted eight 12- pound brass cannon.

It will thus be seen that when Governor Printz arrived there were a few persons at Fort Nassau, a few at the Swedish colony at Christina, now Wilmington, Del., and also a few at the Dutch colony a short distance below Christina. Governor Printz brought out with him his wife and one daughter, a lieutenant-governor and secretary, a chaplain and a surgeon, twenty-four regular soldiers, and officers enough for a considerably larger force. The two vessels he commanded were well filled with stores and provisions, merchandise suitable for traffic with the Indians, and also a few settlers. This colony established by Governor Printz was the first one within the limits of Pennsylvania, and, of course, the first within the earlier limits of Chester County, that was successful.

The Swedes made such rapid progress in the settlement of the lower Delaware, in the State subsequently bearing the name of Delaware, and also in Pennsylvania, that the Dutch became somewhat alarmed lest they should lose the trade of the Indians. The extent and importance of this trade is indicated by the fact that in 1644 they had loaded two vessels, the "Kalmar Nyckel" and the "Fame," with cargoes including 2,127 packages of beaver skins and 70,421 pounds of tobacco. During the year 1646 they erected a church at Tinicum, which they dedicated on October 4, dedicating also at the same time the burying-ground in which the first body deposited was that of Catherine Hanson, daughter of Andrew Hanson, which was laid to rest October 28, 1646.

During and on account of the controversies between the Swedes and the Dutch over the possession of this fertile territory, Governor Stuyvesant of New Amsterdam caused the erection of a fort at the present site of New Castle, Delaware, to which he gave the name of Fort Casimir. To the erection of this fort Governor Printz, although he protested against it for a time, ultimately became reconciled. But his successor, John Rysingh, who arrived and began his administration in 1654, captured the Dutch fort, Casimir, on Trinity Sunday, and called it, in honor of that day, Trefalldigheet. The Dutch in the vicinity of this fort then took the

oath of allegiance to the Swedish government. This capture of
Fort Casimir, as might have been expected, aroused the anger of
the Dutch to such a degree that on September 5, 1655, Governor
Stuyvesant, with seven men of war, and some 600 or 700 armed
soldiers, sent over from Holland for the purpose, arrived in the
Delaware River. The next day Fort Trefalldigheet surrendered
to Governor Stuyvesant, and Fort Christina followed soon afterward, without bloodshed in either case, or a battle of any kind, the
name of the former then becoming New Amstel, which name it
retained until it came into possession of the English, who called it
New Castle, as it has since remained. The capture of these two forts
terminated Swedish authority on the Delaware, which had extended up into Pennsylvania, their most northern settlements
reaching to the present limits of Philadelphia.

But the Dutch did not long remain in possession of the territory they had conquered from the Swedes. Charles II having been
restored to the throne of Great Britain, granted to his brother
James, Duke of York, the territory embracing the whole of the
States of New York and New Jersey, and afterward the State of
Delaware. Articles were drawn up between the Dutch and English, which were signed by eight persons of each nationality, and
approved by Colonel Richard Nicolls, Deputy Governor of New
York, by the terms of which the Dutch surrendered to the English all their rights in New Netherlands, including the settlements
on the Delaware, the date of the affixing of these signatures being
August 27, 1664, old style. Soon afterward the English took possession of the Delaware, which they continued to hold with the exception of a short period in 1673 and 1674.

Passing over several important events of general importance,
but which may be considered of minor interest as pertaining to the
history of Chester County, it may be mentioned that in May, 1675,
Governor Andros of New York visited the settlements on the Delaware, and on the 13th and 14th of that month held a special court

at New Castle, at which it was ordered that "highways should be cleared from place to place within the precincts of the govern- ment." It was also ordered that the church in the town should be regulated by the court, and that the meeting at Crane Hoeck should continue as previously; and also that the church at Tinicum Island should serve for Upland and the adjoining portions of that section of the country. The magistrates of Upland were ordered to have a church built at Wickegkoo, which should serve for the inhabitants of Passayunk and those higher up the river, and these magistrates were empowered to levy a tax for this purpose and to maintain a minister.

This is the earliest record of the proceedings of any court on the Delaware River, and the order with reference to the clearing of the roads from place to place was the first step taken for the estab- lishment of roads in the States of Delaware and Pennsylvania, or in other words, was the first road law in either State.

By the Swedes the territory which afterward, in a somewhat remarkable manner, became Chester County, was organized, if it may be said to have been organized, as Upland County. The name was changed to Chester County by William Penn, or, in better words, William Penn permitted his friend, Thomas Pearson, so to name it in honor of the city of Chester, the county seat of Cheshire County, in the west of England. In this connection it may be interesting to note that the names of many towns in England have this word, Chester, as a part of their composition, as Chichester, for example, and that these places were originally Roman camps. The Roman word castra and the Saxon word ceaster, became in time the Eng- lish word Chester.

From Dr. Smith's "History of Delaware County," published in 1862, the following paragraph is quoted with reference to this change of name: "He (Penn) landed at Upland, but the place was to bear that familiar name no more forever. Without reflection Penn determined that the name of this place should be changed. Turning

round to his friend Pearson, one of his own society, who had accompanied him in the ship Welcome, he said: 'Providence has brought
us here safe. Thou hast been the companion of my perils. What
would thou that I should call this place?' Pearson said: 'Chester,
in remembrance of that city from whence we came.' William Penn
replied that it should be called Chester, and that when he divided
the land into counties, one of then should be called by the same
name Thus, from a mere whim, the name of the oldest town; the
name of the one settled part of the province; the name which would
naturally have a place in the affections of a large majority of the
inhabitants of the new province, was effaced, to gratify the caprice
or vanity of a friend! All great men occasionally do little things."

Reviewing briefly what has been presented above as to the governments which at different times held sway over the west bank of
the Delaware River, it will be seen that what was afterward formed
into Chester County was a part of the following colonies from time
to time: New Netherlands, from 1609 to 1638; New Sweden, from
1638 to 1655; New Netherlands, from 1655 to 1656; New Amstel,
from 1656 to 1664; New York, from 1664 to 1673; New Netherlands,
from 1673 to 1674; and New York, from 1674 to 1682.

This was the year in which William Penn arrived, took possession of his grant and divided his province into three counties:
Chester, Bucks and Philadelphia. The precise date when this division into counties was made is not definitely known, but according to tradition it was November 25, the province having been
granted to Penn by royal charter dated March 4, 1681. The three
counties above named were located on the right or west bank of
the Delaware River, and extended indefinitely to the westward.
The western boundary of Chester County was definitely established
by the erection of Lancaster County, May 10, 1729, and the northern boundary was fixed by the erection of Berks County, March 11,
1752.

Philadelphia County formed the northeast and east boundaries of the original Chester County until Montgomery County was established, September 10, 1784, and Delaware County was established September 26, 1789. The southern limits of the county were determined by the section of a circle of a radius of ·twelve miles and having for its center the court-house at New Castle, so far as the State of Delaware was concerned, and by the famous Mason and Dixon's line, so far as Maryland was concerned, which line is in latitude 39 degrees 43 minutes 26.3 seconds north. The history of this famous line may be found elsewhere in this volume.

The original extent of Chester County may be inferred from the fact that twenty-five counties have been taken either directly or indirectly from its territory as at first organized. Lancaster and Delaware were taken from it directly at the dates above given, and the following have since been taken from it indirectly:

York, from Lancaster, August 19, 1749;
Cumberland, from Lancaster, January 27, 1750.
Bedford, from Cumberland, March 9, 1771;
Westmoreland, from Bedford, February 6, 1773;
Washington, from Bedford, March 28, 1781;
Fayette, from Westmoreland, September 26, 1783;
Franklin, from Cumberland, September 9, 1784;
Dauphin, from Lancaster, March 4, 1785;
Huntingdon, from Bedford, September 20, 1787;
Allegheny, from Westmoreland, September 24, 1788;
Somerset, from Bedford, April 17, 1795;
Greene, from Washington, February 9, 1796;
Beaver, from Washington, March 12, 1800;
Butler, from Allegheny, March 12, 1800;
Erie, from Allegheny, March 12, 1800;
Mercer, from Allegheny, March 12, 1800;
Crawford, from Allegheny, March 12, 1800.
Cambria, from Allegheny, March 26, 1804;
Lebanon, from Allegheny, February 16, 1813.

OCTAGONAL SCHOOLHOUSE.

Perry, from Cumberland, March 22, 1820;

Blair, from Cumberland, February 26, 1846;

Lawrence, from Cumberland, March 20, 1849, and

Fulton, from Bedford, April 19, 1850.

These counties, however, together with the present Chester County, do not embrace all of the original Chester County, for portions of several other counties were taken from the original territory of Chester County.

The first county seat, or seat of justice, of Chester County was at the town of Chester, on the right bank of the Delaware River, at the mouth of Chester Creek. As has been stated elsewhere, the first European inhabitants of this place were for the most part Swedes, who named the place Upland. The first court held there, of the proceedings of which there is any record, was held by justices of the peace, September 13, 1681, and on the ancient record of this court at the February term of 1682 Upland is first named Chester.

However, it should not be inferred that this was the first court held at Upland; for at least ten years previously there had been held a court at that place, Governor Lovelace of New York having in 1672 issued an order respecting a piece of land in Amosland, now in Ridley Township, Delaware County, which order was as follows: "Whereas, complaint hath been make unto him by Jan Cornelis Mattys Mattysen and Martin Martinsen, inhabitants at Amosland, in Delaware River, that after having been quietly possessed of a parcel of Valley or Meadow Ground by the island over against Calcoon Hooke, near their plantacon, Israel Helm did, by misinformacon, obtain a patent for the same, having never possession or pretense thereto before, so that the said inhabitants are dispossessed to the ruin of their plantacons without relief; these are to authorize and empower the court at Upland, with the assistance of one or two of the High Court, to examine into the matter and make report of the truth thereof unto me, that I may make some

order hereupon in equity and good conscience. Given, etc., this
8th day of August, 1672."

The sheriff for the Delaware River for 1672 was Edmund Cantwell, and he was also made collector of quit rents in place of William Tom, resigned. It was in this year that the war broke out
between the English and the Dutch, and a fleet of the latter named
nation appeared before New York August 6, 1673, in the absence
of Governor Lovelave in New Haven. The fort at New York surrendered after a slight resistance, and the country again passed
under the authority of the Dutch. A governor and council having
been appointed, the council held sittings at Fort William Hendrick,
which name the Dutch gave to Fort New York. Before this trib-
unal the Delaware deputies appeared, submitting to the "High
Mightinesses, the Lords States General of the New Netherlands
and his Serene Highness the Prince of Orange," on September 12.
These Delaware deputies obtained in return for their submission
for their constituents the privileges of "free trade and commerce
with Christians and Indians"; freedom of conscience; security in the possession of their houses and lands, and
exemption from all rent charges and excise duties on wine,
beer and distilled liquors, consumed on the South or Delaware
River. This last privilege was to continue until 1676. Three
courts of justice were established at this time on the Delaware—
one at New Amstel, one at Hoorn kill and one at Upland, the jurisdiction of the latter extending provisionally from the east and west
banks of Kristina kill upward to the head of the river.

When the peace was made between the English and Dutch,
February 9, 1674, the possessions along the Delaware were again
restored to the English, and Edmund Andros, appointed governor
of New York July 15, upon his arrival, received possession from the
Dutch governor, Colve.

After 1664 the Dutch did not figure in the history of Pennsylvania, nor did the Swedes, nor did either people in either Pennsyl-

vania or Delaware after 1674. But still that they were present in the State at one time will always be evident from the fact that in several places Dutch names remain. such as Schuylkill, Henlopen and Boomties Hoeck. Schuylkill' means "hidden creek," and was given to the river because its mouth could not be easily seen. That there were Indians here is also evident from names of places still remaining, and which will doubtless ever remain. The Indians called the Schuylkill Manaiung, and Manayunk is now the name of a suburb of Philadelphia near the Wissahickon. While the Swedes were in the early day excellent people and settlers, yet they left very few names of places. After the conquest of the country by the English there were many Swedes still in the country, and sixty years after the arrival of the Quakers there were on the Delaware River nearly a thousand persons speaking the Swedish language.

As stated elsewhere William Penn arrived on the Delaware in 1682. After dividing the province of Pennsylvania into three counties, he divided Delaware also into three counties, and that State has still but that number of counties. The first legislative assembly convened December 4, 1862, at Chester, united the two States of Delaware and Pennsylvania, naturalized the Swedes and other aliens, and established a code of laws. The provincial council was organized in Philadelphia March 10, 1683, and the land purchases of 1682, 1736, 1749, 1758, 1768 and 1784, extinguishing the Indian titles to the land, indicate the progress of the settlement of the province up the Delaware River and westward through Chester County.

In a general way it may be stated that those who settled in the eastern townships of this county were Welsh; those who settled in the southern and middle townships were English Quakers, and those who settled in the northern and western townships were Dutch and Germans. To a considerable extent the population of the several sections exhibits to this day the peculiar characteristics of its ancestors.

Most of the Welsh that came to Pennsylvania in the early day were Quakers. They moved here to have a country of their own. At first they were assisted in this hope by William Penn, with whom, before leaving their native country, they had made an agreement by which they were to have a tract of land containing forty thousand acres set apart for them, on which they could have a little government of their own, and live by themselves. In 1682, when they began to arrive, this forty thousand acre tract was surveyed for them west of the Schuylkill River, and it included that fine stretch of country now so familiar to the people of eastern Pennsylvania and so attractive to them on account of its elegant suburban homes along the Pennsylvania railroad. This is the watershed between the Schuylkill and the Delaware Rivers, rising steadily from the west bank of the Schuylkill for about twenty-five miles, the summit of which is near Paoli, where the elevation is about 630 feet above tidewater, or perhaps it would be better to say, the level of the sea. On the northern side beautiful views are obtained of what is now well-known as the Chester valley, but which the Welsh themselves called Duffrin Mawr, or Great Valley. The tract thus assigned to them was a magnificent domain of hill and dale, covered with splendid oaks, poplars and sycamores. For a time the Quaker meetings ruled this country, but in 1690 the three townships within its limits, Merion, Haverford and Radnor, were organized, and as time went forward the Welsh spread out into Newton, Goshen and Uwchlan, others spreading out into Montgomery County, where places like Gwynedd and Penllyn still remain.

At the present writing (1898) what is said to be the oldest house in Gwynedd Township is being torn down. It was built in 1712, and is thus 186 years old. It is supposed to have been erected by William John, who was certainly Welsh, his name being indubitable evidence of that fact, and the site was within the limits of his tract of land. It was very substantially built of stone.

In 1685 Merion Township was separated from Haverford and Radnor and was a separate township of Philadelphia County. Up to this time they had been the controlling influence in Chester County, but by this division they became a minority of both Chester and Philadelphia Counties, and, though they resisted it, as was natural, yet they were gradually assimilated with or absorbed by their neighbors, and long since became an undistinguishable portion of the great American people. As a general thing their names became Anglicized. Ap Humphrey became Pumphrey; Ap Howell became Powell; Ap Hugh became Pugh, etc. Some of their names were so nearly of English form that no change has ever taken place, as Roberts, Thomas, etc., and some of them still remain as in the original Welsh: Eastcaln, Westcaln, Uwchlan and Tredyffrin. There are also many Welsh names along the Pennsylvania railway, as follows: Merion, Wynnefood, Haverford, Bryn Mawr, Radnor and Berwyn. St. David, which is also retained, was the patron saint of the Welsh.

One of the principal features of the drainage of Chester County, as well as of other counties in the southeast corner of the State, is that most of the streams flow southeastwardly into the Delaware River. No stream enters Chester County from Lancaster County. The northeastern part of the county is bordered by the Schuylkill River for a distance of about twelve miles.

Darby Creek rises near Paoli and flows through Easttown into Delaware County, and so on down to the Delaware River, but before reaching the latter it divides into two branches, which together separate Tinicum Island from the mainland. Crum Creek rises west of Paoli and flows through Willistown in a southerly direction. Ridley Creek rises near Frazer station and flows through East Goshen and Willistown. Chester Creek, east branch, rises in West Whiteland and flows south through East Goshen and Westtown into Thornbury, where it unites with the west branch, which rises near West Chester, and then flows southeast into Delaware

County. These four streams rise along the crest of the South Valley hill, on a straight line which is about ten miles in length.

Brandywine River, east branch, rises in the northwest part of the county, in West Nantmeal Township, flows southward across the valley at Downingtown station, and then past what was once Copesville, Sagersville, opposite Lenape station, and Chadd's Ford, and then passes on into Delaware and enters the Delaware River near Wilmington. It is joined by the west branch about midway between North Brook postoffice and Lenape postoffice. Valley Creek flows west along the valley to near Garland, turns south and unites with the Brandywine about a mile above Copesville. Broad Run flows west into Valley Creek near Harmony. Taylor's Run flows west into Blackhorse Run, which latter flows west into the Brandywine near Copesville. Plum Run rises in West Chester borough and flows southwest into the Brandywine at Sagersville, as also does Radley Run, except that this stream flows into the Brandywine one-half mile further south.

Brandywine River, west branch, rises in the extreme north-western part of the county, flows across the valley and then south-southeast ten miles to the east branch, which it joins between Copesville and Sagersville.

Pocopson Creek flows east into the Brandywine one mile below Sagersville. Ring's Run flows from the west into the Brandywine at Chadd's Ford. Red Clay Creek, east and west branches, drains most of the county west of the Brandywine and flows south into the State of Delaware. White Clay Creek, east branch, rises at and west of Upland and flows south past Avondale. While Clay Creek, middle branch, rises at Londonderry and flows south-south-east eight miles, when it joins the west branch, and then two miles further down this enlarged stream joins the east branch at the State line of Delaware. White Clay Creek, west branch, rises at Kelton and flows south and then east.

Elk Creek rises in the vicinity of Russellville and the Lincoln

University, and flows southeast into Maryland. Little Elk Creek rises at New Prospect and Oxford Borough and flows east and south into Maryland. Northeast Creek rises at Nottingham post-office, and flows southeast and then south into Maryland. Octoraro Creek bounds the county on the west from near Christiana, and flows southwest to the Maryland state line and on into the Susquehanna.

Buck Run and Doe Run drain Highland Township and parts of several other townships, and flows eastward into the Brandywine six miles below Coatesville. Muddy Run rises near Cochranville and flows seven miles into the Octoraro below Hellbank bridge. French Creek rises at the Berks County line and flows southeast, entering the Schuylkill at Phœnixville.

Pickering Creek, with its branches, Pine Run and Pigeon Run, flows east into the Schuylkill, about a mile below Phœnixville. Pigeon Creek flows into the Schuylkill four miles below Pottstown. Stony Run enters the Schuylkill just below Phœnixville.

The fall of the Schuylkill River from Douglasville, four and a half miles above Pottstown, down to Philadelphia, is from 161 feet to 28 feet above sea level, or 133 feet.

The nature of the rocks through which these several streams flow, together with some remarks as to the amount of erosion some of them have caused, will be treated of under the geological description of the county.

The history of the southern boundary of Chester County is of equal interest with that of the southern boundary of the State of Pennsylvania, for the history of the one is substantially that of the other. In order to correctly understand this history it is necessary to begin with the grants to the original English proprietors. The proprietary charter of Pennsylvania was drawn in 1681, and, as was supposed, in plain and simple terms. Prior thereto William Penn was financially interested in the Jerseys, but that interest gradually dwindled until it became of little practical importance.

But it was his experience in the Jerseys that led him to choose Pennsylvania, as it came afterward to be known, as the field for his "holy experiments," the results of which have long been known to the world.

To the father of William Penn, Admiral Penn, the English government was indebted for services to the extent of £16,000, which the Admiral had attempted in vain to collect, either in the form of money or in a grant of land, and he therefore suggested to his son, William, that he, if possible, should secure the grant, which, upon the Admiral's death, William immediately set himself about. On June 1, 1680, he presented a petition to the King outlining the extent of the grant desired in lieu of the £16,000, mentioning, however, only pecuniary considerations.

At length, after long deliberation, and after the Privy Council had held several meetings, at which the counsellor for the Duke of York and the agents for Lord Baltimore played important parts, Penn obtained his desire on March 4, 1681, O. S., and a royal letter was sent to the inhabitants April 2, 1681, commanding due obedience to the proprietary, his heirs and assigns; and the Duke of York was kind enough to execute a quit-claim deed to all the region included in Pennsylvania, though his grant did not extend to the westward of the Delaware River.

This grant of land to William Penn embraced all that section of country bounded on the east by the Delaware River from a point twelve miles from New Castle to the 43d degree of north latitude if the river extended that far, but if it did not, then by a meridian line from the head of the river to the 43d degree, and this region extended westward through 5 degrees of longitude as computed from the eastern bounds. This region was to be bounded on the north by the beginning of the 43d degree, on the south by a circle drawn twelve miles distant from New Castle, northward and westward to the beginning of the 40th degree of north latitude, and by a straight line drawn thence westward to the limit of longitude.

Before proceeding further with the history of the difficulty that existed between Lord Baltimore and William Penn, or, as it perhaps would be better to say, between Maryland and Pennsylvania, with regard to the dividing line between them, it is necessary to quote from the charter granted to Lord Baltimore in 1632, which was nearly fifty years before the grant was made to William Penn. This grant to Lord Baltimore reads in part as follows:

"All that part of the peninsula, or Chersonese, lying in the borders of America, between the ocean on the east and the bay of Chesapeake on the west, divided from the residue thereof by a line drawn from the promontory or headland, called Watkin's Point, situated on the bay aforesaid and near the river, Wighco (Wicomico), on the west unto the main ocean on the east, and between that boundary on the south and that part of Delaware Bay on the north which lieth under the 40th degree of latitude, where New England terminates."

The difficulty about the southern boundary of Pennsylvania was primarily caused by the use of the term "beginning of the 40th degree." Lord Baltimore claimed that his lands extended throughout the 40th degree, that is, from what is always understood as the 39th parallel to what is always understood as the 40th parallel, and that no part of the 40th degree, or the belt of country between these two parallels, was excluded from the grant.

The Penns claimed that the beginning of the 40th degree had reference to the entire space between the 39th and 40th parallels, and thus it will be seen that the claim of the Penns, if allowed, would make the 39th parallel the southern limit of Pennsylvania; but that this could not really have been intended is proven by the charter, which stated that the beginning should be twelve miles from New Castle. But when this place of beginning was first chosen it was supposed that the beginning of the 40th degree was twelve miles north of New Castle. The original intention was that Lord Baltimore should have two degrees in width of latitude, a degree at that time being sixty miles, and that Penn's grant should include three degrees of latitude, from the beginning of the 40th degree to the beginning of the 43d degree.

Had the claims of Lord Baltimore been allowed all the lands on the western side of the Delaware River, from the site of the city of Philadelphia to the capes, would have been given to Maryland, and the Penns would have been deprived of several valuable seaports. Hence it is not surprising that Penn should resist the claim of Lord Baltimore. Had the claims of Penn been conceded the southern limit of Pennsylvania would have extended south to the 39th parallel, and Lord Baltimore would have had a strip of land not much more than sixty miles in width at its eastern end.

In order to settle the matter satisfactorily, all that was needed to be conceded was the fact that the charter itself expressly states that the beginning of the 43d degree and the 43d degree were precisely the same, for it states that the province shall be bounded on the east by the Delaware River from the point twelve miles north of New Castle to the 43d degree, and that on the north it should be bounded by the 43 degree, or, in other words, those who wrote the charter understood the same thing by the beginning of a degree and the degree itself.

The difficulties, it will be seen, were caused by the ambiguities and uncertainties, if not contradictions, of the language used in the grants. Both sides were laid before the King in 1684, and in 1685 an order in council was issued, which said in substance that as the lands granted to Lord Baltimore were originally designed to be only such as were then inhabited by savages, the said Lord was not entitled to the land lying between the river and bay of Delaware and the Eastern sea on the one hand and Chesapeake Bay on the other; but still they decided that this tract of land should be divided into two equal parts by a line from the latitude of Cape Henlopen to the 40th degree of north latitude, the southern boundary of Pennsylvania by charter, and that one-half thereof should belong to his majesty and the other half should remain to Lord Baltimore, as comprised in his charter.

There was much difficulty afterward in the survey of the parallel from Cape Henlopen to Chesapeake Bay, the precise middle of which was to be the starting point for the line to run north.ward to the said 40th parallel, but here it can only be stated that finally, on May 15, 1750, Lord Chancellor Hardwicke pronounced his decree, according to which the survey began November 12, the same year. According to this decree the circle about which there had been so much discussion should have its center at the center of the town of New Castle, and that its radius should be twelve miles. Immediately, however, a curious difficulty arose as to the method of measuring the radii of this circle, the commissioners from Maryland claiming that they should be measured according to the inequalities of the ground, that is, superficially, which would of course make the circle smaller than if the horizontal or geometrical method were pursued, which was the claim of the Penns. The latter, however, finally won their case and the circle was so drawn that all parts of the circumference were, or were supposed to be, equally distant from the center.

This being settled, the survey of the base line from Cape Henlopen to Chesapeake Bay was begun, both sides agreeing that a point should be selected 139 rods due east from a stone already fixed on the northern part of Fenwick's Island, near the former Cape Henlopen, and should run across the peninsula to Chesapeake Bay. The surveyors established the east and west line as far as Slaughter's Creek, when the Maryland commissioners insisted that the line should go no further, and that its length should be 66 miles and 248½ rods, while the Pennsylvania commissioners declared that it should be extended to the shore of Chesapeake Bay, and should be 69 miles 298 rods in length. The deadlock over this question lasted from April, 1751, when the survey commenced, until November, 1754, and the question was afterward in the courts until 1760, when Lord Baltimore succumbed to the contentions of the Penns, the base line was made 69 miles 298 rods long, and its exact middle was 34 miles 309 rods from the fixed point on Fenwick's Island.

Thus it will be seen that the loss to Maryland and the gain to Delaware by the success of the Penns was a strip of land 1 mile 184¾ rods in width, the length of the north and south line from the base line to the northern boundary of Maryland, or rather to the twelve mile circle. And thus it will also be seen the peculiarly shaped point that runs down from the south part of Chester County between the twelve mile circle and the eastern boundary of Maryland was correspondingly affected.

This north and south line from the middle of the base line was required to be run northward up the said peninsula until it should touch the circle above mentioned so as to make a tangent thereto, and there the said straight line should end. Then at the northern point or end of the said straight line, a line was to begin and run due north above the said peninsula, but so far only until it should come into the same latitude as a line running east and west through a point which was fifteen English statute miles due south of the most southern point of the city of Philadelphia. Then a due east and west line was to be run in the manner following: It should begin at the northern point of the due north and south line and should thence run due west across the Susquehanna River to the utmost western extent of the Province of Pennsylvania, that is, through five degrees of longitude from its eastern boundary on the Delaware River.

The running of the temporary southern boundary of the Province of Pennsylvania was an important episode of the history of Chester County, that is, that part of it aside from the drawing of the twelve mile circle, and hence it is treated of briefly in this work. An order in council dated May 25, 1738, provided for the running of this temporary line. On December 5, 1738, the commissioners, on the part of Maryland, Colonel Levin Gale and Samuel Chamberlaine, met the commissioners on the part of Pennsylvania, Richard Peters and Lawrence Growdon, on Society Hill, the mayor of Philadelphia being present, as well as several of the aldermen and prominent gentlemen of Philadelphia, and the most southern point in the city of Philadelphia was ascertained. The commissioners then adjourned to the house of John Postlethwaite, where it was unanimously agreed to settle the variation of the compass by fixing a meridian line by an observation to be made when the Pole Star and the first star in the tail of the Great Bear under the Pole should be in the same vertical circle, or in a perpendicular line, one above the other. But on account of the cloudiness of the weather no observation could be made until the evening of the 8th, and then the meridian line was fixed according to the rule aforesaid.

A theodolite in the possession of Benjamin Eastburn, surveyor for Pennsylvania, was tried and the variation of the needle was found to be 5 degrees 25 minutes to the west, and then a circomferenter in the possession of John Warner was tried, and the variation of its needle was found to be 5 degrees 30 minutes to the west. The variation of the needle of the theodolite was accepted as that by which to run the temporary line. On the 11th of December about two miles of the line were run, but wintry weather coming on it was decided to adjourn until April 5, 1739.

But it was not until April 11, 1739, that work on this survey was found to be 5 degrees 25 minutes to the west, and then a circum-Eastburn's theodolite was precisely the same as before. On April 23 the commissioners proceeded on a line to an old field belonging to John Newlin, within the Society land, on or near its north line, at a distance of about thirty-one miles due west from Philadelphia, where it was agreed that the line had been run far enough to the west for avoiding the large waters of the Brandywine and Christina Creeks, and that the surveyors should begin to set off the

south line of fifteen miles and a quarter, this distance from the east
and west line from the southernmost point of the city of Philadelphia having been agreed upon instead of fifteen miles, between
Lord Baltimore and the Penns, by which the latter gained a strip
one-fourth of a mile in width as far west as the Susquehanna
River, but to the west of the Susquehanna River, the distance between this base line of survey was to be only fourteen and three-
fourths miles.

It was not long after beginning this survey of the south line
before a dispute arose as to whether the superficial or horizontal
method of measuring this $15\frac{1}{4}$ mile line should be employed, the
Maryland commissioners of course insisting on the superficial method and the Pennsylvania commissioners insisting on the horizontal
method. The result of the discussion over this matter was that
the Maryland commissioners yielded to the extent of allowing
twenty-five perches over the fifteen and a quarter miles superficial
measure for the difference between the two methods. On April 24
the two parties, after coming to this agreement, surveyed two miles
of the line, and left off on the ground of Mr. Wickersham in East
Marlboro Township. On the 25th they set off the twenty-five
perches and surveyed seven statute miles, getting to the south
line of the road leading to New Castle, in New Garden Township. On the next day they completed the survey, and drove into
the ground a stake at the distance of twenty perches from the
road leading to Charles Tennent's Meeting House, in Mill Creek
Hundred, New Castle County, Del., and on April 27. they began
the west line at the aforesaid stake.

Before reciting the history of the west line, just mentioned,
it will be of interest to note an instance or two connected with
the survey of the first thirty-one miles of the line running west
from the most southern point of Philadelphia, from which the
distance of fifteen and a quarter miles was laid off to the south..
It will be remembered that the survey of this base line began on

the 11th of April. While it was being surveyed, on the 18th of April, Richard Peters, one of the commissioners for Pennsylvania, reported to Governor Thomas that in the work they had found "a number of Attractions in running the line, so many as to make it a doubt whether the Attractions were not stronger in the spring than in the fall of the year; sometimes the needle will be five degrees to the southward and sometimes to the northward, within a station or two, that is to say, in other terms, the variation will be ten degrees westerly at one time and in an hour or two after that the variation will be half a degree east, or, perhaps, no variation at all. We are got as far as one Weslow Parnell's in Edgemont Township, about 16 miles west of Philadelphia, and in this distance we have crossed the forcer lines, that have been run, several times; and now we are something to the south of the line run by John Taylor, and more to the south of the line run by the Jersey commissioners, and if Ben. Eastburn says truly we shall gain still more and more upon the last line, so as to come very near Elisha Gatchell's plantation. The surveyors go on amicably yet, but Col. Gale is much disturbed to find the line prove so as it does, and as he is disappointed by John Lad, he comes to town to procure another surveyor."

On the 20th of the month Mr. Peters again wrote to Governor Thomas, saying: "He" (Col. Gale) "has been extremely uneasy on account of the line continuing to gain on them, and it being apprehended that the needle in Mr. Eastburn's theodolite might have been altered by some accident in its direction, we this morning compared their theodolite and their two needles with ours, as we had done before on Society Hill, and the variation in all the three needles agreed most exactly with what it was then and now." And Col. Gale being then satisfied that the survey was going on rightly, came to the conclusion that the line they were then running differed from the Jersey line, either because the Jersey commissioners had got into an Attraction that carried them too far north, wihout their being aware of it, or that they had not been careful to fix the index by which the variation was rightly regulated.

The difficulty with reference to the method of surveying the fifteen and a quarter miles has been already mentioned; but there was a peculiar feature of it that does not appear to have been touched upon by writers on local history. After the agreement had been reached on April 25, that an allowance of twenty-five perches should be made in favor of the Pennsylvania claim, or, in other words, added to the length of the fifteen and a quarter miles line, Mr Eastburn, the surveyor for the Pennsylvania commissioners, ascertained that the allowance of twenty-five perches would fully cover the difference between the methods of surveying the line, and, in fact, Mr. Eastburn was satisfied that the difference would not exceed twenty perches. Mr. Peters thereupon wrote to Governor Thomas, "humbly desiring your Honor to keep it private that this is the difference, lest they should come to the knowledge of it." So that by this superior knowledge and skill of her surveyor Pennsylvania was getting five perches in the length of the fifteen and a quarter mile line more than she was in reality entitled to. Or, in other words, Pennsylvania thus gained a strip of land along the southern border of the province eighty-two and a half feet in width for the entire five degrees of longitude, provided the temporary line had become permanent.

It now remains to give a brief account of the survey of the southern boundary line of the State, which is the southern boundary line of Chester County, from the peculiarly formed triangle, or point, so far as Chester County extends to the westward, and which is now famous in history as Mason and Dixon's line.

The commissioners appointed under the deed of 1760 addressed themselves to the work of completing the survey, but their progress was slow. Hence, on August 4, 1763, Thomas and Richard Penn and Lord Baltimore, all of whom were then in

London, made an agreement with Charles Mason and Jeremiah Dixon, two mathematicians and surveyors, "to mark, run out, settle, fix and determine all the parts of the circle, marks of lines and boundaries as were mentioned in the several articles and commissions and were not yet completed." Mason and Dixon landed at Philadelphia November 15, 1763, and at once began their work with more perfect instruments than had been previously used in these surveys. They adopted the twelve-mile radius of their predecessors, and also their tangent point, as sufficiently accurate, and adjourned to Philadelphia to find its southern limit, on Cedar (now South) Street, on which street they erected an observatory that they might ascertain the latitude of this southern limit, this observatory being the first in America used for taking observations of the stars. According to their observations this southern limit was in latitude 39 degrees 56 minutes 29 seconds. They then extended this latitude to the west sufficiently far to be due north of the tangent point, this being accomplished in January, 1764, and the distance run to the westward being thirty-one miles, to the forks of the Brandywine, where they planted a quartzose stone, which was long known in the vicinity as the "star-gazers' stone," which stood on Joel Harlin's land, in Newlin Township, a short distance west of the Chester County almshouse, six miles 264 perches west of the meridian of the West Chester court-house and $446\frac{1}{2}$ perches south of the parallel of the West Chester court-house.

From this "star-gazers' stone" they ran a line south to the latitude of the great due west line, fifteen miles, and there planted a post, from which they ran the due west line a short distance. Then going to the tangent point they ran a line due north to the latitude of the due west line, and at the intersection of the two lines, in a deep ravine, near a spring, they established the corner stone, which thenceforward was to be at the beginning of the due west line, the southern boundary of Pennsylvania, the northern boundary of Maryland, the famous Mason and Dixon's line.

6

This stone which thus stands at the northeast corner of Maryland was ascertained by Mason and Dixon to be in latitude 39 degrees 43 minutes 18 seconds, but was afterward ascertained to be in latitude 39 degrees 43 minutes 26.3 seconds. During the summer of 1764 they ran and marked the north and south line, or the tangent line, which separates Maryland from Delaware, and then started for the stone at the northeast corner of Maryland.

Early in the spring of 1765 they returned to their work, and described that portion of the circle surrounding New Castle which fell to the westward of the meridian line, joining the tangent point with the stone at the northeast corner of Maryland, which meridian line cut off a segment of the circle which is about a mile and a half long and 116 feet wide in the widest part, which segment of the circle, according to the agreement, belongs to New Castle County, Delaware. From the point where this meridian line crosses the circle to the eastward, Mason and Dixon did not survey the circle, as Lord Baltimore had no interest in its location. But this point, which is at the meeting of three States, was carefully marked. From this point north to the northeast corner of Maryland is about three miles and a half, and the distance from the northeast corner of Maryland to the circle in a line running due east is about three-fourths of a mile. These were the distances established by Mason and Dixon, but recent controversies over the circular boundary between Delaware and Pennsylvania have changed the measurements somewhat. These controversies will be treated of briefly later on in this article.

By June 17, 1765, the surveyors had carried the due west line to the Susquehanna River, and received instructions to carry it as far west as Maryland and Pennsylvania were settled and inhabited. By the 27th of October they had reached the North (Cove or Kittatinny) Mountains, ninety-five miles west of the Susquehanna, where the temporary line, run in 1739, terminated. Early in 1766 they again began the survey, and by June 4 they had reached the Little Alleghany Mountains, about 160 miles from the beginning. In 1767 they extended the line to a distance of 230 miles 18 chains and 21 links from the northeast corner of Maryland, or 277 miles 38 chains and 36 links from the River Delaware, near to an Indian war path, ou the borders of Dunkard Creek.

But trouble now began with the original inhabitants of the soil, that is, with the Six Nations, whose consent had to be obtained to the further survey of the line, and soon afterward, with an escort of fourteen stroud-clad warriors, an interpreter and a Mohawk chief, deputed by the Iroquois council, they pushed on from the summit of the Alleghany Mountains down into the valley of the Ohio, whose tributaries they soon crossed. Coming to the western limit of Maryland they still pushed on, resolved to reach the utmost limits of Penn's five degrees of longitude from the Delaware. By August 24 they came to the crossing of Braddock's Ford, and the escort became restless. The Mohawk chief and his nephew left the party, and the Shawnees and Delawares, who then occupied the territory into which the surveying party was penetrating, began to grow hostile, and on September 27, at the distance of 233 miles from the Delaware, twenty-six of the laboring men deserted, leaving only fifteen ax-men with the surveyors, who, however, pushed on, regardless of the danger, until they came to a point a little to the west of Mount Morris, in Greene County, when their Indian escort said to them that they had been instructed by their chiefs not to let the line be run westward of the war path at which they had then arrived—the old Catawba war path.

The instruments used by Mason and Dixon were an ordinary surveyor's compass, to find their bearings in a general way; a quadrant and a four-foot zenith sector, which they brought from England for absolute accuracy. The needle could not be relied upon because of the ferruginous character of the soil over which they had to mark the line. The sector enabled them to be guided by the heavenly bodies, which changed their positions very slowly.

The "visto," as they called it, that is, the opening cut through the woods as they went along, was twenty-four feet in width, and throughout this width they had cut down all the trees and bushes, leaving them to rot upon the ground. Along the middle of this "visto," in the true parallel, monuments were erected at the distance of five miles, each monument consisting of a stone bearing the coats of arms of William Penn on the side toward Pennsylvania, and those of Lord Baltimore on the side toward Maryland, most of these stones having been brought from England. This mode of demarkation was used as far the eastern base of the Sideling Hill Mountain, 132 miles from the northeast corner of Maryland, and from this point to the great Alleghany Mountains the line was denoted by conical heaps of dirt and stones six or seven feet high on the tops of ridges and mountains, and still further to the west as far as they went similar marks were erected at the end of every mile.

As to the length of a degree of longitude on Mason and Dixon's line, it may be said that they made it equal to 53 miles 157.1 perches, hence Penn's five degrees of longitude would extend from the Delaware River westward to a distance of 267.4546 miles. The length of a degree of longitude on the Mason and Dixon arc of the parallel, for which the United States Coast and Geodetic Survey takes the latitude of 39 degrees 43 minutes 20 seconds, is, according to Clarke's spheroid, 53.277 miles, and hence the five degrees of longitude equal 266.385 statute miles. Hence Mason and Dixon made an error in their measurement of these five degrees of 1.096 statute miles.

Another point of interest connected with the lines run by Mason and Dixon is their determination of the length of a degree of latitude, in 1764, on the line separating Delaware from Maryland, known as the tangent line. They made the length of a degree on this line 363,763 feet, or 68,894 statute miles,* for mean latitude 39 degrees 12 minutes, measuring the whole line with deal rods, triangulation, which was brought into use in 1617, being inapplicable in this case. But according to Clarke's spheroid the true length of a meridianal degree at this latitude, 39 degrees 12 minutes, is 68.983 miles, or 469.92 feet in excess of the length as ascertained by Mason and Dixon.†

The circular boundary line is one of interest as to its history and of importance as to the effect its location has had upon the people living in its vicinity. When it was first located it was merely the division line between two counties, but later it came into controversy between two States. The first mention of it is made in the records of Upland Court, November 12, 1678, as follows:

"The limits and divisions between this (Upland) and New Castle County were this day agreed upon and settled by the Court and Mr. John Moll, President of New Castle Court, to be as followeth, viz.: 'This county of Upland to begin from the north side of Oele Francens Creeke, otherways called Steenkill, lying in the voght above the Verdrietege hoeck, and from the said creek ouer to the Singletree Point on the east syde of this river.' "

"Steenkill," otherwise Stony Creek, is now known as Quarry Creek. "It crosses the Philadelphia, Wilmington & Baltimore rail-

---

*It has sometimes been said that this measurement of a degree of latitude by Mason and Dixon was the first ever measured on the surface of the ground; but this is not exactly correct, for, according to the Encyclopedia Britannica, the Caliph Almamoum, in 814 A. D., fixed upon a spot in the plains of Mesopotamia, sent one company of astronomers northward and another southward, measuring the journey by rods until each found the altitude of the Pole Star to have changed one degree, the northern party making a degree 56 miles and the southern party 56 2-3 miles. Again, about the year 1500, a Frenchman named Fernel measured a distance in the direction of the meridian near Paris by counting the number of revolutions of the wheel of his carriage as he traveled.

†These precise figures, according to Clarke's spheroid, were supplied upon request by Henry S. Pritchett, superintendent United States Coast and Geodetic Survey.

road about three and three-quarters miles below the mouth of Naaman's Creek, in Brandywine Hundred, New Castle County." "Verdrietege hoeck," also called Trinity Hook, lay between Stony Creek and Shellpot Creek; and Singletree Point is now known as Old Man's Point of the New Jersey shore, one mile below the mouth of Old Man's Creek.

Stony Creek is there on the dividing line, as at first located, and so remained until the grant to Penn fixed the boundary of his tract "on the south by a circle drawn at a distance of twelve miles from New Castle northward and westward.

Later Naaman's Creek was recognized as the boundary line, and was so laid down by Thomas Holme, surveyor-general of the province, but still the boundary line between the two counties was not fixed, and some of the inhabitants of Chester County petitioned for a division line between their county and that of New Castle. Therefore on the 9th of August, 1693, it was resolved by the Council that the boundary of New Castle County should begin at the mouth of Naaman's Creek and upward along the southwest side of the northmost branch (excluding the townships of Concord and Bethel), and not to extend backward of the said northmost branch above the said two townships.

Still this arrangement did not prove satisfactory, and as there appeared to be danger of the three lower counties separating from the province, a conference was held and a warrant issued dated 28th of the 8th mo., 1701, directed to Isaac Taylor of Chester County, and Thomas Pierson of New Castle County, authorizing them to accompany the magistrates of the two counties interested, and in their presence to "admeasure and survey from the town of New Castle the distance of twelve miles, in a right line," up the River Delaware, "and from said distance, according to the King's letters patent and deeds from the Duke," to survey the said circular line and mark it well two-thirds of the length of a semicircle.

The magistrates agreed upon and established the center of the circle "at the end of the horse dyke next to the town of New Castle," and the survey was accordingly made.

It may be interesting to note the method used in 1701 by Messrs. Taylor and Pierson in surveying this twelve-mile circular boundary line, and hence the following quotation from their report:

"We did begin in the presence of said justices at the said end of the horse dyke and measured due north twelve miles to a white oak marked with twelve notches, standing on the west bank of the Brandywine Creek on the land of Israel Helm, and from the said white oak we ran eastward circularly, changing our direction from the east southward one degree at the end of every sixty-seven perches, which is the chord of one degree at a radius of twelve miles; and at the end of forty-three chords we came to the Delaware River, on the upper side of Nathaniel Lumplugh's old house at Chichester. And then returning to the said white oak on Israel Helm's land we ran from thence westward, changing our course one degree from the west southward at the end of every sixty-seven perches until we had extended seventy-seven chords (which being added to the forty-three chords make two-third parts of the semicircle to a twelve-mile radius), all of which said circular line being well marked on each side of the trees to a marked hickory standing near the western branch of Christina Creek."

It will be observed that this method of marking out a circular was peculiarly liable to error, as a very slight error in running the lines which formed the chords would amount to a considerable error in running one hundred and twenty chords; and it may also be remarked that a very slight error in measuring the "one degree" at each change of direction would also lead to a considerable error, and if all these errors should happen to be in the same direction, the circle would in after years, when more scientific and accurate methods had come into use, be found to be far from its correct position.

This survey of 1701 held good until 1849, when the Legislature of Pennsylvania passed an act authorizing the Governor to appoint a commissioner to act in connection with commissioners appointed or to be appointed by the States of Delaware and Maryland, with power to survey and determine the point of intersection of the three States and to fix some suitable mark or monument whereby its location would afterward be known. Under similar laws passed by the States of Delaware and Maryland commissioners were appointed by the Governors of those States, and the three members of the commission were, on the part of Pennsylvania, Joshua P. Eyre; on the part of Delaware, George Read Riddle, and on the part of Maryland, H. G. S. Key.

At the request of this commission the Secretary of War of the United States detailed Col. J. D. Graham, of the Topographical Engineers, to make the survey. Proceeding to the northeast corner of Maryland the commissioners and Col. Graham found the stone monument set up by Mason and Dixon had been removed, but that a stake was found firmly driven into the ground at the place the monument had occupied, which they ascertained to be correct by subsequent surveys. After establishing this point they planted a new stone of cut granite about seven feet long, set five feet into the ground, marking it with the letter "P" on the north and east sides, and with the letter "M" on the south and west sides.

They also found that the points of tangent and intersection were substantially correct, though according to their measurements the twelve-mile radius was two feet four inches short, and that by errors in the location of the tangent point and the intersection point Maryland had obtained about one and three-fourths acres more than she was entitled to. New monuments were placed at the tangent point, at the intersection point, and at the meridian of the circle, that at the junction of the three States, or the intersection point, being the most important. This was a triangular prismatic post of cut granite seven feet long, inserted into the ground four and a half feet, and marked with the letters "P," "D" and "M," according to the State indicated, and also with the date, 1849, on the north side.

On the 4th of May, 1889, an act was approved by the Governor of Pennsylvania which provided for a resurvey of this circle, and under it commissioners were appointed for Pennsylvania as follows: Hon. Wayne McVeagh of Philadelphia; Hon. R. E. Monaghan of Chester County, and Mr. William H. Miller of Delaware County. The Delaware commissioners were the Hon. Thomas F. Bayard, J. H. Hoffecker and B. L. Lewis.

A meeting of the joint commission was held at Philadelphia, at which a series of four resolutions was adopted, the first one being to the effect that the boundary line between the State of Delaware and the State of Pennsylvania shall be held to commence at the northeast corner of the State of Maryland and to extend due east 4,169 feet to the monument then fixed and agreed upon by the joint commission as the western terminus of the circular boundary line between the said States, said monument being at a distance of twelve English statute miles from the spire of the courthouse in New Castle.

In November, 1891, the joint commission appointed Daniel Farra surveyor for the State of Pennsylvania, and Benjamin H. Smith for Delaware. The commission decided that the most economical means of effecting its object would be to make use of the triangulation stations of the United States Coast and Geodetic Survey, and the positions were furnished by Prof. T. C. Mendenhall, superintendent of the Coast Survey, who offered to detail a competent civil engineer, with the necessary instruments to carry on the work. A preliminary survey developed the fact that no single curve could be made to pass through all the points previously agreed upon, and a compound curve was therefore adopted composed of two arcs of nearly equal lengths, the eastern arc or curve having its center some little distance south and east of the court-house in New Castle, and the western arc having its center somewhat more distant from the court-house in the directly opposite direction. The preliminary survey developed the fact that a circular arc with a twelve-mile radius from the court-house in New Castle as a center would fall entirely within the State of Delaware, would intersect the Delaware River near the mouth of Naaman's Creek, over 3,000 feet below the point agreed upon for the terminal monument, and cut off nearly 5,000 acres from the State of Delaware; and it was also found that a curve from the initial point through the stump at the corner of Kennet Township and a line hickory tree near the corner of Concord would also intersect the river several hundred feet below the terminal point; and a curve from the terminal point through the Concord tree and the corner of Kennet would intersect the east and west line near the corner of Maryland, and thus transfer several hundred acres to Delaware from Pennsylvania. For these reasons a compound curve was determined upon in order to leave the boundary line practically in the same position as it had been since 1701.

Without attempting to present the details of the survey, which would at best interest only those versed in the higher mathematics, it will be sufficient to say that the terminal monument was set up near the Delaware River, December 12, 1892, and the initial monument on December 20, 1892. The stones along the circular boundary line were set every half mile and every mile, the mile stones being so distinguished from the half mile stones as to cause no confusion. The entire length of this circular boundary line as thus surveyed was found to be 23.3619 miles. In this survey the latitude and longitude of many points was determined with greater accuracy than had ever been done before; but only those of three points will be presented here, the three most important points on the line, or indirectly connected therewith. The latitude of the initial monument was found to be 39 degrees 43 minutes 19.91 seconds; the longitude, 75 degrees 46 minutes 26.70 seconds;

the latitude of the terminal monument was found to be 39 degrees 48 minutes 27.92 seconds; the longitude, 75 degrees 25 minutes 31.53 seconds; and the latitude of the northeast corner of Maryland was found to be 39 degrees 43 minutes 19.91 seconds, and the longitude 75 degrees 47 minutes 20.03 seconds.

In still more recent years the question of the location of the circular boundary line has attracted considerable attention. A certain gentleman claiming to live in Delaware refused to pay taxes to a collector for the township of London Britain, in Chester County, Pennsylvania, the name of the collector being Thomas F. Crossan. The former, in order to prevent the collection of the taxes claimed by the Chester County official, secured an injunction against the exercise of his official functions, which injunction was made perpetual by Judge Hemphill at West Chester, January 15, 1897. The judge, in an elaborate review of the boundary line dispute, decided that the lands upon which taxes were claimed to be due lie in White Clay Creek Hundred, New Castle County, Delaware; that they lie "north of the circular arc of the compound curve, his (Mr. Johnson's residence) being 600 feet north of it, and 600 feet south of the traditional curve line of 1701, as established by evidence. His land, therefore, having always heretofore been considered and treated as within the State of Delaware, and the proceedings of the commissioners of 1889 lacking the assent of the two States and of Congress, he is not liable for taxes assessed, and the injunction must be made perpetual."

However, if the assent of the two States of Delaware and Pennsylvania should be obtained to the resolutions of the joint commission, and should the consent of the Congress of the United States also be obtained, then the said land of Mr. Johnson will clearly be within the limits of Pennsylvania, as his land is north of the compound curve, and his residence is six hundred feet north of that curve.

About the year 1786 the people of the southeastern part of

Chester County thought that the county seat, at Turk's Head, was too far away, and consequently petitioned the General Assembly of the State to erect a new county consisting of the borough of Chester and the southeastern part of the county. This petition being regarded as just and reasonable by the General Assembly, that body on September 26, 1789, authorized the division of the county of Chester and the erection of the new county desired. This new county was to be within the following limits:

"Beginning in the middle of the Brandywine River where the same crosses the circular line of New Castle County, thence up the middle of the said river to the line dividing the lands of Elizabeth Chads and Caleb Brinton at or near the ford commonly called or known as Chads' Ford, and from thence, as nearly straight as may be so as not to split or divide plantations, to the great road leading from Goshen to Chester, where the Westtown line intersects or crosses said road, and from thence along the lines of Edgemont, Newtown and Radnor, so as to include these townships, to the line of Montgomery County, and along the same and the Philadelphia County line to the River Delaware, and down the same to the circular line aforesaid, and along the same to the place of beginning, to be henceforth known and called by the name of Delaware County."

By this act the townships of Birmingham and Thornbury were divided; but provision was made that the parts falling in each county should each constitute a separate township, each new township retaining the name of the original township from which it was taken.

CHAPTER II.

THE INDIANS.

CHAPTER II.

WHEN the white man first came to the eastern part of what is now Pennsylvania he found a numerous body of natives here, which he named the Delaware Indians, because they lived on and near the Delaware River. They, however, called themselves Lenni-Lenape, by which they meant the original people. These Lenni-Lenape Indians were usually divided up into small bodies or tribes, each tribe living in some river valley or the valley of a creek. The Nanticokes were one of these smaller tribes, they at one time dwelling and for a long time lingering along the valley of the Brandywine.

It has been said of them by certain historians that when the name Delaware was first applied to them they were displeased, thinking it was given to them in derision; but when they were informed that it was given to them because of a great white chief, Lord De La Ware, they not only became reconciled to it, but took it as a compliment, for they always liked to be named after distinguished people.

In some portions of the county they were more thickly settled than in others, being quite numerous along the Great Valley, and they were quite sparsely settled west of White Clay Creek. In

99

other parts of the county they were quite evenly distributed. They usually located their wigwams in clusters, the numbers in each cluster varying according to circumstances, and when there were a considerable number of them together they were called an Indian town. One of these towns stood in Upper Oxford Township, and another near the Baptist Church, in London Britain Township. Some of their paths leading from point to point have since become public roads. One of these paths led from Pequea, Lancaster County, to the headwaters of Chesapeake Bay, and ran along the ridge dividing the waters which flow into the Susquehanna from those which flow into the Delaware. This is now known as the Limestone Road, which name it has borne for a long period of time, having been mentioned in the records as a public road as early as 1731.

One of their villages was located near two fine springs in Wallace Township. When Daniel and Alexander Henderson, in 1733, purchased their lands, they promised that the burial ground should never be disturbed, and they and their children religiously kept the promise, but now this burial ground is a part of a cultivated field. It was shortly after Braddock's defeat that these Indians removed to that part of the State embraced in Crawford and Mercer Counties.

Some time previous to this time the Shawnese Indians made a settlement in Lancaster County, and after a time spread out into Chester County, they having a large town near the site of the village of Doe Run, and they also had a settlement in the vicinity of Steeleville, on Octoraro Creek.

Among the early tribes of Indians occupying the country bordering the Delaware River was one known as the Okehockings, the members of which tribe had their lodges on the banks of Ridley and Crum Creeks. By a warrant of a survey dated 10th month 15, 1702, it appears that a reservation of five hundred acres of land was granted this tribe near Williston, Chester County, the bounda-

ries of which reservation are shown on the map of the early settlements of the county. It is stated in the minutes of the commissioners of property, under date of 10th month 7th and 8th, 1702,
that the Ockanickon Indians had been removed from their old habitations before the proprietor's departure, by his order, and seated
by Caleb Pusey, Nicholas Pyle, Nathaniel Newlin and Joseph
Baker on the tract in Chester County formerly laid out by Griffith
Jones, but then vacant. The names of the chiefs of this tribe were
Pokkais, Sepopanny and Mattagooppa. Following is the warrant
of survey issued by the commissioners of property to the surveyor
of Chester County:

"Whereas, Pokias, Sepopawny, Mettagooppa and others of the
nation called Okehocking Indians, in Chester County, with their
families, upon their removal from their late settlements near Ridley and Crum Creeks, have, by the proprietor's order and appointment, been seated on another certain tract in the said county, and
on the said Ridley Creek, near the head thereof, formerly surveyed
to Griffith Jones, but by him left and acquitted, and now belonging
to the Proprietary; in which place the said Indians request we
would grant them a certain settlement, under sure metes and
bounds, to them and their posterity, in pursuance of the proprietor's engagement in that case, made before his departure, who
granted them, as it is creditably affirmed to us, five hundred acres
in the said place. These, therefore, are in pursuance of the said
grant, to authorize and require thee to survey and lay out to the
said Pokhais, Sepapawney, Mattagooppa, and others of the said
nation, called the Okehocking Indians, who were lately seated
lower down on the said creeks, and their relations, and to no other
whatsoever, the full quantity of five hundred acres of land in one
square tract, in such place within the aforesaid tract as the said
Indians shall desire; which said five hundred acres we do hereby
grant to the said Pokhais, Sepopawney, Mattagooppa and others of
the said nation called the Okehocking Indians, who were lately

seated as aforesaid, and to their relations, and to no other whatsoever; to take and to hold to them, the said Indians, for settlement, and to their posterity of the same nation of Indians (and to
no other) forever; provided, always, that the said Indians, nor any
of them, shall not give, grant or attempt to sell, or in any way dispose of any of the said five hundred acres of land hereby granted,
to any person whatsoever; but at such time as the said Indians
shall quit or leave the said place, it shall be surrendered to the
Proprietary without any further claim of the said Indians, or any
person whatsoever, by or under them, their title of procurements;
and make returns into the General Surveyor's office.

"Given under our hands and the seal of the Province, at Philadelphia, the 15th of the 10th month, 1702.

"EDWARD SHIPPEN,

"GRIFFITH OWEN,

"THOMAS STORY,

"JAMES LOGAN."

"To ISAAC TAYLOR, Surveyor of the County of Chester."

Five hundred acres were therefore surveyed in the southern
part of the present township of Williston, on the east side of Ridley
Creek, which the Indians occupied for a number of years, leaving
it, however, some time prior to 1737, the lands returning under the
grant to the Proprietary. The proprietary on August 1, 1737,
issued a warrant for the entire tract of five hundred acres abandoned by the Indians to Amos and Mordecai Yarnall, who divided
it between them, Amos taking 196 acres and allowance on the eastern and southern part, and Mordecai taking the remainder, about
276 acres and allowance. Surveys having been returned to the
surveyor's office, patents were granted to them January 29, 1738,
by Thomas Penn.

The famous treaty held or made between William Penn and
the Indians, under an elm tree no less famous than the treaty

itself, was at what is now called Kensington. It was formerly called by the Indians Shackamaxon, or Sachamaxing, Place of Kings, from Sakim, which in the Delaware language means king, or chief. It was held before the meeting of the assembly at Chester, December 4, 1682. The Indian tribes represented at this famous meeting were the Lenni-Lenape, living near the banks of the Delaware; the Mingoes, a tribe which sprang from the Iroquois, otherwise known as the Minguas, and settled at Conestoga, and the Shawnese, a southern tribe, which had removed to the Susquehanna, and which has a most interesting and tragic history.

At this treaty Tamminel announces, through an interpreter, to William Penn, that the nations are ready to hear him. Penn then made his speech, to which an Indian chief replied. Though the treaty then made cannot be found, yet some historians say there is evidence that it was committed to writing. The elm tree under which it was made was blown down in 1810. It was believed to be 283 years old, and was twenty-four feet in circumference. It has been made immortal in a painting by Benjamin West, a former resident of Chester County, whose grandfather was present at the making of the treaty. This was the first time Penn had met the Indian chiefs in council to make with them a firm league and friendship, which was never violated. Voltaire said of it that it was the only league between these nations and the Christians which was never sworn to and which was never broken.

To the Iroquois William Penn was known as "Onas," and to the Delawares as "Miquon," each word meaning quill or pen. However, according to Watson, the treaty under the great elm tree was not a treaty for lands at all, but a treaty of friendship, merely a great meeting for conference and pledge, in which presents were exchanged and mutual civilities extended from either side to the other and reciprocal promises of friendship and good will severally made. He then says that if this assumption of his be true it will account for the absence of any deed or written title to lands and prove that the alleged instrument of writing had no existence at that time, for it would have been wholly unnecessary.

Historians differ among themselves concerning many facts of interest regarding the relations of the whites with the Indians during the early days. One of these points of difference is in regard to the deeds of lands made by the Indians to William Penn, and they also occasionally differ in reference to the same deed. Some say that there was but one deed made by Indians to William Penn, but, however this may be, numerous deeds were executed by the Indians of lands to William Penn, the transactions being conducted either by Penn himself or by his agents. These deeds were often very indefinite as to the boundaries of the tracts sold to Penn, and in many cases the same tract was sold to Penn or his representatives several times by different tribes or bodies of Indians, Penn preferring to satisfy the claims of all who professed original ownership of the lands than to stand upon the rights he had acquired by previous purchases. It is not always easy to state whether the land described in one of these Indian deeds was or was not any portion of what is now Chester County. Some of them evidently covered the whole or a part of this county, others as evidently covered lands quite distant therefrom, and others may or may not have included some portion of the county.

The first deed to William Penn was dated July 15, 1682, ("according to English Accompt"), and conveyed lands east of the creek named in the deed, "Neshamonyes." These lands were a long distance above Philadelphia, and in Bucks County. This deed was confirmed by another made August 25, 1737, and is referred to here because it is known in history as the famous "Walking Purchase," about which there has been considerable difference of opinion as to the real grounds of dissatisfaction on the part of the Indians as to the advantage taken of them by the whites. But the merits of the discussion concern this history still less than does the purchase itself.

The next deed was made June 23, 1683, by King Tammanens,

the original "St. Tammany," to all his lands between Pemmapecka and Neshiminehs Creeks, and is remarkable for that reason, and also more particularly for the terms of the purchase, viz.: "For the consideration of so much wampum, so many guns, shoes, stockings, looking-glasses, blankets, and others goods as he, the said William Penn, shall please to give unto me."

Three other deeds were made on the same day to the same and perhaps to contiguous lands by other tribes or parties of Indians, because they had an interest in this land, to William Penn, and all upon the same terms, "For the consideration of so much wampum, etc., as he, the said William Penn, shall please to give us."

The first deed for lands lying on the Schuylkill River, which borders Chester County, was dated June 25, 1683, and was made by Wingebone, for himself and his heirs, "of all my lands lying on the west side of the Schuylkill River, beginning from the first falls of the same all along upon the said river and backward of the same so far as my right goeth," etc., "for so much wampum and other things as he shall please to give unto me."

The above is probably the first deed that conveyed to William Penn any portion of what is now Chester County, and that it did convey a portion of Chester County is probable for the reason that a line running backward from the Schuylkill River would have to run only a short distance before reaching the eastern limits of the county.

The next deed, made July 14, 1683, certainly covered a considerable portion of Chester County. It reads in part as follows:

"We, Secana and Icquoquehan, Indian Shackamakers, and right owners of the land lying between Manaiunk, als Schuylkill, and Macopanackhan, als Chester Rivers, do this 14th day of the fifth month, in the year, according to English account, 1683, hereby grant and sell all our right and title in the said lands, lying between the said rivers, beginning on the west side of Manaiunk, called Consohockhan, and from thence by a westerly line to the said river Macopanackhan, unto William Penn, proprietor and governor of the province of Pennsylvania, etc., his heirs and assigns, forever, for and in consideration of 150 fathoms of wampum, 14 blankets, 68 yards duffils, 28 yards stroud waters, 15 guns, 3 great kettles, 15 small kettles, 16 pair of stockings, 7 pair of shoes, 6 caps, 12 gimlets, 6 drawing knives, 15 pair of scissors, 15 combs, 5 papers of needles, 10 tobacco boxes, 15 tobacco tongs, 32 pounds of powder, 3 papers of beads, 2 papers of red lead, 15 coats, 15 shirts, 15 axes, 15 knives, 30 bars of lead, 18 glasses, 15 hoes, unto us in hand paid," etc.

Another deed was made on the same day for lands above the Schuylkill, and hence does not concern this work. The deed made July 30, 1685, by the Indians, Shakhoppoh, Secane, Malibore, and Tangoras, covered a considerable portion of Chester County. It reads in part as follows:

"We, Shakhoppoh, Secane, Malibor, Tangoras, Indian Sakamakers, and right owners of the lands lying between Macopanackan, als Upland, now called Chester River or Creek, and the river or creek of Pemapecka, now called Dublin Creek, beginning at the hill called Conshohockin, on the river Manaiunk, or Skoolkill, from thence extends in a parallel line to the said Macopanackan, als Chester Creek, by a southwesterly course, and from the said Conshohockin hill to the said Pemapecka, als Dublin Creek, by the said parallel line northeasterly, and so up along the said Pemapecka Creek so far as the creek extends, and so from thence northwesterly back into the woods, to make up two full days journey, so far as a man can go in two days from the said station of the said parallel line at Pemapecka, also beginning at the said parallel at Macopanackan, als Chester Creek, and so from thence up the said creek as far as it extends; and from thence northwesterly back into the woods to make up two full days' journey, as far as a man can go in two days, from the said station of the said parallel line at the said Macopanackan, als Chester Creek, for and in consideration of two

hundred fathoms of wampum, 30 fathoms of duffils, 30 guns, 60
fathoms of strawed waters, 30 kettles, 30 shirts, 20 gunbelts, 12
pair of shoes, 30 pair of stockings, 30 pair of scissors, 30 combs,
30 axes, 30 knives, 20 tobacco tongs, 30 bars of lead, 30 pounds of
powder, 30 awls, 30 glasses, 30 tobacco boxes, 3 papers of beads,
44 pounds of red lead, 30 pair of hawk's bells, 6 drawing knives,
6 caps, 12 hoes, and do by these presents grant, bargain and sell,
etc., all right, title and interest that we or any others shall or may
have—hereby renouncing and disclaiming forever any claim or pretense to the premises for us, our heirs, and sucecssors, and all other
Indians whatsoever".

Subsequently the following letter was sent out to the above-
named Indian kings by Thomas Holme, in reference to the proposed
marking out of the boundaries of the tract thus purchased:

"To my loving friends, Shakhoppah, Secaming, Maleboro, Tangoras, Indian kings, and to Maskeansho, Wawarrin, Tenoughan,
Tarrecka and Nesonliakin, Indian Sakamackers, and the rest concerned:

"Whereas, I have purchased and bought of you, the Indian
kings and sakamackers, for the use of Governor William Penn, all
your land from Pemapecka Creek, and so backward to Chesapeake
Bay and Susquehanna River, two days' journey, that is to say so
far as a man can go in two days, as under the hands and seals of
you the said kings, may appear; and to the end I may have a certain knowledge of the land backward, and that I may be enabled
and be provided against the time for running the said two days'
journey, I do hereby appoint and authorize my loving friend, Benjamin Chambers, of Philadelphia, with a convenient number of
men, to assist him, to mark out a westerly line from Philadelphia
to the Susquehanna, that so the said line may be prepared and
made ready for going the said two days' journey hereafter, when
notice is given to you that said kings or some of you, at the time
of going the said line; and I do hereby desire and require in the

name of our Governor Penn, that none of you, the said kings, sakamackers, or any other Indians whatsoever, that have formerly been
concerned in the above tracts of land, do presume to offer any interruption or hindrance of the marking of the said line, but rather I
expect your furtherance and assistance if occasion be herein; and
that you will be kind and loving to my said friend, Benjamin Chambers, and his company, for which I shall, in the Governor's behalf,
be kind and loving to you hereafter, as occasion may require. Witness my hand and a seal, this 7th day of the 5th month, called July,
being the fourth year of the reign of our great King of England,
and the eighth of our proprietary, William Penn's government.
A true copy of the original, by Jacob Taylor."

A diagram with the above shows a ground plot of the survey,
it going direct from Philadelphia city to a spot on the Susquehanna, about three miles above the mouth of Conestoga River, near
to a spot marked "fort demolished."

Another sale was made October 2, 1685, the lands conveyed
including a portion of Chester County. The deed referred to, so
far as it is necessary to quote from it, reads as follows:

"This Indenture witnesseth that we, Lare Packenah, Taree-
kham, Sickais, Pettquessitt, Tewis, Essenpenaick, Petkhoy Keke-
lappan, Feomus, Mackaloha, Mellconga, Wissa-Powey, Indian
Sachemakers, Right owners of all the lands from Quing Quingus,
called Duck Creek, unto Upland, called Chester Creek, all along by
the west side of Delaware River, and so between the said creeks
backwards as far as a man can ride in two days with a horse, for
and in consideration of these following goods to us in hand paid,"
etc.

Another deed and a very important one was made October
11, 1736, by eight Indian chiefs of the Onondagas, six chiefs of the
Senecas, four of the Oneidas, two of the Tuscaroras, and three of
the Cayugas, in order to finally settle the ownership to "All the
said river Susquehanna, with the lands lying on both sides thereof to

extend eastward as far as the head of the branches or springs which run into the said Susquehanna," to say nothing of those on the west side of the river, because they do not concern this history, and this is believed to be the last Indian deal made that in any way does concern this work. The lands thus sold may or may not have come within the present limits of Chester County; but they were certainly within the original limits, and to a considerable extent.

With reference to the mode of life and the places in Chester County frequented or occupied by the Indians, the following extract from a paper written by Philip P. Sharpless, of West Chester, who has given much thought to the habits of a race of men now lost to this eastern country, and who in his eighty-ninth year is now living in West Chester, is here presented as being authoritative and concise:

"In selecting a suitable place for his winter quarters, the Indian preferred a south laying land, near to a spring of good water, surrounded and sheltered by wood, and easily accessible to friendly neighbors by a common path.

"Such was the situation where West Chester now stands. On the south side of the town, within one or two hundred yards, ran the great path which left their hunting grounds on the Susquehanna at Peach bottom crossed over to the rapids of the Delaware. Near and on both sides of it are the sites of many of their villages. The Susquehanna was visited early in the spring by whole tribes on arriving of fish from southern waters, as was common at that season of the year; returning to the Delaware as the season advanced.

"The great path, which is still visible in some places, commences, so far as I know it, and is still well marked at that point, in a piece of woods on lands of the late Abraham Williams, formerly known as the southeast corner of the eighty acres. Passing nearly directly west, it enters the small woods formerly of Joshua Darlington, now (1888) belonging to William Smith, where it may

still be traced. Continuing west through the south side of the
Friends' Burial Company's Grounds, thence it passes between the
residences of Smedley and John Darlington. Continuing its westerly course, it now crosses over the hill onto the land of W. T.
Ingram, then to about fifty feet south of the gateway leading to
the dwelling of the late Emmor Davis, crossing the Birmingham
road north of Sconneltown school-house, it runs through the farm
of Paschal Hacker, thence onto the land of William Reid, still continuing the same course its route was up the road on Dr. Price's
farm in front of his greenhouses, and so on through George Little's
woods to the Brandywine, being nearly a straight line from where
it enters the land of Abraham Williams, until it reaches the creek
about one-half mile above the forks.

"On the sides of this great highway I can locate the sites of at
least twenty old camping grounds that have been occupied by the
Indians, not one of which is more than three miles from West Chester.   To find these locations they must be looked for after the
ground has been recently plowed or harrowed, whilst it is still free
from vegetation, and soon after a rain. When a field is in corn or
after it has been cut, it affords the best opportunity to ascertain
the location of an Indian camp, but an amateur, when in the midst
of a town site, will be often disappointed, because of his impatience
and his want of knowledge. He will look for arrow or spear points,
when these may have all disappeared, having been gathered and
sent away, while the spalls under his feet, the hammer, the knife,
or pieces of basin or other worked stone may surround without
attracting notice.

"A little practice with an expert will soon enable him to overcome this difficulty, if he have patience, and of this he will need a
good store, as it may be years before grass lands may be turned
into fallow grounds, and until this is done his labor will be in vain,
as most of the objects he is in search of are buried beneath the sod,
whilst the farmer has removed those that lay on the surface and
sent them away to help macadamize some road.

"There are four well-marked camping sites within the borough of West Chester. The first is in the southwest part, about one hundred yards west of the Philadelphia and West Chester railroad, where it crosses the borough line. The hill faces to the southeast, and the camp extends from top to foot of the same, covering about four acres.

"It is located near a spring of good water. On this ground I have found sixty or seventy arrow and spear points, and many of them have been carried away by others. Among those in my possession is one of black jasper, nearly perfect, made by a good workman, a hammer, several knives, one-half of a banner stone, and those used for heating in the fire to do their cooking with, besides the usual amount of spalls found around an old camp.

"The second camp is on a stream in the south part of the borough, between Darlington Street, extended, and New Street, and where it is proposed in the future to lay Nields Street, on the line between the lands of George Fitzsimmons, Albert Hall and others. On these lots I have picked up a broken red stone hammer, a broken pestle, an axe, a few arrow and spear points, and the usual amount of burned stone and spalls. Others have found here a part of a stone basin, a pestle, several stone ornaments, an axe, tomahawk, and other implements. Most of the ornaments have passed into the collection of Charles H. Pennypacker.

"Number three is on the same stream in the southwest corner of the borough, on the farm of Dr. Jacob Price, near the fine spring which he now uses for dairy purposes.

"The new house west of his barn is near the center of the camping ground. In the field I have found many reliques similar to those already described, and this camp, I think, must have exceeded either of the others in size or contained a greater number of inmates than they did.

"James A. Ingram, a former occupant of this farm, collected many fine specimens here, and still retains them in his cabinet.

This plot of ground is at present in grass. Between numbers two and three are several places.that have been temporarily occupied by the Indians, where their marks are not so distinct as in those named.

"To the north of number three in a lot belonging to M. B. Hickman, between Wayne and Brandywine Streets, and north of Price, around an excellent spring, have been found many good arrow points; but a more thorough examination will be required to ascertain how they came there. If a village stood there at any time, it must have been a small one.

"Number four is on the lands of Hoopes Bros. & Thomas, east of the old borough waterworks. It is undoubtedly the spring from which the savages obtained their supply of water. The center of their camp must have been near where the barn of the company now stands situated northwest of the road leading to the residence of William P. Marshall, and about two hundred yards northeast of the public park. On these grounds was found one of the most perfect stone axes I have ever seen, a hammer of red sandstone, many arrow points and the usual chert chips that mark the site of a camp. These grounds have long been under cultivation, and most of their treasures have been carried away; but there remains sufficient of waste material to mark it as a favorite dwelling place."

Alfred Sharpless, brother of Philip P. Sharpless, in a paper read before the Chester County Historical Society, November 19, 1897, mentions and describes an old Indian fort, which he says was located "less than half a mile above the forks of the Brandywine, on the west bank of the east branch" thereof. This old fort consists of a collection of rocks "at the brow of a sharp hill about eighty feet above the level of the creek, and not more than one hundred and fifty feet from it at the nearest point. * * * The old fort is formed by two or three large rocks that project from the hillside, covering a space about fifteen by twenty feet. Under these is a cave or space, varying in height from five feet to less than a foot, and extending back some twelve or fourteen feet. * * * No doubt this old fort was often a resting place and a shelter for parties of nomads as they passed to and fro between the Delaware and Susquehanna Rivers, as it could not have been far from their great pathway, and having convenient fording places in the vicinity. It may have been the site of many a sanguinary battle, of which we have no record, as the approach to it must always have been very difficult and dangerous to a storming party."

"The only tradition in relation to the fort that we have been able to obtain, comes down to us through one of the old inhabitants of the neighborhood. He states that an alarm came one morning and spread rapidly around among the neighbors that a party of Indians on the war path were coming down the creek road and soon was heard what appeared to be the screaming and yelling of a large party of savages. The neighbors hurriedly assembled with guns and pitchforks at the old fort, as the best place for defense. Later the cause of alarm proved to have come from a farmer's ox cart that was coming down the valley hills making a great screeching, the farmer having failed to grease the axle before starting in the morning. This is said to have been the last Indian scare in Chester County."

While the Delaware or Lenni-Lenape Indians were the only native occupants of the eastern part of Pennsylvania when the white men first settled upon it, yet there were other Indians that occasionally came into this region, sometimes making trouble not only for the Delawares but also for the whites. These were the confederated nations, known as the Five Nations, whose domain extended from Vermont to Lake Erie, and from Lake Ontario to the headwaters of the Delaware, Susquehanna and Alleghany Rivers. By the Delawares these Five Nations were called the Minguas or Mingoes; and by the French they were called the Iroquois. They were composed of the Onondagas, Cayugas, Oneidas, Senecas and Mohawks. In 1712 the Tuscaroras being expelled

from North Carolina were adopted into the family of the Five Nations, the confederation being thereafter called the Six Nations.

At some remote period the Lenni-Lenape Indians had been
conquered by the Five Nations, had been reduced to a state of
vassalage, had been compelled to acknowledge a condition of fealty
to their conquerors, which enabled them to hold their lands only
by permission, and which prevented them from engaging in war.
This was their status among other Indian tribes.when the white
people first visited them.   And although they were the permanent
occupiers of the soil on the shores of the Delaware, they were
frequently subject to intrusion on the part of the Five Nations, who
occupied portions of the country at their own pleasure.

When, therefore, these predatory incursions were indulged
in, there was always more or less apprehension on the part of
the Lenni-Lenapes and the whites.   The Indians with whom Penn
made his first and most famous treaty of friendship. were the peaceful Lenni-Lenapes, but in 1701 he made a treaty with the chiefs of
the Five Nations, and with the Indians from the Susquehanna and
the Potomac, and also with the chiefs of the Shawnese.   In course
of time the Delawares were able to throw off the yoke that had so
long galled them, and at a treaty of 1756 their great chief, Tedyuscung, compelled the chiefs of the Six Nations to acknowledge their
independence.

The Indians that lived latest in Chester County were removed
therefrom in 1757 to the valleys of the Wyoming and the Wyalus-
ing, on the Susquehanna. At the great treaty of St. Mary's in 1820
there were present about twenty chiefs of the Nanticokes, one of
whom was nearly ninety years old.

It is usually the great men of a tribe or nation that make its
history.   One of the great chiefs of the Delawares was Tedyuscung,
who frequently visited Philadelphia and eastern Pennsylvania
from 1750 to 1760.   Another great man among them was Isaac
Stille, who had a good education, had much good sense, was of good

morals and was a professing Christian. He had traveled all over the West and the Rocky Mountain region and had seen the "White Indians," who are said to have lived in the southwestern part of this country. In 1771 he moved into Buckingham County, where he collected together the scattered remnants of his tribe, and in 1775 led them far away to the Wabash country, where he said they would be free "from war and rum."

The Shawnese Indians came to Pennsylvania about 1698, desiring to settle among the Indians and whites of this province as strangers, the Conestoga Indians becoming security for their good behavior. They were also under the protection of the Five Nations, who had set Shakallamy over them as their chief.

The Indians claimed that after they had sold all their lands to William Penn, that is, all in Chester County, that he re-conveyed to them a tract one mile in width on each side of the Brandywine from its mouth up the west branch to its head—but that the writing was accidentally destroyed by the burning of a cabin. In 1706 at the request of the white inhabitants on the Brandywine, the commissioners of property purchased from the Indians their claim to these lands from the mouth of the creek up to a certain rock in the west branch, for the consideration of £100. The rock mentioned was in the line of Abraham Marshall's land, and also in the line of the Society tract purchased by Nathaniel Newlin.

Mr. Newlin soon afterward began disposing of his lands, and within six months had sold off about nine parcels, varying in size from 150 to 300 acres. Some of these parcels were located on the creek. The Indians immediately complained that Newlin was selling their lands; for they were still the owners of the land one mile in width on each side of the creek from the rock mentioned to the head of the creek. As no attention appears to have been paid to the claims of the Indians they carried their cause to the Provincial Assembly in the summer of 1725, and the account of the proceedings before the Assembly is so interesting that it is worth quoting entire:

"13th of 6 mo. 1725. The petition of divers inhabitants of the city of Philadelphia, setting forth that the Proprietary having purchased of the natives all the lands within certain bounds; and that the proprietary did afterward release back to some of the said natives a certain tract of land on the Brandywine, which said land is lately taken up and settled, to the great disturbance of said natives, and praying that this House would take the same into consideration; was read and ordered to be considered this afternoon.

"Then this House was given to understand that the Heads of the said Indian complainants desire to attend the House in person, to set forth their grievances. Ordered, that they wait on the House at three o'clock this afternoon with their interpreters.

"3 p. m., the House met.

"The Indians ordered to attend this afternoon, waited at the door desiring to be heard. Then chairs were placed for them, they were called in, and the Speaker, on behalf of the House, said: 'The House has had information that you have been with the Governor and Commissioners already. Have you received satisfaction?"

"Indians (by interpreter)—'We have not.'

"Speaker—'What it is, then, that you have to offer to the House?'

"Indians—'When William Penn came to this country, he settled a perpetual friendship with us, and after we sold him our country, he re-conveyed back a certain tract of land upon the Brandywine, for a mile on each side of said creek, which writing was, by the burning of a cabin, destroyed; but we all remember very well the contents thereof: That William Penn promised that we should not be molested whilst one Indian lived, grew old, and blind and died,—so another, to the third generation; and now it is not half the age of an old man since, and we are molested, and our lands surveyed out and settled before we can reap our corn off; and to our great injury, Brandywine Creek is so obstructed with

VIEW OF COATESVILLE, LOOKING EASTWARD.

dams, that the fish cannot come up to our habitations. We desire you to take notice that we are a poor people, and want the benefit of the fish, for when we are out hunting, our children with their bows and arrows, used to get fish for their sustenance, therefore, we desire that those dams be removed, that the fish may have their natural course.'

"Speaker—'How did you understand that writing to be? That you should enjoy that land forever?'

"Indians—'Not only we, but all the Indians understood it to be theirs as long as the waters ran down the creek.'

"Speaker—'Have you anything more to say?'

"Indians—'No; but if you hear us not we shall be obliged to come again next spring.'

"Speaker—'The House is inclined to do you all the favor that lies in their power.'

"Indians—'We hope we are all friends, and desire to continue so, as long as we draw breath.'

"Then the Indians withdrew, and after some debate it was ordered that Francis Rawle, John Kearsley, and John Swift, go to James Logan, one of the commissioners of property, and inform him of the substance of said petition, and matter complained of by the Indians; who being returned report that the said commissioner shows a very hearty inclination to accommodate the affair with the Indians, and although their right does not appear so clear, yet they are possessed of such strong notions of it, that there is no divesting them of it; and, therefore, he is ready to do what he can to quiet their complaints, by granting the person who possesses the said lands other lands in the stead thereof.

"Ordered that Francis Rawle and John Kearsley draw up an address to the Governor, on behalf of the Indians. Adjourned.

"6th mo. 14th day, 1725. The House met, etc.

"Then the members appointed yesterday in the afternoon, to draw up an address to the Governor, on behalf of the Indians,

8

brought in the same, which was read and agreed to. Ordered, That the same be transcribed, and then the House adjourned to two, p. m.

"Two o'clock, p. m. The House met, etc.

"The address to the Governor, on behalf of the Indians, according to order, being transcribed, is as follows, viz.: 'The Address of the Representatives of the said Province, in General Assembly met: May it please the Governor, as next to Divine Providence, the peace, happiness, and quietness which this Province first enjoyed, was owing to the wise conduct of the Hon. William Penn, our Proprietary and Governor, by procuring a good friendship betwixt him and the native Indians at his first arrival here, so by diligent care in cultivating and preserving the like friendship, the great happiness of peace hath been hitherto enjoyed among us, when divers of the neighboring colonies have been obnoxious to the insults of the barbarous Indians, to the great damage of their countries; and as the Governor's care and indefatigable pains upon all occasions, has been very conspicuous to that good end, this House do address themselves on an unhappy dissatisfaction some Indians are under (who have always lived very peaceable with the inhabitants of this province) from an opinion that they are likely to be dispossessed of some lands they had long enjoyed on the river Brandywine, as also for being deprived of the benefit of fishing on the said river; all which they have by personal complaint laid before this House. And the House having taken into serious consideration the fatal consequences it may be to the peace of this Province, represented the same to James Logan, one of the Commissioners of Property, who has given the House ample satisfaction of his intentions to accommodate the difference with the said Indians. And we are fully satisfied (were it not for a purchase made of some part of these lands by Nathaniel Newlin, and his too wilful resolution to hold and settle the same), this part of this difference relating to the pretended encroachments on their lands would be immediately silenced. And notwithstanding this obstacle, we have reason to believe that Nathaniel Newlin will, in a very short time, become sensible that it will be as much to his own private interest as to the Province in general, to be more condescending in this affair.

" 'But, whereas there are dams or wares which do obstruct the passage up of fish to the place where the said Indians are settled, without the verge of this government, this House doth humbly request the Governor, that he will be pleased to exert his authority, in such manner as he shall think proper, for quieting and satisfying the said Indians, and preserving the ancient friendship between them and the inhabitants of this Province; and herein we also have that confidence as to hope that the Government of New Castle, Kent and Sussex, will so far think it conducive to their peace and quiet, that they will not fail to do what is necessary on their part, for the full settling and composing this dissatisfaction.

" 'August 14, 1725. Signed by the order of the House.

" 'WILLIAM BILES, Speaker.'

"Ordered, That Thomas Chandler and Elisha Gatchell present the same to the Governor; who return and report that they had delivered the said address according to order, and that the Governor perused the same, and said he was entirely of the opinion of the House, and that he and his Council would use their utmost endeavors to satisfy these Indians, and that he was going down to New Castle, where he would order the persons concerned to move those dams complained of, which, if they did not do, he would give orders to the King's attorney, to prosecute them, and oblige them thereunto by process of law."

The claims of the Indians not being adjusted to their satisfaction they again sought an interview in the spring of 1726, and the following proceedings were had:

"3d month 31st, 1726. The House met, etc.

"The Indians (who claim certain rights on Brandywine Creek)

came to wait upon the House, and by a member sent in a paper they received from James Logan, and likewise a message that they were not satisfied therewith, and therefore made further application to this House for redress, which paper being read, the House went into a debate thereon, and after some time referred the further consideration thereof until to-morrow, and then the House adjourned until to-morrow morning at nine o'clock.

"4th month 1st, 1726, 9 a. m. The House met, etc.

"The House proceeded further on the consideration of the affair relative to the Indians.

"Ordered, That Evan Owen go to the commissioners of property and desire some of them to attend, in order to inform the House what progress hath been made with Nathaniel Newlin toward an accommodation; who returned and reported that he spoke with James Logan, one of the commissioners of property, according to order, and that he was ready to attend the House in order to acquaint them with what had been done in that affair; who, being called in, produced an Indian deed, dated 1685, signed by thirteen Indian kings, which conveys all the lands from Duck Creek to Upland Creek, alias Chester Creek, and as far back as a man could ride on horseback in two days, and says he finds no footsteps of any re-conveyance, neither in the land office nor upon record, but that in 1705 the Indians laid claim to all the lands from the mouth of Brandywine up the west branch to the head, in breadth a mile on each side of that branch; and afterward the commissioners of property purchased of the Indians all the lands from the mouth of Brandywine Creek up to a certain rock by Abraham Marshall's land for the sum of one hundred pounds, seventy-three pounds and eight shillings of which was then paid to their chiefs, and the remainder they paid yesterday, and the chiefs of the Indians signed a release, but said they wanted some instrument given to them that they might know what was theirs and be secure in it. But the commissioners told them it was not at this time in their power to make them any grant of the said lands, but that they should not be disturbed in their quiet possession thereof, neither by Nathaniel Newlin, nor by any other person. That the commis. sioners had told Nathaniel Newlin that it was in vain for him to pretend to that land, let the disappointment be what it would, so long as the Indians laid claim to the same and would continue upon it; that after the Indians came up last year and made the complaint, and a re-conveyance was generally reported to have been given to the Indians, he went down to Chester and took certificates of all those who were reported to have seen and known of such a writing; which certificates being produced and read in the House, none of which did amount to any certainty as to what that writing did contain; but since the Indians had an imperfect idea of it, and a strong resolution to hold it, the commissioners used such means as they thought most likely to satisfy them and continue them in the quiet possession of their claims, and for that end said they had agreed and accommodated the matter with Nathaniel Newlin as far as was in their power to do at present, and then withdrew.

"Then the House, after some debate, was of the opinion that Nathaniel Newlin be sent for to give some further assurance that what is done by the paper delivered yesterday, that he will not molest the said Indians in their claims.

"Ordered, That John Wright send a letter that the House require his attendance to-morrow morning, and then the House adjourned till 3 p. m.

"4th mo., 2d.—The House met, etc., adjourned to 3 p. m.

"3 p. m.—The House met, Nathaniel Newlin not attending, according to the expectation of the House, after some debate a motion was made and the question put that if Nathaniel Newlin come not to town this evening he be sent for by the sergeant-at-arms, and that an order be forthwith issued under the Speaker's hand, and the sergeant be dispatched therewith this evening. Carried in the affirmative. Adjourned till 9 a. m.

"4th mo., 3d, 9 a. m.—The House met.   The sergeant-at-arms reports that Nathaniel Newlin came to town last evening and will attend the House this morning.

"The House being informed that Nathaniel Newlin attended, he was called in, and said that he expected the value, and not the quantity only of land, in lieu of that the Indians claimed of his; and that he was to meet the commissioners of property this afternoon, and then doubted not that they should settle that affair to the satisfaction of the House, and withdrew, and then the House adjourned till 3 o'clock this afternoon.

"3 p. m.—The House met, etc.   Nathaniel Newlin attended, and being called in delivered on the table a paper subscribed with his hand, doth declare and promise that neither he nor his heirs will, by any means, disturb or molest the Indians in their possessions or claims.   Then, after some debate thereon, it was

"Resolved, That the Indians be sent for and the contents of the said paper be explained to them and inquiry made whether it be satisfactory to them.

"Ordered, That John Wright and Samuel Hollingsworth acquaint them thereof, that they may attend forthwith; who return and report that they have been with the Indians, and that they are now attending with their interpreters, who, being called in, the said paper was explained to them by their interpreters, and they declared that they were well satisfied therewith, and they desired that the said paper might remain among the records of this House and a copy thereof be given to them.

"Ordered, That a copy be made out accordingly and delivered to them, and the original lodged in the House, which was done accordingly.

"And the Indians further said that they had been very much disturbed in their minds, but that now they were perfectly easy, since they found that this House would stand by them and see them righted.

"Then Nathaniel Newlin was called in and acknowledged the said writing to them; so they shook hands together and parted fully reconciled, and then the House adjourned."

From this time on until 1729 peace appears to have hovered over the Brandywine; but in the latter year difficulties broke out again, and the Indian chief, Checochinican, under date of June 24, wrote to Patrick Gordon, Governor of Pennsylvania at that time, the following letter:

June 24, 1729.

Honoured Governeur:

It is with regret of mind that I take this opportunity of laying our great grievances before your consideration, hoping that you will be pleased to take care and protect us from any wrongs and injuries done me and our people, whom in the behalf of I now write. In time past we sold our interest to William Penn (our brother); he was pleased to grant us a wrighting for the creek of Brandywine, up to the head thereof, which said wrighting by some accident was lost, with all the land a mile wide of the creek on each side, which afterward we disposed of so far up as to a certain known rock in the said creek, it being in the line of the land belonging to one Abraham Marshall, and of late to the great prejudice and disquiet of us, a people that has done and still desires to do, to continue in peace and love and be as one heart and soul with William Penn and his people, the land has been unjustly sold, whereby we are reduced to great wants and hardships, notwithstanding in the year 1726 application was made to the assembly for relief in that case, and a wrighting was given by Nathaniel Newlin that neither the said Nathaniel Newlin, to whom some of the land was sold, nor his heirs would anyways disturb or molest us in the free and peaceable enjoyment thereof, but contrary to the same it has been sold, and greatly disquieted us; nay, we have been so much interrupted that we have been forbid so much as to make use of timber growing thereon for the convenience of building some cabins, and further, that the town at the head of Brandywine is surveyed to one James Gibbons and many more, and now has an assurance of a conveyance of the same from the commissioners of property, as he himself says, by James Steel, the which grievances we here take freedom to lay before your consideration, hoping that nothing will be wanting more now to cultivate and preserve a good and lasting friendship between us and the descendants of our brother, William Penn, who had shown their love and care so particularly to us as to give it so principally in charge, and as nothing has yet appeared to give us the least umbridge that our cases as before represented will be always neglected. We take freedom to lay it before your further consideration, and subscribe myself your sincere friend and brother.

N. B.—James Logan promised to me that James Gibbons nor anybody else should never have a confirmation thereof, nor any other person within our claim."

Nathaniel Newlin, who seems to have given the Indians so much trouble on the Brandywine, died in 1729. The settlement of the lands went on without apparent interruption by or from the complaints of the Indians, and they not many years afterward removed from the county, when all difficulty growing out of their claims came to an end. The location of the town "surveyed out to James Gibbons," mentioned in the letter, just quoted, is believed to have been about where the "Indiantown Schoolhouse" stands in Wallace Township.

The last of the Lenni-Lenape Indians of Chester County died in 1802, in the person of Indian Hannah. She had her wigwam for many years upon the Brandywine, and was accustomed to travel about a good deal, selling baskets, etc. On such occasions she was often followed by her dog and pigs, and at the time of her death was nearly one hundred years old. She possessed a proud and lofty spirit to the last, hated black people and scarcely brooked the lower class of whites. She often spoke emphatically of the wrongs of her race, and feelingly of their misfortunes, and bestowed her affections on them to the last days of her life. A certain individual, visiting her cabin on the farm of Humphrey Marshall, thus expressed his emotion upon seeing where she had lived in her later years:

"Was this the spot where Indian Hannah
    Was seen to linger, weary, worn with care?
Yes—that mute cave was once the happy home
    Of Hannah, last of her devoted race;
But she, too, now has sunk into the tomb,
    The briars and thistles wave above the place."

Her family consisted of Andrew, Sarah, Jimmy and herself, and she was the "Last of the Lenape." As she grew old she left her wigwam and lived with those who were friendly to her, and at length, on the opening of the poor-house of Chester County, she became an inmate of that institution, the only representative of Newlin Township, and there she died March 20, 1802.

CHAPTER III.

GEOLOGY.

CHAPTER III.

IN this work there is no attempt made to treat of the geology
of Chester County in an exhaustive manner. Such a thing could
not be done for want of space, and, besides, it is only the profes-
sioual geologist that can do such a work in a creditable and satisfactory manner. All, therefore, that will be attempted is to
summarize the leading facts and features of this interesting topic
in such a manner as may lead those who may read this chapter, and
who have not given much thought to the geology of their county,
to turn their attention in that direction and thus become more particularly informed.

Chester County lies principally within what is known as the
Atlantic slope district, which lies between the tide waters of the
Delaware River and the Susquehanna River and the southeast base
of the range of hills known as South Mountain. All of this county
which lies south of the valley, comprising more than half of its
area, is composed of rocks belonging to the primary stratified
group. These rocks consist chiefly of gneiss, but there is a belt of
mica and talc-slate connected with the limestone of the valley,
which belt bounds the gneiss on the north and west.

This limestone valley is the most remarkable feature of the geology of the county, and as it divides the county into two al- most equal portions, it will first be treated.   It is a perfectly straight valley, running nearly east and west through the county, but is inclined slightly toward the northeast and south- west, the divergence being about 18 degrees.   This valley is two miles wide at the Schuylkill River, on the Montgomery County line, which width it practically maintains toward the westward about half across the county, and then tapers to about one mile in width at the Lancaster County line.   This valley separates the northern from the southern townships.   The strata which occupy this Chester County, or Downingtown Valley, are what some geologists have named the Siluro-Cambrian Limestones, and they dip generally from 30 degrees to 50 degrees southward; but small anticlinal rolls run diagonally across their general strike, and the white marble strata, which are confined to the southern edge of the valley, stand almost perfectly vertical. There are other areas of this limestone, lying mainly to the south of this principal valley, in West Marlborough and London Grove Townships.

The North Valley Hill is made by the Potsdam sandstone, No. 1, rising northward from beneath the lowest limestones and spreading in sheets and patches over a considerable gneiss re- gion, embracing Honeybrook, East and West Nantmeal, West Vincent, East and West Pikeland, Charlestown, Upper Uwchlan, East and West Brandywine, and parts of West Caln and Sands- bury Townships; and it is plain that the fundamental gneiss area now exposed was formerly entirely covered by the Potsdam quartzite and the overlying limestone.

The South Valley Hill, on the contrary, is the edge of a low tableland, composed (1) of a belt of magnesian-mica slate; also vertical or dipping at the highest angle southward, apparently in contact and conformity with and over the marble beds of the south

edge of the valley, but possibly overturned and beneath the marble, in which latter case the valley is a synclinal trough, and the
slates south of it are equivalent to the quartzite north of it, or else
a fault runs along the south edge of the valley. The belt of South
Valley Hill slate is only two miles wide at the Schuylkill end,
widens westward to three miles at West Chester, four and a half
miles at the west branch of the Brandywine, and then spreads over
East and West Fallowfield, Highland, Londonderry, Upper and
Lower Oxford, and East and West Nottingham Townships into
Lancaster County. (2) A belt of older and newer gneisses and
mica-schists occupy all the townships to the south and east.
Slight areas of limestone, however, occur in this belt near West
Chester, Doe Run, Kennett Square, Avondale, Landenburg, etc.;
and Potsdam quartzite seems to be observed around London Grove
and at points on the Delaware State line. A long range of serpentine separates the two belts in East Goshen and Willistown
Townships, and another still more extensive serpentine belt
ranges along the Maryland line into Lancaster County and car-
ries deposits of chrome iron sand. A trap dyke enters from Delaware County at the south edge of the slate belt, and extensive out-
spreads of trap boulders occur along the Berks County boundary
in the north, other local exposures of trap being numerous in various parts of the county. Between the Schuylkill River and French
Creek the country is wholly of mesozoic formations, sandstone
and shale, and in the tunnel at Phœnixville through these rocks a
large collection of fossil plants and reptiles was made by Dr. C. M.
Wheatley. Copper, lead and zinc veins have long been mined
to a small extent along the contact line of the mesozoic and gneissic
rocks. The large magnetic iron mines of Warwick connect
with both trap and new red sandstone rocks, but really belonging
to the underlying azoic floor, are still worked. Small quantities
of brown hematite ore have also been obtained from the valley
limestones. The white marble quarries are numerous, but are
none of them large.

The above is a brief summary of the geology of the county by Prof. J. P. Lesley, who, together with Dr. Persifor Frazer, is the best authority on this subject. They must both be consulted by any one who would become tolerably familiar with the scientific and useful features of the geology of the county without themselves making original investigations.

For purposes of convenience of description and a clearer understanding of this important subject it is customary to divide the county into five sections, as follows:

1. The Southern Gneiss region.
2. The Mica-slate region.
3. The Downingtown Valley region.
4. The Northern Gneiss region.
5. The New Red Sandstone region.

The Southern Gneiss region has a general elevation above the level of the sea of about 400 feet, below which general elevation its streams have cut many valleys and ravines to a depth of from 100 to 200 feet, which valleys and ravines are often bounded by steep and rocky slopes. The northern boundary of this southern gneiss region is a line nearly straight, extending east-northeast and passing by West Chester. To the north of this line is a belt of hydro-mica-schist, and south of it spreads a country of syenite rocks, feldspar-porphyry rocks, horneblendic gneiss, micaceous schists, chlorite-schists and quartzite beds. Over this region are to be found patches of serpentine and crystalline limestone, beds of impure limestone, pure kaolin, and often an abundance of corundum. According to Prof. Frazer these rocks were originally sediments of mud, sand and gravel, their real stratification being visible wherever they are quarried.

"Infinitely numerous and rapid variations of constituent character, texture, hue and crystalline contents make the study of these rocks extremely difficult in a structural sense. There are no key rocks to mark geological horizons, and so large a portion of

WILLIAM WAYNE.

the upland is cultivated that the exposures along all the valleys cannot be traced across and identified with those of another valley only a few miles distant."

Without going into a detailed description of the various geological formations, it may be stated that Prof. H. D. Rogers divides this southern gneiss region, which is now passing under review, into three belts, as follows:

1. A northern anticlinal, hard gneiss belt, on which West Chester stands.

2. A southern monoclinal, hard gneiss belt, on which Philadelphia stands

3. The middle synclinal, soft gneiss and mica-slate belt, separating the other two belts.

The prevailing varieties of the northern belt of the southern gneiss region are as follows:

1. Massive feldspathic gneiss, some of it micaceous, some of it like stratified syenite, sometimes porphyroidal, and very much like that at the falls of the Schuylkill. Dark, hard, hornblendic feldspar gneiss, thinly laminated and strongly striped when viewed in transverse sections. In this belt feldspar is in excess; mica is next in abundance, generally black and in minute scales. Hornblende appears mostly in the upper beds.

2. The southern gneisses are usually gray and bluish, finely laminated, metamorphosed strata of white, chalky feldspar, white or transparent quartz, and black or dark brown mica in small plates. The next commonest variety is a dark-bluish gray or greenish black gneiss, hornblende or quartz or a little feldspar. A third common variety is a light gray micaceous quartz, some beds so made up of minute quartz grains as to be whetstones. A fourth variety of coarser gray micaceous gneiss beds, with a preponderance of mica in rather large flakes, and less feldspar and quartz, is unstratified with the other varieties, and makes a transi-

9

tion between common gneiss and common mica-slate. The more micaceous the gneiss the more garnets it contains.

3. The middle or micaceous belt contains four noticeable varieties of rock, as follows:

1. Garnetiferous micaceous gneiss.
2. Wavy, contorted mica schist.
3. Hornblendic gneiss beds, or hornblendic schists.
4. Whetstone schists.

This fourth variety is a schistose, gray, fine-grained mixture of granular quartz and minute mica scales, a kind of whetstone of many layers, breaking up into long, narrow chunks with smooth sides and very ragged ends, like rotten wood.

The most important kinds of rock for economic purposes in this Southern Gneiss section are the serpentine, hydro-mica slates, limestones, sandstones and syenites. The Laurentian syenite areas south of the Chester Valley are the eastern area, which is a continuation of that found in Delaware County, and extends through Easttown, Willistown and East Goshen Townships; an area at the junction of the two branches of the Brandywine, in East Bradford and Pocopson Townships; an area extending through the central portion of Kennett Township into New Garden Township, south of the Philadelphia and Baltimore Central Railroad and Kennett Square, and fourth, a small area bordering the Delaware State line in the south part of Kennett Township; but there is some doubt as to whether this last area belongs to the Laurentian system of rocks.

There are three principal areas of sandstone-quartz, as follows:

1. An area a short distance north of Dilworthtown, along the road to Thornbury postoffice.

2. A small area on the Baltimore Central Railroad, between Norway postoffice and Kennett Square, in Kennett Township, and

3. A larger belt extending through East Marlborough Township into London Grove and West Marlborough Townships.

Limestones exist in so many places that it would be scarcely worth while to attempt to enumerate them all. The Hydro-Mica. Schists belt is well defined from the Delaware County line to Brandywine Creek. Serpentine is found in a large number of places, and is of exceeding value, being used in the construction of many prominent public buildings in various parts of the country, among them the West Chester State Normal School building.

The northern border of the gneiss region is the southern border of the belt of Talc-Mica-Schist, or Hydro-Mica-Schist region, which outcrops along the southern slope and summit of the South Valley Hill and spreads out over the southwestern townships. The northern edge of this region runs along the foot of the hill in contact with the valley limestone or marble.

"The geological relationship of the dark mica belt to the gneiss region south and east of it is not understood by anyone. All that can be affirmed is that the Mica-Slate is of later age and overlies the gneiss. * * * The geological relationship of the dark Mica Slate to the Valley limestone is also in dispute." Both Professor Rogers and Professor Frazer place the mica slate formation beneath the Valley Limestone formation. The former makes it the base of the Palaeozoic system, unconformably resting on the Azoic or Hypozoic gneiss system. But the arguments in favor of these positions are too extensive and intricate for insertion in this work.

The Valley Limestone region is the most striking feature of the geology of the county. The region itself is fifty-five miles in length, extending both eastward and westward beyond the limits of the county. Its eastern termination is at Willow Grove, Montgomery County, and its western end is at Quarryville, Lancaster County. It extends in almost a perfectly straight line from east to west, its direction being about 18 degrees north of east. Its greatest breadth is only two miles, east of Downingtown, and again west of Willow Grove. At Coatesville it is little more than a mile wide, and it tapers rapidly into Lancaster County.

Two opinions are prevalent among geologists as to the geological features of this remarkable limestone valley. Professors Rogers and Frazer regard it as a long, straight, deep basin of limestone, with its northern side sloping southward at angles varying from 30 degrees to 60 degrees, and its southern side turned vertical, or even overturned a little, so as to make the beds on that side of the trough or basin dip from 80 degrees to 90 degrees southward.

Mr. Hall, on the contrary, considers it a monoclinal valley, the whole mass of limestone dipping southward beneath the talc-mica-schists of South Valley Hill.

But there appears to be no difference of opinion as to the age of this deposit. Different geologists have given different names to this formation, but it is sufficient here to say that all of them agree in considering it the same as the Upper Cambrian limestone of Sedgwick, the Trenton limestone of the New York survey, the Lower Silurian of Murchison, and the Siluro-Cambrian of Sterry Hunt. It is the Knoxville limestone of the South and the Magnesian limestone of the West.

It overlies the Potsdam sandstone, which rises from beneath it to form the North Valley Hill, and also appears in anticlinal ridges through it east of the Schuylkill. Professor Frazer shows that this Valley limestone lies on Potsdam sandstone from the Schuylkill to near Coatesville; that here for a short distance thin mica-schist layers come in between the limestone and sandstone, and that west of Pomeroy and all the way to Quarryville, Lancaster County, no sandstone underlies the limestone, but instead the limestone rests on the feldspathic gneiss beds, gneissic mica-schists, etc.

In closing a long, detailed description of the Valley limestone, very interesting and valuable, but occupying too much space for insertion here, Professor Rogers says:

"If, while inspecting the geological map of the State to assist our conceptions, we lift away in imagination the superficial deposits of mesozoic red shale and sandstone concealing a part of the older rocks of the Atlantic slope, we shall perceive this sinking and dying out of the northeastern and southwestern groups and anti-clinals much more obviously.

"It is to this fortunate abatement in amount of vertical uplift of the crust in the district between the Delaware and the Susque-hanna that Pennsylvania is indebted for the inestimable advantage above her sister States to the northeast and southwest of so re-markable an extension southward, or toward the tide, of her fertile and iron-yielding Auroral limestone; and it is to the same cause that she owes her inexhaustible basins of anthracite, nearer to the seaport markets by very many miles than any of the other Appa-lachian coal fields."

Perhaps, however, Professor Rogers would not have said "in-exhaustible basins of anthracite" had he been writing at the pres-ent time.

The Northern Gneiss region is fourth in order of these divi-sions. The northeastern boundary of this northern gneiss region is a gently curving line commencing at the eastern point near Val-ley Forge, passing Wheatley's lead mine, near Pickering Creek. which it crosses at Kenzie's mill, and then passes by the little vil-lage of Kimberton. It then goes nearly straight to Coventry vil-lage, crosses French Creek about two miles northeast of Kimberton, and follows the north side of this valley to Coventry, except for a short distance.

The northwest boundary of the gneiss is traceable from the sources of Pine Creek southwestward along the southern base, first of the eastern spur of Welsh Mountain to Springfield, and thence along the base of the main Welsh Mountain over the Lancaster line north of the little village of Cambridge to within two miles of the western end of the ridge.

The southern limit of the northern belt commences at the east branch of the Brandywine, and running almost due westward fol-lows the south side of the south branch of Indian Run, and after crossing the west branch of the Brandywine it extends along the south edge of the valley cf Two-log Run, beyond which it crosses the county line about a mile and a half south of the village of Cambridge, when it turns northward, and one mile further it again turns westward across the Pequea and runs for three miles further toward the west end of Welsh Mountain to unite with the northwest boundary of the same area of gneiss.

In this Northern Gneiss region there is a great deal of iron ore, which is usually found in a deep, narrow trough, confined between steeply dipping beds of gneiss, or between a hill of granite on the one side and moderately steep southeast dipping strata of the red sandstone on the other, within or behind which no ore is ever found.

Brown hematite iron ore is found in West Pikeland and West Vincent Townships, in the valley of Pickering Creek, and there are other deposits in the vicinity of Yellow Springs which have been developed by mining.

The Mesozoic Red Sandstone region is the last of the five divisions of the county. Of this Mesozoic system it may be said in a general way that it embraces the great division of stratified rocks which lies between the Palaeozoic system on the one hand, lying below the Mesozoic, and the Kainozoic system on the other, which lies above the Mesozoic. The Mesozoic formation contains the fossils which belong to the Middle Ages of geologic time.

According to Professor Rogers this Mesozoic Red Sandstone region has nothing to do with the Old Red Sandstone of Scotland, but consists of sediments deposited after all the Palaeozoic formations (including the Coal measures) had been elevated and folded into what are now the Appalachian and Alleghany Mountains. Then an arm of the sea or ocean stretched across New Jersey, and through Bucks, Montgomery, Chester, Lancaster, York and Adams Counties in Pennsylvania, into Maryland and Virginia, in which arm or estuary many thousands of feet of stratified mud and sands were deposited, which Professor Rogers named Mesozoic Red Sandstone, because they were formed in the Middle Age of geologic time.

But it is believed by geologists that the absence of limestone and sandstone along the edge of the Mesozoic rocks in Chester County indicates that an age of erosion elapsed after the uplift of the continent and before the first Mesozoic sediments began to fill this estuary. If this be correct, then during this age of erosion this estuary could not have been under water. And the first sediments deposited in this estuary after it had become established by the invasion of the sea, were shore gravels or conglomerates, derived from the gneiss country on either side. Then over these conglomerates there were deposited many thousand feet of fine sand and mud, in alternate layers, until the estuary was filled from shore to shore, or from the Philadelphia gneiss hills to the Reading hills, and along the south foot of the South Mountains in York and Adams Counties. This latter species of conglomerates does not anywhere appear in Chester County.

The strange fact that these Mesozoic sand and mud deposits are not horizontal has caused a good deal of perplexity to geologists. The dip is constant to the north-northwest, all the way up to within ten miles of Reading, from Norristown. The explanation coming nearest, perhaps, to the truth, is that which assumes a series of faults, which repeat the stratification at intervals across the belt. While the composition of this Mesozoic sandstone is not by any means of a uniform or homeogeneous nature, yet it is from this material that many beautiful brown sandstone buildings have been erected in cities.

Professor Frazer thus describes the boundary line of this Mesozoic formation in Chester County:

"Passing in a gentle meadering line generally following the road from Valley Forge in Schuylkill Township to Pickering postoffice in Charlestown Township, for two-thirds of that distance, then branching to the northwestward it cuts the township of East Pikeland in almost equal parts by a line deviating but little from straight. It cuts off the northeast end of West Vincent Township,

following up the creek dividing East and West Vincent Townships, it passes then the lower end of South Coventry Township a
short distance to the south of Pughtown and into Warwick, where,
having similarly skirted Knauertown, it is prolonged in a narrow
strip between the dolerite region and the mica-schists south of
French Creek. This narrow strip does not pass the county line,
but dies away, being cut into by the trap and schists a very short
distance west of St. Mary's. The boundary of the larger mass
skirts the above-mentioned dolerite area, makes an abrupt angle
at the point of the thin neck which projects northeast of Harmonyville, incloses the latter hamlet and passes west almost to the
county line, when it suddenly turns, being met by a mass of
Primal, and alters its course to one east of north for a couple of
miles, turns abruptly again and passes into Berks County in a
westwardly course."

It may be remarked in this connection that the principal
exhibitions of trap are for some reason perhaps not yet known to
geologists, confined to the areas occupied by Mesozoic rocks. "In
the midst of the open rolling country of red shale and sandstone
rise high, isolated hills of trap, the eroded outcrops of outbursts
of igneous rocks along cracks which go down to great depths
beneath the floor of older rocks to some profounder reservoir of
lava now extinct, but similar to that which at the present time
underspreads the western part of the United States, feeding active
volcanoes and geysers, and producing earthquakes and fractures
of the crust of the earth. Ancient volcanoes and geysers do not
seem to have existed on the Atlantic border, but outbursts of lava
took place through and between the layers of Mesozoic strata, and
these now constitute the trap hills of the Mesozoic region."

Another remark is appropriate in this connection, and that
is that the trap rocks are of insignificant size in the Gneiss region.
This is explained by the fact that the gneiss country afforded no
facility for wide fissures, while the Mesozoic strata could be lifted

like the lid of a box, and would thus allow of any amount of out-flow. But inasmuch as some of these Mesozoic traps are fre-quently overflows, they must have occurred after lower deposits had been made, and then the upper Mesozoic strata were deposited upon the trap.

MINERALOGY.

It would be a difficult matter to present a better outline of the minerals to be found within the lists of Chester County than that prepared by Dr. George G. Groff, a graduate of the West Chester State Normal School, first president of the Alumni Association of that school, later Professor of Natural Science in the same institu-tion, and at present Professor of Organic Science in Bucknell Uni-versity, Lewisburg, Pa., and which was published in Futhey & Cope's History of Chester County in 1881. That outline or list is, therefore, incorporated in this work. It is as follows:

THE MOST COMMON MINERALS. ORES AND ROCKS OF CHESTER. COUNTY, PENNSYLVANIA.
MINERALS.

Quartz.—Hardness, 7; white, red, blue, yellow; luster, glassy; brittle; form, six-sided crystals and massive; breaks irregularly; composition, silica (SiO); common in all parts of the county; cuts glass readily; infusible; the most common of all our minerals.

Chalcedony.—Hardness, 7; all colors; luster, waxy; tough; form, massive, no crystals; has a curved fracture; composition, silica; a variety of quartz, often translucent, and in beautiful forms; common on serpentine barrens, and in Warwick.

Jasper.—Hardness, 7; red, yellow; luster, earthy; tough; form, massive; has a curved fracture; composition, silica and clay; a variety of quartz, made impure by presence of clay; common on barrens, West Goshen.

Calcite.—Hardness, 3; white, all colors; luster, glassy, pearl;

brittle; form, crystals, rhombs, prisms; cleaves into crystals; composition, carbonite of lime; this is limestone purified and crystallized, same as marble; common in mines and limestone quarries.

Dolomite.—Hardness, 4; white, yellow, red; luster, glassy, pearly; brittle, form, crystal, rhombs, massive; cleaves into crystals; composition, carbonate of lime and magnesia; calcite and magnesia; both effervesce in acids; common in mines and limestone south of Great Valley.

Serpentine.—Hardness, 3-5; shade of green; luster, feeble; brittle; form, massive, no crystals, breaks irregularly; composition, silica, magnesia, water, distinguished by its green color and soft, grassy feel; found in barrens in the southern and western parts of the county.

Talc.—Hardness, 1; white, green; luster, pearly, greasy; flexible; form, in scales and plates; splits into thin leaves; composition, silica, magnesia, water, distinguished from mica by its greasy feel; is not so elastic as mica; common with serpentine.

Hornblend.—Hardness, 5-6; brown, black; luster, pearly, glassy; tough; form, crystals, blades, scales; cleaves in smooth blades; composition, silica, magnesia, iron; the dark mineral in our gneiss and hornblend or trap rocks; found in gneiss rocks and at Knauertown.

Tourmaline.—Hardness, 7; brown, black, red; luster, glassy; brittle; form, long, three-sided, striated crystals, breaks irregularly; composition, silica, lime, magnesia, iron; often resembles hornblend, but usually in long, free, radiating crystals; common in all the southern and western parts of the county.

Mica.—Hardness, 2; whitish; luster, pearly; elastic; form, in plates and scales, splits into thin leaves; composition, silica, potassium, al. fe.; many varieties, but all are in thin plates, elastic, and not greasy; common in the southern and western portions of the county.

Feldspars.—Hardness, 6; white, all colors; luster, glassy,

pearly; brittle; form, usually massive; splits readily in plates; composition, silica, potassium, al.; many varieties; the light-colored constituents of our gneiss rocks; found in gneiss rocks and in the southern and western parts of the county.

Asbestos.—Hardness, 1-4; white, gray, luster, dull, silky; tough; form, in fibers, like linen or wool; splits into fibers; composition, silica, magnesia, lime, etc.; its fibrous nature marks it; common with serpentine. Its value is increasing.

Garnet.—Hardness, 7; all colors; luster, glassy, resinous· brittle; form, round crystals and dodecahedrons; breaks uneven composition, silica, fe., ca. mn.; always in crystals, which are never elongated; common in gneiss or mica schist.

Cyanite.—Hardness, 4-7; blue, green, white, yellow; luster, glassy, pearly; tough; form, in long, flat blades; splits readily one way; composition, silica, aluminum, iron, it is distinguished by its long-bladed crystals and bright blue colors; found in the southern and western parts of the county.

Tremolite.—Hardness, 6; gray, green, white; luster, glassy; brittle; form, massive, fibrous, splits irregularly; composition, silica, lime, magnesia; bladed or fibrous crystals, gray or white color; found in southern part of the county.

Actinolite.—Hardness, 5-6; bright green; luster glassy; brittle; form, crystals, columnar, fibrous; smooth and even; composition, silica, magnesia, lime, iron, bladed or acicular crystals, and bright green or yellow colors; found in southern part of the county.

Magnesite.—Hardness, 4-5; white, yellow; luster, glassy, dull; sectile; form, crystals, granular, massive; even, smooth; composition, magnesia, carbonic acid; radiated crystals on serpentine; foams in acids; found in serpentine quarries.

Apatite.—Hardness, 5; green, all colors, luster, glassy, all colors, brittle; form, crystals, massive; even, good; composition, phosphate of lime; in abundance this mineral would be very valuable for its phosphoric acid; found in limestone in southern part of the county.

Graphite.—Hardness, 1; iron-black; luster, metallic; sectile; form, scales, massive; into scales; composition, pure carbon; soils white paper; is infusible; a valuable mineral, found in gneiss in Uwchlan, Charlestown, Pikeland.

Corundum.—Hardness, 8; blue, gray, brown; luster, glassy; tough; form, crystals, massive; good in crystals; composition, pure alumina; next to the diamond in hardness; very valuable; found in granular albite in Newlin.

Epidote.—Hardness, 6-7; green, yellow; luster, glassy; brittle; form, crystals massive; even, good; composition, silica, lime, iron and magnesia; distinguished by its peculiar yellow green color; found in central parts of the country on hornblend.

Aragonite.—Hardness, 4; white, yellow, red; luster, glassy; brittle; form, crystals, massive; even, good; composition, carbonate of lime; same as calite, but harder; in six-sided crystals; effervesces in acids; found in quarries and mines throughout the county.

Scapolite.—Hardness, 5-6; gray, all light colors; luster, greasy, glassy; tough; form, crystals, massive; even in crystals; composition, silica, alumina, lime; heavier and more fusible than feldspars; with acids gelatinizes; found in New Garden, Kennett, Marlborough.

Jefferisite.—Hardness, 1-5; brown, yellow; luster, pearly; brittle; form, plates and scales; into thin plates; composition, silica, alumina, iron, magnesia and water; swells up in flame; found in Westtown and Newlin, with serpentine. Named after William W. Jefferis, of West Chester, Pennsylvania.

Deweylite.—Hardness, 2-5; yellow, brown; luster, resinous; brittle; form, massive, granular; into curved grains; composition, silica, magnesia, water; known by its peculiar resinous appearance; found with serpentine in West Goshen and West Nottingham.

Fluorite.—Hardness, 4; purple, white; luster, glassy; brittle; from, crystals, massive; even, regular; composition, fluoride of lime;

commonly of a beautiful purple color, and on limestone or culiate, and found in Phœnixville, Newlin and Tredyffrin.

Beryl.—Hardness, 7-8; green; luster, glassy; brittle; form, in hexagonal crystals and massive; breaks unevenly; composition, silica, glucinum, aluminum; is distinguished by its color and its hexagonal crystals; found in Newlin, East Nottingham and Westtown.

Staurolite.—Hardness, 7-8; brown, black; luster, glassy; brittle; form, in crystals, which are never slender; uneven; composition, silica, lime, aluminum, iron; named from crystals which are often cross-shaped, but never slender; found in West Bradford, West Goshen and West Marlborough.

Zoisite.—Hardness, 6-7; green, gray; luster, glassy; pearly; brittle; form, long, fluted crystals; splits smoothly; composition, silica, iron, lime, aluminum; green color and crystals fluted, longitudinally marked; found on hornblend rocks near West Chester and Kennett. .

Ziricon.—Hardness, 7-8; all colors except black; luster, adamantine; brittle; form, crystals and grains; curved fracture; composition, silica and zirconia; hyacinthe, a variety of zoisite; found in South Coventry, West Pikeland, East Bradford, and Unionville.

Kaolin.—Hardness, 1; white; luster, dull; sectile; form, massive; even, earthy; composition, silica, alumium, water; formed by the decomposition of gneiss and feldspar; valuable; found in Newlin, East Nottingham, and Kennett.

Margarite.—Hardness, 4-5; white, gray; luster, pearly; sectile; form, plates, scales; splits into thin scales; composition, silica, aluminum, iron; a micaceous-like mineral, pearly luster implanted on corundum; found in Newlin with corundum.

Chesterlite.—Hardness, 5-6; white, yellowish; luster, glassy; pearly; brittle; form, crystals, very perfect; even, good; composition, aluminum, silica; named from Chester County, and found in poorhouse quarry and Baily's, East Marlborough.

ORES.

Pyrites.—Hardness, 6-7; pale brass yellow; streak, black, brittle; form, in cubes, crystals, massive; breaks irregularly; composition, iron and sulphur; yellow color and striking fire with knife distinguish it; found in most parts of the county.

Limonite.—Hardness, 2-6; brown, yellow; streak, yellow, yellowish-brown; brittle; form, massive, columnar; fracture curved; composition, iron, oxygen, water; marked by a brown or yellow color and yellow streak; this is the common iron ore of the county.

Hematite.—Hardness, 6-7; gray, black, red; streak, red; brittle; form, massive in scales; irregular; composition, iron and oxygen; not common; bright, shining pieces or occasionally in scales; found in Warwick, Phœnixville and East Brandywine.

Magnetite.—Hardness, 5-6; iron-black; streak, black; brittle; form, octahedron crystals, massive; irregular; composition, iron and oxygen; most valuable of the iron ores, but rare; found in Warwick, Newlin and Westtown.

Chromite.—Hardness, 6; iron-black; streak, dark-brown; tough; form, massive; irregular, uneven; composition, iron, chromium; often magnetic, on fresh edge, dull luster; found with serpentine throughout the county.

Titanic Iron.—Hardness, 6; iron-black; streak, black to red; brittle; form, massive usually; uneven, irregular; composition, iron and titanium; often magnetic, infusible, contains rare element titanium; found in Elk, Newlin, Westtown, Thornbury and East Bradford.

LEAD.

Galena.—Hardness, 3; lead-gray; blue; streak, gray-black; brittle; form, cubes, massive, granular; regular, smooth; composition, lead and sulphur, marked by softness and cubical form; found at the mines near Phœnixville.

Pyromorphite.—Hardness, 4; green, brown, yellow, white;

streak, gray to white; brittle; form, columnar crystals; regular; composition, lead and phosphorus; crystals beautiful columnar green; change form on heating; found at the lead mines near Phœ-nixville.

Cerussite.—Hardness, 3-5; white, green, black; streak, gray to white; brittle; form, hexagonal crystals; good and regular; composition, carbonate of lead; fuses very readily; foams in acids; found at the lead mines near Phœnixville.

Anglesite.—Hardness, 3; white; adamantine luster; streak, white, brittle; form, beautiful crystals; regular; composition, sulphate of lead; fuses readily, but does not foam in acids; found in the lead mines near Phœnixville.

COPPER.

Calcopyrite.—Hardness, 4; brass-yellow; streak, green-black; sectice; form, crystals, massive; uneven, irregular; composition, copper, iron, sulphur; resembles iron pyrites; but is much softer; found at the lead mines near Phœnixville.

Malachite.—Hardness, 3-5; emerald green; streak, green; brittle; form, massive, incrusting; smooth, curved; composition, carbonate of copper, colors flame-green; foams in acids, and is a valuable ore; found in Warwick and in the mines at Phœnixville.

Azurite.—Hardness, 4; azure-blue, streak, blue; brittle; form, massive; regular, uneven; composition, carbonate of copper; same as malachite, but blue; found in mines near Phœnixville.

Chrysocolla.— Hardness, 5; sky-blue green; streak, blue; brittle; form, massive; curved fracture; composition, copper and silica; forms jelly with acids; found with copper ores, and in Warwick and mines near Phœnixville.

ZINC.

Calamine.—Hardness, 4-5; white, pale-yellow; streak, gray; brittle; form, crystals, massive; regular; composition, silica, zinc, water, silky tufts and small white or yellowish crystals; a valuable ore; found in the mines near Phœnixville.

Sphalterite.—Hardness, 4; yellow, brown; streak, yellow, brown; brittle; form, crystals, tables, massive; into plates, smooth; composition, zinc and sulphur; bright, glistening appearance, waxy luster, a valuable ore; found at the lead mines near Phœnixville.

Rutile.—Hardness, 6-7; black, red, adamantine; streak, black-brown; brittle; form, crystals, massive; imperfect; composition, titanium and oxygen; brown, red color, mitred crystals; "money stone;" found in Sadsbury, East Bradford, New Garden, Thornbury and London Grove.

Pyrolusite.—Hardness, 2; gran, iron-black; sectile; brittle; form, massive; uneven; composition, manganese and oxygen; infusible; the black oxide of manganese in chemistry; found in Osborne's Hill, East Bradford.

ROCKS.

Gneiss.—A hard, tough or brittle, light or dark rock, composed of quartz, mica and feldspar; found in the southeast part of the county and north of North Valley hill.

Mica Slate.—Constituents same as in Gneiss, but of a slaty structure, owing to great excess of mica. Found in a belt through the central and western part of the county.

Talc Slate.—Same as mica slate, but mica takes the place of talc; soft and greasy feel; associated with mica slate.

Serpentine.—Same as mineral serpentine, in the southern gneiss belt, in the southeast part of the county, in isolated deposits.

Limestone.—Impure calcite, found in many parts of the county, but principally in the great limestone belt, called the Great Valley.

Sandstone.—Small grains of quartz cemented together. A belt of sandstone runs the entire length of North Valley hill.

Red Sandstone.—A soft, shaly sandstone, colored red by the

oxide of iron. It is found in all parts of the county north of French Creek.

Hornblende Rock.—A gneiss in which mica is replaced by hornblende. It is dark in color, hard and tough.

Trap.—An igneous rock of volcanic origin, dark, hard, tough, and consisting of feldspar and hornblende closely mixed.

Quartz.—Same as mineral quartz, rather a rock constituent than a rock, as it never alone forms hills and mountains.

Scale of Hardness.—1. Readily scratched by nail (Talc). 2. Scarcely scratched by nail (Gypsum). 3. Scratched by copper (Calcite). 4. Harder than copper, but will not cut glass (Fluorite). 5. Scratches glass slightly (Apatite). 6. Scarcely scratched by knife (Feldspar). 7. Not scratched by knife (Quartz). 8. Cannot be filed, and scratches 7 (Topaz). 9. Scratches 8 (Corundum). 10. Scratches 9 (Diamond.)

10

CHAPTER IV.

WELSH AND OTHER SETTLERS.

CHAPTER IV.

IT is natural and is also highly commendable for men to take
pride in the achievements of their ancestors; and from the historian each race, nationality and class is entitled to proper credit
for the part it may have played in the great drama of the settlement of a new country, or in the establishment and development
of its institutions, though it is exceedingly difficult for the human
mind, especially when necessarily working within prescribed
limits of space and time, even it is not impossible, to accurately
apportion to each the credit due. These remarks are intended to
introduce a brief account of the introduction of the Welsh into
eastern Pennsylvania by William Penn. These early Welsh are
certainly entitled to respectful consideration, even if their own
claims and the claims of their descendants should not be granted
to the full extent. Many of the early mayors of Philadelphia,
both during Colonial times and for the first half of the present
century, were either Welsh or the descendants of Cymric ancestry,
and it is noteworthy that most of the distinguished physicians of
the earlier days, and even many down to the present time, were
and are of the same descent.

For some time before they came to America William Penn

had professed a friendship for the Cymric Friends, which sentiment was natural, if it be true that he himself was on the
paternal side of his family of Welsh descent. It is certain that
he offered extraordinary inducements to Welsh settlers within
his domains in this country. A conference was held in London
by prominent Welshmen with the proprietor of Pennsylvania,
with regard to the terms of settlement of Welsh people on a tract
of land, in the latter part of 1681, those present being as follows:
Dr. Griffith Owen, Dr. Edward Jones, Dr. Thomas Wynne, John
ap Thomas, Charles Lloyd, John ap John, Richard Davies, Edward Prichard and others. The principal object of the Welsh
appears to have been to establish a barony on a considerable
tract of land in the new country, upon which they could control
themselves, according to the ancient system of baronial government, which, as every student of history knows, was in reality
inimical to individual freedom and equal justice. But the idea
of a Cymric barony within the limits of Penn's province was never
realized, although there is no doubt that the leading Welshmen
who settled on this Welsh tract anticipated such a government
and thought they had good grounds for such anticipation from
the promises of Penn.

The mistake they made at the conference above mentioned
was that they "allowed themselves to be persuaded by the founder
that the powers given to him in his charter, and the general articles of concession to all colonists, which papers were signed by
the Welsh patentees, would be sufficient, with his personal promise, to protect them, and enable them to carry out the plan they
had in view."

So far as known no one questions the sincerity of purpose of
William Penn, but it was found by him utterly impracticable to
carry out all the promises he had made to those whom he induced
to become settlers within his province. Following is the warrant
given in 1684 to Thomas Holmes, the surveyor-general. It is clear
and concise and cannot be misunderstood.

"Whereas divers considerable persons among ye Welsh Friends have requested me yt all ye Lands Purchased of me by those of North Wales and South Wales, together with ye adjacent counties to ym, as Herefordshire, Shropshire and Cheshire, about forty thousand acres, may be layd out contiguously as one Barony, alledging that yt ye number already come, are such as will be capable of planting ye same much within ye proportion allowed by ye custom of ye country, & so not lye in large useless vacancies. And because I am inclined and determined to agree and favor ym with any reasonable Conveniency and priviledge: I do hereby charge thee and strictly require thee to lay out ye sd tract of Land in as uniform a manner as conveniently may be, upon ye west side of Skoolkill River, running three miles upon ye same, and two miles backward, & then extend ye parallel with ye river six miles and to run westwardly so far as this yt sd quantity of land be Compleately surveyed unto you.—Given at Pennsbury, ye 13th 1st mo. 1684."

As a general explanation of the method of disposing of the lands in this tract to the coming Welsh settlers, it may be stated that after they were satisfied as to their safety in proceeding with their arrangements for a settlement in Pennsylvania, they organized themselves into companies of adventurers and selected prominent members among them as trustees, who took out a patent in their own names for all the land for which the company had subscribed. This was in all probability agreed upon at the London conference, with the approval of the proprietor, in order to carry out successfully the proposed plan of a baronial form of government, and it was also necessary in order to obtain a first choice of land.

After the above-named warrant to the surveyor-general was issued, he authorized an order to one of his deputy surveyors, David Powell, under date of 2d mo. 4th, 1684, by which the latter was directed "to survey and set out unto the said purchasers the said quantity of land, there, in manner as before expressed, and in method of townships lately appointed by the governor at five thousand acres to a township," which directions were carried out only in part. Following is an account of the Welsh purchases by David Powell:

"My Respected Friend,

"James Logan:—I hold myself obliged to give thee an account of those lands belonging to the purchases of Thomas Lloyd where David Lloyd is concerned, and likewise Richard ap Thomas: that is, how much is taken up and subdivided to them and sold by them and what remains not disposed of by the said Thomas Lloyd and the said Richard Thomas.

	Acres.
"Thomas Lloyd had a right by his brother Charles to	2,500
took up between Mirion and Harford	1,100
and one 100 acres he ordered in his right to Thomas David the which was laid out to him	100
	1,200
He also bought of Francis Smith Remaining	1,300
the share Margaret Davis reserved to herself:	1,250
	2,550

There is, I think, 100 acres of Liberty land laid out to him   100

The rest is to be yet settled; and warrants to be granted for the subdividing of it within the Welsh tract.

Also Richard ap Thomas: his purchase is,	5,000
out of which he sold to Phillip Howell	700
and one 100 of Liberty land to Hugh Robarts	100

and to Robert William   300
and I think to Edward Joanes   200
                                         ————
                                     1,300

Remaining to him to have warrants to himself for 3,700
As to David Lloyd part there is an imaginary survey made about 1,800 acres, but not perfected.

"When thou art pleased to order warrants for them or any others of the said Welsh purchase, I think there ought to be a recital of the first warrant by which the land was first bounded: and the time of the survey likewise commanding a return of the respective subdivisions within the bounds of the said tract when not already subdivided to any other of the company, the which survey was done on the 28th of the 8th mo. 1684, and finished the — day of the 11th mo. ensuing. I request thee also to put an end to Phillip Howell's business to ease both thyself and the rest of the commissioners of his continual importuning; and I think it were best to let him have that lot on Thomas Joanes' account, and let him pay the money to Joanes, least the warrant granted by the Governor to Nealson takes hold of it, and the Governor forced to pay the 35 pounds to Joanes out of his own pocket; these things I refer to thy consideration, leaving it wholly to thee to order it as thou think best, and desire thy favor in letting me have an end to my one business that my most cordial friend and Governor left me to do; for me else I am afraid that I shall suffer for want of it; who am thy real friend

                                 "D. POWELL.

"Dated 5th, 12th mo., 1701."

Following is "an account of the purchasers concerned in the Welsh Tract granted by the general warrant by which the said tract was laid out, and such lands as hath been laid out by warrants duly executed within the same, and first of the old England purchasers:

"Charles Lloyd and Margaret Davis, 5,000 acres; Richard
Davis, 5,000 acres; William Jenkins, 1,000; John Poy, 750; John
Burge, 750; William Mordant, 500; William Powell, 1,250; Lewis
David, 3,000; Morris Llewlin, 500; Thomas Simons, 500; John
Bevan, 2,000; Edward Prichard, 2,500; John ap John and Thomas
Wynn, 5,000; Edward Joanes and John Thomas, 5,000; Richard
Davis, 1,250; Richard ap Thomas, 5,000; Mordicia Moore, in right
of ———, 500; John Millinton, 500; Henry Right, 500; Daniel
Medlecot, 200; Thomas Ellis, 1,000; Thomas Ellis for B. Roulles,
250; Thomas Ellis on account of Humphrey Thomas, 100; David
Powell, 1,000; John Kinsy, 200; David Meredith, 250; David
Davis, 200; Thomas John Evan, 250; John Evans, 100; John
Jormon, 50; David Kiusy, 200; Evan Oliver, 100; Samuel Mills,
100; Thomas Joanes, 50; David Joanes, 100; John Kinsy, 100;
Daniel Hurry, 300; Henry Joanes, 400; John Fish, 300; John Day,
300; Burke and Simson, 1,000; the whole complement, 50,000
acres."

Among the above names is that of John ap John, who, according to Thomas Allen Glenn, author of "Merion in the Welsh
Tract," from which book numerous facts are taken to complete
this brief outline of the Welsh in Chester County, purchased his
lands September 15, 1681, but who never came to this county.
Of the lands thus purchased John ap John sold as follows to different persons: To Thomas Taylor, 500 acres; to John Roberts,
500 acres; to Treial Reider, 400 acres; to Mary Fouk, 200 acres;
to Richard Davies, 250 acres; to Owen Parry, 150 acres; reserving
for himself, 500 acres; but he rebought the 400 acres sold to
Treial Reider, so that he had at last 900 acres reserved for himself,
which, however, he never saw.

Besides John ap John and Thomas Wynne, the principal
patentees to these lands, that is, those who bought for others in
the capacity of trustees, were as follows: Charles Lloyd and Margaret Davis, who bought 5,000 acres; John Bevan, 2,000 acres;

John Thomas and Dr. Edward Bala, 5,000; Richard ap Thomas, 5,000; Richard Davies, 5,000, and Lewis David, 3,000.

There was considerable land taken up by individuals on their own account, and outside of the 40,000-acre tract there were 10,000 acres taken up by Welshmen, or so reported, previous to 1684. Some of these lands were in Goshen, and some of it as far south as in what is now Delaware.

The first settlement in the township of Merion was made by Dr. Edward Jones, Edward Reese, William ap Edward, and a few others in the latter part of August, 1682, a short time previous to the arrival of William Penn, they having come from near Bala, Merionethshire, Wales. The Haverford and Radnor purchasers came later, those in the former township coming prior to March 2, 1683, and those in the latter township about the same time. As the country became more and more settled by these Welsh immigrants their troubles increased, they suffering not only from the difficulties necessarily incident to the settlement of a new country, but they were discouraged by their failure to establish their barony, as they had confidently expected to do. Other settlers encroached upon their tract, as in the case of the English immigrants, for whom Charles Ashcombe, a deputy surveyor, had laid out lands within the limits of the 40,000 acres; but in this case the Welsh successfully resisted the encroachment, and for a time afterward maintained intact the territory they had purchased.

Afterward there arose a dispute over the Chester County line. On March 25, 1689, Thomas Lloyd appeared before the Council and said that he understood something had been moved about adding the Welsh Tract to the County of Chester, and also said that if anything of the kind were contemplated he desired to speak. To this Governor Blackwell replied that nothing of the kind was yet brought before them; but that if anything should be wherein it were necessary to hear him, he should be notified thereof.

The fact, however, was that the justices of Chester County had already prepared the petition for adding the townships of Radnor and Haverford to Chester County, the purpose being to cut off from Philadelphia County some sixty Welshmen, who, if left in that county, would elect persons to the Council who would oppose the policy of Governor Blackwell. This petition of the justices was presented in the afternoon and came up for argument next day. After earnest discussion and protest on the part of the Welsh, the two townships were set off into Chester County; but, notwithstanding this, the sixty Welsh voters insisted upon voting for their candidate with the inhabitants of Philadelphia County, which caused a long debate, and resulted in an order for a new election. The final result of the contention was that after a long effort to maintain their barony intact, they were obliged to succumb to influences too powerful for them longer to resist. A persistent effort was made by many outside of the tract to break up the Cymric Barony, in 1690 and 1691; but it should be said that the Welsh appear to have departed at that particular time from a determination to be too grasping. They decided that they would not, as asked to do, pay quit-rent on the entire tract from 1684, though they did consent to pay the quit-rent on the entire 40,000 acres. The commissioners of property thereupon resolved that the lands already laid out within the tract to other purchasers should be confirmed to them. Not long afterward the Welsh agreed, or offered, rather, to pay quit-rent from 1684, but the commissioners decided that it was then too late, the matter having been already settled. However, from this time on until about 1700 the Welsh continued their attempts to regain what they had lost, but without success, and the Welsh Barony became a barony only in name The three townships of Merion, Radnor and Haverford continued to be known as the Welsh Tract down to the Revolutionary War, and even into the present century.

John ap Thomas was one of the prominent Welshmen that settled on the great Welsh Tract. He and Dr. Edward Jones were the leaders of the Merion company, they taking out a patent for 5,000 acres of land, one-half of that which was allotted to Thomas in the county of Philadelphia, and the other half in the township of Goshen, Chester County. John ap Thomas' portion was 1,250 acres, $612\frac{1}{2}$ acres being in Goshen. He did not, however, ever reach America, dying in England just when he was on the point of departure for this country. But his wife, Catherine Roberts, as she was called, according to the Welsh custom, came across the sea with her children, after the death of her husband, and set-tled on his lands, some of which are to this day in the possession of her descendants. Besides John ap Thomas, others purchasing lands in Goshen were as follows: Hugh Roberts, 67 acres; Dr. Edward Jones, 353 acres; Edward Jones, Jr., $158\frac{1}{8}$ acres; Robert David, $234\frac{1}{2}$ acres; Richard Rees, 75 acres; John Roberts, 230 acres; Robert William, $76\frac{1}{4}$ acres, and John Roberts, $78\frac{1}{4}$ acres. The sons of John ap Thomas, named respectively, Thomas, Robert and Cadwallader Jones, owned the $612\frac{1}{2}$ acres taken up by their father in Goshen.

An important part of Chester County, which was a portion of the great Welsh Tract and was early settled by Welshmen, was Tredyffrin Township, which is northwest of Radnor Township in Delaware County, and of Easttown Township, in Chester County. The name, Tredyffrin, is, of course, Welsh. It is thus divided: Tre, meaning town, and Dyffrin, meaning "wide, cultivated valley," and the whole meaning is, therefore, the town in a wide, cultivated valley. In the early days an effort was made to Angli-cize the word, it being then sometimes called Valleytown, or Val-leyton. In 1708 a deed was made in which Lewis Walker, the grantor, is referred to as "of the township of Valleyton, in the county of Chester."

As showing the course pursued by William Penn in the sale of his lands outside of the Welsh tract, the dates of several of these sales together with the names of the parties purchasing lands of him, with a few other particulars, are here presented:

Penn sold lands while in England to numerous parties still in England, definite amounts of land for definite prices and quit-rents, but without locating these lands further than to state that they were within the province of Pennsylvania.   As to Bartholo-mew Coppock, of Saltney, in the county Palatine of Chester, Eng-land, March 22, 1681, five hundred acres of land for £10, the quit-rent being one shilling for each one hundred acres of land per year.   This was the second purchase by Bartholomew Coppock of 500 acres on the same terms, the other being on March 21, 1681.

Penn sold to James Dicks 250 acres of land March 3, 1681, which James Dicks sold to Peter Dicks August 16, 1684.   Other purchasers were as follows: Randall Vernon, March 4, 1681, 625 acres; Thomas Vernon, March 3, 1681, 625 acres; Thomas Minshall, March 22, 1681, 625 acres; Robert Vernon, March 7, 1681, 625 acres; William Taylor and others, March 3, 1681, 1,250 acres; Thomas Powell, March 20, 1681, 500 acres; Randall Malin, March 7, 1681, 250 acres; John Pusey, October 11, 1681, 250 acres; Robert Taylor, March 3, 1682, 1,000 acres; John Sharpless, April 5, 1682, 1,000 acres; John Hicks, October 11, 1681, 250 acres; Caleb Pusey, October 11, 1681, 250 acres; Daniel Smith on several different occa-sions bought land in various quantities, from 500 acres up to 2,000 acres, but none of these purchasers were located further than to be within the province of Pennsylvania.   One of the first, if not the first, to be described by metes and bounds, was a purchase by William Hitchcock, a tract of 500 acres: "Beginning at a corner walnut tree of Philip Roman's land, running from thence south-southeast 83 perches, to a corner marked hickory; from thence east-north-east 400 perches; thence east-north-east by land of Nicholas Newlin 480 perches to a corner marked red oak; thence north-north-west 83 perches, to a corner marked red oak; thence west-south-west by land of John Harding, 480 perches to a street in the said town; and thence west-south-west by the land of Philip. Roman, 480 perches, to the first-mentioned walnut tree, containing and laid out for 500 acres," etc.

On the 8th day of the 4th month, 1697, George Willard executed a deed for 500 acres of land lying in Willistown Township to. Peter Thomas, which 500 acres was one-third of 1,500 acres of land formerly surveyed and laid out by the order of the Governor, William Penn, for Thomas Brassie. This 500-acre tract was described in the deed as follows:

"Beginning at a marked red oak, being the corner mark of Francis Yarnell's land; from thence north-north-west 166 perches to a corner post; thence east-north-east to a corner chestnut standing by Crum Creek's side; from thence down the several courses. thereof to a corner maple, being also the corner of Francis Yarnell's land, and thence west-south-west by the said Yarnell's land to the mentioned red oak." It was in the present township of Willistown.

Francis Yarnell had purchased five hundred acres of George Willard, a portion of the same tract, and on the 1st of October, 1708, he sold one hundred and fifty acres of his purchase to John Caldwell for £60.

On the 1st of March, 1690, John Bennett, who had been appointed constable of Birmingham Township in 1686, sold to David Davis fifty acres of land, "Beginning at a marked small hickory, standing in Hugh Henry's line," etc., for £10 current silver money. And on May 8, 1695, Edward Harris sold to John Beckingham fifty acres of land adjoining Samuel Scott's land, for £5, good and lawful silver money.

On the 30th of August, 1705, John Guest sold to Henry Hollingsworth, who was a very prominent man in the early history of Chester County, one hundred acres of land for £20, the land being "situate on the west side of the Brandywine Creek, beginning at a corner black oak, being a corner of a tract purchased.

by the said Henry Hollingsworth from John Budd; thence west by the said Henry Hollingsworth's line 324 perches to a post standing near a corner black oak; thence south 49 perches and a half to a post; thence east 324 perches to a hickory; thence north 49½ perches to the place of beginning; being part of a tract of land held by patent from the commissioners of property." The land mentioned above as having been purchased by Mr. Hollingsworth of John Budd, was purchased in August, 1704, and consisted of one hundred acres.

Among the early purchasers of land in the township of Westtown were Daniel Hoopes, who, in 1697, purchased 300 acres in the east part of the township. Aaron James and Benjamin Hickman were there in 1700, and John Bowater of Middletown purchased land in this township as early as 1704. He appears to have died in this township about the beginning of the year 1705, for, on the 4th of March, 1705, his widow, Frances Bowater, sold to George Smedley four hundred acres of land for £350, the land being described in the deed as follows: "Beginning at a white oak tree standing at the corner of Daniel Hoop, his land; from thence by said land north 24 west, 462 perches to a lyme tree; from thence running by the land of Richard Snead north 66 east, 139 perches to a chestnut tree; from thence by land untaken up south 24 east, 460 perches to a post; from thence extending by the lands of John Wilcox and Joseph Baker south 65 west, 139 perches to the first-mentioned white oak or place of beginning, containing in the whole 400 acres of land."

The Baker family was quite numerous in the early history of the county, and some members thereof very prominent. One of the Bakers, named Joseph, was a member of the general assembly and died in 1716. There is a full genealogy of the Baker family in Dr. Futhey's History of Chester County.

Edward Rees, of the township of Merion, Philadelphia County, sold to Ellis David, of the township of Goshen, Chester County, a

Josiah Hoopes.

tract of land containing 367 acres, which is described as follows in the deed: "Beginning at the corner of Evan Jones & Co.'s land; thence north-north-west 400 perches to a corner post; thence by vacant land east-north-east 147 perches to a post, being a corner of Thomas Jones & Co.'s land; thence by the same land south-south-east 400 perches to another corner post; thence by Griffith Owen's land west-south-west 147 perches to the place of beginning, containing 367 acres."

Griffith Owen was one of the commissioners appointed by William Penn October 28, 1701, the others being Edward Shippen, Thomas Story, and James Logan, who were authorized to grant lands for such sums and quit-rents as they should see fit. His name occurs frequently in the early history of the county, and he was a very prominent and useful man.

On the 24th of April, 1708, Lewis Walker sold to Llewellyn David two parcels of land, one containing 160 acres, the other 400 acres, which are described in the deed as follows: "Beginning at a corner post standing by the land of John David; thence by the land of John Mordent, north-north-west 300 perches to another post set in the ground; thence east-north-east 160 perches to a third post standing in the line of John Havard's land; thence south-south-east 360 perches to the place of beginning."

Lewis Walker, who, as elsewhere stated, is mentioned in this deed as "of the township of Valleyton, of the county of Chester," purchased this land of David Powell, who had purchased it of David Meredith, who had purchased it of the commissioners of property appointed by William Penn.

The Meredith family was a numerous one in the early history of this county, and there is given a full genealogical history thereof in Dr. Futhey's History of Chester County, as also of that of Llewellyn David, the latter of whom was a justice of the peace and a prominent citizen.

On June 5, 1719, James Johnston sold to William Carter two

11

hundred acres of land in New Garden Township, "Bounded east of lands lately owned by William Penn, Jr., northward by Marlboro Township, westward by John M. Cook's land, and south by Robert Tranter's land."

This land had been originally purchased by Thomas Garrett of Evan Evans, who was a most useful citizen, not only to the people who were his neighbors, but also to the country during the Revolutionary War.   Among the first settlers in this township were Mary Rowland, who purchased land here in 1708;   Gayen Miller, who purchased 700 acres in 1712; and in the next year quite a number came into the township, land being bought by John Miller, James Lindley, John Lowden, James Starr, Michael Lightfoot, William Halliday, Joseph Hutton, Abraham Marshall, and Thomas Jackson; and in 1714 Thomas Garnett and Joseph Sharp came in.   These persons paid for their lands £20 per hundred acres.

The next year William Penn, Jr., sold what was left of his lands, originally consisting of 14,500 acres in this township, patented to him May 24, 1706, by the commissioners of property and bounded as follows:

"Beginning at a hickory tree on the west side of a branch of White Clay Creek; thence east 925 perches to a corner of Letitia's Manor (Kenneth); thence by the same 2,314 perches to another corner; thence west-south-west 930 perches to White Clay Creek, west 58 perches and north by land of the London company 2,674 perches to the place of beginning."

Previous to 1715 William Penn, Jr., had sold somewhat more than 5,000 acres of his lands, and in this year he sold the remainder, with the exception of 500 acres, to John Evans, and as a conse-quence this tract so sold was afterward sometimes called Col. Evans' Manor.   The greater part of this, however, reconveyed be-fore the death of William Penn, Jr., which occurred in 1720, and who, when dying, left three children, viz.: Gulielma Maria, Springett and William.. Springett inherited his father's lands in Pennsylvania, but as he died unmarried he was succeeded by his brother William, to whom Col. Evans granted a release to the manor in 1736.

June 9, 1696, George Willard sold to Edmund Butcher one hundred acres of land in the township of Birmingham for £4 down and one shilling quit-rent per year forever. Edmund Butcher on May 4, 1703, sold one hundred and eleven acres to Francis Chadsey, in the same township, for £6 6s.

On September 20, 1718, William Penn, Jr., for £40 sold to James Lindley, "All that piece or parcel of land beginning at a corner marked hickory tree, near the corner of Thomas Garrett's land; thence south by vacant land 160 perches to a small white oak; thence east by north on the top of Taukenemon Hill 239. perches to a black oak; thence north by vacant land 114 perches to a gum tree; thence westerly by vacant land and the line of the said Thomas Garrett's land 234 perches to the place of beginning, containing 200 acres of land, situated in Chester County."

This land was in New Garden Township. The name of the hill given in this description is spelled as above in the deed. In 1700 the surveyor stated that he crossed the Dochcanamon Hill. Other forms of the name are as follows: Tokenamon, Taukenamon, Taughlikenemon, and that in use at the present time, Toughkenamon, the meaning in the Indian language being according to tradition, "Fire-brand Hill." In this same township there were in the early day, besides those already mentioned, the following: Robert Johnson, who owned 200 acres; Evan Evans, 500; Joseph Sharp, 200; John Sharp, 200; Thomas Garnett, 300; William Tanner, 200; Benjamin Fred, 300; John Wiley, 200; Francis Hobson, 200; Gayen Miller, 700; Abraham Marshall, who has been mentioned above, owned 200 acres of land, partly in New Castle County.

Joseph Wood sold to David Phillip for £100, "All that messuage or tenement and plantation where Richard David formerly dwelt, situated in Easttown in the said county of Chester, together with all of a certain tract or parcel of land thereto belonging upon part of said Joseph's purchase, of the said 3,380 acres of land," etc., "containing 200 acres."

With reference to the above purchase, it should be said by way of explanation, that William Wood and William Shardlow had received from William Penn a grant of 5,000 acres, of which 3,380 acres were on December 1, 1684, laid out and surveyed by Charles Ashton, surveyor, in the county of Chester, at the head of the township of Newton, and Joseph Wood, after the death of his father, William, on the 29th of August, 1704, obtained a writ of partition directed to the sheriff of the county to cut into two equal parts the aforesaid 3,380 acres, so that Joseph Wood and William Shardlow should each have 1,690 acres, and it was a part of Joseph Wood's 1,690 acres that he sold to David Phillip.

Joseph Wood on September 1, 1690, sold 250 acres of land to George Simcock, who sold it to Matthew Clomison, who sold it to John Bently, who sold it to William Davies of Radnor, who sold it to John Hugh. Then John Hugh on December 2, 1705, sold this 250 acres of land "Situated and being in Easttown, in the county of Chester, beginning at a corner post of the lands of William Shardlow, and from thence south-south-east by a line of trees 196 perches; thence south 55 west, 202 perches to a corner post; and from thence north-north-west 196 perches, and from thence north 55 east, 202 perches to the place of beginning."

On the 20th of February, 1706, John Guest sold to Daniel Mc-Farson for £60 three hundred acres of land, "The said three hundred acres lying and being in the township of Kennett, in the county of Chester, beginning at a post in the line of Lætitia Penn's Mannor, being a corner of Alexander Frazer's land, and thence east in the line of the said Frazer's land 324 perches to a post; thence south by vacant land 148¼ perches to a white oak; thence west by the land of the said John Guest 324 perches to a white oak; thence north by Laetitia Penn's Mannor, 148¼ perches to the place of beginning."

John Guest on the 21st of November, 1706, sold to Alexander Frazer for £40 two hundred acres of land in the same township of Kennett, which two hundred acres was a part of six hundred and sixty-six and two-thirds acres which he owned by virtue of a warrant from the commissioners of property, laid out and surveyed to him on the 25th of December, 1703, the said two hundred acres adjoining the "Mannor" of Laetitia Penn.

Francis Smith was also one of the early landowners and settlers in this part of the county, he having been probably one of the very first, if not the first, for land was surveyed to him in 1686. Up to 1703, however, the settlement of this township had not made much progress, the following being all, or nearly all, of those who had taken up land therein: Francis Smith, 440 acres; Henry Peirce, 190; Robert Way, 425; Thomas Hope, 310; George Harlan, Israel and the Chandlers, 850; and a few years later the surveyor, Isaac Taylor, estimated the number of acres of land taken up at 12,100, and there were 2,000 acres in Laetitia Penn's Manor not surveyed. The settlers near the Brandywine about this time were the following: Peter Dicks, John Hope, George Harlan, for whom Isaac Taylor surveyed land in 1702, and in 1703 he surveyed for the following: Isaac Few and William Huntley.

The Laetitia Penn Manor may be as well be mentioned here as elsewhere. The tract of land included within this manor was conveyed by William Penn to Sir John Fagg of Sussex County, England, in trust for his wife, Gulielma Maria Penn, the conveyance being dated September 4 and 5, 1682. The land, however, remained unlocated until after the death of William Penn's wife, Gulielma Maria, and also until after the death of all of her children, with the exception of two, William Penn, Jr., and Laetitia. On the 17th of the 12th month, 1699, a warrant was directed to Henry Hollingsworth requiring him to lay out for these two children a tract of land, and on the 25th of the 2d month, 1700, he surveyed for them 30,000 acres. This survey included all of the present township of New Garden, the larger portion of Kennett, and a smaller portion of New Castle County, Delaware.

By a patent dated October 23, 1701, the eastern part of this large tract of land was confirmed to Laetitia Penn, and was described in the following language:

"Whereas, There is a certain tract of land situated on the south side of Brandywine Creek in the province of Pennsylvania. Beginning at a bounded hickory tree standing by a branch of Red Clay Creek, called Burrow's Run, being a corner tree of William Dickson's land, thence by a line of marked trees south and by west over Red Clay Creek at the fork thereof, twelve hundred and eleven perches to a bounded black oak standing in the line of George Reed's land; thence by the said line west forty-two perches to a bounded black oak, being a corner of said George's land; thence south-south-west half westerly thirty-six perches to a bounded hickory, being a corner of William Guest's land; thence by the said Guest's land west 112 perches to a bounded white oak, being a corner of Brian McDonald's land; thence north fifty perches to a bounded poplar; thence west forty-eight perches to a black oak; thence north-west eighty-four perches to a bounded chestnut tree; thence south four degrees westerly one hundred and ten perches to a bounded black oak; thence west one hundred and forty-four perches to a bounded black oak, being a corner of the aforesaid William Guest's land; thence by a line crossing Mill Creek, west-south-west to a bounded tree standing near Peck Creek, six hundred and seventy perches; thence north by a line dividing it from a large tract laid out for the use of my son William Penn, 2,314 perches to a bounded tree; thence east 635 perches to a bounded white oak; hence south 638 perches to a bounded white oak; thence east-north-east 240 perches to a bounded red oak; thence north-east 420 perches to a corner post of George and Michael Harlan's land; thence by the line of their said land east-north-east 427 perches to a bounded black oak; thence south one-fourth westerly ·900 perches to a bounded black oak; thence west-north-west 268 perches to the place of beginning, containing 15,500 acres of land, being one moiety (allowance being first made for lands within the same already taken up) of a tract of thirty thousand acres granted by virtue of my warrant bearing date the 17th of the 12th month, 1699, to my children, William and Laetitia Penn, in right and as part of 50,000 acres by me originally granted to their mother, Gulielma Maria Penn, to hold to her and her heirs forever; which said 30,000 acres being by my order divided, the afore-de-scribed moiety by my will and disposition becomes the lott and share of my said daughter, Letitia, who requesting me to confirm the same to her by patent, Know Ye that as well in due regard to the memory of my dearly beloved wife, her mother, deceased, as for the fatherly love and natural affection I bear to her, my said daughter, Letitia Penn, I have given, granted and confirmed and do by these presents, for mee, my heirs and successors, fully, freely and absolutely, give, grant, release and confirm to the said Letitia Penn, her heirs and assigns forever, all that the said de-scribed tract of 15,500 acres of land, as the same is now set forth, bounded and limited as aforesaid, together with all mines, minerals, quarries, swamps, cripples, woods, timber and trees, ways, water courses, liberties, profits, commodities and appurtenances, what-soever to the 15,500 acres of land, or to any part or parcel thereof, belonging or in any wise appertaining; together with all rents, issues, profits, commodities and advantages, whatsoever, from any part or parcel of the said land heretofore to me, my heirs or successors reserved, arising or in any wise accruing; as also all full and free liberty to and for the said Letitia Penn, her heirs and as-signs, to hawk, hunt, fish and fowl, in and upon the premises hereby granted, or upon any part thereof; reserving always to all persons the fee of any parcel of land which has at any time

been granted or confirmed to them by patents from myself or my
commissioners of property.

"To Have, Hold, Possess and Enjoy the said described tract of
15,500 acres of land with the appurtenances and all other the
premises, to the said Letitia Penn, her heirs and assigns forever,
to the sole proper use and behoof of the said Letitia Penn, her
heirs and assigns. To be holden of mee, my heirs and successors,
proprietors of Pennsylvania, as of our manor of Rocklands in the
said province, in free and common soccage, by fealty only for all
services. Yielding and paying therefor to me, my heirs and successors, a Bever skinn, to be delivered at Philadelphia, at or upon
the first day of the first month of every year, to such person or
persons as shall be appointed to receive the same, and also three
full and clear fifths parts of all Royall mines, which shall from time
to time happen to be found within the limits of the premises
hereby granted, free from all deductions and reprisals for dig-
ging and refining the same. And out of my own further pleasure, free will, certain knowledge, and meer motion, I have thought
fitt to erect the herein before granted tract of land into a manor
by the name of the Manor of Stansing, and so will have it called
henceforth. To have and to hold a Court Baron, belonging and
to have and to hold view of ffrank pledge, for the conservation of
the peace, and the better government of the tenants holding or
hereafter to hold of the said manor, and all other persons that
shall live within the limits thereof, by the said Letitia and
her heirs or by her or by these stewards; and in the same to use all
things that to the view of ffrank pledge do belong. In witness
whereof I have caused these letters to be made patents."

This document was signed by William Penn in Philadelphia.
This manor, named Stansing in the above description, was really
the Manor of Stenning, though in the records it is sometimes
spelled Staning, Steyning, Staining, or Staineing. Letitia Penn
accompanied her father to this country on his second visit, and

returned with him, but while she was in America she signed a power
attorney, November 3, 1701, authorizing James Logan and Edward
Penington to manage her property in the province. After the
death of the latter James Logan was her sole attorney, until De.
cember 24, 1711, she and her husband, William Aubrey, executed
a power of attorney including Samuel Carpenter, who, together
with James Logan, thereafter managed her manor. They surveyed
land to the following persons in the years named: To Gayen Mil.
ler, who has already been mentioned, 200 acres on the east branch
of Red Clay Creek; this including the eastern part of the present
borough of Kennett Square; to Mary Rowland, in 1712, 438 acres
between Mr. Miller's land and the line of New Garden Township;
in 1713, to William Pyle, 280 acres; to Alexander Steward, 350
acres; Silas Pryor, 371 acres; Caleb Prew, 200 acres; John Gregg,
400 acres; John Cloud, 335 acres on the circular boundary line;
in 1715, Ellis Lewis, 293 acres; in 1717, Jacob Bennett, 215 acres; in
1716, Benjamin Fred, 200 acres; in 1720, John Packer, 200 acres;
in 1723, Robert Roberts, 170 acres; and in 1730, William Levis,
100 acres.

That portion of this 30,000 acres designed for William Penn,
Jr., 14,500 acres, was patented to him in May 24, 1706, by the commissioners, Edward Shippen, Griffith Owen and Thomas Story,
and received the same name, Stenning. Its boundaries are much
more briefly described, as follows:

"Beginning at a hickory tree on the west side of a branch of
White Clay Creek, thence east 925 perches to a corner of Letitia's
Manor (Kennett), thence by the same south 2,314 perches to another corner, thence west-south-west 930 perches to White Clay
Creek, west fifty-eight perches, and north by land of the London
company, 2,674 perches to the place of beginning." Settlers
within this manor have been given heretofore.

Francis Yarnell on June 8, 1708, sold to John Cadwallader for
£60 in the township of Williston containing 150 acres, which
had been granted to him by the commissioners of property in 1703.

Edward Hughes on December 20, 1708, sold to Richard Hill for £100 five hundred acres in the township of Easttown, which property was then called "Travelywyn," and on June 13, 1709, Francis Yarnell, as administrator of the estate of Noah Watkins, sold one hundred acres of land in Goshen Township to Mordecai Bean.

William Penn, by his commissioners, Shippen, Owen and Logan, on June 25, 1703, granted to Robert Pennel and Benjamin Mendenhall a tract of land containing six hundred acres on the west side of the Brandywine in Chester County. This land Robert Pennel sold to Benjamin Mead April 18, 1711, with the exception of one hundred acres then owned by William Horne.

Barnabas Wilcox purchased land of the commissioners of property in Westtown late in the last century, and on March 23, 1696, his heirs and successors sold five hundred acres to John Gibbons, which he gave to his son, James Gibbons.

John Blunstone on November 27, 1711, sold to Aaron James two hundred and seventy-six acres of land for £112, which is in the township of Westtown, and which Mr. Blunstone had received from the commissioners of property. This land adjoined land owned by Benjamin Hickman and John Bellows. That John Blunstone was a prominent man in the early history of this county is evident from the fact that when William Penn, on November 1, 1701, went to England, he had established a council of state, composed of ten members, of which John Blunstone and Caleb Pusey were from Chester County.

The land in this township was resurveyed in 1703 by Isaac Taylor, who made a return of lands owned by several parties as follows: William Swarfar, 237 acres; Daniel Hoopes, 470; Benjamin Hickman, 230; Aaron James, 208; Richard Whitepaine's heirs, 1,918; Richard Collett, 1,090. The land of the latter was at the west end of the township, and was probably in charge of the surveyor, at least for a time. It was purchased September 2, 1727, by John Salkeld of Chester, while he was on a visit to England.

On his return to this country he sold one-half of it to his nephew, Joseph Parker, and he also sold three hundred acres to William Harvey of Kennett.

Richard Whitpaine of London, England, bought a large amount of land in the province of Pennsylvania, some of it in Montgomery County. His land in Westtown, Chester County, extended from the Collett tract, above mentioned, to the present School farm. After his death in 1689 his creditors assumed the care of his Pennsylvania lands, and the surviving creditor in 1712 conveyed the property to William Aubrey in trust, who, in 1713 conveyed to Rees Thomas of Merion and to Anthony Morris, Jr., of Philadelphia to whom a patent was granted by the commissioners of property July 10, 1718. On May 28, 1718, these two gentlemen conveyed a one-third interest in the land to John Whitpaine of Philadelphia, grandson of the original owner, and after the death of this grandson his widow disposed of it to settlers. On March 30 and 31 she sold an undivided third interest to James Gibbons, and on the same days Thomas and Morris, mentioned above, sold the other two-thirds to the same man. Land in the same township was also sold: to Thomas Mercer, 401 acres; to Richard Eavenson, 219 acres; to John Yearsley, 290 acres; to Philip Taylor, 200 acres, and to Joseph Hunt, 252½ acres.

Joseph Shippen, then of Westtown, Chester County, in 1792 purchased of Jacob Gibbons two tracts of land, one containing 187 acres and the other somewhat more than 67 acres, parts of 400 acres which had belonged to Joseph Gibbons, father of Jacob, Joseph having received it by will from his father, James, who had purchased it of the widow of John Whitpaine of Philadelphia.

Joseph Shippen was for some time associate judge of Chester County courts, built a mansion on his property, and gave his plantation the name of "Plumley." Richard Thomas on March 30, 1711, sold two hundred acres of land in the township of Goshen to Alexander Beans, which land lay in the vicinity of land owned by Evan

Jones and John Haines and "the reputed land of Thomas Bowater." This two hundred acres of land was a part of 1,665 acres
granted to Richard Thomas by William Penn by patent dated
July 5, 1703, and on the 28th of November, 1711, Mr. Thomas sold
to the same party two hundred acres more of the same tract.

It is stated in Futhey and Cope's History of Chester County
that this John Haines became the owner of all the land in the
borough of West Chester south of Gay street in 1702, of which in
1715 he sold 365 acres to his son John; and that the latter in 1751
sold fifty acres to John Hoopes, and in 1753 to his son David fifty-
one acres and 112 perches, and that he devised one hundred acres
at his death to his grandson John, son of David Haines. John
Hoopes also became the owner of the land sold to David Haines,
mentioned above, and sold the entire quantity to John Patton in
1784. This 101 acres and 112 perches of land formed the southeast
part of the town of West Chester, adjoining the Turk's Head.

The great Welsh Tract was bounded as follows: The northern line is that which separates the townships of Tredyffrin and
East and West Whiteland Townships from Schuylkill, Charlestown and Lower Uwchlan; the western line is that which separates
West Whiteland, West Goshen and West Chester from East Caln
and East Bradford, the northwest corner being thus the northwest corner of West Whiteland Township. The southern boundary does not appear to be now certain, but the survey pretty
surely included the townships of Haverford, Radnor, Merion,
Tredyffrin, Whiteland, Willistown, Easttown, Goshen and a part
of Westtown.

Of these townships Haverford and Radnor are now in Delaware County, though formerly they were a part of Chester County,
and Merion Township is in Philadelphia County. When the division line was run through the Welsh Tract, separating Merion from
Chester County, there was great dissatisfaction among the Welsh,
for this line divided their barony into two parts, but the sequel

has been treated of above and need not be pursued further here, except to note that if the southern and eastern boundaries were parallel respectively to the northern and western boundaries of the Welsh Tract the area thereof would be very nearly 40,000 acres; but the three townships first named above were in part at least outside of these limits, which was made necessary from the fact that others besides the Welsh settled within the limits.

One of the features of early life in Chester County, though not exclusively in Chester County, was that of the indenture of servants, or the binding of them to serve for a term of years. Such advertisements as the following were common in the papers published in the first quarter of the present century:

SIX CENTS REWARD!

"Ran away from the suscribers, living in Sadsbury, Chester County, about five months ago, an apprentice boy turned seventeen years old, named John Watson McCord. I do hereby warn all persons not to harbor said runaway servant about their houses, and any person bringing him home shall be entitled to the above reward, but no expenses paid.

"WILLIAM BRIGGS."

THREE CENTS REWARD!

"Ran away from the subscriber, living in West Brandywine Township, on the 4th of this instant (March, 1819), an indentured servant girl of color, named Hannah Waits, near seventeen years of age. Whoever takes her up and brings her home shall receive the above reward, but no charges.

"HUMPHREY MARSHALL."

As has been stated elsewhere in this work, it was customary in the early history of the province for many who could not pay their passage to this country, to bind themselves out for a term of years to anyone that would pay their way across the sea.

CHAPTER V.

THE REVOLUTIONARY WAR.

CHAPTER V.

ASIDE from the difficulties connected with the boundary line settlement between Pennsylvania and Maryland, which difficulties occurred mainly to the westward of Chester County, there were no warlike demonstrations of interest until the breaking out of the war between England and France, which began in 1744. The declaration of war by England against France was made March 29, 1744, and notice thereof was given to the people of the province of Pennsylvania by the Governor thereof by proclama-tion dated June 11, 1744. While it was fortunately true that Chester County was not the scene of active operations during that war, yet enlistments were made within the county, and petitions were presented to the assembly by James Mather, David Cowp-land, John Salkeld and Aubrey Bevan, travern keepers, of Ches-ter, for feeding a company of soldiers under the command of Cap-tain Shannon, and payment was asked by Dr. Gandouit for medicines and attendance on sick soldiers. In this war the Indians eventually sided with the French, and as the assembly did not make any effective military laws, preparations for defense were necessarily left to the voluntarily action of the people, if made at all. It was this necessity that led to the formation of military bodies or organizations under the name of "Associators," two regiments of his kind being formed in Chester County. One of these regiments was commanded by Colonel William Moore, and its ranks were filled with men from the townships of East and West Nantmeal, Uwchlan, West Caln and Charlestown. The lieutenant-colonel of this regiment was Samuel Flower and the major John Mather. The line officers of the second regiment were Andrew McDowell, colonel; John Frew, lieutenant-colonel, and John Miller, major.

Neither the history of the causes that led to the Revolutionary War, nor the history of that war can be expected or desired in this work; yet it will be serviceable to note a few of the important events in each case for the purpose of introduction to the part played in that great conflict by Chester County. In April, 1770, the British ministry had taken off all the taxes of which the colonists complained except the tax on tea, three pence per pound; and as the result of various movements and disagreements a body of some fifty persons, disguised as Indians, went on board the vessels in Boston harbor loaded with tea and threw the same overboard, December 16, 1773, in the presence of a great crowd of people collected to see this act performed. In March and April, 1774, the British ministry passed a series of acts making an open struggle only a question of time. The Boston Port act closed the port of Boston against all commerce until the tea thus destroyed should be paid for and the town itself should return to loyalty. The Massachusetts act changed the charter of the colony; the Quebec act extended the boundary of Canada over the whole territory of the northwest north of the Ohio River and east of the Mississippi.

The consequence of these acts was to largely crystallize the union elements in the colonies, and the necessity for another congress was widely felt. This congress met at Philadelphia September 5, 1774, all the colonies being represented except Georgia, and it was well known that Georgia was in full sympathy with the movement. This was called the First Continental Congress, the first national body in the history of America. The ultimatum adopted by this congress October 8, 1774, was: "That this congress approve the opposition of Massachusetts Bay to the execution of the late acts of Parliament; and if the same shall be attempted to be carried into execution by force, in such case all America ought to support them in their opposition." Summoning a new congress to meet at Philadelphia May 10 following, this first Continental Congress adjourned.

In February, 1775, Governor Gage of Massachusetts sent a water expedition to Salem to search for powder, but as the day was Sunday a conflict was prevented by the ministers. Another expedition sent out April 19 to Concord, a small village twenty miles from Boston, to seize a stock of powder said to be there stored, resulted in the battle of Lexington, but the troops proceeded nevertheless to Concord, and destroyed the powder, and were so hotly pursued on their return to Boston that had not a rescue party been sent out to their assistance they would all have been taken prisoners. From April 9, 1775, dates the national existence of the United States.

On May 10, 1775, two historic events occurred—the meeting in Philadelphia of the second Continental Congress and the capture of Ticonderoga. This second congress adopted the army around Boston as the "American Continental Army," and Washington appears for the first time on the stage of history, which for so long a time he completely filled. The battle of Bunker Hill occurred on June 17, 1775 and on December 31, 1775, Montgomery fell at Quebec and Benedict Arnold was wounded. In June,

1776, Congress began to issue bills of credit, or continental currency, but it failed to seize the power of taxation to provide for
its redemption, the consequences of which are well known to all
readers of history.   In February, 1776, the first American fleet of
eight vessels sailed, but its work was of but little importance.

During all this time there were two elements at work in
opposition to each other throughout the colonies—one in favor
of reconciliation with Great Britain, the other in favor of independence.   The provincial congress of Massachusetts, the convention of Maryland, the assembly of New Jersey and other colonial
bodies declared in the strongest terms their affection for the
"mother country" and their desire for a reconciliation and harmony between themselves and Great Britain.   What was called
a reunion with Great Britain, on constitutional principles, was
the favorite object of the Continental Congress, whose conduct
was constantly marked with defensive movements, at no time
giving way to revenge or resentment—passions inconsistent with
the dignity of public bodies.   They deeply sympathized with the
distress of their country, and made a redress of grievances and the
protection of America their only care.   Nothing appeared up
to this time to show that independence was what they desired.
Those who opposed any attempt to secure the independence of
the colonies made the statement that outside of the Continental
Congress there were 310,174 people in Maryland represented by
their convention; 372,208 people in Pennsylvania represented by
their assembly; 161,290 people in New Jersey represented by
their assembly, and 124,069 people in New Hampshire represented
by their convention, amounting in all to 967,741 people, nearly
one-third of the population of the entire thirteen colonies, who
were opposed to separation from the mother country, and that
the proportion was as great in the colonies not enumerated.

But notwithstanding such arguments, there were many people
who fully believed that reconciliation was impossible, and these

people were represented in the public prints by able writers, who presented such arguments as the following: Governments should always be considered as matters of convenience, not of right. The Scripture institutes no regular form of government, but it enters a protest against the monarchical form; and a negation of one thing where two things only are offered and one of them must be chosen, amounts to an affirmative as to the other. Monarchical government was first set up by the heathens, and the Almighty permitted it to the Jews as a punishment. "I gave them a King in mine anger," was quoted (but the writer omitted the last part of the same sentence: "I took him away in my wrath.") A republican form of government is pointed out by nature, and a Kingly government by an inequality of power. In republican governments the leaders of the people if improper are removable by vote; Kings only by arms. An unsuccessful vote in the first case leaves the voter safe; but an unsuccessful attempt in the latter, death. Strange! that what is our right in one should be our ruin in the other—from which reflection follows this maxim—that that mode of government in which our right becomes our ruin cannot be the right form of government. A republican form of government has more true grandeur in it than a Kingly government; on the part of the public it is more consistent with freemen to appoint their rulers than to have them born, and on the part of those who preside it is far nobler to be a ruler by choice of the people than a King by the chance of birth. Every honest delegate is more than a monarch. If the history of the creation and the history of Kings be compared the result will be this: That God made the world and Kings have robbed him of it.

While these movements were taking place in the American colonies and while such arguments were being used for and against independence, England was making her preparations for a reconciliation very different from the kind desired even by those whose ties bound them strongest to the mother country. On February

27, 1776, a messenger arrived at St. James's bearing some very important dispatches from the Regency of Hanover, and on the 1st of March he was sent over with several packets for the lords of that electorate. At that time the following forces were agreed to in council to be sent to America: Hessians, 12,000; Brunswickers, 4,000; Waldeckers, 2,000; British, 37,000; total, 55,000. The treaty with the Duke of Brunswick was signed by Colonel William Fawcitt on the 9th of January, 1776. By that treaty 3,964 men were taken into the pay of Great Britain, and also 336 light cavalry, dismounted, while half of them were to be ready to march on the 15th of February and to arrive at the place of embarkation on the 25th of the same month, the other half to be ready to march the last week of March. Levy money to be paid to the Duke of Brunswick was thirty crowns for each man, at the rate of 4s. 9¾d. to the crown, and the King was to pay the Duke a subsidy of 64,500 German crowns a year while in pay, and double that for two years after the troops returned. The treaty with the Landgrave of Hesse was signed at Cassel on the 15th of January and by it 12,000 Hessians were hired, a part of whom were to begin their march on the 27th of February, and the remainder within four weeks thereafter, twenty pounds banco to be paid for levy money for each man, the subsidy to be 45,000 crowns banco per annum at 4s. 9¾d., the treaty to continue one year after the troops arrived back in the Kingdom of Hesse.

The treaty with the Count of Hanau was signed February 5 for 668 infantry, to begin to march on the 20th of March, levy money to be 30 crowns, and the annual subsidy to be 35,000 crowns.

Thus arrayed before the world were the three parties to the coming contest, which has proved so momentous in the history of the world--the patriots, the loyalists and the British nation. And it is now time to turn attention to such events in Chester County that were the natural result of greater movements in the outside world. Immediately after the closing of the port of Boston, as narrated above, meetings were held in Philadelphia, and the committee of correspondence for this city sent out a circular to the principal citizens of each of the several counties in the prov. ince, in which they say: "The Governor declining to call the assembly renders it necessary to take the sentiments of the in. habitants; and for that purpose it is agreed to call a meeting of the inhabitants of this city and the county at the State House on Wednesday the 15th instant. And as we would wish to have the sentiments and concurrence of our brethren in the several coun. ties, who are equally interested with us in the general cause, we earnestly desire you to call together the principal inhabitants of your county and take their sentiments. We shall forward to you by every occasion any matters of consequence that come to our knowledge and we should be glad you would choose and appoint a committee to correspond with us."

This circular was sent to the following persons in Chester County: Francis Richardson, Elisha Price and Henry Hayes. These three gentlemen as a committee, on the 4th of July, 1774, issued a call for a meeting of the freeholders and others, inhabit. ants of the County of Chester, qualified by law to vote for repre- sentatives in the general assembly, to meet at the court-house in Chester on July 13 following, which meeting was accordingly held, and of which Francis Richardson was selected chairman and Francis Johnston secretary. A long series of resolutions was adopted affirming "Allegiance to our lawful and rightful sovereign lord, George III, King of Great Britain," etc., but at the same time condemning the act of Parliament closing the port of Bos- ton as unconstitutional, oppressive and dangerous to the liberties of the British colonies; favoring a Congress of Deputies from the colonies, and expressing the opinion that it would be highly con- ducive to the liberties of America "should the colonies enter into a solemn agreement not to purchase any goods, wares or mer- chandise imported from Great Britain under such restrictions as

be agreed upon by the colonies. We, for our part, sensible of the
great advantages which must arise from promoting economy and
manufacturing among ourselves are determined to use as little
foreign manufactures of what kind or quality soever as our necessities will permit until the several acts of the British Parliament
injurious to American interests be repealed."

The meeting then appointed the following committee to meet
with other similar committees from other counties in the province
to unite them in such measures as should be deemed advisable and
expedient: Francis Richardson, Elisha Price, John Hart, Anthony
Wayne, John Sellers, Hugh Lloyd, Francis Johnston, Richard
Riley, William Montgomery, William Barker, Thomas Hockley,
Robert Mendenhall and John Fleming, the first eight of whom were
present at Philadelphia on the 15th of that month.

At this meeting so held a series of sixteen resolutions were
unanimously adopted, in which they again expressed their
allegiance to the King of Great Britain, condemned the Parliament and urged that a Congress of Deputies from the several
colonies be immediately assembled, which should take such measures as would procure relief for their grievances and restore
harmony between Great Britain and her colonies. John Dichin-
son was chairman of the committee which presented the resolutions and was the author of the resolutions. This committee was
to give instructions to the assembly, which met the week afterward, and request them to appoint a proper number of representatives to attend the Congress of Deputies from the several
colonies, which should meet at some convenient time and place
to carry out the purposes of those having the interests of the
colonies at heart. Chester County's member of the committee
presenting these resolutions was Elisha Price.

The assembly, which met as expected, appointed as members
of the Congress of Deputies: Joseph Galloway, Daniel Rhoads,
Thomas Mifflin, John Morton, Charles Humphreys, George Ross,

Edward Biddle, and later, John Dickinson, John Morton and Charles Humphreys being from Chester County. The congress was composed of fifty-five delegates, and met in Philadelphia on September 5

On December 20, 1774, another meeting was held at the court-house in Chester County for the purpose of choosing a committee to carry into execution the association of the Continental Congress, the committee selected for this purpose being as follows: Anthony Wayne, Francis Johnston, Richard Riley, Evan Evans, James Moore, Hugh Lloyd, Thomas Hockley, David Cowpland, John Hart, Sketchley Morton, Samuel Fairlamb, Isaac Eyre, John Crosby, Nicholas Diehl, Jesse Bonsall, Aaron Oakford, Benjamin Brannan, John Talbot, Joseph Brown, Samuel Price, John Crawford, John Taylor, Lewis Gronow, Edward Humphreys, Henry Lawrence, Richard Thomas, William Montgomery, Persifor Frazer, Thomas Taylor, John Foulke, Robert Mendenhall, Joseph Pennell, George Pierce, Nicholas Fairlamb, Samuel Trimble, Charles Dilworth, John Hannum, George Hoops, Joel Bailey, John Gilliland, Joseph Bishop, Jr., John Kerlin, Edward Bones, William Lewis, Patrick Anderson, Joshua Evans, Thomas Hartman, Dr. Branson Van Leer, William Evans, Thomas Cowan, Thomas Haslep, Patterson Bell, Dr. Jonathan Morris, Andrew Mitchell, Thomas Buffington, James Bennett, Joseph Musgrave, William Miller, Richard Flower, Walter Finney, James Simpson, David Wherry, James Evans, Thomas Bishop, William Edwards, Jonathan Vernon, Jr., Lewis Davis, Sr., Joseph Gibbons, Jr., and Thomas Evans. This committee was authorized to continue until one month after the adjournment of the next Continental Congress, and to transact such business and to enter into such associations as to them might apear expedient.

Of this committee Anthony Wayne was selected chairman and Francis Johnston secretary. The committee then unanimously resolved that any twelve or more of their number should be a quorum, but that nothing should be done except upon the sanction of at least twelve, and that in their opinion it was necessary that a provincial convention should be held as soon as possible. They also resolved that twelve persons of their committee should be appointed to attend as delegates such a convention at such time and place as should be generally agreed upon.

The proposed provincial convention assembled at Philadelphia January 23, 1775, and remained in session until the 28th. Chester County was represented therein by the following ten persons: Anthony Wayne, Hugh Lloyd, Richard Thomas, Francis Johnston, Samuel Fairlamb, Lewis Davis, William Montgomery, Joseph Musgrave, Joshua Evans and Persifor Frazer. The two members elected to attend that could not be present were Thomas Hockley and Thomas Taylor.

A meeting of the Chester County committee was held March 20, 1775, at the house of Richard Cheyney in East Caln, at which meeting it was ordered that Mr. Hockley, Mr. Johnston, Mr. Gronow, Mr. Lloyd, Mr. Frazer, Mr. Moore and Mr. Taylor be appointed a committee to essay a draught of a petition to present to the general assembly of the province, with regard to the manumision of slaves, especially relating to the freedom of infants hereafter born of black women within this province, and to make report of the same to this committee at its next meeting.

At the first meeting of the Chester County committee it had been resolved that subscriptions be taken up for the suffering people of Boston and Massachusetts Bay, in accordance with which resolution the Society of Friends, acting in their meeting capacity, liberally contributed to the object. Chester Monthly Meeting contributed £70, Darby Meeting contributed £33 and Haverford Meeting also contributed to such an amount as was practicable. At the meeting of the committee held in March, above mentioned, it was on motion ordered that each member of the committee use his utmost diligence in collecting the several sums of money subscribed for the use of Boston, and pay the same into the hands of Anthony Wayne, treasurer, at the next meeting of the committee.

The committee held a meeting at Chester May 22, 1775, at which it was resolved, in order to avert the evils and calamities which threatened the country, that they would use their utmost endeavors to learn the military exercise, that they would pay a due regard to their officers, and that they would at all times be ready to defend their lives, liberties and property against all attempts to deprive them of them. On the 25th of September, 1775, a meeting was held at the sign of the Turk's Head in the township of Goshen, at which it was resolved that inasmuch as certain persons inimical to the liberties of America had industriously circulated a report that the military associators in the county, in conjunction with the military associators in general, intended to overturn the constitution by declaring an independency, etc., and as the report could only originate among the worst of men for the worst of purposes, "This committee have thought proper to declare, and they do hereby declare, their abhorrence even of an idea so pernicious in its nature, as they ardently wish for nothing more than a happy and speedy reconciliation on constitutional principles with that state from whom they derive their origin."

On the 23d of October, 1775, the committee, composed in part of new members, met again at the house of David Cowpland in Chester and passed a motion ordering each of its members to immediately make return of the quantity of powder he had already collected or might collect within his district, together with the prices and the name of the owner thereof, that the same might be paid for, and it was also resolved that Anthony Wayne, Francis Johnston, Elisha Price, Mr. Richardson, Mr. Knowles, Mr. Lloyd, and Mr. Brannan be appointed a committee of correspondence for the county.

The assembly, on the 30th of June, 1775, appointed a committee of safety, of which the Chester County members were as follows: Anthony Wayne, Benjamin Bartholomew, Francis Johnston, and Richard Riley. Each county was required to furnish a certain number of firelocks, six hundred being required from Chester County. These six hundred firelocks were manufactured by a Mr. Dunwicke and were ready to be tested by October 6, 1775. Of the committee of safety Benjamin Franklin was made president, William Garrett clerk, and Michael Hillegas treasurer. And among the first labors of this committee of safety was the preparation of articles for the government of those military organizations known as "Associators." In October the committee of safety was reorganized, but the Chester County members were all retained, and Nicholas Fairlamb was added to their number. The Chester County committee held a meeting on December 26, 1775, in order to secure a more perfect organization of the Associators, and it was resolved that Anthony Wayne, James Moore, Francis Johnston, Dr. Samuel Kennedy, Caleb Davis, William Montgomery, Persifor Frazer and Richard Thomas, or any five or more of them, be appointed to represent the county if there should be any occasion in provincial convention for the ensuing year.

At its session in May previous, Congress had resolved to raise a continental army, of which the portion allotted to Pennsylvania amounted to 4,300 men, and the assembly recommended to the several counties that they provide arms and accouterments for this force. At the request of Congress the committee recommended proper persons for officers in the several battalions. The committee recommended Anthony Wayne of Chester County as colonel. of the Fourth Pennsylvania battalion. Francis Johnston was recommended as lieutenant-colonel, and Nicholas Hansecker of Lancaster County as major. Of the three the latter was the only one that went over to the enemy, this being soon after the battle of Trenton.

The Provincial Convention that met in Philadelphia, January

23, 1775, recommended among other things the making of salt-peter, and, in accordance with this recommendation, extraordinary means were adopted to insure a proper supply. Benjamin Brannan, Walter Finney and John Beaton were appointed to attend the saltpeter manufactory in the city of Philadelphia, in order to perfect themselves in the art, and afterward made appointments to meet at several different houses in the county to teach and instruct all persons who might be pleased to apply at the times and places appointed. On February 7, 1776, a powder-maker by the name of Thomas Heimberger engaged to erect a powder mill in Chester County, about thirty-three miles from Philadelphia, a few miles from Yellow Springs, provided the committee advanced him £150 and kept him employed one year. On February 26, 1776, John Beaton advertised that he would be at several places at as many different times to instruct in making saltpeter, and on March 29 an order was drawn by the committee of safety in favor of the committee of Chester County for £500 for the purchase of arms on account of Congress.

Every necessary precaution was taken to prevent any portion of the British navy from passing up the Delaware River to Philadelphia, chevaux-de-frize being sunk in the river, and only persons specially appointed to conduct vessels through the opening in the obstruction permitted to go below Chester. Provincial troops were rapidly organized along the river, and collected in such numbers that there were not houses enough in and around Chester to accommodate them, for which reason the committee of safety on April 13, 1776, resolved that Col. Miles procure for the use of the troops one hundred good tents on the most reasonable terms possible. On April 17, an order was drawn for £1,500 by the committee of safety in favor of the commissioners and assessors of Chester County for the payment of firelocks, etc., made in that county for the use of the province. An application was made to the committee of safety for 850 pounds of powder, in addition to the 400 pounds on hand, and lead enough for the whole, and for 1,500 flints to be distributed among the Associators, in order to supply them with twenty-three pounds per man.

May 7, 1776, Robert Towers was directed to deliver to Col. Samuel Miles, for the use of the Provincial troops under his command, 1,000 pounds of gunpowder and 2,000 pounds of lead, or as great a part thereof as is in store. At the same time 20,000 cartridges for muskets for the use of the Associators of Chester County were directed to be conveyed to Chester, and on the next day the commissary was directed to send down to Chester, for the use of the Provincial troops under Col. Miles, sixty firelocks.

In June, 1776, the powder works in Chester County were as follows: That owned by Cowperthwaite & Biddle on French Creek, about four miles above Moore Hall; that of Thomas Heimberger, on a branch of French Creek about five miles above that first mentioned; one on Crum Creek belonging to Dr. Robert Harris, and besides these there was a small one in Bucks County on Swamp Creek. At this time the number of firearms fit for service, in Chester County, was as follows: First battalion, Col. James Moore, 380; Second battalion, Col. Thomas Hockley, 400; Third battalion, Col. Hugh Lloyd, 300; Fourth battalion, Col. William Montgomery, 450; Fifth battalion, Col. Richard Thomas, 300; total, 1,830.

By order of the committee of safety the commissary, Robert Towers, was ordered to deliver to the colonels of the several battalions of Associators in Chester County the following quantities of ammunition: To Col. James Moore, 2,300 cartridges for provincial muskets; 2,070 cartridges sorted for the other bores of firelocks, and 1,500 flints; to Col. Thomas Hockley, 2,300 of the first kind, 2,300 of the second kind, and 1,600 flints; to Col. Hugh Lloyd, 1,840 of the first kind, 1,610 of the second kind, and 1,200 flints; to Col. William Montgomery, 2,760 of the first kind, 2,415 of the second kind, and 1,800 flints; to Col. Richard Thomas, 1,840 of the first kind, 1,610 of the second, and 1,200 flints. Each of these battalions also received lead and loose powder in the same proportion.

One of the important duties of the committee of safety was the preparation of articles governing the military organizations of the province, which articles are too lengthy and of too general a nature to require introduction here; but they were very rigid. Many of the citizen soldiers refused to subscribe to them or to submit to them, for the reason, as they claimed, that many persons claimed exemption from military service because of conscientious or religious scruples, the citizen soldiers thinking that where the liberties of all were in danger, all should bear their proportionate share of the risk and of the expense of defense. As a result of these objections to the performance of military duty on the part of those who were otherwise willing to perform them, the committee of safety recommended to the assembly that provisions be made that such persons as were opposed to becoming soldiers on account of their conscientious or religious scruples might be permitted to pay an equivalent in money for such services as they would otherwise have to perform. The assembly thereupon resolved that all persons between sixteen and fifty years of age, capable of bearing arms, who did not associate for the defense of the province ought to contribute an equivalent for the time spent by the Associators in acquiring military discipline, except ministers of the gospel and servants purchased bona fide. And the county commissioners were empowered to assess on those not associated the sum of £2 10s. annually in addition to the ordinary tax.

July 4, 1776, was the day that the Declaration of Independence went forth. On the 5th Congress resolved that the declaration be sent to the several assemblies and conventions and councils, and to the several commanders of the Continental troops, that it be read at the head of the army and in each of the United States. Letters were sent out by the committee to the different colonels of the battalions of the counties of Philadelphia, Bucks, Chester and Lancaster, requesting them to have their troops ready to march at an hour's notice. The Associators of the province, divided into fifty-three battalions, met by delegates at Lancaster July 4, 1776, to elect two brigadier-generals to command the forces of Pennsylvania, Daniel Roberdeau and James Ewing being chosen. To this convention at Lancaster, Chester County sent Major Culbertson, Col. Montgomery, Lieut.-Col. Gibson, Captains Wallace, Scott and Gardiner, and Privates Cunningham, Denny, Culbertson and Fulton.

On July 12, 1776, Robert Smith, who had been chosen lieutenant of the county, wrote to Thomas Wharton, Jr., president of the province, that he was under the necessity of applying to him for money to enable him to fill the first class of the militia of Chester County, which had long before been ordered to march, but that only 320 had arrived, of whom 200 were substitutes, and that the class when full would contain 700 men.

The musket battalion composed of 444 men was under command of Col. Samuel John Atlee, the captains of the several companies being Patrick Anderson, Peter Z. Lloyd, Francis Muncy, Abraham Marshall, Abraham Dehuff, Thomas Herbert, John Nice and Joseph Howell. On July 15, Abraham Marshall was permitted to resign and was succeeded by Joseph McClellan. This battalion, along with other troops from Chester County, was present in the campaign of New York. The fourth battalion, of Chester County, which was one of those in the New York campaign, was commanded by Col. Montgomery. One of the companies in this battalion was commanded by Captain James McDowell, the lieutenants being James Thorn and Daniel Hayes, the ensign Abraham Smith, the sergeants Charles Ramsey, John Wallace, Ezekiel Hopkins and John Arnell, and the drummer Neal Crossin. The number of private soldiers in this company was forty-six. Three battalions, including that of Col. Atlee, were formed into a regiment under command of Col. Samuel Miles, and were in the disastrous battle at Flatbush, Long Island, on the 27th of August. Several of Capt. Pat. Anderson's company were killed, one sergeant

and nine privates were missing, and the Captain himself nar-
rowly escaped with his life. Colonels Miles and Atlee were taken
prisoners, and Lieut.-Col. Caleb Perry was killed. The command
of the regiment then devolved upon Col. Daniel Broadhead. On
August 1 there were 397 men in Col. Atlee's battalion, but on September 22, according to a letter from Capt. Anderson, there were
only eighty-three men left, on account of losses in killed, wounded,
prisoners and deserters.

The Pennsylvania troops suffered severely, not only in the battle of Long Island, but also in the reduction of Fort Washington,
Col. Atlee's and Col. Montgomery's battalions, among several
others, being taken prisoners. General Howe then threatened
Philadelphia, to which city Gen. Washington sent Major-General
Israel Putnam to take charge of its defense. In the absence of the
troops from Chester County on the expeditions mentioned above,
the young women followed the plow and prepared the fallow fields
for the fall seeding. All of the coarse blankets, clothing and
stockings in the county were purchased, and the owners of stock,
by order of the committee of safety, prepared to remove their
stock back from the Delaware to a place of security, at least, to a
distance of five miles. The salt in the possession of the committee
was sent to the several counties in the province, Chester County,
receiving eighty bushels, which was to be sold to the people at the
rate of fifteen shillings per bushel. Dr. Robert Harris received
£58 for making powder, and it was proposed by Dr. Thomas Bond
that hospitals be established for the sick at Darby, Chester, Marcus
Hook, Wilmington and New Castle.

The battle of Trenton, won by General Washington December
25, 1776, greatly relieved the drooping spirits of the people and
removed the apprehensions that had been felt by the inhabitants
of Chester County of any immediate attack on the city of Philadelphia, which city was so near to them, and which would bring the
war so near to their homes. On the morning of the 10th of March,

13

1777, a serious accident occurred, in the explosion of the powder mill on French Creek, which, however, may not have been wholly an accident, for Peter Dehaven, who had charge of the mill, wrote to the committee of safety that he suspected the mill was blown up by Mr. Peck or his men, and, as a natural result, Mr. Peck and his men were all taken prisoners and kept under guard until an investigation could be made. One man was so badly burned that he died next day. After the investigation had been made Mr. Peck, who was the powder-maker, and his men were set at liberty.

The cannon cast at Warwick furnace during the year 1776 consisted of 23 12-pounders and 37 18-pounders, 60 in all, and those cast at Reading furnace consisted of 31 12-pounders and 61 18-pounders, 92 in all. On the 11th of November, 1776, Daniel Joy, from Reading furnace, wrote to Daniel Rittenhouse in Philadelphia, that he had sent him two 9-pounder cannon, proved with eight pounds of powder, two shot and three wads, that he intended to cast six more of the same size, and afterward one each day, but they would be somewhat larger.

On the 12th of March, 1777, the officers of the Fifth Pennsylvania regiment were as follows: Francis Johnston, colonel; Persifor Frazer, lieutenant-colonel, and Thomas Robinson, major. On April 3 a requisition for wagons was made upon Colonel Caleb Davis, Chester County; Major Evans, near Yellow Springs; Colonel William Dewees, at Valley Forge, and Isaac Webb, Milltown, now Downingtown.

On April 28, 1777, Lieut. Robert Smith wrote to President Wharton that he had used all the industry in his power in forwarding the business of the militia of Chester County, which had been divided into eight districts or battalions, that the field officers had been elected, and met that day to draw for rank, and he said that the number of persons returnable to him in the county as capable of bearing arms was upward of 5,000.

On July 9 the council made a request that the justices of the peace should nominate proper persons to take an account of all the wheat, flour, grain and other stores in the county of Chester within twenty miles of the Delaware to the westward, and in accordance therewith the justices, namely, Isaac Davis, James Moore, Daniel Griffith, Philip Scott and Robert Smith, made a return as follows:

John Wilson, Isaac Taylor, George Curry, Charles Dilworth, Thomas McCall, Joshua Evans, James Ewing and James Lindsey.

For the purpose of providing for and feeding the poor that might be removed from the city of Philadelphia, in anticipation of an attack on that city by the British general, Howe, the following gentlemen were appointed:

Benjamin Bartholomew of East Whiteland, Daniel John of Charlestown, David Thomas of Vincent, Michael Hallman of Pike-land, Peter Crumbacker of Coventry, William James of East Nant-meal, John Brower of West Nantmeal, Thomas Evans of Uwchlan, George Thomas of West Whiteland, James Thompson of East Caln, John Fleming of West Caln, Joseph Parker of Sadsbury, Thomas Heslip and Samuel Futhey of East and West Fallowfield, William Wilson of Oxford, William Pake of West Nottingham, and David Wherry of East Nottingham.

On August 5, 1877, Lewis Gronow wrote to Timothy Matlack, stating that great dissatisfaction was expressed with the mode of hiring substitutes. The advance of such large premiums as was being made in Philadelphia County for two months' service was unreasonable and absurd. The county had given £25 for several that had been supplied, and the news quickly reached Chester County, which made it necessary to give as much in Chester County, otherwise the men would go elsewhere to enlist; that is, men who were not under marching orders, for which he said they could not be blamed. The question, therefore, was, Mr. Gronow said, whether he should pay such extravagant premiums.

It was about this time that the British fleet approached Delaware Bay, and it was expected that fleet would ascend the bay and river as far as practicable, and make the attack on Philadelphia from that direction. Washington was, therefore, directed to re-pair with his army to Philadelphia, and the militia of Maryland, Delaware and Northern Virginia were ordered to join the Pennsyl-vania troops. Upon Washington's arrival in Philadelphia he first met Lafayette, who had then recently arrived in that city, and Lafayette at once took up his quarters with the commander-in-chief. General Howe, after entering Delaware Bay, found ap-proach to Philadelphia too difficult by that route, so withdrew his fleet to the ocean, and entered Chesapeake Bay. August 25, the British army, consisting of 18,000 men, including a portion of the Hessians, disembarked near the head of the Elk River, and on the 28th the vanguard arrived at the head of the Elk, and the day fol-lowing at Gray's Hill. Here it was joined by the rear guard under General Knyphausen, and the entire army posted itself behind the river Christiana, with Newark on the right and Pencander on the left.

In the month of September two companies of militia of Chester County embodied themselves and applied for ammunition and arms at headquarters, fearing that the enemy would invade the county; but their application was refused, it was thought, for the reason that they were unwilling to join in with the other militia and be taken under the direction of the commander-in-chief. The day be-fore the British army landed, as narrated above, General Washing-ton marched his army through Philadelphia toward the Brandy-wine, and as the means of transportation for the army baggage was inadequate, an order was issued to the justices of the peace of each county of Philadelphia and Chester for twenty-five four-horse wagons. The headquarters were established at Wilmington, and on September 1 the militia called out in Lancaster County were ordered by him to join his forces at that place.

The British army being put in motion, threatened with its right the center of General Washington's position, and with its left extended threatened to turn his right wing. Perceiving the danger, General Washington retired behind the Brandywine and took up a position at Chadd's Ford, as the most practicable of all for defense, and encamped on the rising ground extending from Chadd's Ford in the direction of northwest to southeast. General Maxwell's riflemen scoured the right or west bank of the Brandywine in order to harass and retard the approach of the British army as much as possible, and the militia under General Armstrong was assigned a position on the left or east bank of the Brandywine, about two miles below the principal encampment of Washington, which enabled him to guard two fords, named Pyle's Ford and Corner Ford. In order to fortify the position at Chadd's Ford a line of breastworks was hastily thrown up on the bluff bordering on level ground a little to the north of the main road, and the right wing of the American army lined the banks of the Brandywine higher up, where the passages were more difficult.

Having thus disposed his army Washington awaited the approach of the British, which, on the evening of September 9, entered Chester County in two divisions, one of which, under General Knyphausen, encamped at New Garden and Kennett Square, and the other under Cornwallis, a short distance below Hockessin Meeting-house. The next day the two divisions of the army united at Kennett Square, in the evening the forces under Knyphausen advancing toward Welsh's Tavern, afterward known as the Anvil, those under Cornwallis remaining on the hills north and west of Kennett Square.

On this day Peter De Haven wrote to Vice-President Bryan that Doctor Kanady had requested him to spare one hundred stand of arms at the "Yallo Spring," as there was a suspicion of the "Towrys raising." But Mr. De Haven could not spare any arms or ammunition without an order from the executive council. On the same day Mr. De Haven wrote another letter to the effect that a part of "Mr. Hows armey is within four miles of Downins Town, and I believe they intend for our Magazene, and we are in a very poor situation for defending it. I should be very glad if you would send a proper Gard for this place. I have Rid threw this Naber-hood to Procure Waggons but could get but 8 or 10 to move som of the Powder toward Reddin, but to what place I am a stranger."

By the rapid approach of "Mr. Hows armey," Mr. De Haven was compelled to depart and to burn the mills, removing to Hummelstown.

Early on the morning of the 11th of September General Howe divided his army into two columns, one commanded by General Knyphausen, the other by Lord Cornwallis, the former marching direct to Chadd's Ford by the Philadelphia road, and the other, accompanied by General Howe, taking a circuitous route through the townships of Kennett, East Marlborough, Newlin, West and East Bradford, and Birmingham, on the way crossing the West Branch of the Brandywine at Trimble's Ford, and the East Branch at Jefferis' Ford, and approaching Birmingham Meeting-house from the north. While this movement was being made by Cornwallis' column, Knyphausen's column was making repeated attempts to cross the Brandywine at Chadd's Ford, merely to divert the attention of the Americans from this important flank movement. By furious cannonading on the part of Knyphausen, alternate retreats and eager pursuits of the portions of Washington's army thrown across the Brandywine at Chadd's Ford, the flank movement was kept from General Washington until about noon, when General Howe had crossed both of the upper branches of the Brandywine and was proceeding down the left bank of the main branch with the view of suddenly falling upon and crushing the right wing of the American army. Upon being advised of this movement of the British general, Washington decided on the boldest move possible to be made—to cross the Brandywine with his entire army, fall upon Knyphausen with terrible force and to crush

him before Howe could arrive upon the scene. Had this movement been carried out the fortunes of the day would have been with
the Americans, but when in the execution of this design a second
report arrived at Washington's headquarters that no such movement as previously reported had been made by General Howe, that
he had not crossed the upper branches of the Brandywine, that he
had made a feint of crossing, but that he had really marched down
the right bank of the stream, instead of crossing over, and was
then on the point of uniting his forces with those of Knyphausen;
in which case, Gen. Washington knew that the British army would
be superior to his both in numbers and in the fact of acting on the
defensive, and hence his failure to crush Knyphausen and the loss
to him of the battle of the Brandywine.

In the midst of conflicting reports as to the movements of
Lord Cornwallis' column, a citizen of Thornbury Township named
Thomas Cheyney, a justice of the peace, rode up to the forces under
General Sullivan, and informed that general of the true state of
affairs—that Cornwallis had crossed the Brandywine and was rapidly marching down its left bank. Being rather uncourteously
received by General Sullivan, Mr. Cheyney demanded that he should
be conducted to the commander-in-chief, who at first disposed to
doubt the correctness of the information, was at length convinced
of its truth, and immediately disposed of his troops in such a
manner as best to meet the new and unexpected emergency. The
right wing of the army of Washington was in command of Generals Stephen, Stirling and Sullivan, and under their respective
commanders the three divisions of the right wing advanced to
meet the British coming down from the north. The division
under command of General Anthony Wayne remained at Chadd's
Ford to keep Knyphausen in check, and General Greene's division,
accompanied by General Washington, formed a reserve, taking a
position between the right and left wings, and ready to march
either to the succor of Sullivan or Wayne, as circumstances might
require.

The column of Cornwallis being now in sight of the American forces, General Sullivan drew up his troops on the ground above Birmingham Meeting-house, his left extending toward the Brandy-wine, and his right toward a thick piece of woods. His artillery was advantageously planted, but his division having taken a cir-cuitons route in getting into position, the battle began before he was really ready for it, about half-past four o'clock in the after-noon. The right, having been formed under the enemy's fire, first gave way, exposing that flank of the remaining divisions to a gall-ing fire, and the right continuing to break all along the line, the flight became general. The vanquished soldiers fled into the woods in their rear, the victors pursuing and advancing by the great road toward Dilworth. In order to check the pursuit the Tenth Vir-ginia, under Col. Stephens, and a Pennsylvania regiment, under Col. Stewart, neither of which had participated in the battle, were advantageously posted on the road taken by the fleeing army, and though at length dispersed by Gen. Howe's troops, yet performed good service in checking and putting an end to the pursuit. Gen. Greene also contributed largely to the same end, for, having placed himself at the head of Muhlenberg's Brigade, in the rear of the retreating army, he kept up so destructive a fire from his artillery as to retard the enemy, and arriving at a narrow defile strongly protected on both right and left by woods, he immediately halted his forces, sent forward his cannon, and· formed his troops, de-termined to dispute the pass, notwithstanding the superiority of the pursuing army. Though he was dislodged by Howe, the pur-suit was here abandoned.

While the above movements were in progress General Anthony Wayne was at the defense of Chadd's Ford, with three field pieces and a howitzer, his army for some time standing firm; but learning that the right of their army had been defeated, and seeing some British soldiers coming out of the woods on their flank, they also retired in disorder, leaving their artillery and munitions to the

Hessian general. In their retreat they passed behind the position of General Greene, who still defended the position he had taken, and was the last to leave the field. Finally, after a long and obstinate conflict, darkness coming on, he also retired, and the whole American army retreated that night by different roads to Chester. The next day Washington's army retired to Philadelphia.

The losses of the American army in this battle are stated to have been 300 killed, 600 wounded and about 400 taken prisoners. They also lost ten field pieces and a howitzer. The loss of the British was something over 500, the killed being about 100. The reason for this great disparity of loss is thought to have been that many of the muskets used by the Americans were totally unfit for service. In his report to Congress, dated at Chester, twelve o'clock at night, September 11, 1777, Gen. Washington stated that he believed his loss was much less than that of the enemy.

While the American army was encamped on the Brandywine the headquarters of Gen. Washington were in the dwelling of Benjamin Ring, a mile from Chadd's Ford, and the headquarters of Lafayette were at the dwelling of Gideon Gilpin, who was still living when Lafayette, who was wounded in the leg during the battle of the Brandywine, made his memorable visit to this country in 1824 and 1825. Other Frenchmen who participated in this battle, whose names are worthy of mention, were Baron St. Ouary and Captain De Fleury, the latter of whom had a horse killed under him, and the former being taken prisoner. Count Pulaski, a noble Pole, was also in this battle, and displayed conspicuous bravery at the head of the light horse.

"In the fight at Birmingham Meeting-house a party of the Americans for a time occupied a position inside the rear wall of the graveyard. A number of the British fell here. The killed of both armies who fell in the vicinity of the meeting-house were buried in the graveyard which partly surrounds it, their remains occupying one common grave just inside of the gate and on the side next to the meeting-house.   The meeting-house was used as a hospital while the British army remained in the neighborhood."

A few days after the battle four or five hundred of the American wounded were taken to Ephrata, in Lancaster County, and placed in a hospital, where the camp fever set in, and this, together with the wounds of the soldiers, so baffled the skill of the surgeons that one hundred and fifty of the soldiers died, a fearful mortality. They were principally from Pennsylvania and New England, though there were among them a few British soldiers who had deserted and joined the Americans.

The place where Lafayette received his wound was on the high ground a little northwest of the frame public schoolhouse, and southeast of the residence afterward occupied by John Bennett. It was south of Wistar's woods, a field which for years after the war was strewn with musket balls. In his Memoirs, General Lafayette says: "La confusion devint extreme, et c'est en ralliant les troubes que M. de Lafayette eut la jambe traversee d'une balle. A cette epoque, tout ce qui restait plia. M. de Lafayette dut a Gimat, son aide-de-camp, le bonheur de remonter a cheval."

The story as to Thomas Cheyney's carrying the correct information of the movements of Cornwallis' wing of the army to General Sullivan is thought by some to be wholly apocryphal; but it is given on the authority of a "Lady near West Chester," she relating it in a letter to Dr. A. L. Elwyn of Philadelphia. But whether this story is true or false, it appears perfectly clear that the false information which led to the abandonment by Gen. Washington of his excellent plan for defeating the British army in detail, or at least the crushing of the German wing of it under Gen. Knyphausen, was conveyed to Gen. Sullivan by Major Spear, whom Washington had himself sent out to gain the very information that was needed, and that this false information was transmitted to Gen. Washington by Gen. Sullivan in time to prevent the success of Washington's proposed movement across the Brandywine. This false information was confirmed by Sergeant Tucker before being forwarded to Washington. This is all most remark- able, for the reason that it was in direct contradiction of Gen. Sullivan's opinion of what Gen. Howe would do as a military man, and which, in fact, Gen. Howe did do, and it was this unfortunate communication of Gen. Sullivan to Gen. Washington that led to the loss of the battle of Brandywine, and to many other misfor- tunes which followed in its wake.

A considerable portion of the British army remained in the vicinity of the battlefield from the 11th to the morning of the 16th, the chief portion about Dilworthtown and south of that place. On the 12th a detachment marched to Concord Meeting-house, where it was joined on the 13th by Cornwallis with some light infantry and British grenadiers, and soon after Howe moved his army through Chester County toward the Schuylkill River, with the view of crossing that river and then taking possession of Philadelphia. One of the principal crossing places of that river was at Swede's Ford, near the present southern limits of Norristown, and, as the water was deep lower down the Schuylkill, it was expected the British army would attempt to cross there or higher up the stream. As Washington did not want Philadelphia to fall into the hands of the British, he determined to risk another battle, and on the 15th of September left his camp at Germantown, crossed the Schuylkill with the main body of his army, and marched up the Lancaster road, with the intention of meeting the enemy and giving him battle. The British commander, learning that Washington was advancing on the Lancaster road, resolved to make an attack upon him, and that portion of his army which had been encamped in the neighborhood of Village Green left that point on the morning of the 16th under Cornwallis, proceeding northward toward the Great Valley on the Chester road by the present villages of Glen Riddle, Lima and Howellville, and by Rocky Hill and Goshen Friends' Meeting-house.

The two armies moved to positions between the White Horse and Goshen meeting-houses, on the high ground south of the valley, and began making preparations for a battle. To Gen. Wayne was assigned the duty of leading and opening the battle, and skirmishing began between the advancing forces; but just at this time a sudden and violent thunderstorm came up and put an end to hostilities for the time being. Then, after a consultation, Washington decided to retire and form on the high ground in the Great Valley east of the White Horse, north of the old Lancaster road, where he waited until four o'clock in the afternoon for the advance of the British army. The point where the above-mentioned skirmishing occurred was one and a half miles north of Goshen Meeting-house and about a half mile a little west of south of the old "Three Tuns" tavern, where twelve American soldiers were killed, a few wounded and some taken prisoners.

When Cornwallis moved northward from the Village Green or Seven Stars, the British forces that had remained in camp near the battlefield moved forward under Knyphausen by the way of Turk's Head, now West Chester, with the view of uniting with Cornwallis. A portion of this force under Brig.-Gen. Matthews proceeded from the Turk's Head by the Reading road to the Indian King tavern, and thence to the northeastern part of the farm occupied by James Dunwoody, near the Ship road, and went into camp in order to protect themselves from the rain, while the Hessian line took the road leading from the Turk's Head to the Boot tavern, and proceeded thence northward toward the Ship tavern. On the farm of Daniel Meredith they encountered a detachment of Americans, with which they had a sharp skirmish, a few being killed on both sides, and some prisoners being taken by the Hessians. This engagement, which was likewise interrupted by the rain, occurred about the same as the other between Cornwallis' and Washington's forces, the two skirmishes being about three miles apart. The army of Washington retired to the Yellow Springs, and there an inspection disclosed the fact that on account of the wet condition of the powder there was scarcely a musket in the army that could be discharged. Washington therefore continued his retreat to Warwick furnace, on the south branch of French Creek, where a supply of arms and ammunition was obtained. On the 18th of the month the two divisions of the British army, under Cornwallis and Knyphausen, united their forces and moved down the Lancaster and Swede's Ford road into the township of Tre dyffrin, encamping at the village of Howellville and between that village and Centerville.

On the 17th Gen. Wayne, with his division of about 1,500 men, was ordered to join Gen. Smallwood, in command of the Maryland militia, in the rear of the British army, and to seize every opportunity to annoy the enemy, to cut off his baggage train, and thus arrest his march to the Schuylkill until the American army under Washington could cross the river higher up, pass down the east side and thus be in a position to prevent Gen. Howe from crossing over. On the 18th Gen. Wayne was encamped about three hundred yards to the eastward of the present Paoli monument, securely concealed, as he believed, from all knowledge of Gen. Howe. Wayne thought that he had taken abundant precautions against himself being surprised, and under ordinary circumstances such would have been the case, for the British general did not know the whereabouts of Wayne's forces; but there were Tories in the immediate neighborhood of Wayne's camp, who not only knew of his precise locality and the nature of the approaches, but who also conveyed all the necessary information to the British commander, who at once sent General Grey out to surprise him and cut him off, and Col. Musgrave with the Fortieth and Fifty-fifth regiments was moved up to the Lancaster road in order that if necessary he might aid Gen. Grey, and to intercept any of Gen. Wayne's troops who might attempt to retreat over that route.

Gen. Grey marched from his encampment near Howellville

up the Swede's Ford road and massed his troops as near the camp
of Gen. Wayne as practicable without permitting Wayne to know
of his approach. Several of Gen. Wayne's pickets upon the approach of the British fired upon them and escaped, but others of
the pickets were silently bayoneted in the darkness, and the first
knowledge Gen. Wayne had of the approach of the enemy was from
one of the videttes whom he had sent out. Wayne directed Col.
Humpton, who was second in command, to gain the road leading
toward the White Horse tavern, and a part of the troops took the
right road while others took the wrong one, being thus brought
within the light of their own fires, giving the attacking force a
most important advantage over them. The artillery had taken the
right road and were retreating safely. While General Wayne was
attempted to cover the retreat of the artillery and preparing to
receive the enemy, Gen. Grey approached his position about one
o'clock in the morning of the 21st, under cover of the darkness.
The troops under Wayne fought bravely for a considerable time,
giving the enemy several close and well directed fires, but were
soon obliged to retire before largely superior forces. Wayne thereupon immediately flew to the Fourth Regiment, with which he again
received the enemy's charge, covering the retreat of the rest of his
line, and after being again compelled to retire he rallied those of
Col. Humpton's troops that had taken the right road in their retreat about three hundred yards in the rear of the last stand, where
he formed them ready to renew the conflict. Both parties, however, withdrew without renewing the contest, and Gen. Wayne retired to the White Horse tavern, taking with him his artillery and
ammunition, with the exception of that left upon the field, which
fell into the hands of the enemy.

The attack upon Wayne's men was made with the bayonet
and light swords only, in a most ferocious spirit, Gen. Grey having
ordered his men to remove the flints from their guns in order that
not a single shot should be fired. Many were killed after they had

ceased to resist, and even the wounded and sick were killed. It was this feature of the attack that has stigmatized the conduct of the British in this midnight battle as "barbarity" and "cold blooded murder," and which has given to it the title of the "Paoli massacre." The loss of the Americans was about one hundred and fifty killed and wounded, while the British report a loss of only seven or eight, though it is altogether likely that their loss was considerably larger. Fifty three mangled bodies were found upon the field and decently buried by those living in the vicinity of the battlefield on the very spot where now stands the Paoli monument.

Among the killed was Major Marion Lamar, who fell in the midst of the British on the retreat, and in honor of this martyr in the cause of liberty a township in Chester County was given his name. This attack upon Wayne's forces enabled General Howe to move his army without molestation, that general resuming his march on the morning of the 21st, down the road leading to Swede's Ford, with the intention of crossing the Schuylkill at that point, but as he discovered breastworks on the opposite side of the river occupied by Washington's troops, he turned up the river on the west side with the view of crossing at some of the fords higher up or, as Mr. Pennypacker says in his "Phœnixville and Its Vicinity," he induced Washington to suppose that was his object, or else to seize by a sudden movement the deposit of ammunition and other stores at Reading. Washington, deceived by this movement, hastened up the east bank of the river to the neighborhood of Pottsgrove, when Gen. Howe suddenly wheeled his army on the 23rd of September, marched rapidly down the river and crossed with but little opposition at what was then called Gordon's Ford, now Phœnixville, and at Fatland Ford, a short distance below, and slipped into Philadelphia almost before Washington knew how thoroughly he had been deceived, entering that city on the 26th.

It will have been seen that the army under General Howe

entered Chester County on September 9, and left it on the 23rd, having been within its then limits, including what is now Delaware County, twelve days. This was the only time during the entire period of the Revolutionary War when a British army was in the county, though foraging parties were sent out from Philadelphia while the British remained in possession of that city. In his "Phœnixville and Its Vicinity" Mr. Pennypacker says with reference to the depredations committed on the people of this county by the British army during those two weeks:

"In the course of these maneuvers, on Sunday afternoon, at four o'clock, on the 21st of September, 1777, the British army, numbering about 14,000 men, entered Schuylkill Township and encamped along Nutt's road from Fountain Inn to Fatland Ford. The English occupied the upper side of the road, and upon the other side the Hessians were stationed. The headquarters of Gen. Knyphausen, commander of the Hessians, was at the house of Frederick Buzzard, which, at that time, stood about midway between the Corner stores and the Morris woods. The headquarters of Gen. Howe were at the house of William Grimes, recently occupied by John Acre, and the first house below the Bull tavern.

"No sooner were the men dismissed and ordered to encamp than they commenced depredations upon the surrounding neighborhood. In a little while every house had been visited. All the provisions; clothing, straw and hay that could be found were carried off, and the cattle and horses were driven away. So completely were the people divested of everything which could be used in the camp, that they, in many instances, suffered from the want of food and clothing. The only means by which anything could be retained was by application to the commanding general for a guard. Requests of this kind were usually granted.

"To the residence of Moses Coates, Jr., the Hessians came in droves as soon as the army halted, and they continued their incursions until the next morning, when a guard was obtained. The

BAYARD TAYLOR.   GEN. ANTHONY WAYNE.   T. BUCHANAN READ.
GEN. G. PENNYPACKER.   WAYNE McVEAGH.

garden, cellar and larder were emptied and the hen roosts soon made desolate. Among other things carried away was a large flock of geese. The last of them, an old gander, was pursued through the yard and finally caught around the neck by a huge Hessian, who held the bird aloft as he throttled it and cried exultingly to the members of his family: 'Dis bees goot for the poor Hessian mans.' One of the daughters expressed the hope that it would choke him to death, upon which he began to curse and departed with his prey.

"The family of Patrick Anderson had been informed of their approach, and had removed and secreted as many things of value as possible. The bedding and clothing were locked up in the bureau drawers and the house was abandoned. The English, who knew that Anderson was absent in the American cause, broke open the doors of the dwelling and completely destroyed everything in it. They pushed the locks off from the bureau draw·'ers and closets by thrusting their bayonets through the keyholes, and took possession of the contents. The furniture, which was in good condition, they broke into pieces and used for their fires. Mirrors were thrown upon the floor and paintings and others articles of vertu, with the single rather remarkable exception of a portrait of George Washington, which was left in its place upon the wall, were ruined. The cattle and sheep were slaughtered and the meat was salted and prepared in the parlor for transportation. The bloodstains remaining after this butchery could be seen upon the floors when the house was removed in 1842.

"They came to the residence of Matthias Pennypacker in the night and ransacked it in the search for provisions and clothing. The grain and flour in the mill became a valuable acquisition. The mill was at that time new and in excellent order, and to prevent its future use they hacked the machinery and cut the bolting cloth into strips.

"From the Fountain Inn, where William Fussell then lived,

14

they carried away whatever could be obtained. In order to secure some bed curtains which she considered to have particular value, Mistress Fussell wrapped them about her person and covered them with her dress. Some Hessian women, however, who accompanied the army, having their suspicions aroused, threw the lady unceremoniously on the floor, unwound the wrapping from about her and made it their spoil.

"Lord Cornwallis came himself to the house of Benjamin Boyer after it had been thoroughly stripped. The beehives, for preservation, had been carried into a room in the west end of the house and covered over with sheets. Cornwallis inquired what was concealed there and was informed they were bees. Not to be deceived, however, by what he thought to be a subterfuge, with an impatient movement he removed the covering. The insects, already disturbed by their recent transportation, resented the interference by flying into his face and hair, and they probed him unmercifully. His lordship beat a hasty retreat.

"A horse belonging to a son of Moses Coates, then quite a youth, was taken from the pasture field and it was known that the animal was among the British forces. The young man went to the headquarters of the commanding general and, upon making inquiries of some of the attendants about that officer's person, received only insolent and taunting replies. He insisted, however, upon an interview with their superior and was finally shown into Howe's presence. Upon making his errand known he was treated politely and detained in conversation. The subject of the condition of the American army was adroitly introduced and every effort made to elicit information from him. At length Howe said to him that he could have his horse if he would go over the Schuylkill and learn as accurately as he could the number of Washington's troops. The offer was rejected, and Howe increased it by saying that he would not only return his horse, but give him in addition six guineas in gold. The youth replied with indignation that he could not be bribed to perform an act so base, and when it was found that he would not answer Howe's purposes he was given permission to search through the camp for his horse and to take it away."

Historians generally agree that one of the greatest difficulties with which General Washington had to contend during the entire period of the Revolutionary War was the fact that when the early enthusiasm had in some measure subsided and the war become a stern reality there was a large number of disaffected people always ready to convey correct and valuable information to the British commanders but who made it exceedingly difficult for the American general to procure reliable information of the movements and numbers of the British forces. Had Washington known the intentions of General Howe in moving northward on the west side of the Schuylkill on the 21st of September he might have prevented Howe's crossing that river, and thus have saved Philadelphia. In corroboration of this view of the case the following letter, taken from the Pennsylvania archives, is here introduced:

"BOARD OF WAR TO PRESIDENT WHARTON.

"War Office, October 18, 1777.

"Sir: * * * * * *

"I am directed to communicate to you for the consideration of the Committee of Safety that the board have received satisfactory information that a great number of the inhabitants of Chester County conveyed intelligence and supplied provisions to the enemy during their progress through that county and without such assistance their attempt upon Philadelphia would, in all probability, not have succeeded. These persons can be considered in no other light than as traitors to this state and avowed enemies to the United States, and therefore the great principle of self-preservation requires that the most effectual measures should be forthwith pursued to put it out of their power to persist in their

former mal-practices by taking from them such articles of clothing and provisions, and of the former particularly shoes, stockings and blankets, as might serve for the comfort and subsistence
of the enemy's army, and the acquisition whereof is of absolute
necessity to the existence of our own. The board, therefore,
earnestly requests that the Council will with the utmost dispatch
call forth and send to the county of Chester spirited and determined
militia under the command of discreet and active officers for the
purpose of collecting shoes, blankets and stockings for the use of
the American Army from such of the inhabitants of the said county
as have not taken the oath of allegiance to the state of Pennsylvania and have shown their attachment to the cause of the enemy,
etc.   RICHARD PETERS, Sec."

In accordance with the above suggestion of Richard Peters
the following resolution of the Council of Safety was adopted at
Lancaster, October 21, 1777:

"Ordered.—That Col. Evan Evans, Col. William Evans, Col.
Thomas, Col. Gibbons Capt. Thomas Levis, Capt. William Brooks
and Capt. Jacob Rudolph be authorized and required to collect
without delay from such of the inhabitants of the county of Chester
as have not taken the oaths of allegiance and abjuration or who
have aided or assisted the enemy, arms and accouterments, blankets, shoes and stockings for the use of the army, and that they ap-
praise the same when taken according to their quality, allowing
at the rate of £3 for a new single blanket, and give certificates of
the same to the owners, etc.   TIMOTHY MATLACK, Sec."

On October 31, 1777, President Wharton wrote to Col. Cheney
and Col. Gronow of Chester County to the effect that no time should
be lost in the embodiment of light horse militia in the county, and
urged the immediate formation of three or four troops of light
horse, and that they be put under the command of General Potter.

Having quietly taken possession of the city of Philadelphia,
Gen. Howe considered it a good opportunity to move his fleet up

the Delaware to that city, and while he was engaged at this work, capturing the fort at Billingsport, and driving away the small gar- rison under Col. Bradford, Washington thought he could success- fully attack that wing of the British stationed in Germantown. The result was the battle of Germantown, fought October 4, 1777, and, through a combination of circumstances favoring the British, was won by them, and Washington had to retire from the field. After this defeat, and after the junction of his army and that of Gen. Gates, who had compelled the surrender of Burgoyne at Sara- toga, the combined forces went into camp at Whitemarsh, in Mont- gomery County. Here Gen. Howe made several attempts to draw the American army out of camp into a battle, but failed to do so, and Washington finally decided to go into camp at Valley Forge, the sufferings of his army at that place having become most his- toric. While the army was thus encamped many of the farm houses were selected by its officers for their quarters. Col. Clement Biddle was for some time at Moore Hall; Generals Gates and Mifflin were at the house of Moses Coates, as were also Colonels Davis and Ballard. The house of Edward Lane and also that of Jacob Pennypacker were utilized in the same manner by other officers, and a company of horse soldiers was stationed at the house of Matthias Pennypacker. A number of sick soldiers was taken care of at the house of Philip Rapp, two of whom died and were buried in the woods. The house of Henry Miller was converted into a commissary store, and in the barn of David James delin- quents, deserters and spies were confined, and were continually watched by a guard. The old Varley house was converted into a hospital, and there was also a large hospital on the farm of Joest Smith, where many of the soldiers had the smallpox and camp fever. But the largest hospital was erected on some high ground in a field of the Gwynn farm, and about the hospital about 150 men are believed to have been buried.

Many of the farmers in the vicinity were engaged in teaming for the army, most of them voluntarily, others having to be impressed. All the rails in the immediate neighborhood, and most of the timber, were burned to keep the army warm. The head-quarters of the commanding general were at a stone house on the lower side of Valley Creek, only a few yards distant from the Read-ing Railroad, his wife spending the winter with him. One very cold morning, upon starting away from his house after breakfast, Washington passed the sentry standing in front of his house, who was stamping his feet and clapping his hands in order to keep warm. Washington asked the sentry if he had had anything to eat that morning, and on receiving a negative reply, took the soldier's musket and stood guard in front of his own house while the soldier went inside and ate some breakfast, waited upon by Mrs. Wash-ington.

December 10, 1777, Congress passed a resolution requesting the legislature of Pennsylvania to enact a law requiring all per-sons at the distance of seventy miles and upward from Washing-ton's headquarters and below the Blue Mountains, to thresh out their wheat and other grain within a short space of time, to be fixed by the legislature in its law, and in case of failure on the part of the farmers to comply with the law, to subject the same to seizure at the price of straw. The legislature failed to comply with this request, but the commander-in-chief, on the 29th of the month, issued the following proclamation:

"By virtue of the power and direction to me especially given, I hereby enjoin and require all persons residing within seventy miles of my headquarters to thresh out half their grain by the first day of February, and the other half by the first day of March, next ensuing, on pain in case of failure of having all that shall remain in sheaves after the periods above mentioned, seized by the commissaries and quartermasters of the army and paid for as straw.

"Given under my hand, at headquarters near the Valley Forge, in Philadelphia County, the 20th day of December, 1777.

"GEO. WASHINGTON."

There was an outpost of Valley Forge encampment in Radnor, on property subsequently owned by Tryon Lewis, on which property about seven acres of timber land was cleared near the middle of a large tract of woodland, which was afterward cultivated and known for many years in the neighborhood as the "camp field." During nearly all that winter Gen. Wayne's command was encamped at Mount Joy, in Lancaster County, and aided in securing supplies for the army at Valley Forge.

The encampment at Valley Forge was partly in Chester and partly in Montgomery County. That part of it in Chester County was in Tredyffrin Township, in this township the headquarters of Generals Lafayette, Wayne, Knox and Woodford being located. Count Duportail's headquarters were with Gen. Woodford. General Washington's headquarters were near the mouth of Valley Creek, where it empties into the Schuylkill River, and on the south side of the creek. The winter of 1777-78, during which Washington's army remained in camp at Valley Forge, was uncommonly severe, and the troops suffered intensely from lack of clothing, food and shelter from the storms and wintry winds. But their patience and fidelity to the cause for which they bore arms was sufficient to enable them to bear hardships almost if not quite unparalleled in the history of war. Lafayette, in his old age, said of them: "The patience and endurance of both soldiers and officers was a miracle which each moment seemed to renew."

Thomas Wharton, in the name of Pennsylvania, wrote: "The unparalleled patience and magnanimity with which the army under your Excellency's command have endured the hardships attending their situation, unsupplied as they have been through an uncommonly severe winter, is an honor which will be consid-

ered as more illustrious than could have been derived to them by
a victory obtained by any sudden and vigorous exertion."

Washington's own opinion of his soldiers was thus expressed:
"Without arrogance or the smallest deviation from truth it may
be said that no history now extant can furnish an instance of an
army's suffering such uncommon hardships as ours has done and
bearing them with the same patience and fortitude. To see men
without clothes to cover their nakedness, without blankets to lie
upon, without shoes (for the want of which their marches might
be traced by the blood from their feet), and almost as often without
provisions as with them, marching through the frost and snow,
and at Christmas taking up their winter quarters within a day's
march of the enemy, without a house or hut to cover them till
they could be built, and submitting without a murmur, is a proof
of patience and obedience which, in my opinion, can scarce be
paralleled."

Before taking up other military matters and movements of
interest to Chester County people as being more or less directly connected with their history, it will be well to note the various hospitals used in the county for the benefit of the wounded and sick soldiers after the battle of Brandywine. General Lafayette was cared
for by the Moravians at Bethlehem in their great Inn, called the
Sun. The German Seventh-day Baptists, whigs in sentiment, but
opposed to war, opened their monastic institution at Ephrata, Lancaster County, converting their entire establishment into a hospital.
Joseph Downing's barn at Downingtown was used for hospital purposes, and in the vicinity forty soldiers were buried. The Uwchlan
Friends' Meeting-house was used as a hospital, as was the old
school-house at the intersection of the Valley and Brandywine
roads at the Turk's Head tavern, and also the buildings at Yellow
Springs, now named Chester Springs, where for a time Washington had his headquarters. The wives of Zachariah Rice and Chris-

tian Hench, through their attention to sick soldiers at Yellow Springs, contracted typhus fever and died therefrom.

On the farm of Herman Prizer in East Coventry Township there was a barn that was used as a hospital for sick American soldiers, and there were many churches and meeting-houses in the county which were converted into hospitals, among them being the Brandywine Meeting-house, the German Reformed Church in East Vincent Township and Zion Lutheran Church, on the Schuylkill road in East Pikeland Township, which were about one mile apart, and which continued to be used during the entire winter of 1777-78. Near the East Vincent Church twenty-two of the soldiers that died there were buried on grounds belonging to Henry Hipple, Sr., and in 1831 steps were taken by the military organizations of Chester County to inclose the graves of these soldiers and to erect a monument to their memory. The monument as erected was a marble pyramid about eight feet high, inclosed by a strong wall and standing at the foot of the hill. Appropriate inscriptions were engraved on each of the four sides of the monument. The wall beginning to crumble, a committee was appointed to make the necessary repairs, the grounds were conveyed to trustees, funds were collected and a substantial wall erected on three sides of the grounds, containing twelve and thirty-seven hundredths square perches, and an iron fence was built in front.

On the 14th of November, 1777, the Council of Safety wrote from Lancaster to Robert Smith, lieutenant of Chester County, advising him to be on the watch for Mr. John James of Philadelphia, who had lately been clandestinely sent out by General Howe to promote the views of the invaders. On January 13, 1778, Jacob Dingee and Richard Strode delivered the body of Charles Dingee, late of Chester County, to the Council of Safety, to be committed to the gaol of Lancaster County until he should take the oath or affirmation of allegiance and give security.

On April 2, 1778, an order was drawn on the treasurer in favor of Stephen Cochran for the sum of £2,000, to be paid to Samuel Futhey of Chester County, to purchase horses with which to mount the cavalry. On the 12th of this month the following forfeited estates were noted to be sold: Of Nathaniel Vernon, late sheriff of the county; of Curtis Lewis, blacksmith, and of Richard Swanwick. On April 22, Col. Andrew Boyd wrote to President Wharton that there was a set of tory horsethieves in the county, and he also wrote that in some few instances Quakers insulted and even attempted to fire on two different guards Col. Boyd had out collecting fines.

On May 6, 1778, commissioners were appointed for Chester County, as follows: William Evans, Thomas Cheyney, Thomas Levis, Patterson Bell and John Hannum, and on the 8th orders were issued that Henry Skyles, Thomas Bulla, David Dawson, Jacob James, Joseph Thomas, Nathaniel Vernon, Jr., and John Swanwick, all late of the county of Chester, be required to appear and abide trial for adhering to the enemy.

June 15, 1778, a proclamation was issued by the Supreme Executive Council, designating as traitors nearly 500 persons, of whom sixty-five were named as then belonging·to or having of late belonged to Chester County.

General Joseph Reed, who had been elected President of the state of Pennsylvania, December 1, 1778, wrote on July 28, 1780, to Lieut. Robert Smith, regarding the patriotism manifested by some of the people of Chester County. He said: "It has been observed that less attention has been paid by your county to furnishing volunteers than any other county in the state. We fear that you have not sufficiently attended to the importance of this duty, as we cannot suppose the county would not exert itself if the officers would lead the way. It is unpleasant to suppose that at so critical a season any gentleman in office whose exertions are important would omit them, but there has certainly been a deficiency in your county which we flatter ourselves will be made up," etc.

Thus challenged by the president of the state, Lieut. Robert Smith, who was really a capable and patriotic officer, replied as follows, on September 4, 1780:

"Sir: The particular situation of this county under the late course of the militia induces me to lay before Council the following state of facts, and to request their advice and instruction thereon:

"Our justices at their session in May last rated the average prices of farm labor at $20 per day as the standard of militia fines. This, as I was verbally informed by the president of the court, but no certificate under their hands and seals was received. According to this rate the fines for non-attendance on days of exercise, the former part of the present year were laid, and four companies of the militia were ordered into actual service, were marched before the August sessions under the same circumstances. Upon the militia being called out they expressed great dissatisfaction at their wages being lower than those in the city and other counties; and the court, at their August sessions, rated labor at $30 per day. And in the interim between the marching of the militia and the sitting of the court, some few officers were received at the former rate, as money was much wanted for the purpose of advancing those who marched; and it is now strongly controverted whether we have the right to levy the advanced price of labor upon delinquents, as the militia were ordered out and the fines incurred before the sitting of the court. It is likewise contended by some that as the militia are discharged before the expiration of their two months, the fines now collected should be proportioned to the time of service given. I have taken the liberty to state these circumstances, and would humbly request the advice and instructions of the Honorable Council on the subject, both with respect to the fines upon delinquents and the wages of those who have marched upon the late call, in order that we may proceed in a regular and uniform line of conduct in this matter.

"ROBERT SMITH."

The extent of the ravages committed by the British army in its march through Chester County was very great. It is not deemed necessary in this work to present a detailed statement of the losses of individuals, that having been done in a pretty thorough manner by Messrs. Futhey and Cope, in their "History of Chester County;" hence only the summary of losses by townships will be given, which is altogether likely considerably within the limit of truth, as many people made no return of losses in any way. That recapitulation is as follows:

TOWNSHIPS.	PERSONS.	AMOUNTS.		
		£	S	D
New Garden	8	951	2	8
Oxford	1	500	0	0
New London	2	114	9	0
Londongrove	1	451	7	6
Kennett	4	1,362	1	5
East Marlborough	4	109	4	6
Newlin	4	213	12	6
West Marlborough	5	225	4	0
West Bradford	5	583	9	2
East Bradford	1	125	5	0
Pennsbury	12	894	2	9
Birmingham	20	5,844	6	7
Thornbury	6	787	18	1
Westtown	4	169	0	10
Goshen	29	2,372	13	8
Willistown	13	636	18	4
Easttown	17	420	7	6
West Whiteland	10	1,116	14	4
East Whiteland	18	1,415	14	10
Tredyffrin	30	9,358	13	10
Charlestown	15	1,967	3	2
Pikeland	1	252	7	6

East Nantmeal	1	200	0	0
Coventry	1	18	0	0
West Caln	2	88	0	0
Chester	31	2,742	12	6
Chichester	1	87	17	6
Aston	6	1,245	2	9
Concord	12	961	9	6
Marple	3	217	1	11
Newtown	3	86	3	3
Ridley	6	639	17	10
Edgemont	7	504	16	0
Haverford	22	1,733	1	3
Darby	26	1,475	18	2
Radnor	29	1,499	9	0
	363	41,372	6	10

This sum was equal to $110,326.24. Among the items of loss were 318 horses, 546 cattle, 1,480 sheep, 580 hogs, 9,062 bushels of wheat, 2,324 bushels of rye, 2,881 bushels of Indian corn, 775 bushels of buckwheat, 4,287 bushels of oats, and about 550 tons of hay.

The capitulation of Cornwallis at Yorktown, October 29, 1781, not only gladdened the hearts of all patriots throughout the coun- try, but was the beginning of the end of the war. The treaty acknowledging the independence of the United States was signed November 30, 1782, and on January 20, 1783, the preliminary treaty of peace was signed. On April 11, following, Congress issued a proclamation enjoining a cessation of hostilities, and on the 16th of the same month the Supreme Executive Council announced at the court-house the happy event. And thus at length the long strife and unhappy war were brought to an end. But not so the feelings engendered by differences of attitude, nor the difficulties and settlements that were necessarily of longer con- tinuance.

After the movement in favor of independence of the colonies was fairly launched upon the great ocean of events, there were within each of the colonies at least three classes of people, with regard to their relations to this movement. First of these classes may be enumerated the Patriots, or those who believed in, fought for and sustained, if they did not actually fight for, the movement; second, those who opposed independence, aiding in every way in their power the effort of what they considered the mother country to suppress the rebellion against her authority; and third, those who remained in motive and in action neutral, permitting the other two parties to fight the battle to the end; that is, permitted the attempted suppression of the rebellion to go on with the aid of the second class, who were called tories, while the first class were called whigs. The neutral class was composed in the main of members of the Society of Friends, who could not engage in war, on account of their conscientious and religious scruples against bearing arms. The whigs, however, could not in those active times distinguish between the active participants on the side of the Crown, that is, the tories, and the non-participants on either side; but regarded all who did not take an active part in the establishment of independence as having been enemies, and called both the second and third class tories alike, under the famous saying: He that is not for me is against me.

It is not necessary now to present an analysis of the motives of the individual members of any one of these three classes of men. It is sufficient to know and to admit that generally speaking all men of all classes were conscientious in the course they took. But the sad fact has always existed that it is possible for men to be strictly honest and conscientious and at the same time wrong, and it is altogether probable that this will always be true. Men have always been divided on all questions—political, religious, historical, sociological and even scientific ones, and it appears to be correct to say that every opinion has a right to life, liberty and the pursuit of happiness, as well as men, if it can only convince the world that that right exists. Then it is perhaps true that no system of religious or political thought is entirely without something that is unreasonable, and hence it follows that each and every class of men should look with charity upon what they consider the frailties of all the other classes; and first "pull the beam out of their own eyes before they attempt to pluck the mote out of their brother's eyes."

After the victory was won it was perfectly natural that the state of feeling toward those who had actively or passively opposed the patriot war should find expression, as it did in such resolutions as follow:

"At a meeting of the officers and other respectable inhabitants of the Fifth Battalion district, Chester County Militia, at the house of James Miles, in East Caln Township, on the 19th of June, 1783, Lieut.-Col. John Gardner in the chair,

"Resolved unanimously, That in the opinion of this company it is inconsistent with reason, justice and sound policy that such persons, of every description, as have deserted their country in the time of its calamities, and distress, and joined our enemies, or who have, by a conduct inimical to the Government and laws of their country, been obliged to fly to them for refuge, should ever be permitted to return or remain amongst us, to participate in the blessings of that Freedom and Independence, now so happily established, and which they have done all in their power to deprive us of;

"Resolved, 2ndly, That we highly approve the laudable example of the officers of the militia of the City and Liberties of Philadelphia, and will cheerfully concur with them in carrying their patriotic resolves into execution.

"Resolved, 3rdly, That we will join with others of the community in instructions to our Representatives in Assembly upon the subject, and in the meantime use our utmost endeavors and influence to prevent the return of any of those enemies to their country; and that we will consider all persons who connive at, harbor or entertain them as unworthy the character of Free citizens, and justly liable to the displeasure and resentment of all true Patriots and Friends of Liberty.

"Resolved, 4thly, That the proceedings of this meeting be communicated to the several and respective battalions of the militia in this county as soon as possible, for their concurrence, and likewise published in the Philadelphia newspapers.

"Resolved, 5thly, That a committee of five be appointed to correspond with and meet committees that may be appointed from the other battalions in this county, to draw up a set of instructions to our Representatives in Assembly, on this subject. The persons chosen, Colonel John Gardner, Major John Culbertson, Mr. Samuel Cunningham, Col. Robert Smith and Mr. John Beaton.

"Signed by order of the company,

"JOHN GARDNER, Chairman."

"At a meeting of the officers of the Seventh Battalion of the Chester County Militia, at the house of Ezekiel Webb, in the township of Kennett, on Saturday, the 26th of July, 1783, Lieutenant-Colonel Isaac Taylor in the chair.

"Whereas, During the late cruel and unjust war waged against these United States by the King of Great Britain, a number of persons, lost to all sense of honor and virtue, have deserted their country, joined her enemies and used every means in their power to distress and enslave us. And whereas (our struggles for liberty have been successful and their cruel designs frustratd), there is every reason to fear that these people will endeavor to insinuate themselves into these states: Therefore, to prevent this state from being a harbor for villains of every denomination,

"Resolved, unanimously, That we will use our utmost endeavors to prevent persons of the above description from settling within the limits of this Battalion. And we hereby pledge our-

UNVEILING OF PAOLI MONUMENT.

selves to each other, to unite and stand by each other, in expelling them from amongst us. And as there is reason to think that some of the aforesaid persons are harbored amongst us; Therefore,

"Resolved, unanimously, That we will hereafter inquire into the character, and examine every suspicious person that comes within our knowledge, and that we will assist each other in apprehending and securing them, that they may be brought to justice; and that we will unite in the bringing to condign punishment all persons who aid, abet or harbor any of the said persons.

"Resolved, unanimously, 3rd, That we will concur with other battalions of this county in instructing our Representatives in Assembly, agreeably to the above resolutions; and that Colonel Isaac Taylor, Major John Craig, Peter Bell and Captains William Whiteside and Absalom Baird be appointed as a committee to meet committees which may be appointed from the other battalions in this county, to draw up said instructions.

"Resolved, 4th, That these resolutions be published in the Philadelphia newspapers.

"Signed by order of the meeting,

"ISAAC TAYLOR, Chairman."

Col. Robert Smith, mentioned above as lieutenant of Chester County, was appointed March 12, 1777, and served until March 21, 1785. His sub-lieutenants were Lewis Gronow, Thomas Strawbridge, Thomas Cheyney, Andrew Boyd, Robert Wilson, Thomas Wilson and Benjamin Brannan. The militia of the county was divided into eight classes, and when a class was called out many failed to respond, and it was necessary to make the deficiency good by hiring substitutes, procured by means of a bounty paid by the state, which was to be remunerated by fines imposed on delinquents and ranging from £15 to £50.

Following is a statement of the amount of fines received by Col. Robert Smith and his sub-lieutenants from March 1, 1780, to April 1, 1783:

15

NAMES.	CONTINENTAL MONEY.			STATE MONEY.			SPECIE.		
	£	s	D	£	s	D	£	s	D
Robert Smith	155,336	17	7	67	8	7	1,028	10	8
Lewis Gronow	97,712	17	6	1	0	0	405	16	9
Andrew Boyd	27,634	15	4						
Thomas Levis	89,915	14	9	110	3	6	701	7	0
Robert Wilson	30,075	16	8	6	15	0	186	11	3
Thomas Cheyney	106,279	14	9				410	8	3
	506,955	16	7	185	7	1	2,732	13	11

The methods of the patriots in dealing with traitors are clearly shown by the following proceedings: On August 1, 1779, an advertisement appeared in the Philadelphia papers to the effect that whereas the estates of Joseph Galloway, Nathaniel Vernon, Gideon Vernon, David Dawson, Richard Swanick, William Maddock, Alexander Bartman, Curtis Lewis, Philip Marchinton and Joshua Proctor, late of Chester County, having been by due process of law forfeited and seized to the use of this State, we the subscribers, agents for the said county, do hereby give notice that the plantations heretofore belonging to the above-named persons, which are well watered and wooded, will be sold by public vendue on Saturday, the 4th day of September next.

Signed, THOMAS LEVIS AND JOHN HANNUM.

The estate of Joseph Galloway, thus offered for sale, contained 422 acres; that of Nathaniel Vernon, 244 acres; that of George Vernon, 113 acres, all of them lying near the village of Chester; that of David Dawson, 450 acres, in the township of West Caln; that of Richard Swanick, 300 acres; that of William Maddock, 80 acres; that of Alexander Bartram, 90 acres, his place being known by the name of "Fox Chace;" that of Curtis Lewis, 403 acres, a part of which was near the Ship tavern; that of Philip Marchinton, 400 acres, and that of Joshua Proctor, 80 acres, located in New Garden Township.

At least one of the above-named individuals was hanged on attainder for treason, viz.: David Dawson, who was executed on the commons in Philadelphia, November 25, 1780, which fact was so stated in a letter by Hon. George Bryan to Hon. James Irwin of Philadelphia, the letter being dated October 20, 1784.

In a report to President Reed, dated in 1781, sent by John Shee and Jacob Morris, it was stated that up to that time the amount of sales of forfeited estates in Chester County was £128,030 14s. 7d., the commissions on which amounted to £3,991 2s.

As supplementary to the fact of the sale of forfeited estates it should be mentioned that children were not always deprived of their inheritances because of the treason of their parents. An act was passed by the legislature of Pennsylvania, October 6, 1779, in behalf of Thomas Vernon, Job Vernon, a captain of the Fifth Pennsylvania regiment of Continental troops; Franklin Vernon, a major of the Eighth Pennsylvania regiment of the Continental troops, and John Vernon, all of them being children of Nathaniel Vernon, late of Chester County, one of the persons attainted of high treason by the laws of Pennsylvania, who showed by their petition that no matter how guilty their father might have been of the crime which occasioned the forfeiture of his estate, yet that the petitioners had every one of them demeaned themselves as good citizens, two of them having served in the army of Pennsylvania and having thus aided in establishing the cause of freedom, and they therefore prayed that they might not be reduced to indigence on account of their father's crime or transgressions, and they asked that his estate subject to his debts might be vested and established in themselves. The law passed in accordance with and in answer to their petition gave to them all the estate of their father, except what had already been sold in accordance with the act of attainder, and such as was not needed to pay his just debts.

The officers of the several battalions of militia of Chester County, and the number of men in each battalion, were as follows:

1st.—Lieut.-Col., Thomas Bull; Major, Peter Hartman; number of men, 672.

2nd.—Lieut.-Col., John Bartholomew; Major, Cromwell Pearce; number of men, 873.

3rd.—Lieut.-Col., George Pierce; Major, Edward Vernon; number of men, 510.

4th.—Lieut.-Col., Richard Willing; Major, William Brooke; number of men, 670.

5th.—Lieut.-Col., John Gardner; Major, John Culbertson; number of men, 623.

6th.—Lieut.-Col., David McKey; Major, Samuel Evans; number of men, 484.

7th.—Lieut.-Col., Isaac Taylor; Major, John Craig.

8th.—Lieut.-Col., Joseph Speer; Major, John Boyd; number of men, 570.

The captains who served at different times in the above battalions were as follows: Thomas Carpenter, Joseph Mendenhall, William Whiteside, Joseph Luckey, Hugh Reed, John Boyd, John Bryan, David Curry, Robert Curry, Thomas Taylor, Joseph Johnston, Sampson Thomas, Jonathan Rowland, Evan Anderson, William Harris, Isaac Thomas, Alexander Lockart, John Craig, Thomas Levis, John Flower, Jonathan Vernon, John Lindsey, Edward Vernon, John Pitts, Mordecai Morgan, Joseph Bogg, John Fleming, and others whose Christian names are not at hand, as follows: Cypher, Wilson, Hister, Boylan, Morrell, Moore, Smith, Cochran, Henry, Marsh, McCloskey, Quin, Kirk, Price, Kemp, Pierce, Huston, Dunning, Allen, Graham, Denny, Barker, Elton, Scott, Beatty, Griffith, Carroll, Hollman, Brumback, Barber, Snyder, Evry, Cummings, Jenkins, Kincaid, Corby, Hays, Williamson, Blackburne, Colby, Ramsay, McKee, Fulton, Evans, Black, Ramage and Strode.*

On July 1, 1776, there was a meeting held at the house of Richard Cheyney, in Downingtown, of the Chester County committee, at which the following appointments were made of officers in the battalion of Chester County Flying Camp:

Captains.—Joseph Gardner, Samuel Wallace, Samuel Culbinson, James Boyline, John McDowell, John Shaw, Matthew Boyd and John Beaton.

First Lieutenants.—William Henry, Andrew Dunwoody, Thomas Henry, Benjamin Culbinson, Samuel Lindsay, Allen Cunningham, Joseph Strawbridge and Joseph Bartholomew.

Second Lieutenants.—Robert Filson, William Lockard, Thomas Davis, Samuel Hamill, Jeremiah Cloud, Joseph Wherry, David Curry and Alexander McCarragher.

Ensigns.—William Cunningham, John Grardtrencher, John Filling, Andrew Curry, Thomas James, Lazarus Finney, Archibald Desart and John Llewellyn.

That there were in Chester County, as in other counties in all of the colonies, men who were opposed to the war for independence, can neither be denied nor doubted, and hence it may be permissible to briefly discuss the question as to why they maintained the position which they did. This position was the same as that which for a long time was maintained by the several conventions, assemblies and legislatures of the colonies, and even by the Congress itself, down to the time of the Declaration of Independence, they all apparently preferring and hoping for an honorable adjustment of the difficulties then existing between the colonies and Great Britain, a redress of grievances, the difference being that those who are now, and have ever since been, called "Tories," adhered to that position all through the war, while the patriots became convinced that there could be no redress of grievances while they remained loyal to the crown. The tories feared that no government could be established in this country that would ever be sufficiently strong to preserve order, to protect the citizens against mobs and anarchy. That all parties were equally honest and conscientious in their convictions is now almost universally conceded. But it is altogether likely that the tory part of the population, in addition to their hesitancy to taking up arms against Great Britain for the reason above given, also feared any movement looking toward independence would certainly be crushed out by the arms of the mother country; while the patriots were willing to take the risk of success in war. No one could with any degree of certainty foresee the end. That the issue was for years doubtful is of course well known, and this fact must ever be a partial justification for the hesitancy of the tory in attempting to expel British power from the country.

The situation of the tory after the war he had opposed had been brought to a successful termination was anything but an enviable one. The accounts of the meetings of the militia of Chester County, and the proceedings of the courts in the conviction of individuals of treason, their execution and the confiscation of their estates, proves this fact abundantly. The state of doubt in the mind of the tory as to what was best for him to do in the face of persecution, to which he was frequently subjected for years after the war had closed, is well expressed in the following parody on Hamlet's soliloquy, doubtless written by some patriot poet of the times:

THE TORY'S SOLILOQUY.

"To go or not to go?" that is the question!
  Whether 'tis best to trust the inclement sky,
  That scowls indignant o'er the dreary Bay
  Of Fundy, and Cape Sable's rock and shoals,
  And seek our new domains in Scotia's wilds,
  Barren and bare;—or stay among the Rebels!
  And, by our stay, raise up their keenest rage,
  That, bursting o'er our now defenseless heads,
  Will crush us for the countless wrongs we've done them.
  Hard choice; Stay, let me think, T'explore our way
  Through raging seas to Scotia's rocky coast,

At this dire season of this direful year
Where scarce the sun affords a cheerful ray,
Or stay and cringe to the rude, surly whigs,
Whose wounds, yet fresh, may urge their desperate hand
To spurn us while we sue—perhaps consign us
To the kind care of some outrageous mob,
Who, for their sport, our persons may adorn
In all the majesty of tar and feathers;
Perhaps our necks, to keep their humor warm,
May grace a rebel halter! There's the sting!
This peoples the bleak clime—for who can brook
A rebel's frown; or bear his children's stare
When in the streets they point, and lisp, "A Tory," etc.*

But now, while looking upon the entire question in a calmer
and more philosophical spirit than was then possible for any one,
and while we cheerfully grant honesty and conscientious conviction to all, including the poor, despised tory, yet we must
ourselves have convictions as to the merits of the positions assumed
by each of the several parties to the contest, as well as of those
who refused to range themselves on either side. The patriots
established for themselves, for their immediate descendants, and
it is to be hoped for all generations to come, a form of government
under which a resort to arms for the purpose of securing a redress
of grievances has been so far, is now and must continue to be so
long as that form of government shall remain, not only unnecessary, but even wicked and criminal in the highest degree. While
it may be true, as we are occasionally told, that sometimes in all
places, and perhaps at all times in some places, a portion of the
people suffer from grievances equal to or even greater than any of
which in 1776 the patriots complained, yet under the form of government they established, the people can, if a majority of them so

---

* Published in November, 1783.

desire, quietly remove those grievances, by the simple process of resorting to an election, which shall come at the end of a campaign carried on in a reasonable manner, during which the people may become convinced that they do really suffer from the grievances of which perhaps only a few at first complained, and by which election the majority place in power in the municipality, or county, or state, or nation, men of the same views and convictions with themselves. All that is required on the part of the people is a clear knowledge of what they themselves complain, and of the proper remedy to be applied; and in addition to this knowledge, virtue, intelligence, sound judgment, cultivated reason and self control. The institutions of government which, in order that they may be operated successfully, require such qualities of heart and mind as here enumerated, are most admirably calculated to develop in man the very qualities themselves, and it is this that makes so conspicuous the wisdom of the Fathers of the Revolutionary times, who founded and established the most perfect republican form of government that has so far been established in the world.

September 20, 1817, the Republican Artillerists of Chester County, aided by their fellow-citizens, erected a monument over the remains of those killed at Paoli, September 20, 1777, by the British soldiers under Gen. Grey. On that occasion an address was delivered by Major Isaac D. Barnard, and an account of the massacre was given by Rev. David Jones, who was chaplain of Gen. Wayne's ill-fated army at the time of the massacre, and who at the time of the erection of the monument was in his eighty-second year. Col. Isaac Wayne, son of Gen. Wayne, was present at the time. This monument stood in Willistown Township, less than half a mile southwest of Malvern.

On the one hundredth anniversay of the massacre a new monument was erected at this place, the old one having become injured and defaced to a great extent. On this occasion there were present from 8,000 to 10,000 persons, one of the largest gatherings ever known in the history of the county. On this occasion Capt. William Wayne, a great-grandson of Gen. Anthony Wayne, was present, the captain having been an officer in the Union army during the Rebellion. This new monument is of Quincy granite, twenty-two and a half feet high, and a well-proportioned, chaste and beautiful obelisk. The polished die bears on its four sides appropriate inscriptions, those on the west, north and south sides having been written by Dr. William Darlington, the master spirit in the erection of the first monument in 1817, as Dr. Wood was in the erection of this in 1877, he being the principal mover in the entire enterprise, including the raising of the money.

On the occasion of the dedication of the new monument in 1877, Governor John F. Hartranft and his staff were present. The meeting was organized by Dr. J. B. Wood of Westchester, at 12 o'clock, who named as president, Hon. Washington Townsend, and numerous vice-presidents and secretaries. The exercises were then conducted in the following order:

1. Delivery of the monument by Mr. Van Gunden, on behalf of Messrs. Van Gunden, Young & Drumm, of Philadelphia, the contractors for the construction of the monument, to the committee.

2. Reception of the monument on behalf of the committee by Capt. Robert T. Cornwell.

3. Presentation of the monument by Dr. Wood on behalf of the committee to the president, Hon. Washington Townsend, for dedication.

4. Dedicatory address of the president.

. Unveiling of the monument by Dr. Wood.

National salute of thirty-eight guns by the Griffen battery.

5. Prayer by Rev. Joseph S. Evans.

8. Historical address by J. Smith Futhey.

9. Oration by Hon. Wayne MacVeagh.

10. Benediction by Rev. Mr. Elliott.

The military and citizens then formed in line and marched

round the monument to the solemn music of the bands and the low roll of the muffled drums, which completed the exercises of the day, a day long to be remembered by those who participated in the ceremonies.

The inscriptions on the four sides of this monument are as follows:

West Side:

"Sacred
to the memory of the
PATRIOTS
who on this spot
fell a sacrifice to
British barbarity
during the struggle for
AMERICAN INDEPENDENCE
on the night of the
20th of September, 1777."

North Side:

"THE ATROCIOUS MASSACRE
which this stone commemorates
was perpetrated
by British troops
under the immediate command
of
MAJOR GENERAL GREY."

South Side:

"Here repose
the remains of fifty-three
AMERICAN SOLDIERS,
who were the
victims of cold-blooded cruelty
in the well-known
'MASSACRE AT PAOLI,'

while under command of
GENERAL ANTHONY WAYNE,
an officer
whose military conduct,
bravery and humanity
were equally conspicuous
throughout the
REVOLUTIONARY WAR."

East Side:

"Erected by the citizens of
Chester and Delaware Counties,
September 20, 1877, being
THE CENTENNIAL ANNIVERSARY
of the Paoli Massacre."

"The other inscriptions on this monument are
copied from
the memorial stone
formerly standing here,
which was erected by
the Republican artillerists,
and other citizens of
Chester County,
September 20, 1817."

THE WHISKY INSURRECTION.

What is known as the "Whisky Insurrection" broke out in
1794, in the western part of Pennsylvania, while Washington,
was President of the United States. It was confined to the counties of Fayette, Washington, Allegheny and Westmoreland. Turbulent proceedings continued in these counties for several years
prior to 1794, in which year measures were taken both by the
state of Pennsylvania and the government of the United States to
restore peace. Governor Thomas Mifflin, on the 6th of August,

appointed Chief Justice M'Kean and General William Irvine to proceed immediately to these western counties to ascertain the facts relative to the riots that had then lately taken place, and on the next day President Washington issued a proclamation of warning, commanding all insurgents, on or before the 1st day of September to disperse and retire peaceably to their respective homes. By this proclamation the President also directed the raising of troops, which were to be held in readiness to march at a moment's warning. The quotas of the states from which troops were called out, were as follows:

STATES.	INFANTRY.	CALVA-LERY.	ARTIL-RY.	TOTAL.
Pennsylvania 4,500		500	200	5,200
New Jersey 1,500		500	100	2,100
Maryland 2,000		200	150	2,350
Virginia 3,000		300	...	3,300
	11,000	1,500	450	12,950

On the same day Governor Mifflin issued a proclamation similar to that issued by the President of the United States, directing the quota of the State to be armed and equipped as soon as possible. Of the 5,200 troops required of the State, Chester County was required to furnish 378, to be drawn from the First Brigade of the Third Division of the militia. The entire body of state troops was to be under the command of Major-General William Irvine, and was to be divided into three brigades, the first brigade to be under the command of Brig.-Gen. Thomas Proctor, and to include the Chester County troops. When the command to secure these troops had been given, the Governor himself paid a visit to West Chester to aid in raising them, his influence being immediately felt, and the county's quota was quickly raised. At that time Joseph McClellan was sheriff of the county. He had been a captain of infantry during the greater portion of the Revolutionary War in Gen. Anthony Wayne's army, and when the difficulty arose over the excise tax on whisky in the western part of the State he was soon at the head of a troop of cavalry, and Aaron Musgrave was at the head of a company of artillery. Upon the organization of the troops into regiments Capt. McClellan became major of the regiment to which his company was assigned, and Thomas Taylor became captain of the company in his stead.

This "Whisky Insurrection" was a resistance to the execution of the excise laws passed by the congress of the United States, which were designed to take the place of similar laws by the different colonies; as under the constitution of the United States, "All duties, imports and excises shall be uniform throughout the United States." While it will scarcely be expected that in this work a full history of the legislation in Pennsylvania which affected the minds of the people toward excise laws and which led up to this insurrection, yet that legislation must be mentioned and the reader referred thereto for a full and clear understanding of the conflict between the people and the Government resulting therefrom. The people in the Western counties of this State, within the confines of which the opposition to the excise laws so strongly manifested itself, were of Scotch-Irish ancestry, and had heard of the oppressions and exactions that had been suffered in the old country, under precisely such laws as they were then opposing. They also remembered that the colonies themselves had rebelled against England a few short years before, in part on account of the stamp act and the duty on tea, they themselves having taken active and honorable part in said rebellion, and hence they could not understand how it was that the new government of the United States should so soon after resisting with all their power the enforced use of royal stamps and the payment of the duty on tea, attempt to impose upon her own inhabitants precisely the same kind of injustice, even though the duty was on whisky instead of on tea.

While the insurgents, from the peculiar circumstances in which they were situated and by which they were surrounded, had some show of reason on their side, yet on the whole that provision of the constitution of the United States under which the excise laws were passed that caused this outbreak was wise and necessary, and the government had no recourse but to suppress the insurrection, which it did under the command of President Washington, and it was discovered by all concerned in the incipient rebellion as well as by those who were merely interested spectators from a distance that the Government of the United States was a fixed and established institution, which could not safely be resisted by any State or part of a State, simply because its laws were distasteful to the people of such State or part of State.

The officers of the several companies sent out from Chester County at this time were as follows: Captain, Aaron Musgrave; Philip McAffry, first lieutenant, and William Culbertson, clerk. The captain, first lieutenant and several of the men of this company were from West Chester, the number of men voting for their officers being thirty-six.

Another company made up of men mostly from Tredyffrin Township contained thirty-three men, including officers, who were: Captain, John Parker; first lieutenant, John Lewis, and clerk, David Craig.

Captain Joseph McClellan's comapny of light dragoons contained thirty-nine men, including the officers, who were voters, and who elected Joseph McClellan captain, Thomas Taylor first lieutenant and Joseph Moore clerk. The entire number of men in this company was fifty-four.

Captain George Wersler's company contained thirty voters, who elected the officers, Daniel Shimer being first lieutenant and Yost Smith clerk, and there were fifty-two others in this company.

Captain Harris' company contained forty-one voters, who elected William Harris captain, Stephen Bowen first lieutenant and Thomas J. Bowen clerk.

Captain Alexander Sterrett's company contained twenty-two voters, who elected, in addition to their captain, Samuel McClellan first lieutenant and Jesse Mason clerk.

Captain William Weston's company contained sixteen voters, who elected, in addition to their captain, William Ploughman first lieutenant and Charles Howell clerk.

Captain Isaac Lewis's company contained twenty-six voters, who elected, in addition to their captain, Alexander Nesbit first lieutenant and Robert Darlington clerk.

Captain Arthur Andrews' company elected Ebenezer Kennedy first lieutenant and J. Montgomery clerk. This company contained forty-four voters.

GENERAL LAFAYETTE'S VISIT TO CHESTER COUNTY.

One of the most interesting and historic events connected with the name of any individual was the visit in 1825 of Lafayette to the county. This visit to the United States was made by the general in response to an invitation authorized by Congress and extended in 1824 by the President of the United States. Accompanied by his son, George Washington Lafayette, and his private secretary, Lafayette landed in New York on August 15, 1824, and the news of his arrival reached West Chester on the 17th. A meeting was called to be held at the court-house, of which Colonel Joseph McClellan, who had served in the Continental army under Lafayette as a captain, was made chairman and General Isaac D. Barnard secretary. Judge Darlington delivered a short speech and offered a resolution to the effect that a meeting of the citizens be held at the court-house on Saturday, August 27, "to make arrangements for a suitable reception of that venerable patriot and friend of freedom," if he should be induced to visit Chester County.

At the meeting held August 27 Hon. Isaac Darlington was made chairman and John W. Cunningham secretary, and a committee was appointed consisting of Colonel Joseph McClellan,

Colonel Jacob Humphrey, Colonel Isaac Wayne, Dr. Jacob Ehren-zeller, Colonel Cromwell Pearce, General Isaac D. Barnard, General John W. Cunningham, Dr. William Darlington, General Joshua Evans and Abram Baily, to wait upon the general immediately upon his arrival in Philadelphia and invite him to honor Chester County by a visit and to also visit the battle-field of the Brandy-wine.

When it was learned that General Lafayette and his com-panions would visit the battle-ground of the Brandywine July 26, 1825, and proceed thence to West Chester, preparations were made for his reception in the county, and early in the morning of that day the general was waited upon at the Duponts, where he had passed the night, by General John W. Cunningham, one of the committee of arrangements, and by Samson Babb and William Williamson, two of the marshals of the day, by whom he was con-ducted to Chadd's Ford, which place the general and his party reached at 10 o'clock a. m. Here he was received by the committee from Delaware and Chester Counties, headed respectively by Cap-tain William Anderson and Colonel Joseph McClellan. A large party was in waiting at Chadd's Ford to conduct the illustrious visitor over the battle-ground on which he had proven his devo-tion to the cause of American liberty, and on the battle-ground itself there was a large concourse of people in carriages, on horse-back and on foot, to welcome the nation's guest.

About a mile from Chadd's Ford the general alighted from his carriage to call upon Gideon Gilpin, a very aged man, at whose house during the battle of the Brandywine he had made his headquarters. The procession then moved to Dilworthtown, where another large concourse of citizens awaited the arrival of the distinguished party. It then passed on to the Birmingham Meeting-house, where the general pointed out the spot where he had been wounded, a short distance east and south of the point where the road from the meeting-house comes in at right angles

GENERAL LAFAYETTE, 1824.

with the east and west road. At the meeting-house another large assemblage of people had collected. The party then took dinner at the house of Samuel Jones, a short distance of the meeting-house, and the procession moved to Strode's Mill and thence to the Darlington woods, near the west line of the borough of West Chester. Here the volunteers of the Third Division were drawn up to escort the general and his party into town, the volunteers numbering about seventeen companies. A salute of thirteen guns was fired by the Republican Artillerists, after which the entire party proceeded in to the borough commanded by General Isaac D. Barnard, by way of what is now Rosedale Avenue, to High Street, and thence up High Street. It was estimated that fully 10,000 people were assembled in West Chester to receive the general, and the welcome accorded was both hearty and sincere. The procession moved up High to Market, to Walnut, to Gay, to High, to Market, to Church, to Gay, to High and out to a field owned by Jesse Matlack on the hill east of the Friends' Meeting-house. Here the troops were reviewed by General Lafayette, who complimented them highly on their appearance, and then he was taken to the residence of Ziba Pyle, chief burgess of the borough, for a short rest. Then going to the grand jury room of the court-house he partook of an excellent dinner provided by Eber Worthington, proprietor of the Turk's Head hotel, and was there welcomed by Colonel Joseph McClellan in a neat speech, to which General Lafayette responded in a most happy manner. Toasts were drank and a song, "Lafayette at Brandywine," was sung by Dr. William Darlington. A large number of persons paid their respects to the general at the residence of Ziba Pyle, where he passed the night. Next morning he took breakfast at Humphreyville with Major John Filson, where a great concourse of people had assembled, and whence he was conducted to Lancaster by a committee from that place, the Chester County committee returning home. On the whole, it

16

was an occasion of great joy to the people of the county, such a one as, perhaps, can never occur again.

The love of and veneration for the distinguished patriot and lover of liberty entertained by the ancient inhabitants of Chester County has been in its full strength transmitted to their descendants, which is evident from the fact that in 1895 a movement, started by the Chester County Historical Society, was so nobly responded to by all the citizens of the county, young as well as old, this movement having in view the erection of a monument to mark the spot where the general was wounded in the battle of Brandywine. After the necessary preliminary movements a committee was appointed consisting of James Monaghan, Edwin A. Barber and James C. Sellers to conduct the correspondence and to consider the designs presented. The committee suggested a Roman-Corinthian column, fifteen feet high, to be made of terra cotta, and a sum sufficient to pay for the shaft was quickly raised among the citizens and the school children. The place selected for the erection of this monument is a triangler piece of ground on the north side of a public road leading from Dilworthtown to the Birmingham Meeting-house, at a point where the properties of Mrs. Mardy D. Biddle and Minshall Sharpless join. It is one of the highest points on what is known as "Battle Hill," is in full view of the meeting-house and the hills to the north, over which the British approached on that eventful day. It is a short distance from where Lafayette was wounded.

This monument was dedicated September 11, 1895, a large number of people from all parts of the county being present. The public school children from West Chester were taken there in wagons, others finding other means of transportation or going on foot, the whole number of children present being about 1,000. The entire number of people on the grounds was probably about 7,000. The exercises of the day began at West Chester by the firing of a salute by General George A. McCall Post, G. A. R., of thirteen guns, and were continued throughout the day by different organizations and individuals. They were unusually interesting and will long be remembered. Arriving upon the ground in the vicinity of the monument the meeting was called to order by Dr. George M. Philips, president of the Historical Society, who announced the organization of the meeting, Captain William Wayne being the president and there being seventy-five vice-presidents and twenty-six secretaries. The Phœnixville band furnished music for the day. The opening prayer was made by Rev. Dr. Owen P. Eachus, the address at the unveiling of the monument by M. Louis Vossion, the address of presentation by James Monaghan, the dedicatory address by Dr. George M. Philips, the historical address by Mr. Gilbert Cope, the oration of the day by Charlton T. Lewis and the benediction by Rev. William L. Bull.

The inscriptions on the monument are as follows:

(Front.)

"On the Rising Ground
A Short Distance South of This Spot
LAFAYETTE
Was Wounded at the Battle of Brandywine,
September 11, 1777."

(Right Side.)

"Erected
By the Citizens and School Children
Of Chester County, Pa.,
Under the Auspices of the
Chester County Historical Society
᾿ September 11, 1895."

(Back.)

"The honor of having mingled my blood with that of many other American soldiers, on the heights of the Brandywine, has been to me a source of pride and delight."—Extract from Lafayette's speech at West Chester, July 26, 1825.

(Left Side.)

"May the blood spilled by thousands, with equal merit in the cause of independence and freedom, be to ensuing generations an eternal pledge of unalloyed Republicanism, Federal Union, Public Prosperity and Domestic Happiness."—Lafayette's toast at West Chester, July 26, 1825.

This monument thus erected is now, however, sinking rapidly to decay, the terra cotta not standing the weather as it was supposed that it would. It is becoming evident as time passes that if the historic spot where Lafayette received his wound is to remain marked for the contemplation of coming generations some more substantial monument must be erected in the near future.

On the same day that this monument was dedicated to Lafayette there was dedicated also a monument to Colonel Joseph McClellan, who was also in the battle of Brandywine. The design of this monument was furnished by E. James Dallett, a great-great-grandson of Colonel McClellan. This monument consists of two blocks of Brandywine marble, one above the other, the lower one being about four feet square, the upper one somewhat smaller, and supporting a polished ball bearing the following inscription:

"In memory of Colonel Joseph McClellan, born April 28, 1747. Died October 14, 1834. Served in the brigade of General Anthony Wayne in the Battle of Brandywine, September 11, 1777."

On the lower of the two blocks there is the following inscription:

"Erected by his descendants September 11, 1895."

The total cost of this monument was $285.92. It was unveiled by James D. McClellan of Lancaster, Pennsylvania, a grandson of Colonel Joseph McClellan, and the oration of the occasion was delivered by Colonel Joseph McClellan Bell of Milwaukee, Wisconsin.

CHAPTER VI.

THE WAR OF 1812.

THE MEXICAN WAR.

CHAPTER VI.

IT is well known that difficulties between the United States and England existed for years before war was actually declared by Congress against the latter country, which was done June 18, 1812. But it was on May 12 that Governor Simon Snyder made a call upon the State of Pennsylvania for 14,000 militia, which were to be formed into two divisions, four brigades and twenty-four regiments, the whole to be in the proportion of 11,200 infantry, 1,400 riflemen, 700 cavalry and 700 artillery.

The first offer of Chester County troops was made almost immediately after war was determined upon by the Government, this offer having been made June 24, 1812, by Captain James Ralston of his company of cavalry.

The Ninety-seventh Regiment was mustered in May 5, 1813, rendezvoused at New London cross roads by order of Brigadier-General John W. Cunningham, went to Elkton, Md., and was discharged May 21, 1813. The officers of this regiment were as follows: Colonel, Andrew Thompson; lieutenant-colonel, George W. Thompson; major, Washington Parke; paymaster, Robert Futhey; quartermaster, David Parke; Captains, Thomas Stewart, John Holmes, Robert Ralston, John Wright, J. Skyles, James Alexander, William Steele and John Naglee. There were several men from Chester County in Captain Stewart's company, among whom were Reazin Terry, Samuel Black, Robert Futhey, Archibald

271

Thomas, George W. Parke, Peter Rambo, John Wallace, James Stewart, Israel Hamill, Levi McCormick, Silas Wilson, James Ramsey and Enos Hughes.

After the burning of the Capitol building at Washington by General Ross grave fears were entertained that an attempt was designed upon several Atlantic cities, among them Baltimore and Philadelphia, and Pennsylvania bore an honorable part in the preparations made to prevent such a disaster. The Governor of the State, under date of August 27, 1814, issued a proclamation in order to guard against a surprise and to have ready a force sufficient to meet all emergencies that might arise, ordering and directing the militia within the counties of Philadelphia, Bucks, Montgomery, Delaware, Chester, Lancaster, Dauphin, Lebanon, Berks, Schuylkill, Lehigh, Northampton and Pike to be held in readiness to march at a moment's notice to such place as might be designated in subsequent orders, which were to be issued in case of necessity.

An encampment was formed at Kennett Square called "Camp Bloomfield," the troops there to serve under Colonel Berry, this being on or before September 3. September 10 Governor Snyder reported that General Bloomfield had suggested a camp at Marcus Hook, and on September 12 General Thomas Cadwallader was assigned to the command of the militia at Kennett Square, which were to be formed into one brigade. The next day General Bloomfield ordered that all the troops from Chester and neighboring counties should assemble at Marcus Hook, completely equipped for the field. On September 17 the Governor of the State ordered that an election should be held for officers and that the volunteer troops should be organized into regiments. Isaac Wayne of Chester County was elected colonel of the Second Regiment of volunteer light infantry, but this honor he declined on the ground of previous and sacred engagements with volunteer cavalry. Early in October several regiments of militia marched to "Camp Marcus Hook," then under the command of Major-General Isaac

Worrell, who had command of the First Division of Pennsylvania militia.

Chester County furnished the following general officers: Major-General Cromwell Pearce of the Third Division; Major-General James Steel, same division; Brigadier-General William Harris, same division, Second Brigade; Brigadier-General John W. Cunningham, same division, First Brigade; Brigade Inspector James Park, same division, First Brigade; James Ralston, captain of cavalry.

The companies from Chester County were as follows: The "American Greys," Captain Titus Taylor, with ten non-commissioned officers and forty-one private soldiers; Captain John G. Worsler's company, with seven non-commissioned officers and forty-one private soldiers; Captain Jacob Campbell's company, with nine non-commissioned officers and ninety-two private soldiers; Captain Benjamin Wetherby's company, with eight non-commissioned officers and and one hundred and five private soldiers; Captain James Lackey's company, with eight non-commissioned officers and one hundred and ten private soldiers; Captain George Hartman's company, with eleven non-commissioned officers and one hundred private soldiers; Captain Beerbower's company, Peter Smith as first lieutenant and fifty-one voting members as private soldiers; Captain John Harris' company, with David Rees as first lieutenant and forty-four voting members as private soldiers; Captain Christopher Wigton's company, with nine non-commissioned officers and forty-seven private soldiers; Captain Robert Wilson's company, with nine non-commissioned officers and eighty-three private soldiers; Captain William Stuart's company, with five non-commissioned officers and twenty-seven private soldiers; Captain William Steele's company, with nine non-commissioned officers and sixty-five private soldiers; and Captain John Holmes' company, with nine non-commissioned officers and fifty-nine private soldiers. Captain D. B. Keim's company of volunteer militia had in it Samuel Shaffer and Thomas Baird as voters.

THE MEXICAN WAR.

On May 13, 1846, Congress announced that by the act of Mexico a state of war existed between that country and the United States, and authorized the President to employ the militia and the military and naval forces of the United States in order to bring it to a speedy close. He was authorized to accept the services of 50,000 volunteers. Pennsylvania was asked to furnish six regiments to serve for twelve months, or to the end of the war. Within thirty days ninety companies offered themselves, quite a number of individuals being from the county of Chester, but no company or organization of any kind. The names of a portion of those who went are here appended, it being understood that the list would be much longer could the names of others be ascertained.

Levi P. Knerr served as a lieutenant through the war; William S. Mendenhall, though born at Chadd's Ford, Delaware County, volunteered from West Chester in 1846, he being at the time sixteen years of age, and served two years, taking part in most of the important battles that occurred during that time. He was slightly wounded in the foot in one battle and in the head in another battle, and returned to West Chester when eighteen years of age. Thomas King and John Yocum also went to the Mexican war, and Lieutenant Columbus Penn Evans served in the Eleventh United States infantry was breveted captain and was presented with a sword by the Legislature of the State of Delaware for meritorious conduct in several battles of the war. Irvin Parke was a private soldier in Captain Samuel Hyams' company of the Sixth Louisana Regiment, commanded by Colonel Payton, and Robert Taylor of West Chester was also a private soldier in that war.

CHAPTER VII.

THE REBELLION.

CHAPTER VII.

THE GREAT REBELLION—ITS ORIGIN—FALL OF SUMTER—PROMPT WAR MEAS-
URES—THE FIRST VOLUNTEERS—THEIR DEPARTURE FOR THE FIELD
—CARE FOR THEIR FAMILIES—THE ENTIRE COUNTY AT WORK—
OFFICERS AND COMPANIES—RECRUITING—SERVICE OF THE REGI-
MENTS—AID SOCIETIES—CONTINUED ENLISTMENTS—THE DRAFT—
INVASION OF THE STATE—THE UNION LEAGUE—THE SECOND
DRAFT—THE VETERANS—THE SURRENDER OF LEE AND THE
ASSASSINATION OF LINCOLN—ESTIMATE OF MEN FUR-
NISHED BY THE COUNTY — SPECIAL MENTION
OF DISTINGUISHED OFFICERS.

THE causes of the War of the Rebellion are well known to all and are fully recorded in general history and in many well written biographical works on the great men of that time, both North and South. A few dates of important events immediately pertaining to the beginning of actual hostilities are therefore all that will be represented here in relation to general history, to serve as a mere introduction to the brief narrative given of Chester County's part in that great conflict.

Abraham Lincoln was elected President of the United States November 6, 1860, and was inaugurated March 4, 1861. In the meantime South Carolina passed an ordinance of secession December 20, 1860, other Southern States following with similar ordinances on different dates, until eleven of them had seceded, as they thought, from the Union. Fort Sumter surrendered to the Secessionists April 13, 1861, and on April 15 President Lincoln issued his first proclamation calling for militia from the several States under the act of Congress of February 25, 1795, to the number of 75,000 men, to serve for three months. The number of troops

Pennsylvania was asked to raise was fourteen regiments; but so strong was the feeling throughout the State in favor of maintaining the Union that instead of fourteen regiments enough men offered their services to organize twenty-five regiments almost immediately after the call was made. Out of the excess of men above the fourteen regiments Governor Curtin organized the famous Pennsylvania Reserve Corps, which was the only well organized and well disciplined corps in the Union Army at the time of the battle of Bull Run, July 21, 1861.

So far as Chester County is concerned it is proper to state that no county in the country was more patriotic or prompt to offer soldiers and to equip them for the war, and no county was more prompt to see that the families of the soldiers that went to the front should be provided with the necessaries of life while those soldiers were fighting the battles of their country.

The reception of the news of the bombardment of Fort Sumter, which was on Sunday, April 14, aroused the people of the county to a most remarkable degree. Before night of the next day measures were taken to raise troops for the support of the Government. An immense meeting was held at the court-house, at which Dr. Wilmer Worthington presided, and at which addresses were made by Major Wyck, F. P. Smith, Rev. Mr. Newton, Hon. Townsend Haines, Uriah V. Pennypacker, Hon. John Hickman, Wayne MacVeagh and Captain James Givin. A roll for a company of riflemen was opened, quite a number of young men put down their names and a committee was appointed to raise funds with which to equip the company.

On Tuesday evening a meeting was held in Horticultural Hall at which an election was held, resulting as follows: Captain, James Givin; first lieutenant, Benjamin H. Sweney; second lieutenant, Thomas S. Bell, Jr.; third lieutenant, John H. Babb; orderly sergeant, Walter Hibbard, Jr.; quartermaster, George F. Smith. The services of this company were at once accepted by Governor Curtin and left for Harrisburg on April 23.

On Wednesday, April 17, the National Guards held a meeting at the armory, at which, upon motion of Henry W. Caruthers, the services of the company (A) were offered to the Government. The officers of this company were: Captain, Henry R. Guss; first lieutenant, Francis M. Guss; second lieutenant, Richard D. Townsend, and quartermaster, Galusha A. Pennypacker. Company B of the National Guards was officered as follows: Captain, James F. Andress; first lieutenant, D. W. Clinton Lewis; second lieutenant, William M. Hinkson. And Company C had the following officers: Captain, Samuel Hufty, Jr.; first lieutenant, David Jones; second lieutenant, Joseph T. Barnett. These three companies became parts of the Ninth Pennsylvania Volunteer Infantry, which will be mentioned later on.

A company of soldiers was organized on Saturday evening, April 20, which on that evening elected Henry McIntyre captain, John W. Nields first lieutenant and C. B. Lamborn second lieutenant. This company was named the Brandywine Guards.

At Downington Colonel Ringwalt, Dr. Leech and others made efforts to raise a company of soldiers, and from Valley Forge a number of young men unable to wait for the formation of a company in their immediate neighborhood went down to Philadelphia to join volunteer companies forming there. On April 18 a number of young men of Howellville enlisted with the company then forming at Norristown, and a number left their homes in Oxford for Philadelphia, where they united with regiments forming for the war. At Oxford a meeting was held at Nichols' Hotel, of which 'Squire Sloan was president, at which meeting a committee was appointed consisting of C. S. Riding, E. Newman, J. T. Massey, F. Bowman J. B. Whitcraft, P. F. Ash, Joseph Showalter and H. H. Grubb, for the purpose of collecting money with which to purchase a flag to be raised over the railroad depot.

At Phœnixville David Reeves, president of the Phœnix Iron Works, gave notice that of any of his employes enlisted in the army they should have the houses they lived in, owned by the company, free of rent during their absence in the service of their Government. In a few hours a subscription of $4,000 was raised for the support of the families of such as should enlist. On the 19th of April a meeting of the citizens of West Chester was held at the court-house for the purpose of raising funds for the support of the families of such as should go to the war, of which meeting Joseph Hemphill was the president. A committee was appointed consisting of William Darlington, Edwin Otley, John Marshall, Rev. W. E. Moore, John G. Robison, Rev. John F. Pendergast, Lewis W. Shields, Dr. J. B. Wood and Captain Apple, to solicit and receive the funds contributed for this purpose.

A company was raised at West Chester called the Reserve Guards, composed of men under forty years of age and armed with Sharp's rifles, of which the officers were: Captain, E. L. Christman; first lieutenant, Charles B. Lee; second lieutenant, William Lynch. Another company, raised within the limits of the county, was called the Union Guards, which had the following officers: Captain, John W. Newlin; first lieutenant, George Silvers, and second lieutenant, William Bailey. This company was named the Anderson Light Artillery.

On April 20 a company was fully organized at Kennett Square containing sixty members. This district was inhabited largely by members of the Society of Friends, and the company was named the Kennett Rifles, or the "Quaker Company." Its officers were: Captain, C. F. Taylor; first lieutenant, Chandler Hall, and second lieutenant, Evan P. Dixon. They were equipped with blankets, etc., by the people of their section of the county, $4,000 being quickly raised for this purpose on the day they were organized. On the 30th of the month a company of home guards was raised at Milltown, of which Jesse Matlack was the captain, William B. Hoopes first lieutenant and Eli S. Moore second lieutenant. A company was raised at Kennett Square called the Kennett

MAIN BUILDING, NORMAL SCHOOL.

Square Home Guards, to which a large cannon was presented by Bayard Taylor, to protect the town from invasion.

At Coatesville two companies were raised, one of infantry and one of cavalry, the officers of the infantry being J. T. Minster, captain; Samuel Greenwood, first lieutenant, and Robert Russell, second lieutenant. On the 22d of April there was a meeting at Unionville, in the hall, at which were present many citizens of East and West Marlborough, Pocopson and Newlin townships, for the purpose of forming a company of home guards. One hundred and fifty men enrolled their names and elected William S. Collier captain and D. M. Taylor lieutenant. On this same day there was a meeting at Amity schoolhouse to form a volunteer rifle corps.

The Phœnixville artillerists about the same time offered their services to the Government, their officers being captain, J. R. Dobson; first lieutenant, Joseph T. McCord, and second lieutenant, Joseph Taggart. A company called the Wayne Guards was raised by Captain P. J. Phillips. At West Chester there was organized a home guard company of men over forty-five years of age, to protect Chester County from being overrun by marauders. This company held a meeting April 22, and elected officers as follows: Captain, William Apple; first lieutenant, Maris Frame, and second lieutenant, Richard Townsend. At East Fallowfield a meeting was held April 23 for the purpose of raising a company of home guards, and more than fifty men united with the company, which was named the Fallowfield Guards. A home guard company was formed at Parkesburg, one at Kimbleville, and one at Penningtonville. One of the features of the times, even at that early day, the latter part of April, was the arrival of refugees from the seceding states, many coming into and some passing through Chester County.

On April 27 a meeting was held at the house of James Beale, at which a company was raised and officered, called the Exton Guards. Its officers were as follows: Captain, William Beale;

17

first lieutenant, Charles Jacobs, and second lieutenant, William H. Gunkle. A company of cavalry was organized between Chester and Delaware Counties, called the Chester and Delaware cavalry company, of which Samuel Davis was chosen captain. The New London home guard company was officered as follows: Captain, James M. McDowell; first lieutenant, Lewis Gause, and second lieutenant, Charles Cornell. A company was organized called the Oxford company, with Charles K. McDonald captain.

The Phœnixville Iron Works during the month of April or early in May, 1861, made a number of wrought-iron cannon for the government, six and twelve pounders, for Philadelphia, and turned out several thousand solid 12-pound balls and shells. It was thus in all parts of the county, everyone talking about and preparing for war. The Phœnixville field piece was known as the Griffen gun, the patentee being John Griffen, superintendent of the works at that time.

By the military authorities of the State it was early resolved to establish a military encampment at West Chester, and the managers of the Agricultural Society offered the use of the Fair Grounds for that purpose. The camp here was named "Camp Wayne," in honor of Gen. Anthony Wayne. On Friday evening, May 3, the Ninth Regiment arrived from Harrisburg in a special train, the number of men in the regiment being about 800. The next day brought the Eleventh Regiment, and on that day the two regiments went into camp, although the preparations were far from complete. On Sunday, the 5th, Rev. William E. Moore, by request, held religious services at the camp. The colonel of the Ninth Regiment was ———— Longnecker, the lieutenant-colonel, W. H. R. Hangen, and the adjutant, Thomas S. Bell of West Chester. The colonel of the Eleventh Regiment was Phalen Jarrett, and lieutenant-colonel, Richard Coulter. The Ninth Regiment joined Gen. Patterson's army in June, and through it was attached to the Fourth Brigade of the First Division, and served between Martinsburg and Winchester, Va. It was mustered out July 24.

The Second Pennsylvania volunteer infantry was hastily recruited and organized April 21, 1861, at Harrisburg. Captain James Givin's company, mentioned above, became Company G of this regiment, and he became major of the regiment. The regiment left Harrisburg for Washington on April 21, but was ordered to halt at York, Pa., where it remained until June 1, when it moved to Chambersburg. Here it was assigned to the second Brigade of the Second Division, and on June 16 went to Funkstown, Md., crossing the Potomac July 2, with Gen. Patterson's army, advancing to Martinsburg and thence to Bunker Hill. It was mustered out July 26.

During the month of July, 1861, a general movement took place in many parts of the county to raise a regiment for three years, Henry R. Guss, who had been a captain in the three months' service, being authorized by the Secretary of War to recruit such a regiment. Seven companies of this regiment were raised in Chester County, while three companies, D, G and I, were principally from Delaware County. The several companies rendezvoused at Camp Wayne, after the departure therefrom of the First and Seventh Regiments of Pennsylvania Reserves. Col. Henry R. Guss was at that time proprietor of the Green Tree Hotel, West Chester, and very popular in the county. His regiment was the Ninety-seventh Pennsylvania volunteer infantry, and had the following officers: Colonel, Henry R. Guss; lieutenant-colonel, Augustus P. Duer; major, Galusha A. Pennypacker; Company A, captain, Francis M. Guss; first lieutenant, Lewis Y. Evans, and second lieutenant, William Peace; Company B, captain, William B. McCoy; first lieutenant, Jonas M. G. Savage; second lieutenant, James Hughes; Company C, captain, Isaiah Price; first lieutenant, Emmor G. Griffith; second lieutenant, William Gardiner; Company D, captain, William S. Mendenhall; first lieutenant,

George W. Williams, and second lieutenant, Israel Fawkes; Company E, captain, William McConnell; first lieutenant, John H. Babb, and second lieutenant, John McGrath; Company F, captain, De Witt Clinton Lewis; first lieutenant, Joseph T. Burnett, and second lieutenant, Oliver B. Strickland; Company G, captain, Jesse L. Cummins; first lieutenant, Caleb Hoopes, and second lieutenant, Joshua M. Burrell; Company H, captain, Charles McIlvaine; first lieutenant, Thomas S. Taylor, and second lieutenant, Elwood P. Baldwin; Company I, captain, George W. Hawkins; first lieutenant, Sketchley Morton, Jr., and second lieutenant, Annesley L. Morton; Company K, captain, William Wayne; first lieutenant, John J. Barber, and second lieutenant, ———.

Attached to this regiment there was an excellent band of twenty-two members. While the regiment was in Camp Wayne it was visited by Governor Curtin and his staff, November 12, and on the 15th of that month received marching orders, leaving West Chester on the 16th, marching from camp through the principal streets of West Chester, partaking of a lunch of coffee and sandwiches on Church Street, and leaving the depot on the train for Washington at 11:20 a. m. On December 1, they were encamped about two miles from Fortress Monroe, Va., and from the time they took the field made a most brilliant and honorable record for themselves and for the county which sent them forth to the war. Soon after reaching Fortress Monroe this regiment went to Port Royal, S. C., to Warsaw Sound, and to Florida and Georgia. It participated in the South Carolina campaign and under Gen. Gillmore took part in the assault on Fort Wagner. Afterward it garrisoned the fort at Fernandina and the works at Fort Clinch, Florida. On April 23, 1864, it was ordered to Fortress Monroe to join the Army of the James under Gen. Benjamin F. Butler, under whom it marched on Richmond, and was engaged in severe fighting in front of Petersburg. In the assault on the rebel Fort Gilmore this regiment particularly distinguished itself, Col. Pennypacker being in command of a brigade, which he led on the right of the attacking column. It was in the expedition of Gen. Butler and Commodore Porter against Fort Fisher, North Carolina, and later in Gen. Terry's expedition against this fort, and was engaged in its capture, which was effected after seven hours of the most desperate hand-to-hand fighting in the annals of the war. Here the regiment lost four killed and thirty-seven wounded, among the wounded being Col. Galusha A. Pennypacker, then commanding the Second Brigade. It participated in the capture of Wilmington, North Carolina, February 22, 1865, remaining at Weldon, North Carolina, until August 26, when and where it was mustered out. H. W. Carruthers was adjutant of this regiment, and Isaiah Price, who was at first captain of Company C, was subsequently major.

Turning attention again to what the people at home were doing, it is necessary to note the fact that all through the war there were numerous aid societies within the county that performed important services in the way of making clothing of all kinds and collecting money for the benefit of the "boys" in the field. There was a Central Aid Society at West Chester, and numerous branch societies in all parts of the county. These societies were in the hands of women, who, in their support and management, attested their interest in and loyalty to the cause, the only, or at least the principal, way in which they could serve the government. There was the Ladies' Union Aid Society of Coatesville, Midway and vicinity, which was organized early in 1861, with Mrs. Mary A. Penrose, president; Mrs. Elizabeth Worth and Mrs. Mary Valentine, vice-presidents; Mrs. Elizabeth Morrison, treasurer; Miss Martha J. Morrison, corresponding secretary, and Miss Mary R. Thomas, recording secretary. The meetings of this society were held in the hall of Mr. J. D. Broomall, who permitted the use of it free of rent. In aid of the societies under consideration lectures were given by prominent gentlemen, Wayne

MacVeagh lecturing for the benefit of this society January 14, 1862.

Mortonville Aid Society also performed effective and noble work in the line of making clothing and supplies of various kinds for the soldiers at the front. Of this society Miss Lizzie McFadlen was president, Miss Maggie Moore and Miss Sallie McFadlen secretaries, and about 30 other ladies were members. The East Brandywine Aid Society was not behind similar organizations, nor was the Kimberton Aid Society, nor the Upper Uwchlan Aid Society. Many other societies were equally active and efficient in the work performed. F. Crossby lectured in the Willistown Baptist Church for the benefit of the Soldiers' Aid Society in that part of the county; Dr. I. I. Hayes, the famous Arctic explorer, lectured January 10, 1862, for the benefit of the Soldiers' Fund, and on February 1, 1862, A. K. Warrington of Philadelphia lectured for the benefit of the Union Relief Society. The Central Aid Society of the county at this time had for its officers Mary F. Wyers, treasurer, and E. W. Smith, secretary. This society for the month of January, 1862, received $282.39 in money, besides a large quantity of supplies suitable for men in hospital, a part of which was sent to Louisville, Ky., and a part to hospitals in Missouri. The list of donations for the benefit of this society for February fills half a column in the newspapers. No one seemed ever to tire of doing good in this way. February 15, 1862, Washington Townsend lectured for the benefit of the Union Relief Society at Unionville.

Enlistments were not specially active in the early part of 1862, but there was something done in that line. In January of that year Capt. Price and Sergeant Fithian opened a recruiting office in West Chester, and Lieut. Barber and Jefferson Massey opened a similar office in the borough of Oxford.

On the 27th of February a pleasant incident occurred in the presentation of a handsome saber to Col. Josiah Harlan, who had been commissioned to raise a regiment of cavalry, the committee of presentation being Owen Hamilton, Elwood McFarlan and William D. Pruin. It was about this time that Bayard Taylor was appointed Secretary of Legation to St. Petersburg, one of the reasons being that he was unusually well versed in the modern languages.

When news reached Chester County that Col. Guss's regiment, the Ninety-seventh, had had a severe battle at or near Charleston, South Carolina, the ladies began immediately to prepare articles for the wounded soldiers, and to collect and forward a large quantity of hospital stores, the list of articles filling half a column in the Village Record. It was at this battle in June, 1862, that a remarkable incident occurred in connection with this regiment, that their numerous hairbreadth escapes are "to be accounted for only by the fact that our fire was so rapid and the smoke in consequence so dense as partially to hide our men from view."

President Lincoln, on July 20, made a call for troops, and on the 21st Gov. Curtin issued a proclamation calling for volunteers for nine months and for twelve months, the nine months' volunteers to aid in filling up old regiments, and the twelve months' men to be organized into new regiments. According to the schedule published the quota of Chester County was six companies under this call. In aid of this movement there was a meeting held at the court-house on July 23, Wednesday evening, at which Townsend Haines presided; Capt. William Apple and John T. Worthington were vice-presidents, and Dr. Frank Taylor and John Marshall secretaries. At this meeting it was agreed unanimously that to each and every enlisted man upon his being mustered into the service, a bounty of $40 should be given, and in order to raise the money a committee of seventy gentlemen was appointed from West Chester and vicinity. Meetings were also held in other portions of the county to encourage enlistments. James Whitcraft of Oxford raised a company of men. In West Chester G. C. Marshall was recruiting officer, and Capt. Hawley's company left Downingtown for Harrisburg on August 6. On this same day Capt. Stoll's company came into West Chester, and on the next day Capt. Whitcraft's company from Oxford.

However, with all the activity then manifested volunteering did not fill up the depleted ranks of the troops in the field and the new regiments required fast enough, and it became evident that a draft was necessary to secure the men. The number of men called for from Chester County under the first draft was 1,800, and here, as in all parts of the country, the number was claimed to be too great. It was claimed that as the State, which had a population of 2,900,000, was required to furnish only 42,000 troops, which was one to every sixty-nine persons, Chester County ought to be called upon for only 1,115, as her population was 77,000. In order to aid recruiting and to avoid if possible the necessity for a draft in Chester County, subscriptions were made to a fund to be used in paying bounties to volunteers, and up to August 20, 1862, $30,-000 had been subscribed. In order to secure the requisite number of volunteers, a call was made by James P. Everhart, Francis C. Hooton, William B. Waddell, Isaac McClure, William A. Moore, J. Stuart Leech, Joseph Umstead, John W. Davis, Joshua Kames and David Potts, and to give time for the raising of the requisite number of volunteers, the draft was postponed until September 15. By August 30 Capt. Waddell had 104 men enlisted, Capt. Everhart eighty, Capt. Hooton seventy-five, and other captains about the same average number.

In order to be prepared to go forward with the draft, should the county fail to raise her quota through voluntary enlistments, it was necessary to enroll the inhabitants of the county subject to military service, for which purpose a sufficient number of marshals was appointed. These marshals found the work of enrollment un-expectedly pleasant, there being very little opposition on the part of the people to giving all needed information as to number of men in each family within the ages of eighteen and forty-five. And the marshals reported that even where there was some hesitancy in giving names of those subject to duty in the families of those called upon, they were always willing to give all information about their neighbors. This enrollment commenced on August 25, 1862, under Mr. Barber, chief marshal, and resulted as follows: Total number enrolled, 13,289; volunteers in Pennsylvania regiments, 3,067; volunteers in regiments belonging to other States, 220; total number of volunteers from the county, 3,287.

In connection with the draft, which the county did not succeed in evading, the following extract from the constitution of the State then in force is of interest:

"Those who conscientiously scruple to bear arms shall not be compelled to do so, but shall pay an equivalent for personal services." But each person claiming exemption under this provision of the constitution was required to be sworn or affirmed that he was conscientiously opposed to bearing arms.*

Francis C. Hooton, commissioner of the draft for Chester County, appointed the following places for the hearing and determining of excuses of persons who had been enrolled by the marshals and who claimed exemption from military duty: West Chester, Phœnixville, Buck Tavern, Marshallton, Chatham and Oxford.

On September 10, the danger of invasion by the rebel army having become imminent, Governor Curtin issued a general order calling on all able-bodied men to enroll immediately for the defense of the State and on the 12th of the month, at 8 o'clock a. m., an enthusiastic meeting was held at the court-house in West Chester, at which it was announced that the Governor had called for 50,000 men. Captain Hannum announced that his company

---

* The constitution of 1874 provides that "The General Assembly * * * * * may exempt from military service persons having conscention scruples against bearing arms."

would be ready to move at the call of the Governor. Three volunteer companies were also announced as ready to move, each company containing eighty men. Under this call of the Governor Chester County was among the first to send forward her soldiers to the rescue by September 16, three companies having already left West Chester, one of them going on Sunday morning, September 14. One company, with William Hanna as captain, formed for the emergency, Joel P. Conard being first lieutenant and John Davis second. At Chatham a company of 100 men sprang up in a day, elected Thomas Hicks captain, Joseph Terrell first lieutenant and Enoch Moore second. In East and West Whiteland a company of infantry was organized, with Joseph McMullen captain, and there was a company of cavalry formed under Captain Wayne MacVeagh, the latter leaving Parkesburg September 14.

The time for making the draft was again postponed until September 5 Commissioner Hooton publishing the number required September 23 as 1,330 from Chester County. But once more the draft was postponed until October 16, when it was made, the number drafted being 1,159 men. It was conducted by Commissioner Hooton, assisted by Sheriff Heffelfinger and William McCormick, the latter being blindfolded and drawing the names out of a wheel made somewhat like a churn. The number of men exempted in the county under this first enrollment for physical disability was 1,190 and for conscientious scruples 197. Of the 1,159 drafted men up to October 25, 161 had furnished substitutes, and up to November 1, 79 more had done so. At that time the price paid for substitutes ranged from $100 to $500.

The drafted men and substitutes assembled on Tuesday, October 28, at Camp Wayne, no one else being permitted to enter the camp. Upon arriving inside the camp they were classified under sergeants, sixteen to a sergeant; but as many of the men came already organized through the election of officers to suit themselves the arrangements made by the commissioner of the draft were abandoned. Quite a large number of men did not appear, and upon inquiry in the neighborhood of their homes it was found that the missing ones had not been seen for about a week, and it was generally supposed that they had "skedaddled." The missing ones were in the main substitutes, who had received their pay as such before being sworn in. At 4 o'clock in the afternoon of the day last mentioned the list of the drafted men was called over and 570 found to be absent; but it was known that some of these had merely left camp for the borough, it being late in the day. On Wednesday morning all present in camp, after breakfast, formed into line and marched to the depot of the Pennsylvania Railroad in charge of Colonel John Nields, and at 12:30 p. m., when the cars arrived, all boarded the train and left West Chester for Camp Philadelphia in fine spirits, cheering and singing songs as they were pulled out of the depot. Before leaving camp that morning upon the calling of the roll 810 responded to their names.

Upon arriving in camp at Philadelphia, this camp being the rendezvous for the counties of Philadelphia, Northampton, Monroe, Wayne, Bucks, Delaware, Montgomery, Lehigh, Carbon, Pike and Chester, it was found that still quite a number of substitutes were absent and measures were taken to find them. Two were quickly found in New Jersey and placed in jail in Philadelphia. The drafted men from Chester County were formed into nine companies, which companies elected captains as follows: Peter Colehower, Vincent; Levi Fetters, East Whiteland; Thomas Hicks, Londongrove; Evan P. Dixon, Kennett; Joseph Thompson, East Nantmeal; Theodore Woollens; ———— Rowland of New York, formerly of Chester County; George W. Werntz, Honeybrook; William N. Worthington, West Goshen. On Tuesday, November 11, eight of these companies were mustered into the service of the United States, but none of the companies was full, only 710 answering to their names, the rest being absent on furlough. In order to make a full regiment two companies from Montgomery County joined the Chester County men and thus completed the regiment, which elected Francis C. Hooton colonel, Samuel Dyer of Chester lieutenant-colonel and Isaac McClure of Chester County major.

James H. Bull of West Chester was appointed provost marshal of Chester County early in September, receiving his commission September 8, 1862. The Oxford Guards, Captain James Whitcraft's company, were assigned to the One Hundred and Twenty-fourth Pennsylvania volunteer infantry. Of this company W. C. Dickey was first lieutenant and Levi Crowl second lieutenant. In the Twelfth Pennsylvania volunteer militia there were the Keystone Guards and two other companies from Chester County, one from Whiteland and the other from Lionville. Of the Keystone Guards the captain was William R. Ash; first lieutenant, J. D. Bromall; and second lieutenant, W. H. Gilbert. In the Twenty-fourth Pennsylvania volunteer militia was Captain George B. Thomas' company, of which the first lieutenant was Charles J. Hunt and second lieutenant Isaac Massey.

About March 1, 1863, the recruiting of colored men began in Chester County, those enlisted being taken in charge by a gentle-man from Boston who, as soon as a squad had been secured, took them to Massachusetts to fill the quota of that State. They were paid $13 per month. Twenty-seven men left Chester County on February 26 and twenty-five more were ready to go on March 3. This movement of enlisting colored troops for Eastern States was quite general throughout the eastern and central parts of Pennsylvania.

A few weeks later the most prominent matter in the minds of the patriotic people of the county was the formation of Union Leagues, for the purpose of sustaining the government in suppressing the Rebellion of open and armed foes and also to guard against the machinations of secret foes at home. A call was issued for a meeting of the citizens to take place at the court-house on Wednesday evening, March 25, 1863, for the purpose of forming such a league. This meeting was largely attended and ably addressed by B. F. Brewster of Philadelphia, Governor Cannon of Delaware, Colonel Wilmer of Delaware and Rev. Mr. Jackson of the Methodist Conference, then in session in West Chester. All were in favor of maintaining the Union at whatever cost, no matter what might become of slavery. The result of the meeting was the organization of the West Chester Union League, which adopted a constitution and by-laws, the condition of membership in the league being unqualified loyalty to the government and unwavering support of that government in its efforts to suppress the Rebellion. There was also formed a Union League of Westtown and Thornbury, a meeting for the purpose of organization being held at the house of David H. Taylor, April 25, 1863, at the call of Robert H. Miller, John Q. Taylor, Charles E. Heister, Joseph H. Brinton, Caleb II. Cox and many others.

In May, 1863, the One Hundred and Twenty-fourth Pennsylvania militia, nine months' men, returned home, receiving a warm welcome. The marshal of the day upon which they arrived, Monday, May 18, was Captain William Apple, and the committee of arrangements for the reception of the returning soldiers was composed of Colonel R. Maris Frame, Bentley Worth and S. S. Heed from the borough council of West Chester, and H. S. Evans, Captain William Apple, Colonel T. Hyatt, William F. Wyers, Maris T. Chandler and W. E. Burlin of the Union League. The regiment reached West Chester at 2 p. m. and almost immediately partook of a hearty collation prepared by the patriotic ladies of West Chester and vicinity in the market house and were welcomed home in a neat and eloquent address by Judge Butler. It was an occasion long to be remembered by those present. The Delaware companies remained in West Chester until next day, when they went to Media and had a warm reception in Everett Grove.

Preparatory to another draft Captain E. L. Christman, provost
marshal of Chester County, appointed enrolling officers for each
township and borough in the county and made Lieutenant William
D. Christman of the One Hundred and Twenty-fourth Regiment,
his brother, one of his deputies and George W. Downing and P. W.
Ash clerks. It was not long after this before the entire country was
alarmed by General Lee's invasion of Pennsylvania, in anticipation
of which Governor Curtin, on June 12, called out the entire militia
of the State. On the 15th he sent a telegram to Colonel Joseph W.
Hawley to "Go to work at once! Call out the One Hundred and
Twenty-fourth Regiment," &c. Lee was then invading Pennsylvania and on the 16th there was a grand rally of the people of
Chester County. The bells on the court-house and churches rang
out the alarm, the streets were soon filled with people, farmers
came into West Chester direct from the fields of peaceful labor
and an impromptu meeting was held at the court-house, at which
Judge Butler and Messrs. Darlington, MacVeagh, Everhart, Townsend and others made brief but eloquent appeals to the people to
rush to arms, for it was thought General Lee would cross Chester
County on his way to take and sack Philadelphia. Arrangements
were at once made to enlist and send forward all the troops possible, the captains of the One Hundred and Twenty-fourth Regiment,
just mustered out of service, endeavoring to collect and organize
their former comrades. Early on Wednesday morning, June 17,
men came into town in squads of various sizes from all parts of the
county with their knapsacks on their backs. They kept coming
in all day, and at 5 p. m. several companies left their quarters,
marched to the depot and took the train for Harrisburg, their
numbers being augmented at Downingtown, Coatesville, Parkesburg and Penningtonville. At 5 o'clock next morning they arrived
at Harrisburg. The captains of companies formerly belonging
to the One Hundred and Twenty-fourth Regiment that went out at
this emergency call were C. W. Roberts, W. M. Hinksou, E. F.

James and W. W. Scott, and besides them there were Captains C. W. Thomas of the Second Pennsylvania militia, Wayne MacVeagh of the Pennsylvania cavalry and J. H. Thorp, who also had a company of cavalry. On Thursday Captain J. B. Everhart, then late of the Tenth Pennsylvania militia, left with his company, and the uprising was the same all over the county. At Coatesville, Downingtown, Parkesburg, Penningtonville, Kennett Square, Phœnixville, Oxford and all other towns and villages men and women were alive to the situation and active in taking such measures as they could for the defense of the State. At Coatesville Captain W. R. Ash raised a full company, and Steel & Worth and Pennock & Bro. put out the fires in their rolling mills, marshaled their men and led them forth to do battle for their country. At Downingtown Captain J. A. Eicholtz raised a company and was soon on his way to Harrisburg. Kennett Square was fully alive, the Quakers in that part of the county turned out, organized a company, which immediately took up its line of march. And James Maxton and Isaac Wickersham marshaled the yeomen of the Marlboroughs.

On June 26 Governor Curtin called for 60,000 three months' men and a committee was appointed by the citizens of West Chester consisting of Washington Townsend, William Darlington, David McConkey, W. E. Barber, J. Smith Futhey, Captain William Apple, William Butler, P. F. Smith, James H. Bull, Dr. J. B. Wood, Henry S. Evans, Henry Buckwalter and George W. Pearce, which committee issued a call for volunteers. The commissioners of the county offered each volunteer a bounty of $15, to be paid immediately upon his being sworn into the service of the State, under this call. Several gentlemen began raising companies and almost immediately after the call was made John W. Davis had a company ready, named the Anthony Wayne Guards and belonging in Tredyffrin Township. Under this call for 60,000 men the quota of Chester County was 881 men. Up to Friday, July 3, five full companies of three months' men had left the county for the de-

fense of the State, those of Guss, Cochran, Roberts, Stott and
Davis, and on Saturday, the 4th, the sixth company, that of Captain Strickland of Oxford, left the county. But then, of course,
the emergency that called forth all this activity had passed, for on
that day General Lee was defeated by General Meade at Gettysburg
and was en route for Virginia.

On July 5, Sunday, about 1,500 paroled Union prisoners taken
in the first day's battle at Gettysburg came into West Chester, belonging to the First and Eleventh Corps, a number of them
wounded. The wounded ones were given quarters in the gymnasium at the Normal School, the others being taken to the Agricultural Fair Grounds, where they remained until the 10th, when
they were transferred to the new camp grounds on the new
railroad, about a mile and a half southeast of West Chester.

Some short time before these stirring times a Mr. Beugless
opened an enrollment list for colored soldiers, in two weeks securing nearly 100 names of colored men willing to fight for their country, and took them to the new camp mentioned above on the new
railroad, the camp being on the farm of Abraham Williams. On
July 14 Frederick Douglas delivered an address in the Horticultural Hall in West Chester for the purpose of encouraging enlistments on the part of members of his race.

In the draft which began in West Chester August 4, 1863, and
which was conducted throughout the county at different places at
different times until early in October, there were drawn 1,789, of
which number 1,646 procured exemption from service in one
way or another, either because they were the only support of a
widowed mother, from physical disability, from furnishing a sub-
stitute, or from the payment of the amount required by the Government as an equivalent.

Under the call of February 1, 1864, by the President of the
United States, for 500,000 men, Chester County filled her quota in
large part by re-enlisted men and volunteers. Each man enlisting

1. MARY DOD BROWN CHAPEL.
2. LINCOLN HALL.
3. CRESSON HALL.
4. HOUSTON HALL.
5. UNIVERSITY HALL.

under this call became entitled to a county bounty of $350, this policy being determined on by the county commissioners immediately after the President's call. One hundred dollars of the money was paid in cash, and $250 was given in county bonds. If anyone preferred all cash, he was paid $337.50 in that way, a discount of five per cent. being charged for the payment of the $250. The entire amount of the bounty paid reached somewhere between $350,000 and $400,000. Quite a number of colored men joined the ranks under this call, and were highly pleased at the receipt of the "Greenbacks," so large a pile of which they had never before seen. The commissioners said, after experimenting with this method of raising the county's quota, "Chester County is the first in the State to fill her quota," and of course it was said with no little satisfaction and pride.

As is well remembered, the winter of 1864-65 was the one during which the men at the front re-enlisted, or veteranized, as many of them preferred to call it. This has been hinted at above. The Ninety-seventh Regiment came home to veteranize in April, 1864, reaching West Chester April 9. They were heartily welcomed by the citizens, the address of welcome being delivered by Rev. W. E. Moore. After a month spent at home on furlough those who had re-enlisted left West Chester for the field on May 9. The Brandywine Guards, Co. A of the First Pennsylvania Reserves, reached West Chester from the field June 8, being welcomed in a neat and eloquent speech by Dr. Wilmer Worthington and being afterward addressed by General McCall, who complimented them highly on their services to the government. The ladies of the borough gave them a dinner at the Normal School.

In July, 1864, the rebels made an invasion into Maryland, causing great excitement throughout the State of Pennsylvania. Governor Curtin called for 12,000 men for one hundred days on July 5, and on the 10th of the month a large meeting was held at the court-house, at which a committee was appointed to raise

18

about 700 men for Chester County, this committee consisting of William Darlington, General George A. McCall, Dr. Wilmer Worthington, Henry R. Guss, George F. Smith, Colonel Francis C. Hooton, Galusha Pennypacker, Enoch E. Lewis, Mott Hooton, William McConnell, Washington Townsend, William B. Waddell, Townsend Haines, and Daniel McConkey. Colonel Hooton called on his old regiment, the One Hundred and Seventy-fifth, and Major Everhart made a similar call on the One Hundred and Twenty-fourth, Colonel Henry R. Guss endeavored to rally his battery, and Mr. Beugless was authorized to raise a regiment of colored men, and in order to do this a meeting was held at the court-house July 14, at which Rev. John Brown (colored) presided.

A company of one hundred days' men left West Chester July 22, uniting at camp Cadwallader with a company from Delaware County. On July 18, 1864, the President made a call for 300,000 men, and by October 4, nearly all of the townships in Chester County had their quotas full, only eighty-four men being still required. Under the call of December 19, 1864, for 300,000 men, Chester and Delaware Counties were required to furnish 1,121 men, the proportion from Chester County being 740. This quota was never filled, for after the surrender of Lee on April 9, orders were issued from Washington to discontinue the draft and to stop enlistments, as it was known the war was then practically at an end.

There was great rejoicing throughout Chester County on April 3 and 4, the news having reached there that Richmond had fallen. The court-house bell and the church bells rang out the glad tidings, which spread with great rapidity throughout the county, cannon boomed, flags were thrown to the breeze, farmers rushed into the county seat, to learn the particulars, and crowds surrounded the telegraph office to learn the latest reports from the seat of war. Speeches were made to suit the occasion by Colonel Hooton, Wayne McVeagh, Dr. Worthington, Dr. Taylor and others, and on Tuesday night, April 4, the private and public buildings were illuminated in honor of the event.

On April 10, upon receipt of the news of the surrender of Lee, the provost marshal fired a salute of 200 guns, and Colonel Hyatt's battery, one of 100 guns. The band marched all through the town playing patriotic airs, and everyone was full of gladness. The news of Lee's surrender was brought to West Chester on Monday morning in advance of telegraphic reports, by two colored men, Samuel J. Williams and Alexander Gladman, who left Philadelphia at 2 o'clock in the morning, and William Darlington, chief burgess of the borough, allowed these colored men to first ring the court-house bell, announcing the news to the people.

On April 14, the last day of the draft in Chester and Delaware Counties, four men were drafted in Darby, eighteen in Elk, four in New Garden and eight in West Brandywine.

Then came the news of the assassination of Lincoln, which spread the deepest gloom over a triumphant and happy land. Commenting on this great crime the Village Record said: "In this sudden death of President Lincoln we are forced to the conviction that it is the hand of Providence. By God were the Pilgrim Fathers guided to the shores of America—by God were they protected from savage foes—by Him were they made a great nation, and by Him slavery has now almost been blotted out. Abraham Lincoln was but His instrument. He is now been taken and another great man, Andrew Johnson, takes up the work yet to be done!"

The war was over. Chester County had done her duty nobly during the ordeal through which the country had passed. While there was a large number of persons in the county who were conscientiously opposed to bearing arms, yet most of them without any other thought than the preservation of the Union from disruption, took up arms in its defense, and fought as hard as any, many of them laying down their lives during the conflict. Their zeal and courage were equal to the bravest in the ranks or in com-

mission, and all are to-day proud of the record that they in common with other citizens of the county made. Under the last call
of the President the proportion of the county to be drafted was less
than that of any other county in the State. There had been at
work throughout the war about forty aid societies, through which
the people had contributed clothing, food, nurses, etc., without
complaint and without stint, to the sick and wounded in the hospital and in the field. It is a record of which all will always be
proud so long as history shall be read, and so long as men are willing to die for the preservation of their country and the rights and
liberties which it confers upon them and protects them in enjoying.

While it is impracticable to give the precise number of soldiers
furnished to the army during the war of the Rebellion, yet it
may be stated that, making due allowance for re-enlistments and
recounts, the number of names which appear on the several muster rolls is 6,736. Some of these enlisted twice, some three times,
and some perhaps more than three times, taking into consideration
the numerous emergency cases that arose in Pennsylvania more
than in any other Northern State, occasioned by the invasion
of the State by the rebel armies, and several threatened invasions
where no actual invasion occurred. Then in case of promotions
the same soldier's name necessarily occurs at least twice, in the
same company or regiment, and in such instances the tendency in
counting the names would lead to an excess greater than that due
to re-enlistments. Therefore it may perhaps be stated that the
probable number of different soldiers belonging to Chester County
in the war was not far from 6,000.

This number cannot seem extravagant, for in the Ninety-seventh Regiment alone there were in the aggregate 2,034 men, including volunteers, drafted men and substitutes. Of these sixty-nine
were killed, and sixty-eight died of wounds. One hundred and
sixty-six died of disease, and finally 701 were mustered out

It would seem eminently proper in this connection to make

brief mention of a few of the men that made Chester County fa-mous in the war. Of these, Brev. Major-General Henry R. Guss, first colonel of the Ninety-Seventh Regiment, may well be mentioned first, as he was one of the first to be prominently connected with the movement to raise troops in Chester County. He raised a com-pany of men almost immediately after the President's first call for militia, and became its captain. This was Company A, Ninth Pennsylvania volunteer infantry, three months' men. Upon return-ing from this service he raised the Ninety-seventh Regiment, hav-ing been commissioned colonel in July, and leading his regiment to the field in November, 1861. He was ordered to the Department of the South and was brigaded under Gen. Wright, and com-manded his regiment in the expedition resulting in the capture of Fernandina, Florida, and other important points on the coast of that state. He served through the James Island campaign with marked ability until July, 1862, when he was assigned to the com-mand of Hilton Head, retaining this command until October, when he returned to the command of his own regiment. In April, 1863, Col. Guss was assigned to the command of the First Brigade, Terry's Division, Tenth Army Corps, in the expedition against Charleston, and afterward he was assigned successively to the posts of Edisto, Botany Bay and St. Helena Islands, and later, when the assault on Fort Wagner was ordered, Col. Guss was selected to command the advance storming party, containing 300 men of his own regiment and 300 of the Third New Hamp-shire regiment. The following October the Ninety-seventh was ordered to Fernandina, Florida, and its colonel to the command of the forces at that place, and there he remained until April, 1864, and then received leave of absence to accompany the veterans home on furlough. Rejoining his regiment at Bermuda Hundred in May, he was assigned to the First brigade, Third division, Tenth Army Corps, retaining this position during active operations on the south side of the James. He was then relieved of his command for alleged disobedience of orders, which was never proved and was not true, but on account of this injustice he resigned his commission and returned to his home, his resignation bearing date June 2, 1864.

Charles Frederick Taylor, brother of Bayard Taylor, was another brave soldier from Chester County. Immediately after the attack on Fort Sumter young Taylor raised a company of young men of the vicinity of Kennett Square, who elected him captain, took the company to Harrisburg, and had it incorporated into the famous Bucktail regiment. After the battle of Antietam he was promoted to the colonelcy of the regiment, to fill the vacancy occasioned by the death of Colonel McNeil. He was the youngest colonel in the Army of the Potomac, and General Meade pronounced him one of the most promising young officers in the service. In the battle of Gettysburg, on July 2, 1863, when in advance of his column, encouraging his men to attempt to "take them all prisioners," he was shot through the heart by a rebel sharpshooter. His remains were interred in Longwood Cemetery, where a beautiful monument, purchased by the surviving officers and men of his regiment, was erected over his grave.

Colonel Henry M. McIntyre died at Baltimore, Maryland, from wounds received in the Seven Days' battles, his death occurring January 14, 1863. He was wounded in the ankle, which rendered amputation of the leg necessary. He was a native of Cecil County, Maryland, was a graduate of Yale, began the study of law in New Haven, finishing with Joseph J. Lewis in West Chester, was admitted to the bar and opened an office in the latter place. He joined the Brandywine Guards upon their organization, was made captain of the company, which united with the First Pennsylvania Reserves, of which regiment he was made lieutenant-colonel, and after leaving Camp Wayne, the regiment was joined to the Pennsylvania Reserve Corps under General McCall.

Major-General George A. McCall secured the organization of

the thirteen Pennsylvania regiments, and was invited by Governor Curtin to accept the position of major-general, to which he consented, and was commissioned on May 16, 1861. On the same day he entered upon the command of the Reserve Corps, the history of which is well known to readers of the history of the war. He immediately organized fifteen regiments of troops in the manner provided for the law, and throughout the war for the Union performed valiant and valuable services to the cause.

Lieut.-Col. Thomas S. Bell was another hero of the war. He was born in West Chester, May 12, 1838, and was a lineal descendant of Col. Joseph McClellan, who was a Revolutionary soldier, serving under Gen. Wayne in the battle of Brandywine. He studied law under the instruction of his father, Hon. Thomas S. Bell, and was admitted to the bar in 1859. March 11, 1858, he was commissioned aid-de-camp to the major-general of the Third Division of the uniformed militia of Chester and Delaware Counties, and was appointed paymaster of the same division with the rank of major, October 3, 1859.

When the war of the Rebellion broke out he was among the first to respond to his country's call, and was made adjutant of the Ninth Pennsylvania three months' men. Later he was commissioned by the governor of the State lieutenant-colonel of the Fifty-first Pennsylvania volunteer infantry, and at Roanoke Island had command of a portion of the regiment. At Newbern he had command of the regiment, and being ordered to charge the enemies' batteries, captured the first battery and was the first man to mount it. At Camden he had command of the brigade to which his regiment belonged, the brigade leading the charge. At Antietam he was killed after the capture of the stone bridge, September 17, 1862. His loss was deeply felt, for he was not only a brave soldier, but he had endeared himself to all whose acquaintance he had formed, not only those inferior to him in position, but also to those of superior rank. His remains were brought to West Chester, and lie buried in Oakland Cemetery, where it was his wish to be laid.

Col. Augustus P. Duer entered West Point military academy July 1, 1837, and after leaving that institution aided, as a civil engineer, in laying out the railroad from West Chester to Philadelphia by way of Media. When the war of the Rebellion broke out he promptly responded to the call of duty, and was appointed Lieut.-Colonel of the Ninety-seventh Pennsylvania volunteers, October 7, 1861. He was in command of the regiment a portion of the time while it was in Camp Wayne; at Hilton Head, South Carolina, in September, 1862; at Seabrook Island in May, 1863; and at St. Helena, South Carolina, from June 20, 1863, to September 20, following. He was honorably discharged April 3, 1864, from which time to his death, March 29, 1898, he lived quietly at Atglen, Chester County.

CHAPTER VIII.

THE SPANISH-AMERICAN WAR.

CHAPTER VIII.

WHEN the war broke out between the United States and
Spain Chester County was not less patriotic than in the
wars that had gone before. This war with Spain was brought
about by reason of the failure of President McKinley, through
the most patient and persistent efforts known to diplomacy, to
secure relief to the people of Cuba from the horrible cruelties of
concentration by which they were brought to starvation, disease
and death by the hundreds of thousands, including old men,
women and children, and also by reason of the destruction of the
United States battleship Maine, in the harbor of Havana, by a
submarine mine, on February 15, 1898, two of the officers and 264
of the men of the Maine being crushed and drowned to death.
A Court of Inquiry was appointed by the President, which, after
twenty-three days of continuous labor, reached the conclusion that
the Maine was not destroyed through any interior explosion or
accident, for which any of her officers or men were responsible,
thus fixing the responsibility by implication and inference on
some agent of the Spanish government. On April 11, 1898, President McKinley transmitted this report to Congress, and asked that
he be authorized and empowered to employ the army and navy of

the United States to secure the termination of hostilities between Spain and the people of Cuba, and to carry into effect on the island the establishment of a stable government, capable of maintaining order, observing international obligations, and securing tranquillity and peace. In accordance with a joint resolution of Congress, passed April 19, 1898, the President on April 20 sent an ultimatum to the Spanish government, requiring it to withdraw its land and naval forces from Cuban waters, with which that government declined to comply.

War was therefore formally declared by Congress April 25, and in the meantime the people of Chester County were taking proper measures to enlist their quota of men when the anticipated call should be made. Company I of the Sixth Regiment, National Guards of Pennsylvania, had everything packed ready to move into camp by April 21, and on April 23, the President of the United States issued a proclamation calling for 125,000 troops for two years, unless sooner discharged Under this call the quota of Pennsylvania was 10,762. April 26 Col. Perry M. Washabaugh received orders from Brigadier-General John W. Schall to move the Sixth Regiment to Mount Gretna, on Thursday morning, April 28, and on that morning, an unusually inclement one for the season, Company I of West Chester marched through the streets of that place to the train at the Gay Street crossing, accompanied by about 2,000 people, including 100 veterans of the war of the Rebellion, and the West Chester Band. Following is the roster of the company as it left West Chester:

Captain—Gibbons Gray Cornwell.

First Lieutenant—Granville S. Bennett.

Second Lieutenant—Herman J. Smith.

Quartermaster-Sergeant—G. H. Hazard.

Sergeants—George A. Black, Charles W. Reagan, George B. McCormick.

Corporals—T. Lincoln Ingram, Nathaniel Leaf, William

Thompson, Granville Pratt, Roskell Woodward, Fulton Beatty, Frank Missimer.

Privates—Howard Beatty, P. T. Conner, George Budd, George G. Cardwell, Jr., Joseph Chase, Wm. D. Cornwell, Joseph Cudlipp, William Cudlipp, James Dooley, Thomas Fullerton, George Garrett, Howard Garrett, Joseph Hemphill, E. D. Hemphill, Jr., Frank C. Harp, William Johnson, William Kane, John S. Clark, Paul Ludwick, Alexander McCausland, William McConnell, P. H. Gibbons, W. H. Graham, Charles Murtagh, Harry C. Nields, John Painter, Edmund D. Painter, Warren Sharpe, George Rupert, James McC. D. Ruth, H. T. Lear, Herbert T. Vance, Leon Lyster, Lewis Good, Frank Brown, Edward Manley, Arlington Canizares, Abram Darlington, H. T. Cunningham, C. F. Kellings, Frank H. Diesem, Charles Bennett, George Hoffman, Carl Schrader.

Cooks—Clement Tuck and William Callahan of Wayne; Fred Deery of West Chester. The latter will serve the officers.

Company I, as a part of the Sixth Regiment, left camp at Mount Gretna along with the Eighth, Twelfth and Thirteenth Regiments, on May 19, 1898, for Falls Church, Virginia, which place is within about eight miles of Washington, District of Columbia, and here it is necessary to take leave of the soldiers from Chester County, so far as this work is concerned, for they are undoubtedly to go South, and perhaps to Cuba.

On May 7, 1898, twenty-nine young men left West Chester to unite with Company I, a crowd of several hundred people bidding them adieu at the railway station. The list of those who thus went out to join the company is as follows:

Sanford Singer, Percy S. Darlington, Norman D. Gray, J. Bert Smith, James Rox, Ralph Wood, Eugene Boyles, Martin Echoff, William M. Sager, Jacob S. Smith, Augustus Michiner, Edward H. Musser, James H. Varnum, Harry C. Kugel, Fred W. Guie, Wilfred G. Priest, William S. Baird, Rufus T. Cheyney, William G. Middleton, William Armour, James A. Riley, Henry F. Taylor, Franklin

H. Long, John P. Hayes, Joseph H. Baldwin, Charles B. Heck, William Fisher, Alfred Barry, Bentley Foster and Horace Brinton.

By June 25, 1898, other recruits uniting with this company brought its number up to 110.

Phœnixville sent out Company D to the war, the roster of which was as follows:

Captain—Louis R. Walters.

First Lieutenant—Frank M. Crossman.

Second Lieutenant—Wm. A. Gilbert.

First Sergeant—Wm. A. March.

Sergeants—Horace Seigfried, Ralston Lambkin, James Mortimer, George L. Walters.

Corporals—William Hertinstine, John Wadsworth, Fred Karrer, Wm. Kirkner, James Carlin, Harry McDonald, Charles Barnes, Robert Dunn.

Musicians—Frank Heist, Harry O'Koenig.

Privates—Wm. Ashenfelter, James Barnes, Lewis Benner, James Bitting, Elmer Carruthers, Harry Carter, Jesse Corbet, John Drake, Walter Fulmer, David Fitzcharles, Charles Frick, Samuel Ferguson, Harry Gregory, Wm. Horner, Benj. Hallman, Wm. Kirk, Wm. Kuler, Harvey Mosteller, Abraham Mosteller, Richard March, Luther Moses, Lorenzo Neiman, John J. Robinson, Frank E. Quay, John Swartley, Wm. Swartley, George Shoemaker, John Simmers, Wm. Shaner, John Stewart, Wm. Stern, Julius Sockel, Chas. Sperick, Herman Springer, Ed Shoffner, James Turish, James Winters, Howard McClaskey, Bernard Gillen, Irvin Ziegler, Daniel Ottinger.

Immediately after the departure of Company I for Mount Gretna, Capt. Sharpless M. Paxton and Lieut. St. Julien Ogier, formerly of that company, began to raise a company to take the place of Company 1, and if necessary to make up the State's quota, to take the new company to the front. The following list of members was enrolled in the new company by April 29, 1898:

S. M. Paxson, St. Julien Ogier, J. H. Varnum, Harry C. Kugel,

H. Howard Plank, Edward S. Turner, Frank L. Elliott, Frank R. Burnett, Trevor H. Dawson, Granville T. Mitchell, F. W. Woodward, Wilfred G. Priest, Isaac Lawrence, Joseph H. Hunt, Howard W. Sharpe Jr., Wm. J. Cobourn, J. Hayes Still, W. T. Hunt, Howard Hawley, Jos. H. Baldwin, T. L. Eyre, George W. Griffith, Norris S. Ingram, James B. Fisher, Lewis H. Miller, O. F. Groff, John G. Andress, Unionville; L. Walter Garrett, Harry Cobb, Wm. M. Blenkin, J. F. Shields, John Kerwin, Harry B. Russell, Amos K. Mackie, Edward B. Musser, E. B. Ferrell, Philip H. Smith, Clinton J. Lacey, Thomas M. Hayes, Glen Loch; John F. Hayes, Harry S. Williams, James A. Burns, William A. Webb, W. F. Musser, E. A. Hodgson, Jr., E. M. Boyles, H. B. Moore, Henry R. Guss, Jr., Lemuel H. Kenny, Percy Darlington, John A. Jackson, F. W. Guie, Martin Echoff, David Jones, J. Bert Smith, George C. Guss, John P. Hayes, Edward H. Hayes, John F. Ryan, Bentley W. Foster, James R. Rox, William Miller, Greene Hill, William Armour, John F. Barry, Albert Biles, Clyde S. Hannum, Van Wyck Bull Ralph Wood, H. O. Beaumont, Clarence Beaumont, James A. Riley, Wilmer W. Miller, John F. Woodhouse, Maryatt Paxson, P. W. Hoopes, Jr., E. D. Hoopes, Hamorton, M. P. McFadden, W. S. Snead, Harry Clower, Thomas Ford, Fred Ginceley, Charles McCorkle, John Douglass, Sanford Singer, Ralph Beekman, Melvin C. Musser, Washington Sellers, John C. Brennan, William G. Middleton, Harry D. Lewis, Curtis H. H. Reeder, Addison M. Reeder, Harry Black, Harry J. Wickersham, Glen Hall, Frank A Smith, Jesse W. Dilworth, Fred H. Lewis, George Ford, Willard J. Smith, Howard Hetherington, Joseph W. Clark, Benjamin S. Hughes, William Bartholomew, William M. Hutton, John T. Hazard, Michael F. Marra, Frank H. Long, Thomas S. Lack and Albert M. Ingram.

This company was then drilled for some time in the armory of Company I, in order that if called upon they might be ready to move at a moment's notice. On May 20, 1898, word was received that this company had been accepted and would form a portion of the First Brigade of the new provisional guard, the First Brigade to be commanded by Col. Edward Morrell.

On May 25, 1898, President McKinley issued a call for 75,000 more men, under which Pennsylvania was required to furnish eighteen companies. Under this call Capt. Paxson's company was called upon to join the regiment under Col Morrell of Philadelphia.

On April 29, the next day after Company I left West Chester, a call was made for colored men to enlist in the war by J. S. Prigg, who had his office at the corner of Market and Matlack Streets. A company was raised and became Company L, First Regiment Pennsylvania Colored Volunteers. The famous old Liberty Cornet Band, which has recently acquired a high state of efficiency, also united with the First Regiment, accepting an invitation extended to them by Col. James R. Gillespie of this regiment. This company's enrollment was as follows:

Captain—John S. Prigg.

First Lieutenant—Thomas H. Derry.

Second Lieutenant—John M. Boardley.

Quartermaster-Sergeant—Harry A. Clark.

Sergeants—John Bond, Franklin Curry, Nathan Prigg, Eugene Bell, Joseph H. Jones, George Henry.

Corporals—William E. Curry, George Wilson, William H. Price, Clifford Washington, Isaac Fullerton, John E. Clark, Eugene A. Biddle.

Musicians—Frederick Burton, James Williams.

Privates—L. Sadler, John Dorsey, Wesley Denny, Isaac Harris, H. B. Walker, Thomas Wesley, Newton Richardson, John Wesley, Elwood Spriggs, John Chrisman, Walter Washington, Walter Herod, Fred Goines, Isaac Moore, Jones Wilson, Linford Reed, Jesse Kelly, Wellington Kelly, John L. Price, Percy D. Morgan, George H. Ricketts, Harry Johnson, T. Cheyney Lewis, Jesse Reese,

P.M. Sharples

Eugene Cole, Benjamin F. Spriggs, Chas. E. Pierce, Charles Pennington, William Wilson, L. Willis Denny, Charles Shirley, George Beckett, Wm. T. Fitzgerald, Henry Watkins, Frank Reed, George Trowery, John F. Boyer, Henry Derry, Jos. Jones, Harry Hall, Joseph W. Sharp, Albert Kelly, Harry Thomas, Acre Jacobs, James Davis, John H. Price, Lewis Hickson, George Dennis, John Conway, Chas. Fields, George Boyer, Owen States, Jos. Harrod, Charles Anderson, Harry Fullerton, John Johnson, William Peach, Fred Spence, Jesse Johnson, James Warnick, Thomas Burnett, John Goodwin, Jacob C. Borton, George Young.

Drum major, Herman W. Spence; bandmaster, Wilson Luff; first musician, William T. Burton; second musician, Jacob Milby; sergeant, George Boardley; William Washington, Charles Esley, Frank Bell, William B. Gibbs, Harry M. Petersau, Amos Fairfax, Charles Bostic, Clarence Cooper, Reuben Washington, Fred B. Fry, Richard Thomas, James Miller, Harry Miller, William Spence, Steven Boardley, John Thomas, William Curry, John Clark, Wm. A. Biddle.

On June 14, 1898, twenty-seven young men left West Chester for Camp Alger, near Falls Church, Virginia, their names being as follows, together with the companies to which they were assigned:

Company I—James Kenworthy, John Kelleher, Mayfield Weidler, Charles M. Clark, Charles G. Zook, John C. Kacy, Lawrence A. Sullivan, Hayes Miller, all of Coatesville; Harry L. Esray, William M. Blenkin, John F. Dunleavy, William Burt Brown, James A. Burns, Joseph J. Finegan, James Frank Taylor, West Chester; Darlington F. Hannum, Pocopson; James W. Dorat, Charles A. Lightcap, George W. Berkenheiser, of Downingtown; Warren R. Pechin, Sylvester Detterline, Strafford; James C. Roberts, Bondsville.

Company C—John L. McLear, Lewis H. Shank, Addison M.

19

Reeder, of West Chester; Edward P. Harrison, Eber S. Nethery, Longwood.

Company H—John Francis Barry of West Chester.

John N. Guss, a young member of the Chester County bar, enlisted in Battery A of Philadelphia, stationed at the time, June 14, at Newport News, Virginia, and made up largely of college men.

Scarcely had the soldiers left home for camp when the women of the county, always as patriotic as the men, began the work of preparing such articles of comfort as their husbands and sons would need while away in the service of their country. On April 30 a number of women assembled at the house of Mrs. Charles R. Palmer in West Chester, when a temporary organization was effected by electing Miss Mary I. Stille, chairman, and Mrs. Benjamin Haines, secretary. The object of the ladies present was to secure the making of what they called "housewives" for the soldiers. At an adjourned meeting held the same day at the home of Mrs. L. G. McCauley, the following ladies were present: Mrs. L. G. McCauley, Mrs. Jerome B. Gray, Mrs. Smith, Miss Mary Bogle, Mrs. Chester P. Martindale, Mrs. I. Cary Carver, Mrs. William Hemphill (Chestnut Street), Miss Alice Hoopes, Mrs. Henry C. Wood, Mrs. W. C. Mullen, Mrs. W. K. Thorp, Miss Sallie Fairlamb, Mrs. Sarah K. Ruth, Miss Mabel James, Miss Hettie Strode, Mrs. John J. Gheen, Miss Sarah Bogle, Miss Worstall, Miss Stille, Miss Slonaker, Miss Bessie Rupert, Miss Clara Hemphill, Mrs. John Thorp, Mrs. George W. Conway, Mrs. Charles R. Palmer, Mrs. W. C. Husted, Miss Ella Nields, Mrs. H. C. Cochran, Miss Lillie Hemphill, Mrs. R. M. Scott, Mrs. Benjamin W. Haines.

It was the same throughout the county, the ladies taking as much interest in the war and in the comfort of the soldiers that had gone forth as any of the soldiers themselves. On May 17 there was a meeting of ladies in Library Hall, at which the question of supplying sanitary appliances was discussed, and it was felt that the interest the women of the county were taking in the soldiers' welfare would be helpful to them in every way.

Battery C, National Guard of Pennsylvania, left Phœnixville for the front April 27, 1898. The roster of the battery at that time was as follows:

Captain, George L. Waters, Sr.; First Lieutenant, Francis M. Bean; Assistant Sr. First Lieutenant, Walter Boardman; Sec. Lieut., Q. M., Horace H. Walters; Sec. Lieut., William F. Fulmer; First Sergeant, John W. Shupe; Sergeants, Alexander Wilkinson, Jacob Bartzer, George Schenck, Charles Swier; Corporals, Charles T. Mayer, Lewis Williams, Irwin Yarnall, George F. Clare, John W. Shaffer, Benjamin T. Manley, Charles Newhall and William Swier, Jr.; Musicians, Joseph B. Bailey, Lentz L. Gold and James Lewis.

Private soldiers: Edward F. Allison, Charles A. Bailey, Jacob R. Baum, Mahlon E. Beard, Neal Briley, John J. Byerley, Edward J. Drazel, Charles Davis, George C. Davis, George W. Davis, Isaac J. Decker, William H. Geery, Lewis Dietrich, Sylvester Dawson, Carl. R. Eaby, Norwood G. Elvin, Hiram Fulton, Charles Goelz, Lewis Greer, Frank B. Gundy, Edward Griel, William H. Hallman, William H. Hayes, Joseph L. Hendricks, Joseph R. Jenkins. William M. Koehn, John Kennedy, Da Costa Lightcap, Edward Longaker, Edward T. March, Allen J. Mosteller, Isaac E. Pearson, Harry M. Pharoah, James Patton, John H. Reed, Samuel H. Smith, Daniel S. Smith, Evan G. Speakman, Joseph Sitler, Joseph Showalter, John Clarence Wier, Carl Witmeyer, J. Chester Storey, Frederick Swiss, George H. Swiss, William H. Swier, Sr.; Frederick G. Trunk, Addison M. Vanderslice, John S. Walker, Isaac A. Walters, John P. Williamson, Joseph Wall and Charles Wier.

On May 3, 1898, Captain Waters left Phœnixville, with the following recruits for his company: B. F. Longacre, John Ruckles, Clifford J. Nix, Irvin Everhart, Jesse Hunter, Pierce Pontius, William Davis, Walter Seissinger, John F. Tyson, William Hartman, William Evans, John McKeever, McClellan Curry, George

Beale, Michael McMahon, Irvin Kremer, James O'Donnell, G. W. Whiteside, William Diamond, August Isett, Stephen Donahue, W. E. Kline and George Sassaman.

Phœnixville claimed for itself the credit of raising more soldiers for the war with Spain, up to the time these recruits went out, than any other town of the State, in proportion to population, she having sent out nearly 200, her population being 9,000.

Brevet Major-General Galusha Pennypacker, United States Army, one of the most distinguished soldiers of the war of the Rebellion, was born in Chester County, June 1, 1844. Joseph J. Pennypacker, youngest son of Joseph Pennypacker, was his father, and during the early life of his son, Galusha, resided at Valley Forge. Serving on the staff of General Worth during the Mexican war, he afterward removed to California, and there died a few years ago. The mother of Galusha Pennypacker, a lady of wealth and many accomplishments, was Tamsou A. Workizer, only daughter of John and Sarah A. Workizer of Valley Forge. She died when her son, the only child, was in his infancy. The house at Valley Forge in which he was born was owned by his mother, was known as "Valley Forge Mansion," and was occupied by General Washington's soldiers as a hospital during the war of the Revolution.

Young Pennypacker received a liberal education in Chester County and in Philadelphia, and at the instance of his grandmother entered the office of the Chester County Times at West Chester, with the view of an editorial career, and was entrusted with a column of the paper devoted to matters of interest to youthful minds. But an appointment to a cadetship at the West Point Military Academy having been promised him by Hon. John Hickman, then member of Congress from the Sixth District, through his uncle, Uriah V. Pennypacker, Esq., he would in all probability have entered the academy in 1861 or 1862, but for the breaking out of the war of the Rebellion.

On April 22, 1861, he was mustered into the service of the

United States as quartermaster-sergeant of the Ninth Pennsylvania Volunteer Infantry (declining a first-lieutenancy on account of his youth), and acted as quartermaster of his regiment during the three months' service, serving with his regiment in Major-General Patterson's column in the Shenandoah Valley. When three years' troops were called out he entered the service as captain of Company A, Ninety-seventh Pennsylvania Volunteer infantry, August 22, 1861, and on October 7, following, was promoted to major of his regiment. This regiment joined the Tenth Corps in the Department of the South, and during the years 1862 and 1863 participated in all the movements and engagements in which that corps took part on the coasts of South Carolina, Georgia and Florida.

Major Pennypacker commanded the regiment and the post of Fernandina, Florida, in April, 1864, when that regiment was ordered with the Tenth Corps to Virginia, and became part of the Army of the James. On April 3, 1864, he was promoted to lieut. colonel, and on June 23 following, to colonel. He was in active command of his regiment at Swift Creek May 9; at Drury's Bluff, May 16, and at Chester station, May 18. On May 20 he led his regiment in an assault upon the enemy's lines at Green Plains, Bermuda Hundred, receiving three severe wounds himself and losing 175 men in killed and wounded out of 295 taken into the charge. Returning to duty in August, he was in action at Deep Bottom on the 16th of the month, and at Wierbottom Church on the 25th. In August and September in the trenches before Petersburg. Assigned to command the Second Brigade, Second Division of the Tenth Corps, on the 29th he led his brigade in the successful assault upon Fort Harrison. Here he was again wounded and had his horse shot under him. He was in action October 7, at Chaffin's Farm, and on the 29th at Darbytown Road. With the first Fort Fisher expedition under General Butler, December 1-31, 1864, General Pennypacker's brigade, composed of New York and Pennsylvania troops, formed a portion of the expeditionary corps under command of Major-General Terry, that made the successful and perhaps the most brilliant charge of the war upon Fort Fisher, North Carolina, January 15, 1865. For his distinguished personal gallantry in this assault, in which he was most severely wounded (it was thought for a time mortally), and "for gallant and meritorious services during the war," General Pennypacker received six brevets, or promotions, as follows: Brevet brigadier-general of United States volunteers, January 15, 1865; brigadier-general of United States volunteers, February 18, 1865; major-general of United States volunteers, March 13, 1865; colonel of the Thirty-Fourth (designation changed to the Sixteenth) Infantry, United States Army, July 28, 1866; brevet brigadier-general United States Army, March 2, 1867, and major-general United States Army, March 2, 1867, and besides these six appointments he received the Congressional medal of honor for "bravery at the Battle of Fort Fisher." He was the youngest general officer in the war and the youngest man in the history of the regular army to be commissioned a colonel and brevet major-general. His commanding general made the emphatic statement that General Pennypacker, and not himself, was the real hero of Fort Fisher, and that his great gallantry was equaled only by his modesty.

Since the war, with the exception of two years spent in Europe, General Pennypacker has served in the Southern and Western States, performing the duties pertaining to a regimental and post commander. He was temporarily in command of the District of the Mississippi in 1867; of the Fourth Military District in 1868; the Department of Mississippi in 1870; the United States troops in New Orleans in 1874, and the Department of the South in 1876. He was placed on the retired list of the regular army in 1883, "on account of wounds received in battle," from which he was then and is still suffering. Since his retirement he has lived in Philadelphia, in the enjoyment of the greatest respect from his fellow citizens. The record of his deeds is his sufficient eulogy.

CHAPTER IX.

SLAVERY.

CHAPTER IX.

SLAVERY existed, of course, in the colony and State of
Pennsylvania, as it did in the other colonies of the Crown and in
the other States after the independence of the United States
became established. But in Pennsylvania the enslavement of
Indians, while somewhat common in colonies further to the south,
was very rare. In the early part of the eighteenth century the custom of bringing Indian slaves from Carolina into Pennsylvania
appears to have been so extensive as to be noticeable, and as to
give the Indians of Pennsylvania considerable concern; and in
order to allay the uneasiness of the Indians of this province the
assembly passed the following law, which is somewhat peculiar as
a statute, and which appears to have been misapprehended by certain writers on local history, hence its introduction here:

"Whereas, the importation of Indian slaves from Carolina or
other places hath been observed to give the Indians of this province
some umbrage for suspicion and dissatisfaction,

"Be it enacted, etc., that from the 25th of March, 1707, no person shall import any Indian slaves or servants whatsoever from
any colony or province in America into this province, by land or
water, such only and their children (if any) excepted, as for the

327

space of one year before such importation shall be proved to have
been menial servants in the family of the importer and are brought
in together with the importer's family; every such slave or servant
so here landed shall be forfeited to the government, and shall be
either set at liberty or otherwise disposed of as the governor and
council shall see cause."

At that time laws passed by colonial assemblies had to receive
the approval of the Crown before going into effect, and this law
awaited the action of the Queen of England until 1709, when it
became a law simply because it did not receive the Queen's disap-
proval.   This delay did not serve in any manner to allay the fears
of the Indians, and it is altogether probable that they were ignorant
of its having become a law, even when such was the fact.   Then,
too, it will be observed that it did not absolutely prohibit the
enslavement of Indians within the province, or at least their being
held in slavery here.   And it may be that this fact caused the
apprehension of the Indians, which it is evident that they felt, a
fact proven by the following narrative of an event of much importance at the time of its occurrence:

From this event it is clear that the Indians feared that some
of their young people might be reduced to slavery, as will be seen.
William Dalbo of Gloucester County informed the Governor that a
belt of wampum had come from Mahquahotoni to Conestoga, that
there was a tomahawk in red in the belt, and that the French with
Five Nations of Indians were designed for war and planned to fall
on some of the plantations.   This information was laid by the
Governor before the Council on April 14, together with a letter
from Mr. Yeates, Caleb Pusey, and Thomas Powell, the letter stating that on the next day, April 15, there would be a great concourse
of Indians, those of Conestoga and those of New Jersey, and that in
their opinion it would be a seasonable opportunity for the Governor
to visit them, as the meeting would be the greatest that had been
held in twenty years.

It was the opinion of the board that the Governor with some of the Council should attend, with as many others as could be induced to go, and inquire further about the belt of wampum, and about whatever else might be thought necessary. But if the Governor attended this great meeting there seems to be no record of such visit. On the 29th of April more alarming news was brought to the Council as to the intentions of the Indians, and upon its receipt the Governor proceeded to Conestoga to meet the red men. They appeared to be inclined to the English, but complained of aggresssions committed upon them by the white man. Upon returning from Conestoga the Governor sent Colonel French and Henry Wesley to the Indians in order to ascertain more fully their desires, and on the 16th of June these two gentlemen returned with eight belts of wampum, each belt having a special significance. The import of three of these belts is here given, as bearing somewhat upon the question of slavery of the Indians, now under discussion.

The first of the three belts was from the old women, and signified that they implored the friendship of Christians and Indians, that without danger they might fetch wood and water.

The second belt was sent from their children, born and in the womb, requesting that room to sport and play be granted without danger of slavery.

The third belt was from their young men, fit to hunt, that the privilege to leave their towns and seek provisions for their aged might be granted to them without fear of death or slavery.

Without much research it would be difficult to state just how such Indians as were slaves in Chester County became slaves, and hence it will be stated only that seventy years after the occurrences above narrated, when the registration under the gradual emancipation act of 1780 was made, there were at least two Indian slaves in the county.

Slavery having been abolished in this country and having

become universally considered a crime against mankind, it is but natural that different classes of people should strive to fasten on others the original guilt of bringing the first slaves to America; but history seems to have clearly established the fact that in 1620 the Dutch brought a cargo of negroes from the coast of Guinea and sold a part of their cargo to the tobacco planters of Virginia at Jamestown. This was the beginning of slavery in British America. In 1790, when the first United States Census was taken, there were in Virginia 200,000 negroes.

It appears also that the Dutch and Swedes were the first to introduce slaves into Pennsylvania, bringing them in before the coming of William Penn. But in 1712 the Colonial Assembly of Pennsylvania passed an act to prevent the further importation of negroes into the province, which some time afterward was vetoed by the home government. Subsequently another act was passed with the same object in view, which was also repealed by the Crown. As a general thing the slaves brought into Pennsylvania came from the West Indies, after having undergone a process of seasoning, or gradual acclimation. The history of the movement for the abolition of slavery belongs more to general history than to this work; but it is eminently proper to give credit to the Friends or Quakers for their efforts, which were among the first made for establishment of freedom for all men in this country, and were preceded only by those of the Mennonites. It is only proper here to give the result of the continued agitation of the subject of abolition of slavery by Friends and other large-minded and just men, which came in 1780, in the form of a law for the gradual abolition of slavery within the limits of Pennsylvania. This law provided that all negroes and mulattos born within Pennsylvania after its passage, which was on March 1, that year, should not be deemed or considered slaves for life, and that all servitude for life should be entirely extinguished, taken away and abolished, except that children born within the State after the passage of the act, who would have been, in case the act had not been passed, slaves for life, should be slaves until they became twenty-eight years of age, and should be held in the same manner as were servants then held as bound out for a term of four years.

On the 1st of November, following the approval of the act, every owner of a slave was required by this law to register his slave or slaves in the office of the clerk of the peace of the county; that is, all that were slaves for life or for thirty-one years, according to laws as they then existed, and that all slaves who were not registered were to be free by the failure of the owner to register them on or before November 1. All children born of slaves were required to be registered before they were six months old, and they only were to be slaves until twenty-eight years of age. Subsequently a penalty was provided for forcibly or fraudulently carrying away any negro or mulatto out of the State with the design of selling him or her or to keep him a slave for a term of years.

Inasmuch as in recent years it has been frequently stated by eminent orators and writers that the motive leading to the abolition of slavery in the Eastern and Middle States was wholly selfish and mercenary, the climate and soil of those States not being adapted to that species of civilization; and inasmuch as many thousands of people have charged it upon the people of these States that they first sold off their slaves to the Southern States and then immediately favored the abolition of slavery in the Southern States, it is deemed eminently proper in this History of Chester County and Its People, inasmuch as the sentiment against the crime of slavery was to a great extent awakened and strengthened by the Friends of this county as well as of other portions of the Province and State after it became a State, to set forth in this connection the true motives that did actuate the people of the whole State in the giving of freedom to the enslaved. This can be done in no more forcible manner than in the quoting of the preamble to the act of March 1, 1780, which presents the reasons for the act itself, and bears the strongest possible internal evidence of the sincerity and honesty of those engaged in this most meritorious work. That preamble is as follows:

"When we contemplate our abhorrence of that condition to which the arms and tyranny of Great Britain were exerted to reduce us, when we look back on the variety of dangers to which we have been exposed and how miraculously our wants in many instances have been supplied and our deliverance wrought, when even hope and human fortitude have become unequal to the con- flict, we are unavoidably led to a serious and grateful sense of the manifest blessings which we have undeservedly received from the hand of that Being from whom cometh every good and perfect gift. Impressed with these ideas we conceive it to be our duty, and we rejoice that it is within our power to extend a portion of that freedom to others which hath been extended to us, and release from that state of thraldom to which we were ourselves diabol- ically doomed, and from which we have now every prospect of being delivered. It is not for us to inquire why in the creation of mankind the inhabitants of the several parts of the earth were distinguished by a difference of feature or complexion. It is suf- ficient for us to know that all are the work of an almighty hand. We find in the distribution of the human species that the most fertile as well as the most barren portions of the earth are inhab- ited by men of complexions different from ours and from each other; from whence we may reasonably as well as religiously infer that He who placed them in their various situations hath extended equally His care and protection to all, and that it becom- eth not us to counteract His purposes. We esteem it a peculiar blessing granted to us that we are enabled this day to add one more step to universal civilization, by removing as much as possible the sorrows of those who have lived in undeserved bondage and from which, by the assumed authority of the Kings of Great Britain, no effectual legal relief could be obtained. Weaned by a long course of experience from those narrow prejudices and partialities we had imbibed, we find our hearts enlarged with kindness and benevolence toward man of all conditions and nations; and we conceive ourselves at this particular period extraordinarily called upon by the blessings which we have received to manifest the sincerity of our profession and to give substantial proof of our gratitude."

It would appear impossible to read this statement of the reasons for the enactment of the law to which it is the preamble without being profoundly impressed with a lively sense of the sincerity of its authors. They did actually and in a most effectual manner manifest to the world the sincerity of their profession and give substantial proof of their gratitude, if such a thing were ever done in the history of the world. If they were not sincere it would seem impossible to believe any man or body of men ever to have been sincere or to be sincere at any time or place or under any conditions. The authors of this preamble were the legislators of and for the people of the State, and it is only fair to infer that the people were as much in favor of granting freedom to the slave as were their representatives in the Assembly. Then, too, all of the slaves living at the time of the passage of the act were, according to its provisions, to remain slaves for life, hence no motive of gain could actuate their owners to sell them to prevent loss. Those who were born slaves after the passage of the act were to so remain until twenty-eight years of age, and a penalty was provided by law for anyone taking out of the State any slave to sell him or to hold him in slavery for life. If there were individuals that did this, and it is probably true that there were, such an act cannot be made to reflect upon the body of the people who had specially provided for its punishment; and hence it would seem certain that the verdict of history must always be to the effect that at least in Pennsylvania the emancipation of the slaves was wholly commendable and just and wise, not only in the matter itself but also in the manner.

As has been stated above, every owner of a slave in Pennsylvania was required by the act of March 1, 1780, to register his slaves on or before November 1, that year, and in case he failed to so register any slave, that slave was by such failure made free. In a book provided for such registry in the office of the court of Quarter Sessions of Chester County, the name, age, sex and time of service of every slave was recorded. This book of record, however, appears to have been destroyed within recent years, as it cannot now be found. What is here presented in regard to this registry is therefore taken mainly from the excellent History of Chester County by Judge J. Smith Futhey and Mr. Gilbert Cope, who practically exhausted the subject. The entries in this registry were in the following form:

"Thomas Potts of Coventry Township returns:

"1. A negro man named Cudge, aged fifty-eight years, a slave for life.

"2. A negro man named Ben, aged twenty-four years, a slave for life.

"3. A negro boy named Peter, aged seventeen years, a slave for life.

"4. A negro child named George, aged nine months, a slave for life.

"5. A negro woman named Moll, aged thirty-four years, a slave for life.

"6. A negro woman named Sall, aged nineteen years, a slave for life."

"Evans Evans of London, Britain Township, returns:

"1. A negro woman named Rachel, aged thirty-eight years, a slave for life.

"2. A mulatto boy named Cæsar, aged sixteen years, a slave for life.

"3. A negro girl named Sue, aged thirteen years, a slave for life.

"4. A negro boy named Samp, aged nine years, a slave for life.

"5. A negro boy named Frank, aged seven years, a slave for life.

"6. A mulatto female child named Sal, aged four years, a slave for life."

"Abel Hodgson of East Nottingham returns:

"1. An Indian servant man, till he attains the age of thirty-one years, named Jam, aged twenty-eight years.

"2. An Indian girl named Sarah, aged twenty-four years, a slave for life.

"3. A negro man named Cæsar, aged twenty-five years, a slave for life."

"Samuel Futhey of West Fallowfield Township returns:

"1. A mulatto woman named Jince, aged twenty years, a slave for life.

"2. A mulatto girl named Dinah, aged one year and nine months, a slave for life.

"3. A mulatto girl named Sall, a slave until she attains the age of thirty-one years."

At the time of this registration Delaware County was still a part of Chester County. In Chester County there were 205 slave-holders who made returns, and of these 140 resided in what is now Chester County. According to Dr. Smith, author of the "History of Delaware County," there were in the several townships which afterward were set off into Delaware County the following numbers of slaves registered on or before November 1, 1780:

TOWNSHIP.	SLAVES FOR LIFE.	SLAVES FOR A TERM OF YEARS.
Aston	13	1
Bethel	0	0
Birmingham....	0	0
Chester	16	1
Chichester (Upper).....	0	0

20

Chichester (Lower)............	12	1
Concord	7	0
Darby (Upper)..	2	0
Darby	2	0
Edgmont	5	0
Haverford	24	2
Marple	2	0
Middletown	7	1
Newtown	1	0
Providence (Upper)	0	0
Providence (Lower)...	0	0
Ridley	34	3
Radnor	0	0
Springfield	10	5
Thornbury	3	0
Tinicum	8	2
	146	16

Dr. Smith says that, judging from such records as were accessible to him, there were in what is now Delaware County not less than 300 slaves at the breaking out of the Revolutionary War. The Friends had, between the beginning of the war and the time of the gradual emancipation act, liberated a large number of slaves, but the number so liberated cannot be accurately stated.

According to Judge Futhey and Mr. Cope there were in the entire county of Chester, as then constituted, 495 slaves; hence in what is now Chester County there were 333; but as Futhey and Cope state that there were 335, someone has made a mistake of two slaves. Of the total number of 495, 472 were slaves for life, and 23 until they arrived at the age of thirty-one years. The negroes numbered 410, mulattos 83, and Indians 2. Of the 472 held for life the males numbered 243 and the females 229; and of those held for a term of years the males numbered 13 and the females 10. Of the whole number there were 207 over eighteen years of age, and 228 under eighteen. William Moore of Charles-town (now Schuylkill) Township, owned the oldest male slave, George, who was seventy-five years of age; and John Evans of London, Britain Township, owned Nanny, the oldest female slave, her age being seventy-eight. John Bowen of Goshen Township owned Tom, one month old, the youngest registered slave. There were nine slaves under one year of age and thirteen upward of sixty. William Moore was the largest slaveholder in the county, owning ten. Only eleven of the slaves registered had surnames, the rest being registered only by one name.

A registry of those born after the passage of the act was also made, the number being 85, of whom 47 were males and 38 females. The last return made was by Rev. Levi Bull, of East Nantmeal, afterward Warwick, who returned his negro boy, Andrew, born December 23, 1820.

It is not known when slavery ceased to exist in Chester County, but as there was one slave registered November 1, 1780, that was only one month old, that slave might have lived to 75 or 80 years old, or even older; and as the same thing probably occurred in other counties of the State, there may have been a few slaves in the State and even in Chester County, down to the breaking out of the Rebellion, but there probably were none after about 1840. The number of slaves in Pennsylvania was estimated at 10,000 in the year 1776; and according to the United States census for the different years was in 1790, 3,737; 1800, 1,706; 1810, 795; 1820, 211; 1840, 64.

Following is a list of the townships in what is now Chester County with the number of slaves in each:

Birmingham, 0; East Bradford, 0; West Bradford, 0; Coventry, 9; Charlestown, 24; East Caln, 4; West Caln, 5; Easttown, 1; East Fallowfield, 7; West Fallowfield, 12; Goshen, 13; New Garden, 1; Kennett, 3; New London, 30; London Britain, 19; Londonderry, 20; Londongrove, 4; West Marlborough, 2; East Marlborough, 0;

Newlin, 0; East Nantmeal, 14; West Nantmeal, 19; East Nottingham, 26; West Nottingham, 6; Oxford, 28; Pennsbury, 0; Pikeland,
9; Sadsbury, 13; Tredyffrin, 23; Thornbury, 2; Uwchlan, 7; Vincent,
0; East Whiteland, 8; West Whiteland, 11; Westtown, 1; Willistown, 1.

Besides these there were 13 other slaves registered, the resi-
deuces of whose owners were not given. From the above list it
appears that the townships settled principally by the Welsh, as
Charlestown, East and West Nantmeal and Tredyffrin, and those
largely settled by Scotch-Irish, New London, Londonderry, Oxford
and East Nottingham, had the largest numbers of slaves; while
the townships largely inhabited by Friends, the more central
townships, had the smallest numbers of them.

Of the children of slaves for life registered as servants until
they should become twenty-eight years of age, the returns from the
several townships were as follows: Charlestown, 2; Coventry, 1;
East Fallowfield, 1; West Fallowfield, 4; Goshen, 1; East Caln, 1;
West Caln, 5; New London, 9; West Marlborough, 1; Londonderry,
2; Oxford, 23; East Nantmeal, 4; West Nantmeal, 14; London
Britain, 1; East Notingham, 6; Londongrove, 2; Sadsbury, 2; Tredyffrin, 3; East Whiteland, 2; total, 83.

The Pennsylvania Society for Promoting the Abolition of
Slavery, the Relief of Free Negroes Unlawfully Held in Bondage,
and for Improving the Condition of the African Race, was organized April 14, 1775, was reorganized in 1784, and incorporated by
an act of the Assembly December 8, 1789, with nearly three hundred members. The American Colonization Society was organized
about 1816, and the Pennsylvania Colonization Society in 1826.
County societies, auxiliary to the State society, were formed to the
number of nine within a year, one of which was in Chester County.
In December, 1827, Simeon Siegfried of West Chester published an
eight-page pamphlet containing the constitution and address of the
managers of the Chester County Auxiliary Colonization Society, the
officers being at that time as follows:

President, William Darlington; vice-presidents, Jesse Kersey and Rev. Robert Graham; secretary, Thomas Williamson; treasurer, David Townsend; managers, William H. Dillingham, Townsend Haines, Thomas S. Bell, Jonathan Jones, Gen. John W. Cuningham, Rev. William Hodgson, Dr. Samuel McClean, George Hartman, Jr., Rev. Ebenezer Dickey, Rev. Simeon Siegfried, William Everhart and Jonathan Gause.

In colonial days there were other servants besides slaves, who were known by the names of servants and redemptioners. The master owned the time of the servant for a definite period. In the early settlement of the country, servants were in great demand, and to supply this demand people of more or less wealth who were emigrating to the new country from Europe would bring over with them cargoes of laboring people, such as could not pay their own passage over the sea, and were willing to be bound out for a term of years in order to repay the expense of their transportation and support while on the way over, and dispose of them upon arriving in this province. The indentures were prepared usually in the country whence the emigration took place, binding the servant to serve for a number of years, rarely less than four, after his arrival in Pennsylvania, in consideration of his passage, clothing and provisions. Even mechanics sold their services for a certain length of time. Orphan children were also bound out by the court as servants, the process by which this was accomplished being called "judging" them or "adjudging." At the October court, 1693, Maurice Trent brought into the country eight boys who were called up to be judged, they being according to the opinion of Dr. Smith, negroes. The boys were adjudged to serve their respective masters until they were twenty-one years of age. In 1695 Maurice Trent brought in another set of boys to be judged, their periods of servitude being fixed by the court. In 1697 there were as many as thirty-three orphans who were indentured as servants for different lengths of time. Following are a few samples of entries on the records in connection with cases of this kind:

"Francis Chadsey brought a boy whose name was Alexander Stewart, who was adjudged to serve eight years from the 14th of September last past, to be taught to read and write, or else to serve but seven years; also he had a servant maid whose name is Ann Bearn, who was adjudged to serve five years from this court, to said Francis Chadsey or his assigns."

"William Cope brought a boy whose name is Thomas Harper, who was adjudged to serve five years and three-quarters, if he be taught to read and write, or else to serve but five years to him or his assigns."

"Elizabeth Withers brought a servant girl whose name is Margaret Mongey, who was adjudged to be eleven years of age and to serve ten years to Thomas Withers or his assigns."

"Elinor Clayton, an orphan of the age of fourteen years, was ordered by the court to serve Daniel Hoopes for the term of seven years, on condition that he should teach her to read, knit and sew, and pay £12 according to the order of the court."

In the early part of the eighteenth century captains of vessels brought over persons, selling their time in this country to pay for their passage. These were called redemptioners, and such cases occurred even down into the nineteenth century. Those who imported servants were accustomed to take them in companies through the country and dispose of them to farmers, in some of which cases the masters were outwitted by the servants they were attempting to sell. An anecdote is told of a certain master who had disposed of all but one of his drove, and this one getting up first in the morning sold his master to the landlord of the tavern where the two had remained over night, giving the master an excellent character, except in one respect, that he was in the habit of lying, and that when he should arise he would be apt to try to pass himself off as the master.

Following is the form of an indenture of apprenticeship, in which there is nothing peculiar except the compensation in live stock:

"This Indenture Witnesseth that Elizabeth Hastings, Daughter of Henry Hastings of West Bradford in the County of Chester and Province of Pennsilvania, Yeoman, hath put herself, and by these presents doth voluntarily put herself and of her own free will and accord and with the Consent of her Parents put herself Apprentice to Phebe Buffington of West Bradford afforesaid and after the manner of an apprentice to serve her from the day of the date hereof for and During the Term of Five Years Eight Months next ensuing the date hereof. During all which term the said apprentice her said Mistress faithfully shall serve, her secrets keep, her Lawful Commands everywhere gladly obey. She shall do no damage to her said mistress' goods nor lend them unlawfully to any. She shall do no damage to her said Mistress nor see it to be done by others without letting or giving notice thereof to her said Mistress. She shall not commit fornication nor contract matrimony within the said term. At Cards, Dice, or any other unlawful Game she shall not play whereby her Mistress may have damage. With her own goods nor with the goods of others, without License from her said Mistress she shall neither buy nor sell. She shall not absent herself Day nor Night from her Mistress' service without her leave, nor haunt Ale-Houses, Taverns or Play Houses, but in all things behave herself as a faithful apprentice ought to do, During the said Term. And in Consideration of the said Term the said Mistress shall procure and provide for her said apprentice Sufficient meat, Drink, Apparel, Lodging and Washing fitting for an apprentice both in health and sickness during the said Term, Together with Two Cows and two calves, Each Cow and calf to be worth Four pounds of Current money of Pennsilvania in the following manner—One Cow and Calf to be delivered unto the above named Henry Hastings for the use of said apprentice in the year 1746 and the other Cow and Calf in the spring of the year of our Lord 1748. And the said mistress shall learn her said apprentice to Sew and Knitt so as to know how to make a man's Shirt and Knitt Stocking and to give her one month's schooling in Reading and Writing within the said Term, and at the expiration of said Term said Mistress shall procure for her said apprentice One full Suit of new Apparel besides her working apparel. And for the true performance of all and every the said Covenants and agreements either of said parties bind themselves unto the other by these presents. In Witness whereof they have interchangeably put their hands and seals this ninth day of April, One Thousand Seven Hundred and forty and three. 1743.

"PHEBE BUFFINGTON. (Seal)

"Signed seald and Delivered in the presence of John Buffington, Amy Bate, John McCarty."

While it is true that many of the people of the United States at the time of the adoption of the Constitution in 1789 were opposed to the continuance of slavery, and that though thus opposed to it they yielded their opposition to it in order that the Constitution might be adopted, hoping that with the prohibition of the slave trade after 1808 the sentiment would steadily increase among the people and become so strong that the institution could not exist in its presence, yet they did not for years take any active measures to secure its abolition. But in 1804 cases of kidnapping of free negroes occurred at Columbia, Pennsylvania, which fully aroused this latent anti-slavery feeling among the people in that vicinity, who were mostly Friends, and incited them to do what they could to protect slaves who were attempting by flight to secure the liberty to which nature and nature's God entitled them. One of the most active in this movement was William Wright of Columbia, who assisted all who came to him, and did all in his power both inside and outside of court to aid the fleeing negro to escape. These escaping negroes invariably desired to reach Canada, where there was no fugitive slave law in force, and hence all along the road or route to the British dominion there were agencies established wherever such agencies could be made of service to the cause.

The principal route through this part of the country lay through the counties of York, Lancaster, Chester, Montgomery, Berks and Bucks, to Phœnixville, Norristown, Quakertown, Reading, Philadelphia, and other cities and towns. The principal agents in Lancaster County were Daniel Gibbons, Thomas Whitson, Lindley Coates, Dr. Eshleman, James Moore, Caleb C. Hood and Jeremiah Moore. Those who were most active on this line in Chester County were James Fulton, Gideon Peirce, Thomas Bonsall, Thomas Vickers, John Vickers, Esther Lewis and daughters, Dr. Edwin Fussell, William Fussell, Norris Maris, Emmor Kimber, Elijah F. Pennypacker and Lewis Peart. In Norristown those most active in secreting and forwarding the fugitive were Rev. Samuel Aaron, Isaac Roberts, John Roberts, Dr. William Corson, Dr. Jacob L. Paxon and Daniel Ross (colored), and there were also others. The gentlemen as above mentioned as being active in Lancaster and Chester Counties and in Norristown, were the agents along the northern route through Chester County; but later in the history of this movement the more traveled routes lay through the central and southern parts of the county. It was on these routes that many lively incidents occurred, as they lay, particularly the more southern one, along the boundary of the slave States of Maryland and Delaware. So great was the travel along the southern route that it became necessary to have several branches, and these branch routes interlaced the more northern lines in several places, this being especially the case at the Peirces and Fultons in Ercildoun; Esther Lewis' in Vincent; John Vickers' near Lionville, and Elijah F. Pennypacker's near Phœnixville. From Pennypacker's place many negroes were sent over into Montgomery County— many of them to Norristown. There was a route from Havre de Grace through Penn Township to Ercildoun, by way of Eli, Thomas and Charles Hambleton's, and thence to John Vickers' place, and that of Esther Lewis'.

Generally speaking the negroes were guided when traveling at night (and this was absolutely necessary in many cases in order to elude their pursuers) by the Polar Star, which they knew lay in the direction of liberty, and following this guiding star many of them on the main route from Wilmington passed through the townships of Kennett, East Marlborough, Pocopson, Newlin, and so on to the north. In Kennett they found assistants in the persons of Allen and Maria Agnew, Isaac and Dinah Mendenhall, and Dr. Bartholomew Fussell in Kennett; John and Hannah Cox, Simon and Sarah D. Barnard in East Marlborough; William and Mary Barnhard, Eusebeus and Sarah Marsh Barnhard, in Pocopson; Isaac and Thamsine Meredith, Mordecia and Esther Hayes, in Newlin; James Fulton, Jr., and Gideon Peirce, in Ercildoun; Zebulon Thomas and daughters, in Downingtown; Micajah and William Speakman, in Uwchlan; John Vickers and Charles Moore, in Lionville; Esther Lewis and her daughters, Marian, Elizabeth and Graceanna, William Fussell, Dr. Edwin Fussell and Norris Maris, in West Vincent; Emmor Kimber, at Kimberton, and Elijah F. Pennypacker, at Phœnixville.

There was still another branch which passed through Kennett Township, the station here being at Chandler Darlington's; East Bradford, the agent being Benjamin Price; to West Chester, where the agents were the Darlington sisters and Abram D. Shadd (colored). At West Chester there were two forks to this branch, one leading to John Vickers', on the middle route, and the other to Nathan Evans' place in Willistown, who was a sterling old Friend, and stood almost alone in the work in his neighborhood. Davis Garrett, of the same township, however, frequently aided Mr. Evans. James Lewis of Marple Township, Delaware County, was also an efficient worker on this line, and James T. Dannaker, who lived with Mr. Lewis, was made a conductor on the line.

The great central station at which the Chester County and other southern routes converged was at the anti-slavery headquarters in Philadelphia, which was in charge of J. Miller McKim, assisted by several persons, among whom was William Still, a former slave. In the early part of this combined movement to aid the slave to escape it was very difficult for the master and others in pursuit of the fugitives to trace them beyond Columbia. When the pursuers arrived there all trace of the fleeing slaves was as completely lost as if they had dropped down into the earth, and those in pursuit were accustomed to say, "There must be an underground railroad somewhere," and it was this saying that gave name to the route by which the slaves made their escape. This "Underground Railroad" had many branches in all parts of the Free States, even as far West as Kansas and Iowa, during the later years of the existence of the "peculiar institution."

West Chester was really one of the main stations on one of these routes, and one of those who distinguished himself in the service of the fugitives in this city was George Maris, who, as a lad, drew many a map of the road from there to Elijah F. Pennypacker's place, Mr. Pennypacker having a two-horse wagon in which he used to carry the slaves onward to friends in Montgomery County, or to Daniel Ross's at Norristown. At one time there was an exciting chase of a slave woman in West Chester, she having lived there for some years in a little home on West Miner street. Her master offered a large reward for her apprehension, which tempted one of the citizens of that place to divulge her whereabouts, and when the master, with a constable, had arrested her and carried her into court, before Judge Thomas S. Bell, whose office was at the southeast corner of South Church and Miner Streets, she, by a ruse, got outside the office into the back yard, ran and jumped over a fence, which is said to have been seven feet high, and then running through alleys and streets, finally successfully hid herself, and could not be found by anyone searching for her, though she remained in the town for some days. She at length made her escape in safety and got away to Canada. There were

many incidents of escape from the clutches of the master and the
law which would make interesting reading, which would be inserted in this work but for the fact that there is so much recent
history that has not yet been put in book form, to which the publishers feel in duty bound to give attention; hence only one instance
of this kind will be here inserted, merely to show that lawyers were
then to be found who were as keen in their lookout for technicalities.
as any of the present day, and who would labor like many good
physicians and other good Samaritans, without the hope of pecuniary reward.

About 1838 Robert Purvis, a resident of Philadelphia, and well
remembered even now to many citizens of Chester County, had in
his employ a colored man named Basil Dorsey, who was an escaped
slave, and who was betrayed to his former owner by a brother-in-
law of his wife. This former master, together with a noted slave-
catcher, found Dorsey plowing in a field on Mr. Purvis' farm. They
caught him, handcuffed him and took him to Bristol, where they
had him locked up in the prison cell. Mr. Purvis immediately
followed them and next morning, before the case was brought
before Judge Fox at Doylestown, had enlisted the sympathies of
the entire crowd. Thomas Ross was employed as counsel, and in
order to put up the best possible defense when the case should
come to trial, succeeded in having it postponed a couple of weeks.
Dorsey remained in jail, and the colored population made preparations to rescue him by force in case Mr. Purvis should lose. Mr.
Purvis secured as counsel for the defense David Paul Brown, then
the most noted criminal lawyer in Philadelphia, who would not
accept any fee. The counsel for the claimant, named Griffith,
made a clear statement of the claim, presenting the bill of sale and
other evidence of ownership, and also laws that seemed to seal the
fate of Dorsey. Then Mr. Brown arose, and after admitting the
force of the arguments presented by Mr. Griffith, went on to say:

"But there is one fatal defect in the indictment, and upon that

I take my stand: This is a land of law, this is a court of law, and nothing can be decided in this court without strict sanction of law. You have not shown by proper evidence that under the laws of Maryland a man may be held as a slave, and not showing this, his case goes by default."

Mr. Griffith then demanded a postponement of the case until the necessary proof could be procured, which could, of course, easily have been done; but Brown was unrelenting, as might have been expected he would be, as he had won his case as it then stood, and he demanded the dismissal of the case for want of proper proof. Judge Fox thereupon arose and said, "The case is dismissed." Basil Dorsey went therefore free.

In closing this part of the present chapter it remains only to be said that West Chester was well known far and wide as being friendly to the slave, willing to aid him in securing what was most dear in life, freedom to follow his own inclinations and interests; and it is largely for this reason that so many colored people have made and now make this city their home. They now constitute about one-fourth part of the population, have a ward of the city practically all to themselves, and have had representatives in the Council. They are as well treated here in the way of education as it is possible for them to be in the present condition of civilization, and are working out their own destiny to the best of their ability.

CHAPTER X.

EDUCATION.

CHAPTER X.

THE history of education in Chester County is more or less
directly or indirectly connected with the earliest movements to
educate the young in the Province of Pennsylvania. Hence it may
not be inappropriate to briefly refer to the conditions and ideas
from which the educational systems and institutions since then
established in the present county have sprung.

When the first Swedish colony was planted on the Delaware
River there was no regular, independent educational system in
their native land, that educational system being in the hands of
the church, as agent for the State, and in the hands of heads of
families. The Church, in 1693, forbade the marriage of anyone who
was without a knowledge of Luther's catechism; which shows the
strength of the position of the Church in educational matters.

From Holland, which country is said to have been, in the
later part of the Sixteenth century, the first in Europe to establish
public schools, came a considerable portion of the earlier settlers
of the country on the Delaware; and a still larger portion of the

early settlers of New York were from that country. And it is doubtless true that the Pilgrim Fathers, during their twelve years' residence in Holland, became familiar with the fundamental principles which have made New England famous in the educational and intellectual history of the United States. It was also in Holland that William Penn acquired those broad and liberal ideas in regard to the education of the young which have made Pennsylvania no less famous in educational matters, and far more famous for religious liberty than even New England.

Among the inducements offered emigrants from Sweden to the New World was the promise that "in the same way schools and churches will flourish through it and be sustained, and furthermore those who have learned something will be promoted to dignities and positions."

In planting the Dutch colonies in America the same promise was made. "The patrons of New Netherlands shall also exert themselves to find speedy means to maintain a clergyman and schoolmaster, in order that Divine Service and zeal for religion may be planted in that country, and shall send, at first, a Comforter for the sick thither." This was about 1630.

On July 12, 1656, the city of Amsterdam offered the following conditions to persons settling in its colony at New Castle on the Delaware:

"Said city shall cause to be erected about the market, or in a more convenient place, a public building suitable for Divine Service; item, also a house for a school which can likewise be occupied by a person who will hereafter be sexton, psalmsetter and schoolmaster; the city shall besides have a house built for a minister.

"The city shall provisionally provide and pay the salaries of the minister and schoolmaster."

The same year in which these conditions were prescribed Evert Pietersen, a man of some learning, was sent out to act as schoolmaster, and zieken-trooster, to read the Bible, and to lead the singing until the arrival of a clergyman.

Thus was Evert Pietersen the first school-teacher, or school-master, as such professionals were then called, to take charge of a school in what afterward became for a time a part of the province of William Penn. However, he was not the first European school-master in the colonies, or in North America, having been preceded by several teachers among the Dutch at Manhattan, the first of these being Adam Roelansen, who taught the school of the Dutch Church in 1633, the first school established in what is now the United States, and which is still in existence. But as this chapter does not pretend to be a history of education in the United States, or even in Pennsylvania, it appears appropriate to mention only one more fact in this connection, which item in reality covers in part at least the territory to which it will be necessary to confine this sketch; and that is that along the Delaware River there was not for many years a high school or academy, and it was customary for those who could afford to do so, for some years, to send their children from the Delaware River section, and even from Virginia, to an academy established in 1659 at New Amsterdam, of which, in 1662, Dominie Aegilius Luyck was Latin master.

According to Wickersham, from whose History of Education in Pennsylvania the above facts have been extracted (without pain), there was no schoolhouse on the Delaware up to 1682, nor had there been any regular schoolmaster except Pietersen; and though the colonists were much in favor of the education of their children, yet it was very difficult for them to obtain for those children the proper instruction. On account of the scattered location of the families which rendered it impracticable to sustain schools, as is now done throughout the country districts, it was the custom of the ministers and missionaries, who had the education of the young in charge, to visit individual families scattered about in the settlements, and thus, in conjunction with the parents, to teach the young as best they could; but the difficulties they encountered may be imagined when it is stated, as it rests on good authority,

that in 1697 there were but three books in the entire Swedish colony on the Delaware, and these three books had been passed around
from one family to another in order that all might learn to read.

The above remarks bring this narrative down to the first mention of education within the limits of the present State of Pennsylvania, and the first attempt at education within what was once
Chester County. This is a copy of a record of the court at Upland,
and is the case of Edmund Draufton vs. Dunck Williams:

"March 12, 167 .

"The Pl^t demands of this Deft 200 Gilders for teaching this
Deft children to read one yeare."

"The Co^{rt} haveing heard the debates of both parties as alsoe ye
attestation of ye witnesses, Doe grant Judgment agst ye deft for
200 gilders wth ye costs."

"Richard Ducket sworne in Court declares that hee was p'sent
at ye making of ye bargaine, and did hear that ye agreem^t was
that Edmund draufton should Teach Dunkes Children to Read ye
bybell, & if he could doe itt in a yeare or a half yeare or a quart^r
then he should have 200 gilders."

While the location of this primitive school is not certainly
known, yet there is some evidence to prove that it was at Passayunk. It is not at all likely that Draufton taught a school, the
evidence showing that he taught the children of Williams how to
read "ye bybell," in doing which he probably earned the 200 gilders
thus given him by the court.

It is altogether correct to say that to the doctrines of the
Friends, which will be found treated of briefly under the head of
religious history in this work, much that is noble and ennobling
in education, as well as in religion and jurisprudence, is to be traced.
The Friends fully believed in education, and only feared that
abuse of learning which is sometimes visible in the magnification
of self. They were all fairly well educated, and they had among
them some very learned men, such as William Penn, Robert Bar-

clay, Thomas Loe, Thomas Ellwood, Isaac Pennington and others. And as the Friends were the pioneers in education in the province and also in the county of Chester, it is only appropriate that their proceedings, ideas and institutions should first be dealt with in this work. The first assembly called together by William Penn after his arrival in this country passed what is known in history as the "Great Law," of seventy-one chapters. Chapter LX contains a provision of great significance, as follows:

"That the laws of this Province, from time to time, shall be published and printed, that every person may have the knowledge thereof; and they shall be one of the books taught in the schools of this Province and territories thereof."

The Second Assembly, which met at Philadelphia, March 10, 1683, passed numerous laws, of which the following is the most interesting in this connection:

"And to the end that poor as well as rich may be instructed in good and commendable learning, which is to be preferred before wealth, Be it enacted, etc., That all persons in this province and territories thereof having children, and all the guardians and trustees of orphans, shall cause such to be instructed in reading and writing, so that they may be able to read the Scriptures and to write by the time they attain to twelve years of age; and that then they be taught some useful trade or skill, that the poor may work to live and the rich if they become poor may not want, of which every County Court shall take care. And in case such parents, guardians or overseers shall be found deficient in this respect, every such parent, guardian or overseer shall pay for each such child five pounds, except there should appear an incapacity in body or understanding to hinder it."

Extended comment on this remarkable law is left to the reader. But it may be stated here that it was at once the most comprehensive and strong compulsory educational law ever enacted by any legislative body in America. After it had remained in force ten years it was abrogated by King and Queen William and Mary; but it was re-enacted by Governor Fletcher, "by and with the advice and consent of the representatives," and though never formally repealed so far as anyone knows, yet it was permitted to become a dead letter, not being revived by subsequent forms of government.

As a few of the first teachers in the country have been mentioned, it would be scarcely just to pass over Thomas Makin, the first teacher required to procure a certificate to teach in the Province. Thomas Makin was usher under George Keith, who, for one year, had charge of the Friends' Public School in Philadelphia, and was then succeeded by Makin, who remained in charge of it several years. On August 1, 1693, Mr. Makin was called before the Lieutenant-Governor and Council and told that he must not keep school without a license, and that he must procure a certificate of his ability, learning and diligence from the inhabitants of note in the town (of Philadelphia) by the 16th inst. in order to obtain a license, which he promised to do. Makin lived to be a very old man, wrote a Latin poem descriptive of Pennsylvania in 1729, and on or about November 28, 1733, fell off a wharf in Philadelphia into the Delaware River and was drowned.

Up to the beginning of the Eighteenth century the Friends, throughout the State, continued to work faithfully and well to increase the general intelligence of the people by means of the education of the young; but from that time on to the Revolutionary War little was accomplished by the State in this direction, the work falling back into private hands and into the hands of the several churches. It seems to have been too early in the development of the human race for the universal education of the youth throughout the Province by public authority. The difficulty may have been caused by the fact that the Province of Pennsylvania was noted the world over as being the asylum of those who were persecuted at home for their religious opinions, and that on this account it attracted to its bosom such large numbers of divers opinions that it was difficult for those entertaining these different opinions to work harmoniously together even for the promotion of their best interests. But order must at length come out of chaos, and though there were but few schools established from 1700 to 1776, yet there were a few. In December, 1754, or early in 1755, there was a school established in Vincent Township, Chester County, with John Louis Ache as teacher; Mr. Ache, however, being retired to first qualify himself better in the use of the English language by an attendance, at the expense of the Proprietaries, at the Academy in Philadelphia.

Among the Friends the yearly meeting gave much earnest and practicable advice concerning the establishment of schools, suggesting that in the compass of each monthly meeting there should be ground provided upon which to erect a suitable house and stable, and room for a garden, orchard and pasture, as an encouragement to, and making provision for, a teacher of proper qualifications and good character. The yearly meeting also recommended that funds should be collected for the establishment and support of schools.

In writing the biography of an individual it is often necessary to a correct understanding of the career of that individual to trace, at least briefly, the antecedent members of the family. So in writing of Fagg's Manor Classical School it is at least useful to mention its ancestor in the line of events, the famous "Log College." This college was established by the Rev. William Tennent, in Bucks County, Pennsylvania, in the forks of the Neshaminy, or near there, in 1726; but the land on which stood the building hereafter described, and to which the above name was given, was purchased by Mr. Tennent September 11, 1735, of Mr. John White, of Philadelphia, for £140, the school having been kept at some other location, doubtless near this place, up to that time. Rev. George Whitefield, while on a visit to this country in 1739, was with Mr. Tennent at this log school-house November 22, 1739, and upon his arrival at the academy, where he was expected to preach, "found about three thousand people gathered together in the meeting-house yard." Mr. Whitefield in his journal says: "The place wherein the young men study is, in contempt, called a College."

The purpose of Mr. Tennent in the establishment of his academy was to prepare young men for the ministry of the Presbyterian Church, education then being the handmaid of religion almost exclusively. The log building in which he taught was about twenty feet square, or nearly square, and in this small building were educated many young men who afterward became distinguished in the ministry.

Rev. Mr. Tennent had four sons—Gilbert, William, John and Charles—all of whom, like their father, were born in Ireland, and all of whom became distinguished ministers of the Gospel, and it is the latter's meeting-house that is mentioned in what is said in previous pages about the survey of the north and south line from the Philadelphia parallel down to the southern parallel of Pennsylvania. Rev. Charles Tennent was installed at White Clay Creek Chapel, or meeting-house, in Delaware, in 1737, and remained there as minister until 1762.

Among the distinguished graduates, or perhaps it would be better to say alumni, of "Log College" was the Rev. Samuel Blair, who was born in Ireland June 14, 1712, came early to this country, and was a pupil of Mr. Tennent probably from 1730 to 1735. It was he that established, in 1739, in New Londonderry, or on Fagg's Manor, as it was often called, a school similar to that at the forks of the Neshaminy, his alma mater, for the education of young men for the ministry; and it was in this school thus established by Mr. Blair that many who afterward became distinguished as scholars and divines received their early educational discipline. This school was called Fagg's Manor Classical School, and was the first

classical institution within the limits of Chester County, as those
limits run to-day. Rev. Mr. Blair was considered by his biog-
rapher, Dr. Miller, not only one of the most able and learned, but
also one of the most pious and excellent men that ever adorned
the American church. This school at Fagg's Manor was of a high
order, the pupils being trained in it to a great familiarity with the
ancient languages and the doctrines of the Christian faith. While
they had fewer books than have students of the present day, yet
they mastered those they had, carrying out in their study the
motto, Multum, non multa.

Rev. Samuel Davies, educated at Mr. Blair's school, was licensed
to preach in 1745, and was chosen by the Synod of New York to
accompany the Rev. Gilbert Tennent to England and Ireland for
the purpose of soliciting funds for the College of New Jersey, now
Princeton, of which institution he was elected president to succeed Rev. Jonathan Edwards soon after the latter's death, which
occurred in 1759. Rev. Mr. Davies died in 1761, when nearly
thirty-seven years of age.

Rev. Samuel Blair remained at the head of Fagg's Manor
School until 1751, when he died, being then a little more than
thirty-nine years of age. Soon afterward he was succeeded by
his brother, Rev. John Blair, who took charge of both school and
church at that place, and at the school prepared many young men
for the ministry by instructing them in the languages, philosophy
and theology. After remaining at the head of this school about
nine years he was called to a professorship of divinity in the College of New Jersey, and was elected to the vice-presidency of the
institution, in which position he performed the duties of president
after the death of Doctor Finley and until the arrival of Doctor
Witherspoon, who was elected president.

Among the distinguished men who acquired their education
at Fagg's Manor Classical School were Rev. Alexander Cummings,
Rev. John Rodgers, D. D.; Rev. James Finley, Rev. Hugh Henry,

Rev. Robert Smith, D. D., a noted teacher; Rev. John McMillan, D. D., founder of Jefferson College; Rev. John Woodhull, D. D.; Rev. Hugh McAden, Rev. James F. Armstrong, Rev. James Dunlap, Rev. Nathaniel Irwin, and Rev. John Ross, the latter being one of the first professors of Dickinson College, a noted teacher of the classics, and author of a Latin and Greek grammar.

The next institution of this kind established in Chester County was what was known as New London Academy. Founded in 1743, this school became a famous institution. Rev. Francis Alison was the founder of the school, which furnished many men of distinction to both church and State. Among these noted men were Charles Thomson, secretary of the Continental Congress; Dr. John Ewing, provost of the University of Pennsylvania; Dr. David Ramsey, the historian; Dr. Hugh Williamson, Rev. James Latta, D. D.; Rev. Matthew Wilson, D. D., and three of the signers of the Declaration of Independence, Thomas McKean, George Reed and James Smith. In 1752 Dr. Alison removed to Philadelphia, and was succeeded in the principalship of this school by Alexander McDowell, who removed the academy to Newark, Delaware, where it afterward became the basis upon which was founded Delaware College.

In 1828 another school, by the name of the New London Academy, was established, and was for many years a prosperous institution. Some of its ablest principals were James Magraw, T. Marshall Boggs, William S. Graham, W. S. F. Graham, William F. Wyers, George Duffield and Edward D. Porter.

Next after the early New London Academy came the Nottingham Academy, established in 1744 by the Rev. Samuel Finley, D. D. At this institution were educated some of the ablest men who figured in the early history of the country. Among them may be mentioned Dr. Benjamin Rush, famous all over the civilized world for his scientific attainments; Judge Jacob Rush, his brother; Governor Martin, of North Carolina; Governor McWhor-

·ter, of New Jersey; Governor Henry, of Maryland; Ebenezer Hazard, Colonel John Bayard, William M. Tennent, D. D.; Rev. Joseph Smith, D. D.; Rev. James Waddell, D. D., the blind preacher, who is eulogized for his eloquence by William Wirt in his "British Spy." Dr. Samuel Finley, according to Dr. Benjamin Rush, was one of the wisest and best of men. His school was broken up by his removal to Princeton, New Jersey, to take the presidency of the college at that place; but its place was some time afterward well supplied by the West Nottingham Academy, which was established in 1812 through the instrumentality of Rev. Dr. James Magraw and located in Maryland.

From 1793 to 1816 there was in existence an institution of learning called the Brandywine Academy, near the Manor meeting-house, in what is now West Brandywine Township. Here the classics and the higher branches of science were taught. At different times this institution was under the direction of Rev. M. McPherson, Matthew G. Wallace, John Ralson, John F. Grier and Rev. John W. Grier.

Rev. Nathan Grier was in the early day a prominent educator, his students being principally theological. From 1792 to 1814 he prepared twenty young men for the ministry, among them being Rev. David McConoughey, who was at one time president of Washington College, Pennsylvania; Rev. John H. Grier, Levi Bull and John N. C. Grier.

From 1779 to about 1783 a school was in existence at Upper Octoraro, called the Upper Octoraro Classical School. It was established by Rev. William Foster, and came to an end with the death of its founder.

From 1750 to the end of the Eighteenth century the Friends had in operation numerous schools in Chester County. One was established at Birmingham meeting-house in 1753. Several were established within the limits of Kennett Monthly Meeting, the one near Marlborough meeting-house having two acres of ground, a residence for the teacher, and a fund which in 1886, according to Wickersham, amounted to $3,000. But there was one school in existence long before any of these, that in Willistown Town-the Friends having purchased ground for which as early as 1713.. At an early day there were school-houses connected with the meeting-houses at New Garden, Marshallton, Grove and West Grove and others. In 1779 Goshen, Bradford and Birmingham meetings jointly purchased four acres of ground and erected a school-house thereon one-half mile west of West Chester, and Bradford, New Garden and Kennett Monthly Meetings jointly established a school in 1781. In 1793 Kennett Preparative Meeting purchased a piece of land for a school about two and a half miles west of Kennett meeting-house, alongside the road leading to Nottingham.

But perhaps the most famous of the schools above referred to was that established in 1753 at Birmingham meeting-house by the Friends on the site of the battle of the Brandywine. For many years this school was in charge of John Forsythe, one of the best and most famous of the early teachers of Chester County. One of the most distinguished of the pupils of this school was Dr. William Darlington, who enjoyed a world-wide fame as a botanist. John Forsythe came from Ireland to this country in 1773, when he was nineteen years of age, and on his mother's side of the family was a descendant of the Stuarts. He was a good Presbyterian when he reached this County, was well educated, was a fashionable young man, and a fine performer of the violin. After coming to Chester County he became a Quaker, and for many years was at the head of the Birmingham Classical School. He exerted a powerful influence upon all the young people with whom he came in contact in favor of education, to the great gratification of many a head of a family. For a short time he presided over the destinies of the Westtown Boarding School, a history of which is hereafter introduced, and then he retired to his farm in East Bradford. In

1811 he presided over the first meeting held to promote the establishment of West Chester Academy, was one of the most liberal contributors to that enterprise, which at lenght developed into the present West Chester State Normal School.

Before leaving these early schools of the Friends it is due to the Friends and to the schools they established in this early day to record the fact that they were not merely the elementary institutions that many might suppose. Notwithstanding that they were located in the rural districts, their masters frequently taught the higher branches of learning, such as Algebra, Geometry, Mensuration and Surveying. They also taught, but less frequently, History, Natural Philosophy and Astronomy, and still less frequently Latin and Greek.

About 1790 a prominent Friend named George Churchman established in East Nottingham, Chester County, a boarding school in Chester County; but as the day for this class of schools the higher branches being introduced. This was the first normal school in Chester County: but as the day for this class of schools had not yet arrived, it did not long survive.

It is altogether likely that it was about 1790 that some of the leading Friends began to consider the propriety of establishing a larger and better institution of learning than any they had so far had, for at the yearly meeting held in Philadelphia for Pennsylvania, New Jersey, Delaware, and the eastern parts of Maryland and Virginia, the matter respecting the establishment of a boarding school, which had been brought up from the Philadelphia Quarter in the year 1792, was entered upon and considered. At this meeting a committee of fifty-four Friends was appointed which on October 3, 1794, brought in a report to the effect that inasmuch as many of the Friends had taken into consideration the many advantages to the Society to be derived from one or more such institutions in a suitable place or suitable places within the limits and under the care of the yearly meeting, the use and benefit whereof were to be confined to the children of Friends, etc., they were unanimously agreed in sentiment that an institution of the kind proposed, if managed with religious care and circumspection, might tend to the prosperity of truth by promoting the real good of the rising generation: and they therefore recommended the said proposal to the yearly meeting, and proposed that a committee be appointed to consider and digest the plan and rules for the government and management of the house, school and other parts of the economy, etc. This report was signed on behalf of the committee of fifty-four by Joseph Potts, Thomas Gaskill, Daniel Smith and Robert Kirkbride.

The following committee was then appointed to carry into effect the several matters contained in the report and to submit a full and clear statement of their proceedings at the next yearly meeting: Henry Drinker, Owen Biddle, John Drinker, Thomas Fisher, Jesse Foulke, William Jackson, Humphrey Marshall, Joshua E. Pusey, Warner Mifflin, Jonathan Evans, Jr., Nicholas Waln, George Churchman, John Hoskins, and there were thirty-three others added to the committee on October 2, 1795, among whom were Phillip Price, Jr., James Emlen, William Savery and Eli Yarnall.

Plans having been sufficiently matured, it was determined to name two Friends in each of the quarterly meetings to receive the voluntary contributions and subscriptions of the members of the society. For the Philadelphia Quarterly Meeting Thomas Fisher and Joseph Sansom were appointed, and two others in each of the other quarterly meetings, of which there were nine. Thomas Fisher is believed to have been the first treasurer of the committee. Some of the Friends who were interested proposed to the consideration of the meeting as a suitable situation for the boarding school a tract of land called Langhorne Park, in Bucks County, twenty miles out from Philadelphia, bounded on one side by the Neshaminy Creek, and containing 450 acres. Humphrey Marshall, Jonathan Evans, Owen Biddle and eleven others were named to view this spot and to report at the next meeting, they being also authorized to view any other places that might be thought more likely to answer the purpose.

On December 17, 1794, the Friends above named reported that all of them but three had been to Langhorne Park, but, still having one or more places they desired to view, they wished further time. Eight other Friends were then added to the committee, and at a meeting held on December 10 a sub-committee laid before the committee a description of several tracts of land which they had viewed, and it was ascertained that the general sentiment was in favor of the farm of James Gibbons, in Westtown, Chester County, containing 595 acres of land. Then Humphrey Marshall, John Pierce, Thomas Fisher and Samuel Canby were named to treat with Mr. Gibbons and to confirm the bargain with him if the terms and title should prove satisfactory.

In this case the deed was to be made in trust to Jonathan Evans, Joseph Sansom, Thomas Morris, Thomas Stewardson, John Field and John Wistar. On the 29th of the same month articles of agreement were signed by James Gibbons and his wife, Eleanor, and on the 12th of the 1st month, 1795, the above-named committee was continued to perfect the bargain, with the addition to it of Henry Drinker, John Morton and Roger Dicks.

This James Gibbons was one of the remarkable men of early Chester County history. He was a stanch Friend, a non-combatant, and retired from all public service upon the breaking out of the Revolutionary War. He was a fine scholar, especially well versed in ancient and modern languages, and at his residence opened a school for instruction in Latin, French and Greek. He was a competent surveyor, and was also competent to make deeds and wills. His judgment was so universally respected that his neighbors often submitted their disputes to him, and almost always abided by his decision, feeling satisfied that they had obtained justice as nearly as it was possible for them to obtain it.

The aggregate price he received for his farm was £6,083 6s 8d. In regard to the account in Futhey and Cope's History of Chester County of the attempt of the chairman of the committee that went to visit him to make a sharp bargain for his farm by trying to beat him down £1 per acre, a certain writer in "The Friend," No. 25, Vol. LV, states that there was no Englishman on the committee, all being natives of this country, and that it was not the custom of the Friends to conduct business through a chairman. The four Friends that made the bargain with Mr. Gibbons for this farm were John Pierce, of Thornbury, Delaware County; Samuel Canby, Wilmington, Delaware; Humphrey Marshall, of Marshallton, Chester County, and Thomas Fisher, and to the perfecting of the bargain three others were added, viz.: Drinker, Morton and Dicks, as stated above.

On March, 23, 1795, Thomas Stewardson, Benjamin Sweet, John Drinker and Owen Biddle were desired to attend at James Gibbons' house, on the first of the next month, to get the deed executed. Then, having attended to the arbitration of water rights on Chester Creek with Robert Green and William Ashbridge, the details of which would require too much space for introduction here, it may be next stated that the committee were informed, probably in the fifth month, 1795, that John Elliott, of London, from a desire to promote the institution, had authorized Henry Drinker to draw on him for £100 to be applied for its benefit. A milldam and a mill were then erected northwest of Walnut Hill, not far from the northern boundary of the farm and south of Chester Creek. A meeting of the boarding school committee was held at the farm on August 17, 1795, those present being John Shoemaker, Owen Biddle, John Wistar, Jonathan Evans and eight others, who "viewed the eminence north of the old mansion, remarkable for the fine prospect it affords." On the 18th of the same month the committee of women Friends were invited to procure feather beds, pillows, mattresses, etc., for the accommodation

GEORGE M. PHILIPS.

of such members of the committee, men or women, as might occasionally attend to the duties of their appointment at that place. This is the first mention of women in connection with the proceedings, and at the meeting of September 16 three of the seven women Friends named by the yearly meeting were in attendance.

A road was opened on the east side of the farm to connect with Marlboro Street road and Goshen Township road, and a building committee was appointed consisting of Jonathan Evans, Owen Biddle, Thomas Morris, Thomas Stewardson and Joseph Sansom, the building to stand on the eminence mentioned above, north of the old mansion. The size of the building finally determined upon was 100 feet front, 56 feet deep, and three stories in height.

A notable donation was offered to this school about the first of February, 1796, by John Dawson Coates, a Friend, and then a late banker of Dublin, Ireland, the donation amounting to $500, Irish currency, which was accepted by the committee, Henry Drinker, Thomas Fisher and three others being appointed to receive it. John Pemberton in his will left $22\frac{1}{4}$ pistoles annually to the institution after his widow's death, the annual amount being $80.10. Henry Drinker also made a donation of a tract of land containing $4,989\frac{3}{4}$ acres in Luzerne County, Pennsylvania. Bartholomew Wistar, in his will, left £150 to the school, and James Emlen, in his will, £100. Samuel Walles gave $802\frac{1}{2}$ acres of land in Luzerne County, and on February 15, 1799, Richard and Catharine Hartshorne offered to take charge of the family of the boarding school "without any view to pecuniary satisfaction, which it is stated they cannot agree to receive." This offer was accepted by the committee.

The school was finally opened on May 6, 1799, and on July 19, at the request of the teachers in the school, the following visiting committee was appointed: Benjamin Sweet, Philip Price, Jr., Henry Drinker and Eli Yarnall. On November 15, the number of

22

applicants for admission to the school had reached 300, and it was
decided to discontinue entering names. About this time Richard
Hartshorne desiring to retire from the position of superintendent
of the institution, Jonathan Evans, Eli Yarnall, Philip Price, Jr.,
Abraham Sharpless, Catharine Wistar, Rachel Malin and Margaret Marshall took upon themselves the charge of attending to
the wants of the family. Philip Price is thought to have been
superintendent temporarily until January 4, 1800, when Joshua
Sharpless took charge, receiving for his services £100 per year.
About this time or soon afterward it was deemed necessary, in
order to meet the expenses of the institution, to raise the price
of board and tuition to £30 per year for boys and £25 10s. for girls.

At the opening of the school there were three teachers employed, the principal being John Forsythe, who has heretofore
been mentioned as the popular teacher of the Birmingham school.
On the 19th of the 9th month, 1800, at a meeting at which were
present twenty-one men and ten women, it was agreed to erect a
two-story stone house, 18x28 feet in size, for the accommodation
of a teacher. And it was also decided to erect a building for an
infirmary on the east side of the plantation, 64x27 feet in size.
The original cost of the farm and buildings was about $46,000,
but there have been many additions and improvements since that
time, and it is altogether likely that the expenditures on the property now exceed $300,000.

On January 21, 1811, a stone house having been erected opposite the lane east of the schoolhouse, which it was believed was
designed for a store, with which it was apprehended it would be
difficult to prevent improper communications on the part of the
scholars, it was determined to purchase the property, which included one and one-half acres of land, the price asked being $1,300.
About the same time it was decided to make the salary of the
superintendent of the school $500 per year.

One of the most difficult matters with which the management

had to contend was that of making the income meet the expenditures. The price of tuition and board was often changed to meet changed conditions, but if it were placed high enough to meet the cost then students fell off, and the aggregate income was reduced. If the price were placed low enough to attract plenty of students, then the aggregate cost of board and tuition was so increased that the income was too small. When the charge for board and tuition was placed at $150 per year, the cost of such board and tuition was more than $200, so that there was a deficiency on each pupil's payments to the extent of more than $50 per year. Another difficulty was that teachers would remain in the school only long enough to find other positions at better pay, and hence as early as 1834 it was suggested that the only way to secure the services of competent teachers was to establish a permanent fund, the interest of which should be applied so far as it would go to the payment of salaries to the best teachers that could be obtained by the payment of adequate salaries. Such a fund was afterward established.

In 1844 the farm was carefully surveyed, and found to contain 599 acres, 2 rods and 34 perches.

Early in the history of the institution a library was added to the other educational features, comprising a considerable variety of works on history, biography, science and general literature. Extensive philosophical and chemical apparatus was introduced, and the regular course of study was so arranged and selected as to confer the greatest possible benefit upon the students. This school was established with the view mainly of instructing the young in the doctrines of the Friends, first educating the mind in such a way and to such a degree that it could readily comprehend them and perceive their beauty. This idea was well expressed by William Evans in his journal in 1853, when he said: "There is something of importance that money cannot purchase. It is that Friends should be preserved under a right exercise that the institution may be conducted in such a manner as to support the primitive doctrines and testimonies of the Friends, and educate the children in them. This was the original concern, and that has been blessed," and Mr. Evans expressed his belief that as Friends kept to this ground a blessing would continue to rest upon the school.

From the beginning of this school both sexes have been admitted to its benefits, communication between them being judiciously regulated. Since the division that occurred in the Society of Frinds in 1827, this school has been continuously in the hands of the orthodox branch, and none but children of members of that branch are admitted to its privileges. The school is now heavily endowed, and the cost of board and tuition is much lower than in the earlier days. Many are boarded and instructed entirely without expense. Up to 1872 the number of students that had attended the school was 4,215 boys and 5,396 girls. There has been a very large number of teachers connected with the faculty of this school, and some of them unusually prominent in their respective callings. Among them may be named John Comly, author of Comly's Grammar; Enoch Lewis, author of several works on mathematical subjects; John Gummere, author of Gummere's Surveying, Astronomy, etc.; Joseph Foulke, Samuel Alsop, Emmor Kimber, Joshua Hoopes, at one time principal of a boarding school at West Chester, and a distinguished authority on botanical subjects; Jonathan Gause, a noted Pennsylvania teacher, and Joseph C. Strode, one of the most famous mathematicians in the United States.

The original buildings have been several times added to and enlarged. The main building was 175 feet long and four stories high, and in 1869 a building was erected 68x54 feet in size. In addition to the school and farm buildings there is a gristmill on the place. This school has very largely contributed to the diffusion of knowledge among mankind, and especially among Friends, and many of the private seminaries conducted by Friends may be traced directly or indirectly to this famous institution.

Since 1799 the total number of boys that have entered this school has been 5,350, and the total number of girls 6,425, or a total enrollment of 11,775. Besides these there have been a few children of married teachers in attendance as "day scholars." At the present time (February, 1898), owing to the hard times of the past few years, there are but 90 boys and 70 girls in attendance. The highest average attendance ever reached was in 1840, when it was 244, and in 1867, when it was 243. The lowest average attendance was in 1830, when it was down to 103.

From the beginning down to 1896 the leading officer was always called the superintendent, but in that year the office of principal was created. Other noted teachers, besides those named above, have been Samuel Alsop, Jr., afterward well known at Haverford College; Joseph G. Harlan, also afterward of Haverford; Sarah Bailey, leading teacher of the older girls for thirty-five years; Isaac Sharpless, now president of Haverford College; J. Henry Bartlett, now principal of the Friends' school at Sixteenth and Cherry Streets, Philadelphia, and Thomas K. Brown, still at the school and author of a text book on Algebra. William F. Wickersham was appointed in 1896 the first principal to fill the office then created, a position which he still occupies.

During the year ending March 15, 1897, the expenses of the school were $48,827.65, while the income from the various funds was as follows: From board and tuition, $30,910; from merchandise, $368.85; from farm, $706.94; from income of fund for paying, salaries, $734.88; from income of invested fund for general purposes, $6,825.11; from amount appropriated for use of school from income of Teachers' and Educational funds, $5,145.98, leaving the amount against the institution, $4,135.89.

With reference to the course of study pursued at this institution the following extract from the catalogue of 1896 will be sufficiently specific:

"To suit the requirements of the long and short terms, most

of the subjects are arranged to be completed in three, six, or nine months, the latter time being the whole school year. Three months' work in any subject is technically known as one study. Four studies are generally taken at once and twelve studies constitute a year's work. Three years' work, or thirty-six studies, selected as hereafter explained, will entitle the pupil to the diploma of the school.

"The subjects in the prescribed course are divided into seven sections. Section I embraces English and History; Section II, Science; Section III, Mathematics; Section IV, Latin; Section V, German; Section VI, Greek, and Section VII, French.

"A student may graduate when any three of the first six sections have been completed, and enough additional work has been taken from the other sections to make the whole number of studies amount to thirty-six. Certain subjects, however, are required of all students, and must be included within the three sections taken, or in the additional work. These are marked * in the following list."

Then follows the "Prescribed Course" for three years, which it is not considered incumbent on this work to present; but in order to show the limit of the course the studies for the senior class, or third year, are here appended, with the studies marked * as above mentioned:

"Third Year. Senior Class.

"Section I. English.—Moral Philosophy* (1). Rhetoric* (1). English Literature* (1). Political Economy (1). Psychology (1).

"Section II. Science.—Astronomy (1). Geology (1).

"Section III. Mathematics.—Analytical Geometry (1). Analytical Geometry or Arithmetic (1).

"Section IV. Latin.—Horace (2). Elective Work in Cæsar, Vergil or Cicero (1).

"Section V. German.—William Tell, die Harzreise, etc. Rapid Reading. Narration. Sight Reading.

"Section VI. Greek.—Herodotus. Homer. Plato's Apology."

The first successful movement looking to the establishment of an institution of learning in West Chester was made in 1811, in which year the West Chester Academy was incorporated. It was one of the leading schools of its class for fifty years. The academy was established for the reason that the Chester County Academy, which had then been recently endowed by the State Legislature with $2,000, did not suit many of the citizens of West Chester as to its location. Under the lead of William Hemphill nearly $8,000 was promptly subscribed by the citizens of West Chester and vicinity for the establishment of this institution in their midst. An acre of land was purchased on which, in 1812, a building was erected, and the institution duly launched upon its career. But the war with England which broke out in 1812 prevented the academy from receiving the attention it would otherwise have received at the beginning, and its growth was consequently checked to some extent thereby. The first teachers in the school were Dr. John Gemmil and Jonathan Gause, the former having charge of the classical department, and the latter of the mathematical. Dr. Gemmil died in 1814, and soon afterward Mr. Gause became the principal teacher, holding the position most of the time until 1829, when he resigned to establish a private school. During the time Mr. Gause was principal the academy flourished, in the meantime receiving in 1817 a grant of $1,000. Many men who afterward became distinguished were educated at West Chester Academy while Mr. Gause was in charge, among them Nimrod Strickland, Washington Townsend, John Hickman, Joseph Hemphill, Dr. Wilmer Worthington, William W. Jefferis, James B. Everhart and Dr. George Smith, the latter of whom served in the Legislature of the State, and wrote what is still the best "History of Delaware County."

From 1829 to 1834 the academy had several different principals, but in this latter year a noted individual, Jean Antoine Brunin de Bolmar, a native of France, became principal, and remained in charge until 1840. Mr. Bolmar was one of the most energetic of teachers, and is still remembered with great respect. Under his direction the school reached the zenith of its fame and usefulness, being crowded with pupils. From 1840 to 1854 this academy was in charge of James Crowell, and from 1854 to 1866 William F. Wyers was the principal. During this latter period it became necessary to erect new buildings in order to accommodate the scholars, and when Mr. Wyers withdrew in 1866 he was succeeded by J. Hunter Worrall and Eugene Paulin, they remaining in charge until 1869, when the institution was closed as a separate and distinct school, and merged into the West Chester State Normal School.

This change came about through a proposition made in 1869 by the trustees of the West Chester Academy to the citizens of West Chester, to the effect that the change be made. The citizens responded in a most liberal manner, raising more than $40,000 for the purpose. At the same time the trustees of the Chester County Cabinet of Natural Sciences, which was founded in 1826, merged their property and valuable collections into the enterprise. Altogether there was raised $75,000, and much valuable property in the shape of libraries, museums, etc., was contributed. Ten acres of ground in the southern part of the borough of West Chester were purchased from the Hon. Wayne MacVeagh, and upon this land in 1870-71, the original building, comprising about one-third of the present main building, a cut of which as it now appears is here introduced, was erected.

This building was opened in the fall of 1871, with Ezekiel H. Cook, a graduate of Bowdoin College, as principal, and a strong faculty of teachers. There were about 160 students in attendance during the first year, but from various causes the first year's work was not wholly a success, and at its close the Principal and several members of the faculty resigned. The second year opened with Dr. William A. Chandler, a graduate of the University of Michigan, as principal, and with a decreased attendance. Dr. Chandler resigned at the beginning of the spring term of 1873, having served as Principal about six months. He was immediately succeeded by Professor George L. Maris, also a graduate of the University of Michigan, and who had just completed his term as Superintendent of Public Schools of Chester County. Professor Maris found the school greatly reduced in numbers, and for more than eight years labored diligently and successfully in building up and maintaining the school.

The first addition to the original main building was erected in 1878-79, being the north wing of the building as it is to-day. The first class graduated under Professor Maris' administration in 1874, and he resigned in 1881 to accept a professorship in Swarthmore College as well as the Superintendency of the Friends' schools connected with the Philadelphia Yearly Meeting.

Professor Maris was succeeded by Dr. George Morris Philips, the present Principal of the school. Dr. Philips had previously been connected with the school as professor of higher mathematics from the close of Professor Chandler's principalship in the spring of 1873 until the summer of 1878, when he became professor of mathematics and astronomy at his alma mater, the University at Lewisburg, Pennsylvania, now Bucknell University. This position he resigned in 1881 when he succeeded Professor Maris in the principalship of the Normal school. Upon the accession of Dr. Philips to this position the school at once entered upon a period of growth and prosperity, which has caused it to be generally recognized as the foremost Normal School in the State, and one of the foremost in the entire country. Its students have nearly, if not quite, quadrupled during this period, and its faculty has grown in the same proportion and has been greatly strengthened, until it is now scarcely equaled for scholarship and experience in teaching by that of any other normal school in the country.

The south wing of the main building was begun during the first year of Dr. Philips' incumbency, and it was soon followed by the laundry and boiler building in 1885, the dining-room, chapel and sanitary towers in 1886-87, the gymnasium in 1890, the Principal's residence and infirmary in 1891-92, the recitation hall in 1892-93, the kitchen and storeroom in 1893. Four acres were added to the original MacVeagh lot in 1889, to the northward; five acres were purchased and also a site for the infirmary in 1891; the grounds of the Chester County Agricultural Society in 1895, and a piece adjoining the latter tract in 1898, increasing the original ten acres to forty-six. In 1896 a complete electric light plant and a large elevator were put in, and in the aggregate the property of the school has up to the present time (1898) cost about $500,000.

The enrollment of students each year is about 1,000, and these students come from all parts of Pennsylvania and from other states of the Union, and also some from foreign countries. Each year the school graduates a hundred or more young men and women well equipped for the profession of teaching, which profession, with but few exceptions, they enter upon, and they are almost universally successful. Its graduates now number more than a thousand, almost all of them at present engaged in teaching, winning success in all parts of the country, while its undergraduates number nearly ten times as many as its graduates.

The school is well equipped in all departments; its grounds are ample and handsomely laid out and improved, and its buildings are pronounced by all who have seen them to be the finest State Normal School buildings in the United States. They are constructed of green or serpentine stone from quarries in Chester County, and are substantial and massive. Its gymnasium has long been admitted to be the best and most completely equipped of any of its class in the country, and it is scarcely second to that of any of the first-class universities. Its library is large, well-selected, and is constantly increasing, and it possesses valuable botanical, zoölogical and mineralogical collections. Every department of the school is well equipped with the necessary apparatus, and the school, as a whole, is in a thoroughly first-class and efficient condition. It is now larger and more prosperous than at any time in the past, and gives every evidence of continued and increasing success.

The faculty of the school during the year 1897-98 was as follows:

George Morris Philips, A. M.,
Ph. D., Principal.

David M. Sensenig, M. S.,
Higher Mathematics.

C. B. Cochran, A. M.,
Physics and Chemistry.

Elvira Y. Speakman,
Geography and Spelling.

A. Thomas Smith, Ph. D.,
Pedagogy.

Francis H. Green, A. M.,
English.

Eva J. Blanchard,
Principal of Model School.

C. E. Ehinger, M. D.,
Director of Gymnasium.

Charlotte N. Hardee, Mus. B.,
Music.

Esther M. Groome,
Drawing and Writing.

S. C. Schmucker, A. M., Ph. D.,
Biological Sciences.

Foster H. Starkey, A. M.,
Languages.

Joseph S. Walton, Ph. D.,
History and German.

Cora E. Everett,
Reading.

J. W. F. Wilkinson, A. M.,
Higher Mathematics.

Joseph J. Bailey,
Manual Training.

Lydia A. Martin, M. E.,
Mathematics.

Mrs. A. M. Sensenig, M. E.,
Mathematics.

Sara S. Kirk, M. E.,
English Grammar.

Mrs. C. E. Ehinger,
Physical Culture.

Helen H. Ely, M. E.,
Model School.

Robert Anderson, A. B.,
Mathematics.

William S. Delp, M. E.,
Bookkeeping and Mathematics.

Anna M. Esler, M. E.,
Reading and Grammar.

Elizabeth F. Criley, M. E.,
English Branches.

Elizabeth D. Perry,
  Music.

Ethel M. Davie,
  Model School.

Louis J. Palmer, A. M.,
  Latin and History.

Humphrey M. Carpenter,
  Violin, Flute and Violoncello.

Harriet Baldwin,
  Pedagogy and Latin.

Edgar H. Sensenich, B. E.,
  Secretary.

Carl G. Schrader,
  Assistant in Gymnasium.

Alice Cochran,
  Librarian.

Nathena P. Young,
  Assistant in Gymnasium.

George Morris Philips, Ph. D., Principal of the West Chester State Normal School, was born in Penningtonville (now Atglen), Chester County, Pennsylvania, October 28, 1851. Having received his elementary education in the schools of his native village, and his academic education in the high school there taught by Prof. William E. Buck, he then attended the Lewisburg University, now Bucknell University, graduating from this latter institution in 1871. He was immediately elected professor of mathematics in Monongahela College, and filled that position for about two years, resigning in 1873 to accept a similar position in the West Chester State Normal School, which position he retained five years. Then resigning this latter position he accepted the professorship of mathematics and astronomy in Lewisburg University, which he retained until 1881, when he was chosen principal of the West Chester State Normal School, and has held this position ever since.

During his administration of this office the attendance at the Normal School has trebled, more than $300,000 has been expended in permanent improvements, and the school has come into the first rank of Normal Schools in this country. Dr. Philips is a member of the College and University Council of Pennsylvania; a director of the National Bank of Chester County and of the Dime Savings Bank of West Chester; president of the Chester County Historical Society; a trustee of Bucknell University, and a manager of the Chester County Hospital. He is the author of several popular and widely read text books, is a popular lecturer and institute instructor. In 1888 he was elected president of Bucknell University, and in 1890 was tendered by Gov. Beaver the State Superintendency of Public Instruction of Pennsylvania, both of which, in addition to various other tempting positions, he declined. He is a Son of the Revolution, being a great-grandson of Lieut. John Philips of the Revolutionary Army. In 1877 he was married to Elizabeth M. Pyle, daughter of William H. Pyle, of Chester County, and has two children, Willie P. and Sarah E.

After retiring from the principalship of West Chester Academy in 1829 Jonathan Gause opened a private school, which he named "The West Chester Boarding School for Young Men and Boys." This institution he conducted until 1832, when he was succeeded by Cheyney Hannum. Then, retiring to his farm in West Bradford Township, he opened "The Greenwood Dell Boarding School," which became very popular and)was continued until 1839, when Mr. Gause became principal of the Unionville Academy, which he conducted until 1847, when he reopened the Greenwood Dell Boarding School and was its principal until 1865 Then, having been a teacher for more than fifty-seven years, he retired to a well-earned private life.

Joshua Hoopes established "The Downingtown Boarding School for Boys" in 1817, and continued it until 1834, when he removed to West Chester, and there opened "Hoopes' Boarding School for Boys," which he continued until 1862, when, on account of advancing age, he ceased to teach.

Edward Sparks in 1816 established "The East Bradford Boarding School for Boys," and was succeeded in the principalship thereof in 1818 by Joseph C. Strode, who remained its principal, with an occasional interval, until 1846. Lewis Levis then became the principal and conducted the school until 1857, when Mr. Levis closed the school and became a teacher in the school being conducted by Mr. Bolmar.

Mrs. Phelps' Young Ladies' Boarding School was established in 1838, by a joint stock company, the company erecting an elegant edifice in West Chester for the accommodation of young ladies. This school was in charge of Mrs. Almira H. Lincoln Phelps, an accomplished lady, and well known as the author of a work on botany. Townsend Eachus was the principal mover in the establishment of this school, which flourished abundantly while in charge of Mrs. Phelps. However, at length the company failed, and the property was sold by the sheriff, being purchased in 1840 by Anthony Bolmar, who is often referred to as the Napoleon of teachers. Mr. Bolmar converted the school into a boarding school for young men and boys, and it became widely known, attracted numerous pupils even from the Southern States and West Indies, and was, in fact, one of the most flourishing institutions of the kind in the land. The school was noted for its thoroughly systematic and exact discipline, and its principal was too watchful ever to be outwitted by any of his pupils. He was the author of several educational works for the instruction of pupils in French. He remained at the head of the institution until 1859, when business required his presence in France, and during his absence from this country the school was closed. Upon his return he made an attempt to reopen it, but his health was too badly shattered, and he died February 27, 1861, at the age of sixty-four years, leaving a widow and six children.

From 1862 to 1865 the property was occupied by the Pennsylvania Military Academy, under the presidency of Col. Theodore Hyatt, in the latter year being removed to Chester. The property was then purchased by another of Chester County's noted teachers, William F. Wyers, who in 1866 opened a school therein, called by him "Wyers' Scientific and Classical Institute for Boys." This school Mr. Wyers conducted until his death in 1871. Mr. Wyers was succeeded by Robert M. McClellan, who conducted the school for two years, when the property was purchased for the Catholic

Convent of the Immaculate Heart, and a school established therein entitled "Villa Maria Academy for Young Ladies," which has since been conducted by the Sisters of the Immaculate Heart. Under their efficient management the original property has more than trebled in value, and several spacious additions have been made to the buildings, among them an exquisite building of Avondale stone containing chapel and commencement hall. A fifth story has been added to the entire main building, and an extensive north wing, for the use of the community, raised to an equal height.

Villa Maria has an attendance of about one hundred and twenty resident pupils, and the course of study is arranged on a modern basis, conducive to a most thorough training. The departments are four in number, viz.: primary, intermediate, senior and academic. The instruction includes a systematic course in English, mathematics, elementary sciences, Latin, German, French, history, bookkeeping, drawing and music, the latter in all its branches.

In December, 1894, a purchase of four acres was annexed to the convent property upon which, in September, 1895, a boarding school for small boys was opened under the title of St. Aloysius Academy, the present number of pupils here being twenty-seven, and the lads are laying a first-class foundation for a future business or college course.

Mr. McClellan, above mentioned, moved his school to the Evans school property, on West Union Street, which is now partly occupied by the Reformed Episcopal Church, where he continued to teach a few years longer.

Emmor Kimber in 1817 established the French Creek Boarding School for Girls, the name of which was changed to the Kimberton Boarding School when a postoffice was established there, named Kimberton, January 15, 1820, Mr. Kimber being made the first postmaster. This school was conducted on principles quite different from those usually in operation in such schools, there-being no rules in operation, the entire plan of government being based on the Golden Rule. In the management and teaching of the pupils attending this school, Mr. Kimber was aided by his accomplished daughters, and all of them, father and daughters, had the faculty of maintaining an invisible government, which was none the less effective because it was based entirely upon the sense of honor of the pupils, who came not only from other States, but also from the West Indies. Mr. Kimber died in 1850, and the school was closed after a most useful career of thirty-three years.

Afterward a school was conducted at the same place by the Rev. J. R. Dimm.

George Pierce established the Brandywine Boarding School in 1816, and conducted it until 1823, when it was closed.

Rev. Francis Alison Latta established Moscow Academy, a classical and literary institution, in Sadsbury Township, in 1826, and it was a successful institution for some years, though under different principals. It closed its career in 1840. Rev. Mr. Latta was a fine scholar, especially in the classics and theology, and was a Presbyterian minister. He died April 21, 1834.

Rev. James Latta in 1830 opened Mantua Female Seminary, a sort of companion school to Moscow Academy, and located only a short distance from it. For several years it had a successful career.

Unionville Academy was established in 1834 by the liberality of citizens in the vicinity, who donated the land and erected the buildings. It was for many years one of the best known and most successful private schools in the county. Among its principals were such men as Milton White, Gaylord L. More, Cheyney Hannum, James Fling, Jonathan Gause, Milton Durnall, Henry S. Kent, Jacob W. Harvey, A. A. Meader, and among its illustrious pupils were Bayard Taylor and James P. Wickersham.

Evan Pugh opened a school for young men in 1847 in East Nottingham Township, which was known as Jordan Bank Acad-

A. Gibbons

emy. This school he conducted until 1853, when he went to Europe, graduated at the University of Heidelberg, which conferred upon him the degree of Doctor of Physical Science, and upon his return home in 1859 he at once became president of the Agricultural College of Pennsylvania.

At Rockville in Honeybrook Township there was established in 1848 a school by the name of Howard Academy, under the principalship of Prof. James McClune, LL. D., and the same school was afterward conducted by Rev. S. Ogden, A. Kirkland, and others, until 1862.

Benjamin Price conducted a school in East Bradford from about 1842 to 1847, which was known by the name of Prospect Hill Boarding School.

Philip and Rachel Price in 1830 opened Price's Boarding School for Girls in West Chester, and this school was conducted by their daughter, Mrs. Hannah P. Davis, until 1852, when it was purchased by Miss P. C. Evans and her sisters. The school then became the West Chester Female Seminary, and was conducted in the same building until 1872, which in that year was purchased by Robert M. McClellan, who established therein McClellan's Institute for Boys, which was discontinued some years later.

Mary B. Thomas and her sisters in 1839 opened a boarding school for girls, in Downingtown, which they conducted for many years.

Carl Heins had a similar institution in the same town for boys, which he conducted from 1860 to his death, in 1865.

F. Donleavy Long in 1871 opened in Downingtown the Chester Valley Academy for Boys, which he conducted for many years.

Alexander Moore opened the Downingtown Academy for Boys in 1872, and conducted it for some years.

Moses Coates conducted a boarding school in Coatesville from 1834 to 1838, and a select school was carried on there for some years, beginning in 1871, by Francis Parke and Benjamin I. Miller.

23

The Coatesville Academy, under several different principals, was in operation at Coatesville from 1853 to 1868.

The Eaton Institute for Girls was established in 1843 at Kennett Square, and this school was for a long time an excellent institution. It was afterward under the principalship of Evan T. Swayne. Joseph B. Phillips had a noted school for some years at Kennett Square, having among his pupils such men as Bayard Taylor, Dr. Howard Pugh, Dr. Elisha Gatchell and Dr. John B. Phillips.

Dr. Franklin Taylor, Dr. Elwood Harvey and Prof. Fordyce A. Allen in 1852 opened a normal school in West Chester, Professor Allen soon afterward becoming sole proprietor, and opening in 1860 a female institute in connection therewith. These schools were continued until 1864. Dr. Franklin Taylor in 1875 opened Kennett Academy, and conducted it for some years. Dr. Taylor had previously had charge of the Young Ladies' Academy, in West Chester, from 1867 to 1870, a school which, under the name of the Young Ladies' Select School, was established in 1860 by Miss Lamborn and Miss Worrall, and it was conducted by them until 1867.

The Oxford Female Seminary was established by Rev. J. M. Dickey about 1835, always had a large number of students from Maryland and Delaware, received the State appropriation in 1838, and for many years was an excellent institution of learning.

Rev. Alfred Hamilton in 1847 established at Fagg's Manor an institution which, in honor of the old school of the Blairs at that place, he named "Blair's Hall." It was in operation about eight years.

A school for females was in operation at Parkesburg from 1853 for some years, and was in charge of Miss Hannah Cooper, and later of the Misses Kelley and Johnson.

Benjamin Swayne established Londongrove Boarding School for Young Men and Boys in 1849, and it was successfully con-

In the same place Rebecca B. Pugh's Boarding and Day School for Children was opened in 1848, removed to West Chester in 1854, conducted there until 1874, when it was discontinued.

Thomas H. Harvey had a school for young men in Penn Township from 1840 to 1855, and sent out into the world many well-educated young men, among them the celebrated Isaac I. Hayes, Arctic explorer.

Thomas Berry, for some years prior to 1835, conducted a school near Fairville, named Harmony Hill Boarding School for Girls.

Jesse D. Sharpless established Fairville Institute, for pupils of both sexes, in 1854, and it was in operation until 1868, as many as ninety students being sometimes in attendance.

Fremont Academy in East Nantmeal Township was conducted from 1847 to 1858 by Jesse E. Phillips.

Oakdale Academy was conducted from 1855 to 1875 by David Phillips, and then by J. C. Guilden, being located at Pughtown.

Ivy Institute for Girls, at Pughtown, was under the charge of Jesse Hawley and his daughters there from 1856 to 1870, in the latter year being removed to Phœnixville.

Rev. J. E. Bradley was in charge of the Grovemont school at Phœnixville from 1856 to 1866.

The Ridge Road Academy was in operation from 1852 to 1853. The Springville Academy from 1858 to 1872; Johnson's School at Guthrieville from 1870 until a few years ago. Malvern Boarding School, for both sexes, under Jane M. Eldridge, was established in 1860. Thomas Conard and Thomas P. Conard were successively principals of West Grove Boarding School for Girls from 1853 to 1869. Henry S. Kent had a boarding school in Benn Township from 1860 to 1863. Hannah M. Cope's Toughkenamon Boarding School was established in 1867. Abraham Fetters established Edgefield Institute in Upper Uwchlan in 1867. Cheyney Hannum taught a school in West Chester from 1832 to 1838. Mrs. Sarah Fales also had a school there from 1838 to 1842. Miss Sarah Edmunds had one in the same city from 1842 to 1850. J. W. Pinkerton taught a school for girls, and Thomas B. Jacobs one for boys, in West Chester for some years. James M. Hughes had a school for girls there from 1854 to 1858. Miss Barclay's select school was located at No. 96 West Miner Street. Miss Emma Dennis' primary school was at 64 West Gay Street. Miss Hannah Embree's primary school was at the northeast corner of Church and Barnard Streets. Miss Mary C. Pratt's day school for young ladies was in the rear of the Chester County Cabinet. Miss E. W. Richards' Young Ladies' Boarding School was at No. 96 East Gay Street. The Student's Home, kept by Isabella B. Butler and Sarah Hughes, was at the northeast corner of Market and High Streets, where is now the Turk's Head Hotel.

Edward E. Orvis conducted a female seminary for two or three years in New London called the New London Female Seminary, beginning May 16, 1853.

J. William Thorne began his boarding school in Sadsbury Township, four miles north of Parkersburg, in the summer of 1856, and there taught the Latin and French languages and lectured on English classics, history and astronomy. This school was discontinued in 1866.

In 1857 the citizens of Parkesburg and its vicinity had determined to establish an academy at the village named, and organized a board of seven trustees for the purpose. Three acres of ground immediately north of the Pennsylvania railroad shops were purchased, and the school was opened in November, 1857, in the basement of the Baptist Church, by W. W. Woodruff, a graduate of Oberlin College, Ohio, he being the only teacher. In the summer of 1858 a large building was erected suitable for a boarding school, costing, together with the grounds, about $7,000, to which the school was transferred. In this new building Mr. Woodruff taught until the spring of 1860, having an average attendance of about thirty-five students, all boys. Professor Woodruff, being a friend of the co-education of the sexes, proposed to lease the academy property for five years, provided he were permitted to receive both sexes into his school; but his proposition being declined by the trustees, he removed to West Chester, and was soon after elected Superintendent of Schools for the county. Several attempts were subsequently made to revive the academy, but with only partial success, the property being finally sold and a private school for both sexes established and kept up for a few years. The property then passed into the hands of a private citizen, and is now occupied as a dwelling. In Professor Woodruff's academy were taught algebra, geometry, trigonometry, Latin, Greek and French. Those who succeeded Professor Woodruff in the management of this school were Rev. David X. Junkin, J. Morgan Rawlins, Rev. J. Landis, William W. Rupert and Milton R. Alexander.

In 1854 an institution was incorporated by the Legislature of Pennsylvania, under the name of the Ashmun Institute, for the education of young men of negro parentage, in response to a resolution passed by the New Castle Presbytery, October 5, 1853. This resolution, introduced and advocated by the Rev. Dr. John Miller Dickey, pastor of the Presbyterian Church at Oxford, Pennsylvania, was as follows:

"Considering the many Christian congregations of colored people in this country which are unable to secure educated ministers of their own color; considering the communities of such people in many parts who need educated men amongst them to fill the places of teachers and other responsible situations; considering the wants of Liberia and the importance to its present and future welfare of having suitably qualified men to fill its offices and posts of authority, instruction and influence; considering the vast missionary work yet to be done in Africa, and to be mainly done by persons of African descent; considering how extremely difficult it is for colored youth to obtain a liberal education in this land, arising from want of schools for that purpose, and their exclusion from all regular institutions of learning of a higher grade; considering the strong recommendation to that effect from our board of education and its full indorsement by the General Assembly of our Church, and considering the favorable indications of Providence at this time apparently calling us to such a work:

"This Presbytery, trusting in God, and under Him, depending on the Christian liberality of the friends of the African race throughout our country, do determine as follows:

"1. That there shall be established within our bounds and under our supervision an institution to be called the Ashmun Institute,* for the scientific, classical and theological education of colored youth of the male sex."

Doctor Dickey was in reality the founder and the animating spirit of the enterprise, and continued to be so until his death, which occurred in March, 1878. From the day of the inception of the institute he continued to labor for its success with abiding faith. When it was in need of funds, and there was no other way to raise them, he mortgaged his own property to secure the necessary resources.

Ashmun Institute existed as such for ten years, during which period it did good work without a fixed curriculum or a graded course of study. Theology was taught with the classics and other studies, and about thirty young men whom it had instructed were sent out into the field, twelve of whom became ministers, and two of whom went as ministers to Africa. At the close of the year, 1865, when nearly 4,000,000 slaves were suddenly freed and thrown upon the compassion of the church and the country with almost no education, with few schools, few churches, few teachers and few preachers, it was at once evident that Ashmun Institute was wholly inadequate to the work needed to be done, and the charter secured in 1854 was so amended as to grant new and enlarged

---

* Named after Jehudi Ashmun, well known for his labors in Liberia.

powers to the board of trustees and faculty, increasing their right to hold property, and authorizing them to confer degrees. The name was changed to that of the "Lincoln University," to indicate the broader scope it had acquired and to honor the great Emancipator.

In 1870, when the two branches of the Presbyterian Church, "Old and New school," were reunited, New Castle Presbytery, which up to that time had had control of this institution, was deprived of all ecclesiastical control north of Mason and Dixon's line, another change in the charter became necessary, and by this change the control of theological instruction was transferred to the General Assembly of the Presbyterian Church of the United States, this relation between the institution and the General Assembly still continuing. The Theological Department, which provides a full three years' course, has been from the first the heart of the university's work, but in 1871 it was rearranged and enlarged. In connection with this course there is a more limited one, in English only. In 1871 two other courses or departments were organized, Medicine and Law, which in 1874 were discontinned on account of the financial depression then existing.

The catalogue of 1897 states that more than 500 young men had then been sent out from the Preparatory Department and the lower classes in the Collegiate Department, and that from the Collegiate Department 554 had been graduated, after a course of instruction extending over four years, and in many cases over seven years, including the preparatory and the regular collegiate course. Most of these graduates are engaged in educational and professional labors in the Southern States. Two hundred and thirty-five of the students had received ordination as ministers of Evangelical Protestant denominations, and thirteen had gone to Africa as missionaries.

This university has eighty acres of land in Lower Oxford, Chester County, and its buildings consist of a Chapel, the Vail

Memorial Library building, University Hall, a building for general purposes; Livingston Hall, for commencement assemblies and capable of seating 1,000 persons; the Harriet Watson Jones Hospital; Ashmun Hall, Lincoln Hall, Cresson Hall, and Houston Hall, the four containing dormitories for students, and there are besides, nine residences for the professors. The value of the entire property of the university is now $250,000; the professorship fund bearing interest is $140,000, and the fund for scholarship is $50,000.

At the present time the corps of professors numbers ten, though through the death of Rev. Gilbert T. Woodhull, February 11, 1898, one chair became vacant. The nine professors remaining are as follows: Rev. Isaac N. Rendall, D. D., president and professor of logic, psychology and ethics since 1855; Rev. John B. Rendall, A. M., professor of Latin since 1871; J. Craig Miller, M. D., professor of natural science; Rev. R. L. Stewart, D. D., professor of pastoral theology, evidences of Christianity and Biblical antiquities; Rev. J. Aspinwall Hodge, D. D., professor of Biblical instruction; Walter L. Wright, Jr., A. M., professor of mathematics; Rev. William Deas Kerswill, B. D., professor of Hebrew and history; Rev. George B. Carr, D. D., professor of rhetoric; Rev. William R. Bingham, D. D., instructor in systematic theology.

Rev. Edward Webb, financial secretary of this institution from 1873 until his death, was born in Lowestoft, Suffolk, England, December 15, 1819, and was at different times pastor of Presbyterian Churches at Darby, Glasgow, Delaware, Andover and the Ashmun Church at Lincoln University. His death occurred suddenly from heart disease just after he had taken the train at Oxford, Chester County, his place of residence, for Philadelphia, on the morning of April 6, 1898.

Ercildoun Seminary is noted in part for having been destroyed by a tornado or whirlwind July 1, 1877. This institution of learning was established in 1851 by Smedley Darlington, as a boys' academy, but in 1854 it was changed to a school for girls. The building was a four-story structure and capable of accommodating about fifty pupils. It was conducted by its founder as a girls' school for about seven years, and then it passed into the hands of Richard Darlington, brother of Smedley. Richard Darlington, after viewing the ruins of his property caused by the storm, amounting to $9,500, decided that it would be best to change the location of his school, and purchased a valuable property, containing twenty-six acres of land, in the vicinity of West Chester, twelve miles east of its former location. Upon this property he erected buildings of the most approved character, and had more room for pupils than before. It was also believed that other advantages besides additional room would accrue to it, from its being more easy of access, and because of its being near to such a beautiful and well-situated town.

The grounds embrace twenty-seven acres of land, lying about three-fourths of a mile southwest of the court-house in West Chester, and are surrounded by a fine privet hedge. The buildings are four in number—one of stone, two of brick and one frame building containing the gymnasium. They are all connected by interior halls. The main school building is 45x60 feet in size and three stories high. The second building contains the dining-room, capable of seating from sixty to seventy pupils. The stone building contains the double parlors and office of the seminary, and the fourth or frame building, as stated, the gymnasium. The buildings, which are altogether 180 feet long, were erected expressly for school purposes, and contain all necessary modern improvements. They are all supplied with pure spring water by means of a windmill, which fills a tank in the upper part of the buildings. Excellent spring water is also forced up by a hydraulic ram to all the buildings.

The course of instruction comprises a thorough English education, together with the Latin, Greek, German and French languages. Music, drawing, crayoning, painting, in oil and water colors, are all taught. The Fuller Literary Society holds its meetings every week, and there is an excellent library of about 1,000 volumes, to which all students have access.

The electric railway (Lenape Branch) passes the grounds on the south, and has a station near and on purpose for the seminary.

Richard Darlington, Ph. D., is the Principal of the school, and is assisted by nine other teachers, seven of whom are ladies. The number of graduates since 1888 has been as follows: 1888, 6; 1889, 7; 1890, 10; 1891, 3; 1892, 10; 1893, 6; 1894, 6; 1895, 7; 1896, 10; 1897, 7.

The entire number of pupils that have attended this well-known institution since it was founded is about 2,500, some of whom have attained a wide reputation in the professions of teaching, medicine, law and literature, and they are living in nearly every State of the Union. The value of the school buildings, grounds and private dwellings on the property is more than $35,-000. This school has prepared a large number of pupils for admission to some of the leading colleges of the country, such as Wellesley, Vassar, Bryn Mawr, Swarthmore and others. It has all the features of a home school, yet its numbers give it the advantage of a large seminary. Regular courses of lectures are given on scientific and literary subjects, which are well attended and valuable. This is one of the oldest private institutions of its kind in Eastern Pennsylvania, a section widely known for its excellent private schools.

In 1865 William E. Buck of New Hampshire opened an academy at Atglen under the name of the Penn High School, which he conducted with constantly increasing success and efficiency for about five years. At first this school was kept in the basement of the Presbyterian Church, but, outgrowing its accommodations, it was found necessary by Mr. Buck to purchase adjoining grounds, which he did, and upon which he erected a two-story building, which gave ample room for his school during the remainder of his stay. Mr. Buck was an excellent scholar and a fine teacher and disciplinarian, and many young people for miles around were educated by him. After the death of his wife he gave up the school and returned to his native state, and has been for many years and is now the efficient superintendent of the city schools of Manchester, New Hampshire.

For a short time his school at Atglen was owned and conducted by a Mr. McClellan, who sold the property to the school directors of the village, and recently a new and modern-graded school building and school has taken the place of the former academy.

Still another private school was maintained at Penningtonville for many years by the late John M. Philips, father of Dr. Philips of the Normal School at West Chester. There being no public school in or near the village he erected a building at his own expense, and for a number of years engaged and paid a teacher for his own and for his neighbors' children. This school has been superseded also by public schools of more recent date.

The history of the public schools in Chester County must be briefly traced. Some of these common schools were at first kept in the session-houses of the churches, but at a later period houses were built on purpose for their accommodation. These early district school-houses were either of logs or stone, and sometimes they were in octagonal form, and then were called eight-square school-houses. The desks were placed around the outside of the interior of the building, the children sitting with their faces to the walls. Benches without backs were placed in the middle of the room for the smaller pupils, there was a desk for the teacher, a large stove in the middle of the room, and there was a "pass," which was a small paddle with the words "in" on one side, and "out" on the other. The early teachers were often characters in their way. One of them named Abel Wickersham was the proprietor of a remarkable book, called "Synopsis Mathematica Universalis," or

"Brief System of Mathematics for Young Students." It included chapters on Arithmetic, Geometry, Trigonometry, Astronomy, Dialling, Chronometry, Geography, Optics, Catoptrics, Dioptrics and Statics. It was printed in London, England, in 1729. There were in these early public schools no female teachers, young women scarcely considering it respectable to teach school, or at least they avoided the profession, in part possibly because of the difficulty of governing the boys in those earlier days. The teachers were then paid by the parents and guardians of the pupils, the schools being conducted upon the subscription plan.

The earliest schools of this kind were established by the Friends. In 1753 they purchased an acre of ground in Willistown for school purposes, and there was a school set up by the Bradford, New Garden and Kennett Monthly Meetings, jointly, sometime before 1781. There was also a joint school established about the same time by Goshen, Bradford and Birmingham meetings, these meetings purchasing four acres of ground one-half mile west of West Chester, where the walls still stood until recently, to mark the spot where the school-house was erected more than one hundred years ago. There was also a house for a public school of this kind erected on the northwest corner of the property belonging to the Brandywine Manor Presbyterian church, which was 28x18 feet in size, had two doors in front, which faced the south, and was divided by a swinging partition. One division of the room was used for the common school and the other for the classical school. It stood within three hundred yards of where three townships joined, these three townships constituting the eighth election district, and elections were held therein from 1798 to 1814. This was the first stone school-house built in that part of Chester County, most school-houses being built of logs.

While the history of the efforts of the State to establish common schools supported out of the State Treasury is exceedingly interesting, yet it cannot be traced in this work, except very briefly, and, in fact, can be scarcely more than referred to for want of propriety and space. The constitution of 1790 contains the following section:

"The Legislature shall, as soon as conveniently may be, provide by law for the establishment of schools throughout the State, in such a manner that the poor may be taught gratis."

This section was incorporated into the constitution of 1838, and is the basis of the common school system of the State. The first law under this provision of the constitution was enacted in 1802, but it was soon found inadequate to the requirements of a system of public education, and another act was passed in 1804. This act was but little better than the former, and in 1809 another act was passed, which was more carefully drawn, and found to work out better results. This act required "the assessors in each and every township, ward and district to receive from the parents the names of all children between the ages of five and twelve years, who reside therein, and whose parents are unable to pay for their schooling." These names were to be placed on the township transcripts, and the lists, after revision, were returned to the assessors, whose duty it was to notify the parents of the children to what schools they should be sent.

The townships which are here named reported poor children in 1810: Brandywine, 3; East Bradford, 15; West Bradford, 2; London Britain, 4; East Caln, 6; Charlestown, 39; Coventry, 5; Londonderry, 6; West Chester, 7; East Fallowfield, 8; Goshen, 15; Londongrove, 3; New Garden, 5; Honeybrook, 12; Newlin, 5; East Marlborough, 16; East Nottingham, 3; Upper Oxford, 7; Lower Oxford, 21; Pennsbury, 1; Sadsbury, 3; Easttown, 4; Westtown, 11; East Whiteland, 6; West Whiteland, 20. The following reported in 1811 as follows: Birmingham, 4; West Marlborough, 3; Thornbury, 3; Tredyffrin, 10; Uwchlan, 3, and Willistown, 2. In 1812: West Caln, 3; New London, 18; East Nantmeal, 12; West Nantmeal, 7, and West Nottingham, 2. In 1813: West Fallowfield reported 3 and Kennett 8. In 1811 East and West Vincent reported 8, and in 1812, East and West Pikeland reported 4. The total number thus reported in the county was 304.

The law under which such reports as the above were required to be made was unpopular, as it compelled the parents to publicly record their poverty and to send their children to "pauper schools." Even public schools, to which all the children were permitted to be sent, have thus been branded, while the people were prejudiced against them. And it is altogether likely this act of 1809, together with those enacted previously, tended to increase the prejudice against public education than otherwise. At any rate the struggle for and against such a system was maintained with vigor for many years, and it was not until 1834 that an act was passed that had in it the elements of success. It is not unreasonable to attribute a part of the opposition to a system of public education to the various religious denominations that were in those days sustaining schools in which children were being taught at the least possible expense. These semi-public schools were maintained in large part for the purpose of inculcating certain religious tenets in the minds of the young, and it was clear to many of those who desired their children to be brought up Friends, or Presbyterians, or Baptists, or Episcopalians, or Methodists, that in a public school, where children of parents of various denominations were collected together, that no one particular system of religion or faith could be taught to the exclusion of others; for this would be unjust to those who entertained the other system of belief, and it would be equally impracticable to teach all systems, for that would be to divert the entire school system from an educational force to a religious one, and would result in the greatest possible confusion even in this field of instruction. The only possible course, therefore, with reference to religious instruction, would be to exclude everything of a sectarian or denominational nature, which would render the schools non-religious, to say the least, and it might render them even irreligious.

But as time passed on it became more and more evident to the most intelligent of the citizens that a public school system was a real necessity. Free schools were in the public mind, and they must be established. In 1833-34 therefore the State took more active measures than before to put such a system into operation. At the commencement of the session of those years, on motion of Samuel Breck of Philadelphia a joint committee was appointed, which was charged with the duty of framing a general system of education for the commonwealth. Dr. Wilmer Worthington was the Chester County member of this committee from the lower house, and at the same time Elijah J. Pennypacker was a member of the Legislature from Chester County. The act framed by this joint committee was passed by the Legislature, and was entitled, "An Act to Establish a General System of Education by Common Schools." It was approved April 1, 1834, but it did not get into operation without long and bitter opposition. The details of this struggle cannot be here traced, but it may be stated further with reference to the opposition with which it met that different classes of the people fought it for widely different reasons, and what is perhaps what is most remarkable is that those needed free schools the most fought it with the greatest bitterness.

At that time there were 987 school districts in the State, and when the question of accepting the law was submitted to a vote, of these 987 districts 502 accepted it, 264 rejected it, 57 were not represented and 164 made no return. Chester County was then divided into forty-four districts, of which seventeen accepted the law and twenty-seven rejected it. But the Governor of the State, George Wolf, was a firm and steadfast friend of the law, and did much in aid of its proper enforcement.

During the succeeding session of the Legislature petitions went up from all over the State for the repeal of the law, and for its modification, as well as many remonstrances against its repeal or modification. Chester County was on both sides of this question, as might naturally be expected; but it was found by careful count that in the entire Commonwealth about 32,000 persons petitioned for repeal, and 2,084 for some modification of the law. It was also found and given out as a curious fact that "not more than five names in every hundred were written in English," and most of those signed to the petitions for repeal were very illegibly written. Chester County sent up forty petitions, containing 2,261 names, asking for repeal, but the final result was that a bill was passed strengthening the act of 1834, and from that time on there was never any doubt as to the attitude of Pennsylvania on the free school question. It was a great, even a magnificent, victory that was won for free schools, for the intelligence of the people at large, instead of for the education of classes, and it appears to be generally conceded that to no man is more credit due than to Thaddeus Stevens, then a member of the lower house of the Legislature, who then for the first time gave an exhibition of his masterly strength. This is the opinion of Elijah J. Pennypacker, mentioned before as one of the members from Chester County, who was himself also a steadfast friend of free education in the State. The following paragraph presents the number of children reported in each township in Chester County in 1835, and the year in which each township adopted the free school law :

East Caln, 68, 1836; Schuylkill, 43, 1836; West Bradford, 37, 1837; East Fallowfield, 68, 1837; West Caln, 71, 1837; West Nantmeal, 51, 1837; in 1838, West Chester 115, Honeybrook 80, East Marlborough 50, East Whiteland 30, West Marlborough 59, Willistown 49, West Nottingham 31, West Fallowfield 76, West Vincent 22; in 1839, Goshen 101, Londongrove 21, New Garden 87. East Nottingham 108, Uwchlan 45, East Nantmeal 126; in 1840, London Britain 22, Coventry 92, Thornbury 9, Tredyffrin 87, East Vincent 36; in 1841, Brandywine 111, Charlestown 48, Londonderry 26, Newlin 37, Upper Oxford 74, Lower Oxford 51, Pennsbury 51, Sadsbury 110, West Whiteland 43, Birmingham 16, New London

ROXBOROUGH HOME FOR WOMEN.

84, Kennett 45, Penn 45, East Pikeland and West Pikeland 45; in 1843, East Bradford 79, Westtown 31, Easttown 48.

From the time of its successful establishment on through the years public sentiment steadily and even rapidly grew and strengthened in its favor; and it was further seen, or at least thought, that the State could afford to aid higher institutions of learning. In this movement Chester County was not behind other counties in the State. Her representative, William H. Dillingham, introduced a bill in the house, as did also Thaddeus Stevens of Adams County, making a liberal appropriation for ten years to incorporate colleges and academies, that is, such as were able to comply with certain easy conditions.

Chester County was the birthplace of Townsend Haines, who was secretary of the Commonwealth, and Superintendent of Common Schools during the latter portion of the term of Governor Johnston. As Superintendent of Common Schools Mr. Haines made two reports, in which he objected to the short terms of the district schools, then less than five months in the year; and to the low salaries paid teachers, male teachers receiving then on the average $17.27 per month, and females $10.25 per month. He suggested for the evils then existing an increased school tax, and to cure the apathy of the people he suggested periodical conventions of teachers in the several counties. In his second report he complained among other things of the incapacity of the teachers, and of the improper selection of school books, of the want of funds, and of the absence of some direct and intelligible communication between the school directors and the State Superintendent of Schools. To remedy these defects he suggested the establishment of the county superintendency of schools, and the normal school connected with central high schools.

But, notwithstanding all the work that had been done up to 1848, and the widespread public sentiment that had by that time grown up in favor of the system, yet there were still in Chester

24

County a few districts that had not accepted it. These districts were East Bradford, North Coventry, Kennett, Westtown and West Vincent. In this year, a provision of the law making appropriations, repealed all laws concerning non-accepting school districts, and made the common school law applicable to every school district in the State. Afterward one by one of the nearly two hundred non-accepting school districts put schools into operation within their limits, and by 1868 there were only twenty-three districts in the State, with about 6,000 school children, that had no common schools in operation.

The law of 1849, while it marked no new departure with reference to educational affairs, was yet a step in advance, as it prohibited teachers from teaching without a certificate enumerating the branches they had been found capable of teaching, the certificate to be signed by a majority of the board of directors conducting the examination; and it increased the minimum length of time during which schools should be kept open from three to four months. It also fixed the school age as being from five years to twenty-one. This bill was introduced into the House by Henry S. Evans of Chester County.

"In 1855 an act of Assembly was passed establishing a teachers' institute in Chester County, requiring one to be held each year at the county seat, and appropriating from the county treasury annually two hundred dollars for that purpose. This was a step in advance of any other county, and has rendered the institutes more efficient than they otherwise would have been." *

From the beginning of the public school system the Secretary of State was the Superintendent of Common Schools for the State up to 1857, on the 18th of April of which year an act was approved which provided for the separation of the two offices, and for the appointment of a Superintendent of Common Schools, who should hold his office for three years.

---

* Futhey and Cope's History of Chester County.

Previously to this time it became apparent that more efficient county superintendency was required, if the people were to receive the full benefits of the system in the thorough education of the young, and as a consequence an act was approved May 8, 1854, "For the regulation and continuance of a System of Education by Common Schools," Section 37 of which is as follows:

"Section 37. That there shall be chosen in the manner hereafter directed an officer for each county, to be called the County Superintendent. It shall be his duty to visit as often as practicable the several schools of the county, and to note the course and method of instruction and branches taught, and to give such directions in the art of teaching and the method thereof in each school as to him, together with the directors or controllers, shall be deemed expedient and necessary; so that each school shall be equal to the grade for which it was established, and that there may be, as far as practicable, uniformity in the course of study of the several grades respectively."

Section 38 provided that it should be the duty of each county superintendent to see that in every district there were taught orthography, reading, writing, English grammar, geography and arithmetic, "as well as such other branches as the board of directors or controllers may require."

Section 39 provided that the school directors of each county should meet in convention at the seat of justice of their respective counties on the first Monday (5th) of June, 1854, and on the first of May (in 1866 changed to the first Tuesday of May), in each third year thereafter, and select viva voce, by a majority vote of those present, one person of literary and scientific acquirements and of skill and experience in the art of teaching as County Superintendent for three successive school years. The school directors by a majority vote in such convention were also authorized to fix the salary of the superintendent.

Section 41 made it the duty of the County Superintendent to

examine all the candidates for the profession of teaching, in the presence of the board of directors, should they desire to be present, and to give each person found qualified a certificate setting forth the branches said candidate was found capable of teaching.

Under this law the following gentlemen have been County Superintendents of Schools in Chester County: R. Agnew Futhey, 1854 to 1857; Dr. Franklin Taylor, 1857 to 1860; W. W. Woodruff, 1860 to 1869; George L. Maris, 1869 to 1872; Hiram F. Pierce, 1872 to January, 1877, when he died; Jacob W. Harvey, appointed February 1, 1877, and served until 1887; Joseph S. Walton, 1887 to September, 1896, when he resigned and F. P. Bye was appointed and has served ever since.

As in the case of the Common School System itself, when it was first proposed, it was strongly opposed, so in case of the county superintendency, it likewise met with lively opposition. It would appear that in the economy of human nature, all innovations have to demonstrate their fitness before they become acceptable to mankind. Those who opposed the county superintendency were divisible into two classes—First, those who considered themselves fully competent to examine the teachers, and who were jealous of the new officer; and second, those who thought the office useless and that the salary of the new official should be added to the school fund.

Through the judicious conduct of the first County Superintendent the opposition gradually subsided. He gradually surmounted all the difficulties that he encountered, held the first county institutes and left the ground comparatively clear for Dr. Taylor, his immediate successor. Mr. Futhey held seven teachers' institutes, each lasting a week. There were then in the county sixty-two school districts, and 292 schools.

So far as the County Superintendents are concerned it would appear that Dr. Taylor held the first special Normal School in the county, opening it on Monday, May 3, 1858, in connection with

F. A. Allen and Dr. E. Harvey, in the borough of West Chester. This normal school lasted twenty weeks, and there were forty-six teachers in attendance.

In 1860 there were still twenty-four private schools in existence, attended by 1,250 students. Phœnixville that year completed two very superior school buildings, capable of accommodating 800 pupils. In 1861 two graded schools were established, one at West Chester, the other at Phœnixville. In 1862 there were in the county 172 male teachers, the number in 1859 having been 174; and in 1862 there were 223 female teachers, the number in 1859 having been 175. In 1863 two school-houses in the county were heated from below, the stoves being placed in the cellar and surrounded by non-conducting substances. During this year there were engaged only 152 male teachers, on account of so many of them having gone off to the war, and there were 243 female teachers. In the year 1868, besides the two graded schools mentioned above, there were such schools in Coatesville, Downingtown, Kennett Square, and Oxford, and there were schools partially graded in Marshallton, Sugartown, Unionville and Waynesburg. In October, 1867, the most useful institute so far held was held in the county.

During the nine years of Professor Woodruff's incumbency of the office of County Superintendent there were erected 100 new school buildings, at a cost of about $150,000; during that period the number of schools increased from 304 to 335; the pupils increased from 16,032 to 17,628; the length of the school year increased from 7.41 months to 8 months, and the average salary of the male teachers increased from $26.22 to $36.50 per month, while that of the female teachers increased from $22.09 to $33.04 per month. The highest salary paid any teacher in the county in 1860 was $80 per month, while in 1869 the highest salary paid any male teacher was $111.11. The highest salary paid any female teacher in 1860 was $30 per month, while in 1869 it had increased to $110.

During the school year 1869-70 there were erected eleven new school-houses in the county, the finest one of the eleven being at Kennett Square. This was a two-story structure, with four large assembly rooms and the same number of convenient class-rooms. The yard contained two and a half acres of gently-sloping land, and according to Mr. Maris, then superintendent, the building was better suited to its purposes than any other in the county. The entire property was worth $10,000. Of the eleven erected that year the one at Waynesburg came next, worth $5,100.

The high school at West Chester in June, 1869, graduated a class of seven members, the course of study embracing Latin, German, French, algebra, geometry, botany, physiology, and natural philosophy. This event marked a new era in the educational history of Chester County. Phœnixville, Coatesville and Oxford had adopted similar courses of study. A teachers' institute was held in West Chester in October, 1869, at which there were present 492 teachers, and there were present as instructors, among other distinguished men, Theodore Tilton, Wayne MacVeagh, and Dr. Isaac I. Hayes.

The schools of Honeybrook, West Nantmeal and Sadsbury were graded during the year ending June 5, 1871. The annual institute for that year was held in October, 1870, and among the distinguished instructors and lecturers present were Hon. E. E. White of Ohio, Prof. Lewis B. Monroe and Prof. E. D. Cope. There were numerous local institutes held, at which among other distinguished men were present Prof. James McCosh, Bayard Taylor, M. Brosius, W. W. Woodruff and T. Clarkson Taylor.

During the winter of 1873-74 there was opened a night school for the factory children of Bondsville, Fisherville and the vicinity, in the Chestnut Dell school, of Caln District, ladies and gentlemen of the neighborhood volunteering their services as teachers.

About 1883 the question of teaching temperance in the public schools began to attract attention, and has since then been continned. There were then 380 public schools in the county, and forty-eight private schools having an attendance of 1,900 students. During the year 1887-88 originated the formation of directors' as sociations, and the attempt was made to form a teachers' organization by dividing the county into thirteen districts, and the thorough introduction of a graded course of study in the rural schools. The school directors effected a permanent organization, which was to meet semi-annually, the first chairman being William W. Parker, and the first secretary being Edwin J. Durnall. It had an executive committee of nine, the principal of the Normal School and the county superintendent being members ex-officio. By 1889 seven of the rural districts had adopted the graded course of study. The Berwyn School-house, built this year, was considered the model school-house of the county. By 1890 fifty-two of the sixty-eight school districts in the county furnished the text books free of cost, and all but three or four of the remainder furnished them at not more than one-half or two-thirds cost. By 1891 manual training had been introduced into eleven of the schools, mostly in the country districts.

By 1893 Tredyffrin had established a township grammar school, and had given the local supervision of the schools in the township to the principal, Richard S. Macnamee, who holds the position at the present time. Easttown has done the same thing, and at the present time J. Alexander Clarke of Berwyn is the district superintendent. The West Chester Public Schools are in charge of a superintendent, at present Addison Jones, and the Phœnixville Public Schools are managed in the same manner by H. F. Leister. The rest of the borough schools in the county are conducted by supervising principals.

The graded school system during the past twenty years has been slowly but steadily gaining ground, and at the present time the demand for systematizing the work is stronger than ever before. A general outline prepared under the direction of the

County Directors' Association is used over the greater part of the county. Each township makes such modifications in the general plan as are necessary to adapt it to its special needs. Graduates in the elementary course are given diplomas which are uniform throughout the county, the examinations sent out from the office of the County Superintendent having been satisfactorily passed. A feature of the work lately introduced which is giving general satisfaction is the requirement of some specific work in English. Besides a general knowledge of American and English literature each candidate is required to be familiar with certain English classics announced at the beginning of the year.

The Chester County Teachers' Association is a purely representative body, its work being to direct the operations of the district association throughout the county. Of these there are thirteen, each of which reports annually to the general association. This organization has in it great possibilities, which are being developed and appreciated more and more as time goes on.

The Chester County School Directors' Association was organized in February, 1888, Isaac A. Cleaver of Berwyn being the first president and Edwin J. Durnall the first secretary. This is an exceedingly strong organization, and is a powerful instrument in the work of unifying and advancing the schools of the county. It is one of the most efficient associations in the State, and has received special mention by the State Superintendent of Common Schools. The two meetings held each year are well attended, all parts of the county being represented. The efficiency of the present officers, President Isaac Richards of New Garden and Secretary John L. Balderston of Kennett Township, is sufficiently attested by the fact that they are now serving a third term.

Several years ago a few of the principals of the county held a meeting to discuss methods of school supervision, as it had been felt for years that the local and county institutes did not reach the duties of the principal. It was thought, too, that all would be benefited by an interchange of views regarding the courses of study, methods of teaching, means of supervision and discipline. As a result of the meeting mentioned there is now the organization known as the Principals' Association of Chester County, which meets at stated intervals during the year, at which subjects of interest are discussed. Someone is appointed to open the discussion with a short paper, and the members make reports or ask questions as they see fit. A prominent feature of all the meetings is the absence of set speeches, while the topics placed before the association are such as to prompt nearly all the members to take part in the discussion. All the principals of the county are eligible to membership.

The Chester County Teachers' Association, at its annual meeting during the Institute week in the autumn of 1896, organized the Teachers' Professional Society for the improvement of its members, and through their improvement the improvement of the county schools. Although many of the teachers of the county take Saturday work at schools in West Chester and Philadelphia, and under tutors, yet there are many to whom these means of self-improvement are not available, and to those who cannot reach the professional school the school has been taken. A committee of leading local educators conducts a correspondence course in professional study, in which the tuition fee is but twenty-five cents per year, and each teacher taking the course invests in two or three good books bearing on the work of the course taken. During the school year 1898-99 the County Institute and the Professional Society will be merged along the same lines of work, thus turning the entire corps of teachers in the county, four hundred and fifty in number, into a great professional society. In other words the themes of the Institute lectures will follow lines laid down by the society, and the society, on the other hand, will amplify and re-enforce the work of the County Institute. Four courses will be open to the teachers from which they may select their professional line of work. Subjects for themes will be announced by the instructors who will examine the papers prepared by the teachers. The preparation of these themes will form a part of the work of the society. At the end of each year the society faculty issues a certificate setting forth the work done by the holder thereof.

The Circulating Library is the result of an agitation carried on of late years within the county, but there was no general movement looking toward a solution of the problem until the summer of 1897. A plan was evolved by the present County Superintendent, Frank P. Bye, which combines a maximum of circulation with a minimum of cost. At a meeting in the office of the superintendent in West Chester, representatives from nearly all parts of the county being present, an organization was effected under the name of the Public School Circulating Library of Chester County and Superintendent Bye's plan adopted. The fundamental principle on which it is based is that of co-operation in the purchase or use of books. David C. Windle of West Chester was made president; Watson W. Dewees of Westtown, treasurer, and Superintendent Frank P. Bye, secretary and librarian. The headquarters are in the Superintendent's office in the court-house, where books may be obtained or exchanged at any time. The reading itself is to a considerable extent directed from this office. This library system has met with general approval and has been endorsed unanimously by the Directors' Association.

From the annual report of the County Superintendent of Schools for 1897, the following statistics are obtained: Whole number of schools, 436; average number of months taught, 8.59; number of male teachers, 63; number of female teachers, 396; average salary of male teachers, $54.48; average salary of female teachers, $39.42; number of male scholars, 9,191; number of female scholars, 8,767; average number attending school, 12,549; average per cent. of attendance, 86; cost per month of educating each pupil, $1.37; total amount of taxes levied for school and building purposes, $181,736.25; receipts from State appropriation, $89,-977.77; receipts from taxes and all other sources aside from State appropriation, $250,507.90; total receipts, $340,485.67; teachers' salaries, $169,339.58; total expenses, $320,337.84.

In 1895 what is known as the "Massachusetts System" of consolidating country schools and transportating pupils to a central school at public expense, was introduced into Tredyffrin Township.

The system has for its purpose the closing and abandoning of one-teacher-country schools, and supplying in their place large, well-equipped buildings, in which thoroughly graded and classified consolidated schools may be established, to the end that rural education may be broadened, the usefulness of country schools greatly increased, and many of the educational advantages now enjoyed almost exclusively by towns and cities may be extended to rural sections.

This movement had its origin in the generally recognized fact that the demand upon ungraded country schools are increasing more rapidly than it is possible to meet them in the old way; that the small, ungraded school is an expensive one, and that there is not only economy in "centralization," but that it furnishes the only means by which sufficient numbers can be brought together in the country to make proper grading and thorough classification of pupils possible.

The circumstances leading to its adoption by Tredyffrin Township were as follows: An increasing population in the neighborhood or vicinity of Devon led to the establishment of a new public school in a private dwelling; but in 1893 a new double school building was erected at Strafford on the site of the old Eagle school, which had then recently been destroyed by fire. The Devon school and the old Eagle school were then consolidated in this new double building, and the school was henceforth called

"Strafford School." But on account of the distance of this school from Devon, and of the fact that there was a sufficient number of children in that vicinity to support a school, the school board was asked, two years later, to re-establish a school at or near Devon.

The friends of consolidation advocated the enlarging of the Strafford school building instead, and the establishment of the free transportation of the Devon pupils, in order that by the employment of another teacher and the establishment of another division in the Strafford school, the advantages to be derived therefrom might be enjoyed by both sections. The directors, fully impressed with the merits of the latter plan, adopted it, and during the first week in September, 1895, the transportation of the pupils from the Devon district was begun. It is worthy of note that while the entire school board was sufficiently imbued with the spirit of progress to favor this important step in the educational affairs of that township, yet it was due largely to the intelligent advocacy of the plan by the secretary of the board, S. C. Weadley, that sufficient sentiment was molded to carry the system into successful operation.

Three years' experience with the system in that township has confirmed the wisdom of those directors in its adoption; for it has not only proved itself to be practicable, and shown that in point of economy, grading, classification and teaching facilities it possesses the merits claimed for it by its friends, but it indicates the way to a satisfactory solution of the great problem of improved rural school facilities, which problem is forcing itself more and more persistently, year by year, upon the minds of those who have the interests and welfare of the country school districts at heart, and upon whom the responsibility of their continued and increasing usefulness rests.*

---

* This article of Transportation was prepared for this work by Professor R. S. Macnamee, of Strafford.

Miss Susan Gorgas, born in Wilmington, Delaware, April 23, 1845, is a member of a family long noted for their philanthropic and charitable deeds. Her father, John Gorgas, was born May 11, 1804, and her mother, Ann (Wills) Gorgas, December 17, 1807. The latter died August 6, 1848, and the former, July 30, 1869. Both lie buried in Brandywine Cemetery, Wilmington, Delaware. Samuel Gorgas, grandfather of Miss Susan Gorgas, died October 2, 1857, and her grandmother, Susanna Gorgas, died April 18, 1845. Her uncle, Samuel Gorgas, Jr., died April 3, 1868, at the age of fifty-seven years, and her aunt, Margaret Gorgas, died July 30, 1884, in her seventy-seventh year. Her uncle, Matthias Gorgas, died January 3, 1885, and her aunt, Susan Gorgas, died March 29, 1892.

Mr. John Gorgas removed from Wilmington to West Chester in 1864. His daughter, Susan, attended the school of Miss W. Anna Hoopes, at 1409 Locust street, Philadelphia, and remained there six years, returning to West Chester in 1864. In 1874-75 she made a tour of Europe, visiting the British Isles, France, Germany, Switzerland and Italy. Miss Gorgas has lived mostly with her aunt, Miss Sarah W. Wills, at No. 100 South High street, West Chester, Miss Wills being eighty-one years old July 4, 1898.

It is not an uncommon thing to find generous and large-hearted women, who, blessed with abundant means, take delight in helping those who are needy. Miss Gorgas lives an unostentatious and quiet life, devoting herself to the service of others. The ancient home at Roxborough has been occupied by four generations of her family, and is still owned by her. It is a beautiful and romantic spot, full of Revolutionary memories, fragrant with Philadelphia and Germantown associations. In this home Miss Gorgas spends a portion of every summer, where the Wissahickon waters her fruitful lands. The stone house in which her maternal great-grandfather, Andrew Wood, once lived still stands in Roxborough, and the barn attached thereto was occupied by the British soldiers during their sojourn in Philadelphia.

Samuel and Margaret Gorgas (brother and sister), uncle and aunt of Miss Susan Gorgas, gave an endowment fund of $160,000 to the Roxborough Home for Indigent Women, and which was erected in 1887. To the erection of this building Miss Gorgas gave $15,000, and has always taken a deep interest in its success. Seventeen women, mostly residents of the neighborhood, find therein a comfortable and secure retreat in their declining years. The Home occupies a beautiful site upon Levering Avenue, overlooking the waters of the Wissahickon. Miss Gorgas is the president of the Board of Managers.

Miss Gorgas also takes a warm interest in the work of Lincoln University, and secured the erection of Livingston Hall. In this hall commencements are held, and it has been a most useful adjunct to the school. The Home for Incurables, and the Episcopal Hospital, in the city of Philadelphia, have each a bed endowed by Miss Gorgas.

Gorgas Park on Ridge Avenue, Roxborough, containing about five acres of ground, was presented by her in 1893 to the City of Philadelphia. This park has since been enlarged by the addition thereto of adjoining properties. Miss Gorgas is a member of Holy Trinity Episcopal Church, West Chester, and has ever been a generous patron of its charities and has contributed largely to its building fund.

CHAPTER XI.
POLITICS.

CHARLTON LEWIS.

CHAPTER XI.

POLITICS—GOVERNMENT UNDER PENN—THE COLONIAL ASSEMBLY—THE SEVERAL
CONSTITUTIONS—MEMBERS OF THE ASSEMBLY—THE EARLY CONGRESSES—
REPRESENTATION OF CHESTER COUNTY—MEMBERS OF CONGRESS—
JOHN MORTON—SENATORS—PROMINENT POLITICIANS OF
THE COUNTY—ELECTORS—POLITICAL CHANGES—
CONVENTIONS—MEMBERS OF THE COUNCIL
—COUNTY OFFICERS—RECENT CON-
VENTIONS—POPULATION OF
THE COUNTY.

THE form of government prepared by William Penn for the government of his Province was somewhat unique, especially as compared with the forms of government now in existence in the several States and in the United States itself. Under Penn's form of government there was to be but one legislative body, which was called the Assembly, and the executive branch consisted of a Governor and a Council. The Assembly was to consist of not less than 200 nor more than 500 persons. The first Assembly elected under writs issued by William Penn to the sheriffs of the several counties convened at Chester, December 4, 1682, and this is the only meeting of the Assembly within the ancient limits of Chester County.

The second Assembly, which convened at Philadelphia, March 12, 1683, consisted of nine members from each county, in the writ calling for the election of members of this Assembly, Penn having directed the election of twelve members of the Council. Each county, however, sent twelve persons, requesting that nine of them might serve in the Assembly and three in the Council. During the

25

session of this second Assembly a new frame of government was prepared, according to which the Assembly was to consist of not less than thirty-six persons, six from each county, nor more than two hundred, and that it should meet annually on May 10.

From this time to 1703 the number of members from Chester County in the Assembly varied from three to six, and from 1703 to 1776 the number was usually eight. Under the constitution adopted in 1776 the number of members from each county for the years 1776, 1777 and 1778 was six, and afterward according to the population, to be determined by the Assembly itself. In 1779 the number was increased to eight, so remaining until 1786, when it was again reduced to six, and in 1789, on the creation of Delaware County, Chester County had four members, while Delaware County had two.

A new constitution was adopted in 1790, which provided that within three years after the first meeting of the General Assembly there should be an enumeration of the taxable inhabitants of each county, and that the members of the two houses created by that constitution should be apportioned according to the number of taxables. This enumeration and apportionment were to be made every seven years thereafter, the number of members from each county to remain the same until the first enumeration and apportionment were made. Chester County therefore had four members in the Assembly until 1895, and under the first apportionment she had five. In 1822 the number was reduced to four; in 1843 it was reduced to three, and in 1871 to two. In 1874 the number again became four.

The members from Chester County in the Assembly, so far as can be ascertained, have been as follows from 1682 to the present time:

1682.—John Simcock, Thomas Brassey, Ralph Withers, Thomas Usher.

1683.—John Hastings, Robert Wade, George Wood, John Blunston, Dennis Rochford, Thomas Brassey, John Bezer, John Harding, Joseph Phipps.

1684.—Joshua Hastings, Robert Wade, John Blunston, George Maris, Thomas Usher, Henry Maddock.

1685.—John Blunston, George Maris, John Harding, Thomas Usher, Francis Stanfield, Josiah Fearn.

1686.—Robert Wade, John Blunston, George Maris, Bartholomew Coppock, Samuel Lewis, Caleb Pusey.

1687.—John Blunston, George Maris, Bartholomew Coppock, Caleb Pusey, Edward Bezer, Randall Vernon.

1688.—John Blunston, James Sandelands, George Maris, Robert Pyle, Edward Carter, Thomas Coeburn.

1689.—James Sandelands, Samuel Levis, John Bartram, Robert Pyle, Michael Blunston, Jonathan Hayes.

1690.—John Bristow, William Jenkin, Robert Pyle, Joshua Fearn, George Maris, Caleb Pusey.

1692.—Philip Roman, George Maris, Bartholomew Coppock, Robert Pyle, Caleb Pusey, Thomas Withers.

1693.—John Simcock, George Maris, David Lloyd.

1694.—David Lloyd, Caleb Pusey, Samuel Levis.

1695.—John Blunston, Bartholomew Coppock, William Jenkin, Robert Pyle, Walter Forest, Philip Roman.

1696.—John Simcock (Speaker), John Blunston, Caleb Pusey.

1697.—John Blunston (Speaker), Bartholomew Coppock, Thomas Worth, Jonathan Hayes.

1698.—Caleb Pusey, Samuel Levis, Nathaniel Newlin, Robert Carter.

1699.—John Blunston (Speaker), Robert Pyle, John Worrilow, Robert Carter.

1700.—John Blunston (Speaker), Robert Pyle, Richard Ormes, John Hood, Samuel Levis, Henry Lewis.

1700.—Elected October 14: Joseph Baker, Samuel Levis, Nathaniel Newlin, Nicholas Pyle.

1701.—John Blunston, Robert Pyle, Nathaniel Newlin, Andrew Job.

1703.—Nicholas Pyle, John Bennett, Andrew Job, David Lewis, Nathaniel Newlin, Joseph Baker, Robert Carter, Robert Wood.

1704.—Nicholas Pyle, John Bennett, Nicholas Fairlamb, Joseph Coebourn, John Hood, Richard Hayes, Joseph Wood, Isaac Taylor.

1705.—Robert Pyle, Richard Webb, Caleb Pusey, Nicholas Fairlamb, John Bennett, Isaac Taylor, Nathaniel Newlin, Joseph Coebourn.

1706.—Samuel Levis, Richard Hayes, Francis Chadds, Joseph Baker, Evan Lewis, John Hood, George Pearce, William Garrett.

1707.—Francis Chadds, William Smith, Samuel Levis, Richard Hayes, John Hood, William Garrett, John Bethell, Evan Lewis.

1708.—Daniel Williamson, Samuel Levis, Henry Lewis, Richard Hayes, John Hood, Thomas Pearson, William Bartram, Daniel Hoopes.

1709.—Samuel Levis, John Maris, John Hood, Henry Lewis, Daniel Williamson, Daniel Hoopes, Richard Hayes, William Smith.

1710.—Nicholas Pyle, Joseph Pyle, William Lewis, John Wood, Nathaniel Newlin, Ephraim Jackson, Caleb Pusey, Isaac Taylor.

1711.—Francis Yarnall, John Bezer, Caleb Pusey, Nicholas Pyle, Nathaniel Newlin, Joseph Baker, Nicholas Fairlamb, David Llewelin.

1712.—Caleb Pusey, David Lloyd, William Davis, Nicholas Fairlamb, John Wood, George Harlan, Isaac Taylor, John Maris.

1713.—David Lloyd, William Davis, Joseph Baker, Nathaniel Newlin, Nicholas Fairlamb, Richard Hayes, William Brinton, John Blunston, Jr.

1714.—David Lloyd (Speaker), Nathaniel Newlin, Nicholas Pyle, Evan Lewis, John Miller (died and was succeeded by Gayen Miller), Benjamin Mendenhall, Samuel Garrett, Richard Maris.

1715.—David Lloyd, Samuel Garrett, Henry Lewis, Henry Hayes, William Pyle, Edward Bezer, Philip Taylor, David Lewis.

1716.—David Lloyd, John Blunston, Jr., Henry Hayes, Joseph Pennock, David Harry, John Maris, John Worrall, Henry Oborn.

1717.—David Lloyd, Nathaniel Newlin, Richard Hayes, Samuel Garrett, James Gibbons, John Wood, George Maris, Henry Miller.

1718.—David Lloyd, Richard Hayes, Nathaniel Newlin, John Wright, James Gibbons, Henry Lewis, William Lewis, Henry Oborn.

1719.—Isaac Taylor, Joseph Pennock, Moses Key, John Bezer, Nathaniel Newlin, John Maris, James Gibbons, Evan Lewis.

1720.—Joseph Pennock, Samuel Levis, Jr., Isaac Taylor, Israel Taylor, John Maris, Ralph Pyle, Daniel Williamson, David Lewis.

1721.—Samuel Levis, Jr., William Pyle, Daniel Williamson, Isaac Taylor, David Lewis, Henry Oborn, Nathaniel Newlin, Israel Taylor.

1722.—Samuel Levis, Jr., Joseph Pennock, David Lewis, William Pyle, Daniel Williamson, Israel Taylor, Nathaniel Newlin, Isaac Taylor.

1723.—Thomas Chandler, Samuel Levis, Jr., Samuel Nutt, John Crosby, Moses Key, William Webb, Joseph Pennock, David Lloyd.

1724.—Moses Key, Joseph Pennock, William Webb, William Pyle,

Thomas Chandler, Elisha Gatchell, John Parry, John Crosby.

1725.—David Lloyd (Speaker), Thomas Chandler, William Webb, John Wright, Samuel Hollingsworth, William Pusey, George Ashton, William Paschall.

1726.—David Lloyd (Speaker), Samuel Nutt, Samuel Hollingsworth, John Wright, Richard Hayes, Joseph Pennock, Thomas Chandler, William Pusey.

1727.—John Parry, Samuel Hollingsworth, David Lloyd, Thomas Chandler, John Carter, Daniel Williamson (died and was succeeded by Philip Taylor), Simon Meredith, William Webb.

1728.—David Lloyd (Speaker), Thomas Chandler, Samuel Hollingsworth, John Parry, William Webb, Philip Taylor, John Carter, Henry Hayes.

1729.—Caleb Cowpland, Richard Hayes, Joseph Brinton, Thomas Chandler, William Webb, Samuel Gilpin, James James, Joseph Pennock.

1730.—Henry Pierce, John Taylor, Samuel Lewis, John Parry, Thomas Chandler, Samuel Gilpin, William Webb, Henry Hayes.

1731.—Joseph Harvey, John Parry, Samuel Lewis, Caleb Cowpland, John Taylor, Joseph Brinton, Henry Pierce, Evan Lewis.

1732.—Caleb Cowpland, Joseph Harvey, Joseph Brinton, Thomas Thomas, William Webb, Joseph Pennock, John Davis, William Hughes.

1733.—Caleb Cowpland, Joseph Harvey, Joseph Brinton, John Davis, Thomas Thomas, Joseph Pennock, John Owen, William Moore.

1734.—Joseph Harvey, Joseph Brinton, Caleb Cowpland, John Evans, William Moore, William Webb, John Owen, Joseph Pennock.

1735.—Joseph Harvey, William Moore, Joseph Pennock, Caleb Cowpland, John Evans, John Parry, Joseph Brinton, Thomas Cummings.

1736.—Joseph Harvey, Thomas Cummings, John Evans, Caleb Cowpland, William Webb, William Moore, Thomas Chandler, John Parry.

1737.—Thomas Chandler, Joseph Harvey, John Evans, Thomas Cummings, William Moore, James Gibbons, William Hughes, Richard Hayes.

1738.—William Moore, James Gibbons, Thomas Chandler, Joseph Harvey, John Owen, Thomas Tatnall, William Hughes, Jeremiah Starr.

1739.—James Gibbons, Thomas Chandler, Joseph Harvey, William Hughes, Jeremiah Starr, William Moore, Samuel Lewis, John Owen.

1740.—Thomas Chandler, Joseph Harvey, James Gibbons, William Hughes, Samuel Levis, John Owen, Jeremiah Starr, Thomas Tatnall.

1741.—Joseph Harvey, Thomas Chandler, James Gibbons, John Owen, Thomas Tatnall, Samuel Levis, William Hughes, Jeremiah Starr.

1742.—James Gibbons, John Owen, Samuel Levis, Jeremiah Starr, Thomas Chandler, Joseph Harvey, William Hughes, Thomas Tatnall.

1743.—Jeremiah Starr, James Gibbons, Thomas Chandler, Joseph Harvey, Samuel Levis, Joseph Pennock, George Ashbridge, Jr., Francis Yarnall.

1744.—George Ashbridge, Francis Yarnall, Joseph Pennock, Samuel Levis, James Gibbons, Joseph Harvey, Thomas Cummings, Thomas Chandler.

1745.—Joseph Pennock, Thomas Cummings, George Ashbridge, Francis Yarnall, Joseph Harvey, Samuel Levis, Robert Lewis, Thomas Chandler.

1746.—Francis Yarnall, George Ashbridge, Robert Lewis, Thomas Worth, Samuel Levis, Peter Dicks, Thomas Chandler, John Owen.

1747.—Samuel Levis, Francis Yarnall, George Ashbridge, Thomas Worth, Peter Dicks, John Owen, John Davis, Thomas Chandler.

1748.—Thomas Worth, George Ashbridge, Francis Yarnall, John Davis, John Owen, Joseph James, Thomas Chandler, Joseph Gibbons.

1749.—Joseph Gibbons, George Ashbridge, Henry Hockley, Thomas Chandler, Nathaniel Grubb, Nathaniel Pennock, Roger Hunt, Thomas Cummings.

1750.—Joseph Gibbons, George Ashbridge, Thomas Cummings, Henry Hockley, Thomas Chandler, Nathaniel Grubb, Nathaniel Pennock, Peter Dicks.

1751.—Joseph Gibbons, Thomas Cummings, George Ashbridge, Nathaniel Grubb, Peter Dicks, Nathaniel Pennock, Henry Hockley, Thomas Chandler.

1752.—Joseph Gibbons, Thomas Cummings, Nathaniel Pennock, George Ashbridge, Peter Dicks, Nathaniel Grubb, William Peters, Jacob Howell.

1753.—Thomas Cummings, Nathaniel Pennock, George Ashbridge, Joseph Gibbons, Nathaniel Grubb, William Peters, Peter Dicks, Joseph James.

1754.—George Ashbridge, Joseph Gibbons, Thomas Cummings, Peter Dicks, Nathaniel Pennock, Nathaniel Grubb, Joseph James, William Peters.

1755.—Thomas Cummings, George Ashbridge, Nathaniel Pennock, Joseph James, Joseph Gibbons, Nathaniel Grubb, William Peters (resigned and was succeeded by John Morton), Nathaniel Grubb.

1756.—Joseph Gibbons, John Morton, Roger Hunt, George Ashbridge, Hugh Trimble, Nathaniel Grubb, Peter Dicks,

Nathaniel Pennock (the latter two resigning and being succeeded by Isaac Wayne and Ralph Pyle).

1757.—Joseph Gibbons, George Ashbridge, John Morton, Roger Hunt, Isaac Wayne, Nathaniel Grubb, Hugh Trimble, Joshua Ash.

1758.—Joseph Gibbons, John Morton, George Ashbridge, Roger Hunt, Hugh Trimble, Joshua Ash, Nathaniel Grubb, Isaac Wayne.

1759.—John Morton, George Ashbridge, Joshua Ash, Joseph Gibbons, Hugh Trimble, Roger Hunt, Peter Dicks, Isaac Wayne.

1760.—George Ashbridge, John Morton, Roger Hunt, Joshua Ash, Joseph Gibbons, Nathaniel Pennock, William Boyd, Isaac Wayne.

1761.—Joseph Gibbons, George Ashbridge, Nathaniel Pennock, Joshua Ash, John Morton, Isaac Pearson, Roger Hunt, Isaac Wayne.

1762.—Nathaniel Pennock, George Ashbridge, Joshua Ash, Isaac Pearson, John Morton, Joseph Gibbons, John Jacobs, Isaac Wayne.

1763.—George Ashbridge, Joshua Ash, Isaac Pearson, John Morton, Nathaniel Pennock, John Jacobs, Charles Humphreys, Isaac Wayne.

1764.—George Ashbridge, Nathaniel Pennock, John Morton, Joshua Ash, Isaac Pearson, Charles Humphreys, John Jacobs, John Fairlamb.

1765.—George Ashbridge, John Morton, John Jacobs, Nathaniel Pennock, John Fairlamb, (died and was succeeded by John Minshall), Charles Humphreys, Isaac Pearson, Joshua Ash.

1766.—George Ashbridge, Nathaniel Pennock, John Jacobs, Charles Humphreys, Isaac Pearson, Joshua Ash, John Minshall, John Morton (accepted the office of sheriff and Jonas Preston took his place).

1767.—Isaac Pearson, Charles Humphreys, George Ashbridge, John Minshall, Jonas Preston, John Jacobs, John Sellers, Nathaniel Pennock.

1768.—John Jacobs, Nathaniel Pennock, George Ashbridge, Charles Humphreys, John Sellers, John Minshall, John Crosby, Isaac Pearson.

1769.—George Ashbridge, Charles Humphreys, Isaac Pearson, John Sellers, John Jacobs, John Minshall, John Crosby, John Morton.

1770.—Charles Humphreys, Isaac Pearson, John Minshall, John Morton, John Jacobs, John Crosby, John Sellers, George Ashbridge.

1771.—John Morton, John Jacobs, John Sellers, John Minshall, John Crosby, Charles Humphreys, Isaac Pearson, George Ashbridge.

1772.—Charles Humphreys, Isaac Pearson, John Morton, John Jacobs, John Minshall, James Hockley, George Ashbridge, Benjamin Bartholomew.

1773.—Isaac Pearson, Benjamin Bartholomew, John Jacobs, Charles Humphreys, John Morton, James Gibbs, John Minshall, Joseph Pennock.

1774.—Benjamin Bartholomew, John Jacobs, Joseph Pennock, James Gibbons, Isaac Pearson, Charles Humphreys, John Morton, Anthony Wayne.

1775.—John Morton (Speaker), Benjamin Bartholomew, James Gibbons, Isaac Pearson, John Jacobs, Charles Humphreys, Joseph Pennock, Joseph Pyle.

1776.—John Jacobs, Caleb Davis, Joseph Gardner, John Fulton, Samuel Cunningham, John Sellers.

1777.—Joseph Gardner, John Fulton, Samuel Cunningham, John Culbertson, Lewis Gronow, Stephen Cochran.

1778.—Joseph Gardner, John Fulton, John Culbertson, Stephen Cochran, John Fleming, Patrick Anderson.

1779.—John Fulton, David Thomas, Henry Hayes, James Boyd, Patrick Anderson, Joseph Park, William Harris, Sketchley Morton.

1780.—David Thomas, Henry Hayes, Joseph Park, William Harris, James Boyd, Patrick Anderson, John Culbertson, Evan Evans.

1781.—John Culbertson, Evan Evans, James Moore, Persifor Frazer, Thomas Maffat, Patrick Anderson, John Hannum, John Lindsay.

1782.—Persifor Frazer, James Boyd, Evan Evans, Thomas Strawbridge, Benjamin Brannan, David Thomas, John Lindsay, Thomas Maffat.

1783.—David Thomas, Evan Evans, John Hannum, Joseph Park, Richard Willing, Thomas Potts, Thomas Bull, Edward Jones.

1784.—Richard Willing, Anthony Wayne, Edward Jones, Robert Ralston, James Moore, Thomas Potts, Persifor Frazer, Joseph Strawbridge, Charles Humphreys.

1785.—Anthony Wayne, Robert Ralston, James Moore, Thomas Bull, John Hannum, Robert Smith, Samuel Evans, Jonathan Morris.

1786.—Robert Ralston, Richard Willing, James Moore, Samuel Evans, Richard Thomas, Townsend Whelen, and in 1787 the same members.

1788.—Richard Thomas, James Moore, Mark Wilcox, John McDowell, Caleb James, Richard Downing, Jr.

1789.—Richard Thomas, John McDowell, Caleb James, Richard Downing, Jr.

1790.—Richard Downing, Caleb James, John McDowell, James Boyd.

1791.—Richard Downing, Caleb James, James Boyd, Samuel Evans.

1792.—Dennis Whelen, Charles Dilworth, John Hannum, Samuel Sharp.

1793.—Dennis Whelen, Thomas Bull, John Ross, Joseph Pierce.

1794.—Thomas Bull, John Ross, Robert Frazer, Roger Kirk.

1795.—Thomas Bull, Robert Frazer, Roger Kirk, Joseph Pierce, Abiah Taylor.

1796.—Thomas Bull, Robert Frazer, Roger Kirk, Abiah Taylor, James Hannum.

1797.—Thomas Bull, Roger Kirk, Abiah Taylor, James Hannum, Joseph Hemphill,

1798 and 1799.—The same as in 1797.

1800.—Thomas Bull, Roger Kirk, Abiah Taylor, Isaac Wayne.

1801.—Thomas Bull, John McDowell, Abiah Taylor (died and was succeeded by Isaac Anderson), Isaac Wayne, William Gibbons.

1802.—Joseph Park, James Fulton, Edward Darlington, Thomas Taylor, Methuselah Davis.

1803.—James Fulton, Edward Darlington, Methuselah Davis, John Boyd, Hezekiah Davis.

1804.—The same members.

1805.—John Boyd, Methuselah Davis, James Kelton, Francis Gardner, John G. Bull.

1806.—Same members re-elected.

1807.—Joseph Park, James Kelton, William Worthington, Isaac Darlington, George Evans.

1808.—James Kelton, John G. Bull, Isaac Darlington, George Evans, Abraham Baily.

1809.—James Steele, John W. Cunningham, John Ramsay, Jacob Clemmons, Roger Davis.

1810.—James Steele, John W. Cunningham, John Ramsay, Jacob Clemmons, William Harris.

1811.—Edward Darlington, Jacob Clemmons, William Harris, John Reed, James Brooks.

1812.—John G. Bull, Abraham Baily, John Menough, Nathan Pennypacker, Lea Pusey.

1813.—Edward Darlington, John Harris, John Reed, James Brooks, James Hindman.

1814.—Nathan Pennypacker, John Menough, Lea Pusey, Jacob Humphrey, James Roberts.

1815.—John Menough, Jacob Humphrey, James Roberts, Joseph Sharp, John Jones (died and was succeeded by Isaac Darlingtou).

1816-17.—John Menough, Thomas Ashbridge, Evan Evans, Joseph Sharp, Samuel Cochran.

1818.—Thomas Ashbridge, Wallace Boyd, John G. Parke, Joseph Sharp, Joshua Hunt.

1819.—James Kelton, Thomas Ashbridge, Joshua Hunt, Abraham Baily, Thomas Baird.

1820.—James Kelton, Joshua Hunt, Thomas Baird, Stephen Webb, Joshua Evans.

1821.—Wallace Boyd, Timothy Kirk, Jonathan Jones, Elijah Lewis, Stephen Webb.

1822.—Wallace Boyd, Timothy Kirk, Elijah Lewis, Jonathan Jones.

1823.—Elijah Lewis, Joshua Hunt, David Potts, Jr., John Chandler.

1824.—Joshua Hunt, David Potts, Jr., John Chandler, William Thompson.

1825.—Same.

1826.—William Thompson, Townsend Haines, Robert Miller, Matthias Pennypacker.

1827.—Same members re-elected.

1828.—Robert Miller, John Morgan, Isaac Trimble, Dr. Samuel McCleane.

1829.—Joshua McMinn, Jesse James, Jesse Pugh, Gen. Matthew Stanley.

1830.—Thomas Ashbridge, Matthias Pennypacker, Arthur Andrews, Dr. Benjamin Griffith.

1831.—Thomas Ashbridge, Arthur Andrews, Dr. Benjamin Griffith, Elijah F. Pennypacker.

1832.—Same members.

1833.—Oliver Alison, Dr. Samuel McCleane, Dr. Wilmer Worthington, Dr. Thomas I. ————.

1834.—Elijah F. Pennypacker, Charles Brooke, John Hutchinson, John Parker.

1835.—Same members re-elected.

1836.—John Parker, Abraham R. McIlvaine, Maurice Richardson, Isaac Downing.

1837.—Abraham R. McIlvaine, Maurice Richardson, William H. Dillingham, Benjamin J. Passmore.

1838.—Maurice Richardson, Richard M. Barnard, William K. Correy, Beynard Way.

1839.—Joseph Baily, Joshua Hartshorne, John Morgan, Joel Swayne.

1840.—John D. Steele, Robert Futhey, William K. Correy, Dr. John B. Chrisman.

1841.—William K. Correy, Robert Futhey, Emmor Elton, Robert Laverty.

1842.—Emmor Elton, Robert Parke, Jesse C. Dickey, John Beidler.

1843.—Robert Parke, Jesse C. Dickey, Joseph Whitaker.

1844.—Robert Parke, Jesse C. Dickey, William Price.

1845.—William Price, William D. Thomas, George Ladley.

1846-47.—George Ladley, Henry S. Evans, Thomas K. Bull.

1848.—Henry S. Evans, Thomas K. Bull, David J. Bent.

1849.—David J. Bent, John S. Bowen, John Acker.

1850.—David J. Bent, John S. Evans, James M. Dorlan.

1851.—John Acker, William Chandler, Jesse James.

1852.—William Chandler, Jesse James, Dr. Joseph Hickman.

1853.—Robert E. Monaghan, Henry T. Evans, William Wheeler.

1854.—Dr. Matthias J. Pennypacker, Mark A. Hodgson, William R. Downing.

1855.—Andrew Buchanan, Joseph Dowdall, Robert Irwin.

1856.—Dr. Ebenezer V. Dickey, James Penrose, Paxon Vickers.

1857.—John Hodgson, Eber W. Sharpe, Morton Garrett.

1858.—Isaac Acker, William T. Shafer, Caleb Pierce.

1859 and 1860.—The same.

1861-62-63.—P. Frazer Smith, William Windle, Robert L. McClellan.

1864-65-66.—William B. Waddell, Nathan J. Sharpless, Dr. Nathan A. Pennypacker.

1867.—John Hickman, James M. Phillips, Dr. Stephen M. Meredith.

1868.—James M. Phillips, Dr. Stephen M. Meredith, Archimedes Robb.

1869.—James C. Roberts, Joseph C. Keech, Abel Darlington.

1870.—Joseph C. Keech, Levi Prizer, Samuel H. Hoopes.

1871.—Joseph C. Keech, Levi Prizer.

1872.—Levi Prizer, Dr. E. W. Baily.

1873.—The same two members re-elected.

1874.—Dr. E. W. Bailey, Peter G. Carey, John P. Edge, George F. Smith.

1876.—Samuel Butler, William T. Fulton, Jesse Matlack, John P. Edge.

1878.—Samuel Butler, William T. Fulton, Jesse Matlack, John A. Reynolds.

1880.—John A. Reynolds, Theodore K. Stubbs, John T. Potts, William Wayne.

1882.—John T. Potts, Theodore K. Stubbs, William Wayne, Levi Fetters.

1884.—Theodore K. Stubbs, William Wayne, Levi Fetters, Levi B. Kaler.

1886.—Lewis K. Evans, W. W. McConnell, John W. Hickman, D. Smith Talbot.

1887.—William Evans.

1888.—Lewis H. Evans, John W. Hickman, W. W. McConnell, D. Smith Talbot.

1890.—David H. Branson, William P. Snyder, Dr. J. G. West.

1892.—D. Smith Talbot, J. H. Marshall, T. J. Phillips, D. F. Moore.

1894.—D. Smith Talbot, J. H. Marshall, T. J. Phillips, D. F. Moore.

1896.—J. H. Marshall, T. J. Phillips, D. F. Moore, Plummer E. Jefferies.

On the first Tuesday of October, 1765, the first American Congress convened in the city of New York, composed of delegates from nine of the colonies, and originating in a call by the Legislature of Massachusetts to take into consideration the oppressive measures of the British Parliament. The result of the deliberations of this Congress was a declaration of rights, a memorial to Parliament, and a petition to the king, in which they objected to being taxed except by their own representatives. Their proceedings were approved by the assemblies of the several colonies, and thus for the first time a semblance of a federal union was formed or at least prefigured. In this first Congress Chester County was represented by John Morton, who resided in what is now Delaware County, and who afterward signed the Declaration of Independence.

In the second Congress, usually known in history as the "First Continental Congress," which met September 5, 1774, in Carpenter's Hall, Philadelphia, Chester County was represented by John Morton and Charles Humphreys, and eight of the fifty-five members were from Pennsylvania. In the next Continental Congress, usually known as the Second, Chester County was represented by the same two members, and this was also the case in the next Congress, which met in 1776. In this Congress, when the vote was taken on the adoption of the Declaration, John Morton voted in its favor, and Charles Humphreys against it. Only two other members from Pennsylvania voted against the Declaration, John Dickinson, its ablest opponent, Thomas Willing of Philadelphia County, and these three gentlemen were succeeded in the Congress by

Colonels George Ross and James Smith, Dr. Benjamin Rush, George Clymer, and George Taylor, all of whom signed thé Declaration of Independence as they had opportunity.

Chester County was represented in Congress from 1777 to 1779 by William Clingan of West Caln Township, and in 1784 and 1785 by Dr. Joseph Gardner, who resided near Sadsburyville. Previous to the adoption of the Constitution of the United States members of Congress were elected by the legislatures of the several states, and at the first election for members of Congress held under that Constitution they were elected on a general ticket, the votes cast in Chester County for delegates to the first Congress under the Constitution being as follows: Henry Wynkoop, 904; Thomas Hartley, 903; Frederick A. Muhlenberg, 901; Thomas Fitzsimmons, 900; John Allison, 896; Thomas Scott, 895; George Clymer, 890; Stephen Chambers, 890.

When the State was divided into congressional districts by act of March 16, 1791, Chester and Montgomery Counties became the Third district, and at the election held in October following, Israel Jacobs of Montgomery County was elected to represent it in Congress. On April 7, 1792, an act was passed providing for election of congressmen on a general ticket, and under this arrangement the candidates for Congress in the State who were elected and the votes cast for them in Chester County were as follows: Frederick A. Muhlenberg, 2,034; William Irvine, 2,011; Daniel Heister, 2,009; William Findley, 2,003; John Wilkes Kittera, 1,999; Thomas Hartley, 1,973; Thomas Fitzsimmons, 1,843; Henry Wynkoop, 1,801; Thomas Scott, 1,787, and Samuel Sitgreaves, 1,721.

The State was divided into twelve congressional districts by an act passed April 22, 1794, Chester and Delaware Counties forming the Third district, and this arrangement lasted until 1802, in which year the State was, as it has been in every tenth year since then, districted according to the number of members to which it was entitled under the several censuses of the United

26

States. Since 1802 the districts to which Chester County has belonged, and the number of members of Congress the district has been entitled to, have been as follows:

1802.—Third district, Chester, Berks and Lancaster, three members.

1812.—Second district, Chester and Montgomery, two members.

1822.—Fourth district, Chester, Delaware and Lancaster, three members.

1832.—Fourth district, Chester, Delaware and Lancaster, three members.

1842.—Seventh district, Chester County, one member.

1852.—Sixth district, Chester and Delaware, one member.

1862.—Seventh district, Chester and Delaware, one member.

1872.—The same, and 1882, the Sixth, as it still remains.

When the vote on the Declaration of Independence was first taken, the colonies, aside from Pennsylvania, were equally divided, and the vote of Pennsylvania was itself divided equally in the absence of one of Chester County's representatives in the Congress. John Morton, coming into the hall, turned the tide in favor of the Declaration, for, with his vote in favor of it, Pennsylvania was ranged on its side, and thus there was a majority in the colonial vote. At least this is the way this important point of history has usually been written and understood. And it is for the reason that John Morton was of such importance at a most critical juncture that an exception is made in his case, and a full sketch of his life here introduced.

The first mention of the name of Morton in the history of ancient Chester County is in the list of names attached to the oath of allegiance of the Swedes to the Dutch in 1655, where it was spelled Martin Martens. In an old book of service at Harrisburg, dated 1675, may be found the following: "Laid out for John Cornelis and Marton Marteson (Morton Mortonson) one piece or parcel of land where they now dwell, situate, lying and being on the west side of the Delaware River, and on a creek which cometh out of said river, said creek commonly known and called Amsland, or Mill Kill," etc. Morton Mortonson as early as 1655 lived on his plantation at Ammesland in Ridley Township, old Chester (now Delaware) County. He is always spoken of as "of Ammesland." There was a Morton Mortonson of "Calking Hook," whose will is dated November 1, 1718. Whether these two Morton Mortonsons were one and the same individual, or whether there were two individuals of the same name, appears not yet to have been settled by local historians. But the Morton Mortonson of "Calking Hook" had children as follows: David, Andrew, John, Matthias, Katharine and Margaret.

John Morton, the third of the above-named children, married Mary Archer, daughter of John Archer of Ridley, by whom he had but one son, also named John, born after his father's death, early in the year 1725. The widow married John Sketchley, an Englishman, yeoman, who came from England in 1718, and settled in Ridley Township in 1724, and died in 1753 without children. His stepson, John Morton, in remembrance of his kindness, named one of his sons Sketchley, who became a major in the Revolutionary army, and a man of note in his day.

John Morton, the signer, married Ann Justis, by whom he had three sons and five daughters. He was a member of the Provincial Assembly for eleven years from 1756; was a justice of the peace for Chester County in 1757; was sheriff in 1767 and 1768; was a member of the Congress that sat in New York in 1765; and was re-elected in 1774 and again re-elected in 1776; was a member of the first convention to frame a constitution for the State of Pennsylvania in 1776. He was appointed associate judge of the Supreme Provincial Court of Pennsylvania, and was the last appointment to that court under the old order of things. He died in December, 1777, in the fifty-fourth year of his age.

His children were Aaron, Sketchley, John, Mary, Sarah, Lydia, Ann and Elizabeth. Major Sketchley Morton married Rebecca Taylor of Tinicum, and had children as follows: Charles, Rebecca, Ann, Aaron Taylor, and John S., the latter of whom was born February 21, 1780. He married Susannah Crosby, June 30, 1803, and had the following children: Ann Crosby, Rebecca Taylor, Susan Crosby, Sketchley, John Crosby, Ellen Elizabeth, Crosby Peirce, Franklin H., and Catharine Plummer. Of these Sketchley Morton was born October 12, 1810, and married Annesley Newlin, by whom he had John S., Benjamin N., Elizabeth N., Sketchley, Annesley, Susan, Mary, Crosby. and Hattie, the latter two twins.

That patriotism is inherent in the family is shown by the fact that Sketchley Morton, Jr., son of Judge Sketchley Morton of Springfield, Delaware County, Pennsylvania, enlisted in the Ninety-seventh Pennsylvania volunteers, becoming first lieutenant of a company, and serving until his death by yellow fever November 12, 1862, at the age of twenty-one years. Upon his death a poem was written as has been thought by Rev. John Pleasanton du Hamel, at one time rector of the Church of the Redemption, Philadelphia. The poem in part is as follows:

"A noble youth, a noble lineage,
  Descent of man whose patriot deed
  Gave Independence to our glorious Union;
  Aye, set his State, the Keystone.
  Of this loved temple of our Liberties.

"The name of Morton—when the Nation's fate
  Poised in dubious scale of destiny,
  (Who doubts may read) the balance shook, and to
  The side of Freedom sent the quivering beam," etc.

Chester County has been represented in the Senate of the United States by one of her distinguished citizens, viz., Gen. Isaac

D. Barnard, who was elected to that high office in 1828, took his seat March 4, 1829, and served until 1831, when he resigned on account of failing health. He died at West Chester in 1834. General Barnard was born in 1791 at Chester, Pennsylvania, and was admitted to the bar at West Chester in 1816. He had been a gallant soldier and officer in the war of 1812, being under the command of Winder at Sackett's Harbor. He was promoted to the rank of major in the year 1813, and descended the Saint Lawrence River with Wilkinson and heard the firing at Chrysler Farm, unable to be present on account of illness. He greatly distinguished himself for bravery at the battle of Lyons' Creek, conducting the charge and driving the enemy from their ground. After the conclusion of the war he applied himself to the practice of the law in West Chester, becoming unusually popular on account of his courage and high character. In 1820 he was elected to the State Senate from the district composed of Chester and Delaware Counties, and in 1824 he was elected major-general of the Third district of the militia, in which capacity he aided largely in the hospitalities extended to the Marquis de Lafayette on his visit to Chester County. In 1826 he was appointed Secretary of the Commonwealth, and in 1828 he was elected to the Senate of the United States, as above stated. In 1829 his friends made the attempt to nominate him for Governor of the State, but on account of a factional fight in Chester County, the attempt was not successful. As a lawyer he was eminently successful, notwithstanding the many interruptions in his practice, by his engagements in military and political life, and the many able competitors then practicing at the Chester County bar. On October 19, 1854, his remains were removed from the Friends' graveyard on High Street, to the Oaklands Cemetery, where a monument to him had already been erected, Dr. William Darlington delivering an oration on this occasion, which was made a very imposing military pageant, the procession reaching from the court-house to the cemetery.

Following is a list of the members of Congress from Chester County, together with the number of the Congress in which they severally served, and the year in which they were elected, since 1794:

1794-96-98.—IVth, Vth and VIth congresses, Richard Thomas, West Whiteland.

1800.—VII, Joseph Hemphill, West Chester.

1802-04.—VIII and IX, Isaac Anderson, Charlestown.

1806.—X, John Heister, Coventry.

1808.—XI, Daniel Heister, West Chester.

1810.—XII, Dr. Roger Davis, Charlestown.

1812.—XIII, the same.

1814.—XIV, Dr. William Darlington, West Chester.

1816.—XV, Isaac Darlington, West Chester.

1818-20.—XVI and XVII, Dr. William Darlington, West Chester.

1822.—XVII, Col. Isaac Wayne, Easttown.

1824-26.—XIX and XX, Charles Miner, West Chester.

1828-30.—XXI and XXII, Joshua Evans, Tredyffrin.

1830-32-34-36.—XXII, XXIII, XXIV and XXV, David Potts, Jr., East Nantmeal.

1838-40.—XXVI, XXVII, Francis James, West Chester.

1843-44-46.—XXVIII, XXIX and XXX, Abraham R. McIlvaine, West Nantmeal.

1848.—XXXI, Jesse C. Dickey, New London.

1850.—XXXII, Dr. John A. Morrison, West Fallowfield.

1852.—XXXIII, William Everhart, West Chester.

1854-56-58-60.—XXXIV, XXXV, XXXVI and XXXVII, John Hickman, West Chester.

1862-64-66.—XXXVIII, XXXIX and XL, John M. Broomall, Delaware County.

1868-70-72-74.—XLI, XLII, XLIII and XLIV, Washington Townsend, West Chester.

1876-78-80.—XLV, XLVI and XLVII, William Ward, Delaware County.

1882-84.—XLVIII and XLIX, James B. Everhart.

1886-88.—L and LI, Smedley Darlington.

1890-92-94.—LII, LIII and LIV, John B. Robinson, Delaware County.

1896.—LV, Thomas S. Butler.

Hon. John Hickman, elected four times to Congress from Chester County, was one of the historic personages of his times. While he was a youth he was noted for his uncommon intellectual ability, and it was this that led his parents to secure for him the best education obtainable. Having read law with the Hon. Townsend Haines, he was admitted to the bar in 1832, and being a good speaker he soon won a prominent position in the Democrat party of Chester County. In 1844 he was a delegate to the National Convention that nominated James K. Polk for President, but was himself in favor of Andrew Jackson. In that year he was nominated by the Democrats of his district for Congress, but was defeated by Hon. Abraham R. McIlvaine. In 1845 he was appointed district attorney, and was again appointed to the same office about the first of the year 1847. In 1854 he was again nominated for Congress by the Democracy, and was elected by a majority of 2,656, securing the vote of the Know Nothings, "through some influences which have never been satisfactorily explained." In Congress Mr. Hickman was an opponent of slavery, notwithstanding which he was again elected to Congress in 1856 by the Democracy of his district. Though he supported Mr. Buchanan for President that year, yet in a speech delivered in the House on January 28, 1858, he declared that the President had broken faith with the party in his Kansas policy, and he could no longer support him. In 1858 he was again elected to Congress by a large majority over both the regular Republican and Democratic nominees, and aided the Republicans to break the deadlock in the famous contest of

Speaker of the House, the result of which was the election of Mr. Pennington.

During the two years that followed Mr. Hickman made for himself a world-wide reputation by his able and sarcastic speeches against slavery. In reply to the threat of disunion, he said that the North would never tolerate a division of territory, because "eighteen millions, reared in industry, with habits of the right kind, will always be able to cope successfully, .if need be, with eight millions of men with these appliances" of art.

In 1860, when Mr. Lincoln was nominated for the Presidency, Mr. Hickman confidently anticipated the nomination for Vice-President; but failing in this he was again elected to Congress, and at the end of this term declined re-election. He gave his district a national reputation, and was much in advance of the times in regard to the freeing of the slaves, the right of the President to confiscate all kinds of property of the rebels in arms, including slaves, and the arming of the blacks as soldiers in the Union army, his views at length being acted upon.

It is presumed that all know how Presidential electors are chosen, hence all that is deemed necessary to do in this connection is to present a list of the Pennsylvania Presidential electors that have been residents of Chester County. Though it is proper to state that the electors who voted for General Washington when he was first elected President of the United States were appointed by the Legislature of the State. Following is the list since 1792, including two from Delaware County, representing the Congressional district:

1792, Washington's second election, Thomas Bull; 1796, John Adams' election, James Boyd; 1804, Thomas Jefferson's second election, James Boyd; 1808, James Madison's first election, George Hartman; 1812, Madison's second election, James Fulton; 1816, James Monroe's first election, Isaac Anderson; 1820, Monroe's second election, William Clingan; 1824, John Quincy Adams' election,

Cromwell Pearce; 1828, Andrew Jackson's first election, John W. Cunningham; 1832, Jackson's second election, Oliver Alison; 1836, Martin Van Buren's election, Oliver Alison; 1840, William Henry Harrison's election, A. R. McIlvaine; 1844, James K. Polk's election, Jesse Sharp; 1848, Zachary Taylor's election, John D. Steele; 1852, Franklin Pierce's election, N. Strickland; 1856, James Buchanan's election, John H. Brinton; 1860, Abraham Lincoln's first election, J. M. Broomall; 1864, Lincoln's second election, Robert Parke; 1868, U. S. Grant's first election, Francis C. Hooton; 1872, Grant's second election, John M. Broomall; 1876, Rutherford B. Hayes' election, Joseph W. Barnard; 1880, James A. Garfield's election, David F. Houston; 1884, Grover Cleveland's election, Horace A. Beale; 1888, Benjamin Harrison's election, Joseph R. T. Coates. Delaware County: 1892, Grover Cleveland's second election, Maxwell Clower; 1896, William McKinley's election, Joseph H. Huddell.

Gen. Anthony Wayne, one of the most famous soldiers of the Revolutionary War and in the Indians wars in the West, whose rapid movements and fearless courage led to his being styled "Mad Anthony Wayne," was born in Easttown, Chester County, Pa., January 1, 1745. Having received a good academic education he began life as a professional surveyor at the age of eighteen years, and when he was twenty years old he was sent to Nova Scotia to locate lands for a company. After a two years' residence there he returned to Chester County, married, and resumed the business of a surveyor. In 1773 he was elected to the Assembly, and in 1775 he was appointed to a command in the Continental Army, proceeding to Canada with General Thomas, and remaining there one year. He was then promoted to brigadier-general, and was actively engaged with General Washington in the battles of the Brandywine, Germantown and Monmouth. In 1779 he made a determined attack by night on Stony Point on the Hudson, making the entire garrison prisoners. After conquering the Western Indians in 1794, he died at Presque Isle, now Erie, Pennsylvania,

December 14, 1796, and his remains were there buried; but they were removed in 1809 to the family lot in the cemetery connected with St. David's Church, Delaware County, where they now repose.

Washington Townsend, formerly a member of Congress from Chester County, was born in Chester County, January 13, 1813. He was a son of David and Rebecca (Sharpless) Townsend, and was educated by such old-time teachers as Jonathan Gause and Joseph Strode at West Chester Academy. While occupying the position of teller in the Bank of Chester County he began the study of the law, reading with William Darlington, and was admitted to the bar May 7, 1844. From that time until his death he was success-fully engaged in the practice of his profession, though he served from 1848 to 1857 as cashier of the bank, resigning this position in the latter year in order that he might devote himself more closely to the law. He served as prosecuting attorney from October, 1848, to April, 1849; was a delegate to the National Whig Convention of 1852 and to the National Republican Convention of 1860, which nominated Abraham Lincoln for the Presidency of the United States. He served in Congress from 1868 to 1876, during which time he warmly advocated a tariff for the protection of American industries, the national banking system, the appropriation of the public lands for educational purposes, and an improved policy with reference to the Indian wars of the nation. Succeeding John H. Ketcham as chairman of the Committee on Public Lands, he was also a member of the committee on education, the com-mittee on Freedmen's affairs and of the committee on finance and commerce. He strenuously opposed the bill, by the passage of which the members of Congress voted themselves back pay to the amount of $2,500 to each man, and after the bill became a law he refused to accept the sum to which, under its provisions, he was entitled. Returning to Chester County from Congress he was elected president of the National Bank of Chester County, filling the office until his death, March 18, 1894.

Hon. James Bowen Everhart, a man of rare ability, highly distinguished for his public services, was the third son of Hon. William and Hannah (Matlack) Everhart. He was born in West Whiteland July 26, 1821, and received his education at Anthony Bolmar's Academy and at Princeton College, graduating from the latter institution in 1842. He was admitted to the bar in 1845, and took special law courses in the universities of Edinburgh and Berlin. Returning to the United States, he practiced his profession until 1861, and then served bravely and faithfully in the army of the Union. He was a popular Republican leader in Chester County, and served as a member of the State Senate from 1876 to 1882, during which time he pronounced eulogies on Bayard Taylor, William Penn and Anthony Wayne, which have been pronounced the finest memorials ever heard in the State. Having in 1882 been elected to the Forty-eighth Congress, he resigned his seat in the State Senate, and was re-elected to Congress in 1884. He was a noted author, and his "Miscellanies," his "Poems," "The Fox Chase," and his "Speeches," are volumes of great usefulness and interest. He died August 23, 1888, honored and mourned by all that knew him.

Hon. Wayne MacVeagh was born in Phœnixville in 1833, and is a son of Major and Margaret (Lincoln) MacVeagh. He was educated at Freeland's Seminary in Montgomery County and at Yale College, graduating from the latter institution in 1853, the class of that year being rendered famous by many of its afterward distinguished members, among whom, besides Mr. MacVeagh, were Chauncey M. Depew, Andrew D. White, Charlton T. Lewis and Isaac Bromley of the New York Tribune. Mr. MacVeagh read law with Hon. Joseph J. Lewis of West Chester and was admitted to the bar in 1856. He was made district attorney in 1859, and was chairman of the Republican State Committee in 1863, in which Governor Curtin was elected to the office of Governor the second time. During the Civil War he served on the staff of General Couch, with the rank of major, was appointed by President Grant Ambassador to Turkey, and in the constitutional convention of 1872-73, and was appointed by President Hayes as a member of the Louisiana Commission, which decided in favor of seating Governor Nichols as against Packard, some of the other members of that commission being ex-Gov. Joseph Brown of Georgia and Joseph Hawley of Connecticut. He was solicitor for the Pennsylvania Railroad Company for a number of years, and was made Attorney-General of the United States under President Garfield. By President Cleveland he was appointed in 1894 Ambassador to Italy, and is now engaged in the practice of the law in Washington the winters, and resides on his farm at Bryn Mawr in summer seasons.

Mr. MacVeagh is noted for scholarship, and is in great demand as an orator on public celebrations, as at college commencements and other educational occasions. For years he has been president of the Pennsylvania Civil Service Reform Association, and in politics, though acting most of his life with the Republican party, is in favor of the Democratic doctrine of tariff for revenue only.

His first wife was a daughter of Joseph J. Lewis, and his second wife a daughter of Gen. Simon Cameron. By his first wife he has two sons living, one of whom is practicing law in New York City, and the other residing in Philadelphia. By his second wife he had two children, a son and daughter, the former of whom is dead, but the second, Margarretta, is living.

Major Levi G. McCauley, auditor-general of the State of Pennsylvania, was born in Chester County, September 2, 1837, and is a son of John and Lydia (Gheen) McCauley. He was educated in the public schools and at Abington Center and at Wyoming Seminary. Prior to the late Civil War he was a practical mechanical engineer. He was the eldest of four brothers who joined a battalion of 200 men raised by their father in Susquehanna County in the latter part of April, 1861, and as the father was refused a commission on account of his age, by Governor Curtin, Levi left the battalion and joined a company of soldiers at Wilkesbarre, commanded by Col. E. B. Harvey, this company afterward becoming Company F, Seventh Regiment Pennsylvania Reserves, and going into camp at Camp Wayne, West Chester, as a private soldier. He was promoted to first sergeant at Camp Wayne, and to first lieutenant in November, 1862. At the battle of Charles City Cross Roads Mr. McCauley was severely wounded, in consequence of which his right arm had to be amputated. Taken prisoner by the rebels, he was taken to the famous Libby prison, where he was confined seventy days, and being at length paroled he was taken to David's Island Hospital, New York, remaining there until the following November, when he was ordered to Harrisburg for duty in the recruiting service. Notwithstanding his maimed condition he rejoined his regiment in January, 1863, and in February, 1864, he was promoted to captain of his company and performed his duty with his regiment until the next December, when he was transferred to the Veteran Reserve Corps. He was breveted major in 1865 for gallant and meritorious services, and on January 30, 1866, was discharged because his services were no longer needed by the Government.

Ever since the close of the war Major McCauley has been an active leader in the Republican party. He was elected register of wills in the fall of 1869; was chairman of the Republican committee from 1866 to 1890, and has been a delegate to numerous county, state and national Republican conventions. He was nominated by the Republican State Convention in August, 1897, for auditor-general of the State of Pennsylvania, and in November following was elected by a vote of 412,652 as against 268,341 given to his Democratic opponent. His majority over all opponents was 79,456, and he led his ticket by a vote of 40,214. He was elected a delegate to the Republican State Convention in the spring of 1898.

Major McCauley was married October 6, 1870, to Miss Isabel

Darlington, daughter of the late Hon. William and Catherine P. Darlington.

For more than one hundred years, or from 1681 to 1790, the frame of government under which the Province of Pennsylvania prospered provided for a Governor, a Council and an Assembly, the Council being a portion of the time appointed by the Governor and a part of the time elected by the people of the several counties. But all of this time it was a portion of the executive branch of the government, instead of being as the Senate has been since 1790, a part of the legislative branch. It has often been a matter of uncertainty as to where those constitution builders of Tennessee, in 1796, found a form of government after which to pattern, who attempted to provide the then new State with a legislative body, consisting of but one branch, or part; but they may have had the frame of government in vogue in Pennsylvania for the then past one hundred years in mind.

At first, in the Province of Pennsylvania, it was directed that the freemen on the 20th of the twelfth month (February) should elect seventy-two persons as councilors, one-third for three years, one-third for two years and one-third for one year, next ensuing, and that on the 20th of the twelfth year afterward twenty-four persons, instead of seventy-two, should be so elected. The first election for councilors was therefore held on the 20th of February, 1682, and the Council elected met on the 10th of the next month, the sheriffs making their returns and presenting petitions from the inhabitants on that day. Thomas Usher presented a petition from Chester County, to William Penn, proprietary and governor of the Province, to the effect that the freeholders of Chester County had chosen twelve persons for delegates to serve in the Provincial Council, and asking that, in consideration of the fact that there were but few people in the county acquainted with public business, and of the further fact that the county was unable to support greater elections and assemblies, three of the twelve elected might serve as councilors, and that the other nine might serve in the Assembly. This arrangement was agreed to, the three men selected for the Council by the voters of Chester County being John Simcock, for three years; Ralph Withers, for two years, and William Clayton, for one year. By a new frame of government the number of councilors was reduced to three from each county, which number was subject to changes by the Governor, Council or Assembly, but was never to exceed the limitations of the charter.

Governor Fletcher of New York, being placed in charge of the Province in 1693, chose his own Council of twelve persons, who served two years. Under Governor Markham the plan of electing the Council was resumed, but in the next year, 1796, the Governor selected his own Council. In this latter year a new frame of government went into operation, under which there were two councillors from each county, who served for one year. In 1700 the number of councillors from each county again became three, but the charter was surrendered in May of that year, and a new one granted, under which the councillors were appointed by the proprietary or his lieutenant. In 1702 John Finney, son of Capt. Samuel Finney, was selected as the member from Chester County, to serve in the Council, and from this time on until the Revolutionary War there were but few members chosen from Chester County.

In January, 1775, the Revolutionary convention appointed a "Council of Safety," as did the convention of 1776, the latter convention finding it necessary for them to usurp the entire government, and to form a constitution, which went into immediate effect without having been submitted to a vote of the people, a high-handed proceeding, which would not be submitted to at the present time, and only justified by the overpowering necessities of the time. The members of Chester County to this convention were Benjamin Bartholomew, John Jacobs, Thomas Strawbridge, Albert Smith, Samuel Cunningham, John Hart, John Mackey and John Fleming.

This constitutional convention originated in an assembly called a "Provincial Conference," convened in pursuance of a resolution of Congress, recommending a change in the form of State Govern-ments. Of this provincial conference, which met at Philadelphia, June 18, 1776, the members from Chester County being Col. Rich-ard Thomas, Maj. William Evans, Col. Thomas Hockley, Maj. Caleb Davis, Elisha Price, Samuel Fairlamb, Col. William Montgomery, Col. Hugh Lloyd, Richard Riley, Col. Evan Evans, Col. Lewis Greno, Maj. Sketchley Morton and Capt. Thomas Levis.

Under this constitution the power of legislation was vested in a general assembly of one house, and the supreme executive power in a council of twelve persons, elected in fours for a term of three years, and the council and assembly elected a president annually by joint ballot. This constitution remained in force until 1790.

Following is as complete a list as could be made of the mem-bers of the Council from Chester County:

1681.—Robert Wade, James Sandelands, William Woodman-see, William Clayton.

1683.—William Clayton, Ralph Withers, John Simcock.

1684.—William Clayton, William Wood, Christopher Taylor.

1685.—Nicholas Newlin.

1686.—John Simcock, Francis Harrison.

1687.—John Bristow.

1688.—Bartholomew Coppock.

1689.—John Blunston, declined to serve, and William Howell elected in his place.

1689.—John Simcock.

1690.—John Blunston, declined to serve, and William Howell elected in his place.

1691.—John Bristow. ·

1692.—Samuel Levis, John Simcock. · ·

1693-94.—George Foreman.

1695.—George Maris, one year; Caleb Pusey, two years, and David Lloyd, three years.

John A. M. Passmore

1696.—Jasper Yutes.

1697.—John Simcock, Caleb Pusey.

1698.—John Simcock, David Lloyd.

1699.—Caleb Pusey, David Lloyd.

1700.—David Lloyd, three years; Caleb Pusey, two years, and John Simcock, one year.

After the Surrender of the Charter.

1700.—Caleb Pusey, continued until 1715.

1702.—John Finney.

Committee of Safety.

1775.—Anthony Wayne, Benjamin Bartholomew, Francis Johnston, Richard Riley, and after October, the same, with Nicholas Fairlamb added.

1776.—Council of Safety, Benjamin Bartholomew.

Supreme Executive Council.

1777.—John Evans and John Mackey, from November 21.

1779.—Dr. Joseph Gardner; 1782, Dr. John McDowell; 1785, Evan Evans; 1788, Col. Richard Willing.

In 1789 Dr. Thomas Huston was elected, by 1,586 votes, but his claim to a seat was rejected.

In 1790 the Legislature was for the first time in this State made to consist of two bodies, a Senate and a House of Representatives, and by the Constitution under which this form of government was established, the Senate was to consist of not less than one-fourth nor more than one-third of the House. Upon its organization the Senate was composed of eighteen members; but in 1801 the number was increased to 25, in 1808 to 31, in 1822 to 33, and in 1874 to 50.

Under the Constitution of 1790 the term of service was four years; under that of 1838, three years, and under that of 1874, four years. In the division of the State into districts, Chester County, from 1790 to 1808, was a district in itself, and had one

27

member; in 1808 it was united with Delaware County in one district, which was allowed two members; in 1836 Montgomery County was added to the district, which had three members; in 1843 Montgomery County was placed in another district, and Chester and Delaware were allowed one member; in 1864 Montgomery County was again added and the district was allowed two members, and in 1871 Delaware and Chester again became a district, with one member.

Following is a list of the members of the senate from Chester County:

1790.—Richard Thomas, elected for four years.

1794.—Dennis Whelen, three years.

1797.—Joseph McClellan, one year.

1798.—Dennis Whelen, four years.

1802.—John Heister, four years.

1806.—Isaac Wayne, four years.

1810.—Isaac Wayne, one year.

1811.—John Gemmill, three years.

1814.—Abraham Baily, four years.

1818.—Samuel Cochran, four years.

1820.—Isaac D. Barnard, four years.

1822.—James Kelton, four years.

1826.—Joshua Hunt, four years.

1830.—William Jackson, four years.

1834.—Francis James, four years.

1838.—Nathaniel Brooke, four years.

1842.—Joseph Baily, three years.

1845.—William Williamson, three years.

1851.—Henry S. Evans, three years.

1857.—Thomas S. Bull, three years.

1863.—Dr. Wilmer Worthington, 3 years.

1866.—Dr. Wilmer Worthington, three years.

1870.—Henry S. Evans, served until his death in February, 1872.

1872.—William B. Waddell, for balance of term.

1874.—Robert L. McClellan, two years.

1876.—James B. Everhart, four years.

1880.—James B. Everhart, four years.

1884.—A. D. Harlan, six years.

1892.—S. E. Nevin, served one day.

1892.—William P. Snyder, four years.

COUNTY OFFICES.

The county offices, those of the Prothonotary, Register of Wills, Recorder of Deeds, Clerk of the Orphan's Court, Clerk of the Court of Quarter Sessions and Clerk of the Court of Oyer and Terminer, were, under the Provincial Government, filled by appointment by the proprietary government. Under the Constitution of 1776 these appointments were made by the Supreme Executive Council and General Assembly. Under the Constitution of 1790 they were made by the Governor, and under the Constitution of 1838 they became elective.

From 1777 to 1821 the offices of prothonotary and clerk of the Orphans' Court and of the Courts of Quarter Sessions and Oyer and Terminer were filled by the same persons, and from 1821 to 1824 one person was prothonotary and clerk of the Court of Oyer and Terminer, and one person was clerk of the Court of Quarter Sessions and of the Orphans' Court. From 1777 to 1824 the same person held the offices of register of wills and recorder of deeds. From 1824 to 1836 the same persons held the offices of prothonotary and clerk of the Courts of Quarter Sessions and Oyer and Terminer, and from 1824 to 1828 the same person held the offices of clerk of the Orphans' Court and register of wills. From 1828 to 1836 the office of clerk of the Orphan' Court was separate from any other office.

From 1824 to the present time the office of recorder of deeds has been separate from other offices, and the same is true of the office of register of wills since 1828. From 1836 to the present time the office of prothonotary has been separate from others, and the offices of clerk of the Orphans' Court and of the Courts of Quarter Sessions and Oyer and Terminer have been filled by the same person.

PROTHONOTARY.

Previous to 1777 the prothonotary was generally the clerk of the Quarter Sessions and of the Orphans' Court. Robert Assheton was commissioned prothonotary in 1712; Joseph Parker, prothonotary and clerk of the peace, in 1733, and Henry Hale Graham, prothonotary, clerk of the Courts and recorder, in 1770. Since 1777 the prothonotary has been as follows:

Benjamin Jacobs, March 22, 1777, to April 4, 1777; Caleb Davis, appointed June 20, 1777; William Gibbons, appointed in 1791; Daniel Heister, January 6, 1800; Jesse John, February 1, 1809; John G. Wersler, March 25, 1818; Thomas Davis, February 29, 1821; William Williamson, January 17, 1824; David Townsend, August 3, 1827; Dr. William Darlington, August 17, 1827; John W. Cunningham, February 15, 1830; Benjamin I. Miller, January 26, 1836; Samuel Pinkerton, appointed February 2, 1839, elected under Constitution of 1838, and commissioned November 4, 1839; Abner M. Chamberlain, November 12, 1842; James Davis, November 17, 1845; Samuel B. Thomas, November 25, 1848; William Wollerton, November 22, 1851; James Bayard Jefferis, November 10, 1854; Jacob Gillough, November 10, 1857; Emmor B. Lamborn, November 19, 1860; Franklin Haines, November 16, 1863; Alfred Rupert, November 16, 1866; Seneca G. Willauer, November 20, 1869; John A. Rupert, November 19, 1872; Hannum Baldwin, December 28, 1875; James Lynch, December 28, 1878; Davis K. Loomis, in 1881; Jeremiah T. Carpenter, in 1884; William P. Snyder, in 1887; David C. Windle in 1890; Elisha G. Cloud, in 1893, and E. D. Baldwin, the present incumbent, in 1896.

REGISTERS OF WILLS.

Previous to 1714 all wills made in Chester County were taken to the office of the register-general in Philadelphia and there filed. In 1712 an act of assembly directed the appointment of deputies in each county; but even such appointments were made many wills from Chester County, especially from the northeastern part, continued to be taken to Philadelphia, almost down to the time of the Revolution. Following are the names of the deputy-registers for Chester County for the times given:

John Simcock, from 1714 to May, 1716.

Joseph Parker, August 14, 1716, to January 12, 1759.

Henry Hale Graham, March 5, 1759, to February 13, 1777.

Following is a list of the Registers of Wills from March 25, 1777, to the present time, together with the dates of their several commissions:

Thomas Taylor, March 25, 1777.

John Beaton, April 6, 1782.

Persifor Frazer, April 8, 1786.

Stephen Moylan, April 7, 1792.

John Hannum, Dec. 13, 1793.

Richard M. Hannum, December 6, 1798.

John Christie, January 6, 1800.

James Bones, Feb. 22, 1804.

John Smith, January 12, 1806.

Charles Kenny, Jan. 12, 1809.

Jesse Sharp, March 25, 1818.

Daniel Heister, Feb. 28, 1821.

Joseph Pearce, Jan. 17, 1824.

Eber Worthington, April 23, 1828.

Robert Ralston, Feb. 15, 1830.

Nimrod Strickland, April 20, 1833.

James Walker, Jan. 26, 1836.

Jesse Coulson, Feb. 2, 1839.

George W. Parke, November 12, 1842.

Henry Buckwalter, November 17, 1845.

William Baker, Nov. 25, 1848.

Alexander Leslie, November 22, 1851.

Hickman James, November 10, 1854.

Amariah Strickland, November 10, 1857.

Dr. Charles L. Seal, November 10, 1860.

George C. M. Eicholts, November 17, 1863.

Hampton S. Thomas, November 14, 1866.

Levi G. McCauley, Nov. 20, 1869.

Lewis H. Evans, Nov. 19, 1872.

George H. Paxton, December 28, 1875.

William S. Underwood, December 30, 1878.

1881, B. Frank Widdicombe.

B. Tevis Hoopes, in 1884.

Nathan J. Waitneight, in 1887.

Frank A. Thomas, in 1890.

Jesse J. Hickman, in 1893, and William Eachus, the present incumbent, in 1896.

RECORDERS OF DEEDS.

The first deed recorded in Chester County was a grant from Urin Keen for a lot on which stood Chester Meeting-house, the date of the deed being March 1, 1688, and "Inrooled" on the 10th of the same month. There were but few documents recorded previous to July 1, 1688. Following is a list of those who have held the office of recorder of deeds from 1688 to 1898:

John Bristow, about March 10, 1688.

Robert Eyre, March 26, 1693.

Henry Hollingsworth, October 10, 1700.

Joshua Fearne, March 25, 1691.

John Childe, January 3, 1695.

Peter Evans, April 17, 1706.

John Simcock, January 28, 1707, and on the 24th of February, 1707-08, his commission was read in open court. At the session of the assembly of 1714-15 an act was passed, making the prothonotary or county clerk of Chester County the recorder of deeds until he should be removed by the Court of Quarter Sessions, his bond being fixed at £200. At this time John Simcock, who, it will have been seen, filled at one time or another most of the offices in the county, was still recorder of deeds, and it is thought he was succeeded in 1716 by George Yeates, he being clerk of the courts in 1717. Richard Marsden, who was employed in the office as clerk as early as 1716, was either clerk or deputy clerk from 1719 to 1723, and in 1724 Joseph Parker became clerk and continued in office until 1766, when he died. Henry Hale Graham then became recorder and held the office until 1777. Since then the following persons have held the office, the dates of their commissions being given in connection with their names:

Thomas Taylor, March 25, 1777.

Persifor Frazer, April 8, 1786.

John Hannum, Dec. 13, 1793.

John Beaton, April 6, 1782.

Stephen Moylan, April 7, 1792.

Richard M. Hannum, December 6, 1798.

John Christie, January 6, 1800.

James Bones, Feb. 22, 1804.

John Smith, January 12, 1806.

Charles Kenny, Jan. 12, 1809.

Jesse Sharp, March 25, 1818.

Daniel Hiester, Feb. 28, 1821.

Nimrod Strickland, February 15, 1830.

Robert Ralston, April 29, 1833.

Stephen Marshall, Jan. 17, 1834.

Edward Bartholomew, January 26, 1836.

George Hartman, Feb. 2, 1839.

Abner Williams, Nov. 12, 1842.

William McCullough, November 17, 1845.

Edward H. Hibbard, Nov. 25, 1848.

Thomas Walter, Nov. 22, 1851.

Robert F. Hoopes, Nov. 10, 1854.

Thomas S. Taylor, Nov. 10, 1857.

Jonas G. Bossart, Nov. 19, 1860.

David Andrews, Nov. 17, 1863.

Dilwyn Parker, Nov. 14, 1866.

John A. Groff, Nov. 20, 1869.

C. Burleigh Hambleton, November 19, 1872.

Edwin Bateman, Dec. 22, 1875.
Franklin P. Ash, Dec. 18, 1877.
Harry Sloyer, Dec. 13, 1880.
Richard H. Plank, in 1883.
Sharpless M. Paxson, in 1886.

Hugh Kenworthy, Jr., in 1889, and
Samuel Ivison, Jr., in 1892.
Thomas D. Grover, the present incumbent, in 1895.

CLERK OF COURTS.

The first sitting of the Upland Court, of which there is any record, was held November 4, 1676, and at this time it was ordered that Mr. William Tom, the former "clarke," should deliver unto the clerk at that time, Ephraim Herman, the records and other public books and writings belonging to the court.

Since March 4, 1681, the date of the charter for Pennsylvania, the following have been clerks of courts:

Thomas Revell, September 13, 1681, to August 22, 1683; October 17, 1683, to December, 1689; Joshua Fearne, September, 1690, to April 18, 1693; John Childe, June 13, 1693, to March, 1699-1700; Henry Hollingsworth, June 11, 1700, to February 22, 1708-09; John Simcock, May 24, 1709, to about 1716; George Yeates, 1717; Richard Marsden, clerk or deputy, 1719 to 1723; Joseph Parker, 1724 to about 1766; Henry Hale Graham, 1766 to 1777.

Since that time the dates of the commissions of those holding office have been as follows:

Caleb Davis, clerk of all the courts, July 1, 1777; William Gibbons, the same, 1791; Daniel Hiester, the same, January 6, 1800; Jesse John, same, February 1, 1809; John G. Wersler, same, March 25, 1818; Thomas Davis, of Oyer and Terminer, February 28, 1821; Henry Fleming, of Orphans' Court and Quarter Sessions, February 28, 1821; William Williamson, Oyer and Terminer and Quarter Sessions, January 17, 1824; Joseph Pearce, Orphans' Court, January 17, 1824; Joseph Pearce, Orphans' Court, December 21, 1826; David Townsend, Oyer and Terminer and Quarter Sessions, August 3, 1827; Dr. William Darlington, Oyer and Terminer and Quarter Sessions, August 17, 1827; Simeon Siegfried,

Orphans' Court, April 23, 1828; John W. Cunningham, Oyer and Terminer and Quarter Sessions, February 15, 1830; George Fisher, Orphans' Court, February 15, 1830; John W. Cunningham, Oyer and Terminer and Quarter Sessions, April 29, 1833; George Fisher, Orphans' Court, April 29, 1833; P. Frazer Smith, Orphans' Court, May 2, 1835; Horatio G. Worrall, of all the courts, January 26, 1836; James M. Kinnard, of all the courts, February 2, 1839; James M. Kinnard, elected and commissioned November 14, 1839; Cheyney Nields, commissioned November 12, 1842; Alexander Marshall, November 17, 1845; Thomas P. William, November 25, 1848; James Sweney, November 22, 1851; Thomas W. Parker, November 10, 1854; Addis M. Ayars, November 10, 1857; Thomas P. Evans, November 19, 1860; Thomas H. Windle, November 17, 1863; James E. McFarlan, November 16, 1866; William H. Guie, November 20, 1869; James H. Wynn, November 19, 1872, died October 31, 1874; William W. Scott, appointed to the vacancy, February 17, 1875; William W. Scott, elected in November, 1875, commissioned December 22, 1875; Pierce Hoopes, Jr., December 30, 1878; Edward Paist, in 1881; Davis O. Taylor, in 1884; Thomas W. Taylor, in 1887; H. Morgan Ruth, in 1889; Elias Bair, in 1893, and R. Jones Patrick, the present clerk, in 1896.

SHERIFFS.

The Dutch, while they exercised jurisdiction on the Delaware, had an officer which they called a "schout," who performed offices similar to those of a sheriff under the English system of government. And Governor Lovelace granted a commission to Herman Frederickson as schout at the Hoare-Kill, and notwithstanding that at a council held at Fort James May 17, 1672, it was agreed that the office of schout should be converted into that of a sheriff for the corporation, and that the sheriff should be chosen annually, yet the name was not dropped, for on August 1, 1672, Governor Lovelace signed the following order:

"Upon the return of a double number from the inhabitants at the Whorekill, in Delaware Bay, for Schout and Comisary, I do approve of Hermans Frederick Wilbank to be Schout, and of Ottho Wolgast, William Claessen, and Isaac Savo to be Comisarys for the space of one year ensuing, after which time they are to make a new return."

And as Edmond Cantwell was one of the two persons returned to the Governor of whom to choose the high sheriff, Mr. Cantwell was chosen for that office, and appointed to be high sheriff in place of the schout, and he was to enjoy all the perquisities and priv- ileges of a schout. This appointment was made August 2, 1672.

Captain Cantwell was also authorized to receive the arrears of rents, in the place of William Tom, who had been commissioned receiver of quit-rents August 10, 1669, but had resigned. The Dutch having resumed control on the Delaware in 1673, Peter Alrichs was appointed schout; but this arrangement did not last more than a year before the English again became rulers on the Delaware and Captain Cantwell was appointed sheriff, serving from 1676 to 1681, when Governor Markham arrived and John Test became sheriff, and served until the arrival of William Penn.

Under the "Charter of Privileges," granted by Penn in 1701, each county was authorized to present two persons to the proprie- tary for the office of sheriff, one of whom he was to commission for three years, which arrangement continued until the adoption of the Constitution of 1776, which provided that in each county two per- sons should be annually elected, one of whom should be commis- sioned by the President of the State. Under the constitution the commission to the sheriff was issued by the Governor for three years. Under the amended Constitution of 1838 one person was elected in each county.

Following is a list of the sheriffs of Chester County, believed to be nearly correct, from 1676 to the present time:

Capt. Edmund Cantwell, 1676.
John Test, 1681-82.
Thomas Usher, 1682-83.
Thomas Withers, Dec., 1683-84.
Thomas Usher, June, 1686, to April, 1687.
George Foreman, 1689 to 1692.
Joseph Wood, 1693 to 1697.
John Hoskins, 1701 to 1708.
John Hoskins, 1709.
Nicholas Fairlamb, 1717 to 1719.
John Taylor, 1721 to 1728.
John Parry, 1732 to 1734.
John Parry, 1738 to 1739
John Owen, 1743 to 1745.
John Owen, 1749 to 1751.
John Fairlamb, 1755 to 1758.
John Fairlamb, 1762 to 1763.
John Morton, 1766 to 1768.
Henry Hayes, 1772 to 1733.
Robert Smith, 1777.
Robert Smith, Nov. 21, 1778.
John Gardner, October 19, 1780.
Ezekiel Leonard, Oct. 13, 1786.
Joseph McClellan, Oct. 13, 1792.
William Worthington, October 13, 1798.
James Kelton, October 21, 1801.
Titus Taylor, October 22, 1807.
Jesse Good, October 22, 1813.
Samson Babb, October 21, 1819.
Jonathan Jones, Oct. 29, 1825.
Peter Osborne, Oct. 28, 1831.
Joseph Taylor, Oct. 24, 1837.
Nathan Frame, Nov. 1, 1843.
James Bayard Wood, November 7, 1844.
David Bishop, Oct. 30, 1850.
David McNutt, Oct. 20, 1856.
Rees Welsh, November 7, 1862.
De Witt Clinton Lewis, November 2, 1868.
William B. Morrison, January 2, 1875.

George E. Hoopes, Dec. 30, 1880.
Benjamin Irey, in 1886; killed on his first day's work.
William Gallagher, in 1887.
Jeremy Collett, 1684-85.
Joshua Fearne, 1687 to 1689.
Caleb Pusey, 1692 to 1693.
Andrew Job, 1697 to 1701.
John Simcock, 1708.
Henry Worley, 1715.
John Crosby, 1720.
John Owen, 1729 to 1731.
John Owen, 1735 to 1737.
Benjamin Davis, 1740 to 1742.
Benjamin Davis, 1746 to 1748.
Isaac Pearson, 1752 to 1754.
Benjamin Davis, 1759 to 1761.
Philip Ford, 1764 to 1766.
Jesse Maris, 1769 to 1771.
Nathaniel Vernon, 1774 to 1775.
Charles Dilworth, Oct. 17, 1778.
David Mackey, October 16, 1779.
William Gibbons, Oct. 20, 1783.
Charles Dilworth, Oct. 17, 1789.
Ezekiel Leonard, Oct. 17, 1793.
James Bones, April 17, 1801.
Jesse John, October 16, 1704.
George Hartman, Oct. 25, 1810.
Cromwell Pearce, Oct. 19, 1816.
Jesse Sharp, October 15, 1822.
Oliver Alison, October 30, 1828.
Robert Irwin, October 25, 1834.
William Rogers, Nov. 9, 1840.
Clinton Frame, March 20, 1844.
Brinton Darlington, October 21, 1847.
Lewis Heffelfinger, November 4, 1853.
Jacob Heffelfinger, November 8, 1859.
Pusey J. Nichols, Nov. 3, 1865.
Davis Gill, November 1, 1871.
James E. McFarlan, December 31, 1877.
William Baker, in 1883.

George R. Hoopes, appointed in 1887.
James G. Parker, in 1890.

Alexander H. Ingram, in 1893.
Robert L. Hayes, the present incumbent, in 1896.

The several coroners, or, as they were sometimes called in early days, the "crowners," so far as has been ascertained, have been as follows since 1684:

CORONERS.

James Kenela, 1684.
Henry Worley, 1710.
Robert Barber, October 4, 1721.
Robert Parke, October 3, 1728.
John Wharton, October 3, 1730.
John Wharton, October 4, 1734.
Aubrey Bevan, October 4, 1738.
Joshua Thomson, Oct. 3, 1751.
Joshua Thomson, Oct. 3, 1753.
Davis Bevan, October 4, 1763.
John Trapnall, May 27, 1766.
John Crosby, Jr., Oct. 5, 1771.
David Denny, Nov. 21, 1778.
Benjamin Rue, October 12, 1782.
Isaac Thomson, Oct. 14, 1785.
John Underwood, Oct. 15, 1787.
James Bones, Dec. 19, 1794.
Jacob Righter, Nov. 4, 1800.
Ephraim Buffington, October 31, 1805.
Joseph Pearce, Dec. 2, 1811.
Joel C. Bailey, October 23, 1817.
Emmor Bradley, Nov. 25, 1823.
Davis Brooke, Nov. 5, 1829.
Thomas Ervin, Nov. 6, 1835.
Hezekiah Jackson, in 1841.
Thomas Walker, in 1847.
Hashabiah Clemons, in 1853.
Benjamin F. Smith, in 1859.
William H. Turner, in 1869.
Joseph B. Smith, in 1872.
Barclay Lear, in 1878.
Ernest White, in 1884 and 1887.

C. G. Troutman, the present incumbent, in 1896.
Jacob Simcock, 1696.
Henry Hollingsworth, 1707.
Jonas Sandelands, commission dated October 3, 1717.
John Mendenhall, Oct. 4, 1726.
Abraham Darlington, October 4, 1729.
Anthony Shaw, October 3, 1732.
Stephen Hoskins, Oct. 4, 1737.
Isaac Lee, October 4, 1746.
John Kerlin, October 4, 1752.
Philip Ford, May 22, 1761.
Abel Janney, October 4, 1765.
Joseph Gibbons, Jr., October 4, 1768.
John Bryan, October 4, 1773.
Allen Cunningham, October 19, 1780.
John Harper, October 20, 1783.
John Harper, October 13, 1786.
Nathan Scholfield, October 17, 1789.
Joshua Weaver, July 16, 1798.
Robert Miller, October 27, 1803.
Jacob Righter, Dec. 8, 1808.
Jesse McCall, Dec. 15, 1814.
Emmor Bradley, Nov. 9, 1820.
Anthony W. Olwine, 1826.
Benjamin J. Passmore, November 3, 1833.
William Taggart, Oct. 30, 1838.

Daniel Nields, in 1844.
David Williams, in 1850.
Robert McNeely, in 1856.
Joseph W. Barnard, appointed
in 1862, and elected in 1863
and in 1866.

William V. Rambo, 1875.
William Mercer, in 1881.
J. Jones McFadger, in 1890 and
1893.

Of the above-named coroners it is proper to note that John Harper was in office when the county-seat was removed from Chester to West Chester, an account of which is presented in another portion of this work, and that he was opposed to the removal, because he had property in Chester and naturally preferred to remain there. It is also said that he had command of the belligerent forces that came over to the Turk's Head, with the view of demolishing the county buildings then in course of erection. Afterward he removed to West Chester, and for some time kept the famous Turk's Head Hotel.

COMMISSIONERS.

It is probable that the officers called "commissioners," in the early history of the county, performed duties somewhat different from those performed by the county commissioners of the present time. The earliest legislation found regarding commissioners was an act passed February 28, 1710-11, entitled "An act empowering commissioners to compel the collection of all arrearages of former taxes, of which the following language is a part:

"Be it enacted by the honorable Charles Gookin, Esquire, by the Queen's Royal approval Lieutenant-Governor under the honorable William Penn, Esquire, absolute proprietary and governor-in-chief of the Province of Pennsylvania, etc., and by and with the advice and consent of the freemen of the said Province in general assembly met, and by the authority of the same, that in each respective county.of this Province the persons hereafter named shall be commissioners for putting this act into execution: That is to say * * * for the county of Chester, Nathaniel Newlin, Richard Webb and Isaac Taylor, who are hereby empowered and required to meet together on the 13th day of the month of March, 1710, at the place where the respective courts of the county are held," that is, at the county seat, and they were empowered to call before them all collectors and receivers and all other officers and persons whatsoever who had been employed in the assessing, levy-ing and gathering the rates and assessments aforesaid, and to cause them and every one of them to make and give a true and perfect account of all and every the aforesaid rates and assess-ments, etc.

On the same day an act was passed entitled, "An act for rais-ing a supply of two pence per pound and eight shillings per head," under which for Chester County Jasper Yeates, Caleb Pusey, Nicholas Pile and Henry Peirce, or any two of them, were ap-pointed to put the act into execution.

An act was passed February 22, 1717-18, entitled, "An act for the more effectual raising of the county rates and levies," ap-parently never submitted to the consideration of the crown, under which for the County of Chester, David Lloyd, Nathaniel Newlin, John Wood and Henry Miller were appointed commissioners to put the act into execution; and still later an act was passed, March 20, 1724-25, which was apparently not considered by the Crown, entitled, "An act for raising the county rates," which pro-vided "that the present commissioners for putting the said act into execution together with the assessors of the respective counties of Philadelphia, Chester and Bucks, now in being, shall continue in their several places and execute the powers and authorities given and required of them by the same acts for and during all the time they were respectively appointed to serve according to the direc-tion of those acts."

The duties of commissioners in the first place was probably the same as those performed by justices and the grand jury, and later by the grand jury and assessors. It is also probable that four commissioners were elected to serve one year, for in January, 1721-22, when a supplementary tax bill was under consideration it was ordered that the three eldest commissioners in Philadelphia County, the two first named in Chester County and the first named in Bucks County, should be discharged on September 30, 1722, and that on October 1, that year, one commissioner should be elected to take their places.

A petition from Chester County was read February 28, 1721-22, praying that the county levy might be repealed, or that three commissioners might be elected yearly. On March 1 (the next day), petitions from the other counties were read, and the bill was read for the third time. And it was enacted that three commissioners should be elected annually on October 1. The act as finally passed enacted that one commissioner should be elected annually. And the act referred to above, passed March 20, 1724-25, provided that the newly elected commissioner and the assessors should take the following qualification of oath:

"Thou shalt well and truly cause the county debts to be speedily adjusted and the rates and sums of money by virtue of this act imposed, to be duly and equally assessed and laid according to the best of thy skill and knowledge; and herein thou shalt spare no person for favor nor affection, nor grieve any for hatred nor ill-will."

By this act the commissioners were required to issue precepts to the constables, requiring them to make return to the assessors of the names and estates of the inhabitants, and the assessors were required to lay the rates thereon.

Following is a list of the commissioners since 1721, with the dates of their appointment or election:

1721, David Lloyd, John Wood, Nathaniel Newlin, Henry Miller; 1722, Robert Pyle; 1723, Nathaniel Newlin; 1724, Samuel Hollingsworth; 1725, Robert Pyle; 1726, Isaac Taylor; 1727, William Webb; 1728, Henry Miller, Evan Lewis; 1729, Samuel Nutt;

1730, Evan Lewis; 1731, Jacob Howell; 1732, Samuel Lewis; 1733, George Aston; 1734, John Davis; 1735, Richard Jones; 1736, Samuel Lightfoot; 1737, John Parry, Jr.; 1738, William Jefferis; 1739, John Davis; 1740, John Parry, Jr.; 1741, John Yarnall; 1742, John Davis; 1743, Jacob Howell; 1744, Joseph Mendenhall; 1745, John Davis; 1746, Thomas Pennell; 1747, Joshua Thompson; 1748, Isaac Davis; 1749, Thomas Pennell; 1750, Edward Brinton, Samuel Buntium, vice Thomas Pennell, deceased; 1751, William Lewis; 1752, John Fairlamb; 1753, Robert Miller; 1754, Thomas Pearson; 1755, Joseph Ashbridge; 1756, Joseph Davis; 1757, Joseph James; 1758, John Hannum; 1759, Jonas Preston; 1760, Joseph Pennock; 1761, John Griffith; 1762, Lewis Davis; 1763, John Brice; 1764, Benjamin Bartholomew; 1765, Richard Baker; 1766, John Davis; 1767, Robert Pennell; 1768, John Webster; 1769, John Evans; 1770, Jesse Bonsall; 1771, Robert Mendenhall; 1772, John Fleming; 1773, Thomas Levis; 1774, Thomas Taylor; 1775, William Evans; 1776, Sketchley Morton; 1777, David Cloyd; 1778, Andrew Boyd; 1779, Benjamin Brannan; 1780, John Bartholomew; 1781, Joseph Strawbridge; 1782, Caleb James; 1783, John Davis; 1784, Joseph McClellan; 1785, Caleb James; 1786, Caleb North; 1787, John Worth; 1788, Joseph Gibbons; 1789, James Moore; 1790, Elijah McClenachan; 1791, John Mecham; 1792, Wiliam Trimble, Jr.; 1793, Samuel Cochran; 1794, George Davis; 1795, George Miller; 1796, James Kelton; 1797, William Rogers; 1798, Even Evans; 1799, John Menough; 1800, Titus Taylor; 1801, John Rinehart; 1802, John Ramsey; 1803, Thomas Taylor; 1804, James Lockhart; 1805, John G. Parke; 1806, Joshua Gibbons; 1807, David Denny; 1808, Jesse Good; 1809, William Evans; 1810, David Wilson; 1811, James Ramsey; 1812, Eber Worthington; 1813, David Townsend; 1814, Alexander Chandler; 1815, Jesse Mercer; 1816, Samuel Baldwin; 1817, Maris Taylor; 1818, Joshua Weaver; 1819, Benjamin Thomas; 1820, Jesse Pugh; 1821, Isaac Trimble; 1822, James Davis; 1823, Abisha Clark; 1824, Ezra Cope; 1825, Joseph Hughes; 1826,

Benjamin Parker; 1827, Isaac Thomas; 1828, Melchi Happersett; 1829, James Alexander; 1830, George Gregg; 1831, Evan Evans; 1832, Joseph Wood; 1833, Walker Yarnall (Eber Worthington appointed in place of George Gregg, deceased); 1834, John Malin; 1835, Alexander Correy; 1836, Elijah Lewis; 1837, John Beidler; 1838, John W. Passmore; 1839, Hibbard Evans; 1840, John Templeton; 1841, Hatton Mercer; 1842, John Worth; 1843, Mordecai Lee; 1844, Enos Pennock; 1845, Smith Sharpless; 1846, David Byerly; 1847, Daniel Thompson; 1848, John Hannum; 1849, Rees Welsh; 1850, Joel Thompson; 1851, Thomas Vendever; 1852, Jacob Kulp; 1853, Newton I. Nichols; 1854, Albert Way; 1855, William G. Martland; 1856, Joseph Russell; 1857, Titus W. Gheen; 1858, Benjamin Hartman; 1859, Caleb Windle; 1860, Thomas Bateman; 1861, Joseph G. King; 1862, Andrew Mitchell; 1863, Lorenzo Beck; 1864, Levi H. Crouse; 1865, Thomas H. Charlton, by appointment to fill vacancy caused by Andrew Michell's death, and in 1865, Thomas M. Charlton by election for three years; 1866, Joseph F. Hill; 1867, Joseph Doan; 1868, Washington Haggerty; 1869, C. Marshall Ingram; 1870, Nathan G. Grimm; 1871, Alfred Wood; 1872, Matthew Barker; 1873, John Irey; 1874, David Ramsey; 1875, David Ramsey, John Irey, John McWilliams; 1878, Jacob M. Zook, William M. Elliott, Edwin Otley; 1881, Joseph T. Reynolds, Wellington C. James, Walter McFeat; 1884, Thomas Mercer, Samuel Whitson, G. Washington Beerbower; 1887, Thomas Mercer, Samuel D. White, Ebenezer D. Johnson; 1890, Samuel D. White, J. Harrison Rennard, D. Morgan Cox; 1893, Davis W. Entrekin, R. Thomas Garrett, John S. Mullen; 1896, R. Thomas Garrett, D. E. Chambers, Townsend Mouler.

COUNTY TREASURERS.

Following is a list of the county treasurers since 1695:

1695, Jeremiah Collett; 1697, Walter Marten; 1704, Caleb Pusey; 1706, Walter Marten; 1720, Henry Pierce; 1724, Philip

M. S. Way

Taylor; 1740, Joseph Brinton; 1756, Robert Miller; 1761, Humphrey Marshall; 1765, Jesse Maris, Jr.; 1766, Lewis Davis; 1770, James Gibbons; 1775, Philip Taylor; 1776, John Brinton; 1778, Thomas Levis; 1779, William Evans; 1780, Persifor Frazer; 1781, David Cloyd; 1785, Andrew Boyd and David Cloyd; 1786, William Evans; 1788, Andrew Boyd; 1786, William Haslitt; 1791, John Hannum; 1793, Elijah McClanachan; 1794, John Mecham; 1795, William Trimble; 1796, Samuel Cochran; 1797, George Davis; 1798, Robert Miller; 1799, James Kelton; 1801, Evan Evans; 1802, John Menough; 1803, Titus Taylor; 1804, William Worthington; 1806, John Rinehart; 1807, James Lockhart; 1808, John G. Parke; 1809, Joshua Gibbons; 1810, David Denny; 1811, Jesse Good; 1812, William Evans; 1813, David Wilson; 1814, John Ramsey; 1815, Eber Worthington; 1816, David Townsend; 1817, Alexander Chandler; 1818, Jesse Mercer; 1819, Samuel Baldwin; 1820, Maris Taylor; 1821, Joshua Weaver; 1822, Benjamin Thomas; 1823, Jesse Pugh; 1824, Robert Miller; 1826, James Davis; 1827, Abisha Clark; 1828, Ezra Cope; 1829, Joshua Hughes; 1830, Benjamin Parker; 1832, Melchi Happersett; 1833, James Alexander; 1834, Abraham Darlington; 1835, Joseph B. Jacobs; 1837, William Embree; 1840, Samuel M. Painter; 1842, S. C. Jefferis; 1843, Samuel M. Paiter, appointed in place of S. C. Jefferis, deceased; 1844, Morgan Reese; 1846, James M. Hughes; 1848, Samuel Davis; 1850, George W. Pearce; 1852, Henry Beidler; 1854, Samuel Wickersham; 1856, Townsend Walter; 1858, Charles Fairlamb; 1860, Joseph I. Tustin; 1862, Reuben Bernard; 1864, C. H. Kinnard; 1866, John T. Potts; 1868, Philip Price; 1870, Edwin Baker; 1872, Frank Shellady; 1874, Jesse E. Phillips; 1875, John G. Moses; 1878, John H. Buckwalter; 1881, Emmor G. Griffith; 1884, David Cope; 1887, Robert L. Hayes; 1890, Wilmer E. Pennypacker; 1893, Joel B. Pusey, and 1896, E. Vinton Philips.

The Prohibition County convention held meetings May 10, 1898, with John Flint, chairman. They named Richard T. Ogden

28

of Swarthmore, Delaware County, as their candidate for Congress, and the following executive committee was chosen: Harry L. Skeen, Downington; Granville Tyson, Spring City; James D. Peck, West Whiteland; J. H. Earp, Kennett Square; Dr. Levi Hoopes, West Chester; Rev. Alford Kelley, Frazer; J. H. Broomall, Upper Oxford; Mordecai T. Bartram, Willistown, and J. E. Diverty, Phœnixville. The convention expressed themselves as being in favor of Dr. Silas C. Swallow for Governor, and adopted the following platform:

"We, the members of the Prohibition party of Chester County, Pennsylvania, in County Convention assembled, renewing our acknowledgment of and allegiance to Almighty God as the rightful ruler of the universe, declare as follows:

"First. We reaffirm our approval of the platform and declarations of the National and State Conventions.

"Second. We declare ourselves as opposed to all forms of wrong everywhere, and hope suffering Cuba may gain her freedom and independence, and that our flag may soon cease to protect the saloon and all other evils.

"Third. We instruct the delegates to-day elected to the State Convention to use their best endeavor to secure the nomination of Rev. Dr. Silas C. Swallow for Governor, believing he eminently represents the principles of the Prohibition party, and commands the entire respect and confidence of all good citizens of our State, to the end that his election would secure an honest and economical administration of State affairs."

In closing this chapter on the politics of the county it is necessary to present the result of the Republican Convention held in West Chester, June 7, 1898. It is well known that the Republican party in Pennsylvania is divided into two factions—Quay and Anti-Quay—and this is, of course, the case in each county. The convention was held in the opera-house and was under the control of the Quay faction. The ticket nominated was as follows:

Congress, Thomas S. Butler, West Chester; Legislature (Eastern District), D. Smith Talbot, West Chester; Northern District, William P. Corwell, East Coventry; Western District, James G. Fox, Caln Township; Southern District, Evan B. Evans, Penn Township; Recorder of Deeds, Oscar E. Thomson, Phœnixville; Director of the Poor, Samuel Wickersham (Anti-Quay), New Garden, and county surveyor, Walter A. McDonald, West Chester.

Following is the platform adopted by this convention:

First. The Republican party of Chester County at the convention assembled ratifies and reaffirms the doctrines enunciated by the Republican National platform adopted at St. Louis in 1896 and the Republican State platform adopted in Harrisburg in 1898.

Second. We declare our emphatic approval of the wise and patriotic course of President McKinley in his general administration of the affairs of the Government, and we pledge to the administration and to Congress our universal support in the wise and proper course which they are pursuing in the defense of humanity and the honor of the nation.

Third. We congratulate Pennsylvania's representatives in the United States Senate and our member of Congress from the Sixth Pennsylvania District upon the support which they are giving to the National Adminstration during this critical period.

Fourth. We congratulate the Republican State Convention upon its selection of standard bearers of unimpeachable personal character and worth to lead the party to victory in the coming campaign and pledge to the Republican party the usual majority from Chester County.

POPULATION OF CHESTER COUNTY.

The following table shows the population of the county from 1790 to 1890, both years inclusive, according to the various censuses:

Year.	White.	Colored.	Total.
1790......	27,249	688	27,937
1800......	30,902	1,191	32,093
1810......	37,775	1,821	39,596
1820......	41,710	2,741	44,451
1830......	47,911	2,999	50,910
1840......	53,372	4,143	57,515
1850......	61,215	5,223	66,438
1860......	68,671	5,907	74,578
1870......	71,569	6,233	77,802
1880......	76,402	7,073	83,475
1890......	81,695	7,682	89,377

According to the Census of 1830 there were then five slaves in Chester County, three of whom were under twenty-eight years of age. This was somewhat of a surprise to a portion of the people, although it need not to have been, for from 1780 to 1830 was only fifty years, and in 1780 there were slaves that were very young, one at least that was only one month old, and female slaves of this age in 1780 might have become mothers late enough to have had children not yet twenty-eight years old in 1830.

Following is the census table for the townships, boroughs and a portion of the villages of the county in 1880 and 1890:

Townships, etc.	1880.	1890.
Atglen......	347	397
Birmingham......	503	458
East Bradford......	1,480	1,043
West Bradford......	1,620	1,281
East Brandywine......	1,011	995
West Bradford......	874	723
Caln......	863	1,053
East Caln......	539	256
West Caln......	1,275	1,146
Charlestown......	902	790
Coatesville......	2,766	3,680
East Ward.... 1,426		
Middle Ward.... 1,630		
West Ward..... 624		
East Coventry......	1,259	1,219

Township, etc.	1880	1890.
North Coventry	1,441	1,605
South Coventry	569	495
Downingtown	1,480	1,920
East Ward	872	
West Ward	1,048	
Easttown	845	1,082
Elk	830	789
East Fallowfield	1,461	1,505
West Fallowfield	1,048	1,039
Franklin	966	791
East Goshen	724	684
West Goshen	1,133	1,111
Highland	896	910
Honeybrook Township, including		
borough	1,849	1,876
Honeybrook Borough	470	514
Hopewell	216	213
Kennett Square	1,021	1,326
Kennett	1,247	1,185
London Britain	621	607
Londonderry	727	671
Londongrove	2,148	2,613
Malvern		641
East Marlborough	1,337	1,327
West Marlborough	1,146	1,041
New Garden	1,942	2,126
Newlin	779	680
New London	891	789
East Nantmeal	936	837
West Nantmeal	1,027	995
East Nottingham	1,351	1,305
West Nottingham	864	817
Oxford	1,502	1,711
Lower Oxford	1,429	1,384
Upper Oxford	1,696	1,096
Parkesburg	817	1,514
Pennsbury	795	773
Penn	739	632
Phœnixville	6,682	8,514
Ward 1	1,801	
Ward 2	1,086	
Ward 3	2,127	
Ward 4	1,724	
Ward 5	1,176	

Township, [etc.	1880.	1890.
Pocopson	564	513
East Pikeland	804	823
West Pikeland........	1,005	664
Sadsbury	749	843
West Sadsbury......	693	774
Schuylkill	1,416	1,254
Spring City......	1,112	1,797
Thornbury......	262	251
Tredyffrin......	1,975	2,549
Upper Uwchlan	848	824
Uwchlan	698	684
Valley......	1,072	1,187
East Vincent......	1,252	1,285
West Vincent......	1,238	1,081
Wallace	711	662
Warwick	1,267	1,487
West Chester......	7,046	8,028
East Ward 2,157		
North Ward 1,324		
South Ward 2,314		
West Ward 2,233		
Westtown	848	895
East Whiteland	1,273	1,157
West Whiteland	1,345	1,096
Willistown, together with Malvern.	1,620	1,390

CHAPTER XII.

ROADS.

CHAPTER XII.

THE making of roads in any country is a matter of great
importance. In the United States good roads have, as a matter of
necessity, come slowly, because of the great extent of the country,
of the poverty of the people and the great cost of such highways.
The first roads in the country were the Indian trails, and in many
cases more modern roads, even the railroads, have, to a considerable extent, followed the ancient paths of the Red Man.

Early in the history of Chester County the question of the
laying out and the establishment of better roads attracted the attention of the authorities. In 1678 the court at Upland ordered
that every person should, within two months, so far as his land
reached, make good and passable ways from neighbor to neighbor,
with bridges where they were needed, to the end that neighbors
might on occasion come together. Those who failed to comply
with this order were to forfeit twenty-five guilders.

Later the manner of making roads was prescribed, and was
in effect as follows: That the road should be made clear of standing and lying trees, and to be at least ten feet wide; stumps and
shrubs to be cut close to the ground, and sufficient bridges to be
be made over all marshy and difficult places. The earliest ap-

489

pointment of overseers of roads, or supervisors, was made October 13, 1680, and the court, under the government of William Penn, continued to appoint overseers of roads and fence-viewers for different precincts and townships until 1692, when the authority to so appoint these officers was conferred upon the townships themselves.

In the early days of the Province public roads were laid out by the grand jury, which was continued until 1699, and after this time the practice was that six persons were appointed by the court upon application. The first appointment of this kind was on December 12, 1699, and the first report of a jury specially appointed by the court was made in December, 1700. This jury was composed of John Worrell, Randall Malin, William Edwards, George Smedley, Robert Pennell and Daniel Hoopes.

In 1703, upon the petition of Humphrey Ellis, Daniel Lewis and fifty-eight others, to the Council, that council appointed Samuel Richardson, David Lloyd, Rowland Ellis, William Howell, William Jenkins and Richard Thomas to view certain roads which had been laid out, and to survey and lay out one direct road fifty feet wide leading from William Powell's ferry on Schuylkill and passing Haverford Meeting-house to the principal part of Goshen Township, and thence continued in a direct course to the upper settlements on the Brandywine.

In 1716 a petition was presented for a road leading from the west side of William Fleming's land to Caln Mill, and thence to William Brinton's in Birmingham, and James Gibbons, Richard Woodward, John Yearsley, Richard Thomas, Thomas James and David Davis were appointed to view. In 1717 a road was laid out from Ellis Lewis' mill southeast to the county line. And the same year a road was laid out from the land of Griffith Owen on King's Road from Goshen to Edgemont and Chester, S. 60 E. 80; east a little south through Owen and George Ashbridge, 440 perches to mill; thence through Ashbridge, William Hudson, in Willistown, Thomas Garrett, east and east by north, 352 perches to road from mill to Chester, and across to corner of Thomas Garrett's land and Samuel Lewis' land, 60 perches E. ½ N., between Lewis and Thomas James, and through James and Thomas Mary, 220; east somewhat southerly to road from Chester to Valley, 100 perches to end of road formerly laid out from Newtown to Philadelphia. Also in the same year a road was laid out from Joseph Pennock's to west end of Marlborough Street, and along the same 1,120 perches, and then north 52 east, along Thomas Wickersham's and Moses Key's land 132 perches to road running from Henry Hayes' to Brandywine Creek.

In 1717-18 a road was laid out from John Mendenhall's in the valley to the forks of the Brandywine, by way of Edward Clayton, George Carter, Abraham Marshall, Thomas Buffington, William Buffington, William Baldwin and Jacob Taylor.

In 1719 a road was laid out from Goshen to Philadelphia, commencing at the intersection of the Goshen Mill Road with the Providence Road, this road passing by what had been known as the "Old Square," in Newtown Township, and a short distance beyond that point it entered the great road leading to Philadelphia.

In 1736 a road was laid out from the Susquehanna, near the house of John Harris, and falling into Conestoga Old Road near Edward Kinnison's in Whiteland, passing near Uwchlan Meetinghouse, and was about 68½ miles in length.

According to S. W. Pennypacker, in his "Phœnixville and Vicinity," "An early road entered the township at the French Creek Bridge, and pursued a southeasterly course until it reached the trail," this trail extending from the Indian village near the mouth of Pickering Creek, to a large and permanent settlement called Indiantown. In the other direction it passed over Green Hill, reaching the Schuylkill at the old fording place near Perkiomen Junction. "It remained the only thoroughfare in that direction until a jury in 1735 opened a road on a line between the properties of Coates and Starr. From the active participation of Samuel Nutt in obtaining and locating this road, it received and has since borne his name.

"The road leading from the village of Charlestown to the Fountain Inn and Starr's Ford, was opened in August, 1731, and at one time was called the 'Egypt Road,' because it connected two settlements, one in Chester County, the other in Philadelphia County, respectively honored with the suggestive names of Upper and Lower Egypt.

"The White Horse Road, southward from the Long Ford, in the direction of Cedar Hollow, was laid out in the early days of the settlement to accommodate the residents of the valley on their way to the Schuylkill fisheries.

"The road leading from Phœnixville northward to the Black Rock Bridge, was opened about the year 1730."

On February 25, 1762, the county was divided into fifty-one districts, each township to be one road district.

The following extract from a communication of Ziba Darlington to the Jeffersonian furnishes some interesting history connected with the laying out of the Street Road.

"William Penn laid out a public road in Marlborough Township, and named it Marlborough Street. It ran nearly, if not quite, straight its whole distance, a stretch of some five miles, beginning in the Pennsbury line, east of the present Red Line Tavern, and ending at Marlborough Friends' Meeting-house.

The highway from the end of Market Street, Philadelphia, was laid out in sections, as settlements extended westward in the colony. It was not known as the Street Road. Long after these old colonial times and ways, in 1815, the Legislature of Pennsylvania authorized a State road to be laid out from Market Street Bridge, Philadelphia, to McCall's Ferry on the Susquehanna River. Governor Snyder appointed John Thompson of Delaware

County, Edward Darlington of Chester County, and Samuel An-krim of Lancaster County, commissioners for such purpose. They, with their corps of target-bearer, chain-carriers, axmen and assistants, began the work at Market Street Bridge, but made no change in the existing road thence to Marlborough Friends' Meeting-house. From thence to McCall's Ferry the road laid out was pretty much a new one. Burr, a noted bridge-builder, had got the heavy timbers for the bridge at McCall's Ferry ready, and during the winter of 1815 moved them on the ice to their position. The floor was not laid when the commissioners arrived there, and the target-bearer recollects walking out on the timbers over the Susquehanna River. The commissioners would have cut off an angle in the road at the Marlborough Meeting-house premises had it not been for an old burial ground; so the right angle turn there yet remains.

"The Street Road is the name applied to the highway from Market Street Bridge to McCall's Ferry, and got it from the old Marlborough Street of Penn."

The above survey was made in 1815, John Thompson acting as surveyor, and Ziba Darlington of Chester County as target-bearer.

At an early period a public road was laid out from Philadelphia to Lancaster, which was known as the "Old Lancaster," or "Provincial" Road. In Chester County it passed the present Eagle Station on the Pennsylvania Railway, Paoli, Admiral Warren, White Horse, Moore's Mill, Ship, Caln Friends' Meeting-house, Wagon and Mariner's Compass. A portion of the bed of this road is now occupied by the Lancaster Turnpike, but the greater portion is still used as an ordinary public road.

The Swede's Ford Road ran from a fording over the Schuyl-kill just below Norristown, westward joining the old Lancaster Road in East Whiteland Township. The road known as the "Boot Road" ran from the ferry at Philadelphia by way of the "Boot

Tavern," in Goshen, to Moore's Mill (Downingtown). The Great Chester Road, running north from Chester, intersected this road at the "Boot," and is said to have been laid out on an old Indian trail. A road ran from Moore's Mill westward, a continuation of the Boot Road, crossed the west branch of the Brandywine near Coatesville, and Buck Run at Pomeroy, and running northward of the valley to the Gap.

The Strasburg Road dates from 1794 and was laid out at different times. Part of the original road is what is now known as "Goshen Street," forming the northern line of the borough of West Chester, and in its westward course it unites with the present Strasburg Road at the foot of Black Horse Hill, in East Bradford, passing eastwardly by the residence of William P. Marshall and Fern Hill Station on the railway leading from West Chester to Frazer.

The road from Wilmington to Reading, passing through West Chester, is a very old one, and there was a road running from Downingtown, by way of Waynesburg, to the Conestoga settlements. On the bed of this last mentioned road runs for a portion of its length the "Horseshoe Turnpike." The road from Philadelphia by way of Concord, Chadd's Ford, Hamorton, Kennett Square and New London, and on to Baltimore, is also an old one, and was long a leading stage route between Philadelphia and the Southern States. There was also a road from Wilmington to the Pequea Valley, by the way of Hamorton, Unionville, Doe Run, Ercildoun, Humphreyville and Sadsburyville. This last mentioned road was intersected at Humphreyville by another road which led past Upper Octorara Church and the old Black Horse Tavern northward. The "Gap and Newport Road" led from the "Gap" in Lancaster County to Newport, Delaware, and was long a leading road from Lancaster to Wilmington.

There was a road leading from West Chester in a southwest direction, crossing the Brandywine at Jefferis Ford, which was known as the "Oil-mill Road," from an oil-mill which stood on a farm lately owned by Edwin James. This road was superseded by a State road laid out in 1830 from New Hope, on the Delaware River, through Doylestown, Norristown, West Chester, Unionville, White Horse and Oxford to the Maryland line. The "Limestone Road," in the western part of the county, which passes through Oxford, was at one time an old Indian trail. The Valley or Mc-Call's Ferry Road, which runs from Parkesburg to McCall's Ferry, on the Susquehanna River, was authorized in 1809 by an act of the Assembly of the State.

Much might be written on the history of early staging on all of these roads did space and time permit. A brief sketch of the first turnpike in the United States is here introduced.

The Philadelphia and Lancaster Turnpike Road was the first of its kind constructed in America, and hence is worthy of special mention. It was in 1790 or 1791 that it was agreed in the Assembly of the State to cause a survey to be made between Philadelphia and Lancaster, with the view of ascertaining the most eligible route for a turnpike road between the two cities. A company was incorporated under the name of the "Philadelphia and Lancaster Turnpike Road Company," April 9, 1792, and the eagerness of people to subscribe for stock in this company was remarkable, it being necessary to resort to the drawing of lots in order to determine who should first subscribe. This road as it was constructed has a length in Chester County of thirty-six miles, nearly seventeen miles along the Great Valley. It was a very expensive undertaking, on account of the inexperience of the engineers. The entire length of the road is sixty-two miles, and it was formed of three highways between its terminal points, the King's Highway of Lancaster County being extended to join the two lower sections. It was opened to travel in 1795 and immediately became the leading thoroughfare between Philadelphia and the West. The road was made of hard stones broken small, the pavement being twenty-four feet wide, eighteen inches thick in the middle. and twelve inches thick at the sides. The cutting down of hills to the limits of four degrees elevation and the leveling of the platform was very expensive, the total cost of the road, including the construction of the bridges and aqueducts, being $465,000, or $7,500 per mile. For the first twenty-five or thirty years the corporation had at its head Mr. Ellison Perot, of Philadelphia. For many years the travel upon it was enormous, which is one of the strongest evidences of the value to the community of good roads. It was lined with public houses, these houses being in some parts of its course through Chester County not more than one mile apart. At night the yards of these public houses or taverns were filled with teams, the horses standing on each side of the wagon-tongue, on which a trough was placed for their feed. The teamsters spread their beds, which they carried with them, on the barroom floors or on the floors of other rooms. These taverns were usually conducted by their owners and were remarkable for their good order.

But the glory of this great route of travel and of its hotels were doomed to disappear, for when the Pennsylvania Railroad went into operation about forty years after its construction, it took away the travel and the transportation of merchandise over this turnpike, and its income from tolls diminished and the number of its hotels as gradually, or perhaps it would be better to say as rapidly, decreased, until at the present time the use of the road is only local, and the traveler may pass over many a mile of it without seeing a single sign inviting him to refreshment or to rest.

Other early turnpikes were as follows: The Downingtown, Ephrata and Harrisburg, otherwise known as the Horseshoe Pike, chartered March 24, 1803; the Gap and Newport, taking the place to a great extent of the old Gap and Newport Road, chartered April 7, 1807; the Little Conestoga, running from the Philadelphia and Lan-

caster Turnpike, near the Warren Tavern, to a point in Berks County, where the Reading Road intersects the Morgantown Road, chartered March 16, 1809.

In 1811 a survey was made for a turnpike from the Philadelphia and Lancaster Turnpike at or near the twenty-sixth milestone through Westchester to Wilmington, laws being passed by both Pennsylvania and Delaware authorizing the work; but the people of Delaware declined to take stock in the enterprise and the people of Pennsylvania then felt justified in abandoning the project. The people of Delaware then constructed a turnpike from Wilmington to the State line, a distance of about six miles, in the direction of West Chester.

The West Chester and Wilmington Plank Road Company was organized in 1854 and a plank road constructed from West Chester to Dilworthtown, and in 1858 this road was converted into a macadamized road.

Much of this information on early roads, with the exception of what is presented on the Philadelphia and Lancaster Turnpike Road, has been derived from Judge Futhey's excellent "History of Chester County," due credit for which is thus given.

In the early day there were the following stage routes extending out of West Chester:

One leading to Reading, over which a stage coach was run from West Chester every Tuesday, Thursday and Saturday, and leaving Reading every Monday, Wednesday and Friday, by way of Oakland, Lionville, Eagle, Wallace, Loags, Morgantown, Joanna Furnace and Beckersville, the fare to Reading being $2. Of this line John G. Dunwoody was proprietor in 1857.

One to Cochranville, leaving West Chester on the same days, and Cochranville also on the same days as the above, the fare to Cochranville being $1. Of this line Francis Conway was the proprietor in 1857.

One to New Holland, leaving West Chester on the opposite

29

days from the above, as well as New Holland, passing Downingtown, Gallagherville, Brick, Brandywine Manor, Rockville and
Waynesburg, the fare each way being $1.87½, and the proprietor
of the line being R. Fox.

One to Wilmington, leaving both West Chester on every Tuesday, Thursday and Saturday, the fare to Wilmington being $1, the
proprietor of this route being George Court, in 1857.

One to Philadelphia, leaving West Chester every morning, and
leaving Philadelphia every afternoon, the fare each way being
62½ cents, and the proprietor being Stackhouse & Co., in 1857.

RAILROADS.

Chester County is well supplied with railroads. The Pennsylvania Railroad passes through the county from east to west;
the Wilmington and Northern Railroad crosses it from north to
south, passing down the valley of the Brandywine; the West Chester and Philadelphia Railroad connects West Chester with Philadelphia, and the West Chester Railroad connects the latter railroad with the Pennsylvania Railroad at Frazer. The Pennsylvania and Delaware Railroad runs from the Pennsylvania Rail-
road at Pomeroy Station with Delaware City; the East Brandywine and Waynesburg Railroad runs from Downingtown northwesterly to Waynesburg; the Chester Valley Railroad runs from
Downingtown eastward to Norristown; the Pickering Valley Railroad runs from Uwchlan to Phœnixville; the Wilmington and
Western Railroad connects Wilmington with the Pennsylvania
and Delaware Railroad at Landenburg; the Reading Railroad
passes along the eastern boundary of the county, and the Perkiomen Railroad connects with the Reading Railroad between
Phœnixville and Valley Forge.

Previous to the introduction of the railroad in Chester County,
travel and transportation across the county and the country were

principally by stages and wagons. Passengers and freight were carried from Philadelphia to Pittsburg and from Pittsburg to Philadelphia by means of these vehicles drawn by four or six horse teams, all owned by farmers of Chester and adjoining counties. The wagons were large and high, on high wheels, strongly built, and covered over with canvas, supported by hickory hoops or bows. In this State these vehicles were known as Conestoga wagons, while farther to the west they were frequently called Pennsylvania wagons, and are still thus referred to, though, as things of the past. A half dozen or more teams were in those early days frequently seen traveling in company along the Lancaster Pike, on which a line of four-horse stages was run, which became quite popular with the traveling public and profitable to their owners. This pike was almost invariably taken in fine weather when the roads were good; otherwise both stages and wagons would take the Strasburg Road passing through West Chester. In addition to these two roads there were numerous others passing through West Chester. In addition to these two roads there were numerous others passing in different directions through the county, and at their intersections villages grew up and postoffices were established. The trip from Philadelphia to Pittsburg and return usually occupied from four to six weeks, the average value of a trip one way was one hundred dollars, and in case a load was found from Pittsburg back to the east it was $150.

About 1823 the public mind began to be exercised over the question of railroads, but the ideas entertained as to what a railroad was were not always clear. From that time until 1828 several attempts were made to organize a company to build a railroad to connect with the canals of the State, by which means it was expected to form a through line for both passengers and freight from Philadelphia to Pittsburg; but capitalists, being like the rest of the world, ignorant of what a railroad was, were slow to invest, as they always have been and always will be in a new thing. Each of these attempts therefore came to naught.

But at length, in 1828, the Legislature of the State passed an act providing for the construction of a railroad from Philadelphia to Columbia, in Lancaster County, to be styled the "Pennsylvania Railroad," and directed that twenty miles at each end of the road be built at once. Soon after this the people of West Chester began to take up the question of building a railroad and to discuss the question of how much more a horse could draw on such a road than on a common dirt road; for the idea of steam being used as a motive power on such a road had then entered the minds of but few people, at least in the United States.

In this connection it may be proper to state that according to Dr. George Smith, in his History of Delaware County, the first railroad constructed in this country was in what was once a portion of Chester County—in Ridley Township, Delaware County, in 1806. This railroad was built by Thomas Leiper, who had seen a road of the kind in either England or Scotland, and before building his road in Delaware County he had constructed for him an experimental road on a vacant lot in the Northern Liberties in Philadelphia, at a grade of one and a half inches to the yard, which on the day of trial proved to be a great success. This rail road in Delaware County was constructed by Mr. Leiper for the purpose of transporting stone from his quarry on Crum Creek to his landing on Ridley Creek, a distance of about one mile, the ascent being a graded incline plane, and the superstructure being made of white oak, with cross-ties and string-pieces. The wheels of his cars were made of cast-iron, and had flanges to keep them on the rails. This short railroad was afterward superseded by the Leiper Canal, built in 1828 by Hon. George G. Leiper, son of the builder of the railroad, the canal being in use until 1852.

The great event which startled the country from one end to the other, and which really determined the merchants of Philadelphia and the people of Pennsylvania to build the railroad to Columbia, was the completion of the Erie Canal in 1826. They were quick to perceive that unless something were done to prevent it their previously obtained and profitable Western trade, which had up to that time been carried by means of the great Conestoga wagons, would go by way of the Erie Canal to the city of New York; hence the passage of the act above referred to, to build the railroad from Philadelphia to Columbia. Thence it was thought travel could go by canal to Hollidaysburg, whence a railroad would pass over the mountains, and from Johnstown a canal would extend to Pittsburg. By such a route it was thought practicable to compete with the Erie Canal, as there would be a gain of time over the two stretches of railroad which this plan contemplated.

In the construction of this first railroad from Philadelphia to Columbia many experiments were made in order to ascertain what kind of rail would be suitable. From the head of the inclined plane at Philadelphia to White Hall a heavy stone sill was laid, with a flat bar of iron spiked upon it; but this proved a failure. Then flat bars of iron were laid, which were two and a half inches wide by one-half an inch thick; but these proved too light. They would draw loose, and in one or two cases the bars curled up at the end and pierced the bottom of the car. Then even these rails had to be imported from England at a great expense, and were very poor, there being then no American mills in operation. American mills came later on.

The Columbia Road was completed into Philadelphia in 1833, entering the city at Vine Street, whence a city track laid on stone sills was extended down Broad, Market and Third to the foot of Dock. Upon the completion of this road, although it would not by any means compare with railroads of the present day, the competition of the Conestoga wagon was soon extinguished, and the drivers and their horses were transferred to the railroad. The first cars for passengers which, as intimated, were for a time drawn by horses, were four-wheeled vehicles, the body being similar to but much larger than that of a Troy coach.

It is now time to turn attention to the construction of the first railroad that entered West Chester. It was in 1830 that this matter was taken up in earnest, the question being, or rather, perhaps, one question being, at what point should a' railroad from West Chester connect with the Columbia Railroad, then well under way. A public meeting was held December 11, at the Turk's Head Hotel, at which a committee was appointed to confer with Major John Wilson, and as a result of this conference, with the consent of the canal commissioners, Major Wilson sent a corps of engineers to make a preliminary survey, the Major himself making an estimate of the probable cost. A second meeting was held December 22, at which a general town meeting was called for December 24, to take further and definite action. Dr. William Darlington of the committee made a report which was accepted, and the following resolutions adopted:

"Resolved, That it is expedient to construct a railroad from the borough of West Chester to intersect the Pennsylvania Railway at such point as shall be found most eligible.

"Resolved, That Dr. William Darlington, William H. Dillingham, Thomas Williamson, Ezra Cope, David Townsend, Thomas S. Bell and John H. Bradley, Esq., be a committee whose duty it shall be to take the necessary steps to obtain a law authorizing the incorporation of a company to construct the said railway."

Major Wilson reported on January 8, 1831, that he had located a satisfactory route and submitted an estimate of the cost of the road, which he had placed at $88,021.29. The charter was granted July 18 following, with all the privileges and concessions asked for by the petitioners.

Anticipating the granting of the charter subscription books were opened in Philadelphia at the Merchants' Coffee House, at West Chester, at the Paoli Tavern and at the Washington House, on March 22, 1831. There was a grand rush made by those who wished to subscribe to the stock of the company, and in a very short time more than double the amount of stock authorized had been subscribed; but this amount was later reduced, as provided for in the charter. The first board of directors, elected March 28, was composed of the following gentlemen: Dr. William Darlington, Ziba Pyle, William Williamson, S. C. Jefferis, Jonathan Jones, Joseph Hemphill and Elihu Chauncy, Esq. On May 3, 1831, Major John Wilson was appointed chief engineer, and John P. Bailey, assistant, and on May 26, the grading of the line was let out in one mile sections, and the work pushed rapidly to completion. A meeting of the board of directors was held September 18, 1832, at which it was announced that John P. Bailey had completed the construction of the entire line in sixteen months. The track laid at that time consisted of chestnut cross ties, supporting yellow pine string pieces, on which were laid flat iron bars two and a half inches wide by one half an inch thick, and the road was so ballasted between the rails as to make a good pathway for horses.

The first superintendent of the road was J. Lacey Darlington, who was paid a salary of one dollar per day, when he was engaged in the service of the company, and the first general agent, Hickman James, received for his services $500 per year. The second annual meeting of the Board of Directors was held January 23, 1833, and it was then announced that the road had been opened pro forma September 13, 1832, and horses placed on the road, making partial trips for the accommodation and entertainment of the friends of the enterprise. On the 18th of October, 1833, the Canal Commissioners had completed a line of rails to the head of the inclined planes, and the cars of the West Chester Railway Company were at once run to that point, whence passengers were conveyed into Philadelphia in stages and omnibuses, a drive of about four miles down the west side of the Schuylkill River.

On January 1, 1834, the company declared the first dividend

and the stockholders were made happy with the prospect of future earnings of their road. During the year following it was deemed advisable by the West Chester Company to construct a connecting road from Kirkland Station across to Whiteland, in order to reach the limestone and marble quarries in that section, and to shorten the distance to Columbia, where lumber was then obtained. The capital stock was increased $10,000 and the road was built. This road, however, was but very little used and went to decay for want of repairs, proving an almost total loss to the company.

During the year 1835 a lot was purchased in Philadelphia, on Broad Street, south of Race Street, on which lot was built a hotel called the West Chester House, with tracks for the company's cars under it. In July, 1836, William P. Sharpless was appointed superintendent of the road and property to reside in Philadelphia, whence it was thought a better supervision could be had of the property. Soon afterward adjoining lots were purchased on the southeast corner of Broad and Race Streets, upon which lots was built a large warehouse suitable for a forwarding and commission house, and from this house the freighting to West Chester was done for several years.

About this time the railroad boom that had so excited the entire country subsided, times becoming hard, and there was but little done for some years. The times continuing hard it became difficult for people to meet their obligations, and the West Chester Railway Company was no exception to the general rule. There was no relief until after the passage of the tariff act of 1842. In order to meet the difficulties of the situation the company was compelled to raise the fare from one dollar to one dollar and twenty-five cents for the single trip. Then, too, the road had enemies, and an opposition company put four-horse coaches on the road to compete with the railroad, carrying passengers at reduced rates, and getting the carrying of the United States mails at about half what had been formerly paid to the railway company. Besides all this the Canal Commissioners were endeavoring to induce the State Legislature to appropriate money in order to enable them to go down the Chester Valley from Downingtown, thus avoiding the inclined planes, as it had been discovered that these planes were a great obstruction to travel, and must be avoided. Had the Canal Commisioners accomplished their object the West Chester Railway Company would have been left high and dry at Malvern, but the State was in debt to the extent of some $40,000,000 and the Canal Commissioners failed of their object.

At the annual meeting held January 15, 1844, the following gentlemen were elected directors: Joseph J. Lewis, Isaac Thomas, Philip P. Sharpless, Edward Hoopes, James Martin, George Campbell and William M. Spencer. Philip Sharpless and Isaac Thomas became members of the executive committee and at once determined that if possible they would lift the road out of its difficulties. One of these difficulties was the exorbitant charge made by the Canal Commissioners in the shape of tolls over their road, and it was resolved that because of these excessive charges they would, in case they could not secure a reduction of these tolls within three months, suspend the running of all cars, and call a meeting of the stockholders to consult upon the best means of disposing of their property. In a few weeks, however, the demands for a reduction of tolls were conceded and the fare to Philadelphia was reduced to seventy-five cents. Efforts had been made at various times to induce the State authorities to furnish steam power to haul the company's cars, and on January 31, 1844, the executive committee reported that they had appointed Samuel M. Painter, superintendent, and that an agreement had been made with the Canal Commissioners by which the company's cars were to be hauled from the head of the inclined planes to the intersection at the rate of fifteen dollars per day for each train. This agreement went into operation May 25, 1844, at which time two second-hand eight-wheeled passenger cars were purchased for the service.

Afterward two new passenger cars were ordered built, which had a compartment for baggage underneath the body of the cars, to save wheel toll on the baggage car. These were for a time the best equipped and the most highly ornamental cars on the road. Previously only horse cars had been used, and horse cars were still to be used from the inclined planes to the city and on the West Chester Railroad. On May 26, 1845, the Canal Commissioners agreed to haul the cars of the company from the inclined planes into the city of West Chester for $6,000 per annum, and horses were continued to haul the cars into the city of Philadelphia from the foot of the inclined planes.

In 1846, a turntable was constructed at West Chester, and the fare, which had been raised to $1 to Philadelphia, was again reduced to seventy-five cents. Although the locomotives used at this time were very light, yet they were too heavy for the light irons on the road, and it was determined to lay a heavy T-rail as early as possible. Money was raised and the road rebuilt more permanently in 1847.

About this time the Canal Commissioners were having a great deal of difficulty with the properties under their management. They were confronted with a deficit every year, and appeared determined to prevent the railroad now under consideration from making any better showing. And the officers of the railroad began to consider the question of a new route to Philadelphia by which it would be possible to avoid the State works altogether. An engineer, with a small corps in charge, was sent out to find a new route and to make a rough survey of such route when found. It was found that the cost of a railroad over this route would be about $1,000,000, and it was decided that the interest on this sum could not be earned if the road were built. Then some of the ablest professional men of West Chester, together with a few sound business men of Delaware County, determined to make a trial survey of a route through the northern end of Delaware County, and engaged Edward F. Gay to make the survey and estimate the cost. His estimate footed up $768,829.03, which was too high for the gentlemen contemplating the enterprise. T. G. Sickles was therefore engaged to make an estimate, and, seeing where the dif-ficulty lay, and knowing that none of those by whom he was em-ployed knew anything about railroading brought in an estimate about $100,000 less than that of Mr. Gay. This estimate was satis-factory, and a public meeting was at once called for the purpose of organizing a company to build what became afterward known as the West Chester and Philadelphia Railroad. Of this com-pany John S. Bowen, a lawyer of West Chester, was elected presi-dent; T. C. Sickles was the engineer-in-chief, and work was com-menced to locate the road. This was in 1851.

About this time the old West Chester Railroad Company made an exchange of their Broad Street Depot in Philadelphia for a lot at the southwest corner of Eighteenth and Market Streets, upon which they erected a passenger and freight depot, and in the mean-time earnest efforts were made to effect a union between the old road and the direct West Chester road. But the owners of the old road, finding that their property was steadily increasing in value and promised dividends in the near future, rejected all overtures, advising all people to take warning by the experience they had had. However, after a fierce newspaper war, the West Chester Direct succeeded in getting a single track laid down to Glen Mills, where, for a time, the company was stranded. West Chester, by a popular vote, had invested to the amount of $20,000 in the stock, which was sold a few years afterward for $4,000, and some of the original stock sold as low as $1 per share. But at length, in 1858, a great effort brought the road through to West Chester, it having been chartered about ten years before. The road, having thus been completed, was transferred by the trustees, J. and I. T. Thomas, to the company, it having at the time $1,000,000 worth of bonds outstanding and all stock sunk. The road had cost about

$2,000,000, and several of the original projectors had been ruined and had passed out of the management. In the meantime the old West Chester Company had been improving and strengthening their road and reserving their income for the contest with the new road for the business of West Chester, which they realized must come.

The Pennsylvania Railroad Company was chartered April 13, 1846. This company was authorized to construct a railroad from Harrisburg to Pittsburg, a distance of 248 miles. The work of construction began at Harrisburg in July, 1847, and the division from Harrisburg to the junction with the Portage Railroad (then a State work) at Hollidaysburg at the eastern base of the moun-tains, being opened September 15, 1850. The western division, from the western end of the Portage Railroad to Pittsburg, was opened September 10, 1852; the mountain division, and with it the whole line, being opened February 15, 1854.

From Harrisburg to Philadelphia, a distance of 105 miles, the road was made up of the old Philadelphia and Columbia Railroad (originally a State work), and the Harrisburg, Portsmouth, Mount Joy and Lancaster Railroad, chartered in 1832, opened in 1838. and leased in 1849. The Philadelphia and Columbia Railroad was purchased in 1857, with the main line of a system of public works in the State. This system of public works was inaugurated in 1826, and contemplated the canals along the leading water courses. In this year the Legislature passed an act providing for a canal to be constructed at the expense of the State, and to be styled the Pennsylvania Canal. This canal was to extend from the Swatara River, at or near Middletown, where the Union Canal commenced, to the mouth of the Juniata, and from Pittsburg to the mouth of the Kiskiminetas and the Allegheny River. The design appears to have been to make the Juniata and the Kiski-minetas navigable by slackwater, and to use the Union Canal as the eastern end of the line, connecting with Philadelphia.

In 1827 the Canal Commissioners were authorized by the Legislature to make examinations through Chester and Lancaster Counties preliminary to the construction of a railroad to connect with the canal, and in 1828 the Commissioners were directed to locate a railroad from Philadelphia through Chester County, and on to Columbia, via Lancaster, the road to be completed within two years. This road was completed to Columbia with a double track in 1833. When this great public system of internal improvements was first undertaken it was supposed that a canal from the waters of the Susquehanna to those of the Allegheny was practicable. The Portage road across the summit was worked by a series of inclined planes, which was abandoned upon the completion of the Pennsylvania Railroad. For the work purchased of the State between Philadelphia and Pittsburg the company paid $7,500,000 in its five per cent. bonds, payable at the rate of $460,000 per year, the balance of this payment, after the interest had been taken care of, to apply on the principal debt.

In 1833 besides the completion of the road to Columbia the Portage was completed with a single track, and the main line of the canal was also finished. In 1834 the entire line between Philadelphia and Pittsburg was opened to travel. The first train of cars that passed over the Columbia Railroad from Columbia passed over it on Wednesday, February 26, 1834. On March 6, 1834, the Whig, a newspaper published in West Chester, contained an account of this first trip, a portion of which account is as follows:

"One track of this important State improvement being completed, arrangements were made by Mr. S. R. Slaymaker of Lancaster for passing a train of cars from that city to Philadelphia on Wednesday. The members of the Legislature from the city of Philadelphia and the counties adjacent to the line of the road, with others, arrived at Columbia on Tuesday evening, by the canal-packet from Harrisburg, and were immediately conveyed to Lancaster in a train drawn by the locomotive, 'Black Hawk.' The engine performed the trip in fifty-five minutes.

"On Wednesday morning" (February 26) "a train of cars was
again attached, and left North Queen Street at eight o'clock, arrived at the Gap at ten, passed with ease the works there constructed, and arrived at the head of the Inclined Plane, near the
Schuylkill, at half-past four in the afternoon, having made the
trip in eight hours and a half, all stoppages for taking in water,
receiving and discharging passengers and incidental delays included. * * * * *

"Throughout the whole line the progress of the train was
hailed with hearty acclamations by crowds of persons collected
to witness the novel spectacle. An immense concourse of citizens
was also assembled at the head of the inclined plane to greet its
arrival at that point. The locomotive was there detached, the cars
passed down without obstruction or serious difficulty, and were
thence conveyed to Broad Street and other points in the city."

The locomotive Black Hawk, built in England, was the first put
on the road. This was in 1832. In 1835 there were three locomotives, and in 1837 forty, horses being then relieved of the duty of
hauling cars on the railroad.

An offer having been made by the Pennsylvania Company for
a lease of the old West Chester Railroad, an agreement was entered
into by the two companies April 6, 1859, by which the former
company agreed to run trains on satisfactory terms for five years.
The manner in which the road was operated under this lease was
not satisfactory to the old company, as there was no apparent
effort put forth by the Pennsylvania to increase the value of the
property, and the impression gained strength that the operating
company intended to permit the property to run down and its
value to become so impaired that they would be able at the end
of their lease to purchase it at a merely nominal figure. But notwithstanding this the old company were able to pay dividends
and to lay aside a considerable surplus.

In the meantime the direct line to Philadelphia by way of

Media was doing a fair and increasing business through the ener-getic management of its president, Marshall B. Hickman. A short time previous to the expiration of the lease referred to above, Mr. Hickman made an offer to purchase the old line. Terms were agreed upon and the transfer of the road made without consulta-tion with the Pennsylvania Company, the old line thus passing into the possession of the Media Company. The Pennsylvania Company was not satisfied with this arrangement, as it needed West Chester as a local station to and from Philadelphia, and the result was that this company purchased both roads, since which time the old and new lines from West Chester to Philadelphia have been parts of the Great Pennsylvania System.

The East Brandywine and Waynesburg Railroad Company was incorporated March 3, 1854, the road originally extending from Downingtown to Waynesburg, a distance of eighteen miles. The road was leased to the Pennsylvania Railroad Company for ninety-nine years, November 1, 1876, and was reorganized after foreclosure, June 7, 1888. The name of the road was then changed to the Downingtown and Lancaster Railroad, and now extends from Downingtown to Conestoga Junction, a distance of 37.58 miles.

The Wilmington and Northern Railroad is the result of sev-eral consolidations. The Berks and Chester Railroad Company was incorporated April 20, 1864, and in 1866 it was consolidated with the Delaware and Pennsylvania Railroad Company, under the name of the Wilmington and Reading Railroad Company. The road from Wilmington to Birdsboro' was opened in 1870, and was extended to Reading in 1874. On May 8, 1876, the road was placed in the hands of trustees, A. Gibbons, George Brooke and George Richardson, by order of court, and by them operated until it was sold December 4, 1876. The Baltimore, Philadelphia and New York Railroad Company, successor to the State Line and Juniata and Maryland, and Pennsylvania Railroad Companies, having the

right to build a railroad from Baltimore to Philadelphia, was
absorbed by the Wilmington and Reading, and the purchasers
of the road organized as the Wilmington and Northern, January
18, 1877. The extension of the road to Reading was sold separately; but during the year 1887 the Reading branch was consolidated with the main line, of which it still forms a part. The
total length of line operated on June 30, 1896, was 92.30 miles, and
the total number of miles owned by the company was then 88.41
miles.

The Philadelphia and Delaware Railroad Company was incorporated under the name of the Doe Run and White Clay Creek
Railroad Company, March 24, 1868, the road to extend from the
Pennsylvania Railroad at Pomeroy to Delaware State line, where
it was to connect with a road running to Delaware City. Subsequently the name of the company was changed to the Pennsylvania and Delaware Railroad Company, and in 1873 the road was
leased by the Pennsylvania Railroad Company, by which it has
since been operated. It connects with the Baltimore Central
Railroad at Avondale, with the Wilmington and Western at Land-
enberg, and with Philadelphia, Wilmington and Baltimore Railroad near Newark. The road extends from Pomeroy to Delaware
City.

The Wilmington and Western Railroad connects Wilmington
with the Pennsylvania and Delaware Railroad at Landerberg, its
length within Chester County being between two and three miles.
It was opened October 19, 1872.

The Pickering Valley Railroad Company was incorporated
April 3, 1869, and was leased for ninety-nine years from September
1, 1871, by the Pennsylvania and Reading Railroad Company for
thirty per cent. of its gross earnings. Its capital stock is $95,655.
The road extends from Phoenixville to Byer's Station, a distance of
11.3 miles.

The Perkiomen Railroad Company was chartered March 23,

Geo. G. Groff.

1865, and the road was opened May 8, 1868. It was leased from August 16, 1868, to May 14, 1879, to the Philadelphia and Reading Railroad Company, the road having been completed October 11, 1875. It extends from Perkiomen Junction to Emaus Junction, Pennsylvania, a distance of 38.5 miles, the track of the East Pennsylvania Railroad Company being used from Emaus Junction to Allentown. The company was reorganized in 1887.

The Philadelphia and Chester Valley Railroad Company was chartered May 7, 1888, as the successor of the Chester Valley Railroad Company, which was chartered April 2, 1850, reviving the charter of an old company by the name of the Norristown and Valley Railroad Company, incorporated April 15, 1835, to construct a railroad from some point on the Philadelphia and Columbia Railroad east of Brandywine Creek to a point on the Philadelphia, Germantown and Norristown Railroad near Norristown; but this company, after expending $850,000, became unable to complete their road within the time prescribed. The road is 21.50 miles in length, from Downingtown to Bridgeport, and is operated by the Pennsylvania Railroad Company, in 1891 the latter company paying for its use 45 per cent. of the gross earnings up to $30,000 and 50 per cent. on all above $30,000. The road cost $1,073,613.88.

The Philadelphia and Reading Railroad was constructed previous to 1842, being opened for business January 10 of that year. The bill incorporating the company was introduced into the Legislature by Elijah F. Pennypacker, during the session of 1832-33. This was a difficult and expensive railroad to build, at least through Chester County, for bridges were required over the Valley, Pickering and French Creeks, besides one over the Schuylkill River. There is also a tunnel cut through solid rock, 1,932 feet long, and which was originally 19 feet wide and 17 feet high. This tunnel, begun in December, 1835, was completed in September, 1837.

The Philadelphia and Baltimore Central Railroad Company

30

was incorporated March 17, 1853, and on April 6, 1854, was authorized to form a union with a corporation chartered by the State of
Maryland. The main line of this road from West Chester Junction
to the junction near Port Deposit with the Columbia and Port Deposit Railroad, is 46 miles in length, of which 36¾ miles is in Pennsylvania.   From West Chester Junction to Lamokin is seven miles.
The road was opened to Oxford in 1859, to Rising Sun, Maryland,
in 1865, and to River Junction in 1869.   It had been brought into
use to Chadd's Ford and soon afterward to Avondale, some time
previously.   Among the men who carried forward this enterprise to success may be mentioned John M. Dickey, Samuel
Dickey, Dr. E. V. Dickey, Samuel J. Dickey, Ebenezer Dickey,
Dr. Franklin Taylor, John M. Kelton, James R. Ramsey, Mark A.
Hodgson, Isaac Watkins, John Richards, Samuel Martin, James
A. Strawbridge, Job H. Jackson, Daniel Stubbs, Milton Conard and
David Woelpper.   Each of these men served for a time during the
construction of the road as a member of the board of directors.

      The West Chester Street Railway Company was chartered
August 4, 1890, with a capital of $60,000, divided into shares of $50
each.   The officers of the company since its organization have been
as follows: William Hayes, president; William S. Harris, secretary, and F. W. Worthington, treasurer.   The directors have been
as follows: William M. Hayes, R. T. Cornwell, M. H. Matlack,
J. Carroll Hayes and A. G. McCausland. That part of the railway
within the limits of West Chester was commenced in November,
1890, and the cars began running on it September 28, 1891.   It
consists of one track on High Street, extending from Virginia Avenue to Rosedale Avenue, and one track on Market Street, extending from the Pennsylvania Railway to New Street, down New
Street to Sharpless Street, the intersection of the two branches
being at High and Market Streets.   That part of the road extending from Sharpless Street to Lenape Station on the Wilmington
and Northern Railway, a distance of nearly five miles, was built

during the month of June to November, inclusive, 1891, and the cars began running on this line November 10, 1891. Power to propel the cars on the lines of this company is derived from the West Chester Electric Light and Power Company.

The Philadelphia, Castle Rock and West Chester Railway Company was organized December 15, 1892, and chartered with an authorized capital stock of $1,000,000, of which $100,000 has been subscribed. This company has already constructed an electric railway from Philadelphia to Ridley Creek on the Philadelphia and West Chester Road, and on March 31, 1898, it passed a resolution to the effect that in order to increase its business and accommodate the travel of the public it was necessary to construct its railway from its western terminus, as above given, to the line of the borough of West Chester, and into the said borough along Market Street to Adams Street, then north on Adams Street to Gay Street, and then on Gay Street to Walnut. Permission being asked of the borough council of West Chester to so construct its railway inside the borough, a resolution was passed by the Council on April 11, 1898, granting the privilege asked. The president of this railway company is John N. M. Shriner and the secretary, William S. Taylor.

CHAPTER XIII.

THE COURTS.

CHAPTER XIII.

THE first court of Chester County, after William Penn's ar-
rival, met at Chester February 14, 1682: John Simcock, president;
Thomas Brasy, William Clayton, Robert Wade and John Bezer,
justices; Thomas Usher, sheriff; and Thomas Revell, clerk; Will-
iam Rawson, James Browne, Jeremiah Collett, William Hewes,
Walter Martin, Nathaniel Evans, Joshua Hastings, William
Woodmanson, Thomas Colborne, Albert Hendrickson, Joseph
Richards, and Edward Carter, jurors.

There was also a Tribune established called the Peace Makers,
consisting of three persons holding their appointment from the
court. The duties of the Peace Makers appear to have been to
arbitrate upon such questions as were brought before them. They
were appointed for a specified time and held meetings regularly.

At a court held June 27, 1683, it was ordered that the Peace
Makers are to meet on the first Fourth-day every month, and at a
court held August 5, 1684, the Peace Makers made the following
order:

"According to the order of the court to us directed we have
seriously considered the premises between the plaintiff, Richard

523

Crosby, and the defendant, George Andrews, whereby we, the Peace Makers, do give, grant, judge and allow that the said defendant, George Andrews, his heirs and assigns, shall pay or cause to be paid unto the said plaintiff, Richard Crosby, or his assigns, such full and just sum, eighteen pounds, in lawful money of this province, at or upon the twentieth day of this instant, December, at the now dwelling house of James Saunderlaine, at Chester, one-half of said eighteen pounds, the said defendant, George Andrews, or his assigns, is to pay the said plaintiff, Richard Crosby, or his assigns, as aforesaid in ready money, the other half as aforesaid, in good and merchantable wheat or rye at the common market price of this river. To which conclusion we, the Peace Makers, for this County of Chester, have set our hands at the aforesaid Chester, the 17th of the 10th month, 1683.

"JOHN HASTINGS,

"JOHN HARDING."

At a court held August 22, 1683, a most interesting case was tried, a case involving the title to the whole of Tinicum Island. This island had been given by deed of November 6, 1643, to Governor John Printz, and the Governor's daughter, Mrs. Papegoya, in 1662, had sold it to Jost De Lagrange, receiving in part payment a bill of exchange which was protested. After returning from Sweden she brought suit to recover that portion of the consideration represented by the bill of exchange. The case was taken from the High Court of the Delaware to the Court of Assizes of New York, where, on October 2, 1672, a verdict was rendered for the plaintiff for £350 and costs. Jost De Lagrange having died, his widow married Andrew Carr, and at the time of this verdict Andrew Carr and his wife were in possession of the island. The sheriff was ordered to put Mrs. Papegoya in possession of the island and of the stock in payment of the debt, which was done, and Mrs. Papegoya afterward sold the island to Otto Ernest Cock.

To trace this case further would scarcely be interesting to the general reader, hence it is here dismissed.

At a court held in December, 1684, Joseph Cookson was presented by Robert Wade "for taking a wife contrary to the good and wholesome laws of this Province," and was ordered to find security in the sum of ten pounds, which, so far as could be ascertained, was the end of the case.

A most interesting case came before the court which met January 6, 1685, entitled, "Justa Anderson vs. Laurentius Carolus and James Saunderlaine." It appeared that Justa Anderson a few years before had purchased of Laurentius Carolus, the Swedish priest, his house and land, about 200 acres, for which he gave or agreed to give 800 guilders. It was probably in 1684 the Swedish priest had sold the same land or tried to do so, with the exception of the house and a small piece of land on which it stood, to John Grubb, and hence the suit against Carolus and Saunderlaine, for weakening the title to land. The verdict was in favor of the plaintiff, but the defendants carried the case to the next court of assizes held at Chester.

Thus proceedings were held in the courts for many years, the recital of the details of which would be both tedious and uninteresting to the general reader.

The first Court of Equity for Chester County was held in March, 1685-86, the record being:

"Att a court of equity held att Chester, the 5th day of the 1st week of the 10th month, 1686:

"Commissioners present:—John Blunstone, John Simcocke, George Maris, Bartholomew Coppock, Samuel Levis, Robert Wade, Robert Pile.—Robert Eyre, clerk."

The first Orphans' court was held at Chester on the 3rd day of the 1st week of the 8th month, 1687.

The first court-house in the county, called the "House of Defence," was erected about 1678, and soon afterward a prison was erected. A new prison was provided for in 1691, which was de-signed as a work-house for felons. It was to be of stone and 18x26 feet in size. This order was not, however, carried out, and an-other order was made in 1692, a poll-tax being levied to provide for the expense, this being the first poll-tax levied in the county in which no distinction was made between freemen and servants. This levy not being made, a new order was issued in December, 1693, and early in 1694 an assessment was authorized for raising £150 for defraying the expense of the building of the new jail "at the true value of two pence per pound upon the real and personal estates of all the inhabitants of the county, seasable by the first act of the new laws—all freemen 6s per head." In 1693 the num-ber of taxables in the ten townships in what is now Delaware County was 140, and in 1696 this number had become 182.

In 1697 a new court-house had been erected, and in 1700 the necessity for a pair of stocks and a whipping-post had become evi-dent. In 1703 this necessity was again presented. In 1724 an-other new court-house was erected in Chester, which served until after the separation of Delaware from Chester County, and for many years served as a town hall in Chester Borough.

Under the Constitution of 1790 the State was divided into dis-tricts, each district to contain not less than three counties nor more than six. There was to be appointed by the Governor of the State a president judge for each district and associate justices for each county, not less than three nor more than four. In the divi-sion of the State into districts, Chester County came in the second, along with Lancaster, Dauphin and York. The first president judge of this district, William August Atlee, was appointed by Governor Thomas Mifflin. He presided over the courts of his dis-trict from November, 1791, to August, 1793. John Joseph Henry was also appointed by Governor Mifflin, and presided from Febru-ary, 1794, to May, 1800. John D. Coxe was the next president judge, serving from May, 1800, until May, 1805. William Tilghman presided from August, 1805, to February, 1806, both terms.

By an act of the Legislature passed February 24, 1806, the State was redistricted, Chester County being placed in the Seventh District, along with Montgomery, Delaware and Bucks; and soon afterward Bird Wilson, otherwise referred to in these pages, was appointed president judge of this district, remaining from February, 1806, until November, 1817, when he became a clergyman in the Episcopal Church.

In 1818 John Ross became president judge, remaining in that office until May, 1821. A new district was then formed, composed of Chester and Delaware Counties, and named the Fifteenth Judicial District, over which Isaac Darlington presided from May, 1821, until his death, April 27, 1839. Thomas S. Bell was then appointed, and presided over the district from 1839 until he was elevated to the Supreme Court, November 18, 1846. John M. Forester, of Harrisburg, was then appointed, and served from December, 1846, to March, 1847, and then James Nill, of Chambersburg, was appointed, presiding from March 23, 1847, until March 18, 1848. Henry Chapman, of Doylestown, succeeded Judge Nill, and presided from March 18, 1848, until December 2, 1851, the office then becoming elective, and though Judge Chapman was solicited by both political parties to become a candidate for election to the office, he declined, because it was not convenient for him to reside within the district, as the law required.

Under the elective system Townsend Haines was elected in October, 1851, was commissioned November 6, and presided over the district until December 2, 1861. William Butler was elected to this office in October, 1861, was commissioned November 20, 1861, and served until February 24, 1879, when he resigned, having been appointed United States district judge for the Eastern District of Pennsylvania. On February 27, 1879, J. Smith Futhey was appointed by Governor Hoyt to serve during the remainder of Judge Butler's term, or until January 5, 1880, and was elected in November, 1879, there being no opposing candidate. Judge Futhey served until his death, which occurred November 26, 1888. During the greater part of his term he was the only judge, the associate judges having been legislated out of office, as will be seen later on, in 1876, and it was doubtless due to the fact of the great amount of labor performed by Judge Futhey on the bench that his life was terminated as early as it was. It was also due to this great amount of labor performed by him that an additional law judge was provided for by an act of Assembly approved June 15, 1887, under which William B. Waddell was appointed by the Governor to fill the vacancy caused by the creation of this office, Judge Waddell's commission being dated July 7, 1887. Judge Waddell was elected to the office of additional law judge in the fall of 1887, and was commissioned January 3, 1888.

Upon the death of Judge Futhey, Judge Waddell was appointed president judge, his commission as such being dated December 4, 1888, and in February, 1889, Thomas S. Butler became additional law judge. Judge Waddell served until his death, which occurred June 3, 1897, when Joseph Hemphill, who was elected additional law judge in November, 1889, became president judge, and is serving as such at the present time. William Butler, Jr., was appointed additional law judge August 29, 1897, and was subsequently elected, and on January 3, 1898, was commissioned for a term of ten years.

Previous to 1790 the Court of Oyer and Terminer was held by the justices of the Supreme Court, who at stated times made a circuit of the counties. A sitting of this court was held at Chester October 3, 1698, before Joseph Growdon and Cornelius Empson to hear an appeal in a suit between Thomas Thomas and Morgan James, and another session was held October 2, 1705, before John Guest and Jasper Yeates, at which time the Governor's commission to John Guest, Joseph Growdon, Jasper Yeates, Samuel Finney and William Trent, or any two of them, was read. At this time David Lloyd, who was attorney for the defendant, showed that the Governor's commission was defective, and consequently nothing could be done. The members of this court came, of course, from all parts of the State, the following being from Chester County: John Simcock, who served in 1690, and David Lloyd, who served from 1717 to 1726, both of whom were citizens but not natives of Chester County; and Thomas McKean, who was a native of Chester County and one of the ablest men of his time. He served in 1777.

Under William Penn's form of government murder was the only capital crime; but about the time of his death the counterfeiting of bills of credit and current coin were made capital. After the Revolutionary War a revised penal code was adopted, in the preamble of which it recited the provisions of the royal charter, that the English laws on felony should be in force in Pennsylvania until altered by the Proprietor and freemen. And it was enacted that high treason, murder, robbery, mayhem, witchcraft, arson and six other crimes should be capital crimes, and fines, whipping, branding and imprisonment were provided for crimes of lesser grade.

Since then, however, one by one these crimes have been dropped from the list of capital ones, and at present the State has returned to the more humane code of William Penn, only one crime, that of murder, being now capital.

Isaac Darlington, one of the foremost lawyers of the early part of the present century, was born in the township of Westtown, Chester County, December 13, 1781, and it is said of him that probably no young man in Chester County was trained to more laborious habits in early life than he. He was instructed in the rudiments of an English education by the celebrated John Forsythe, the best schoolmaster of that period, and for two or three years he taught a country school, acquitting himself with remarkable success. When nearly eighteen years of age he began reading law in the office of Joseph Hemphill, a distinguished member of the

Chester County Bar, and he was admitted to the bar a short time before he was twenty-one years of age. In 1807 and in 1808 he was elected to the Legislature, and declined a re-election, but at a special election held in February, 1816, to fill a vacancy, he was again chosen to that body.

At the general election in 1816 he was elected to a seat in the Fifteenth Congress, to represent Chester and Montgomery Counties, and in 1820 he was appointed deputy attorney-general for Chester County, holding the position until 1821, when he was appointed president judge of the district composed of Chester and Delaware Counties. This position he held until his death, which occurred April 27, 1839.

Hon. Thomas S. Bell, formerly a distinguished attorney, and president judge of the district composed of Chester and Delaware Counties, was born in Philadelphia, October 22, 1800. Having studied law under James Madison Porter, he was admitted to the Philadelphia Bar April 14, 1821, and in May following removed to West Chester. In 1823 he was appointed deputy attorney-general for Chester County, and held the office until August, 1828. Continning in practice until May, 1837, he then became a member of the convention to revise the Constitution of the State, and in 1838 he was elected a member of the State Senate, but owing to some alleged errors in the returns his seat was contested and awarded to Nathaniel Brooke.

On May 16, 1839, he was appointed president judge of the district composed of Chester and Delaware Counties, which position he filled until November 18, 1846, when he was appointed a member of the Supreme Court of Pennsylvania, holding this position until December 1, 1851, when the tenure of office was changed by the Constitution. He represented Chester and Delaware Counties in the State Senate in 1858, 1859 and 1860, and in all the public positions he held was able and faithful in the discharge of his duties. His mind was remarkably active and correct in its operations, and he mastered his subjects, as it were, almost by intuition. A fluent speaker, a clear and forcible writer, uniformly courteous and honorable in his dealings and associations with men, he was missed greatly by all at his death, which occurred in Philadelphia, June 6, 1861.

Hon. Persifor Frazer Smith, born in Philadelphia, January 23, 1808, was a son of Joseph and Mary (Frazer) Smith, the former being a son of Robert Smith, of Uwchlan, Chester County, and lieutenant of the county during the Revolutionary War. Persifor Fraser Smith was educated in Philadelphia, principally in the classical schools of Dr. Samuel B. Wylie and Joseph P. Engle, and graduated from the University of Pennsylvania July 31, 1824, and immediately removed with his father to East Whiteland, Chester County. In October, 1826, he began the study of the law in the office of William H. Dillingham, and was admitted to the bar of Chester County in 1829. In December, 1831, he was admitted to the Supreme Court of the State, and in October, 1832, to the Circuit Court of the Third District of Pennsylvania. In May, 1835, he was appointed clerk of the Orphans' Court of Chester County, and on February 25, 1839, he was appointed prosecuting attorney for Delaware County. In February, 1849, he was admitted to practice before the Supreme Court of the United States, and became widely known as an able and honest practitioner by both lawyers and jurists. He was well skilled in the intricacies of the law, and his opinion was frequently sought by his professional brethren.

In 1861 he was elected a member of the State Legislature, and was returned in 1862, 1863 and 1864. During the Civil War he was one of the strongest sustainers of the Union cause in its struggle with armed rebellion, and in 1866 he was appointed State Reporter of the Supreme Court of Pennsylvania, a position which he filled with ability for ten years, resigning in May, 1876. Almost every law library in the State of Pennsylvania contains the thirty-two volumes of State Reports compiled and arranged during the ten years he held the office of State Reporter. He was also the author of a valuable legal text-book entitled "Forms of Procedure."

He was a man of wide and varied reading, keeping fully abreast of the progress of the age in which he lived in scientific and literary matters, and he was always closely identified with every good work calculated to promote the prosperity of his town and county.

Hon. J. Smith Futhey, who became president judge in 1879, and died while still holding that office, November 26, 1888, was one of the most distinguished men of Chester County. He was possessed of unusual ability, was of independent thought and action, and of great and untiring industry. He was the only judge of his district for about eight years. It was stated that his death was largely due to overwork, and in 1887 the Legislature enacted a law providing for an additional law judge, in order that the president judge might be to some extent relieved.

Besides performing his duties as judge, Mr. Futhey spent most of his leisure hours in historical research and other literary work, and it is to him that the people of Chester County, as well as historians generally, are mainly indebted for information in regard to the early history of the county in all its varied lines. His genius for and appreciation of detail in matters of this kind was very great.

Mr. Futhey was undoubtedly one of the most upright and faithful of the common pleas judges of the State, and it may be truthfully said of him, and without the least disparagement of others, that no one preceded him or has succeeded him who was or has been of more sterling integrity or possessed of a higher appreciation of the value of justice. Soon after his death the Bar of Chester County adopted the following memorial address:

"The death of Hon. J. Smith Futhey is a serious loss to the bench and bar of this county. When stricken down he had nearly completed a ten years' term as president judge of this district.

J. Smith Futhey

The absence of so prominent a personage from our midst leaves a void which will be long felt and mourned. He was worthy of the ermine—able, industrious, merciful and just. In the trial of cases he knew no parties, and followed implicitly where the law and the evidence led. He was uniformly courteous and exceedingly tender and considerate of the feelings of others. His denials left no sting; his judgments no offense; his inflictions no wound. Taking him all in all, he will be hard to follow and his place difficult to fill.

"As a member of the bar for nearly forty-six years, he was endeared to us by all the ties that can unite professional brethren. He was proud of his profession, and had a high sense of the integrity, honor and courtesy essential to it. His ability, industry and worth won for him a large, devoted and influential clientage. He was a consistent Christian gentleman, and was highly esteemed as a citizen. A friend of popular education, he labored assiduously for its promotion. His historical and other researches and publications are valuable contributions to the literature of the times and have been widely read. As husband, father, citizen, author, lawyer and judge, his life has been an exemplary one and full of good works."

These eulogistic words were signed by William B. Waddell, president, and by J. Newton Huston, secretary.

Hon. William Bell Waddell, formerly president judge of the District Court, was born in Philadelphia, September 21, 1828. The family was of Scotch-Irish origin and traced its ancestry back to the north of Ireland, peopled by the Scotch after the native inhabitants had been driven out by King James I of England. One member of the family, born in Ireland, has been rendered famous by William Wirt as the "Blind Preacher," in the History of Virginia, and another member, grandfather of the judge, whose name was William, was also born in Ireland. His son Robert married Mary Bell, and they were the parents of Judge William Bell Waddell.

31

Judge Waddell pursued his academic studies in the private school of James Crowell, and entered Princeton College in 1846, graduating therefrom in 1849. Returning to West Chester, he read law with Joseph Hemphill, father of Judge Joseph Hemphill, and he was admitted to the bar March 2, 1852. From this time on until his death he was almost continuously engaged in the practice of his profession in West Chester, until 1887, when he was elevated to the bench.

In 1864 he was elected to the House of Representatives of the State Legislature, serving until 1867. In 1871 he was elected to the State Senate, and served until the close of his term in 1873, when he returned to the practice of law. In 1887 he was appointed to serve as additional law judge until the election in the fall of 1887, when he was elected for the term of ten years, from 1888 to 1898, but, upon the death of Judge J. Smith Futhey, he was appointed president judge, his commission being dated December 4, 1888. This position he filled untl his death, which occurred June 3, 1897.

He was always courteous as a jurist, was an able, honorable man and an upright judge. He was well respected by his fellow-citizens, and was widely and sincerely mourned at the time of his death.

Hon. Joseph Hemphill, president judge of Chester County, was born at West Chester, September 17, 1842. After attending private schools at West Chester he went to Williston Seminary at East Hampton, Massachusetts, where he remained until compelled by sickness to return to his home. Entering his father's law office in 1860 as a law student, he read law there three years, and then spent one year in the law department of Harvard University, under the special instruction of Parsons and Washburne, well-known authorities on American law. He was admitted to the bar October 31, 1864, and the law partnership then formed with his father lasted until the latter's death, February 11, 1870. From 1864 to at the time of his election as additional law judge he was in constant practice.

Judge Hemphill is a democrat, and in 1872 served as a member of the Constitutional Convention, rendering valuable service in framing the present constitution of the State. This led to his nomination by the Democratic party of the county for additional law judge in 1889, and in the fall of that year he was elected over Thomas S. Butler, by a majority of thirty-two votes. Taking his seat January 6, 1890, he discharged the duties of his office to the satisfaction of all, and upon the death of President Judge William B. Waddell, succeeded to that position, which he is now filling.

As stated above, the Constitution of 1790 provided that in each county there should be associate judges, not less than three nor more than four, to hold their offices during good behavior. The first associate judges in Chester County were appointed by Governor Thomas Mifflin, August 17, 1791. They were Joseph Shippen, of Westtown; Walter Finney of New London; and James Moore of West Nantmeal. Benjamin Jacobs of West Whiteland was appointed the fourth associate judge July 3, 1792.

Judge Shippen held the judgeship until December 28, 1792, when he resigned, and on January 5, 1793, Samuel Evans was appointed first associate judge in his place. Samuel Evans, having removed to Lancaster County, resigned his office, June 29, 1793, and was succeeded by James Boyd, of what is now Penn Township, November 1, 1793. These four associate judges, Walter Finney, James Moore, Benjamin Jacobs and James Boyd, presided together until 1802, in which year Judge Moore died, and was succeeded by John Ralston of Vincent, who was appointed April 7, 1802. Judge Jacobs served until March 31, 1803, and was succeeded by John Davis of Tredyffrin. From this time on until September, 1820, Judges Finney, Boyd, Davis and Ralston were associates, Judge Finney dying in that month, and no appointment was made to fill the vacancy, because the Legislature in 1803 has passed an act providing that when a vacancy should thereafter occur, there should be no appointment until the number of associate judges had been reduced by death, resignation or otherwise, to less than three.   In 1806 an act was passed providing for the reduction of the number of associate judges to two.   Judge Boyd died August 10, 1821, and the number was thus reduced to two.

Judge Ralston died September 1, 1825, in the eighty-first year of his age, and was succeeded by Cromwell Pearce of East Whiteland, his commission being dated September 5, 1825.   Judge Davis died in 1827, and was succeeded by Jesse Sharp, who was commissioned January 26, that year.   Judges Pearce and Sharp were associate judges until 1839, when, on account of defective hearing, Judge Pearce resigned, and was succeeded by Thomas Jones of East Whiteland, for the term of five years, in accordance with the Constitution of 1838.

Judge Sharp's term having expired February 27, 1841, he was re-appointed for the constitutional term of five years, and on the expiration of this term he was again re-appointed for another term of five years.   But on account of his age he resigned in December, 1847, and was succeeded by Nimrod Strickland of West Chester, whose commission was dated January 31, 1848.

Upon the expiration of Judge Jones's term of five years, February 19, 1844, he was re-appointed, and at the expiration of his second term, in February, 1849, he retired from the bench.   Samuel Shafer was appointed to succeed Judge Jones, and Judges Strickland and Shafer served until the expiration of their terms of office, December 1, 1851, the office being made elective by amendments to the Constitution.

At the election of 1851 Samuel Shafer and Joseph Hodgson were elected for five years, and took their seats December 6, 1852. Judge Hodgson was a resident of Penn Township, and at the expiration of his five years' term declined a re-election.   Judge Shafer, who was an unusually popular man, filled the office until his death, April 26, 1866, and was succeeded by Robert Parke of Sadsbury Township, commissioned by the Governor May 9, 1856, for the remainder of Judge Shafer's term.

At the general election in 1856 Nimrod Strickland and William Wollerton were elected, and commissioned for the term of five years from December 7, 1857, but in October, 1857, Judge Strickland was elected canal commissioner, and to fill out his unexpired term John P. Baily of West Chester was appointed, and was commissioned January 21, 1858. In October, 1858, Robert Parke was elected in opposition to Judge Baily, and took his seat on the bench December 6, 1858. In October, 1861, John P. Baily was elected to succeed Judge Wollerton, who had declined a re-election and was commissioned for the term of five years commencing December 2, 1861. In 1866 he was re-elected for another term of five years.

In 1863 Benjamin J. Passmore of West Chester was elected to succeed Judge Parke, and was commissioned for the term of five years commencing December 7, 1863. He was subsequently re-elected twice, and served until his death, March 4, 1875. In 1871 Joel Hawley of Uwchlan was elected to succeed Judge Baily, was commissioned by the Governor and held the office until the expiration of the term, December 4, 1876. On the death of Judge Passmore in 1875, no successor was elected, the new Constitution of 1874 having provided for the abolition of the office on the death, resignation or termination of the office of any incumbent. Judge Hawley was the only associate judge, therefore, until the expiration of his own term of office, December 4, 1876.

For a period of 110 years previous to 1793 the criminal business of Chester County was conducted by the attorney-general in person, on account of the prosecution. In 1793 the first deputy attorney-general was appointed, and from that time to 1850 the pleas of the Commonwealth were prosecuted by deputies appointed by the attorney-general, with the exception of a brief period. In 1850 an act of Assembly was enacted creating the office of district attorney, and since then these officers have been elected by the people.

Among the attorneys-general of the Province, whose names it is not deemed necessary to present in this work, was Thomas Clarke, who, at a Court of Quarter Sessions held May 25, 1708, "appeared in open court and was qualified attorney-general for the county of Chester according to law. Of these attorneys-general, some of them were very able and distinguished men. One of them, Andrew Hamilton, is said to have been one of the greatest lawyers of his time, and filled several public stations with conspicuous ability and integrity. His son, James, was several times Governor of Pennsylvania between 1748 and 1771. Tench Francis, attorney-general from 1741 to 1755, was one of the most eminent lawyers of the Province, and a relative of Sir Philip Francis, the one-time reputed author of the celebrated Junius Letters. Benjamin Chew, attorney-general from 1755 to 1769, was in 1774 appointed chief justice of Pennsylvania, but being opposed to the Revolution, he retired from the bench in 1776, being thus the last chief justice of the Crown in Pennsylvania. Andrew Allen was the last attorney-general under the King of England, was also opposed to the Revolution, placed himself under the protection of Gen. Howe at Trenton, and lost his estates by confiscation by the new government. He died in England at the age of eighty-five. He was a grandson of Andrew Hamilton above mentioned.

Following is a list of the deputy attorneys-general from May, 1793, to the year 1850: Robert Frazer, May, 1793, to February, 1800; John Sergeant, May, 1800, to May, 1803; Thomas Sergeant, August sessions, 1803; William Hemphill, November, 1803, to November, 1808; John Duer, Jr., February, 1809, to April, 1816; Robert Frazer, July and November sessions, 1816; Isaac D. Barnard, January, 1817, to November, 1820; Isaac Darlington, January and April sessions, 1821; William H. Dillingham, July, 1821, to November, 1823; Thomas S. Bell, January, 1824, to May, 1828; Henry H. Van Amringe, August, 1828, to August, 1829; and from May, 1830, to February, 1835, the interim between August, 1829, and May, 1830, there being no deputy; Joseph J. Lewis, May, August and November sessions, 1835; William Darlington, 1836, 1837 and 1838; Joseph Hemphill from 1839 to 1844, six years; John Hickman, during 1845 and the sessions in January and April, 1846; Joseph J. Lewis, July and October sessions, 1846; John Hickman, January sessions, 1847; John H. Brinton, April, 1847, to July, 1848; Washington Townsend, October sessions, 1848, and January sessions, 1849; J. Smith Futhey, from April sessions, 1849, to November sessions, 1850, both inclusive, being the last of the deputy attorneys-general who prosecuted in Chester County.

In 1850 an act of Assembly created the office of district attorney, elected by the people, and the following gentlemen have since then filled this office:

Paschall Woodward, November, 1850, to September, 1853; J. Smith Futhey, at October sessions, 1853, the remaining session of Mr. Woodward's term, and then by election from November, 1853, to November, 1856; William Butler, November 1856, to November, 1859; Wayne MacVeagh, from November, 1859, to November, 1862; Henry M. McIntire, elected in October, 1862, to January, 1863, when he died from wounds received in the service of his country; James J. Creigh, appointed in January, 1863, to serve until the election, and was elected in November, 1863, and served until November, 1866; Francis C. Hooton, November, 1866, to November, 1869; George F. Smith, November, 1869, to November, 1872; Abraham Wanger, November, 1872, to January, 1876; James H. Bull, January, 1876, to January, 1879; Thomas W. Pierce, January, 1879, to 1882; Francis Windle, 1882 to 1885; John J. Gheen, 1885 to 1888; Thomas W. Baldwin, 1888 to 1891; E. D. Bingham, 1891 to 1894; Joseph H. Baldwin, 1894 to 1897, and W. W. MacElree, 1897 to 1900.

It is not deemed necessary in this work to present a detailed account of the various crimes that have been committed within the county; but it is necessary, as a matter of history, to note the degree and nature of the punishment meted out to criminals in the different periods of the county's history. In the earliest times the most common punishment for ordinary offenses was the infliction of fines. But from 1714 to 1759 most of the sentences embraced whipping as the chief feature of punishment for offenses of this kind, and usually consisted of "twenty-one lashes on the bare back well laid on." During this period there was no imprisonment, and rarely was standing in the pillory resorted to.

One of the noted crimes in the early day was the murder of Jonathan Hayes of Chester County by Hugh Pugh and Lazarus Thomas, the murderers being immediately apprehended and lodged in jail. This was in 1715, but their trial did not begin until near the beginning of the year 1718, when the Supreme Court was so constituted as to hold a Court of Oyer and Terminer for the purpose. Being found guilty they were sentenced to be executed. On May 18, 1718, asserting three legal defects in their conviction, they petitioned the Governor for a reprieve until the pleasure of the King could be ascertained, these three defects being that the jury had been composed of Quakers, who affirmed instead taking an oath; that the act for the proper qualification of judges, juries and witnesses was passed after the supposed commission of the murder, and that the said act was contrary to the statutes of Great Britain. The Governor rejected the petition, and in so doing was sustained by a majority of his council. The two murderers were ordered to be executed May 9, 1718.

In April, 1728, John Winter and Walter Winter killed an Indian and two squaws in the upper part of Chester County; warrants were issued for their arrest, and they were soon safely lodged in jail at Chester. On June 19, 1728, they were guilty by a jury of twelve men, and sentenced to "be hanged by the necks until they and each of them be dead."

On August 1, 1752, John Thomas and Eleanor Davis were cruelly murdered in Tredyffrin Township by Bryan Doran, James Rice, alias Dillon, and Thomas Kelly. Rice and Kelly were soon afterward arrested, and tried November 27, 1752, the latter pleading guilty. Rice was executed December 9, 1752, and Kelly on the 16th of the same month.

In 1764 a slave named Phebe, belonging to Joseph Richardson, was sentenced to be hanged for burglariously entering the house of Thomas Barnard and stealing divers goods.

On March 23, 1772, Patrick Kennedy, Thomas Fryer, Neal McCarriber and James Dever were convicted of a rape on Jane Walker, committed November 30, 1771, and they each sentenced to death. Kennedy was ordered to be executed May 2, 1772, but the others were reprieved.

On September 26, 1778, James Fitzpatrick was executed for burglary and larceny, of which he had been regularly convicted.

In May, 1780, William Boyd, while in the discharge of his duty, as tax collector in Chester County, was murdered by John and Robert Smith, and on May 13, the Governor of the Commonwealth, Joseph Reed, offered a reward of $20,000 for their apprehension. They were captured while en route to join the British army, by David Furman, sheriff of Monmouth County, New Jersey, and were tried in Chester County, June 26, and executed July 1, 1780.

On November 2, 1784, Joseph Chalk, John McDonnell, and John Varnum, alias Benson, were executed for burglary.

Since 1789, when Chester County was reduced to its present limits, the following executions have been had:

Hannah Miller for the murder of her infant child, tried at the May session, 1805, sentenced June 1, and executed in public August 1, 1805, under the direction of the sheriff, Jesse John.

Edward Williams (colored), for the murder of his wife, tried at the November sessions, 1830, sentenced November 30, and executed in public December 31, 1830.

Charles Bowman (colored), for the murder of Jonathan Mc-Euen, a blind fiddler, tried at the August session, 1834, sentenced August 25, and executed November 21, 1834.

Jabez Boyd, for the murder of Wesley Patton, fourteen years old, tried at the July sessions, 1845, sentenced August 8, and executed November 21, 1845.

George Pharaoh, for the murder of Rachel Sharpless, tried at the January Sessions, 1851, sentenced February 12, 1851, and executed August 29, 1851.

Lewis Green (colored), for the murder of Jacob Marks, a peddler, generally known as Dutch Jake, tried at the August Sessions, 1861, sentenced November 1, 1861, and executed March 7, 1862.

George Grant (colored), for the murder of Mrs. Amanda Spence (colored), tried at the October Sessions, 1871, sentenced January 31, 1872, and executed November 13, 1872.

William Eachus Udderzook, for the murder of Winfield Scott Goss, tried at the October Sessions, 1873, sentenced December 13, 1873, and executed November 12, 1874.

This was one of the famous murder trials of the country. Udderzook and Goss were brothers-in-law, having married sisters. They entered into a conspiracy to defraud insurance companies, Goss securing insurance on his life in several companies for $25,-000. A dead body was then introduced into a frame shop in which Goss worked by himself near Baltimore, and the building fired and burned to the ground. Goss disappeared; it was given out that he was last seen in the burned building, and the charred remains of the body of a man was found in the ruins. These remains Udderzook stated were those of Goss, and they were buried as such.

The insurance companies were not satisfied that the remains were those of Goss, and instituted inquiries with such success that they learned of a man whom they believed to be Goss in hiding under the assumed name of A. C. Wilson, and as it was impossible to keep Goss in hiding Udderzook determined, in order to conceal his part in the attempt to defraud, to take the life of his brother-in-law. Accordingly he decoyed him to Jennerville, Chester County, stabbed him to death, and buried the body in the woods. The body was discovered through the agency of buzzards. Udderzook, suspected, was tried and executed as above stated.

Since the execution of Udderzook there has been no one hanged in Chester County; but the probabilities are that there will· be an execution for murder in the near future. Jonas Preston, Jr., was tried at the April Sessions, 1898, for the murder of his wife, Ella Preston, in Penn Township. The defense set up was that of insanity, but Preston was convicted on April 28, of murder in the first degree, and if a new trial should not be granted, or if an appeal to the Supreme Court should be without avail, he must be sentenced to hang.

Robert Emmet Monaghan, formerly one of the leading members of the Chester County bar, was a son of James and Catherine (Streeper) Monaghan. He was born in West Whiteland Township, Chester County. James Monaghan was engaged in the rebellion with Robert Emmet, and this rebellion failed young Monaghan was compelled to flee to the United States, and died on his farm in Chester County in 1841.

It was on this farm that Robert E. Monaghan was born and on it he remained until he was nearly twenty-one years of age. Receiving his preliminary education at the academies at Unionville and at New London in Chester County, and at the Strasburg Academy in Lancaster County, he then began life for himself as a school teacher, at twenty dollars per month. Being offered a position as collector on the Pennsylvania Canal at Liverpool, Perry County, he retained it three years, in the meantime reading law with Hon. Hamilton Aldricks of Harrisburg. He was admitted to the Chester County bar at West Chester, and there began the practice of the law, continuing in practice up to the time of his death, which occurred June 29, 1895.

He served as a member of the borough council of West Chester, and as a trustee of the West Chester State Normal School, for a few years being president of the board. He also served as president of the Chester County Agricultural Society, and was in all the positions he filled faithful and efficient and trustworthy. In 1890 he was appointed by Governor Beaver a member of the joint commission from the States of Pennsylvania and Delaware, composed of himself, Hon. Wayne MacVeagh, W. H. Miller, from the former State, and Thomas F. Bayard, Dr. B. L. Lewis, and Hon. John H. Hoffecker from the latter State, the duties of these commissioners being to define, settle and mark the dividing line between the States, this subject being fully treated in the chapter on the boundary lines of the State.

William H. Dillingham, one of the foremost lawyers of Chester County during the period he devoted to the profession, was born in Lee, Massachusetts, August 3, 1791. His preparatory educated was received at Lenox Academy, and when fifteen years of age he entered the sophomore class of Williams, remaining there as a student about a year and a half, and although he did not graduate, yet in 1815 his alma mater conferred upon him the honorary degree of Master of Arts. In 1808 he began reading law in the office of Charles Chauncey of Philadelphia, and in 1811 was admitted to the bar. Removing to West Chester in 1817 he there rapidly rose in his profession, and was always prepared for trial. In 1821 he was appointed prosecuting attorney, holding the office a little more than two years. He was employed as solicitor of the Bank of Chester County for more than fifteen years, and in 1837 was elected to the State Legislature, and in the fall of 1841 after a residence of nearly twenty-five years in West Chester, he returned to Philadelphia, and there spent the remainder of his days.

Mr. Dillingham was a man of public spirit, and aided every good work that needed aid, the public schools, charitable institutions of all kinds, and scientific and literary societies always found in him a friend. Although the productions of his own pen were not numerous, yet he contributed judicious essays to the leading journals of the times. His literary taste was refined, and his style was polished and terse. And it has been truly said of him that he touched nothing that he did not adorn.

Townsend Haines, one of the most able and distinguished of the earlier citizens of Chester County, was born at West Chester, January 7, 1792. He was a son of Caleb Haines, a member of the Society of Friends, and one of their number that took the side of Great Britain in the Revolutionary War, after its close becoming a refugee in Nova Scotia, and remaining there until an act of Congress provided an amnesty for all cases of the kind. Then returning to West Chester he married Ann Ryant early in 1791, Townsend Haines being their eldest son. In October, 1809, young Townsend entered the school of Enoch Lewis at New Garden, where he improved his knowledge of the various branches of higher mathematics up to and including trigonometry, and by this means became familiar with the processes of abstract reasoning, by which, if the premises are true, the conclusion is irresistible. In his latter life while engaged in the practice of the law he became fully convinced of this means of intellectual discipline, and to it was largely due his great measure of success. From his mother, who was a woman of taste and culture, he acquired a knowledge of elocution and rhetoric, which in his forensic efforts was of use to him, as was the development of his reasoning faculties in the preparation of his cases.

Removing to West Chester in 1815 he took lessons in Latin of Mr. Glass, with the view of entering the profession of the law. After a dilligent course of study in the office of Judge Isaac Darlington, he was admitted to the bar February 7, 1818, but for sometime the law practice of the county was divided up among the older professionals, and he was compelled to be content with a small amount of business in the Orphans' Court, and with such

criminal practice as came to him. This latter class of practice
brought him fame and popularity and led to the trial of jury cases
in the Court of Common Pleas. In 1826 Mr. Haines was elected
to the Legislature of the State, and was re-elected in 1827. Mr.
Haines was a good lawyer, excellent in the examination of witnesses, and powerful in the presence of a jury. He always ap-
pealed to the better nature of a witness and not to his fears, framing his questions in such a way as to elicit the truth without producing the feeling of humiliation even in a witness that was unwilling. He was equally considerate of the feelings of his fellow-
attorneys, his conduct being so uniformly courteous and fair that
no resentment was ever awakened. Mr. Haines was an able man.
The position he attained at the bar was the result of spontaneous
action on his part; but the position he might have attained and
which he knew he might attain, he studiously declined to strive
for. He thought he could not afford the sacrifices such a struggle
would involve. He felt sure that his profession would sustain
him, and for distinction, which he knew was practically in his
grasp, he did not care. The prominence he acquired came to him
unsought, and simply from the force of circumstances, whether
that prominence were in the legal or political field.

In 1846 Mr. Haines was a candidate for Congress on the Whig
ticket, but was defeated by a single vote, his defeat being the nat-
ural result of his opposition in previous years to Anti-Masonry.
When William F. Johnson became Governor, he offered to Mr.
Haines the position of Secretary of the Commonwealth, which
offer was accepted, and in 1850 he was appointed by President
Taylor, Treasurer of the United States, and in the fall of 1851 he
was elected to the position of president judge of the Fifteenth
Judicial District, composed then of the counties of Chester and
Delaware, filling the office most acceptably for the ten years of the
term.

In February, 1865, his wife died, and he felt her loss very

severely. In September following he was himself taken ill, and rapidly sank to his death in October, in the seventy-fourth year of his age, respected and honored by all for his great ability, and for the uprightness and kindliness of his life.

Hon. Joseph J. Lewis, one of the ablest men of his time, and a lawyer of distinction, was born October 5, 1801, at Westtown, Chester County. His education was received at the Westtown Boarding School, and in Philadelphia, where he studied Latin and Greek under Thomas Dugdale, and afterward he took charge for some time of the Chester County Academy in the Great Valley. In 1822 he was invited by Jonathan Gause to assist him in teaching mathematics in West Chester Academy. In 1824 he went to New York to complete his legal studies, and remained some time under the direction of Chancellor Kent, returning to West Chester in April, 1825, being admitted to the bar May 1, of that year. In 1835 he was appointed deputy attorney-general for Chester County, and in 1844 he was again appointed to the same position. He took a leading part in politics and in 1860 aided largely in securing the nomination of Abraham Lincoln for Presidency of the United States. From March, 1863, to July, 1865, he held the office of commissioner of internal revenue, and drafted many important acts necessary for the efficient working of the internal revenue system.

Taking him all and all there were few men more useful to their fellow-citizens than was Mr. Lewis, and his death was sincerely mourned by all that knew him.

Joseph Hemphill, formerly a lawyer of Chester County, and one of the deputy attorney-generals for Chester County, was a worthy descendant of honorable ancestry. Alexander Hemphill, great-grandfather of Joseph Hemphill, came from the north of Ireland in the early part of the Eighteenth Century, and settled in Thornbury Township, Chester County. Joseph Hemphill, the eldest son of Alexander, married Amy Wills, and by her had eight children, the eldest of whom was also named Joseph. The latter

Joseph Hemphill was an able lawyer, and served as a member of the Seventh, Sixteenth, Nineteenth and Twenty-first Congresses, and for fourteen years presided over the district court for the county and city of Philadelphia.

Joseph Hemphill, father of the present president judge of Chester County, was a prominent and distinguished member of the Chester County bar. He was born in West Chester December 7, 1807, and received his classical education at the hands of such teachers as Jonathan Gause, and Joshua Hoopes of Chester County, and James W. Robbins of Lennox, Massachusetts. He read law with his brother-in-law, Hon. Thomas S. Bell, was admitted to the bar August 3, 1829, and immediately afterward began the practice of the law. Being an industrious and an honest man he rapidly rose in his profession and soon won a place among the most prominent and successful members of the Chester County bar. His career extended from his admission to the bar in 1829 to 1870, and while he was always watchful of the interests of his clients, yet he was at the same time always fair to his opponents. From 1839 to 1845 he was deputy attorney-general for Chester County, and he was nominated by the Democrats in 1861 for president judge in a district then composed of Chester and Delaware Counties, but was defeated at the polls, though no one doubted his peculiar fitness for the place. His death occurred February 11, 1870, and on that day numerous deserved tributes of respect were paid to his memory, by Wayne MacVeagh, William B. Waddell, Robert E. Monaghan and others. His loss was greatly felt by all that knew him.

Hon. William Darlington, born October 19, 1804, studied law with his brother, Judge Isaac Darlington, and was admitted to the bar January 31, 1826. From this time until his death, which occurred December 6, 1879, he was devoted to his profession, which has always been looked upon as "a jealous mistress." While he occasionally engaged in the trial of cases before the

District Court of the United States at Philadelphia, yet his principal practice was confined to the county courts of Eastern Pennsylvania. He served as deputy attorney-general for Chester
County from 1835 to 1838, but he preferred legal science to criminal jurisprudence, and as a consequence enjoyed a lucrative practice. In 1837 he was elected a member of the State convention to
remodel the Constitution, and he was also elected to represent the
people of his county in the Constitutional Convention of 1873.
His leading characteristics were courage, sagacity, equanimity,
aptness, precision, brevity and force, an array of qualities which
should make any man a formidable antagonist, and at the same
time a powerful friend. He was most emphatically a scorner of
cant, bigotry and hypocrisy, and though he had a birthright in
the Society of Friends, yet beyond that he had no connection with
any religious denomination. He was not in the ordinary accepta-
tion of the term an educated man, but his success in life demon-
strates the fact that college training, though of inestimable value
to a man of sound mind and of lofty ambition, is not always essential to the attainment of distinction among one's fellow men. But
without natural ability no man can greatly distinguish himself.
He was the youngest child in a family of twelve, but notwithstanding this he acquired the greatest estate of them all. While he
did not, as many men do, mingle with the masses of the people,
yet he was unusually and deservedly popular and highly respected
by all.

Uriah V. Pennypacker, third son of Joseph and Elizabeth
(Funk) Pennypacker, was born in Schuylkill Township, Chester
County, October 6, 1809. His father was a farmer and the family
were Mennonites, descendants of a Dutch emigrant, Heinrich Pen-
nebaker, who had settled in Montgomery County about 1716.
Uriah was a pupil at the Union School-house in Charlestown Township during the winter seasons, and was an interested listener to
all debates held therein in the evenings. At eighteen years of age

32

he spent one session at the West Chester Academy, taught then by Jonathan Gause, and the following year began the study of law with his uncle, Matthias Pennypacker, a member of the Chester County bar, and he was admitted to the bar after three years' study. He possessed a prodigious memory, and in a short time was noted for his vast and exact knowledge of the law and where to find it. He could repeat, verbatim, every definition in Blackstone. In 1834 he married Mary Fisher Wheeler, of West Chester. About that time the First Baptist Church of West Chester was founded, Mr. Pennypacker being a charter member. He was active in the formation of the Central Union Association of Baptist Churches. In politics he was an energetic Whig and retained during all his life an intense interest in public affairs. His rise in his profession was rapid, and for more than twenty years the Reports of the Supreme Court attested his zeal, his skill and his learning. His manner was easy and graceful and his presentation of a case to a court or a jury was clear, concise and convincing. He enjoyed the marked confidence of his friends and neighbors, and was so liberal and considerate in his views that all parties supported him when he was twice elected chief burgess of West Chester. He was six feet seven inches in height, and used to remark facetiously that he "stood highest at the bar." His love of humor was great and his sayings and his stories were the delight of many a Chester County audience.

Ill health diminished his ability to work, and the last ten years of his life witnessed a gradual relinquishment of business cares. He died August 16, 1867, and was buried at Oakland Cemetery, surviving his wife six years. He was one of a group of great lawyers, who had made the bar of Chester County famous for learning, integrity and ability, and for a high sense of personal and professional honor. In all the relations of life he was careful and exact, and at his death he was mourned by the bar, by the church and by the community of which he had so long formed a conspicuous part. His son is Charles H. Pennypacker.

Charles H. Pennypacker, one of the ablest members of the Chester County bar, was born in West Chester, April 16, 1845. Having received his preliminary and preparatory education in the public schools of his native city and in West Chester Academy, he then attended Philips Exeter Academy, at Exeter, New Hampshire, which he left in 1862. In December, 1863, he married Mrs. Elizabeth A. Passmore, widow of Levis Passmore, formerly of West Marlborough, Chester County. Mrs. Pennypacker, while a young lady, attended and graduated from the Friends' Westtown Boarding-school, and she has been for nine years a school director in West Chester.

Mr. Pennypacker studied law with his father, Uriah V. Pennypacker, until his father died, and then with William B. Waddell, and was admitted to the bar in 1869. He was admitted to the Supreme Court of Pennsylvania in 1870, and to the Supreme Court of the United States in 1888. He has tried hundreds of cases in all the courts mentioned, and the first case argued by him before the Supreme Court of the State is reported at length in Twentieth P. F. Smith. In 1873 he was counsel for the insurance companies in the celebrated Udderzook murder trial.

His uncle, after whom he was named, was a distinguished lawyer of South West Virginia, having studied law with William Rawle of Philadelphia. His maternal grandfather, Dr. Thomas Ruston, was a graduate of the college of Nassau Hall, Princeton, New Jersey, and was the first American graduate of the medical department of the University of Edinburgh, Scotland.

Mr. Pennypacker has devoted many years to the study of several of the modern languages, especially the English. He has lectured in several of the States of the Union, and has written many articles for leading magazines and other periodicals. During his entire life he has taken great interest in natural science, especially mineralogy, conchology and chemistry, and has had correspondence with reference to these subjects with leading scientists in all parts of the world, who have furnished him material for the purposes of examination and identification. Mr. Pennypacker is a member of the Microscopical Society of Liverpool, England, and of the Academy of Natural Sciences of Philadelphia. He was one of the founders of the West Chester Philosophical Society, and has lectured before it many times.

Mr. and Mrs. Pennypacker have had four children, as follows: Levis Passmore, a graduate of the Rensselaer Polytechnic Institute at Troy, New York, in the class of 1888, and now a civil engineer engaged in his profession in Guatemala, where he has resided five years; Henry, a graduate of Harvard University in the class of 1888, and now a Master in the Boston Latin School, Boston, Massachusetts, where he has resided for the last five years; Joseph Albert, accidentally killed when twenty years of age while residing in Salvador, Central America, and Blanche, who died in infancy.

Alfred P. Reid, one of the most prominent members of the bar of Chester County, was born in Highland Township, Chester County, September 3, 1842, and grew up on his father's farm. His early education was secured at Parkesburg, Coatesville and West Chester, and he then entered Lafayette College, graduating from this institution in 1864. Reading law with Judge J. Smith Futhey he was admitted to the bar August 14, 1866, and has ever since been engaged in the successful practice of his profession in West Chester, though that practice extends into the adjoining counties and thus brings him in contact with the ablest legal minds in the State. Possessed of a fair, logical and judicial mind, his arguments are always of weight with the court and his influence is felt by all the judges on the bench. Outside of his regular profession Mr. Reid has given much time to banking, and is recognized as an able financier. He has been president and vice-president of several different banks, among them the First National Bank of West Chester, to the presidency of which he was elected soon after the death of President Wollerton. By his ability, energy and in-tegrity he has won for himself a distinguished position in the pro-fession of the law and also in the financial world.

Col. Hamilton H. Gilkyson, of Phœnixville, one of the most successful members of the Chester County bar, is a son of James and Anna (Henry) Gilkyson, and was born in December, 1848, at Doylestown, Bucks County, Pennsylvania. James Gilkyson, his father, was of Irish ancestry, and was for many years a prominent practitioner at the bar of Bucks County, and served for a number of years as district attorney of that county.

Hamilton H. Gilkyson received his education at private schools in Doylestown and at Pennington Seminary in New Jer-sey, graduating from the latter institution in 1864. For several years afterward he was engaged n the West as a teacher and in business as a merchant. Returning to Pennsylvania he read law in the office of his father in Doylestown, being admitted to the bar in 1872. He immediately afterward established himself in prac-tice in Phœnixville and has there been successfully engaged ever since, practicing in the courts of Montgomery and Philadelphia Counties, and is well known in all three counties as a careful, painstaking and able attorney, always thoroughly preparing him-self for the trial of cases before going into court.

During the early history of Chester County, or say prior to 1750, there were but few attorneys at law within its limits. The method of bringing cases into court also seems to have been dif-ferent from what it is at the present time, the parties interested being permitted to make their presentations in person or through a friend. In June, 1677, it was ordered in the Upland Court that all declarations must be entered at least the day before the court, and that no person be admitted to plead for any other person as an attorney in court without first having his admittance of the court or a warrant of attorney for so doing from his client.

While many persons appeared in behalf of others, those appearing not being familiar with the law, yet there were the following who were admitted to practice or who practiced in the courts of the county prior to 1750: In 1683, John White and Abraham Mann; in 1698, John Moore and David Lloyd; in 1726, Ralph Assheton, John Kinsey, Peter Evans, Francis Sherrard and Joseph Growdon, Jr.; in 1730, Alexander Keith; in 1734, William Rawle; 1735, John Ross, James Hamilton, John Robinson, Thomas Hopkinson; 1736, Alexander Piercey, James Keating and Andrew Hamilton; 1738, William Assheton; 1739, William Peters; 1740, John Webb; 1741, Tench Francis, Edmund Ackworth, Neil Harris; 1742, Robert Hartshorne, Richard Peters, John Mather and James Read; 1743, John Moland and Townsend White; 1744, David Edwards; 1745, Benjamin Price; 1747, John Lawrence; 1748, Edward Shippen, Jr.; 1749, Joseph Galloway and John Evans.

Following is a list of those admitted from 1750 to 1776:

1752, David Finney; 1753, Thomas Otway, John Price, William Morris, Jr.; 1754, Benjamin Chew; 1755, Samuel Johnson, Thomas McKean, David Henderson, William Whitebred; 1756, George Ross, John Armond; 1760, John Morris; 1763, Nicholas Waln, James Tilghman; 1764, Hugh Hughes, John Currie, Elisha Price, Lindsay Coates; 1765, Andrew Allen, Alexander Porter, Nicholas Vandyke, Alexander Wilcocks, Joshua Yeates, Stephen Porter, Richard Peters, Jr., James Biddle, James Allen, Henry Elwes, James Loyre; 1766, Isaac Hunt, David Thompson, James Vandyke; 1767, William Hicks, James Wilson; 1769, Jacob Rush, Miers Fisher, Daniel Clymer, John Ruley, Stephen Watts; 1770, Abel Evans, Thomas Good, James Lukens; 1771, Joseph Read, George Noarth, Jacob Bankson, Francis Johnson, Asheton Humphreys; 1772, Richard Tilghman, John Lawrence, Peter Zachary Lloyd; 1773, Christian Hook, William L. Blair, Phineas Bond, John Stedman, John McPherson, William Lewis; 1774, Edward Tilghman, Gunning Bedford; 1775, Andrew Robeson, John Vannost; 1776, William Prince Gibbs, Collinson Read.

Of those above named Benjamin Chew was one of the most prominent. In 1755 he became attorney-general of the Province and he was president judge of the Court of Common Pleas of Philadelphia. From 1774 to 1776 he was chief justice of the Supreme Court of the Province, and from 1790 to 1806 he was president of the High Court of Errors and Appeals, this court being abolished in 1806, upon the reorganization of the judiciary department.

Another prominent man whose name is in the above list was Thomas McKean. He was born in New London Township, Chester County, March 19, 1734, and in 1757 was elected to the Assembly of the Province. From 1762 to 1769 he was a member of the Assembly from New Castle County, in 1765 assisting in framing the address of the colonies to the House of Commons of England. He was elected a delegate to the first Provincial, or "Stamp Act," Congress, which was dissolved October 24, 1765. In 1774 he was elected a member of the Continental Congress, and was annually re-elected until 1783. In 1778 he was a member of the convention which framed the Articles of Confederation, and in 1781 he was president of Congress. He was a member of the Pennsylvania convention which ratified the Constitution of the United States. He had signed the Declaration of Independence and had served during a part of the War of the Revolution under Washington, in command of a battalion. He was Governor of Pennsylvania from 1798 to 1808, and was distinguished as one of the ablest men of his time. His death occurred June 24, 1817.

One more of the above-named attorneys was an unusually able man, Hon. James Wilson, and was distinguished as being both a great lawyer and a great orator. He was a signer of the Declaration of Independence, was a member of the convention which framed the Constitution of the United States, and in 1789 he was appointed by President Washington an Associate Justice of the Supreme Court of the United States, holding the office until his death in 1798. One of his sons, Rev. Bird Wilson, LL. D., D. D., was one of the most prominent lawyers and divines of the early day. He was born in 1777, and in 1806 was appointed by Governor McKean president judge of the judicial district composed of Chester, Delaware, Bucks and Montgomery Counties, holding the office until 1818, when he became a clergyman of the Episcopal Church. Ordained deacon by Bishop William White, D. D., March 12, 1819, he became a priest in 1820. After about a year's rectorship of the Episcopal Church at Norristown he became a professor in the Theological Seminary of the Episcopal Church in New York, and occupied this position twenty-nine years. He died April 14, 1859, aged eighty-two years.

Following is a list of the attorneys admitted to the bar of Chester County from 1776 to 1800, some of whom it will be seen were readmitted after the Revolutionary War, none being permitted to practice law except those who supported the order of things brought about by that war:

1777.—John Morris, Andrew Robeson, William Lewis, William L. Blair, John Kaley.

1778.—George Ross, Jonathan Dickinson Sergeant, Jacob Rush, Elisha Price, Alexander Wilcocks, Gunning Bedford, John Pancoast.

1779.—Edward Burd, Francis Johnston, Henry Osborne, George Campbell, Jacob Bankson, Jared Ingersoll, William Bradford, Jr.

1780.—Moses Levy.

1781.—Nicholas Vandyke, John Coxe, William Moore Smith, John Lawrence, Nathaniel Potts.

1782.—Joseph Reed, John F. Mifflin, Daniel Clymer, John Vining.

1783.—John Wilkes Kittera, Henry H. Graham, William Rawle.

1784.—William Ewing.

1785.—Peter Zachary Lloyd, Jacob R. Howell, Thomas Ross, James Hanna, John Andra Hanna, Joseph B. McKean, John Todd.

1786.—Robert Hodson, Charles Smith, John Young, Benjamin Chew, Jr., B. R. Morgan, Jr., Richard Wharton, Thomas Memminger.

1787.—David Smith, James Wade, John Joseph Henry, William R. Atlee, W. Montgomery, Sampson Levy, James Hopkins, Samuel Roberts, Samuel Bayard, Matthias Baldwin, James A. Bayard.

1788.—Thomas Armstrong, Peter S. Duponceau, Jasper Yeates, Peter Hoofnagle, Joseph Hubley, William Graham.

1789.—John Hallowell, Joseph Thomas, Robert Porter, Charles Healty, Anthony Morris, John Craig Wells, John Cadwallader, John Moore.

1790.—Thomas B. Dick, Abraham Chapman, John Thompson, Marks John Biddle, David Moore, Isaac Telfair.

1791.—Robert Henry Durkin, Seth Chapman.

1792.—Miles Merion, Robert Frazer, John Price.

1793.—Thomas W. Tallman, John H. Brinton, Evan Rice Evans, Joseph Hemphill, Michael Kepple, John Shippen, Henry Kelmuth, A. W. Foster.

1794.—Jacob Richards, Joseph B. Hopkinson, William Martin.

1795.—J. Harvey Hurst, James Hunter, Jr., James Milner, James Lattimer, Jr., John Cloyd, Joseph Reid, Isaac Wayne.

1797.—W. Lee Hannum.

1798.—C. Chauncey, Jr.

1799.—Jonathan T. Haight, John Taylor, William Hemphill.

Jacob Rush, mentioned above as having been admitted in 1778, was a brother of Dr. Benjamin Rush. He was president judge of the Court of Common Pleas of Philadelphia, of the Court of Errors and Appeals, and also of the Supreme Court. John Lawrence and John Coxe were judges of the Court of Common Pleas of Philadelphia, and Moses Levy was president of the District Court of Philadelphia. Jonathan D. Sergeant was a member of the Provincial Congress, and was attorney-general of the State from 1777 to 1780.

William Bradford, after whom Bradford County was named, became attorney-general in 1780, and was one of the judges of the Supreme Court of the State from 1791 to 1794, becoming in the latter year attorney-general of the United States by appointment by President Washington. Jared Ingersoll, admitted to the Chester County bar in 1779, was twice attorney-general of Pennsylvania, and was president judge of the District Court of Philadelphia at the time of his death. Joseph B. McKean, a son of Governor McKean, succeeded Jared Ingersoll as attorney-general, and also served as president of the District Court of Philadelphia. Jasper Yeates became one of the judges of the Supreme Court of the State, and Seth Chapman became a district judge.

Following is a list of the attorneys admitted to the bar of Chester County from 1800 to the breaking out of the War of the Rebellion in 1861:

1800.—Jonathan W. Condy, John Sergeant, T. Barton Zantzinger and William Dewees.

1801.—Isaac Darlington.

1803.—James D. Barnard, Thomas Sergeant, Samuel Jacobs, John Ewing Porter.

1804.—John Duer.

1806.—John Edwards, Charles W. Humphrey.

1807.—Reuben Eachus.

1808.—Ziba Pyle.

1809.—Jefferis Moore, Matthias Morris and Daniel Addis.

1810.—Blaithwaite J. Shober, Archibald T. Dick.

1811.—Philip S. Markley, Michael W. Ash.

1813.—Benjamin Tilghman, Thomas Breintnall.

1814.—James Madison Porter, William B. Smith, Clement B. Buckley, Henry Shippen, John Kerlin, Benjamin Evans.

1815.—George B. Porter, Samuel Edwards.

1816.—George C. Willing, William H. Dillingham, Isaac D. Barnard, Thomas Kittera, Thomas A. Maybin.

1818.—Townsend Haines.

1819.—Jesse Conard.

1820.—William Williamson.

1821.—William S. Haines, David Paul Brown, Thomas S. Bell, Edward Darlington, Henry H. Van Amringe, John Freedley and Samuel Parke.

1822.—Abraham Marshall.

1824.—Daniel Buckwalter, John D. Pettit.

1825.—Matthias Pennypacker, Francis James, Joseph J. Lewis, Lewis G. Pearce, Owen Stover.

1826.—Benjamin Bartholomew, William Darlington, James M. Kinnard, Davis H. Hoopes.

1827.—John K. Zellin, Levi B. Smith.

1828.—William McK. Ball, John H. Bradley, Robert B. Dodson, James A. Hemphill, James S. Tongue.

1829.—Mark Denny, Joseph Hemphill, Richard Bailey, P. Frazer Smith.

1830.—Lea Bennett, John Rutter.

1831.—Volney Lee Maxwell, Uriah V. Pennypacker.

1832.—John H. Brinton.

1833.—John Hickman.

1834.—Horatio G. Worrall.

1835.—Addison May.

1836.—William Wheeler.

1839.—Ferdinand E. Hayes.

1840.—William Penn Miner, James H. Bull, B. Franklin Pyle.

1842.—John S. Bowen, George W. Pearce, Matthew A. Stanley.

1843.—J. Smith Futhey, James Davis, Joseph B. Townsend, William M. Bull, Howard Darlington.

1844.—John M. Broomall, Isaac D. Pyle, Washington Townsend, John P. Baily, Edward H. Williamson, Samuel B. Thomas, Thomas H. Speakman.

1845.—James B. Everhart, Joseph P. Wilson, James A. Gilmore, William G. Smith, William Parker Foulke, William Butler.

1846.—William E. Barber, William Nicholson, Thomas P. Potts, W. Ross Cunningham, Henry C. Townsend.

1847.—James P. Fleming, Paschall Woodward.

1848.—Robert E. Monaghan, Joseph R. Morris, Samuel Rush, Robert Frazer, James M. Meredith, James L. Jones.

1849.—Ezra Lewis, Edward Shippen, Jesse Landis, John F. Roberts, Charles H. Garber.

1850.—Franklin Pennington, Clinton Auge.

1851.—Francis Darlington, A. Herr Smith.

1852.—William Bell Waddell, William L. Marshall, Jesse Bishop, Levi Kimes.

1853.—Edward J. Lewis, Charles D. Manley, William H. Darlington.

1854.—B. Markley Boyer, James Merrill Linn.

1855.—W. Arthur Jackson.

1856.—Wayne MacVeagh.

1857.—James J. Creigh, Egbert K. Nichols, George W. Conarroe, Samuel M. Du Bois, Francis C. Hooton.

1858.—George M. Roberts, Cheyney W. Neilds, Henry M. McIntire.

1859.—Thomas S. Bell, Jr., George M. Rupert.

1860.—William T. Haines, Henry W. Carruthers, John J. Pinkerton, W. M. Hinkson, Gardner Furness, George W. Wollaston and J. C. Price.

Following is a list of the attorneys admitted to the bar since 1860:

1861.—William T. Fulton.

1862.—Oliver Sidwell, Henry C. Bergstresser.

1863.—John J. Pyle, Abraham Wagner, Elbridge Meconkey, David Ruth.

1864.—Rees Davis, Joseph Hemphill, George F. Smith, William W. Hayes, John A. McCaughey.

1865.—Joseph Beale, William J. Gibson, William H. White-head, James Allen Morris.

1866.—Augustus J. Feather, Nimrod Strickland, Jr., Alfred P. Reid, Robert T. Cornwell.

1867.—William T. McPhail, Joseph W. Barnard.

1869.—Charles H. Pennypacker.

1870.—Joseph T. Perdue, D. Smith Talbot.

1871.—Abner Pyle, Thomas W. Pierce, Samuel D. Ramsey, William S. Windle.

1872.—Andrew C. Fulton, William B. Reid, Henry H. Gilky-son, Charles Wesley Talbot, Francis Windle, B. F. McAtee.

1873.—George L. Maris, Robert J. Monaghan, Isaac Newton Wynn, Frederick S. Dickson, John B. Kinnard.

1874.—William E. Dingee, Curtis H. Hannum.

1875.—Theodore K. Stubbs, Thomas B. Taylor.

1876.—Ezra Evans, John A. Groff, William T. Barber.

1877.—Thomas S. Butler, Archibald D. Thomas, H. T. Fairlamb.

1878.—John Jay Gheen, J. Newton Huston, Edward D. Bingham.

1879.—James Monaghan, William N. Needles, Jr.

1880.—Samuel H. Holding, George B. Johnson, Wilmer W. MacElree.

1881.—John Austin Purcell, Benjamin Miller, Leonard R. Thomas.

1882.—William Rhoads Murphy.

1883.—J. Frank E. Hause, Thomas W. Baldwin.

1884.—Archibald McCall Holding, Arthur T. Parke.

1885.—Robert Scott Waddell, Wallace Scott Harlan, William Butler, Jr., Barton Darlington, N. Warren Talbot.

1886.—Henry P. Waitneight.

1887.—S. Duffield Mitchell, William S. Harris.

1888.—R. E. M. Strickland, William W. Montgomery, Wilbur S. Yearsley.

1889.—Gibbons Gray Cornwell, Joseph H. Baldwin.

1890.—Joseph McClellan Bell.

1891.—Thomas Lack, John Russell Hayes.

1892.—J. Carroll Hayes.

1893.—John Noble Guss, Hector Lee Ball.

1897.—Isabel Darlington, Carroll Brinton Jacobs.

1898.—George S. Dewees.

The Chester County Law and Miscellaneous Library Association was organized December 4, 1861, by the members of the Chester County bar. The first meeting of the association was held at the office of Joseph J. Lewis, who presided over the meeting, and William B. Waddell was the secretary. After the adoption of the constitution Joseph J. Lewis was chosen president of the association, and George M. Rupert, secretary, treasurer and librarian. The first executive committee was composed of J. Smith Futhey, William B. Waddell and Washington Townsend.

January 22, 1877, at an annual meeting Joseph J. Lewis, William Darlington and William B. Waddell were appointed to secure the grand jury room for the use of the association, reporting to the association on the 25th of the same month at a special meeting that an arrangement had been effected with the commissioners of the county for the use of the room. This room was in the northwest corner of the old court-house, and is now used for the courts of Judges Hemphill and Butler.

At an annual meeting of the association held June 5, 1891, a motion carried in favor of the enlargement, the initial movement having this object in view, and on January 4, 1892, the committee on enlargement reported that the plans had been completed and the erection of the addition or annex begun. May 13, 1893, at a special meeting, William B. Waddell announced that the room assigned to the library association, which is in the south end of the annex, was ready for occupation, and the books were soon afterward removed thereto.

The library at the present time contains the following classes of books: The statutes of the State of Pennsylvania from the earliest times down to the present; all the Pennsylvania State reports, and most of the side bar reports from the earliest times; all the British common law and equity reports commencing with Lord Coke in 1562 and coming down to the present time; the reports of the States of New York, New Jersey, and Massachusetts; reports of the courts of various other States; a complete series of the reports of the Supreme Court of the United States; numerous editions of general reports covering the entire jurisdiction of the United States and Great Britain; and editions of text books covering all branches of the law. This also contains numerous curiosities of legal literature in the form of old black letter volumes setting forth the functions of justices of the peace, etc., as they were defined in the earliest times, obtained by Judge Hemphill from the British Museum. There are also bound volumes of the American Republican from its earliest issues down to the war of the Rebellion, and numerous miscellaneous works. The number of volumes of all kinds now in the library is 6,745.

The officers of the association at the present time are as follows: William M. Hayes, president; Thomas Lack, secretary and treasurer, and A. M. Holding, librarian. The executive committee consists of A. P. Reid, J. J. Pinkerton and J. Frank E. Hause.

CHAPTER XIV.

MINING AND MANUFACTURING.

CHAPTER XIV.

IT appears to be certainly true that one of the first miners of
lead in Chester County, if not the first, was Charles Pickering,
after whom, as stated elsewhere in this work, Pickering Creek
was named, and also Charlestown Township. Charles Pickering
was an Englishman, and owned land in the above-named township and also in Schuylkill Township. He had for his principal
assistant a man named Samuel Buckley, whose house was situated
on Zachariah Acker's farm in Schuylkill Township. These two
men in addition to mining lead also obtained silver to some extent, by melting the galena in an ordinary forge, and from the
silver thus obtained they manufactured silver coins, using copper
as their alloy, or "allay," as it was called at that time. For this
offense Messrs. Pickering and Buckley were tried before Governor
William Penn and a council, consisting of Thomas Holmes, Lasse
Cock, William Biles, William Clayton, Chr. Taylor, and John Sym-
cock, the trial commencing on the 24th of the 8th mo., 1683.

On this day Governor William Penn informed the board that
it was convenient that warrant should be sent from the board
to apprehend some persons upon suspicion of putting away bad
money. The first person called on to testify was Robert Felton, to
whom the question was put as to whether he had received any

silver of Charles Pickering "to Quine for him." He answered: "Yes, twenty-four pounds of Bard silver." He also said that he made the scales and that Charles Pickering and Samuel Buckley helped him. The next question asked him was: "What did they add to the allay of the 15 lb. 2 oz. of silver?" He answered: "About 4 oz. of copper." "And what to the 9 lb. of silver?" "About 3 or 4 oz. of copper," but he could not be exact, however, as to the allay, because they did sometimes put in more than he knew of. Robert Felton also said that he had no silver brought to him but by the persons above named, and he "scroopled to do it, the silver having already been allayed, and if they did not put more copper in it they would lose by it, and they said they would Bare him out in what he did for them."

The Governor then told Charles Pickering and Samuel Buckley of their abuse to the government in "Quining" of Spanish bitts and Boston money, to the great damage and abuse of the subjects thereof, and he asked them if they were guilty of the fact. They confessed they had put off some of those new bitts, but they said that all their money was as good silver as any Spanish money, but they denied that they had any hand in the matter of "quining." Charles Pickering said he would stand by and be tried, and he declared that he had heard John Rush swear that he spent half his time in making the bitts.

The Governor then asked Samuel Buckley if he had not helped to melt money and to put in some of the copper allay into the silver more than should be, and to have been at the stamping of new bitts and striking on the stamp. Samuel Buckley confessed that "he had been guilty of somewhat of that," and also that he had knowledge as to the amount of copper put into the silver that was melted. He also admitted that he had helped Charles Pickering's man to melt the silver and to strike the hammer and to see the silver, and to disperse some of the bitts, more or less. He also confessed that there was more copper put into the silver than there should be.

Charles Pickering and Samuel Buckley were then required to give bail in the sum of £500 each to appear at the next opening of the court, which was the next day, when it was ordered that an indictment be brought against them both. Griffith Jones testified against Mr. Pickering, as also did Mary Bartholomew. The grand jury brought in the indictment, and the petit jury taking the case, in a short time brought in a verdict of guilty as they were indicted.

The Governor then imposed sentence on Charles Pickering to the effect that he should make full satisfaction of good and current pay to every person that should within one month bring in any of this false, base and counterfeit "coyne," according to their respective proportions, and the money should be melted down into gross before it was returned to him, and that he should pay a fine of £40 into the court toward the building of a new court-house in that city, and should stand committed until the fine was paid, and that afterward he should find security for his good "abearance."

Then Samuel Buckley was sentenced, but "being considered more Engenious than he that went before, they hath thought fit to fine thee £10 toward the public court-house, and that thee find good security as to thy good abearance."

Robert Felton was sentenced to stand in the stocks one hour the next morning.

The proclamation of the Governor notifying all that held any of the spurious or counterfeit coin to bring it in within one month was issued on the 27th of that month.

As stated above, Pickering Creek was named after Charles Pickering. It had been formerly named "Vincent River." French Creek was also called Vincent River, but at what time the change in name was made in ether case is not now known. Sir Francis Vincent was a large land owner in that part of the county in those days, and the two streams must have been named after him.

The most valuable mineral in Chester County is its iron ore, which is found in various parts of the county and has been mined for many years. This industry began in 1716, Thomas Rutter establishing the industry at Pool Forge, three miles above Pottstown. In 1718 Samuel Nutt took out patents for 400 acres of land in one place and 800 acres in another, on French Creek. The 400 acres here mentioned is believed to be the property now owned by I. J. Brower and Dr. Z. Taylor Chrisman. In 1719 there were surveyed 650 acres at Warwick Furnace; in 1720 there was laid out 300 acres in Coventry, and in 1721 Mr. Nutt purchased 300 acres in Coventry.

There were in operation at this early day several forges and furnaces in the northern part of the county; as the Pool Forge and Warwick Furnace above mentioned. On French Creek there was a forge in operation before 1720, which was assessed in 1722 in Nantmeal, and in 1724 in Coventry, so that it must have been on the line or very near it. Nutt's road was laid out in 1726 from the iron-works on St. Vincent River in the township of Coventry leading to Uwchlan Meeting-house, beginning at the forge and passing over Mt. Austrie at the distance of four miles. In 1736 Mr. Samuel Nutt and W. Branson agreed with John Potts to carry on Redding Furnace, then recently built near Coventry. Soon afterward the widow Nutt and her daughter built Warwick Furnace. Another furnace was built one and a half miles further up the creek, and the interests of all parties were consolidated by Rutter & Potts, of the Warwick Furnace, which consolidation lasted from 1778 to 1783.

An iron-works was established on Crum Creek, in what is now Delaware County, but in what was then Chester County, in 1742, by John Crosby and Peter Dicks, and as one of the consequences Thomas Dell complained that the dam overflowed his land. Sarum Forge on Chester Creek was owned by John Taylor and was worked from 1745 to 1751, at least. In 1748 the Swedish naturalist, Peter

Kalm, passed through the lower part of Chester County, spend-ing some time at Chichester, "a borough on the Delaware, where travellers pass the river in a ferry, and where they build every year a number of small ships for sale, and from an iron-work which lies higher up in the country they carry iron bars to this place and ship them. About two English miles behind Chester I passed an iron forge, which was to the right hand by the road-side. It belonged to two brothers, as I am told. The ore, how-ever, is not dug here, but thirty or forty miles hence, where it is first melted in an oven and then carried to this place." This must have been the forge on Crum Creek, mentioned above, and the ore must have been dug in what is now Chester County.

A most remarkable fact connected with the early iron indus-tries of this and other counties in Pennsylvania and the other counties must be mentioned here. James Hamilton was then Deputy Governor, serving from 1748 to 1754, and in pursuance of an act of Parliament having for its object the restriction of the manufacture of iron in the colonies, Governor Hamilton issued his proclamation requiring the sheriffs of the several counties to make a réturn to him of "every mill or engine for slitting or rolling iron, every plating forge to work with a tilt hammer, and every furnace for making steel which were erected within their several and respective counties," the date of this proclamation being June 24, 1750. In response to this proclamation John Owen, then sheriff of Chester County, certified "that there is but one mill or engine for slitting and rolling iron within the county aforesaid, which is situate in Thornbury Township, and was erected in the year 1746 by John Taylor, the present proprietor thereof, who, with his servants and workmen, has ever since the 24th day of June last used and occupied the same." Sheriff Owen also certified that there was not any plating forge to work with a tilt-hammer nor any furnace for making steel within the county of Chester.

What had become of the iron-works within two English miles of Chester, as seen by Peter Kalm, above mentioned, can only be guessed at. They must have gone into disuse, for Peter Kalm was too careful an observer to make a mistake in such a simple and important matter, and Sheriff Owen was too honest to certify to a misstatement.

The partnership between Branson and Anna Nutt, widow of Samuel Nutt, who died about the close of the year 1737, and Mrs. Nutt's nephew was continued as if Mr. Nutt had not died, for several years, terminating probably about 1740, after which the Warwick and Reading estates were conducted independently of each other. Warwick Furnace was built on land devised to Mrs. Anna Nutt by her husband for that purpose, and the property remained in the possession of her descendants, by the name of Potts, except that in 1771 a half interest was purchased therein by Thomas Rutter.

William Branson erected a second furnace in what is now Warwick Township, about a mile and a half above Warwick Furnace, which, according to tradition, melted ore before the Reading Furnace. William Branson obtained a warrant for 2,000 acres of land on French Creek near the iron-works on July 12, 1733, and on November 29, 1736, he obtained another warrant for 1,500 acres in the township of Nantmeal, near French Creek. William Branson died in 1760 and his grandchildren, fifteen in number, inherited his property. The interests of all these heirs were purchased by Rutter & Potts, by several conveyances, from 1778 to 1783, as stated above.

In his "History of New Sweden" (1759) Acrelius writes of iron-works in Chester County as follows:

"Friends' (French) Creek, in Chester County, near the Schuyl-kill. The mine is rich and baundant, from ten to twelve feet deep, commencing on the surface. Its discoverer is Mr. Nutt, who after-ward took Mr. Branz (Branson) into partnership. They both went to England, brought workmen back with them and continued together. Each has his own furnace—Branz at Reading, Nutt in Warwick. Each also has his own forges—Branz in Windsor. Nutt supplies four forges besides his own in Chester County.

"Sarum belongs to Taylor's heirs; has three stacks, and is in full blast.

"Crum Creek belongs to Peter Dicks; has two stacks, is worked sluggishly, and has ruined Crosby's family.

"Two others are in the Great Valley.

"At French Creek, or Branz's works, there is a steel furnace, built with a draught-hole, and called an 'air-oven.' In this iron bars are set at the distance of an inch apart. Between them are scattered horn, coal-dust, ashes, etc. The iron bars are thus covered with blisters, and this is called 'blister-steel.' It serves as the best steel to put upon edge-tools. These steel works are now said to be out of operation."

It will also be of interest to note that on January 18, 1745, John Taylor, mentioned above as the owner of Sarum Forge, made an agreement with Thomas Wills, forgeman and finer, who was to work in the forge two years, making anconies at 22s. 6d. per ton, and with Rees Jones on June 10, 1746, to coal 200 cords of wood in Middletown for 11s. 8d. per 100 bushels. In 1851 John Taylor sent an invoice of bar-iron to Mr. Plumsted of Philadelphia, for shipment to Boston, asking for the returns to be made in oil, loaf-sugar and rum.

After its purchase by Rutter & Potts, Reading Furnace was permitted to fall into decay and was replaced by a forge, which in 1788 was owned by Captain Samuel Van Leer, a grandson of William Branson, the forge being carried on successfully for many years by Captain Van Leer & Sons, but at length it had its fall and decline.

Mordecai Peirsol, about 1764, built Rebecca Furnace, which

was supplied with ore from Jones' mines. In 1793 this furnace was owned by Jacob Vinance, Thomas Rutter, Sarah May and Samuel Potts, but in 1794 it was discontinued because farmers refused longer to sell wood for charcoal.

In 1786 Jesse Potts was assessed in Coventry for a steel furnace, which in 1787 appears to have been operated by Ellis Jones & Co., and in 1788 by North & Evans. In 1786 David Moore had a forge in West Nantmeal, which in 1788 appears to have belonged to James Moore, together with 564 acres of land. At Warwick Furnace, during the year 1776, sixty cannon were cast, of twelve and eighteen-pound caliber.

Vincent Forge existed during the later years of the last century, and was owned by John Young, who in his will March 2, 1781, devised it to his son, John, upon his becoming of age. In 1788 it appears to have been operated by James Templin.

Valley Forge was built originally about five-eighths of a mile from the mouth of Valley Creek, in Chester County. From the spring of 1757 it was operated by members of the Potts family until its destruction by the British, in 1777, about two months before the American army encamped at this historic place. Col. William Dewees, a son of Sheriff William Dewees of Philadelphia, became associated with the Pottses in 1771, and probably purchased an interest in 1773. Warwick Furnace furnished the iron for this forge. After the close of the Revolutionary War a slitting mill was erected in Chester County by Isaac and David Potts, brothers. In 1786 this mill and a forge across the Schuylkill, in Montgomery County, were operated by Isaac Potts & Company, the "Company" consisting of David Potts and his son James. In 1814 these works were sold to John Rogers and Joshua Malin, the latter being a cousin of the former, and the manager of the works. On April 1, 1816, Rogers bought Malin's half interest in the property, and in the following autumn James Woods became a partner of Rogers and manager of the works. Wood completed certain improvements began by Malin and converted it into a saw factory mainly, but also manufactured shovels, spades, files and other implements of industry. At the rolling-mill boiler-plate, sheet-iron and band-iron were made. A portion of this output was slit for the nail-mill at Phœnixville, at which place there were no such facilities. The iron used by Wood was obtained from Laurel Forge, Coventry Forge and Springton Forge.

Not long after 1818, several experiments having been made, cast-steel was successfully made here by Wood, clay for crucibles being brought from Perth Amboy. Early in 1821 Brooke Evans, of Sheffield, England, leased the property from Rogers, converted the gun factory and rolling-mill into gun factories, raised the roof of the rolling-mill and added two stories to it, and at Valley Forge made 20,000 muskets. Subsequently this building was destroyed by a freshet, but the building on the Montgomery County side, after serving its purpose as a gun factory, was enlarged and converted into a cotton and woolen factory.

Mary Ann Forge was built in 1785 and was located on the north branch of the Brandywine, two miles north of Downingtown. Springton Forge was built in 1766 and was five miles north of Mary Ann Forge, on the same stream. Hibernia Forge was built in 1793 on West Brandywine Creek, four miles north of Coatesville. A small rolling-mill was added in 1837, and both were abandoned in 1880. Rokeby Rolling-mill was built in 1795 on Buck Run, four miles south of Coatesville, and Brandywine Rolling-mill was built at Coatesville in 1810. Sadsbury Forges were built in 1800 and 1802 on Octoraro Creek, near Christiana. Ringwood Forge, also near Christiana, was built in 1810, was in operation as late as 1856, since which time it has been abandoned. Pine Grove Forge on Octoraro Creek, was built in 1800, and in 1844 a small rolling-mill was added on the Chester County side of the line, but these enterprises have been abandoned. Pleasant Garden Forge was built about 1806 and was about two miles southwest of New London, and a small rolling-mill was built about 1845, both of them being abandoned soon after this later date.

Kentgen's Works, which obtained considerable celebrity from the attempts made there to manufacture German steel, were situated in Pikeland Township. They were established in 1793, and in Swank's history of iron manufacture it is stated that Kentgen, on November 17, 1796, obtained a patent for forging round-iron, and that on June 27, 1810, he obtained a patent for rolling-iron in round shapes.

The Phœnix Iron Works were started some time late in the Eighteenth Century for the manufacture of nails. In 1828 they were bought at sheriff's sale by Reeves & Whitaker, the partners being Benjamin and David Reeves and James and Joseph Whitaker. Reeves & Whitaker greatly enlarged and improved the works and added new machinery, building a new and improved rolling-mill and introducing self-heading nail machinery, thus more than quadrupling the product of the establishment. They also erected a charcoal blast-furnace, which they ran until wood could no longer be obtained, and in 1845 they began the erection of two anthracite coal blast-furnaces, and in 1846 the erection of a rolling-mill for the manufacture of railroad iron. This rolling-mill was at the time it first went into operation at least equal to any other rolling-mill in this country, and the quality of its output was equal to that of any similar mill in England. Still later another and larger blast-furnace was erected, the mills again enlarged, and the machine shop also increased in capacity, so that not only the quality of the mills was improved, but the quantity was considerably increased.

Up to the close of the war railroad rails were a large part of the product of these mills, but since then attention has been given more to the manufacture of higher and finer qualities of iron. The manufacture of nails was transferred from these works to other works owned by the same firm at Bridgeton, New Jersey, in 1848, the nail-mill being at that time burned down at Phœnixville.

Since 1828 the owners of the works have been Reeves & Whitaker, Reeves, Buck & Co., and the Phœnix Iron Company, the Messrs. Reeves being from 1828 to 1881 the largest owners. The new mill, erected some time previous to 1881, was fire-proof, having an iron frame, iron sides and slate roof. It was in the last named year the largest single mill in the country. At these works are manufactured all kinds of structural iron, such as is used by architects, engineers, bridge builders, fancy iron workers, including iron beams and joists used in buildings, and the ribs and decks of iron ships. These works rolled out most of the iron used for ribs and decks of ships built on the Delaware River, including iron steamers running in the interest of the Pennsylvania Railroad Company to Liverpool, and those built at Chester for the Pacific Mail Steamship Company. They also made for the government large numbers of wrought-iron guns during the war of the Rebellion, these guns being an invention of Mr. John Griffen, general superintendent of the company for twenty-five or thirty years, dying in 1884. The number supplied was about 500, and they were the most efficient field guns in the service.

The presidents of this company have been as follows:
David Reeves, Samuel J. Reeves and David Reeves.
Secretaries—James Milliken, Robert B. Aertsen and George G. White.
Treasurers—Samuel J. Reeves, and James O. Pease.

The Phœnix Bridge Company is practically the same as the Phœnix Iron Company, taking contracts for the construction of bridges and then making contracts for the materials with the latter company.

As above narrated, iron mining began at a very early day. It is now of interest to note where it has been mined in more recent times. According to Professor H. D. Rodgers, there were in 1853 several excavations for iron ore in the narrow limestone valley south of Bethel Hill, two of these excavations being east of the gorge by which Gulf Creek passes through that hill. At that time one group of pits was about a mile southwest of this hill, and about 150 yards south of the road running along the north side of the valley. The ore was smelted in Merion furnace. An old pit, near the fork of the road at the Baptist meeting-house, had a shaft seventy-six feet deep, the ore from which was of a superior quality, and there was another opening further east on the southwest side of the road.

For some time there had been an ore-bank of considerable size, not far from the marble quarry owned by a Mr. Henderson of Upper Merion, which up to about 1854, yielded excellent ore, but which at length became unprofitable to mine. About 1,250 feet northeast of this bank there was another bank, then mined by George Fisher, and which contained good ore, the ore being used by the Phœnixville Iron Works. The average amount of dirt in this bank was about three to one of ore. Thomas Widdart's bank, Milliton's bank, Otto's bank, and Hughes & Jones' banks were all in this vicinity, and all yielded tolerably good ore.

Ore was also mined in Tredyffrin Township, south of the village of Howellville, and there was a small ore-bank northwest of Howellville, on the Swede's Ford Road. Woodman's ore-bank was about 500 yards west of the Valley Forge Road, where the ore was in the proportion of two to one of dirt. Nathaniel Jones, Charles Beaver, and Buck & King had ore mines about half a mile from Centerville, and Samuel Beaver had one about half a mile from the head of Valley Forge dam, which was of considerable size, and yielded good ore. Holland's Bank, the ore from which was smelted at Phœnixville, was located about one and a half miles northwest of Howellville.

Then, too, to the westward of the meridian of Paoli, there was another district of ore mines, in which were located William Buchanan's Ore-bank, about 400 yards north of Oakland Hotel, the ore from which was taken to Jones' Furnace on the Schuylkill; G. W. Jacob's bank, between the North Valley and the Columbia Railroad, about two miles east of Oakland, and two other banks belonging to the same party, about one-fourth of a mile of Ship Tavern; Maguire's bank, about one mile north of the Ship Tavern, was of considerable size and furnished good ore. A Mr. Evans had a bank three-fourths of a mile east of Ship Tavern, which yielded good ore, and was a large deposit; Frederick Neal had ore-banks in the vicinity which also yielded good ore, and about a mile northwest of Downingtown there was an ore mine near the foot of North Valley Hill, which had not been extensively opened, and which was not very promising. West of Coatesville there had been two or three openings for ore toward the southern side of the valley, between the west branch of Brandywine and Buck Run.

Two extensive excavations developed large deposits of iron ore about a half mile northeast of Yellow Springs, one of which was formerly known as the Fegley mine, the valley in which these excavations occur being separated from the valley containing the Lewis mine by a narrow belt of gneissic hills, the main body of the ore being in loose earth. The principal excavation at Fegley's Mine in 1853 was about 200 feet long, 100 feet wide and 50 feet deep, the irregular ore bed itself being only about 40 feet wide. A short distance to the northeast of Fegley's Mine there was one still larger, where the ore dipped to the southeast and reposing against a slanting wall of altered (Mesozoic) red sandstone. The ore here was about twelve feet thick at the bottom of the bed. About the time mentioned Fegley's Mine was yielding 2,400 tons of ore per annum, which was taken by the Phœnix Iron Works. The other mine in the near proximity was yielding 2,000 tons per annum.

The Latschaw Mine was situated about three-fourths of a mile southwest of Yellow Springs, and there was another mine owned by Reeves, Buck & Co., of Phœnixville, known as the Stite-

ler Mine, or Ore-bank, which was about three-fourths of a mile
further to the southwest of Yellow Springs. It was situated
five-eighths of a mile from the West Vincent line, was about 300
yards long by 200 yards wide, and at one time yielded from 5,000
to 8,000 tons of ore per annum. It has been abandoned for many
years. Jones' Mine was near the Latschaw Mine, or, as it was
otherwise called, the Harvey Mine, upon another rupture of the
strata.

Iron ore occurred also on the West Chester and Pottsgrove
State Road, one-fourth of a mile north of Little Eagle Tavern, in
Uwchlan Township. Similar iron ore was also found on the farm
of Morgan Hoffman, and there was a small ore pit on the farm
owned by William Parker. In 1853 the principal ore-banks being
operated were the Stauffer, seven-eighths of a mile southeast of
Pughtown, which was leased in October, 1880, by the Phœnix
Iron Company, and afterward abandoned, they exhausting the
ore when they had taken out about 4,000 tons; the Morris Russell
Mine, one mile north of Chester Springs, in West Pikeland Township, and owned by the Phœnix Iron Company; the Jones Mine,
one-half mile northwest of Chester Springs, in West Pikeland
Township, and worked by James Harvey; the Old Prizer Mine,
one-fourth of a mile north of Chester Springs railway depot,
and one-eighth of a mile off the line of the railway to the northwest, leased in July, 1865, by thePhœnix Iron Company, and later
by the Monocacy Furnace Company, which took out a large
quantity of ore, but abandoned it because the ore extended to
too great a depth; the Isaac Tustin Mine, a quarter of a mile
south of Chester Springs, first explored in 1851, and leased to
the Monocacy Furnace Company, and in 1864 to the Phœnix
Iron Company, which took several hundred tons of surface ore
from it, and then abandoned it, because the ore did not extend
to any depth.

The Raby Mine was owned by Rev. Mr. Raby, and situated

Joseph B. Jacoby-

one mile southwest of the Kimberton railway station, and was worked in 1882, several hundred tons of ore going to the S. Tilton's Plymouth Furnace at Conshohocken. The Orner-farm Mine lay one-half a mile due west of the old Fegley Mine, and was owned by the Phœnix Iron Company. The Acker Mine, one-fourth of a mile due west from the Harvey Mine, was worked for some years by the Phœnix Iron Company, under a lease dated January 1, 1863, but in 1883 it was being worked by Mr. Acker for the Monocacy Furnace Company. The John Mosteller Mine of brown hematite iron ore, about one-eighth of a mile south of the Eagle and Kimberton Road, was in 1883 being worked by the Phœnix Iron Company, and was yielding about fifteen tons of surface ore per day.

The Hopewell Middle Mine, in Warwick Township, was one of the most famous in the county. It was originally owned and run by Mr. Hopewell and by him worked by the open-cut method of mining, until the workings became too deep for this method. He then sank a shaft, and after the mine passed to the possession of the Pottstown Iron Company in 1873, that company sank another shaft, which passed down through the ore at the depth of 150 feet, where the vein averaged from twelve to fourteen feet in thickness. In 1882 the miners were robbing the pillars, and cutting away about thirty tons per day.

St. Mary's Mines, in 1882, were being worked by the E. & G. Brooke Iron Company, the mining being done by shafts, and the yield being about twenty tons of magnetic iron ore per day. Steel's Iron Ore-pits were about one-half mile north of St. Mary's village in Warwick Township, but it had not been worked for many years. The Leighton Iron Ore-mine was a little to the south of the village of St. Mary's, from which, before its abandonment, more than 20,000 tons of ore had been taken. Knauertown Iron-mine lay a little to the north of Knauertown, the iron found here being very similar to that of the Warwick Mine, but there was

34

not enough ore to encourage mining to any considerable extent.
Crossley's Iron Ore-pits were worked at one time, but were aban-
doned previous to 1854, their location being about one mile north of
Knauertown.

Lead and copper ore come next in point of value to iron ore
in the minerals of Chester County, but are far less extensively
found. The Wheatley and Brookdale Lode in the Pickering Creek
district is the best known and most valuable. This lode cuts
at least three of the trap dykes of that region, and the metallifer-
ous lodes which extend from the Perkiomen Mines in Montgomery
County to the Charlestown Mines of Chester County are situated
not far from the boundary line which separates the gneissic rocks
of this region from the Middle Secondary formation of the red
shale and sandstone, some of them lying on one side of this
boundary line and some on the other; and some are partly within
the gneiss and partly within the shale. Then, too, it is a curious
fact that as a general thing those veins which are confined entirely or mainly to the gneiss bear lead principally, while those
veins that are confined entirely within the red shale formation contain principally the ores of copper. But the zinc ores,
as zinc-blende or calamite, prevail in both sets of veins, though
perhaps to a relatively larger amount in the copper-bearing lodes
of the red shale. The Perkiomen and Ecton Lode, the United Mine
Lode, the Shannonville South Lode, the small French Creek Lode,
the Port Kennedy Lode, and the Morris Lode, near Phœnixville,
are genuine copper veins, and with no single exception are within
the red-shale formation; while on the other hand the Wheatley
and Brookdale Lode, the Chester County Lode, the Montgomery
Lode and the Charlestown Lode all lie within the gneissic formations and are all genuine lead veins.

The following paragraph from Prof. Rodgers shows the rich-
ness of these lodes and the variety of minerals which they contain:

"Selecting the Wheatley Lode as presenting, perhaps, the

greatest diversity of species, and as that which has received alto-gether the closest study, we find the mineralogy of these veins represented by the following large and interesting catalogue: Sulphate of lead, carbonate of lead, phosphate of lead, arseniate of lead, molybdate of lead, chromate of lead, arsenio-phosphate of lead, sulphuret of lead, antimonial sulphuret of lead and silver, sulphuret of zinc, carbonate of zinc, silicate of zinc, sulphuret of copper, green malachite, blue malachite, black oxide of copper, native copper, oxide of manganese, native sulphur, native silver, quartz, cellular quartz, oxide of iron containing silver, hæmatite iron, brown spar, sulphate of barytes, iron pyrites, and two or three other species."

The Brookdale Lode, an extension of the Wheatley Lode, was a remarkably regular silver lead vein. On May 1, 1853, there had been wrought a total length of 1,111 feet, and between the Wheatley and Brookdale engine shafts there was a further open-ing by an adit level of 456 feet, and there was but little if any doubt that the vein was much more extensive than its openings showed. In width the vein varied from one foot to two and a half feet and it was very productive. In the Wheatley vein the aver-age width was about eighteen inches, while in the Brookdale vein it was about two feet. The latter vein was rather fuller of quartz than the former. The main shaft at the Wheatley Mine was, in 1853, 234 feet deep, and the lode was very productive in ore, as was also the Brookdale end.

The Elizabeth Copper Mine was at one time a noted one. It was situated on the Knauertown Copper Lode, not far from Cross-ley's ore-pits, previously mentioned. The vein, according to Prof. Rodgers, consists largely of crystallized calcareous spar, in which occur crystallized oxide of iron, many brilliant octahedral crystals of sulphuret of iron, and some copper pyrites. The width of this vein or bed was about forty-five feet, an engine shaft descended 140 feet, and there was an interior underlay shaft descending from the bottom of the main shaft forty-five feet deeper. Active work was suspended there in May, 1854.

Sulphurets of copper and iron were found in the French Creek Magnetic Ore-mines, situated half a mile south of Harmonyville, where there were in 1854 two shafts about 250 feet deep, with hoisting and pumping engines at both, and the capacity of the mines was about 15,000 tons per annum. They were then worked by the E. & G. Brooke Iron Company.

Valuable marble is found in various parts of the county. About three and a half miles east of Downingtown, just south of the Valley Turnpike, is an extensive quarry of superior marble, which for years supplied Philadelphia with the beautiful white marble of which so many of her public and private buildings were constructed. The beds of this quarry were slightly contorted, the portion worked for marble separating into two beds. These beds were massive, mainly white, sometimes with a bluish tinge, and were quarried with ease and great facility. It was much used in the construction of Girard College and other public buildings in Philadelphia and neighboring towns.

There have been opened extensive quarries of marble or limestone in the vicinity of the Valley Church, where the limestone is very similar to that quarried two or three miles below Valley Forge, and on the road from Glassley to Valley Forge, near the county line, there is a small hill over the east end of which the road passes, which hill is composed of slaty talcose calcareous rock. Near Valley Forge there is a stratum of feldspathic rock exposed in the creek and occasionally appears overlying the primal white sandstone at the foot of North Valley Hill. Near the White Horse Tavern the limestone is talcote and slaty, but near the Steamboat Tavern the limestone is of the more usual granular structure. The limestone at Downingtown is compact and of a light color, several quarries of compact and granular limestone having been opened in the vicinity of this place.

A blue limestone quarry near Downingtown was opened in 1831, the rock being stratified, with regular jointing and fine texture. It was used for building, lime burning and ballast. It was used in building Villanova College, Villanova railway station, railway bridge, abutments and piers. At Bell's Quarry, Midway, the limestone is of a light color, and in the vicinity of Buck's Run and Parkesburg it becomes darker and more slaty.

Graphite and chrome are both extensively mined in Chester County, the latter mineral being found in considerable quantities in the southwest part of the county in both rock and sand. Dug and shipped to Europe it commands a high price. For many years the trade in chrome was under the exclusive control of Isaac Tyson of Baltimore, who procured from the farmers the right to dig and remove the mineral found on their farms. In this manner Mr. Tyson amassed a considerable fortune, and it doubtless was a profitable proceeding for the farmers, as the lands where this mineral is found are comparatively valueless for agricultural purposes.

Graphite or plumbago of a superior quality is found apparently in inexhaustible quantities in Upper Uwchlan and adjoining townships, near the line of the Pickering Valley Railroad.

Corundum has been mined for many years, especially in Newlin Township, and formerly in numerous quantities. This material existed in a narrow vein of hard white albite. An attempt to mine it regularly, made some years ago by D. Lewis Williams, was not persisted in. But loose blocks of corundum rocks were at one time collected to the amount of six or seven tons and exported to Europe. By geologists corundum is said to be a metamorphose of the gneiss composed more largely of alumina than the rest of the same rock, and while it is seldom found pure in nature, yet where found pure it is pure alumina. In the spring of 1866 John Leslie took up about five tons of corundum, which he sold at $60 per ton.

It is remarkable that during the last century there were several persons within the county who were engaged in the manufacture of clocks. The brass works were probably brought across the sea, and fitted together in the county, the cases being generally made where the clock was needed. Among the earlier workmen in this line were the Chandlees, of Nottingham, Benjamin Chandlee being the pioneer, and removing from the neighborhood in 1741. His son, Benjamin, manufactured not only clocks, but also compasses and a general line of mathematical instruments. His son, Ellis, also carried on the same lines of manufacture, and is said to have been the most ingenious of the family.

Isaac Thomas of Willistown made clocks during the later years of the Eighteenth Century, his residence being on the Boot Road, near Crumb Creek. Caleb Hibberd, living a mile east of Sugartown, in the same township, made clocks during the early part of the present century. Isaac Jackson of New Garden is remembered as a man of ingenuity, working in the finer materials, and being a maker of clocks. Benjamin Garrett began to make clocks about the year 1800, importing the castings, and his work was carried on quite extensively for twelve of fifteen years. Joseph Cave, of West Chester, made clocks and watches from about 1824 to 1834, his cases being made by Thomas Ogden. Others carried on the work until about 1835, when the Yankee clocks began to be introduced, and the home-made clocks were from that time on gradually superseded.

The Thorndale Iron Works were erected in 1847, J. & J. Forsythe & Sons erecting the mill and sixteen dwelling houses. Soon afterward Horace A. Beale purchased the establishment, and he in turn sold them to J. B. Moore of Philadelphia, from whom they passed into the hands of William L. Bailey in 1868. Mr. Bailey, in connection with J. B. Hayes, ran the works about eight years, under the firm name of William L. Bailey & Co., and still later they passed into the hands of a stock company, of which

Charles L. Bailey of Harrisburg was president; Abraham S. Patterson, of the same city, vice-president; and William L. Bailey, treasurer. They manufactured plate-iron, such as is used in the construction of locomotives, boilers, bridges, ships, and tanks, in 1880 turning out 6,495,777 pounds of finished iron. These works ceased to operate several years ago.

It has been stated that the first mill in Pennsylvania was located on Cobb's Creek, near the Blue Bell Tavern, erected about 1643. In 1683 the "Chester Mills" were erected on Chester Creek, not far above the present manufacturing village of Upland, in Delaware County. Richard Townsend about 1730 set up a mill on Chester Creek, "which served for grinding corn and sawing boards," he being a tenth owner in the mill.

Some of the earliest mills in Chester County, as at present bounded, were as follows: In Birmingham, Francis Chadds', in Tredyffrin, Thomas Jerman's, both mentioned as early as 1710; at Avondale, John Miller's, in 1714; in Kennett, Gayen Stevenson's in 1715; at Downington, Thomas Moore's 1716; in Goshen, George Ashbridge and others in 1717; in Kennett, Ellis Lewis' same years; in Birmingham, James Huston's 1719; in Bradford, Abiah Taylor's, in 1719; in Coventry, Thomas Miller's, in the same year; in Sadsbury, John Jones' 1721; in East Bradford, Carter, Scott and Willis', 1721; in Pocopson, Joseph Taylor's, 1724; in New London, Abraham Emmit's, on Big Elk Creek, and Henry Hollingsworth's on Little Elk Creek, in 1724; in London-grove, William Pusey's, 1730; in Sadsbury, James Hamor's, in 1722; in Whiteland, "Vale Royal" Mill, Richard Thomas, Samuel Phipps, William Williams and Magdalen Howell, in 1730; Jones' Mill, where afterward was erected Sager's Mill, on the Brandywine, in 1744.

In West Nantmeal, in the west branch of the Brandywine, there was a mill erected in 1840, a litle above Beaver Dam. This mill went to decay after the erection of Mackelduff's Mill, this being in 1762, there not being water enough for both. Mordecai Piersol built a mill in 1762, and in 1766 there was a mill built at Glen Moore. In 1770 Ackland's Mill was built, and White's Mill near Cupola Station, was erected in 1811. In this same year there was a mill on Naaman's Creek, owned by John Bellach, who "paid the highest price for grain," and Benjamin Jeffries owned a mill near Kennett Square.

Pennypacker's Mill was located in Pikeland Township, at least as early as 1812, this being for carding, spinning and weaving. The prices were as follows: Carding into "roles," 10 cents per pound; spinning, 12 cuts to the pound or less, 1½ cents per cut; all over 12 cuts to the pound, 2 cents per cut. This mill was owned by Harman Pennypacker and William Stidham.

Levi John and William McFarlan, in April, 1813, erected "a pair of machines for carding wool," at the mill, then lately occupied as a clover-mill in Vincent Township, near William Reed's Mill. Wool-carding was also carried on by John Woodward, at the mill of William Woodward in East Bradford, by Mordecai Thomas at his own mill in Willistown, and by Joseph H. Downing in Downingtown. At this same time John Taylor had a grist-mill in East Bradford, run by water from Brandywine Creek.

In 1817 James Hance built a mill in West Whiteland, which mill, in 1831, was purchased by George Hoopes, and later became the property of his son, Robert F. Hoopes. The Charlestown Woolen Mill was owned by Hood & Sandham, who manufactured both broad and narrow cloth, cassimeres, satinets, flannels, linsey and plaid, as well as broad and narrow blankets, carded and and wove woolen goods, and purchased wool. In West Chester, in 1818, Joseph Jones began the making of chairs, fancy, windsor and rush-bottom, carrying on the business for several years.

The Bloomfield Factory, located near Kennett Square, was operated by John P. Chambers, who manufactured woolen cloths at the following prices: Blankets, 1 yard wide, 8 cuts to the pound, 55 cents; flannels, 1 yard wide, 12 cuts to the pound, 75 cents; thick flannels, ⅞ of a yard wide, 12 cuts to the pound, 90 cents; cloth, ¾ of a yard wide, 12 cuts to the pound, $1; cloth ¾ of a yard wide, 16 cuts to the pound, $1.25; carding common wool into rolls, 10 cents; spinning, from 8 to 12 cuts per pound, 20 cents per dozen; from 12 to 20 cuts per pound, 24 cents per dozen; all under 8 cuts, 10 cents per pound.

There was a Union Woolen Manufactory in Sadsbury, Township, manufacturing wool into broad and narrow cloth, cassimeres, cassinettes, coarse and fine flannel, etc. Andrew Wilson carried on the carding and fulling business "at the stand formerly occupied by Calvin Cooper, deceased," in West Bradford Township. Seneca Warner carried on wool carding at J. Buffington's Tilt-mill in East Bradford Township, and himself owned a grist-mill in East Marlborough Township. The fulling business was also carried in by Elisha Davis, in West Bradford, on the road leading from Downingtown to the Center House. Jeremiah Bailey made fans, wire screens, rolling screens, etc., at his mill near Kennett Square. And that there was brick-making early in the history of the county is shown by the fact that in 1818 Joseph Townsend of West Chester offered 50,000 bricks for sale, and also some draining tile. For several, if not for many years, William Work carried on coach-making in West Chester, commencing about 1824, and he had for sale the "highly approved patent C springs."

The Doe Run Woolen Factory, located in West Nantmeal Township, was owned by Abel I. Thomas, and the Downington pottery, which, in 1824, was managed by Eber James, was previously owned and managed by Jesse Kersey. Caleb Jackson at this time carried on coach and Dearborn-wagon making about half a mile west of Kennett Square, at the place then lately occupied by Isaac Philips.

In 1825 Samuel Bellerjeau carried on cabinet-making in

Downingtown, as did Thomas Ogden in West Chester, and Jonathan Rowland was a wool carder at Lapp's mill, near the Fox Chase Tavern in Tredyffrin Township. Townsend Eachus carried on wool-carding at his clover-mill in West Goshen Township, about one and three-quarter miles from West Chester, as also did Joseph Painter in East Bradford. George S. Downing had a tan-yard in East Caln Township, three miles west of Downingtown, and in 1826 Robert and Canby Steel manufactured hats in West Chester. This year John Tweddle managed the Downingtown Brewery, at which he brewed porter, ale and small beer.

The Platinum Works of J. Bishop & Co. are located at Sugartown, in Willistown Township, six miles east of West Chester and three miles south of Malvern, on the main line of the Pennsylvania Railroad. The founder of these works was born in Portugal in 1806, where his father, an Englishman, was temporarily residing, and where he was director of the Royal Fabrics. Joaquin Bishop, the founder, came to the United States with his parents in 1810, settled in Philadelphia in 1811, and was there apprenticed to a jeweler in 1826. In 1832 he became instrument maker and assistant chemist of the University of Pennsylvania, under Dr. Robert Hare, and in 1839 he began to work in platinum, in 1842 establishing what is now the firm of J. Bishop & Co. In 1845 he drew first premium at Franklin Institute for platinum work. In 1858 he removed his business to Radnor, and in 1865 to its present location. In 1876 he received first premium and diploma from the Centennial Commission, and in 1881 he associated with himself in partnership Edwin T. Cox, under the firm name of J. Bishop & Co. After a life of activity and usefulness he died August 4, 1886, leaving his interest in the business to his grandson, Joaquin B. Matlack. Mr. Matlack and Mr. Cox have since then carried on the business under the old firm name. Their work consists of refining and melting platinum ore or scraps, and manufacturing said metal into assaying apparatus vessels

and tubes of all decriptions, and all kinds of experimental instruments in use by analytical chemists, and in short anything made
of platinum. For these goods a market is found in the labora-
tories of universities, colleges, steel and iron manufactories, and
among all kinds of professional and scientific men in the country,
in Canada, Mexico, and to some slight extent in Europe.

The Lukens Iron and Steel Company was originally established in 1790, though not under its present name. In that year
Isaac Pennock, great-grandfather of Mr. A. F. Huston, present
president of the company, built a mill and began the manufacture
of iron at a place called Rokeby, on Buck Run, Chester County,
about four miles south of Coatesville. This mill was called the
"Federal Slitting Mill," charcoal slabs being heated in an open
charcoal fire, rolled out into plates, and then slit up into rods for
general blacksmith use. In 1810 he bought a saw-mill property
on the Brandywine, at Coatesville, which he converted into an iron-
mill. This mill was called Brandywine, and afterward developed
into the large plant now in operation, covering many acres of
ground and furnishing employment to a large number of men.

Rebecca W. Pennock, daughter of Isaac Pennock, married
Dr. Charles Lukens, the latter leasing Brandywine of his father-
in-law in 1816 and carrying on the business of iron-making until
his death in 1825. It was between 1816 and 1825 that steam
boilers first came into use, and the first boiler plates produced in
this country were made in this mill by Dr. Lukens. After the
death of Dr. Lukens, his widow, in accordance with his request,
continued to carry on the business, greatly increased the plant
and continued successfully for many years, and it was as a tribute
to her memory that the name of the works, after her death, was
changed to the "Lukens Rolling-mills." The works have been
continuously operated by the family from 1810 to the present
year, 1898.

After the death of Mrs. Lukens the business was conducted

by her sons-in-law, Abraham Gibbons and Dr. Charles Huston. In 1855 Mr. Gibbons retired after a short but prosperous and honorable business career. The works then remained in Dr. Charles Huston's hands, who, together with his partner, Mr. Charles Penrose, who joined him a few years later, carried on the manufacture of iron until the death of Mr. Penrose, in 1881; in the meantime Dr. Huston's two sons, A. F. and C. L. Huston, upon their graduation from college, in 1872 and 1875, having joined the company. The company was known from this time until 1890 as "Charles Huston & Sons." In this latter year a stock company was formed and chartered under the title of "The Lukens Iron and Steel Company," the officers of which were as follows: Dr. Charles Huston, president; A. F. Huston, vice-president; Charles L. Huston, general manager; R. B. Haines, secretary, and Joseph Humpton, treasurer. Not long afterward Mr. Haines resigned the position of secretary, and Mr. Humpton was appointed to this position, since then filling both offices of secretary and treasurer. Upon the death of Dr. Charles Huston, in 1897, A. F. Huston succeeded to the presidency and Charles L. Huston became vice-president.

Originally the boilers plates were made from single charcoal blooms, the blooms being made in the old-fashioned forge fire, then reheated over an ordinary grate fire and rolled into plates. These plates were shipped without being sheared. Later shears were introduced and the shearings were cut into nails. Afterward a reverbatory heating furnace was introduced, enabling the scrap to be worked up. The plate-rolls at this time were from sixteen to eighteen inches in diameter, and from three to four feet long between the housings, and were driven by an overshot water-wheel. Many a time, when it looked as if the mill would stall, the workmen would rush to the water-wheel, climb upon its rim, and by their weight help the pass through the rolls. In this way a "sticker" was often prevented, which, whenever it came, meant fire-cracked rolls and later on broken ones.

Owing to the constant increase of business the overshot water-wheel was superseded by the breast-wheel, so geared as to convey more power to the rolls, and in addition, a heavy fly-wheel was introduced, geared to a high speed for the storage of power. The use of larger rolls was thus permitted, those now introduced being twenty-one inches in diameter and sixty-six inches long. In 1870 a modern steam plate-mill was erected with chilled rolls twenty-five by eighty-four inches, the old mill becoming a puddling mill. At length there was put in position a three-high mill, with solid chilled rolls, 34 inches in diameter by 120 inches long, weighing eighteen tons each. At that time this was the largest mill of its kind ever erected in the United States.

The capital (and surplus) employed in the business is over $1,000,000, the capacity of the works being 75,000 tons per year. The number of men on the pay roll is 500, and the amount of money paid out annually to employes is $250,000. The plant covers nearly fifty acres of ground, and the quantity of freight, both in and out of the works, is 175,000 tons per year. Connected with the plant at the present time are six open-hearth furnaces—in three of which is used the basic process, and in the other three the acid process. The heating furnaces number nine and the trains of rolls three. A machine-shop, a fitting-shop, a carpenter-shop, a blacksmith-shop, a turning department, a supply building and an electric apparatus constitute portions of the equipment. An electric charging machine performs the work of several men, and two small locomotives move material from place to place. Hydraulic handling cranes are placed wherever they can be used to advantage, the largest lifting eighteen tons. Four hydraulic cranes in the shipping house, which is 240 feet long, are each capable of lifting five tons. Two large flanging machines, capable of turning the largest sized boiler heads, machines for making flue holes in boiler heads, one of them a hydraulic machine with

a cylinder 48 inches in diameter, and machines for manufacturing patent steel boiler braces, of which latter Mr. A. F. Huston
is the patentee, are in position.   One of the engines is 60x36
inches, having an indicated horse power of 2,000, and another
engine is 48x28 inches.   The twenty-five large gas producers supply the steel plant and the plate mills, the four reverberatory furnaces using coal.   The mill across the Brandywine has four furnaces.

The officers of this company at the present time are A. F.
Huston, president; C. L. Huston, vice-president, and Joseph Humpton, secretary and treasurer.

This history of the Lukens Iron and Steel Company cannot
well be closed without at least brief reference to the man to whose
efforts, since the death of Mrs. Lukens, its success and present
standing in the industrial world are mainly due.   Dr. Charles
Huston was born in Philadelphia in 1822, graduated at the University of Pennsylvania in 1840, finished a three years' course in
medicine at the Jefferson Medical College in Philadelphia in 1843,
and supplemented this course in medical study by an eighteen
months' special course in Europe.   He began the practice of his
profession in Philadelphia, married Miss Isabella Lukens of
Coatesville, and settled down to the laborious life of a practicing
physician.   In 1848 he moved to the country, and in 1849 became
engaged in the iron business, which he continuously followed until his death in January, 1897.   In 1875, when the government
of the United States began requiring that plates used in the construction of steamboat boilers should be stamped with their
tensile strength, Dr. Huston promptly purchased a testing machine, and began investigating the properties of iron and steel,
and in 1877, when the manufacturers of boiler plates were requested by the Treasury Department of the United States government to send a committee to Washington to advise with the
Board of Supervising Steamboat Inspectors in framing a proper

standard of tests, Dr. Huston was chosen chairman of the committee, and because of his practical knowledge of the character of metal and his experience in testing, his recommendations were adopted by the Board of Inspectors. In later years his counsel was frequently sought by the Government of the United States, and his views were also sought and followed by the leading steam boiler inspectors and insurance companies in this country. Dr. Huston was one of the leading authorities in the United States upon the iron and steel industry, and in 1878-79 he published revised articles in the journal of the Franklin Institute upon the behavior of iron and steel under varying conditions of heat and stress. These articles attracted the attention of engineers abroad years afterward, when they began this line of investigation.

In 1895 Dr. Huston was selected by Chauncey M. Depew as the man best qualified by ability and experience to write the article on the iron and steel industry in his comprehensive history of "One Hundred Years of American Commerce." The natural ability of Dr. Huston and his scientific acquirements permeated every department of the Lukens Works, and the influence of his high personal character was always felt, not only throughout these works, but also throughout the community in which he lived.

The Coatesville Boiler Works were started in 1886 by Frederick Sotter, A. J. George, H. C. Smith and Cyrus Shank, who rented the old planing-mill property of William T. Hunt's estate, and began making boilers under the firm name of Sotter, George & Co. The entire amount of capital invested in the business at first was less than $700, but each member of the firm was a skilled mechanic, and by turning out first-class work at moderate prices they gradually built up the business which amounted the first year to $11,000.

In 1887 Messrs. Smith and Shank withdrew from the partnership, and were succeeded by Frederic and George E. Reif,

Frederic Reif selling his interest in 1890 to Charles Edgerton, a mechanical engineer of Philadelphia. This year the firm purchased the old round-house property of the Wilmington and Northern Railroad Company, and erected their present shops. The main building is 60x160 feet, with additional buildings for the engine and tool rooms, and an annex for the flanging department.

September 15, 1891, the Coatesville Boiler Works were incorporated, with a capital stock of $50,000, and since the enterprise has grown to its present large proportions. The machinery in this plant cost $20,000, and among the most important pieces is a pair of bending rolls 18 feet 6 inches between housings, with double engines attached, capable of bending plates 18 feet wide to a circle of 38 inches. These rolls cost $6,000 and weigh thirty-five tons. There are also large machines punching five-inch holes in ⅜-inch plates with perfect ease. There is also other necessary machinery, which it is not necessary to describe.

The products of these works consist of boilers of various sizes, smoke-stacks, stand-pipes, all kinds of tanks, including congealing tanks for ice plants, as well as other articles of iron. The number of men employed is about sixty, the annual pay roll amounting to more than $20,000. The volume of business amounts to something over $125,000 per year, and the business has been so prosperous that the stock of the company is usually at a premium.

The officers of the company at present are as follows: F. Sotter, president; Charles Edgerton, vice-president, and A. J. George, secretary and treasurer.

Ridgway's Foundry of Coatesville, manufacturing water-wheels and cranes, was established in 1863, the main business for many years being that of keeping in repair the rolling-mills of the town and neighborhood, and the manufacture of the old Tyler water-wheel. In 1879 William H. Ridgway was admitted to partnership with Mr. Craig Ridgway, and soon improved the Tyler wheel, bringing out the now celebrated Perfection water-wheel,

J. B. Everhart

which was a success from the start, and which is in use in Asia, Africa and all parts of Europe, as well as in the United States. In 1888 Mr. Ridgway produced, in the invention of his Balanced Steam Crane, one of the most notable inventions of the day. This is one of the most successful enterprises of its kind in the country.

The Coatesville Casket Company was organized at a stockholders' meeting held February 20, 1896, the directors elected then being Joseph N. Woodward, L. B. Henson, Charles W. Ash, John W. Thompson, W. P. Moore, O. A. Boyle, W. S. Young, J. L. Lovett, and J. H. C. McClure, and these directors elected J. N. Woodward president, John W. Thompson treasurer and H. C. McClure secretary. The company was incorporated in March, 1896' with a capital of $25,000, at which it still remains. They purchased an old shoe factory building at the corner of Main Street and Sixth Avenue, to which they made some improvements and additions, and which they still use. The product of the factory consists of all kinds of caskets, the specialty being those made of oak and mahogany. The first year's output was worth about $40,000, the capacity of the works being about $50,000 worth of products. The officers of the company at the present time are the same as those mentioned above.

The Viaduct Iron Works were purchased at sheriff's sale about 1853 by Hugh E. Steel and S. B. Worth, under the firm name of Steel & Worth. They were then known as the Tridelphi Iron Works, but the name was changed by the new owners to the Viaduct Iron Works, they being situated in the borough of Coatesville, directly underneath the high Pennsylvania railway bridge spanning the Brandywine. At this time the mill consisted of two small trains of rolls, driven by water. Steel & Worth immediately increased in size both sets of rolls, using all the water power to drive one set, and introducing a steam engine to drive the other. In 1861 they erected another steam mill, and in 1868 still another and larger mill was erected. Since 1872 all the rolls have

35

been operated by steam. In 1874, owing to the death of S. B. Worth, the firm was dissolved, and later the works were continued by Hugh E. Steel and the heirs of S. B. Worth, under the name of Steel & Worth Company, the same being incorporated. In 1880 the Worths withdrew from the corporation, and the name was changed to the Coatesville Iron Company. In 1888 the works were purchased by J. S. & W. P. Worth, who have since continued it under the firm name of the Coatesville Rolling Mill Company. The present capacity of the works is about 15,000 tons annually.

The Brandywine Rolling Mills was erected in 1880 by Worth Brothers (J. Sharpless and William P.). Upon its commencement the product of the mills was about 3,000 tons of finished plates annually, and this capacity was increased from time to time, as occasion demanded. In 1895 the firm was incorporated as Worth Brothers Company, the Worths being the principal stockholders, the capital stock being placed at $250,000. Radical improvements were made and the works generally enlarged. An open-hearth steel plant and a large three-high plate-mill, including rolls eleven feet wide (the largest in Pennsylvania), were established. These works are located in East Fallowfield Township, about one-half a mile from the borough line of Coatesville, and contiguous to the Wilmington & Northern Railway. ·The business consists mainly in the manufacture of open-hearth steel-plates and sheets. Steel is manufactured by both the basic and the acid process, and all the improvements in the methods or processes of making steel are here in use. The mills have a capacity of about 40,000 tons of finished steel per year, and this capacity is being increased by the addition of more furnaces.

Hoopes Bros. & Darlington, manufacturers of wheels of all kinds, established themselves in business in West Chester in 1868, though, at the beginning, only William and Thomas Hoopes were in the firm. Shortly afterward Stephen P. Darlington became a member of the firm, and the name given above was adopted.

The business at first consisted of the manufacture of spokes, but in 1870 the manufacture of bent rims was added, and in 1872 the manufacture of wheels. From that time on the manufacture of spokes gradually was discontinued, as the timber fit for such purposes diminished in quantity, and the manufacture of wheels as gradually increased, until, at the present time, it is almost exclusively the business of the company. All kinds of wheels are made, from those on the lightest wagons up to those on wagons which carry twenty-five tons. The market for the product of this establishment, which is located on Market Street, just east of the railroad, is confined mainly to a radius of three hundred miles, but still a portion of the product is shipped to England and other European countries. The floor space of the buildings is equal to about two acres; the capital employed is about $200,000; the force ranges from 140 to 175 men, and the product of the works ranges from $250,000 to $300,000 per year. The members of the firm at the present time are William and Thomas Hoopes and Edwin S. Darlington, the two brothers having been continuously in the company.

The Sharpless Separator Works were established in 1885 by Philip M. Sharpless in a building where the stocking factory now is located, with five men and less than $200 capital, the success with which he has met being attributable to the mechanical knowledge acquired in various manufactories of steam engines and other factories of a similar nature and to industry and determination to succeed. The business which Mr. Sharpless owns and manages has grown in sixteen years to be one of the most successful in the country, turning out a product that goes extensively into every dairy country of the earth. Many carloads of machinery were shipped in 1897 to Australia, New Zealand, Africa, South America, Europe, and other foreign countries.

The special product is the Cream Separator, an implement which, within the last few years, has revolutionized the dairying business of the country. Thousands of machines are annually put into the hands of dairymen and farmers, who, though not skilled in the handling of machinery, yet have no difficulty in managing a separator which makes 25,000 revolutions per minute, day after day, with an expense that is merely trifling, with rarely a breakdown and never a life endangered. The buildings are located in the immediate vicinity of the Villa Maria Academy, on the railroad, thus possessing every needed shipping facility. The works spend $20,000 per year in advertising, and in connection with its branch houses at Dubuque, Omaha, and at Elgin, employ about 300 people, and over half a million dollars of capital, and on January 1, 1898, there was not a dollar outstanding against them anywhere. The success of Mr. Sharpless in building up and conducting this business has been most remarkable, and is a valuable object lesson to those who may feel that they have within them the enterprising spirit necessary to success, but yet hesitate to put it into practical operation.

The Edison Electric Illuminating Company of West Chester was organized in 1885, and erected in that place the third plant of the kind in the State of Pennsylvania. The directors of the company at first were R. T. Cornwell, H. C. Baldwin, E. H. Hemphill, T. Brown, Dr. Isaac Massey, A. Hoopes, R. E. Monaghan, W. Hoopes and F. P. Darlington. The officers of this company from its organization to the present time have been and are as follows: R. T. Cornwell, president; John A. Rupert, secretary, and D. M. McFarland, treasurer.

The object for which this company was organized was the manufacture of light and power, and for this purpose it purchased a building at the northwest corner of Chestnut and Walnut Streets, into which the first plant, which was much less in completeness and effectiveness than that at present in use, was placed. The present building is a two-and-a-half-story brick, 50x120 feet in size, and there is a boiler-house one story high. The equipment at the present time consists of five boilers and six engines, with an aggregate of 750-horse power. All of the engines are high-speed automatic ones, three of them straight lines, one of the others being made by the McEwen Company, one by the Beck Company, and one by the Ames Company. The dynamos are as follows:

Four 30-kilowatt dynamos, with 125 voltage, the first introduced in 1885, for the purpose of incandescent lighting and furnishing power to manufacturers of West Chester.

Two 50-kilowatt dynamos, introduced in February, 1887, for the same purpose.

Two 60-kilowatt railway generators of 500 voltage, for the purpose of furnishing power to the street railway company, introduced in the early part of 1891.

One Edison series-arc thirty-five lights machine, for supplying commercial lights to stores, introduced in 1891, and another for the same purpose, introduced in 1892.

One Thomson-Houston series-arc fifty lights machine, for supplying arc lights for the streets, introduced in 1893, and a similar machine, introduced in 1895.

It may be proper to state in this connection that a kilowatt is a thousand watts, and that 746 watts is equal to one horse-power.

The present directors of this company are as follows: R. T. Cornwell, H. C. Baldwin, T. Brown, J. S. Evans, F. P. Darlington, P. E. Jefferis, Abner Hoopes, and Samuel Marshall.

Damon & Speakman were engaged for several years in the manufacture of various implments that are used on or about the farm, their foundry and machine shop being located in West Chester, where now stands the artificial ice plant. They began business about 1855, making horse-powers, corn-shellers, lime-spreaders, etc. In 1858 they began making the Hubbard mowing machine, then the best in use. They also made one-horse power machine, for running the churn, and the butter worker, all of these before the war of the Rebellion.

The Parkersburg Iron Company's Works were started in 1873, by Horace A. Beale, and afterward the firm became Horace A. Beale & Co. by the admission of William H. Gibbons of Coatesville to partnership. In 1882 the present company was organized and incorporated with a capital of $125,000. The first officers were Horace A. Beale, president; William H. Gibbons, vicepresident; Amos Michener, secretary, Samuel R. Parke, treasurer, and A. J. Williams, general manager. These persons remained in their respective offices until the fall of 1897, when Horace A. Beale died, and Mr. Gibbons became president, Horace A. Beale, Jr., vice-president; William C. Michener, secretary; George Thomas (3), treasurer, and the general manager remaining the same, though an assistant general manager was provided in the person of E. H. Brodhead.

The product of these mills consists of boiler tube-iron skelp, the annual output being about 10,000 tons. The buildings consist of three mill buildings, one forge building, two charcoal houses, two scrap houses, a machine shop, two trimming houses and other necessary buildings. The mill consists of three twohigh plate lines driven by a horizontal slide-valve engine; one three-high muck-bar roll-train driven by a vertical slide-valve engine; three puddling furnaces with double-acting upright hammer; nine heating furnaces; twelve forge fires, and two horizontal hammers. The machine shop is fitted up with all necessary machinery. There are employed at these works about 300 men.

Capt. Horace A. Beale, deceased, former president of the Parkesburg Iron Company, was born in Philadelphia, January 25, 1827. The first member of the Beale family to settle in Chester County was William Beale, a son of Thomas and Catherine Beale, of Calne, in Wiltshire, England. Horace A. Beale was a son of Joseph and Margaret (McDowell) Beale, the former of whom died on his farm near Downingtown, in 1841, his wife having died in 1834.

Reared mainly in Chester County, Horace A. Beale received his education in the old Philadelphia Academy and at the University of Pennsylvania. In 1846 he became a clerk at the Laurel Iron Works, and there gained his first knowledge of the iron business. Going to Phœnixville soon afterward, he became a clerk in the Phœnixville Iron Works, and there acquired a knowledge of the iron business in all its details. In 1852 he purchased the Thorndale Iron Works, and while occupied in the management of these works made himself familiar with everything connected with the industry in which he was engaged. In 1882 he established the Parkesburg Iron Company, of which he was president the remainder of his life, and which he made an unusual success. One of the results of the location of the works in this place was the growth of Parkesburg from a population of about 300 to one of nearly 2,000, as it is at the present time. While Capt. Beale encoutered many obstacles, yet he overcame them all, and achieved a very substantial success.

One of the features of Mr. Beale's character was his uniform courtesy and kindly disposition. He was in reality the idol of his employes, all of whom he knew by name, and all of whom he always treated with the greatest interest and sympathy. The result of this kindly interest was that every man in his employ labored diligently for the interest of his employer, and strikes in his works were unknown. This is believed to be the true secret of success in the treatment of the laboring man. He is entitled to justice under the bare contract for the surrender of his time and the expenditure of his energy, and he is in a certain sense entitled to more than justice, in order that he may be in some degree contented with his lot. And no one can appreciate more than he such kindly sympathy as was always extended by Capt. Horace A. Beale. When he died November 3, 1897, he was sincerely mourned by all, family, friends, employes, all that knew him.

The Downingtown Manufacturing Company (Limited), was organized as a stock company under the act of June 2, 1874, on November 20, 1884, though the business had been carried on from 1881 by Guyon Miller and A. B. Tutton as a private concern. When the stock company was formed it was authorized to have a capital of $33,500, which was subsequently increased to $50,500. The first officers of the company were A. B. Tutton chairman, and Guyon Miller secretary and treasurer. The works are located on Washington Avenue and the Pennsylvania Railroad, and consist of several buildings such as are needed in an establishment of the kind. The products of the works consist of patent beating engines and fourdrinier and cylinder paper machines. The annual capacity of the works is $125,000 worth of these goods.

S. Austin Bicking's Paper Mills, Nos. 1 and 2, are located in Downingtown, No. 1 having been started in 1881 by Mr. Bicking at the corner of Brandywine and Lancaster Avenues. No. 2 was started in 1895, a flour mill formerly belonging to Mr. Shelmire being converted into a paper mill. At the present time Mr. Bicking's sons are in partnership with him in the operation of the mills, which manufacture wrapping, roofing and rosin-sized building paper, and binders' and trunk boards.

F. P. Miller manages a paper mill as agent, and William Kerr also has a paper mill in the southern part of Downingtown.

The Downingtown Brick Works are located in East Downingtown, and are owned by W. Logan Rogers and Lewis Miller, under the firm name of Rogers & Miller. They were established in 1892 by Rogers & Kerr, who ran them about one year, when the firm became Rogers & Parke. In 1897 the firm became Rogers & Miller, as it is at present. Twenty-one acres are occupied by the firm, who employ an average of about thirty men, and manufacture about 3,500,000 brick per annum.

James Florey's brick yard is also in East Downingtown, and was established in 1895. He owns fourteen acres of land, employs from twenty-five to thirty men, and makes about 5,000,000 brick per year.

The Chalfant Manufacturing Company's business, located at Atglen, was established in 1873 by Isaac P. Chalfant, who carried on the business alone until the company was incorporated in 1890, under the above name. Isaac P. Chalfant was the first president of the company, and T. S. Chalfant secretary. The business of Isaac P. Chalfant and of the company has been and is the manufacture of the Potts sad-irons, invented by Mr. Potts. These sad-irons are known all over the world, and since the patent expired in 1888 have been manufactured largely in most civilized countries. At the present time the headquarters of the company are at Lancaster, the establishment at Atglen being only a branch, and being located on a small branch of Octoraro Creek, about half a mile above the borough of Atglen.

The American Road Machine Company was organized March 1, 1886, with the following officers: Samuel Pennock, president; George W. Taft, vice-president; C. J. Pennock, secretary, and Edward Lewis, treasurer. From 1881 to 1886 the business was carried on under the name of S. Pennock & Sons' Company, and from 1877 to 1881 under the name of S. Pennock & Sons.

Samuel Pennock is the patriarch of Kennett Square. From a farmhouse just beyond the borough limits this now venerable man came to the place, and together with his brothers, Morton and Barkley, erected the machine shops now owned by J. M. Worrall, and engaged in the manufacture of agricultural implements. Moses Pennock and his son, Samuel, invented the first practical grain drill in America, and also a corn-sheller. Samuel Pennock's harvesting machine was the first machine of the kind which enabled the operator to manipulate it while remaining seated upon it. In the establishment where these implements were manufactured there were employed about thirty men. In 1858 or 1859 the car shops were built by the Pennocks, in which freight cars, principally, were made, and about 125 men were employed.

Mr. Pennock invented the road-machine which gives its name to the American Road Machine Company, in 1877, without knowing of the existence of any similar invention in the country, but others were at work on the same idea, and many thousands have been sold, but the combined inventions of several companies have given the public the perfection of such a machine. For the past eighty-one years Mr. Samuel Pennock has been a resident of Kennett Square, with the exception of two years spent in Unionville, one year with the Pusey & Harlem Company of Wilmington, Delaware, and four and a half years in Ithaca, New York. He has been an anti-slavery man, a prohibitionist and a equal suffragist, and is in favor of more light being thrown on every phase of socialism.

In 1886 George W. Taft, of Abington, Connecticut, made a consolidation with the firm in Kennett Square, and the capital of the new company was increased to $250,000. Then about half of the buildings now in use had been erected, their elegant brick office building having also been erected since then. This company manufactures road-machines, rock-crushers, road-rollers, and other valuable inventions. The officers of the company at the present time are: George W. Taft, president; Edward Lewis, vice-president; S. Jones Philips, secretary and treasurer, and the board of directors consists of the above-named officers and Henry C. Davis and Wilfred Lewis.

Cassel's Terra Cotta Works at Kennett Square were located in this place in 1894, but had been in existence previously for about twenty years, for fifteen of which years in Philadelphia. In Kennett the building is a three-story brick, 40x80 feet in size, and here all kinds of rustic terra-cotta are made. The goods find a market in all parts of the United States and in Europe. The office of the works is at 709 Arch Street, Philadelphia.

Joseph R. Gawthrop is engaged in the manufacture of fertilizers of all kinds in Kennett Square, succeeding his father, James Gawthrop, who died in 1887, his factory being located in the southern part of the village.

The Fiber Specialty Company was organized June 8, 1898, with officers as follows: George W. Taft, president; Ishael Marshall, vice-president; C. J. Pennock, secretary, and S. Jones Philips, treasurer. The capital stock of the company is $50,000, and the plant is located on West Cedar Street and the railway. The building is a two and a half story brick, 40x120 feet, and contains all the machinery for the proper carrying on of the business. The boiler is a forty-horse power one, and the engine is of fifteen-horse power. All kinds of fiber goods are manufactured, such as trunks, valises, traveling bags, etc.

The Kennett Foundry and Machine Works, of which J. Eli Crozier is the proprietor, were established in 1887, by Mr. Crozier. They are located on South Union Street and the railway, the building consisting of a brick-machine shop, a large brick foundry, and several others necessary to such an enterprise. Mr. Crozier turns out about $25,000 worth of products each year, which consist in part of parts of the rock-crusher and of the road-machine made by the American Road Machine Company, and he employs on the average twenty-two men.

The Oxford Milling Company was organized in March, 1888, with a capital of $25,000. The company manufactures high-grade winter wheat flours, their mill being equipped with the latest improved roller process machinery. The leading brands of flour made are the "Passmore Fancy," the "White Daisy," the "White Plume," and the "Arbutus." The officers at present are W. F. Dowdall, president; H. P. Passmore, secretary and manager; D. M. Taylor, treasurer, and J. Hannan, superintendent. The mills are adjacent to the tracks of the Central Division of the Philadelphia, Wilmington & Baltimore Railroad, and they have a large export trade to Cuba and European countries.

Wilson, Pugh & Wilson, successors to Bailey & Wilson, have been in the business of manufacturing carriages, buggies, etc., for more than thirty-five years. Their buildings on Pine Street are conveniently arranged, the main building being 30x100 feet, two stories above the basement, and is used as a repository. Three other buildings are in use, a smith-shop, a wood-shop and a two-story building used both as a repository and a paint and trimming shop. The territory over which the trade of this firm extends embraces the surrounding country in Southern Pennsylvania and Northern Maryland, and such large cities as Philadelphia, Baltimore, Chicago, and portions of the states of Maine, New York, Ohio, and states intermediate between Ohio and Alabama. The firm is now composed of Samuel W. Wilson, A. Louis Pugh and J. Henry Wilson, the last named being the son of the first named. In 1897 this firm began the sale of agricultural implements.

Chandler & Andrews operate the only planing-mill in Oxford.. The building consists of a two-story brick, 60x40 feet, with an "L" 18x24 feet, and is well designed for rapid and perfect work. Every description of sash, doors, blinds, moldings, and finishing materials are turned out, and the firm deals extensively in lumber, flour, feed, grain and hay. F. G. Andrews became a member of the firm in September, 1895. In the planing is one large planer and several joiners, the machinery being propelled by a thirty-horsepower engine.

The Oxford Caramel Company was incorporated according to the laws of Pennsylvania November 1, 1894, with a capital of $100,000. The officers at first were as follows: President, W. F. Parker; secretary and treasurer, H. U. Williams; directors, W. F. Parker, H. U. Williams, D. M. Taylor, J. E. Ramsey and W. T. Donald. At the present H. U. Williams is president, H. L. Shumway, secretary and treasurer, and the directors are as follows: H. U. Williams, D. M. Taylor, J. E. Ramsey, H. L. Shumway and W. H. Wieting.

The business was founded in 1882 in Philadelphia by W. F. Parker. On January 1, 1892, Mr. Parker and H. U. Williams formed a co-partnership under the firm name of W. F. Parker & Co., removing the business to Oxford in April following. The establishment has always been distinguished for enterprise and its business has steadily and rapidly increased. The daily capacity of the works is between seven and eight tons, caramels being manufactured under fifty or sixty different forms, and special novelties are being constantly added. These caramels being made of the best materials to be had command a steady preference wherever introduced. About three hundred hands are employed and the products of the factory are shipped all over the United States, Canada, Mexico, South America, Europe and Australia.

The Johnson Carriage Company, Limited, was organized in 1880, and manufactures a full line of carriages, buggies, phaeton, road carts, spring wagons, etc. A specialty is made of the three-spring handy milk-wagon, and prompt attention is given to repairing. The officers of the company are as follows: Joseph Leeke, president; John H. Kimbell, treasurer; Joseph E. Johnson, general manager. Mr. Johnson has had many years' experience in every department of carriage building, and his experience is of much value to the enterprise.

The Oxford Machine Works, formerly the Woodside Manufacturing Company, were established in 1895, by John W. Woodside, the name being changed to the Oxford Machine Works in 1897. The factory is located on Fourth and South Streets, and manufactures flour and feed mill machinery, as well as other kinds of machinery. The officers at the present time are: John W. Woodside, president; J. H. Dawson, vice-president; J. C. Worth, secretary, and R. G. Woodside, treasurer.

The Chester Pottery Company, Limited, was incorporated June 1, 1894, with the following officers: E. L. Buckwalter, president; H. I. Brownback, secretary and treasurer, and David Smith, general manager. The officers have remained the same to the present time, except that David Smith died in May, 1896, and was succeeded by William M. Chantry. The capital stock of the company was at first $20,000, and is now $25,000.

The business carried on by this company was started in 1865, by a Mr. Shriver, who made yellow ware. L. B. Beerbower & Company had the works from about 1872 to 1874, when Mr. Beerbower sold out to Griffen, Smith & Co., who were the proprietors until 1884, and then Griffen, Love & Co. succeeded to the business retaining it until 1890. Then the Griffen China Company came into possession of the property and business, running it about one year. From 1891 to 1894 the works remained idle, and then the present company purchased the property, and have since been manufacturing all kinds of pottery, employing from eighty-five to one hundred hands, and turning out from $60,000 to $70,000 worth of product per year. The works are located at the corner of Church and Starr Streets.

Byrne, Parsons & Co., the firm being composed of Thomas F. Byrne and William H. Parsons, proprietors of the largest knitting works in Phœnixville, began the business in which they are now engaged in 1885. At first they were located in a small frame building on Jackson Street, remaining there until 1890. Then, after being on Hall Street until 1896, they removed to their present three-story and basement building, which is 140x46 feet in size, and fully equipped with knitting and sewing machines, the machinery being propelled by a seventy-five-horse power engine. The company manufactures hose and ladies' underwear, employs about 175 hands, and turns out annually about $175,000 worth of goods.

The Phœnixville Knitting Mills were established in 1891, by the present firm, Davis, Russell & Co., composed of Amber Davis, William Russell and Jonathan Davis. Their building is on Breckenridge Street, is two stories high, and at first was 32x60 feet in size, an addition of the same size being erected in 1894. These works are well equipped with knitting and sewing machines, which are run by a ten-horse power steam engine. The company employs about eighty hands and manufactures about $70,000 worth of hose and ladies' underwear, the latter feature of the business being added in 1894, when the second building was erected.

The Perseverance Knitting Company was organized in the spring of 1896 at Spring City, and moved down to Phœnixville in September, 1897. This company is composed of William Rice, Annie R. Davis and Hiram Buckwalter. The business is on Vanderslice Street, and is in the same building with the Schuylkill Valley Illuminating Company. This company manufactures ladies' underwear, employs about thirty hands, and turns out about $25,000 worth per year. Mrs. Annie R. Davis is president of the company and William Rice secretary and treasurer.

William J. O'Donnell began the business of knitting ladies' underwear in February, 1896, in the upper story of a two-story building owned by himself on Hall Street, the lower story being used for the manufacture of paper boxes. He employs about ten hands and manufactures from $6,000 to $10,000. Power for propelling the machinery in this factory is derived from the Schuylkill Valley Illuminating Company.

Parsons & Angstadt, proprietors of knitting mills at the corner of Hall Street and Lincoln Avenue, Phœnixville, the firm being composed of Lewis Parsons and Peter Angstadt, began business in August, 1897. Their building is a two-story brick, and is fitted up with machinery suitable to the knitting of ladies' fine hosiery. The firm employs about twenty hands, and turns out from $7,000 to $10,000 worth of goods per year. Power is derived from a steam engine in the first story of the building.

The Union Knitting Company, composed of H. W. and E. E.

Walters, began business in April, 1897, renting a two-story brick building on Main Street, near Church. They carry on the business of knitting ladies' underwear, their machinery being propelled by electric power derived from the Schuylkill Valley Illuminating Company, about twenty-five hands being employed, and from $60,-000 to $70,000 worth of product being manufactured annually.

The Phœnixville Industrial Association was incorporated under the laws of the State of New Jersey March 22, 1898, with a capital of $100,000. The stockholders numbered about 150, and the first board of directors and officers were as follows: Paul S. Reeves, president; Amos G. Gotwals, treasurer; Dr. J. P. Eldridge, vice-president; C. H. Howell, secretary; Thomas D. Grover, David Schmutz, V. N. Shaffer, Thomas L. Snyder, John S. Dismant and J. F. Starkey, Jr.

Five acres of land was donated to the enterprise by John Gallagher of Phœnixville, the land being located on Franklin Avenue at the corner of Grant Street. Ground was broken for the erection of a building June 15, 1898, the building to be of brick, and 50x300 feet in size, and there is to be also a boiler and engine building and a good sized office besides. The purpose of the association is to manufacture silk ribbon, and the works are to be operated by Johnson, Cowden & Co. of New York City. When in full operation it is expected this company will employ 400 hands.

The Schuylkill Valley Illuminating Company was organized in 1892, and purchased its present plant of a construction company. It is located at No. 413 Vanderslice Street, the building being of brick. The equipment consists of three steam engines, one of 125, one of 85 and one of three hundred and fifty-horse power; one fifty-light arc dynamo; one 65 kilowatt and one 25 kilowatt machine; two alternating dynamos, one of 60 amperes and the other of 30 amperes; the steam for the three engines being supplied by three boilers of an aggregate of five-hundred-horse power. This company have on their circuit at present 55 arc lights in Phœnixville, and about 3,000 incandescent lights. They have about 100 miles of wire, and besides lighting Phœnixville, they light Spring City and Royer's Ford with both arc and incandescent lights, and Mont Clare with incandescent lights alone. They also supply electricity for direct and alternating fans, and for ten electric motors.

The Schuylkill Iron Works were established in 1873 by Denithorne Brothers. The business consists in the manufacture of bridges, standpipes, tanks and boilers and passed into the hands of John Denithorne, Sons & Co. in 1886. The plant covers about two acres of ground, one of the buildings being 50x60 feet, and another 90x105 feet, the latter erected in 1892. The line of manufactures consists of roadway bridges, roof trusses, standpipes, railway bridges and iron roofing, and many contracts are taken for work in all parts of the county.

The Ahwaga Manufacturing Company of Phœnixville was incorporated under the laws of New Jersey for the purpose of manufacturing parlor, sulphur and other matches. Its officers are Edward M. Lockwood, president; Allen W. Poucher, treasurer, and George R. Moore, Jr., secretary. The board of directors consists of the above-named gentlemen and Prof. I. B. Poucher, Oswego, New York; W. A. Poucher, Oswego, New York; Paul S. Reeves, Phœnixville, and Alexander Duer, Camden New Jersey. This company has the exclusive right to use new, improved, patented and exceedingly valuable machinery for manufacturing matches, thus effecting a great saving in the cost of production, and besides improved methods in the manufacture of matches, the matches after they are made are counted and boxed by machine and are delivered for shipment directly from it. The earning capacity of the plant of twenty machines working ten hours per day is $187,500, and the cost of the plant was $250,000.

36

William Walter Jefferis is the son of Horatio Townsend and Hannah (Paul) Jefferis, and was born in West Chester, January 12, 1820. At an early age he became interested in mineralogy, from hearing a lecture on the subject, and at once took up the hammer, proceeding to investigate the minerals to be found within walking distance of his home. Two older experts, Lewis White Williams and Dr. William Hartman, rendered him valuable assistance, and through the industrious use of all his spare time his collection grew to respectable dimensions, many fine specimens from local quarries adorning his shelves.

His education was derived at the old West Chester Academy and principally under the instruction of Jonathan Gause, and on leaving school he was offered a clerkship in the Chester County Bank, in which his father had long been teller. After filling this position some years he was called to the cashiership of the bank, and in all positions held by him he was ever faithful to the interests of his employers, devoting still his spare time to his favorite study, mineralogy.

Mr. Jefferis in his early researches discovered a mineral somewhat similar to mica that had not yet been named, and on its being submitted to the best authorities it was named Jefferisite, in honor of its discoverer. Mr. Jefferis made the acquaintance of several eminent foreign mineralogists, and with them made many profitable exchanges, thereby greatly increasing the value of his own collection.

After retiring from the cashiership of the bank he made two voyages to England and the Continent of Europe, making a thorough examination of the cabinets of minerals of those countries. He was handsomely treated by scientists wherever he went, his name having already become familiar to mineralogists throughout the world. Having retired from all business and settled in Philadelphia in 1882 he there took an active interest in the Academy of Natural Sciences, particularly in its mineralogical section, and he has ever since then added much to the beauty and strength of that department.

His own private collection, still retained in West Chester, is a monument to his energy and perseverance, and though there may be larger collections in this country, yet there are probably no private ones to excel it in the quality or beauty of its specimens. His collection of local minerals cannot now and probably never will be duplicated, at any price. In the pursuit of his favorite study Mr. Jefferis was thrown more or less into contact with other natural scientists, and having the advantage of an intimate acquaintance with Dr. William Darlington, Benjamin M. Everhart and other eminent botanists, he became familiar with and took delight especially in the flora of his native county.

Abraham Gibbons, a history of whom is a part of the history of Coatesville, was born in Leacock Township, Lancaster County, Pennsylvania, on December 29th, 1812. He was the son of William and Hannah Gibbons, the sixth in descent from John and Margery Gibbons, who as early as 1634 had immigrated from Warminster, in Wiltshire, England, and settled in Delaware County.

His early life was spent on his father's farm in Lancaster County. In 1841 he removed to Coatesville, having married Martha Pennock, the daughter of Dr. Charles and Rebecca W. Lukens. He became associated with Mrs. Lukens in the management of the Brandywine Iron Works. In the course of a few years, about 1846, Mrs. Lukens having retired from the business, he associated with him his brother-in-law, the late Dr. Charles Huston, under the firm name of Gibbons & Huston, and continued actively and sucessfully in the iron business until 1857, at which time, the Bank of Chester Valley being organized, he retired from the iron business and was elected president of the bank, occupying that position continuously for twenty-five years, until 1882.

Desiring to be relieved from the arduous duties connected with this office, he then resigned his position as president, and was soon chosen as president of the Mutual Insurance Company of Chester County. He continued to occupy that position until declining health, in 1893, caused him to give up all active pursuits.

He was one of the members of the first council of Coatesville, and was the means of securing for that borough the splendid supply of water that it still enjoys. In many ways he labored for the good of the community of which he was a part.

We have spoken of his character as a public man and a citizen. As a friend, and in his domestic relations, his was an ideal nature.

Absolutely just, his wise counsel and advice were sought by all sorts and conditions of men. His fine judgment, knowledge of human nature, and keen sense of humor made him a very delightful companion. His manners were so genial and courteous, he made friends wherever he went. His temper so equable, those who had known him for years said no angry word had ever passed his lips.

An earnest and sincere Christian, his charities were numerous but unobtrusively bestowed; and no deserving person ever left his presence without the help they had asked for. While he was known to be a consistent member of the Society of Friends, he was broad-minded, and found good in all men. His friendship was most highly prized, and those who mourned his loss felt that of him they could truly say, "The path of the just is as a shining light." He died May 24th, 1895, full of years and beloved and regretted by all who knew him.

THE PRESS AND LITERATURE.

CHAPTER XV.

THE first attempt to publish a weekly newspaper in Chester County was made near the close of the Eighteenth Century by three young men named Jones, Hoff and Derrick. They called their paper the West Chester Gazette. After finding their venture to be premature they discontinued its publication, a few numbers only being presented to the community. The latter of the above-named three young printers was Philip Derrick, father of William S. and Alexander H. Derrick, who for many years were connected with the State Department at Washington, District of Columbia, and he was the father-in-law of the Hon. Townsend Haines and of William H. Price.

Philip Derrick was also connected with the first attempt to supply Chester County with periodical literature, he and Nathan H. Sharpless establishing a monthly paper, entitled the Literary Museum or Monthly Magazine, in January, 1797. It was printed in a frame building on South High Street, West Chester. For the times it was an ambitious publication, containing fifty-six octavo pages of excellent reading matter, and selling for twenty-five cents per number. Being like the weekly, in advance of the requirements of the age, it was published only six months, from

January to June, 1797. Some of the numbers were illustrated with copper-plate engravings.

The next paper to be established in this county was the Temperate Zone, a weekly paper started in August, 1808, at Downingtown, by Charles Mowry. Downingtown was then a village of some note, situated on the Philadelphia and Lancaster Turnpike, a thoroughfare running through the very heart of the then settled portion of Eastern Pennsylvania, and quite extensively traveled. Having been published one year under the title given above, the Temperate Zone, its name was then changed to the Downingtown American Republican, and with the change of name came a change in the political complexion of the paper, from neutral to Democratic. This change in politics was occasioned by the establishment at West Chester in 1809 of a paper called the Chester and Delaware Federalist, the politics of which is indicated by its name, and of course it was necessary to have a paper on each side of the political questions as they then shaped themselves in the public mind.

In those days a Democrat was a Republican and a Republican was a Democrat, but the term of Republican was more often used than the term Democrat to indicate an individual opposed to the Federal Party.

This paper was continued under the name of the Downingtown American Republican until August 13, 1813, when the first word of the title was dropped, and it was afterward called the American, and it was published by Mr. Mowry until November 28, 1820, when he sold out to William Schultz and William J. Marshall, who, under the firm name of Schultz & Marshall, commenced a new series of the paper, which they published one month, when the interest of Mr. Schultz reverted to Mowry, and from that time until June, 1821, the paper was published by Mr. Mowry and Mr. Marshall under the firm name of W. J. Marshall & Co. At this time Samuel Johnson purchased Mr. Mowry's interest, and he and

Mr. Marshall published the paper under the firm name of Marshall & Johnson, until May 29, 1822, when Mr. Marshall sold his interest to Mr. Johnson, who thus became sole proprietor.

In the meantime Mr. Mowry, who was a vigorous writer, was selected by the leaders of the Democratic-Republican Party to go to Harrisburg to assume editorial control of the Pennsylvania Intelligencer. .This selection was made because Mr. Mowry, as editor of the American Republican at Downingtown, had used his pen in such a vigorous manner in defense of William Findlay, then candidate for Governor, who was assailed for some alleged malfeasance in the office of State Treasurer, which he had previously held.

In the meantime, also, the American Republican was removed to West Chester, the removal occurring April 9, 1822, because of the opportunities afforded by a county seat than by a mere town in the county, but not because of any dissatisfaction with the town of Downingtown. November 17, 1824, Mr. Johnson sold the paper to Simeon Siegfried, who was sole proprietor until May 12, 1829, when he sold a half interest to Edgar S. Price, they two publishing it under the firm name of Siegfried & Price until August 18, following, when Mr. Siegfried sold the half interest he had retained to Robert B. Dodson, and from that time on until July 11, 1832, it was published by Dodson & Price. At this time Mr. Dodson sold his interest to Mr. Price, who was then sole proprietor until January 29, 1833.

On January 29, 1833, the American Republican was united with the Chester County Democrat, a paper which had been started by George Fisher and George W. Crabb, and which paper in reality succeeded a paper called the Independent Journal, which will be mentioned later on. The first number of the Chester County Democrat was published April 20, 1830. In 1831 Mr. Fisher purchased the interest of Mr. Crabb, and continued the publication of the paper until 1832, when he removed it from

Downingtown to West Chester, and it was united with the Ameri-can Republican, as stated above.

Upon the consolidation the firm became Fisher & Price, and the name of the paper became the American Republican and Chester County Democrat. The motto adopted for this united paper was "In Union there is Strength." March 31, 1835, Mr. Fisher sold his interest to Caleb H. Kinnard, who had been connected with the American Spectator at Downingtown, the firm name becoming Price & Kinnard. May 7, 1839, Mr. Kinnard sold his interest to Nimrod Strickland, the firm name becoming Price & Strickland. March 24, 1846, Mr. Price sold his interest to Henry Bosee, the latter of whom had been editor of the Delaware Gazette, and the new firm was known as Strickland & Bosee. This firm published the paper until October 11, 1853, when they sold it to George W. Pearce, who published it until his death, April 14, 1864, from which time until November, that year, it was published by his estate, and then it was sold to Caleb H. Kinnard, who published it until January, 1866, when he sold it to Major Edward B. Moore, who remained its proprietor until June 1, 1878, when he sold it to Walter E. Hall. On April 1, 1881, Robert P. Sharpless became part proprietor, and it was then published by Walter E. Hall & Co. until 1884, when the West Chester Publishing Company was formed, which continued its publication until ————, when it was purchased by its present editors and proprietors, Messrs. Donath & Temple.

During the time this paper was conducted by George W. Pearce, from 1853 to 1864, the Democratic Party became divided in sentiment, and the paper joined itself to the Douglas Democrats, losing many subscribers in consequence. As a result of the changes going on in the political sentiments of the people the Republican and Democrat became a Republican publication in the modern sense of the word Republican, and so remained.

Until July 29, 1876, this paper was a weekly publication, and then it became a semi-weekly, which was continued until July 1, 1878, when it again became a weekly, and at the same time a daily issue was started, which has since continued. The daily was issued in the afternoon until November 1, 1878, since which time it has been issued in the morning.

The next paper established in the county was the Chester and Delaware Federalist, started by Dennis Whelen June 8, 1809. Its publication was probably suggested by the fact of the publication of the Temperate Zone at Downingtown; the size of this paper was ten by sixteen inches, and its establishment as a party organ led to the conversion of the Temperate Zone into a Democratic paper. The Chester and Delaware Federalist continued under the charge of Dennis Whelen until August 6, 1817, when he sold the paper to Charles Miner, who changed the name to the Village Record. January 1, 1818, but continued to use the former name of the paper, Chester and Delaware Federalist, as a sub-title. He also enlarged his printed page to one twelve by eighteen inches. For a part of the year 1824 the paper was conducted by Miner & Bryan, and for some time after July, 1825, Asher Miner, a brother of Charles, was associated with the latter in the management of the paper. In 1830 the paper was again enlarged, the page becoming fourteen by nineteen inches, and the sub-title And General Advertiser was substituted for Chester and Delaware Federalist. The Miner brothers conducted the paper until April 1, 1834. when they sold it to Henry S. Evans, and both went to Wilkesbarre, where Asher Miner had, previously to coming to West Chester, published a paper for a time, and where they both died, the latter in 1841, the former in 1865.

From April 1, 1834, until February 9, 1872, Henry S. Evans published the Village Record, a period of twenty-eight years, during which time it was, under Mr. Evans' management, the most influential paper in Chester County. In 1854 Mr. Evans purchased the Register and Examiner from John S. Bowen, and united it with the Village Record, using the term Register and Examiner as a sub-title. Mr. Evans died on February 9, 1872, and from that time on until 1894 the Village Record was published by his sons,. Barton D. and Willie D. Evans. In 1854, when the consolidation above mentioned was effected, the paper became a semi-weekly one, and on August 8, 1878, the sons of Mr. Evans added a daily to the weekly and semi-weekly editions.

In 1894 the property passed into the hands of S. Edward Paschall, of Bucks County, the daily and semi-weekly editions being then discontinued. Mr. Paschall changed the entire appearance of the paper by converting it into a pamphlet form of sixteen pages. For some time it was under the editorial management of W. W. Woodruff, formerly county superintendent of common schools, and was devoted almost exclusively to agricultural topics, its news feature being made quite a secondary matter. Under its new form and managment, however the paper failed to thrive, and in the fall of 1895 Mr. Paschall disposed of his interest to H. C. Boyer, of Pottsville, Pennsylvania, who restored it to its original form; but he did not long retain the proprietorship. About this time the stalwart,. or Quay wing of the Republican Party was casting about for a recognized organ, and in February, 1896, the Village Record was purchased by T. Lawrence Eyre, the leader of that wing of the party, James B. Fisher, formerly of the morning Republican, being installed as editor. The Record then became a vigorous champion of the principles of the Quay Republican organization, and during the following two years aided in winning three of the most notable battles ever fought within the Republican Party ranks in Chester County.

Originally the Village Record was a supporter of the Federalist policy so long as that party existed. It then became a Whig publication, and when the Whig Party was disbanded and the Republican Party organized, it became an aggressive organ of the latter party, and while under the direction of Henry S. Evans was a powerful factor in Chester County politics.

In recognition in part of the influence of Mr. T. Lawrence Eyre, the present publisher of the Village Record, he has been appointed by the Federal Government Deputy Collector of Customs of the port of Philadelphia.

Charles Miner was one of the prominent citizens of Chester County from 1817 to the time of his removal, or rather return, to the Wyoming Valley in 1834, and it is eminently appropriate that brief mention should be made of him in this work. He was born February 1, 1780, in Norwich, Connecticut. In 1802 he became associated with his brother, Asher Miner, in conducting the Federalist in Wilkesbarre, Pennsylvania, which they sold in 1809 to Steuben Butler and Sidney Tracy, who in 1811 enlarged it and changed its named to the Gleaner, Charles Miner becoming a few months afterward associated with Mr. Butler in the place of Mr. Tracy, and it was in the columns of the Gleaner that Mr. Miner made himself celebrated as a writer.

In 1807 and 1808 and in 1816 he represented Luzerne County in the Legislature of the State, in the latter year taking charge of a paper in Philadelphia called the True American, conducting it one year. Removing to West Chester in 1817, he purchased the Chester and Delaware Federalist, the name of which he changed to the Village Record. He conducted it with signal ability until 1837, when he sold it to Henry S. Evans. From March, 1825, to March, 1829, he was a member of Congress from the district of which Chester County formed a part, and in this body he took great interest in the subject of slavery, to which institution he was greatly opposed, and made efforts to have slavery and the slave trade in the District of Columbia abolished.

Mr. Miner was the associate of the great men of his day, and he was intelligent, social and attractive, his abilities and usefulness being recognized by Henry Clay, at that time Secretary of State, and Mr. Clay looked to Mr. Miner, nearly as much as to any other member of the Lower House of Congress, to carry into effect his views on the tariff, internal improvements, and the United States Bank. From 1834 to October 26, 1865, the date of his death, he continued to reside in the beautiful Wyoming Valley, dying at the great age of eighty-five.

On September 25, 1833, appeared the first number of a paper established in Waynesburg, now Honeybrook, by the name of the Waynesburg Press and Chester, Berks and Lancaster Advertiser, by Henry S. Evans and William Jenkins. After the expiration of six months Mr. Evans purchased the Village Record, of West Chester, which fact has already been narrated, the management of the Press and Advertiser devolving upon Mr. Jenkins, who conducted it until May 28, 1834, when Mr. Evans sold his interest therein to Caleb H. Kinnard. Mr. Jenkins and Mr. Kinnard then removed the paper to Downingtown, where on June 10, 1834, started the American Spectator and People's Friend, which was published until April 1, 1835, when it was purchased by Mr. Evans and merged by him into the Village Record. It was at this time that Mr. Kinnard purchased the interest of George Fisher in the American Republican.

Nathan Blackman, Jr., a native of New England, established in 1814 a weekly paper by the name of the Eden Star in the village of Edentown, in Upper Oxford Township, the first number of which appeared March 28 that year. The village at that time consisted of a store-house, a public house and the building in which the Star was printed, the village being owned and the tavern and store being kept by John Downing. At the expiration of two years the building in which the Star was published was accidentally burned down, and as there was no other building in which it could be published it was removed to Russellville, about one mile away, and was there published for some time longer under the name of the American Star. Soon after this it was discontinued, and the publisher took Horace Greeley's advice and went to the West.

On August 29, 1827, the first number of the Independent Jour-

nal appeared, published in Downingtown by Dr. George A. Fairlamb and George Plitt. It was a Democratic paper of the Jack-
sonian kind, and from the first advocated the election to the Presidency of Andrew Jackson. In addition to being a Jackson paper
it advocated the nomination of George Wolf for the governorship
of Pennsylvania, another portion of the Democratic party being
in favor of the nomination of General Isaac D. Barnard, a citizen
of Chester County. After a very bitter contest two sets of delegates were sent to the convention from Chester County, those in
favor of Mr. Wolf being admitted, and this determined the nomination of Mr. Wolf. Had those in favor of General Barnard been
admitted to seats in the convention he would have been nominated
by a majority of one vote, and would have been elected Governor
of the State.

Dr. Fairlamb died April 10, 1829, and the Independent Journal
was then conducted by George Plitt until April 13, 1830, when he
sold out to George Fisher and George W. Crabb, the latter gentleman having for some time been associated with Mr. Plitt in the
editorship. Discontinuing the Independent Journal, Fisher &
Crabb established in its stead the Chester County Democrat, the
first number appearing April 20, 1830. In 1831 Mr. Fisher purchased the interest of his partner, Crabb, continued the publication of the paper until 1832, when he removed it to West Chester,
and there, on January 29, 1833, it was united with the American
Republican, as has been stated earlier in this chapter.

The Literary Casket and General Intelligencer was started
at Yellow Springs, now Chester Springs, in March, 1829, by Alexander Marshall and Nathan Siegfried. After a few months Mr.
Siegfried retired, Mr. Marshall becoming sole proprietor. This
paper was published in the Washington House, a building erected
for a hospital during the Revolutionary War. This paper let politics entirely alone, confining itself exclusively to the literary field,
and many of the first essays of young writers of Chester County

appeared in its columns. In February, 1830, this paper was sold to Morris Mattson and Cheyney Hannum, who removed it to West Chester. Soon afterward Mr. Mattson sold his interest to James A. Hemphill, and the firm of Hannum & Hemphill conducted it until the fall of 1830, when it was merged into the National Republican Advocate and Literary Gazette, a new weekly paper established at West Chester by them for the purpose of advocating the principles of the National Republican Party as against the Democratic Party, the first number of this paper appearing November 30, 1830.

Hannum & Hemphill published the Advocate until April 3, 1832, when the former sold his interest to John Hickman and William Whitehead, and the paper was then published by the firm of Hannum, Hickman & Co. until July 31, 1832, when John T. Denny and William Whitehead became editors and proprietors. Mr. Denny retiring June 18, 1833, he was succeeded by John Bicking, the firm then being Bicking & Whitehead until April 8, 1834, when the paper was sold to a company of gentlemen who were in favor of the supremacy of the Whig Party, then beginning to attract attention.

The name National Republican Advocate was dropped and that of Whig substituted, the first number of the Whig appearing April 15, 1834, and it was ostensibly edited by Simeon Siegfried, formerly one of the proprietors of the American Republican; but the editorial matter was furnished by such prominent gentlemen as Dr. William Darlington, William H. Dillingham, Townsend Haines and William Williamson. The motto of this paper was "True to the principles of '76." Previous to taking editorial charge of the Whig, Mr. Siegfried had always been a Democrat, but as he differed from General Jackson on the subject of the National Bank, he was willing to publish a paper which advocated the continuance of the National Bank, as the Whigs very generally, if not universally did. He remained with the Whig until May, 1835.

But Mr. Siegfried was in principle a democrat, and when it was suggested to him that he should discontinue the Whig, he readily consented to do so, especially as it was not self-supporting, there being two other papers in the county of the same political pro-clivities. He therefore removed the Whig establishment to Down-ingtown and there in May of that year established the Republican Standard and Democratic Journal, which advocated the election to the governorship of George Wolf, who had then served as Governor six years, and who was opposed by Henry A. Muhlenberg, another Democratic candidate, and by Joseph Ritner, the Whig candidate, the latter of whom was elected through the division in the ranks of the Democratic party. This paper was published by George W. Mason & Company, Mr. Siegfried being the "com-pany," and it was edited by Nimrod Strickland and others. Upon the election of Mr. Ritner, the publication of the paper ceased, and Mr. Mason removed to Elmira, New York, where he for some years published the Elmira Gazette with gratifying success. The next year after the election of Mr. Ritner to the Governorship of Penn-sylvania, Martin Van Buren was elected to the presidency of the United States, and the divisions in the Democratic party were healed.

Simeon Siegfried in September, 1831, began the publication in West Chester of the Temperance Advocate, conducting it in West Chester until May, 1835, when he removed it to Downingtown, continuing it there until September, following, when it was merged into the Philanthropist, a paper published in Philadelphia.

The General Advertiser and Journal of the Times was started March 1, 1836, by William Jenkins, whose name has been mentioned in connection with the publication of earlier newspapers in Chester County. After two years this paper was discontinued, and the materials of the office were purchased by John S. Bowen and Benjamin I. Miller, who in May, 1838 started the Coatesville Star, which was published in the interest of those who favored a

37

distinct organization for the Whig Party. Mr. Bowen was the editor of this paper. At the expiration of about one year this paper was removed to West Chester and the name changed to the American Star, with George Shidell, formerly foreman in the office, as editor and proprietor. In June, 1839, Townsend Haines became its owner and editor and published it in an office which stood where the First National Bank of West Chester now stands. The party sustained by the American Star formed an independent Whig ticket in the autumn of the last-mentioned year, forming their ticket on Monday, the other Whig Party being made up of Whigs and Anti-Masons, forming theirs on Tuesday. One of these wings of the Whig Party was called the "Monday" Whigs and the other the "Tuesday" Whigs, and the result of their running separate tickets was that the Democrats carried the county. The American Star was published until August 23, 1841, when everything connected with it was sold to Asher M. Wright and Alfred J. Creyon, who discontinued the Star was established the Independent Journal and Workingmen's Advocate, the first number of which appeared August 31, 1841. This was considered a new series of the Independent Journal published in Downingtown, which has already been mentioned. As a neutral in politics it was soon found that it could not succeed, and hence on October 4, 1842, it was discontinued, and the Jeffersonian established in its stead, which was devoted to the interests of the Democratic Party.

On October 3, 1843, after a suspension of five months, the Jeffersonian was united with the West Chester Herald, which first appeared on September 5, 1843, and the consolidated paper was named the Jeffersonian and Democratic Herald, the latter name being used as a subtitle. It was published by John Hodgson and Asher M. Wright until February, 1845, when Mr. Wright retired and Mr. Hodgson became the sole proprietor, and so remained until 1866, when he was succeeded by his son, William H. Hodgson, who still owns and publishes it, though in changed and enlarged form. For several years the Jeffersonian was published in the basement of the building east of the Mansion House, whence it was removed about the year 1860 to the west side of South High street, and where it still remains.

The Anti-Masonic Register was established in West Chester October 1, 1829, by Joseph Painter, and the Anti-Masonic Examiner was started in Coatesville about the same time by Dr. John D. Perkins. As there was not sufficient support for two Anti-Masonic papers in the county, Joseph Painter, in 1831, purchased the Examiner, united it with the Register, under the name of the Anti-Masonic Register and Chester County Examiner, and in January, 1836, when the Anti-Masonic Party united with the Whigs, Mr. Painter dropped the "Anti-Masonic" from the title of his paper, and published it under the name of the Register and Examiner until January 1, 1851, when he sold it to John S. Bowen and James M. Meredith, who enlarged it and improved it, and sold it in 1854 to Henry S. Evans, who published it a short time under its old name, under the firm name of William Baker & Co., but it soon became absorbed into the Village Record, which then became a semi-weekly paper under the name of the Village Record and Register and Examiner, the latter part of the title, however, being soon discontinued.

The Pennsylvania Farm Journal was published for some time by John S. Bowen and James M. Meredith, but upon the dissolution of their partnership Mr. Bowen became proprietor of the Register and Examiner and Mr. Meredith of the Pennsylvania Farm Journal. Later Mr. Meredith removed his paper to Philadelphia, where for some time he continued its publication.

On January 1, 1854, Henry Bosee began the publication of the Independent Herald in West Chester. One year afterward he sold it to Lewis Marshall, who conducted it from January 1, 1855, to

May 1, 1856, when he sold it to William L. and Edwin F. James, who then published it until February 6, 1857, under the title Independent Herald and Free American. At the date last mentioned they disposed of it to Samuel R. Downing and John J. Pinkerton, who conducted it under the same name until April 25, 1857, when they changed it to Chester County Times. Mr. Pinkerton retired from the paper March 20, 1858, Mr. Downing then becoming sole proprietor, and on August 1, 1858, Mr. E. W. Capron becoming editor. On July 9, 1861, the paper, which had previously been a weekly, became a semi-weekly under the name of the Chester County Semi-Weekly Times. January 1, 1863, the Times was sold by Mr. Downing to George W. Pearce, who consolidated it with the American Republican, which he was then publishing, started in Coatesville about 1836.

A paper was established in Coatesville about 1836 called the Colonization Herald, for the purpose of sustaining the cause of the colonization of the negro as against the doctrine of the abolition of slavery, the publisher being named Walton; but only a few numbers of the paper were issued.

In December of this year a paper was started by Jason M. Mahan in Sadsbury Township, Mr. Mahan being interested in the silk culture, the name of his paper being the Silk-Growers' Instructor and the Farmer's Friend; but as knowledge on the culture of silk did not seem to manifest itself, the paper did not have an extended career. It was in the form of a sixteen-page octavo pamphlet, and was issued monthly as long as it lasted.

For about six months during the year 1839 a temperance paper was published at the office of the Register and Examiner, under the editorial supervision of Cyrus P. Painter and others, but it had too little support to be continued.

Another temperance paper, called the Crystal Fountain, was started in 1847 by Caleb N. Thornbury, and was continued about one year.

Samuel Moses and John Lewis began the publication in Phœnixville of the Phœnix Gazette, the first number appearing October 6, 1846. After a short time Mr. Moses withdrew, selling his interest to Benjamin P. Davis. On December 29, 1846, Mr. Lewis and Mr. Davis sold their paper to Bayard Taylor and Frederick E. Foster, they changing the name to the Phœnixville Pioneer. This venture not being pecuniarily satisfactory, Mr. Taylor withdrew from it on January 4, 1848, and became assistant editor of the New York Tribune, from which time to February 21, 1849, the Pioneer was published by Mr. Foster, in conjunction with S. L. Hughes, the latter date being that of its last number.

The Phœnix Ledger was then published for a short time by Messrs. Hughes & Greene, but it ceased to exist in 1850. During the same two years, 1849 and 1850, the Iron Man was published, but ceased to exist about the same time with the Ledger. With the Iron Man a poet, A. J. H. Duganne, was associated. Mr. Duganne was the author of a notable patriotic poem entitled "Bethel," beginning with the line: "We mustered at midnight, in darkness we formed," and contained the following stanza:

"When our heroes, like bridegrooms, with lips and with breath,
Drank the first kiss of Danger and clasped her in death,
And the heart of brave Winthrop grew mute with his lyre,
When the plumes of his genius lay molting in fire—
"Column! Forward!"

John Royer and his son, John H., on April 4, 1857, issued the first number of the Weekly Phœnix, which name they changed to the Phœnix, and later to the Independent Phœnix. This paper in 1871 became the property of Vosburg N. Shaffer, who changed the name to that of the Phœnixville Independent, and also published a daily edition called the Daily Independent.

Col. J. H. Puleston started the Pennsylvania Guardian in 1860, but discontinued it on being appointed by Governor Curtin State agent for Pennsylvania at Washington, District of Columbia.

Marshall is credited with the discovery of gold in California in 1847, and the semi-centennial of this supposed discovery was celebrated in 1897. But the first number of the Phœnixville Gazette, published October 6, 1846, contains the following paragraph, which shows that history needs correction in regard to this matter:

"A correspondent writing from Upper California says: 'Near the Town of the Angels is a large sandy plain at the foot of some mountains, in which they have discovered quantities of gold. A common laborer can gather to the amount of $2 per day. The plan of getting the ore is to wash the sand in a flat basket. They have introduced ounce currency of the metal.' "

Col. J. H. Puleston, formerly a resident of Phœnixville, was born in Wales, coming to the United States in 1857, and establishing himself in New York as a physician among the Welsh. The story is that in this occupation he failed, and that, making the acquaintance of Horace Greeley, he was sent by the latter gentleman to the Wyoming Valley during the campaign of 1858 to speak to the Welsh of that region in favor of the Republican candidates. Colonel Puleston was interested in the first charter granted to a street railway company in Pennsylvania.

In 1860 he went to Phœnixville and there started the Pennsylvania Guardian, ran it through the campaign in favor of Gen. John C. Fremont for President of the United States, dropping the publication of the paper at the close of the campaign. In February, 1861, Colonel Puleston was in Washington, and was made assistant secretary of the famous Peace Convention, presided over by ex-President John Tyler, and when the secretary of the convention, S. C. Wright, was compelled to return to his home on account of serious illness in his family, Colonel Puleston became secretary of the convention. Later he was made agent for the Pennsylvania troops at Washington, with the rank of colonel. Still later he studied law and practiced in the courts of the District of Columbia.

Afterward he became a member of the banking firm of Hugh Mc-Cullough & Co., of New York City, and was sent to London, England, as the representative of that company. He was then elected a member of Parliament for Plymouth, and, running again for the same position as the candidate for a constituency in Wales, was defeated. Subsequently he was knighted by Her Majesty, Queen Victoria, and is now Sir John H. Puleston, a member of the House of Lords. ˙

Wilmer W. Thomson on October 17, 1868, began the publication in Phœnixville of an advertising sheet entitled Everybody's Business, continuing it as a weekly three months, and on January 23, 1869, Mr. Thomson began the publication of another advertising sheet called the Legal Tender, which on August 21, 1869, became a regular subscription weekly publication, published by Price & Thomson.

John Pawling in 1870 published one number of a paper called the Phœnixville Republican.

David Euen and Hadley Lamborn in January, 1871, began the publication of the Messenger, which in January, 1873, became the property of John O. K. Robarts. Mr. Robarts changed the name to the Phœnixville Messenger, and has since continued to conduct it. Mr. Robarts was born in Plymouth, England, in 1835; came to the United States in 1850, landing in New York. After residing in Reading, Pennsylvania, five years he removed to Phœnixville, Chester County, and has since then been a continuous resident of that place.

The Downingtown Archive was established in 1872 by Potter & Cordery, from New York, as a weekly publication, and in December, 1874, it was purchased by its present proprietor and editor, Harry L. Skeen. At first it was a six-column paper; was soon enlarged to a seven-column, and is now an eight-column paper, published weekly, and advocating the legal prohibition of the liquor traffic. In other matters it is independent.

The Chester County Journal was established at Downingtown by a company at the head of which was Joshua Kames, the Journal being managed by Joseph Pepper, who on August 29, 1868, became the proprietor. Later it was owned by Potter & Cordery; was for some time managed by W. H. Hineline, and still later by William S. Kames, and, though a large and well-edited paper, it proved unprofitable, and its publication was discontinued in 1873.

Henry S. Evans, under the direction of the Chester County and Delaware County Medical Societies, published at West Chester the Medical Reporter, a quarterly journal, from July, 1853, until some time in 1856. It was a thirty-two-page octavo, of suitable size for binding, and contained matter of interest to the medical profession.

The Children's Friend, a monthly juvenile magazine, was commenced in May, 1866, by Mrs. Esther K. Smedley, wife of Dr. R. C. Smedley, at the request of some of the members of the Society of Friends. It was an illustrated octavo of twenty-four pages at first, but afterward was twice increased, both as to the size of its page and the number of its pages. In 1872, owing to failing health, Mrs. Smedley sold the magazine to her sister, Mrs. Anna F. Bradley, of Coatesville, who continued its publication until November, 1879, when it was sold to Mary Y. Hough, of Philadelphia, who continued its publication there.

Lydia H. Hall, who for a short time assisted Mrs. Dr. Smedley in the publication of the Children's Friend, began the publication of an illustrated monthly called Scattered Seeds, which was designed for the use of children and was circulated largely in schools. In 1881 its circulation had reached 5,700 copies, indicating an exceptional popularity. Though edited by a Friend, it was strictly non-sectarian, and was welcome in all families.

In September, 1880, The Student was established in connection with the Haverford College and the Westtown Friends' Boarding School. It was an octavo of twenty-four pages, and was edited by

Isaac Sharpless, a professor in Haverford College, and by Watson W. Dewees, a teacher in the Boarding School.

The first number of the Chester County Reporter appeared April 6, 1880. It was a weekly legal journal devoted to the publication of the proceedings and decisions of the Chester County bar, and for some time was edited by James Monaghan, of the West Chester bar.

The Oxford Press was established in Oxford February 14, 1866, by Henry L. Brinton. January 1, 1870, he sold a half interest to George D. Hayes, and it was published until the next year by the firm of Brinton & Hayes. Then Mr. Brinton sold the other half interest to E. Howard Rollins, the name of the firm becoming George D. Hayes & Co. Mr. Rollins, on September 1, 1875, sold his interest to John I. Moore and R. Frank Cochran, the firm name remaining the same, and in March, 1876, they sold their half to Henry L. Brinton, who had been engaged in editing the paper since the fall of 1872, the firm name of the proprietors then becoming Hayes & Brinton. This paper has always maintained a high moral tone, and has been well supported. January 1, 1892, Mr. Brinton and his sons, Douglas E. and William G., purchased Mr. Hayes' interest, and since then the paper has been owned and published by them under the name of H. L. Brinton & Sons. It is a weekly paper, in form half folio and half quarto, the subscription price being $1.50 per year, and holds the leading place among the weekly papers of the county.

In October, 1871, Franklin P. Levre started a monthly journal under the name of the Farmers' Club, which was devoted to agriculture, and which he published about three years.

George C. Stroman & Co. published a weekly paper called the Oxford Republican from March 28, 1874, to July 25, 1874.

The Kennett Square Free Press was established July 21, 1855, by B. F. Coles, at Kennett Square, the first paper published in the place. The paper was devoted to literature and local news. The first number contained a poem by Bayard Taylor, sketches of Scandinavia, and translations from Hans Christian Andersen by Barclay Pennock. Dr. Franklin Tayor was its editor, and the paper was well printed, as well as being conducted with exceptional ability. October 16, 1855, D. J. Godshalk became associated with Mr. Coles, they continuing its publication for about three years.

The Weekly Leader was published at Kennett Square by H. M. Worth & Co., the first number appearing January 14, 1871, Swithin C. Shortlidge as editor. In July, 1872, it was enlarged from a seven-column to a nine-column folio, and was published by the "Leader Association," semi-weekly, one edition at Kennett Square on Saturday morning, the other edition at Oxford on Wednesday morning, the edition published at Oxford being called the Oxford Leader, that published at Kennett Square being called the Kennett Leader. The first number of the Oxford Leader appeared March 20, 1872. This journal was Republican in politics until the Presidential campaign of 1872, when it supported Horace Greeley for the Presidency. When the panic of 1873 came on the Leader Association became financially embarrassed, and the paper was suspended in February of the latter year. The Kennett Leader was revived by William W. Polk in April following, and was conducted by him until July, when he abandoned its publication.

The next paper to be published in Kennett Square was the Kennett News and Advertiser, started in January, 1877, by Theodore D. Hadley and J. Frank Holton, the latter of whom withdrew on July 1 of the same year. Mr. Hadley, thus becoming sole proprietor, enlarged it to a seven-column folio, twenty-four by thirty-eight inches, and continued its publication until January 1, 1894, when his son, Charles C. Hadley, who had been in the office ever since it was started, became publisher and editor, as he still continues. This paper has been published in the same place since 1880, in Swayne Block, on State Street, near Union Street. In politics the paper is neutral, and is mainly devoted to local news. It is now an eight-column folio, 26x44, and is printed on a cylinder press by hand. Its circulation in 1,400, and the subscription is $1 per year.

The Chester County Democrat was established in West Chester September 11, 1879, the second paper of the name published in the county. For some time it was published by J. Henry Long & Company, the "company" being George R. Guss. In September, 1880, Mr. Guss purchased the interest of Mr. Long, and was thereafter sole proprietor until the time of his death, which occurred January 24, 1897. As the name of the paper indicates, it was published in the interest of the Democratic Party, and after the death of Captain Guss its publication was discontinued.

Captain George R. Guss was a son of Colonel Henry R. Guss, and during General Lee's invasion of Pennsylvania raised an independent battery, securing his men in and around West Chester, commanded it in the service of the United States from July 1 to August 24, 1863, when it was discharged. He also was captain of a section of the Griffin Battery of Phœnixville, which performed good service in connection with the Pittsburg riots in 1877.

Edward E. Orvis commenced the publication at New London in March, 1853, of the Day Spring, a weekly paper devoted to general news, literature and temperance. John Larkin soon afterward became associated with Mr. Orvis, they publishing the paper until October 29, 1853, when they sold it to Pearsol & Geist, of the Saturday Express, a temperance paper published in Lancaster.

From 1853 to 1856 Mr. Orvis, who was a minister or elder of the Christian Church, conducted at New London the Christian Union and Religious Review, a monthly periodical of thirty-two pages, devoted to the interests of the religious denomination to which he belonged. Mr. Orvis had charge of a congregation of Christians near New London.

Mr. Larkin in December, 1855, purchased the printing office

and materials that had been used by Bayard Taylor and Frederick E. Foster when they were publishing the Phœnixville Pioneer, and carried on a job printing office in Phœnixville until 1856, when he removed his outfit to East Brandywine and there carried on job printing until May, 1870.

In 1870 Mr. V. N. Shaffer purchased the Independent Phœnix and changed the title to Phœnixville Independent, and on January 3, 1881, he began the publication of the Daily Independent, the first daily paper published in Phœnixville. Later he sold the Daily Independent to R. P. Sharpless, who changed the title to The Star. In 1888 Mr. Shaffer sold the Phœnixville Independent to the Phœnixville Republican Company, the name of the paper being again changed to suit the corporation name. The Star having ceased to exist the Daily Republican took its place, In 1890 the weekly edition of was discontinued and the daily became the paper of Phœnixville.

The Daily Republican was purchased December 1, 1893, by John H. Miller and Mark F. Sullivan, who are still the proprietors. It is now a seven column folio, the columns being twenty-two inches long. In politics it is Republican, and is devoted to literature and local news. It is the only daily paper in Chester County outside of West Chester. It has a circulation of about 3,000 copies, and the subscription price is $3 per year. While Mr. Sullivan is at the present time the nominal editor of the paper, yet the editorial work is being done by H. C. Gillingham, during the absence of Mr. Sullivan in college. Mr. Gillingham was born in Bucks County, Pennsylvania, May 25, 1858, became a Presbyterian minister, and preached for churches in Wisconsin, Iowa and California from 1884 to 1891, and in 1896 became editor of the Daily Republican, a position he still retains. Mr. Miller is the business manager. This paper has connected with it one of the finest job offices to be anywhere found, all kinds of job work being done, even to half-tone printing. There are employed on this paper and in the job office twenty people, thirteen of the compositors being girls.

The Chester ιValley Union was established in Coatesville, June 6, 1863, by William J. and J. C. Kauffman. It was a four page, six column weekly paper, and was printed on an old fashioned Washington hand-press. The above-named gentlemen were editors and proprietors until September, 1866, when the latter sold his interest in the paper to John P. Brooke, the firm name then becoming Kauffman & Brooke, and one year later Mr. Kauffman purchased Mr. Brooke's interest, thus becoming sole proprietor, which he still remains.

The Coatesville Weekly Times was established in 1879 by William R. Ash, then an attorney-at-law in Coatesville. The paper was begun as a four-page, six-column sheet, and has been enlarged from time to time until at the present time it is an eight-column paper. Mr. Ash was soon offered a position on the Philadelphia North American, and sold his paper to Clarence F. Jenkins, who conducted it until 1882, when he sold it to Joseph F. Perdue, who was then practicing at the West Chester bar. On February 18, 1884, Mr. Perdue sold the Times to E. H. Graves, of Uniontown, Pennsylvania, who also purchased the printing office from A. H. Potts & Co., of Parkesburg, and engaged F. L. Campbell as local editor. Mr. Graves remained sole proprietor of the paper until December 1, 1890, when, on account of having been appointed post master of Coatesville, he sold a half interest to D. H. Weaver, the firm name becoming Graves & Weaver, which continued until May 1, 1891, when F. L. Campbell purchased a one-third interest, and the business was then carried on under the firm name of E. H. Graves & Co.

William W. Polk and William H. Phillips, the former being the editor, established the Kennett Advance, a weekly paper, the first number coming out August 4, 1877. It is especially devoted to the publication of home news, is Republican in politics, and in size is twenty-four by thirty-eight inches. Mr. Phillips, on June 1, 1878, sold his interest to Mr. Polk, who has since been sole proprietor, and who soon after enlarged the paper from seven to an eight-column folio, and continues its publication until the present time. During the year 1897 the Advance was published every other day, on Mondays, Wednesdays and Fridays, but was returned to a weekly in January 1898.

The Rural Economist was started in West Chester April 1, 1861, by Dr. Edmund C. Evans, who published it until April 1, 1862, as a monthly of thirty-two pages. It was devoted to rural affairs, horticulture and agriculture. It lasted only one year.

Nelson P. Boyer & Co. in September, 1864, founded at Gum Tree in Highland Township, the American Stock Journal, a thirty-two page octavo monthly. The office was removed to Parkesburg in 1868, where the publication of the Journal was continued until June, 1871, when it was taken possession of by the American Stock Journal Company, and published by them under the management of Robert A. Young, until January, 1875, when it was purchased by Potts Brothers. Suspended by them until October of that year, it was then revived and published until December, 1878, when its publication ceased altogether.

Robert A. Young in 1874 established the Parkesburg Herald, published it one year and then sold out to A. H. Potts & Co., who changed the name to the Chester County Times, under which title, as a four-page, eight column weekly, they continued its publication.

The first number of the Local News was issued November 19, 1872. At the head of its columns it had the name of W. H. Hodgson, proprietor, and that of W. W. Thomson, editor. Those names have remained there ever since, a period of nearly twenty-six years. At first the paper was a four-column folio, the size of each page being $12\frac{1}{2}$x$8\frac{3}{4}$ inches. Preceding and leading up to the establishment of this little daily was the publication of a programme of the Teachers' Institute held in West Chester from

November 11 to 15, inclusive, Monday to Friday, 1872, this programme being a neatly printed four-page sheet, the first page of which was devoted to the programme of the Institute for the day, and the other three pages being given up to the proceedings of the previous day, to local and general news and to advertisements.

Learning that the business men of West Chester would miss the visits of the little sheet, the editor suggested to the proprietor the establishment of a daily, which was at once determined upon, and on Saturday morning and on Monday morning, the 16th and 18th of the month, the Local News was distributed gratuitously throughout the city. On Tuesday morning, the 19th, carriers were put on the streets. Prosperity appearing to dawn, the paper was enlarged February 3, 1873, by the addition of a column to each page, the page itself being correspondingly lengthened, so that each page was after this first enlargement 15x11 inches in size. By June the paper had eight hundred subscribers. At this time the machinery in the office consisted of a small vertical engine and a good Campbell press. At the time of the murder of W. S. Goss by Udderzook the subscription list suddenly sprung up to 5,600 names, which number, however, died down to about half when the law had been vindicated by the punishment of the murderer. November 19, 1873, the paper was again enlarged to a page seventeen inches long, and on June 20, 1874, one of Hoe's three-revolution presses was put in, at a cost of $3,500, and a short time afterward a ten-horse power engine was set up with which to run the new press. Another enlargement was deemed necessary May 1, 1876, each page being then made 18¼x13 inches, which enlargement was not justified by immediate events, was yet maintained. October 8, 1878, still another enlargement was made, each page being 19½x13 inches, and on October 23, 1886, each page was made 21x13 inches. This enlargement rendered it necessary to put in another press, and one of Hoe's Type-Web Perfection presses was purchased at a cost of

$16,000. This new press had a capacity of 12,000 per hour, each paper being neatly printed and folded, which fact was a marvel to contemplate. But even this fast press was deficient in capacity by the fall of 1895, and in December of that year one of Hoe's fast perfecting presses was purchased at a cost of $25,000, including four of the celebrated Mergenthaler Linotypes, or type-setting machines, and a complete stereotyping outfit. About the same time the reporters began to use type-writers in the preparation of their copy, which greatly facilitates the labor of the linotype operator. At the present time the office of the Local News is probably as well equipped as any newspaper office in any inland town in the State, if not in the country. The circulation at the present time is about 13,000 in Chester and adjoining counties, and it is mainly devoted to local news, although there appears each day a generous amount of general news.

Mr. Hodgson and Mr. Thomson have been respectively proprietor and editor ever since the first number was issued, and the present business manager, John G. Moses, has been at his post since 1880. The foreman in the composing room, Walter Clark, has been with the paper now twenty years, and the pressman and engineer for a period of more than thirteen years.

The Local News is independent in politics and aims to treat all parties with that impartiality that leads to correct opinions and views on the part of its readers.

On April 19, 1898, a number of leading Democrats of Chester County held at a meeting at the Green Tree Hotel to plan for the founding of a new paper, which should be the organ of the Democratic party in the county. Editor P. Gray Meek, of the Bellefonte Watchman, made a proposition to the Democrats of the county to the effect that if they would insure him a subscription list of 2,000, he would start a paper in West Chester, conducting it as his own enterprise, but in the interest of the Democrats of Chester County. The proposition was generally favored, and the county chairman, John Cavanaugh, was instructed to issue a let-ter to the various county committeemen and other prominent Democrats, asking them to solicit subscriptions for the proposed paper, and to secure aid from all the Democrats possible.

Among those who were present at the meeting and who promised their aid to the enterprise were the following: Bur-gess William H. Bitting, Phœnixville; Harry B. Schofield, Paoli; J. Harry Hoskins, Paoli; Joshua E. Hibberd, Malvern; Theodore Bye, Franklin; Thomas Rettew, Nantmeal; John Ecker, North Coventry; Thomas Rettew, Brandywine; Jury Commissioner Jesse B. Ramstine, Upper Uwchlan; Wayne L. Battin, Pocopson; Dan-iel Sheehan, New Garden; Harry C. Hall, West Bradford; Pat-rick McCormick, Darlington's Corner.

This project has not, however, up to July 1, 1898, been re-alized.

The West Grove and Chester County Mirror, published at West Grove, was started there by Morris Lloyd in 1884. It is a four-page paper, 24x36 inches, is independent in politics, and mainly devoted to local affairs. The circulation at the present time is 1,000, and the subscription price, $1 per year.

The Avondale Herald was established in 1894, and was a very small paper at first. In 1896 it became the property of Charles C. Hadley, and was then, and is now, managed by Charles W. Pierson. It is a seven-column folio, and is devoted to local news, is neutral in politics, has a circulation of 800, and the sub-scription price is $1 per year. The Kennett News and Advertiser was established January 1, 1877, by Hadley & Holton, Thomas D. Hadley and J. Frank Holton. The latter retired from the paper at the end of six months; and from that time on Mr. Hadley has been sole proprietor. He continued its publication until January 1, 1894, at which time his son, Charles C. Hadley, who had been connected with the office from the beginning, took charge as publisher and editor. Since 1880 it has been pub-

38

lished in the Swayne Block, on State Street, near Union. In politics it is neutral, and is devoted exclusively to local news. It is an eight-column folio, 26x44, and is printed on a cylinder press by hand. It has a circulation of 1,400 copies, and the subscription price is $1 per year.

LITERATURE IN CHESTER COUNTY.

In what is said under this head it will not be expected that an exhaustive review of the writings of Chester County people can be attempted, for the reason that the county has been so prolific in authors of merit that any such attempt, if made in good faith, would require a volume of itself. All that can be done, therefore, is to present the names of most of the authors, with the titles of their respective works.

Caleb Pusey was one of the prominent settlers in the earliest history of the county, was a Quaker, and wrote much in defense of the doctrine of his sect or denomination, but more particularly in contravention of the doctrines of George Keith. The principal works of Caleb Pusey were as follows:

1. A Serious and Seasonable Warning Unto All People Occasioned by Two Most Dangerous Epistles to a Late Book of John Falldoe's, subscribed by Richard Baxter and others, printed in 1675.

2. A Modest Account from Pennsylvania of the Principal Differences in Point of Doctrine Between George Keith and those of the People Called Quakers, etc., printed in 1696.

3. Satan's Harbinger Encountered, etc., printed in 1700.

4. Daniel Leeds Justly Rebuked for Abusing William Penn, etc., printed in 1702.

5. Proteus Ecclesiasticus, or George Keith Varied in Fundamentalls, etc., printed in 1704.

6. George Keith Once More Brought to the Test, and Proved a Prevaricator, etc., printed in Philadelphia about the same time.

7. The Bomb Searched and Found Stuffed with False Ingredients, etc., printed in 1705.

Rev. David Evans, pastor of the Presbyterian Church in Tredyffrin Township, known as the Great Valley Church, was the author of a work called: "Law and Gospel," in which he attempted to show that man is ruined by the Law and recovered by the Gospel.

Rev. Samuel Blair wrote numerous sermons on religious subjects, which he collected and published. Rev. John Blair, brother of the above, wrote three works, all on religious subjects.

John Churchman published "An Account of the Gospel Labours and Christian Experiences of a Faithful Minister of Christ."

John Churchman, grandson of the preceding, published a Map of the Peninsula between the Bays of Delaware and Chesapeake, etc., and

The Magnetic Atlas or Variation Chart of the Whole Terraqueous Globe, the object of which was to determine with greater accuracy the longitude.

Humphrey Marshall published two works of merit, one entitled Arbutum Americanum, and Alphabetical Catalogue of Forest Trees and Shrubs, and the other called Observations on Botany, as Applicable to Rural Economics, etc. Humphrey Marshall was one of the earliest botanists of Chester County.

James Ross, A. M., LL. D., published a Latin Grammar, which by 1829 had reached its ninth edition. Also a Greek Grammar, which reached its second edition in 1817. He also published the Select Colloquies of Erasmus; A Select Century of the Colloquies of Corderius, Selectæ Profanis Scriptoribus Historiæ, Æsop's Fables, Latin and English, and Ciceronis Epistolæ.

Thomas Huston, M. D., published two works, one an Essay on Inoculation for Small Pox, and the other a Collection of Facts and Observation on Yellow Fever.

Hugh Williamson, M. D., LL. D., wrote on Civil History, on

the Climate of Different Parts of America, A History of North Carolina, and An Essay on Comets.

John Gummere wrote a Treatise on Surveying, which passed through many editions and was extensively used in schools.

Francis Glass wrote a life of Washington in Latin prose.

Hezekiah Niles wrote Principles and Acts of the Revolution in America and published Niles' Weekly Register, the latter well known to the reading public of his times throughout the United States, and containing much valuable historical matter. He edited fifty volumes and his son, William Ogden Niles, twenty-six.

John Jones wrote "The Power of Deception Unveiled and the Man of Sin Revealed."

Thomas L. Smith, M. D., wrote "The Chronicles of Turkey-town; or the Works of Jeremy Peters," etc.

Alexander Maitland wrote "The Political Instructor and Guide to Knowledge," etc.

Joshua Jones wrote "English Grammar in Two Parts," etc.

Jesse Conard wrote two novels, one called "Stephen More-land," the other, "The Secrets of Mount Echo."

Enoch Lewis was a very prolific writer, among his works being A Revised Edition of Simpson's Trigonometry, A Revised Edition of Bonnycastle's Algebra, A Treatise on Arithmetic, A Familiar Introduction to English Grammar, A Treatise on Plane and Spherical Trigonometry, all of which passed through several editions and were used extensively in the schools. Mr. Lewis also wrote A View of the Militia System of Pennsylvania, A View of the Present State of the African Slave Trade (1824), Vindication of the Society of Friends (1834), A Work on Domestic Slavery (1837), A Dissertation on Oaths (1838), Observations on Legal and Judicial Oaths (1846), Essay on Baptism, showing that the Baptism of the Spirit is the true baptism, and not Water Baptism (1839), A Life of William Penn (1844 and 1845), and edited the African Observer and the Friends' Review.

Joseph J. Lewis wrote twenty-seven letters on the early history of Chester County, published in the Village Record in 1824.

Anthony Bolmar was a prolific writer on language and literature. He wrote A Collection of One Hundred Fables, Les Adventure de Telemaque, par Fenelon, with a key, etc., A Collection of Colloquial Phrases, A Complete Treatise on the Gender of French Nouns, A Book of the French Verbs, both regular and irregular, A Theoretical and Practical Grammar of the French Language, and the Institutes of Morality for the Instruction of Youth.

Charles Miner, one of the ablest minds ever engaged in literary work in Chester County, wrote Essays from the Desk of Poor Robert the Scribe, and a History of Wyoming, which is the standard History of the Wyoming Valley.

William Darlington, M. D., one of the most industrious and successful laborers the county has produced in the botanical field, wrote Florula Cestrica, and Flora Cestrica, the latter a revised edition of the former. He also wrote a work which he called Reliquiæ Baldwinianæ, an Essay on the Development and Modifications of the External Organs of Plants, a work on Agricultural Botany, on American Weeds and Useful Plants, the latter being a revised edition of the former; Memorials of John Bartram and Humphrey Marshall, Sesqui-Centennial Gathering of the Clan Darlington, and aided in the compilation of Notæ Cestrienses, Notices of Chester County Men and Events, a series of biographical and historical papers, published in the Village Record in 1860-62, J. Smith Futhey being the compiler of about one-third of the numbers and Dr. Darlington of the remainder.

Ezra Michener, M. D., wrote A Retrospect of Early Quakerism; A Brief Exposition of the Testimony to Peace; Christian Casket, or the Pearl of Great Price, the latter being the Sermon on the Mount, combined from Matthew and Luke, with notes, and a Manual of Weeds, or the Weed Exterminator.

William D. Hartman, M. D., and Ezra Michener, M. D., together wrote a work entitled Conchologia Cestrica, the Molluscous Animals and Their Shells of Chester County, and Dr. Hartman has published papers: On the Opercula of the Family Strepo- natidæ; A Bibliographical Catalogue of the Genus Partula Fer- russac; On the Duplicates of the same genus; and also a Catalogue of the same genus, the latter printed in 1881.

Jesse Kersey has written Letters on Agriculture, A Treatise on the Fundamental Doctrines of the Christian Religion, and A Narrative of the Life, Travels, and Gospel Labors of Jesse Kersey.

Thomas Woodward wrote the Columbian Plutarch, a work containing twenty-eight biographical sketches of persons con- nected with American History.

William Gibbons, M. D., wrote a work entitled Truth Vindi- cated, in defense of the Doctrines of the Society of Friends; and An Exposition of Modern Skepticism.

Rev. George I. Miles wrote a work entitled A Glance at the Baptists.

Halliday Jackson wrote a work on the Civilization of the In- dian Natives, in which he gave a brief view of the friendly con- duct of William Penn toward the Indians in the early settlement of Pennsylvania.

Dr. William Johnson wrote a work entitled The Good Sa- maritan; or, Sick Man's Friend.

Gen. Josiah Harlan wrote a Memoir of India and Afghan- istan; and A Personal Narrative of General Harlan's eighteen years' residence in Asia.

Henry H. Van Amringe wrote a work entitled The Seals Opened; or A Voice to the Jews.

Morris Mattson, M. D., wrote: The Patriot, A Story of the Revolution; Hours of Devotion; Paul Ulric; and The American Vegetable Practice, or A New and Improved Guide to Health.

Bayard Taylor was the most prolific and distinguished man of letters that may be claimed by Chester County, and his name and fame will always be cherished by her people. Only a portion of his numerous works need be here named, which is more to recognize his value as an author than to give a complete catalogue of his writings. Among them were Ximena, or the Battle of the Sierra Morena, and other Poems; Views Afoot, or Europe seen with Knapsack and Staff; Eldorado, or, Adventures in the Path of Empire; A Journey to Central Africa; The Lands of the Saracens; A Visit to India, China and Japan, in 1853; Northern Travel, Summer and Winter Pictures, Sweden, Lapland; Hannah Thurston, a Story of American Life; The Story of Kennett; By-Ways of Europe; The Ballad of Abraham Lincoln; Goethe's Faust, Parts I and II, Translated into English; The Masque of the Gods; Egypt and Iceland in the Year 1874; School History of Germany; Boys of Other Countries; Bismarck, his Authentic Biography; Prince Deukalion, and besides the above-named works Mr. Taylor edited numerous volumes, and wrote extensively for newspapers and magazines, as the Atlantic Monthly, Harper's Monthly Magazine, North American Review, and Scribner's Monthly. Since his death his widow, Mrs. Marie Taylor, has edited "Studies in German Literature," which has been published with an introduction by Hon. George H. Boker.

Barclay Pennock wrote a work entitled The Religion of the Northmen.

Rev. John Crowell, at one time pastor of the First Presbyterian Church of West Chester, wrote a work entitled Republics Established and Overthrown by the Bible.

Thomas Baldwin compiled three works entitled: A Universal Pronouncing Gazetteer; A New and Complete Gazetteer of the United States, and a Complete Pronouncing Gazetteer, or Geographical Dictionary of the World.

Rev. William Newton, at one time rector of the Holy Trinity Church of West Chester, wrote Lectures on the First Two Visions of the Book of Daniel.

Gilbert Cope, the author of many genealogical works and joint author of Futhey & Cope's History of Chester County, was born August 17, 1840, in East Bradford Township, at the present residence of George B. Mellor, near the old Black Horse tavern. He is a son of Joseph and Eliza (Gilbert) Cope, and, like his father and grandfather, he was the youngest of eight children. His father owned the land now comprising the two farms of George B. Mellor and Herman Hoopes, and in 1852, having erected new buildings on the hill, removed thereto, leaving his eldest son in charge of the homestead.

Joseph Cope was a son of Joseph and Ann (Taylor) Cope of East Bradford, and grandson of John and Charity (Jefferis) Cope of the same township. Eliza Gilbert was a daughter of Abner and Ann (Cooper) Gilbert, of Westmoreland County, Pennsylvania, and granddaughter of Benjamin and Elizabeth (Walton) Gilbert, who, with her father and some of their other children, were taken captives by the Indians from their home in Northampton County, Pennsylvania, in 1780, and carried to the St. Lawrence River. A narrative of their captivity has passed through several editions.

Gilbert Cope received his education in a family school at home and at a neighbor's, taught by a sister; at a Friends' School in West Chester, and at the Friends' Boarding School in Westtown Township; but as was common with farmers' boys at that early day, attended only in the winter months, and his school education ceased before he was seventeen years old. When about fourteen he became interested in botany, and in succeeding years spent many happy hours in becoming familiar with the vegetation of his native county. At seventeen the subject of genealogy was brought to his attention, and after the publication of a work on the Cope family in 1861, he turned his attention to other families from which he is descended, and also began to collect data for local history. After his father's death and the sale of the homestead he became a resident of West Chester in 1872, and has continued there to reside ever since.

Before the collection of family and local history he has been much interested in the preservation of public and private records and manuscripts, and has put into book hundreds of volumes of manuscripts for the Pennsylvania Historical Society, Philadelphia Library, College of Physicians and of Chester County records. His own collections demanded a place of security, and a fireproof vault has been added to his residence for their storage. Believing that future generations would justify the measure, he has endeavored to secure the passage of an act for the recording of old and unrecorded deeds within the county.

Gilbert Cope is a most industrious compiler of genealogies, among his works being a Record of the Cope Family; a Genealogy of the Dutton Family of Pennsylvania; The Browns of Nottingham, besides numerous other works of a similar nature.

In 1880 he married Anna Garrett, daughter of David and Mary Ann (Hoopes) Garrett, late of Birmingham Township, and by her has had four children, viz., Herman, Ellen, David G., who died in infancy, and Joseph.

Thomas Buchanan Read is one of the most famous authors to whom Chester County can lay claim. His writings, mostly poetic, are numerous, and of the several volumes some of them are entitled merely "Poems." They may be named as follows: Poems, Boston, 1847; Lays and Ballads, Philadelphia, 1848; The Female Poets of America, 1848; The Pilgrims of the Great St. Bernard, published in the successive numbers of a magazine; Poems, London, 1852; Poems, Philadelphia, 1853; The New Pastoral, A Poem, 1855; The House by the Sea, 1856; Sylvia, or the Lost Shepherd 1857; Rural Poems, London, 1857; The Wagoner of the Alleghenies, a Poem of the Days of Seventy-Six, 1862; A Summer Story, Sheridan's Ride, etc., 1865; Poems, New and Enlarged Edition, 1865; and Good Samaritans, a Poem, published in Cincinnati.

Eli K. Price was a prolific writer, among his works being the following: Memoir of Philip and Rachel Price; Memorial of Our Daughter; Discourse on the Family as an Element of Government; Discourse of Trial by Jury; Of the Limitations of Actions and Liens Against Real Estate in Pennsylvania; The Act for the Sale of Real Estate; and the History of the Consolidation of the City of Philadelphia.

James P. Wickersham wrote several works, among them: School Economy; Methods of Instruction, and The Common School Laws of Pennsylvania, and Decisions of the Superintendent, with Explanations, Forms, etc.

Edward H. Williamson wrote several volumes, among them being: The Scout, a Story of the Revolution; The Quaker Partisans, a Story of the Revolution; Philip Morton; The Book of Deeds, and The List of Notaries.

Daniel G. Brinton, M. D., wrote: The Floridian Peninsula; The Shawnees and Their Migrations; The Myths of the New World; A Guide Book of Florida and the South; The National Legend of the Chahta-Muskokee Tribes; The Phonetic Alphabet of Yucatan; Grammar of the Choctaw Language; The Arawack Language of Guiana in its Linguistic and Ethnological Relations; Contributions to a Grammar of the Chahta-Muskokee Language; The Religious Sentiment, Its Source and Aim; and the Brinton Family.

Gen. George A. McCall wrote a series of Letters from the Frontier, covering a period of thirty years' service in the army.

Isaac I. Hayes, M. D., the great Arctic explorer, wrote: An Arctic Boat Journey in the Autumn of 1854; The Open Polar Sea; The Land of Desolation; and Cast Away in the Cold.

J. Smith Futhey wrote: History of the Upper Octorara Presbyterian Church; History of Educational Institutions in Chester County; and an Address on the One Hundreth Anniversary of the Paoli Massacre. Judge Futhey and Gilbert Cope wrote a History of Chester County, which was published in 1881.

Major Isaiah Price wrote a history of the Ninety-seventh Regiment, Pennsylvania Volunteer Infantry, during the war of the Rebellion.

Samuel W. Pennypacker was the author of the Annals of Phœnixville and Its Vicinity; The Pennypacker Reunion; Abraham and Dirck Op Den Graeff, and the Settlement of Germantown.

Charlton T. Lewis, son of Joseph J. Lewis, in company with Marvin R. Vincent, professor in Troy University, translated John Albert Bengel's Gnomon of the New Testament; and Mr. Lewis wrote A History of Germany from the Earliest Times, and Harper's Latin Dictionary, with the exception of the first 216 pages.

Mrs. Mary D. R. Boyd has written largely in the line of Sunday-school literature; Fannie H. Bent is also a writer of literature designed for the use of Sunday-schools.

Isaac D. Johnson, M. D., of Kennett Square, has written a Therapeutic Key, and a Guide to Homeopathic Practice.

Joseph T. Rothrock, M. D., has written a Sketch of the Flora of Alaska; a Work on Botany; the sixth volume of the United States Geographical Surveys West of the One Hundredth Meridian; A Catalogue of Trees and Shrubs, Native and Introduced in the Horticultural Gardens Adjacent to Horticultural Hall, Fairmount Park, Philadelphia, and a work called Medical Botany of America.

John Russell Young, at present Librarian of Congress, has written Around the World with General Grant.

George L. Maris, A. M., is the author of a work entitled The Normal English Grammar.

Prof. George G. Groff, M. D., has written on the Common Minerals, Ores and Rocks of Chester County; The Common Minerals and Ores of Pennsylvania, New York, Delaware and Maryland; The Chemical Elements; Geological Chart; Plant Description; Elements of Animal Physiology; Elements of Mineralogy; Elements of Agricultural Chemistry; and A Manual of Accidents and Emergencies.

Francis C. Hooton is the author of a work on The General and Special Pennsylvania Road Laws, and The Supervisor's Guide.

Hon. P. Frazer Smith wrote a work on the Forms of Procedure in the Courts of Pennsylvania, and Pennsylvania State Reports, comprising cases adjudged in the Supreme Court of Pennsylvania from 1865 to 1876.

Thomas Louis Ogier is the author of two books, one a pamphlet of 26 pages on Capital Punishment, and the other a Life of the Hon. James Bowen Everhart, of 156 pages, published in 1889.

George M. Philips, Ph. D., in connection with President Isaac Sharpless of Haverford College, wrote an Elementary Astronomy and an Elementary Natural Philosophy, and also a key to the latter, published in a separate volume. Dr. Philips also wrote a work on the Civil Government of Pennsylvania, and a Supplement to Mowry's Civil Government. He also wrote a work on the Geography of Pennsylvania which was published as a supplement to Rand & McNally's Grammar School Geography.

Professor James McClune wrote a History of the Brandywine Manor Presbyterian Church; A Comprehensive Calendar, a Calendar for all time indexed for two hundred and fifty years; a Report on the Solar Eclipse of August 7, 1869; a Biography of the Class of 1825, Princeton College, compiled by four of the class, including himself.

Howard M. Jenkins wrote an address on William Penn, his character and career, and prepared Historical Collections relating to Gwynedd Township, Montgomery County, Pennsylvania, settled in 1698 by the Welsh, together with data referring to the adjoining township in the same county.

Frank M. Stauffer wrote a work entitled The Queer, the Quaint, the Quizzical, a Cabinet for the Curious, 367 pages, published in 1882.

Col. Isaiah Price wrote an account of the Reunion of the Ninety-seventh Regiment, Pennsylvania Volunteers, October 29, 1884, on the old camp ground at Camp Wayne.

Thomas D. Ingram, M. D., wrote a work on Representative Government, * * * ᛜ The Civil Evil and its Remedy.

Pennock Huey wrote A True History of the Charge of the Eighth Pennsylvania Cavalry at Chancellorsvile.

Benjamin Moran wrote The Footpath and Highway, or Wanderings of an American in Great Britain in 1851 and 1852.

Samuel W. Pennypacker wrote a choice work entitled Historical and Biographical Sketches, published in 1883.

James Grier Ralston wrote an Historical Sketch of the First Presbyterian Church of Norristown, Pennsylvania, with Biographical Sketches of its Ministers, etc., and a work entitled Solar Hieroglyphics.

James Monaghan prepared The Chester County Reports, cases decided by the Supreme Court of Pennsylvania and the several courts of the Commonwealth, arising chiefly in the courts of Chester County, and also Pennsylvania County Court Reports, cases decided in the courts of the several counties of the Commonwealth.

Horatio McLean Jones compiled Missouri State Reports, volumes 21 to 30, published 1856 to 1861.

George L. Maris and Annie M. Maris prepared a volume on The Maris Family of the United States; a Record of the Descendants of George and Alice Maris, 1683-1885.

Edwin Atlee Barber prepared a Genealogical Record of the Atlee Family: The Descendants of Judge William Augustus Atlee and Colonel Samuel John Atlee, of Lancaster County.

Thomas Maxwell Potts wrote a Bi-Centennial Memorial of Jeremiah Carter, who came to the Province of Pennsylvania in 1682, published in 1883.

Edward H. Williamson wrote in addition to the works mentioned above several other works, some of them as follows: Ancestral Brief: A Brief of Lineage of the Descendants of William

Williamson of Thornbury Township, Chester County; The Clipping of the Osprey's Wings, and other Tales of Battle and Adventure on Sea and Land; After Work Hours; State Laws Relating to Wills; and The Scout, a Legend of Old Thornbury Township.

Cyrus Stern wrote a work entitled Our Kindred—The McFarlen and Stern Families.

Mrs. Sarah Louisa Oberholtzer wrote Violet Lee and Other Poems; Come for Arbutus; Daisies of Verse, and Hope's Heart Bells.

Frances Lavinia Michener wrote Prose and Poetical Works, octavo, 386 pages, published in 1884, third edition in 1888.

Ann Preston wrote Cousin Ann's Stories, a book of poems for children.

Mrs. Levi G. McCauley wrote Stories for Little Ones, 1886.

Thomas Elwood Garrett wrote the Masque of the Muses.

Mrs. Isabella P. Huston wrote Superficial Glimpses of Travel, published in 1888.

Fenelon Darlington wrote A Short History of Great Inventions and Discoveries, and A Token of Esteem and Remembrance for My Young Friends at School.

Rev. James Roberts, D. D., wrote a Memorial of the Rev. James W. Dale, D. D., for private circulation.

Rev. William H. H. Marsh wrote The Modern Sunday-school, and Two Theories of the Visible Church.

Rev. Francis J. Collier, D. D., wrote Quarter Century Reunion of Jefferson College, and Temperance Truth for Young and Old.

Rev. Samuel Fulton wrote Golden Promises Selected from God's Word; Compend of Chronology, and A Family Manual, Seven Don'ts.

Rev. Robert P. Dubois wrote a Sketch of the Life and Character of the Rev. James Latta, D. D.

Rev. David Evans wrote The Minister of Christ and the Duties of His Flock.

Rev. John Duer wrote a Memorial of Rev. John Duer, his father.

Rev. J. W. Hood wrote The Negro in the Christian Pulpit, or the Two Characters and the Two Destinies.

Rev. Mathias Sheeleigh, D. D., wrote numerous works, the principal ones being as follows: Outlines of Old Testament History, for Youth; Outlines of New Testament History, for Youth; Brief Life of Martin Luther, the Great Reformer; The Relation of the Sunday-school to the Church; and the Conservation of Our Church's History.

Thomas K. Brown wrote an Academic Algebra, designed as an Advanced Algebra for High Schools.

Esther J. Trimble wrote a Handbook of English and American Literature, Historical and Critical.

William M. Rupert wrote a Guide to the study of History and the Constitution of the United States.

William Vogdes, A. M., wrote a United States Arithmetic, designed for Schools and Academies, a Key to the same and a Treatise on Mensuration.

Joshua Jones wrote an English Grammar, founded on the natural principles of speech, and a Lecture on English Grammar.

David M. Sensenig, M. S., wrote a work entitled Numbers Symbolized: An Elementary Algebra.

Elijah W. Beans wrote a Manual of Practical Surveyors.

Samuel Sloan wrote the Model Architect: a Guide for the Builder and Carpenter; City and Suburban Architecture; Homestead Architecture; Constructive Architecture; and Architectural Review and Builders' Journal.

Marie Hansen Taylor and Horace E. Scudder wrote the Life and Letters of Bayard Taylor, two volumes, 1884.

T. B. Read wrote Paul Redding, a Tale of the Brandywine.

Alfred L. Elwyn, M. D., compiled a Glossary of Supposed Americanisms.

George Lippard wrote an Original Revolutionary Chronicle and the White Banner.

Rev. Edwin McMinn wrote Rambles in Mineral Fields.

Stephen P. Sharpless wrote a work entitled The Woods of the United States.

William McClay wrote Sketches of Debate in the First Senate of the United States, most interesting reading. William McClay was born in Chester County, was educated in the famous school of Rev. John Blair at Fagg's Manor, and was a Senator in Congress from Pennsylvania, and it has been often stated that he, and not Jefferson, was the father of the Democratic party.

Benjamin M. Everhart has written much for the Journal of Mycology, or the Science of the Fungi. Mr. Everhart has given much time to the study of botany, and is at the present time one of the foremost authorities on this department in the world.

Edwin Atlee Barber wrote a Genealogical Record of the Atlee Family, 1884; a Genealogy of the Barber Family, 1890, and The Pottery and Porcelain of the United States, 1893.

John Vanderslice wrote Around the World, Sketches of Travel Through Many Lands and Over Many Seas, 1876.

William Whitehead wrote Etoile and Other Poems, 1872.

Brinton W. Woodward wrote Old Wine in New Bottles, 1890.

Dr. J. T. Rothrock wrote Vacation Cruising in Chesapeake and Delaware Bays, and has also written a large number of scientific articles, which have been embodied in government reports, mainly on forestry.

Judge Samuel Whitaker Pennypacker wrote Annals of Phœnixville and Vicinity; Historical and Biographical Sketches, 1883; Pennsylvania Supreme Courts, four volumes, 1882 to 1886; Weekly Notes of Cases argued and determined in the Supreme Court of Pennsylvania, 1875 to 1891; and the Descent of Samuel Whitaker Pennypacker, 1898.

· Dr. William Darlington compiled a Directory of West Ches-

F. Gutekunst Co

GILBERT COPE.

ter in 1857, in which he published a short History of West Chester up to that date.

Gilbert Cope is also author of the following works: Genealogy of the Sharpless Family, descended from John and Jane Sharpless, settlers near Chester, Pennsylvania, 1682; together with some account of the English ancestry of the family, including the results of researches by Henry Fishwick, F. H. S., and the late Joseph Lemuel Chester, LL. D.; and a full report of the Bi-Centennial Reunion of 1882. Compiled by Gilbert Cope of West Chester, Pa. Published for the Family, under the auspices of the Bi-Centennial Committee. Philadelphia, 1887. pp. xvi., 1333.

This contains the names of over 19,000 descendants of John and Jane Sharpless, with several thousand others connected with the family by marriage. The Grubb Family of Pennsylvania and Delaware, 1893. This is a pamphlet of twelve double-column pages, reprinted from the Daily Local News; Ancestral Chart. This is a blank for filling up with the names of all a person's ancestors covering eight generations; first published in 1875, with a second edition in 1879. This is much in demand by those interested in their ancestry; Genealogical Records of the ancestry of William Hood Dunwoody, of Minneapolis, Minnesota. Now in press; Darlington Genealogy, nearly ready for the press, and to be published this year (1898); Smedley Genealogy, in preparation—a large work, which will probably appear in 1899.

Thomas Buchanan Read was born about four miles from Downingtown, Chester County, on March 12, 1822, and died in New York City, May 11, 1872. His mother, a widow, apprenticed him to a tailor, but he ran away, learned in Philadelphia the trade of cigar-making, and in 1837 made his way to Cincinnati, where he found a home with the sculptor, Shobal V. Clevenger. He learned the trade of a sign painter, and attended school at intervals. Not succeeding in Cincinnati, he went to Dayton, and

39

obtained an engagement in the theater. Returning to Cincinnati in about a year, he was enabled by the liberality of Nicholas Longworth to open a studio as a portrait-painter. He did not long remain in Cincinnati, but wandered from town to town painting signs when he could find no sitters, sometimes giving public entertainments, and reverting to cigar-making when other resources failed. In 1841 he removed to New York City, and within a year to Boston. While there he made his first essays as a poet, publishing in the Courier several lyric poems in 1843-44. He settled in Philadelphia in 1846, and visited Europe in 1850. In 1853 he went again to Europe and devoted himself to the study and practice of art in Florence and Rome until 1858. He afterward spent much time in Philadelphia and Cincinnati, but in the last years of his life made Rome his principal residence. While in the United States during the Civil War he gave public readings for the benefit of the soldiers, and recited his war songs in the camps of the National army. He died while making a visit to the United States.

His paintings, most of which deal with allegorical and mythological subjects, are full of poetic and graceful fancies, but the technical treatment is careless and unskillful, betraying his lack of early training. The best known are The Spirit of the Waterfall, Undine, The Lost Pleiad, The Star of Bethlehem, Longfellow's Children, Cleopatra and her Barge, and Sheridan's Ride. He painted portraits of Elizabeth Barrett Browning, the ex-queen of Naples, George M. Dallas, Henry W. Longfellow, Leigh Hunt, Tennyson, and others. His group of Longfellow's daughters was popular in photographs. He turned his hand occasionally to sculpture, producing one work, a bust of Sheridan, that attracted much attention. He possessed a much more thorough mastery of the means of expression in the art of poetry than in painting. His poems are marked by a fervent spirit of patriotism and by artistic power and fidelity in the description of American scenery and rural life. His first volume of Poems (Philadelphia, 1847) was followed by Lays and Ballads (1848). He next made a collection of extracts and specimens from the Female Poets of America (1848), containing also biographical notices and portrait drawn by himself. An edition of his lyrics, with illustrations by Kenny Meadows, appeared in London in 1852, and 1853 a new and enlarged edition was published in Philadelphia. A prose romance, entitled The Pilgrims of the Great St. Bernard, was published as a serial. The New Pastoral, his most ambitious poem, describes in blank verse the pioneer life of a family of immigrants, (1854). The more dramatic and imaginative poem that followed, entitled The House by the Sea (1856), gained for it more readers than had been attracted by its own superior merits. Next appeared Sylvia, or the Lost Shepherd and Other Poems (1857) and A Voyage to Iceland (1857), and the same year a collection of his Rural Poems was issued in London. His Complete Poetical Works (Boston, 1860) contained the longer and shorter poems that had been already published. His next narrative poem was The Wagoner of the Alleghenies, a tale of Revolutionary times (Philadelphia, 186). During the Civil War he wrote many patriotic lyrics, including the stirring poem of Sheridan's Ride, which was printed in a volume with A Summer Story and other pieces, chiefly of the war (Philadelphia, 1865). His last long poem was The Good Samaritans (Cincinnati, 1867). The fullest editions of his poetical works were printed in Philadelphia (3 vols., 1865 and 1867).

Bayard Taylor, one of the most widely known literary writers of America, was born at Kennett Square, Chester County, January 11, 1825, his father and mother (Joseph and Rebecca (Way) Taylor, both living after his death. Robert Taylor, a rich Quaker who came to Pennsylvania in 1681 with William Penn, was his ancestor, and a part of the land taken up by this rich Quaker is now the site of Cedarcroft. The grandmothers of Bayard Taylor were both of South German descent. The name Bayard was given him in honor of James A. Bayard, the United States Senator from Delaware at that time, and Bayard was "his only and true name." In 1829 the family moved to the farm a mile from Kennett Square, and there continued to live until the building of Cedarcroft. "The education which he received at home and under the impulse of his own nature took precedence of the more formal culture of school life. Especially was he indebted to his mother, who understood well the refinement of his nature." And he says of himself that the books he read came from the village library, and the task of helping to fodder on the dark winter evenings was lightened by the anticipation of sitting down to Gibbon's Rome or Thaddeus of Warsaw. He derived the greatest satisfaction from books, and the eagerness with which he read was measured by the retentiveness of his memory of those early readings, and before he was twelve years of age he had "devoured" the contents of the circulating library of the little town of-Kennett Square, and Cooper's novels, and the histories of Gibbon, Robertson and Hume. But his chief delight was in books of travel and poetry.

His earlier education was supplemented by a regular course of study in the school, which was a great delight to him. The influence of the writings of others upon the tender mind is aptly illustrated by that upon his mind of a certain stanza of poetry, which in writing later to his old teacher at Kennett Square had cheered and encouraged him a thousand times when his prospects seemed gloomy.

"O, why should we seek to anticipate sorrow,
　By throwing the flowers of the present away,
And gathering the dark rolling cloudy to-morrow
　To darken the generous sun of to-day?

In addressing old Quaker friends it was easy for him to throw his letters into the Quaker form, for his family, though not formally Quakers, yet generally adhered to the principles of the society. His mother was reared a Lutheran, yet she became attached to the Quakers in early life, and taught her children the fundamental doctrines of the society. At fourteen he began the study of Latin and French, and at fifteen Spanish. At sixteen his schooling practically ceased, but he kept on until he was nineteen with Latin and French. In 1837 his father was elected sheriff of Chester County, and moved to West Chester, remaining there three years, and it was during this time that young Bayard attended Anthony Bolmar's school. Shortly afterward he attended the academy at Unionville, and there completed his formal schooling in 1842.

It was in this latter year that he became apprenticed for a term of four years to Henry E. Evans, publisher of the Village Record, and it was during this apprenticeship that he began to write poems. One of these poems, to which he had given the name of "Rosalie," he afterward named Ximena. He believed that poetry owns as its true field the happiness of mankind. Quoting Channing, he said, "its use is to lift the mind out of the beaten, dusty, weary walks of life, to rouse it into a purer element, and to breathe into it a more profound and generous emotion."

The first journey he ever made was to the Catskill Mountains, and his first purpose in publishing his volume of poems, Ximena, was to secure money enough to carry out a plan of going to the West Indies. After reading Howitt's Rural Life in Germany he became convinced that it was possible for him to see Europe on foot, after once having crossed the Atlantic. In order to accomplish this object he purchased the remainder of his apprenticeship time from Mr. Evans, and made arrangements with certain editors of magazines for letters from abroad, some of them paying him in advance as much as $50 for twelve letters. In this way he secured $140, a sum which he thought sufficient to carry him to the ends of the earth. He made an agreement with Horace

Greeley by which he was to write for the Tribune letters descriptive of German life and society, Mr. Greeley admonishing him not to write until he knew something.

Bayard Taylor reached the old world July 26, 1844, and spent there two years in travel and study, which comprised his university education. While he ardently desired to travel in Greece, yet Rome was the end of his journey toward the East. Upon returning home in 1846 his anxiety was great to undertake some occupation which should yield him a fixed income so that he might marry and settle down in life. Determining, therefore, to establish a weekly paper in Chester County, he was joined by Frederick E. Foster, and they located in Phœnixville, purchasing the Phœnixville Gazette, and changing its name to the Phœnixville Pioneer. The first number of this paper appeared December 29, 1846, but its career was not what he anticipated. The inhabitants of the village of Phœnixville were mostly workmen in the several manufacturing establishments, and the country people were conservative farmers, and they preferred local news to anything he felt like preparing for publication in the Pioneer. His neutrality in politics made him enemies in both parties, and after one year's experience he gave up the business in despair and went to New York, "weighed down with a debt, the paying of which cost me the earnings of the next three years."

Remaining in New York until 1849 his prosperity was so great that he was enabled to buy into the New York Tribune, which laid the foundation of his pecuniary fortune. Mr. Greeley and he became very friendly, and in 1850 he went to California for the Tribune. In 1851 he went to Egypt, traveled up the Valley of the Nile, and saw much of the country. After traveling in Syria, Palestine and Asia Minor he reached Constantinople in July 12, 1852, and reached Catania in Sicily in time to see the grand festival of St. Agatha, which takes place only once in a hundred years.

After this he went to the Farther East, reaching Bombay

December 27, 1852, went to Agra, Delhi, Landowr, Dehra, Meerut, Cawnpore, Allahabad and Calcutta. In 1854 he returned home to find himself famous, and invitations to lecture poured in upon him. Though he found this field of labor profitable, yet he also found it very irksome. In 1856 he went to Scandinavia, being present before returning home in 1858 at the three hundredth anniversary of the University of Jena.

In 1859-60 he built Cedarcroft, and at the breaking out of the war of the Rebellion, when his brother Frederick enlisted, he sold a share of his stock in the Tribune and devoted a thousand dollars to the cause of the Union. Then after a short tour in Germany he returned to his native country to aid in the prosecution of the war. In 1862 he was sent with Simon Cameron to Russia, as secretary of legation, and upon Mr. Cameron's return from St. Petersburg he was made charge d' affaires, and in this position was eminently useful to his country in preventing Russia from uniting with England and France in an intervention in American affairs, by showing Gortchakoff that the United States was abundantly able to suppress the Rebellion.

Bayard Taylor was engaged in literary work, novel writing and poetry from 1863 to 1867, most of the time at Cedarcroft. After this he spent a year in Europe, and then another year, 1869, at Cedarcroft. In 1872 he again went to Europe, where his translation of Faust made him a man of mark and interest. From Germany he returned to America in the fall of 1874, in October of which year he removed to New York City with the view of making that his permanent home, leaving his parents in possession of Cedarcroft. In 1876 he wrote the National Ode, and early in 1878 he was appointed by President Hayes minister to Germany. He was greatly honored by his fellow-citizens of Kennett Square and West Chester on the occasions of his visits to those places when on his way to take passage to Germany. His last great work was "Prince Deucalion," and the last verse he wrote was called

"Epicedium," written in September, 1878, and read at the Century Memorial to William Cullen Bryant. He died November 19, 1878, and his remains, after lying in the cemetery at Jerusalem, reached America March 13, 1879.

It is needless to say in conclusion more than that Bayard Taylor was one of the most industrious and illustrious writers of his day, and taken in every way one of the best of men, high-toned, honorable and unselfish to an unusual degree.

In the early spring of 1863 Bayard Taylor had the good fortune to intercept dispatches from Secretary of State Bejamin of the Confederate States Government to Mr. Lamar, who had been appointed agent of the Confederate States at St. Petersburg. These dispatches instructed Mr. Lamar not to permit the introduction into any treaty of amity and commerce which the Confederate States might make of a clause prohibiting the African slave trade. In transmitting these dispatches to Hon. William H. Seward Mr. Taylor caustically remarked:

"It is a curious illustration in the combat of the powers of light and darkness for the possession of the world, that on this 3d day of March, 1863, the day of the jubilee on which twenty millions of serfs became forever free, that I forward to you an insidious document in favor of human slavery."

Upon the appointment of Hon. Cassius M. Clay as minister to Russia, Mr. Taylor immediately resigned as secretary of legation, and upon learning of the death of his youngest brother, Frederick, who fell at Gettysburg, he at once returned to America.

CHAPTER XVI.

THE MEDICAL PROFESSION.

CHAPTER XVI.

THE first medical society in Chester County was organized in West Chester in 1809, by the physicians of the place and the vicinity. It was not sufficiently well attended to be maintained. Another was organized in 1828, which included the entire county. This society flourished for a number of years and then suffered a period of suspended animation, when it was revived, and by about 1850 it was in a flourishing condition.

The society organized in 1828 was named the Chester County Medical Society, and its first meeting appears to have been held February 5 that year, Dr. Isaac Thomas being the chairman and Dr. Wilmer Worthington, secretary. A committee to prepare a constitution was appointed, consisting of Drs. William Darling-ton, George A. Fairlamb, William Harris, Samuel McClean, Ezra Michener, Joseph Griffith and John Kennedy. In addition to those named above the following participated in the forming of the society: Jacob Sharpless, Isaac L. Coffman, Bartholomew Fussell, Isaac Pennington, Charles W. Parish and John B. Brinton. The constitution as adopted provided for a president, two vice-presidents, a recording and a corresponding secretary, and a treasurer. The by-laws made it incumbent on the members to report to the society all remarkable cases of disease within their knowledge. A permanent organization was effected by the election of Dr. William Darlington, president; Drs. George A. Fairlamb and William

Harris, vice-presidents; John Kennedy and Wilmer Worthington, secretaries; Thomas Seal, treasurer, and Samuel McClean, orator. During the next three years the new members added were Drs. Enoch P. Hoopes and Gideon G. Palmer. From 1831 to 1847 no meetings were held. In the latter year six of the old members and thirteen other members met June 8, in the hall of the Chester County Cabinet of Natural Sciences, and effected a reorganization. At the next meeting, held in December, 1847, the society adopted the code of ethics then recently adopted by the American Medical Society and also a fee-bill, which it was hoped would "be found to approach as near as may be to the views and practices of the physicians of the county, and furnish no just grounds of complaint to patients."

At the same December meeting resolutions were introduced by Dr. Wilmer Worthington and adopted by the society, having in view the formation of a State Medical Society, and directing the corresponding secretary to invite the coöperation of the various medical associations and schools of the State. The result of this correspondence was the organization of the Medical Society of the State of Pennsylvania, which held its first meeting in Lancaster, in April, 1848.

In 1849 the stated meetings of the Chester County Medical Society were made semi-annual instead of quarterly, and the plan was adopted of holding an adjourned meeting in some other part of the county about a month after the stated meeting. In 1850 the Delaware County Medical Society was organized, the members of Chester County Medical Society living in Delaware County withdrawing to unite with their own society. This left in the Chester County Society somewhat more than forty members. In 1852 Drs. William Darlington, Charles W. Parish and Wilmer Worthington were appointed a committee to prepare and report biographical sketches of deceased physicians of the county, which biographies were published in the Medical Reporter, a quarterly journal published under the direction of the Chester and Delaware County Medical Societies, its first number appearing in July, 1853. This journal was published for three years, and was in charge of five editors, viz.: From Chester County, Drs. Wilmer Worthington, Isaac Thomas and Jacob Price, and from Delaware County Drs. J. T. Huddleston and George Martin. Previously to the time of the Medical Reporter the proceedings of the society were published in pamphlet form, first in 1848, and again in 1852. All other publications authorized by the society have been made through the transactions of the State Medical Society.

In 1857 the State Medical Society held its annual meeting in the West Chester Court-house, and for several years after 1860 the Chester County Medical Society was in an inactive condition, for the reason that the War of the Rebellion attracted from it its most active members. The society in other ways showed the patriotism of its members by offering, in April, 1861, in a unanimous resolution, and to attend the families of those who should volunteer in the service of the Union, in cases of sickness, so long as those volunteers should remain in the service, without charge. In 1869 the membership was thirteen and in 1880 it was thirty.

Since 1880 the officers of this society have been as follows:

Presidents—J. D. W. Henderson, E. V. Swing, George R. Spratt, E. Hopkins, William B. Brinton, R. B. Carey, Thomas D. Ingram, E. V. Swing, William R. Perdue, James Fulton, Thomas D. Dunn, J. K. Evans, R. B. Ewing, W. T. Sharpless, Charles J. Roberts, J. H. Stubbs, U. Grant Gifford, Mrs. Elizabeth H. C. Howell, Benjamin Thompson, Ida V. Reel, who fills the office at the present time.

The corresponding secretaries have been as follows: Ephraim Hopkins, W. R. Perdue, Thomas D. Ingram, S. H. Wollerton, J. R. McClurg, P. C. Hoskins, both corresponding and recording secretary from 1885 to 1896, when S. H. Scott, the present official, succeeded.

The recording secretaries have been as follows: Ephraim Hopkins, Edward Jackson, James Fulton, and P. C. Hoskins as above.

The treasurers have been as follows: Charles E. Woodward, until 1895, when Wilhelmina T. Nelson of West Chester became treasurer, holding the office until the present time.

Dr. James Anderson, one of the early physicians of Chester County, was born in Charlestown Township, April 11, 1782, and in 1804 began the study of medicine under the instruction of Dr. Roger Davis. After attending lectures in the University of Pennsylvania two years he received his degree in 1806, and he was actively engaged in the practice of his profession in the county for upward of thirty years. He died June 1, 1858, in the seventy-seventh year of his age.

Dr. Nathan Hayes, one of the older physicians of Chester County, was born in the township of West Marlborough, February 5, 1787. He commenced the study of medicine with Dr. T. Griffith, a practitioner in the village of Unionville, completing his study with Dr. William Baldwin of Wilmington, Delaware. In the spring of 1808 he received the degree of M. D. from the University of Pennsylvania, the subject of his thesis being the "Modus Operandi of Medicine." He immediately located in Edgemont Township, Delaware County, but at the end of a year he removed to Unionville, where he continued the practice of medicine during the remainder of his life. He died of consumption in July, 1819.

Dr. Frederick William Heckel, Sr., was born in Saarbruck, Germany, in January, 1800, and came to the United States in 1823. In 1825 he settled in East Vincent Township and immediately began there the practice of medicine, and continued in the practice of his profession until his death, which occurred June 30, 1861.

Dr. Frederick William Heckel, Jr., was born February 24, 1829, and began reading medicine with his father and Dr. Charles

Fronefield, of Philadelphia. After attending lectures at the University of Pennsylvania he was graduated from that institution April 7, 1849, and thereafter spent one year in practice with his father. Then setting up for himself he continued in practice with increasing success until 1858, when he removed to his farm near Phoenixville, when he removed to East Vincent Township, and continued there to reside. In September, 1862, he was commissioned assistant surgeon in the Fifth Pennsylvania, and in December following promoted to surgeon, and was ordered to take charge of the medical department of the One Hundred and Sixty-fifth Pennsylvania Regiment, with which he served until it was mustered out. He has been always unusually successful as a physician, and highly respected as a citizen and as a man.

Dr. Roger Davis was born in Charlestown Township, October 2, 1762, and pursued his medical studies under the direction of Dr. Duffield of Philadelphia, afterward taking three full courses of lectures at the University of Pennsylvania, though he took no degree. From 1785 to his death, which occurred November 20, 1815, he continued the practice of medicine in his native township, with gratifying success.

Dr. Samuel Kennedy, one of Chester County's early physicians, and one of its most sterling patriots during the Revolutionary War, was descended from the Kennedys of Ayrshire, Scotland. On January 3, 1776, he offered his services as a surgeon to the Continental Congress, and on the 19th of the same month it was resolved in Committee of Safety that he be appointed surgeon to the Fourth Battalion of Pennsylvania troops in the service of the United Colonies. In May, 1777, he was appointed senior surgeon in the military hospitals, and in November following he was appointed senior surgeon and physician in the General Hospital of the Middle Department.

The general hospital had been erected at the Yellow Springs, on which property the American army was quartered for a time, while the British occupied his homestead in the Great Valley, the occupation by the one being equally with that of the other. Dr. Kennedy went with Wayne to Long Island, was at Ticonderoga, and on the borders of Canada. He was also at the battle of the Brandywine, and of Germantown, and superintended the hospital at Bethlehem. For his invaluable services he received nothing from the public treasury. In his will he bequeathed a sum of money to be expended in the building of a stone wall around the graveyard of Charlestown Meeting-house, where a neat monument commemorates his virtues and his services. His death occurred June 17, 1778, in the forty-eighth year of his age.

Dr. Thomas Ruston Kennedy, son of the above, was born in Chester County in 1763, studied medicine under Dr. Morgan of Philadelphia, and graduated from the University of Pennsylvania. By Governor Mifflin he was appointed surgeon of Major Denny's battalion which was to relieve the garrison at Le Bœuf, near Lake Erie, the appointment being made November 17, 1794. He was subsequently surgeon to the troops under charge of Andrew Elli-cott, who constructed a fort at Presque Isle (Erie), and whose daughter Dr. Kennedy married. When Crawford County was organized in 1800 he was appointed prothonotary and clerk of the courts, and died in Meadville, March 24, 1813.

Dr. Thomas Kennedy was born in Wallace Township, Chester County, then, however, a part of Nantmeal Township, in 1766. Having attained his majority he began the study of medicine with Dr. Harris of Indiantown and graduated from the University of Pennsylvania. Entering upon the practice of his profession in his native township, he became in 1797 the successor of his preceptor, Dr. Harris. He had a large practice, and was strongly opposed to amputation whenever there was a chance of saving the limb. He died in April, 1814.

Dr. John Kennedy was born in Baltimore February 13, 1800. Having graduated from the University of Maryland in 1820, he became resident physician of the Baltimore City Hospital, and in February, 1822, located in Oxford, Chester County, where he rapidly acquired an extensive practice and rose to deserved eminence in his profession. He was a charter member of the Chester County Medical Society, organized June 7, 1828, and which was the first institution of the kind in the State. He died May 28, 1838.

Dr. William Darlington, LL. D., one of the most noted physicians and citizens of Chester County, widely known as a botanist, was the first student to graduate from the Medical Department of the University of Pennsylvania. While he gave much time to the practice of his profession, yet he gave more of it to botanical research. In 1826 he published his "Cestrica," and in 1847 his "Agricultural Botany." He also published many papers upon the science of botany, and served in the Fourteenth, Sixteenth and Seventeenth Congresses, and was always an active man. His death occurred April 23, 1863, and a monument erected to his memory bears the following inscription, written by himself twenty years before his death:

"The plants of Chester which he loved and described,
May they bloom forever above his tomb."

At a meeting held April 22, 1898, Dr. William T. Sharpless spoke in part as follows, concerning the effect of Dr. Darlington's life on the people of Chester County:

Dr. William Goodell, who once practiced medicine in West Chester, and who afterward became an eminent professor of a branch of surgery in the University of Pennsylvania, a man of great skill, fine scholarship and wide experience with the world, says in his book published in 1887: "I once knew a man, a member of our profession, a general scientist and withal a great botanist, who so molded the tastes of his fellow townsmen that there is, I venture to assert, no other town in this country which in pro-

40

portion to the number of its inhabitants contains so many excellent botanists, geologists, mineralogists, conchologists and entomologists. Few farmers in that county have not had a liberal education, and scores there are who can show a well arranged hortus siccus or give the botanical names of the indigenous plants and weeds. The town in which he lived has at this moment more successful schools, normal, public and private, than any other of its size in the United States."

Dr. John Bowen Brinton, one of the most distinguished physicians of his day, was born in East Bradford Township, Chester County, on the banks of the Brandywine, in 1804, and graduated from Jefferson Medical College in 1825, and also from the University of Pennsylvania, 1826. His preceptor was the celebrated surgeon, Dr. George McClellan, father of Gen. George B. McClellan. Almost immediately after his graduation he located in West Chester, and there practiced his profession until his death, which occurred October 13, 1881, when he was seventy-seven years of age. "His urbanity and professional skill, ere the lapse of many years, enabled him to rank among the prominent physicians of the county. The bent of his mind was in the direction of surgery, and he became well and widely known for his skill in surgical operations. During his professional career he performed many difficult and highly important operations previous to the introduction of anæsthetics. At that time, however, the patient was frequently stupefied with laudanum."

Dr. Brinton was devotedly attached to his profession, and he was scrupulously observant of its ethical code. He was one of the founders of the Chester County Medical Society, and remained deeply interested in its proceedings until advancing age compelled that interest to decay. His death occurred, as above stated, October 13, 1881, and his loss was deeply felt not only by his immediate relatives and friends, but also by the profession itself.

Dr. William B. Brinton was born November 30, 1842, in West Chester, was educated in Wyer's Academy and afterward at the University of Pennsylvania, graduating with honors from the latter institution. From this time on until his death he success-fully followed his practice in medicine until his death, which oc-curred March 7, 1883. The cause of his death was determined by his physicians to have been uræmia of the most positive kind, his system being weakened by overwork in his profession, to which he was much attached. Dr. Brinton was appointed assistant sur-geon of the Fourth Regiment, Pennsylvania Reserves, on March 14, 1863, and was transferred to the One Hundred and Eighty-fourth Pennsylvania Regiment March 3, 1864. He was mustered out with this regiment July 14, 1865. In 1881 he succeeded his father as physician of the Chester County prison, the vacancy be-ing occasioned by his father's death. Dr. William B. Brinton mar-ried a daughter of Judge J. Smith Futhey, and by her had two children.

Dr. Isaac Hayes, known all over the world as a famed Arctic explorer, was born in Chester County, March 5, 1832. After re-ceiving his education at the public and private schools of the county, and at the Westtown Boarding School, he entered the University of Pennsylvania, graduating from that institution in 1853. Soon after graduating he accompanied Dr. E. K. Kane on his Arctic expedition as surgeon, and in 1860 started with an expedition of his own to the polar regions, being absent about a year and a half. In these northern regions he reached a point within 480 miles of the North Pole, which was a point further north than had previously been reached. For this distinguishing feat he received gold medals from the leading societies of the world, besides numerous decorations. He became a surgeon of United States volunteers, with the rank of major and brevet rank of colonel, and he built and commanded until the close of the war the army hospital at West Philadelphia, capable of accommo-dating 4,000 patients.

Dr. Jacob Rickabaugh was born in Chester County, February 6, 1815, read medicine with Dr. James Francis Latta of Tredyffrin and attended lectures in the Medical Department of the University of Pennsylvania, graduating from this institution in March, 1842. Then, immediately locating at his old home in Tredyffrin Township, he still remains there in the practice of his profession.

Dr. James Bayard Wood, once one of the prominent and honored citizens and physicians of Chester County, was born in New Castle County, Delaware, November 5, 1817. While his educational advantages were only such as were afforded by the common schools of the day, yet through persistent private study he acquired much useful learning, and it was during the period from 1849 to 1853, while he was postmaster at West Chester, he studied medicine, graduating from the Homeopathic Medical College of Pennsylvania, in March, 1854, from which time on he devoted his energies to the practice of his profession, which was quite extensive and in which he was unusually successful. He was president of the Chester County and the State Homeopathic Medical Societies, and in civil life was highly honored. It was through the instrumentality of Dr. Wood that in 1877 the present enduring monument was erected on the grounds of the "Paoli Massacre." His only son, Dr. Henry C. Wood, also practiced medicine in West Chester.

Dr. William Dell Hartman was born in Pikeland, Chester County, December 24, 1817, and was educated by such teachers as Joseph C. Strode, Jonathan Gause and Anthony Bolmar, in the West Chester Academy, and later read medicine with Dr. Wilmer Worthington, and attended lectures at the University of Pennsylvania three full years, and then had to wait some months until he came of age before he could graduate, his graduation occurring in 1839. Locating immediately in West Chester, he has been continuously in practice since that time, a period of fifty-nine years.

Dr. Hartman, outside of his regular practice, is one of the distinguished men of Chester County, having by his own exertions made himself known as a scientist in all parts of the civilized world. He has given great attention to the conchology of Chester County, to herpitology, to ichthyology, to ornithology and entomology, and his publications on these subjects are numerous and valuable. Among these works may be mentioned Bibliographic and Synonimic Catalogue of the Genus Partula, and also a Bibliographic and Synonimic Catalogue of the Genus Auriculella, and also a paper on a new species of Partula.

Dr. I. D. Johnson, homeopathic physician of Kennett Square, was born at Elkview, August 10, 1827, and began the study of medicine with Dr. C. Harlan of Wilmington, Delaware. In 1852 he graduated from Hahnemann Medical College at Philadelphia and practiced medicine one year between West Grove and Jennersville, and one year in Wilmington, locating in Kennett Square in 1855, where he has been engaged in practice ever since. His "Therapeutic Key" is largely used as a text-book in colleges in the United States and in Europe; his "Homeopathic Guide" has been translated into German and French, and his "Counsel to Parents" is largely used and is dedicated to the National Woman's Christian Temperance Union.

Dr. Morris Hughes, homeopathic physician of Kennett Square, was born in Marshallton in 1854. Receiving his elementary and higher education in the public schools and in Eaton Academy in Kennett Square, he then attended Hahnemann Medical College at Philadelphia, graduating in 1884. After practicing medicine one year in Philadelphia with Dr. Middleton, he located in Kennett Square in 1885, and has been there ever since.

Dr. H. Graham, homeopathic physician of Kennett Square, was born in Chester County in 1852. He was educated at Cambridge, Massachusetts, and attended Hahnemann Medical College in Philadelphia, graduating in 1891. Then locating in Kennett Square, he has been engaged there in the practice of his profession ever since, with the exception of two years, 1894 and 1895, spent in Ohio.

Dr. Levi Hoopes, homeopathic physician of West Chester, was born in Chester County in 1842, was educated in private schools mainly, and graduated from Hahnemann Medical College of Philadelphia in March, 1871. On June 1, 1871, he located in Pottstown, remaining there in the practice six years. Removing then to Downingtown, he was there engaged in the practice of his profession ten and a half years, and removed to West Chester January 5, 1888, where he has since been engaged in practice. At the present time he is surgeon for the Pennsylvania Railroad Company.

Dr. Charles Rees Palmer was born in West Chester July 10, 1870, was educated in the public schools of that place, in the West Chester State Normal School, attended the biological department of the University of Pennsylvania, and graduated from Hahnemann Medical College of Philadelphia April 19, 1893. Immediately afterward he located in West Chester, where he has since been engaged in the general practice of medicine.

Dr. S. A. Mullin was born in Downingtown in 1857, was educated in the public schools of that place, at Long's Academy of Downingtown, and graduated from Hahnemann Medical College of Philadelphia in 1880. Since then he has been engaged in the general practice of medicine in West Chester. He is a member of the Homeopathic Medical Society of Chester, Delaware and Montgomery Counties, and also of the Homeopathic Medical Council of Philadelphia.

Dr. Joseph E. Jones was born in West Chester in 1832, was educated at the University of Lewisburg, now the Bucknell University, and graduated from the University of Pennsylvania in 1856. Then, after spending a year as resident physician at the Alms House in Philadelphia, he entered Hahnemann Medical College of that city, and graduated therefrom in 1859. Since that time he has been engaged in the practice of his profession in West Chester.

Albert Weeks, M. D., read medicine with Dr. D. D. Richardson, then of Philadelphia, and graduated from the Jefferson Medical College of Philadelphia in 1880. Then becoming assistant physician in the insane department of the Philadelphia Hospital, he remained there until April 1, 1882, when he removed to Phœnixville, opened an office and has been engaged in the practice of his profession there ever since, with more than ordinary success, owing to his superior and knowledge and skill.

Percy C. Hoskins, M. D., was born in East Goshen Township, Chester County, December 17, 1852. Having been educated in West Chester Academy and the State Normal School at West Chester, he read medicine with his father, Dr. John R. Hoskins, who was engaged in practice first at Sugartown, and later at East Goshen, but who removed to West Chester in 1877, remaining there in practice until his death in 1884. Dr. Percy C. Hoskins completed his medical education at Jefferson Medical College of Philadelphia, graduating therefrom March 13, 1875, and immediately opened an office at East Goshen; but in 1883 he removed to West Chester, and has since been engaged in practice there.

Frank D. Emack, M. D., received his literary education at Columbia College at Washington, D. C., and graduated from the Medical Department of the University of Maryland in 1875. Almost immediately afterward he was appointed resident physician of the Bay View Asylum of Baltimore, resigning shortly afterward to locate in Schuylkill County, Pennsylvania. Removing to Phœnixville in 1881 he soon acquired a large and active practice. He is a member of the Chester County Medical Society and of the American Medical Society, and his standing among physicians is deservedly high.

G. D. Armstrong, M. D., one of the prominent physicians of Chester County, graduated from Jefferson Medical College in 1839, having previously read medicine with Dr. H. F. Askew of Wilmingtou, Delaware. He began practice at New London, Chester

County, at which place he has been ever since engaged in a large and successful practice.

Charles S. Horning, M. D., began the study of medicine in the office of Dr. Thomas L. Pratt of Norristown. After he entered the Hahnemann Medical College of Philadelphia, graduating from that institution in the spring of 1881. Beginning practice · at Phœnixville, he remained there until 1886, when he removed to Shannonville, Montgomery County, but still continuing his practice in Phœnixville.

James Rea Maxwell, M. D., began the study of medicine in the office of Dr. John B. Martin, at Bart, Lancaster County, and afterward entered Jefferson Medical College at Philadelphia, from which institution he graduated in 1888. He immediately located at Parkesburg, where he has since continued in practice, and where he is deservedly popular. He is a member of the Chester County Medical Society.

Charles E. Woodward, M. D., was born at Marshallton, Chester County, January 8, 1846. Having received a liberal education at the Westtown Boarding School, he attended the College of Pharmacy of Philadelphia, graduating therefrom in 1867. In 1872 he entered the Medical Department of the University of Pennsylvania, from which he graduated in 1874. Immediately he located in West Chester, where he has since been actively engaged in the practice of his profession, is now a member of the United States Pension Examining Board that meets at Malvern, the other members of the board being Dr. Swizer and Dr. I. K. Evans.

Dr. Sumner Stebbins, who died July 12, 1884, was one of the prominent men of Chester County. Born in 1809, his boyhood was passed in a manner common to boys of that day. After a careful schooling he entered upon the study of medicine, and as a physician ranked second to none in the county. For several years prior to his death he lived a retired life, but many of the older citizens yet remember his many acts of mercy and kindness. In all matters he was a man of advanced ideas, being no less prominent in public than in social life, the temperance cause finding in him a warm advocate, and his influence in this direction was widely felt.

During the fifties he removed to Iowa, and there read law, but never practiced that profession to any great extent. After a time he removed to Michigan, where he achieved considerable prominence as editor of the Marshall Statesman, and in 1860 he returned to Chester County, resuming the practice of medicine, his home being in Unionville. Dr. Stebbins was a man of rare attainments and left the impress of his character for good upon the people of the county and was highly respected by all with whom he came in contact. He married Mary Ann Pierce, by whom he four sons and one daughter.

Dr. Edward Penn Worrall, formerly one of the prominent dentists of Chester County, was born in Baltimore, Md., July 14, 1820, and died in West Chester on his birthday, 1880. After the death of his mother, when he was yet a lad, he went to live with his grandparents in Bucks County, Pennsylvania, and was educated at Westtown, Chester County. He studied dentistry in Philadelphia, and there practiced his profession, and was the first to administer ether in that city or in West Chester. In Philadelphia he married Miss Sarah Foster, a native of Baltimore, and located in West Chester in 1847, residing there until his death.

Dr. Worrall was a Christian in spirit and in deed, a great reader, an ever earnest student, and his writings for the press on religious and other subjects were widely read and as widely approved. For many years he prepared lessons for Sunday-schools. Accumulating considerable property, he believed that half what he earned should be bestowed to charity, and this idea he carried out to the end. He and his wife were the parents of five children, Thomas being the only one now living. Few better men have ever lived than Dr. Edward Penn Worrall.

Septimus Augustus Ogier, M. D., born in Charleston, South

Carolina, September 17, 1821, was the seventh child of Thomas and Sarah Ogier, of Huguenot extraction, the family being forced to flee from France during the reign of Charles IX. In 1840 he began reading medicine with his brother, Dr. Thomas Louis Ogier, in Charleston, and in 1842 he graduated from the State Medical College of South Carolina, at Charleston. In 1843 he entered Jefferson Medical College in Philadelphia, graduating from that institution in 1844. In 1846 he settled in Philadelphia and engaged in the business of an apothecary, but this business not being suited to his tastes he removed to Glenloch, then called "The Steamboat," and succeeded Dr. Stephen Harris in the practice of medicine in 1849. Dr. Ogier was one of those physicians who practice in part at least for the love of doing good, and was always at the post of duty, whether in the humble home of the poor or in the mansion of the rich. He soon became a member of the Chester County Medical Society, was its president one year, and on several occasions represented it in State and National Associations. In 1856 he was elected one of the secretaries of the Pennsylvania State Medical Society, and so remained until his death, which occurred in East Whiteland Township November 26, 1857.

Dr. William Brower, an eminent physician of Chester County, was born in East Coventry Township, February 25, 1842. Having received his academic education at Oakdale and Freeland Seminaries he entered the Millersburg State Normal School in 1862 and left there in 1863 as a member of the senior class. After reading medicine with Dr. A. R. Savidge of Parker Ford, he entered Jefferson Medical College, graduating therefrom March 9, 1867, and immediately afterward located at Spring City, Chester County, where he has since been actively and successfully engaged in the practice of his profession. He is an affable and agreeable gentleman, and is well versed in the principles of medicine, and is skillful in his practice.

Dr. Notman Catanach was born in Philadelphia in 1872, was educated at the Episcopal Academy in Philadelphia, and professionally at Jefferson Medical College, graduating from this latter institution in 1896. After a year's practice in Jefferson hospital he located in West Chester, where he is now engaged in general practice.

Dr. Wilhelmina T. Nelson, a native of Rhode Island, was educated first at Mount Holyoke Seminary, graduating from this institution in 1871, taught school ten years, and graduated from the Woman's Medical College of Pennsylvania at Philadelphia in 1891. Then locating in West Chester, she has been since engaged in the general practice of her profession.

Dr. Mary B. Cheyney was educated at the Woman's Medical College of Pennsylvania at Philadelphia, graduating with the class of 1885, and located in West Chester in 1886, where she has since been engaged in general practice.

Dr. H. U. Umstad of Phœnixville was born in Lower Providence Township in 1828. Having been educated at Norristown Seminary and at the Jefferson Medical College, graduating from the latter institution in 1851, he immediately began practice in the vicinity of Phœnixville, removing into the city of Phœnixville in 1887. Here he has been engaged in practice ever since.

Dr. George B. R. Umstad, son of the above, was educated at Ursinus College and at Jefferson Medical College, graduating from this institution in 1888. Since then he has been engaged in practice in Phœnixville and its vicinity.

Dr. I. Z. Coffman was at one time one of the most prominent physicians in Chester County. He began practice in Phœnixville more than fifty years ago. He was born in 1805, and at his death was eighty-seven years of age, and at this time was the oldest graduate of the University of Pennsylvania.

Dr. R. C. Sharp of Atglen was born in Weymouth, England, coming to the United States when six weeks old. He read medicine with Dr. J. D. Schoales, then graduated from the Philadelphia College of Pharmacy, and later from Jefferson Medical College in 1881. Locating immediately in Atglen, he has been there engaged in the practice of his profession ever since.

Dr. E. V. Swing of Coatesville was born in Pittsgrove, New Jersey, February 26, 1840. His education was received in the public schools and under a private tutor, and then, teaching four years and reading medicine meanwhile, he afterward attended the University of Pennsylvania, and graduated from that institution March 14, 1867. Locating in Compassville, he practiced there fifteen years, and removed to Coatesville in 1882, and has been there ever since. He is a member of the American Medical Society.

Dr. Ida V. Reel of Coatesville graduated from the Woman's Medical College of Philadelphia, and was afterward in Norristown as a physician in the State Asylum for the Insane for some time, locating in Coatesville in 1889, and has been there engaged in practice ever since.

Dr. S. H. Scott of Coatesville was born in Chester County in 1865. After reading medicine at Coatesville he attended Jefferson Medical College, graduating therefrom in 1889. Ever since then he has been engaged in practice in Coatesville.

Dr. D. P. Rettew of Coatesville graduated from the University of Pennsylvania in 1890, locating in Coatesville that year. After being relief surgeon for two years he returned to Coatesville in 1894, and has been there ever since.

Dr. J. W. Pratt, homeopathic surgeon, of Coatesville, was born in Chester County in 1850, was educated at the public schools of Coatesville, took a commercial course at Poughkeepsie, and graduated from the Hahnemann Medical College in 1873. After practicing in Downingtown from May 11, 1873, to August, 1876, he removed to Coatesville, and has been there ever since.

Dr. H. E. Williams, homeopathic physician, of Coatesville,

graduated from Hahnemann Medical College of Philadelphia in 1868, and has been in practice in Coatesville since that time.

Dr. George R. Spratt was born in Northumberland County, Pennsylvania, in 1839, graduated in 1864 from the University of Pennsylvania, and was second assistant surgeon of the Forty-ninth Pennsylvania Regiment during the rest of the war, being mustered out as surgeon. After practicing at Corry, Pennsylvania, for a couple of years, he removed to Chautauqua County, New York, and remained there in practice for six years. In 1873 he removed to Coatesville and has been there engaged in the practice of medicine ever since.

Dr. John Ivison was born in Philadelphia July 16, 1847, was educated in the public schools and the high schools of that city, and then, entering the University of Pennsylvania, he graduated from that institution in 1874. From that time until 1889 he practiced in Philadelphia, and then removing to Coatesville, he has been there ever since.

Dr. Edward Kerr of East Downingtown was born in East Bradford, Chester County, November 16, 1868. After receiving his literary education at the Normal School at West Chester he attended the University of Pennsylvania, from which he graduated in 1890. Ever since then he has been engaged in the practice of medicine in Downingtown.

Dr. James Stuart Leech of Downingtown was born in Harrisburg, December 11, 1812, graduated from Jefferson College at Canonsburg, Pennsylvania, in 1836, and from Jefferson Medical College at Philadelphia in 1841. Immediately afterward he located in Downingtown, where he has been ever since engaged in the practice of his profession, though in 1841, after establishing himself in the regular practice, he read homeopathy and has since practiced that system of medicine.

Isaac Massey, M. D., was one of the most successful and popular practitioners of Chester County. Born in West Goshen Township, he was to all intents and purposes a native of West Chester, which place was his home from the close of the war. He was a son of John and Jemima (Garrett) Massey, was born February 15, 1838, and was of English ancestry. His grandfather, Israel Massey, was a lifelong resident of Valley Forge, and owned the land upon which were located the headquarters of General Washington while at that celebrated camping ground with his Continental Army. John Massey, father of Dr. Isaac Massey, was born at Valley Forge in 1798, and died while a resident of West Chester in 1893, at the age of ninety-five. His wife, Jemima Garrett, was born in 1800, and died in 1883.

Dr. Isaac Massey was educated at Ercildoun and Norristown Academies. In 1859 he became professor of English and higher mathematics in the William F. Myers Academy, West Chester, holding this position five terms. In the meantime he read medicine preparatory to a regular course of study at Jefferson Medical College, from which institution he graduated in 1864. Then, becoming assistant surgeon in the army of the United States, he served in this capacity until the close of the war. Returning then to West Chester he opened an office, and there he ever afterward remained in the successful practice of his profession. He was a member of the Chester County Medical Society, of the College of Physicians and Surgeons in Philadelphia, and of the Pennsylvania State Medical Association. For the last ten years of his life he was physician to the Westtown Boarding School, and he was a member of the Board of Health of West Chester. For several years he served as physician and surgeon for the Pennsylvania Railroad Company and for the Philadelphia, Wilmington and Baltimore Railroad Company at West Chester, and from 1873 to 1890 he was a member of the West Chester Borough School Board, in that position having much to do with building up the excellent school system of which West Chester is justly proud. From 1881 to 1883 he was a member of the board of trustees of the State Normal School at West

Chester, and he was a director in the Dime Savings Bank from the beginning of its career. But the institution in which he took especial pride was the Boys' House of Refuge at Glen Mills. He was a member of General George A. McCall Post, No. 31, G. A. R., and also of the Union League, Philadelphia.

Belonging to that class of physicians who practice largely for the love of the profession and the good they can do, often with full knowledge that there is no possibility of pecuniary compensation for their labors, and being one of the most kind-hearted of men, he was highly regarded by all who knew him, and was devoutly loved by those who had intimate knowledge of his character and career. His death occurred suddenly of apoplexy while on a visit to a patient at the State Normal School, on January 31, 1898, which caused a great shock to the community and especially to his relatives and intimate friends.

Dr. Thomas D. Dunn, one of the most popular physicians of West Chester, died in that city as the result of an accident with which he met at Westtown about two months previously, May 6, 1898. He was born in Crawford County, Pennsylvania, January 30, 1855, and was of Scotch ancestry, his paternal great-grandfather coming to the country from Scotland and settling in New Jersey. His parents were Rev. Thomas H. Dunn, a Seventh-Day Baptist preacher, and Diantha M. Curtis, a daughter of Miles Curtis of New York.

Dr. Thomas D. Dunn entered the office of Dr. Jacob Price of West Chester, later entering the Medical Department of the University of Pennsylvania, from which he graduated in 1881. Immediately afterward he entered the University Hospital as resident physician, serving one year, and then spent six months at the Children's Hospital in Philadelphia. Then, settling in West Chester, he was continuously in practice there until his death. He shared the office of Dr. Jacob Price on South Church Street, the latter having every confidence in his judgment, and knowing him to be an excellent physician and surgeon, in which capacities he was for years in great demand. Dr. Dunn was frequently called upon to give expert testimony in the county courts, and in the courts of other counties of the State, and it was to him, perhaps, more than to any other man that the Chester County Hospital became an established success, and it was at this hospital that he died, and at the time of his death he was president of its medical staff. He was a member of the Philadelphia Pathological Society, the College of Physicians of Philadelphia and of the Pennsylvania State Medical Society, and during the first year of President Harrison's administration he was appointed one of the Board of Examiners of applicants for pensions, Dr. Woodward and Dr. Patrick of West Chester being the other two. During the four years of his service he gave excellent satisfaction.

Dr. Jacob Price, born in East Bradford, Chester County, in 1826, is a son of Benjamin and Jane (Paxson) Price, the former of whom was a son of Philip Price, founder of Price's Boarding School for Girls, at which school many a Chester County girl was educated. Dr. Price was educated in the Friends' School in West Chester, and at the academy of John Gummere in New Jersey, John Gummere being an eminent mathematician of the day in which he lived. Engaging next in a survey of New Castle County, Delaware, he made a map of that county, and later of the State of Delaware, by which means he earned the money to pay his expenses while pursuing the study of medicine. Entering Jefferson Medical College in the fall of 1848, he graduated from that institution in September, 1850, and then locating in West Chester he has ever since been engaged in the practice of both medicine and surgery. At first he purchased the house at the southwest corner of South Church and Miner Streets, which he occupied until 1863, and then purchased the property at No. 114 South Church Street, formerly owned by Dr. Wilmer Worthington. Here he resided and had his office until 1885, when he sold his residence to Dr.

Jesse C. Green

Dunn, now deceased, and removed to a farm in the south corner of the borough of West Chester, where he still resides, retaining his office at No. 114 South Church Street. Dr. Price is still actively engaged in the practice of his profession.

Since 1850 he has been a member of the Chester County Medical Society, and has been twice vice-president of the Medical Society of the State of Pennsylvania. He is also a member of the American Medical Association, and of the College of Physicians of Philadelphia. In 1851 Dr. Price married Rachel L. Thomas, daughter of Col. Philip D. Thomas, who at one time represented Chester County in the Legislature of the State.

Dr. Isaac A. Pennypacker, one of the early physicians of Chester County, was born in Schuylkill Township, July 9, 1812, and was a son of Matthias and Sarah (Anderson) Pennypacker, the latter being a daughter of Isaac Anderson. Isaac A. Pennypacker read medicine with his uncle, Isaac Anderson, and also with Prof. William E. Horner, and graduated from the Medical Department of the University of Pennsylvania, March 26, 1835. In 1836 he established himself in the practice of medicine in Phœnixville, continuing to follow the profession until 1854, when he became Professor of the Practice of Medicine in the Philadelphia College of Medicine.

In this professorship he displayed all the energy, manliness, integrity and sagacity which had previously distinguished him in his country practice, and as a professor as well as a man won the love and regard of his pupils to a high degree. In his manners he was mild and agreeable and in deportment affectionate and kind, and his wide and varied experience and reading of the best authorities fitted him admirably for the duties of life which he was called upon to perform.

Dr. Nathan A. Pennypacker of Schuylkill Township was born October 20, 1835. During the war of the Rebellion he was captain of Company K, Fourth Pennsylvania Reserves, and in 1865, 1866 and 1867 was elected to the Legislature of the State. In 1877 he was one of the commissioners to erect the State Hospital for the Insane at Norristown, and he also served as lieutenant-colonel on the staff of Governor Hoyt. His practice of medicine was carried on for many years successfully when not otherwise engaged.

The history of dentistry in Chester County is practically the same as in other counties in the State and in the cities throughout the country. Progress has been made sometimes slowly, and at other times sudden developments have come along to surprise and delight the profession and the public, by which the filling of teeth and the extraction of them when they could not be saved has been more successful and less painful. Among the very first dentists to visit the county was Dr. A. M. Freeman, or at least he was among the first to advertise in the local papers. This was in 1824. Dr. Freeman appears to have been located at Lancaster and to have visited West Chester, Wilmington, Delaware, and other places on his regular tours. There were two dentists in Philadelphia who advertised in the Chester County papers, one of whom was then recently from London, England, and who had a tooth powder that would almost instantly cure the toothache. The other cleaned teeth and blocked them. This dentist said in his advertisement that "if the teeth are not preserved by the above operations they will fall into a state of decay, unless the mouth is very large and the teeth grow irregularly." He also built up teeth on stumps. Dr. Freeman continued to visit Chester County as late as 1829.

It is believed that the first resident dentist in West Chester was Dr. Jesse W. Cook, who came to the place in 1835, and was a physician as well as a dentist. For some time subsequently he was president of the Young Ladies' Seminary, located where is now the Catholic School for Young Ladies. He left here about 1839, first going to Baltimore, and then became instrumental in founding the Ohio College of Dental Surgery, in 1842 or 1843, in Cincinnati, Ohio.

Dr. S. Sherburne Smith came to the county about 1838, and was a man of considerable note as an operator.

Dr. William Whitehead, who studied dentistry with Dr. Smith, began to practice in West Chester in 1840, and continued to follow his profession there many years. He was also prominent in many other ways, as in literature and in temperance work.

About the same time came Dr. Mahlon J. Gallagher, who was for that age a first-class dentist. He remained in West Chester until 1845. Besides dentistry he gave considerable attention to mechanics, and was somewhat of an inventor, inventing a self-priming hammer for the rifle and also a breech-loading rifle.

Dr. Jesse Cope Green was one of his pupils in 1842 and 1843. Dr. Green began the practice of dentistry in West Chester in August, 1843, and has ever since been continuously engaged there, besides being engaged in multifarious other lines of mental activity, believing that every man owes it to himself first to keep himself busy about something useful to mankind. He received his degree of D. D. S. from the Pennsylvania College of Dental Surgery in Philadelphia in the year 1865, and was elected a member of the Pennsylvania Association of Dental Surgeons in 1855. He took an active part in effecting the organization of the State Dental Society in 1868, was treasurer thereof in 1880 and president in 1883. He held a membership in the American Dental Association, which was organized in 1859, for many years, and was active in forming the first national convention of dentists in Philadelphia in 1855.

In 1876, upon the enactment of the law requiring the organization of a State Dental Examining Board, Dr. Green was made secretary, a position which he has filled ever since. While the limits of this sketch preclude mention of almost everything else connected with Dr. Green's career, yet it must be stated that since 1855 he has been a volunteer observer of meteorological phenomena for the Smithsonian Institution, and also for the Weather

Bureau at Washington since its establishment, and also for the State Weather Service since its establishment in 1887.

Dr. William Smedley graduated at the Pennsylvania College of Dental Surgery and located in West Chester about 1866. There he practiced six years, when he went to Denver for the benefit of his health and is living there at the present time.

Dr. Joseph Eldridge succeeded Dr. Smedley in 1872, purchasing his professional business, remained in practice in West Chester until 1882, when he sold out to Dr. Justin E. Harlan, son of State Senator Harlan, and who continued in practice in West Chester until 1897, when he went to China for the purpose of pursuing his profession there, returning, however, to West Chester early in 1898, and is there now engaged in successful practice.

Dr. John M. Surgison followed Dr. Price, practiced in West Chester some time and then removed to Marietta, Ohio.

Dr. J. Lewis Baker graduated from the Philadelphia Dental College in 1866, and soon afterward began the practice of dentistry in Coatesville, remaining there until 1881. Then going to Philadelphia he was there one year, and located in West Chester in 1882 . and remained in practice until his death in 1889.

Dr. Charles McCowan located in West Chester in 1882, having graduated from the Pennsylvania College of Dentistry in 1881. Remaining in West Chester three or four years he then removed to Richmond, Virginia, where he remained a short time, and then returning to Chester County located in Malvern, where he remained until the death of Dr. Baker, when he immediately returned to West Chester, where he has since enjoyed the confidence of the public, and has a successful practice.

Dr. Robert M. Scott graduated from the Dental Department of the University of Pennnsylvania in 1883, and located in West Chester in 1883, going there from Gettysburg. He succeeded to the practice of Dr. Baker and has been unusually successful.

Franklin Pierce Coburn graduated from the Pennsylvania

Dental College in 1885, beginning the practice of his profession in West Chester the same year. In West Chester he has continued to reside and practice dentistry ever since. In May, 1892, Dr. Coburn gave the first demonstration of local anæsthetics, by means of hypodermic injections, as applied to dentistry, in Chester County, and in 1892 and 1893 he successfully demonstrated before the University of Maryland the value of local anæesthetics in the painless extraction of teeth. In 1894 and 1895 he was honored with a judgeship in the gold medal contest given by the University of Maryland to the student performing the best work in operative dentistry, and has met with unusual success.

Dr. D. G. Snyder was born in Chester County in 1867, graduated at the West Chester State Normal School in 1890, and from the Philadelphia Dental College in 1895. Locating in West Chester this same year, he is still engaged in the practice of his profession in that place.

Dr. John Anderson commenced the practice of dentistry at Kennett Square about 1842, and was for years an unusually noted and successful practitioner, commencing life as a blacksmith, he later acquired knowledge of dentistry, which seemed to be better suited to his tastes, and he therefore followed this profession for many years with great success and popularity.

Dr. Robert L. McClellan, a member of the noted McClellan family of Chester County, began the study of dentistry in April, 1847, with Sharpless Clayton. After spending fifteen months in this way he became an assistant alternately with William H. Thompson of Coatesville and Robert W. McKissick of Cochranville until the death of Dr. McKissick in the early part of 1851, when he began the practice of dentistry for himself. After being for some time in practice he attended lectures in dentistry and in the Philadelphia School of Anatomy, graduating from the Dental College with the degree of D. D. S., and returning to Cochranville for the practice of his profession. Dr. McClellan was successful not only in his profession, but also in politics, being a member of the lower house of the State Legislature during the years 1862 and 1863.

Dr. George M. Yard came to West Chester from Philadelphia about 1843, was a fair dentist, and remained until 1849, when he went to California. For some time he was postmaster in West Chester.

Dr. Chalkley M. Valentine was another student of Dr. Gallagher, and located first in Coatesville in 1843. Removing to West Chester in 1847 he remained there until his death in 1883. He was a son-in-law of Joseph Painter.

Dr. Elwood Penn Worrall located in West Chester in 1847 and practiced dentistry until his death in 1878. He was a good and successful practitioner, and was in other ways a prominent citizen.

Dr. Isaiah Price graduated about 1853 from the Philadelphia College of Dental Surgery. He practiced in Chester County until the breaking out of the war of the Rebellion, when he raised a company for the Ninety-seventh Regiment, Pennsylvania Volunteers, became its major and was breveted colonel of United States volunteers. He was the husband of Lydia H. Price, a prominent minister among the Friends, and is now living in Philadelphia, but is not in the practice of his profession.

Dr. George G. Cardwell located in West Chester in 1860. He graduated from the Second Philadelphia College of Dental Surgery, and pursued a most successful career as dentist in Chester County until his death, May 1, 1898. He was Demonstrator of Dentistry duding the years 1895-96-97 in the Pennsylvania Dental College, and was well known and highly esteemed as a professional gentleman and citizen.

Dr. Meta T. Haley, the only lady dentist in Chester County, is a native of Virginia, and graduated from the Pennsylvania College of Dental Surgery in 1892. In April, 1893, she opened an office in the Assembly building in West Chester, and has been in active practice ever since. In 1897 she was quiz master in the Pennsylvania College in the Department of Operative Dentistry and Dental Physiology, and in 1898 she was Demonstrator of Operative Dentistry in the same college.

Dr. C. I. Reese was born in Atglen (then Penningtonville) September 17, 1849, was educated at the public schools of Atglen and professionally at the Pennsylvania College of Dental Surgery; graduating from the latter institution in 1874. He immediately located in Atglen, and has been there engaged in the practice of his profession ever since.

Dr. J. H. McClure of Coatesville was born in Chester County in 1860. He studied dentistry with Dr. J. L. Baker, and afterward attended the University of Pennsylvania, graduating with the class of 1881. Immediately locating in Coatesville, he has been there engaged in practice ever since.

Dr. Joseph Huggins, dentist of Downingtown, located there in 1897, immediately after graduating from the University of Pennsylvania.

Dr. David Z. Sahler, dentist, of West Chester, was born in West Whiteland, Chester County, was educated at the West Chester State Normal School, and at the Pennsylvania College of Dental Surgery, graduating from the latter institution in 1887. Locating immediately afterward in West Chester, he has since then been engaged there in the practice of his profession.

Dr. Wendell P. Lamborn, dentist, of West Chester, was born in Newlin Township, Chester County, December 24, 1862. Upon the home farm in that township he was reared, obtaining his education principally in the public schools. Then he attended Edgefield Academy in Chester County two years, and entered the dental office of Frank P. Coburn of West Chester, and graduated from the Pennsylvania Dental College of Philadelphia February 26, 1888. In January, 1891, he located in West Chester, and has there successfully followed the profession of dentist ever since.

Dr. F. Barnard, dentist, of Kennett Square, was born in Chester County, was educated in Chester and Lancaster Counties, and attended the Baltimore Dental College, and began practice in Kennett, in 1879. Since then he has been continuously engaged there in the practice of his profession.

Dr. E. L. Coffman, dentist, of Phœnixville, is a native of that city. He is a son of the late I. Z. Coffman, mention of whom is elsewhere made in this work. After learning the science and acquiring the art of dentistry he established himself in his profession in Phœnixville, and has been there successfully engaged therein ever since.

The Chester and Delaware County Dental Society was organized at the house of Dr. Jesse C. Green, October 27, 1894, Dr. S. Blair Luckie of Chester, Delaware County, being made president; Dr. James L. Paish of Avondale, Chester County, vice-president; Dr. Meta T. Haley, of West Chester, secretary, and Dr. Harry Leedom Smedley, of Media, treasurer. The society meets in January at Media, in April at Chester, and in October at West Chester. It has now twenty-five active members and three honorary members. The officers of this society at the present time are as follows: Dr. J. L. Paist, president; Dr. Ellen MacMurray, secretary, and Dr. H. L. Smedley of Media, treasurer.

George G. Groff, A. M., M. D., was born on the Welsh Tract, in Tredyffrin Township, Chester County, April 5, 1851. Until he reached his twenty-second year his home was on his father's farm, and he was educated at the public schools, at the Norristown Seminary and at the West Chester State Normal School, at Michigan University and the Long Island College Hospital, Brooklyn, New York. He taught in the public schools, in the West Chester State Normal School, and since 1880 has been professor of Organic Science in Bucknell University at Lewisburg, Pennsylvania. He takes an interest in public affairs, has been coroner of his county and assistant surgeon in the Pennsylvania State National Guard.

He has been a member of the State Board of Health since 1886, and of the State Board of Agriculture since 1889, and is now (1898) president of the State Board of Health. He is a member of the State Medical Council, and of the State Dental Council. He is author of a series of school physiologies and of numerous papers and pamphlets on hygiene and sanitary science.

The Chester County Homeopathic Medical Society was organized in West Chester, July 21, 1898, with the following officers: President, Dr. H. E. Williams, of Coatesville; Vice-president, Dr. Hamilton Graham, of Kennett Square; Secretary, Dr. Charles R. Palmer, of West Chester; Treasurer, Dr. S. A. Mullin, of West Chester, and Board of Censors, Drs. Hoopes, Taylor and Hughes. The new society meets bi-monthly.

CHAPTER XVII.

BANKING AND INSURANCE.

CHAPTER XVII.

The National Bank of Chester County has a history of unusual interest. At the session of the Legislature of 1812-13 a movement was made to establish twenty-five new banks in the State. The reason for this movement lay in the fact that the United States Bank in Philadelphia, the fate of which had been decided by the casting vote of Vice-President Clinton in the Senate of the United States, was about to wind up its affairs. The bill authorizing the establishment of these twenty-five new banks was passed by the House of Representatives of Pennsylvania by a vote of 43 to 42, and by the Senate by a vote of 14 to 13. Rev. John Gemmil, then the Senator from Chester County, and a Democrat, voted against the bill. On March 19, 1813, this bill was vetoed by the Governor. It did not provide for a bank in Chester County, no request having been made for one. The members of the lower house from Chester County, all Democrats, voted against the bill.

At the next session of the Assembly a bill was passed entitled "An Act Regulating Banks," authorizing the establishment of forty-one new banks, one of which was to be in Chester County, al- though, curiously enough, no one had asked for it, and the mem- bers from this county in the lower house, John Harris, John Reed, Edward Darlington, James Brooke and James Hindman, all Demo- crats, voted against the bill, which is all the more remarkable, as members of the Democratic Party have, throughout the entire his-

715

tory of the United States, been generally in favor of local as against national banks. On the 19th of the month (March, 1814), the Governor returned the bill with his objections; but it passed the Senate by a vote of 20 to 10 and the House by a vote of 66 to 24, and became a law on the 21st of the month.

The commissioners for taking the stock named in the act for the Bank of Chester County were Dr. William Darlington, John W. Cunningham, Jesse John, James Kelton, Joseph Taylor, Henry Chrisman, Matthew Stanley, and Joshua Evans, Jr. Henry Chrisman declining to serve, the Court of Common Pleas appointed Joseph Pearce to serve in his place. Books for subscription to the stock of the bank were opened June 8, 1814, at West Chester, Downingtown, Tredyffrin, New London, Cross Roads, and Cochranville, the commissioners distributing themselves among the several places named. A few persons promptly subscribed for as much of the stock as they could conveniently carry, but soon the subscriptions fell off, the people generally being somewhat shy of the proposed new institution. Up to near the time for subscriptions to close the indications were that the new institution would fail to have a career; but then Charles Rogers and Daniel Hiester came forward and each subscribed for 1,000 shares, which left but little of the stock to be taken, and that little was then quickly subscribed. The bill provided for a capital stock of 4,500 shares at $50 per share, and as soon as the subscription books were closed the stock was immediately in demand.

The charter was obtained August 2, 1814, and at a meeting of the stockholders held September 8, 1814, thirteen directors were chosen, as follows: Jesse Mercer, Jesse John, Joseph Taylor, Charles Rogers, Daniel Hiester, Joseph McClellan, James Keton, Dr. William Darlington, John W. Townsend, Jesse Good, Isaac Darlington, Joshua Weaver and James Jefferis. The next day Joseph McClellan was chosen president and Daniel Hiester, cashier. Mr. Hiester then resigned as director of the bank, and

Thomas Hoopes was appointed in his stead. Rooms over the county offices at the northwest corner of Market and High Streets were obtained, which were opened for business November 11, 1814. On November 21, 1814, the second board of directors was chosen as follows: Joseph McClellan, Jesse Mercer, Jesse John, Dr. William Darlington, Charles Rogers, David Dickey, Isaac Darlington, Jesse Good, Thomas Hoopes, Joseph Taylor, John W. Townsend, Thomas Worth and David Townsend.

At that time on account of the fact that West Chester was not widely known the directors thought it wise to state on the face of the circulating notes that the bank was "between Philadelphia and Lancaster," in order that holders might know where the bank was located. The following is the form of the note first issued:

THE BANK OF CHESTER COUNTY,
Between Philadelphia and Lancaster,

Promises to pay to bearer on demand
FIVE DOLLARS.
West Chester, Penna.

DANIEL HIESTER,
Cashier.

JOSEPH McCLELLAN,
President.

FIVE.

PENNSYLVANIA.

On January 6, 1818, it was resolved to erect a banking-house and a committee previously appointed to select a site for the proposed building was directed to offer William Townsend $500 for a lot forty feet front on Gay Street at the corner of Walnut, asking for a positive answer within a week. On January 20, 1818, it was resolved to purchase a lot thirty feet front on High Street for $500, and on the 23d the committee produced a deed for the lot therein described, but for some reason the project was not carried out. On March 17, 1818, it was ordered that the house and lot on High Street opposite the Court-house, belonging to Nathan H. Sharpless, be purchased for the use of the bank for $5,250, and the banking-house was fitted up at a cost of $1,426.19, and Joseph McClellan, president of the bank, was allowed $250 for his wages for the year then closing. The bank was re-chartered March 22, 1824, and during the next few years the business of the institution was exceptionally good. So rapid indeed did the business increase that it became necessary to erect a new building, which was done about 1836, the funds for its erection coming out of the profits of the bank, which would otherwise under the law have been turned over to the State, as a dividend of more than six per cent. could not be declared. This building is a large and substantial one, built of Chester County marble, and having a noble Doric portico in front, there being four large fluted columns, four feet in diameter at the base and tapering to three feet at the top, and being twenty-five in height. The architect of this building was Thomas U. Walter of Philadelphia, one of the most noted architects so far produced by the United States. The cost of the building was about $30,000. To this building the business of the bank was transferred in 1837.

On May 30, 1843, the capital stock of the bank, which had then increased to $360,000, was reduced to $225,000, and the par value of the shares became $25. This reduction was made by deducting from the capital stock the following loans: Union Canal Loans, $25,000; Chesapeake & Delaware Canal Loans, $25,000; Susquehanna & Tide-water Canal Loans, $35,000; Loans to individuals, $23,548.50; Loans to the State, $26,451.50; total, $135,000.

On October 11, 1864, when it was in contemplation to change to a National bank, Joel Hawley, Joseph Dowdall, and P. G. Carey, not holding sufficient stock to warrant them in retaining their positions as directors, resigned. And on October 14, 1864, a series of resolutions was adopted providing for the surrender of the State charter, which had been renewed in 1837 for fifteen years and in 1852 for the same length of time, and organizing under the National Banking Law of 1863. The name of the bank then became the National Bank of Chester County, and the capital stock of the bank was fixed at $225,000, with authority to increase it to any amount not to exceed $450,000. The number of this bank among the National banks is 552, the certificate of authorization bearing this number being signed by Hugh McCullough, October 25, 1864. On November 1, following, P. P. Sharpless, Joseph Dowdall, William Darlington and M. B. Hickman were appointed to fill vacancies in the board of directors occasioned by the resignations of others. The other members of the first board of directors of this as a National bank were as follows: John Marshall, Thomas S. Cox, Brinton Darlington, Walter Hibbard, Samuel H. Hoopes, Eusebius H. Townsend, Dr. Isaac Thomas, Dr. George Thomas and William B. Waddell.

Among the prominent men who were directors of the old Chester County Bank were the following: William Darlington, who was the last survivor of the original board at the time of his death, April 23, 1863; Isaac Darlington, Joshua Weaver, William Williamson, Isaac D. Barnard, W. H. Dillingham, Joseph Hemphill, Enoch Harlan and John Smith Futhey.

The other members of the board of directors since the organization of this as a National bank have been as follows: Lorenzo Beck, Henry P. Sharpless, Charles Fairlamb, Washington Townsend, Milton Conard, Robert Neely, Francis J. Darlington, H. T. Fairlamb, James Smith, M. Shaner Chrisman, William P. Marshall, J. Preston Thomas, Edwin James, William F. Dowdall, Joshua E. Hibbard, William B. Sharpless, Thomas W. Marshall, G. Morris Phillips, D. M. McFarland, Thomas S. Chambers and Thomas Hoopes, the last eleven of whom constitute the board at the present time, the number of directors having been reduced October 5, 1897, from thirteen to eleven.

In 1874 the interior of the bank was entirely remodeled and new vaults put in, all at a cost of $10,048.73. In 1889 safety deposit vaults were put in at a cost of $15,223.62, and in 1898 a new floor was laid, of iron joists and iron lining, in order to render the building entirely fire-proof.

42

The presidents of this bank since its organization have been as follows:

Joseph McClellan, September 9, 1814, to November 25, 1816, and from November 24, 1817, to November 22, 1819; James M. Gibbons, November 25, 1816, to November 24, 1817; Richard Thomas, Jr., November 22, 1819, until his death in February, 1830; Dr. William Darlington, February 23, 1830, until his death April 23, 1863; John Marshall, May 1, 1863, until his death June 22, 1873; Walter Hibbard, June 27, 1873, to his death July 31, 1879; Washington Townsend, August 5, 1879, to his death March 18, 1894, and William P. Marshall, March 27, 1894, to the present time.

The cashiers of the bank have been as follows:

Daniel Hiester, September 9, 1814, to October 1, 1817; David Townsend, October 1, 1817, to April 10, 1849; Washington Townsend, April 10, 1849, to October 30, 1857; William W. Jefferis, October 30, 1857, to June 12, 1883; Paul F. Whitehead, July 1, 1883, until his death, October 14, 1884, and I. Cary Carver from November 1, 1884, to the present time.

The present charter of this bank will expire October 12, 1904.

Methods of transacting banking business were in the early days quite different from those now in vogue. The directors of this bank, thirteeen in number, were selected in such manner as to give each part of the county a representation on the board, and these directors in coming from their homes to West Chester were entrusted with the money which their neighbors desired to deposit in the bank. When a depositor desired to use money in the transaction of his business it was customary for him to withdraw it in specie or paper and pay it out direct to his creditor. The great advantages of the check system had not then dawned upon the minds of the people, whereas now from ninety to ninety-five per cent of the transfers from debtor to creditor, including the payment of foreign bills, that is, debts in Philadelphia, New York and other distant places, are paid by the debtor sending his personal check on his own bank. The deposits of this bank have steadily in creased, they being in 1850 from $215,000 to $250,000; in 1860 from $175,000 to $247,000; in 1870 from $300,000 to $600,000; in 1890 from $430,000 to $645,000, and in 1898 from $750,000 to $950,000. Semi-annual dividends have been declared by this bank as follows: From 1850 to 1860, 5 to 6 per cent; 1860 to 1890, 6 to 8 per cent and from 1890 to 1898, from 6 to 7 per cent.

The First National Bank of West Chester had its origin in the following manner: On November 13, 1863, the following-named gentlemen met in the banking-house of Brinton & Wilson in West Chester, to consider the expediency of establishing a national bank in said borough, viz.: George Brinton, David Woelffer, Joseph Hemphill, William Wollerton, Wellington Hickman, John Smith Futhey, and William S. Kirk. The following resolution was adopted:

"Resolved, That we associate ourselves together for the purpose of carrying on the business of banking under the act of Congress entitled: "An Act to provide a National Currency secured by a pledge of United States stocks, and to provide for the circulation and redemption thereof," approved February 25, 1863."

The name adopted for this new financial institution was the First National Bank of West Chester, and the capital stock was fixed at $50,000, each share to be $100. Articles of association were entered into November 13, 1863, and on November 17, 1863, an election for directors was held, resulting in the election of the above named seven gentlemen. At the first annual election the same gentlemen were re-elected, and George Brinton was chosen president and William S. Kirk cashier. On November 17, 1863, Joseph Hemphill, William Wollerton and John Smith Futhey were appointed a committee to procure a building in which to carry on the business of banking, and on December 11 reported in favor of the house then owned by David Meconkey, which stood immediately north of the Bank of Chester County, which was leased for five years. December 16 the capital stock of the bank was increased to $100,000, and on January 2, 1864, the business of banking was regularly commenced. On January 9 the number of directors was increased to nine, and the following gentlemen were elected: George Brinton, William Chalfant, John Smith Futhey, Joseph Hemphill, Wellington Hickman, Andrew Mitchell, Robert Parke, David Woelffer and William Wollerton.

On May 24, 1864, it was resolved to erect a building for the use of the bank, and a lot was purchased of James D. McClellan, on which the present bank building stands, and the building was erected at a cost of $25,000. Into this building the bank moved March 15, 1865. On August 9, 1864, the capital of the bank was increased to $200,000.

The presidents of this bank have been as follows: George Brinton, from the organization as given above to January 15, 1869; William Wollerton, January 15, 1869, until his death, April 29, 1898; Alfred P. Reid elected president May 21, 1898.

The cashiers have been as follows: William S. Kirk, from the organization until April 16, 1867; James G. McCollin, April 16, 1867, to February 14, 1868; Thomas W. Marshall, February 14, 1868, to December 17, 1872; Enos E. Thatcher, December 17, 1872, to January, 1887; F. W. Wollerton, from January, 1887, to the present time.

In 1897 the interior of the building was remodeled and improved, safety deposit vaults being put in containing 300 private boxes, the capacity of the vaults being upward of 600, the entire cost being about $11,000. These private boxes rent for from $3 to $12 per year, making it one of the most convenient banking rooms in the county.

The First National Bank of Honeybrook was organized January 1, 1868, with the following directors: Joshua Kames, E. D. White, R. W. Morton, Thomas Millard, William Corbit, Joseph C. Davis, Samuel Lemmon, James C Roberts, and Thomas S. Ingram.

Joshua Kames was the first president and Richard D. Wells first cashier. The bank was opened for business at Honeybrook February 8, 1868, and on April 9, 1868, both the president and cashier resigned their positions. E. D. White then became president and R. W. Motton, cashier. January 11, 1877, Samuel Lemmon became president, serving until his death in February, 1892. Then he was succeeded by John S. Galt, who has served ever since.

Mr. Morton served as cashier until January, 1892, when he died and was succeeded by John E. Tinger, who has served ever since.

The capital of this bank was at first $100,000, at which it remains. The present directors are John S. Galt, Theodore M. Stoob, Jacob Hertzler, John A. Lemmon, Thomas Millard, William Martin, John Stauffer, Jacob Hartz.

E. D. Haines & Co., private bankers of West Chester, began business in 1868. The members of the firm at the beginning of and up to 1883, when Mr. Haines died, were E. D. Haines and J. T. Murtagh, their place of business being No. 19 North High Street.

Pyle & Brown (Abner Pyle and Thomas B. Brown), private bankers of West Chester, began business in February, 1871, each of them having been in business separately in West Chester for two years. They moved into their present building in 1872, Nos. 111 and 113 North High Street. The business is of the nature of general banking, loan, real estate and insurance.

D. M. McFarland, banker of Wester Chester, has been engaged in this business since 1868. It was established in 1820 by a Mr. Warren, who was succeeded therein by Thomas Williamson, and he was succeeded in 1834 by David Meconkey. The latter gentleman carried on the business until 1868, when Mr. McFarland took charge. The business includes in addition to banking, conveyancing, and the drawing up of legal papers of all kinds, and Mr. McFarland has acted as administrator for many estates. The office of the bank is on North High Street, opposite the Court-house.

The Downingtown Bank was organized as a State institution September 3, 1860, beginning business May 16, 1861, with a capital of $50,000, which in 1863 was increased to $100,000. It was changed to a National bank December 30, 1864, under the name of the Downingtown National Bank of Pennsylvania, with the following directors: William Edge, Jonathan C. Baldwin, Samuel Ringwalt, Peter Dampman, David Shelmire, Dr. John P. Edge, Leonard F. Roberts, William Rogers, Jacob Edge, Samuel P. Miller, and Jonathan P. Butler.

The presidents of this bank have been as follows: Charles Downing, November 23, 1860, until his death, May 3, 1863; David Shelmire, June 1, 1863, to November 3, 1863; William Trimble, November 23, 1863, to his death, December 18, 1863; William Edge, December 28, 1863, to May 29, 1865; Jacob Edge, May 29, 1865, to March 13, 1889; Joseph R. Downing, April 4, 1889, to the present time.

The cashiers have been: Mordecai T. Ruth, from the organization until December 1, 1863; Joseph R. Downing, December 1, 1863, until April 4, 1889; Thomas W. Downing, April 11, 1889, to the present time.

The Parkesburg National Bank. On April 14, 1869, Parke, Smith & Co., a private firm, established themselves in the banking business, with a capital of $50,000, and a board of directors consisting of Robert Parke, Robert Baldwin, Robert Fairlamb, John N. Chalfant, John A. Parke, and Ezekiel R. Young. Robert Parke was president, and Samuel R. Parke, cashier. The name of this private institution was the Parkesburg Bank. On April 22, 1873, Robert Parke resigned as president, Samel R. Parke becoming president, and Robert Agnew Futhey, cashier. On March 30, 1880, this institution became a National bank, under the name at the head of this article, with the same president and cashier, and the following directors: Samuel R. Parke, Robert Parke, Robert Fairlamb, John A. Morrison, M. D., John Y. Latta, and James B. Kennedy. At the present time the directors of this bank are as follows: John A. Morrison, John Y. Latta, James B. Kennedy, Robert Futhey, John A. Parke, and A. T. Parke, the officers being Samuel R. Parke, president, and M. F. Hamill, cashier.

The National Bank of Chester Valley, at Coatesville, was organized first as a State bank, May 1, 1857, with the following board of directors: Abraham Gibbons, Nathan Rambo, Enoch S. McCaughey, William Dripps, Henry G. Thomas, Caleb Pierce, Lewis Maxton, Hugh E. Steele, Isaac Hayes, Charles Downing, John W. Wagoner, Samuel Slokum and James King Grier. Abraham Gibbons was the president and Francis F. Davis cashier.

On November 17, 1864, it became a National bank, the same officers remaining in charge until 1882, when Mr. Gibbons resigned and was succeeded by William Mode. Cashier Davis died in 1883 and was succeeded by John W. Thompson. In 1893 Mr. Mode resigned the presidency and was succeeded by Mr. Thompson, H. J. Branson becoming cashier. The first directors of this bank when it changed to a National bank were the following: Abraham Gibbons, Samuel Slokom, James Penrose, Hugh W. Robinson, Alexander Moore, Jr., Joseph Davis, Levis Pennock, Jr., James King Grier and Dr. Charles Huston. The present board of directors is as follows: H. Preston Baker, William H. Gibbons, Lewis B. Henson, A. F. Huston, Alexander Mode, Jesse Shallcross, J. H. Schrack, Brinton Walker and J. W. Thompson.

In 1895 the building was enlarged and improved, and a large fire and burglar proof vault was put in, containing 210 small safes of various sizes, which are rented at a merely nominal cost.

The Octoraro Bank at Oxford was chartered by the State in 1857 and organized in July, 1858. The first board of directors of this bank was as follows: Samuel Dickey, John M. Kelton, John B. Harlan, Dr. D. W. Hutchinson, J. C. Taylor, G. W. Lefevre, A. F. Eves, David Hayes and Daniel Stubbs. Dr. E. V. Dickey, the first president, died soon after his election, and was succeeded by

Rev. Samuel Dickey, who remained president until his death, January 14, 1884, when he was succeeded by S. R. Dickey.

On February 19, 1865, the State charter was surrendered and the bank was opened as a National institution under the name of "The National Bank of Oxford," with the following directors: Samuel Dickey, John M. Kelton, J. C. Taylor, R. H. Kirk, A. F. Eves, Alexander Turner, D. W. Hutchison, Newton I. Nichols, P. W. Housekeeper, James R. Ramsey, James A. Strawbridge, William R. Bingham and Daniel Stubbs. The present directors are: S. R. Dickey, William R. Bingham, William T. Fulton, G. D. Armstrong, R. B. Patterson, Edgar F. Fulton, T. J. Foulk, J. M. C. Carhart and J. E. Ramsey. The capital of the bank, which at first was $100,000, is now $125,000, the surplus fund is $25,000 and the undivided profits $25,000, and the total amount of dividends paid since it became a National bank is $276,000.

Dr. James H. Cunningham was cashier of the Octoraro bank and of the National bank until May, 1866, when he was succeeded by John Janvier, who died in July, 1878, and was succeeded by by James E. Ramsey, who is still cashier.

The Farmers' National Bank of Oxford was established in 1868 as a private bank by Kirk, MacVeagh & Co. In 1870 it became a State bank under the name of the Oxford Banking Company, was incorporated March 11, 1872, and was chartered as a National bank in 1883. The president of the Oxford Banking Company was James Wood, president, and David M. Taylor, cashier. The officers at the present time are as follows: President, D. M. Taylor, and cashier, R. A. Walker. The board of directors is as follows: H. A. Menough, J. Dickey Smith, J. D. Nelson, Eber Heston, M. D., C. Blackburn, Amos K. Bradley, Levi B. Kirk, D. M. Taylor and Henry Cope. The capital stock is $75,000; deposits, $170,672.45; discounts, $205,460.32, and the surplus fund and undivided profits, $32,000.

J. A. Watt & Co., bankers at Oxford, began business here in

1873, and carry on a general banking business in all its branches. J. A. Watt is sole proprietor of the business and C. N. Lawrie is the cashier.

The Dime Savings Bank of Chester County, located in the Assembly Building, at West Chester, was incorporated April 22, 1890. The purposes of the bank are indicated by the act under which it was organized, which was approved May 20, 1889. It receives deposits from all classes in any amount, from ten cents to $5,000, and allows interest at the rate of three per cent. per annum on all deposits aggregating two dollars remaining on deposit three calendar months or more. The net earnings of the bank are also divided among the depositors. The officers of this bank at present are Alfred P. Reid, president; William P. Marshall, vice-president; Thomas E. Parke, second vice-president; Joseph S. Evans, secretary, and John A. Rupert, cashier.

The following statement shows the condition of this bank at the close of business May 14, 1898: Mortgages, $195,675; municipal bonds and premiums on same, $55,944.75, and money in bank and cash on hand $4,194.99. Total resources, $255,814.74; liabilities, to depositors, $250,344.89, and undivided profits, $5,469.85.

This bank has issued altogether 6,756 bank books, and at the present time there are 4,500 open accounts. The board of trustees of this bank are as follows:

R. T. Cornwell,	S. D. Ramsey,	Henry C. Baldwin,
L. J. Brower,	Wallace S. Harlan,	J. Frank E. Hause,
Davis W. Entriken,	Marshall H. Matlack,	Joseph S. Evans,
Lewis C. Moses,	Alfred P. Reid,	Geo. Morris Philips,
J. Preston Thomas,	Plummer E. Jefferis,	Addison Jones,
William P. Marshall,	Michael J. Murphy,	Elisha G. Cloud,
J. Comly Hall,	Thos. E. Parke, M. D.	Evan T. Pennock.

The National Bank of West Grove was organized in 1882, with a capital of $50,000. The officers have been as follows: President, Samuel K. Chambers; cashier, Walter W. Brown; vice-presidents,

Samuel C. Kent, 1882-94; Menander Wood, 1894-97; Robert L. Pyle, 1897 to the present time. The first board of directors was as follows: Samuel K. Chambers, Samuel C. Kent, Henry Cope, Charles Dingee, David Mercer, Robert L. Pyle, William H. Pyle, Mordecai V. Taylor and Menander Wood. The present board is as follows: Samuel K. Chambers, Henry Cope, Alfred P. Conard, Joel P. Conard, Alonzo B. Criswell, William B. Harvey, David Mercer, Robert L. Pyle and Emmor B. Wood.

The bank is located on Exchange Place, owns its building, and rents rooms to the postoffice authorities and to private parties. The capital remains as at first, the surplus is $22,000, deposits, $125,000, and with the exception of the first six months, a dividend of three per cent. has been declared semi-annually.

The National Bank of Avondale was established June 25, 1891, with the same officers as at present, except the vice-president, viz.: Samuel Wickersham, president; M. B. Kent, vice-president, and E. Pusey Passmore, cashier, then the youngest cashier in the State. The vice-president since 1894 has been W. J. Pusey. The first board of directors was as follows: S. Wickersham, S. John Pyle, W. J. Pusey, M. B. Kent, Edwin C. Cloud, Augustus Brosius, William Willard, Harry C. Taylor, I. Frank Chandler, W· F. Vernon and Z. Lamborn.

The present board is as follows: S. Wickersham, W. J. Pusey, S. John Pyle, Augustus Brosius, B. H. Chambers, Samuel Sharpless, William Willard, Thomas H. Marvel, M. G. Brosius, John T. Alexander, and Solomon J. Pusey.

The bank building, one of the most neat and elegant little buildings in the county, stands on Pennsylvania, No. 116. It is of Avondale limestone, and cost $13,000. There is in it a safety deposit vault of modern construction, which contains seventy-two boxes which rent from $2.50 to $6 per annum. The business was transferred to this new building, which is heated by a water heater, in October, 1896. The capital of this bank is as at first, $50,000, the surplus on May 5, 1898, was $15,000, the deposits then amounted to $127,000, and beginning in 1894, it has declared a dividend of two and a half per cent. semi-annually.

The Farmers' National Bank of West Chester was organized December 5, 1882, and was chartered January 11, 1883, with a capital of $100,000. It commenced business in a rented room in the building standing on the southwest corner of Market and High Streets, West Chester, but purchased the building January 1, 1897. Its presidents have been as follows: Samuel Butler, H. B. Buckwalter and A. P. Hall, and its cashier has been and is William Dowlin. The directors at the present time are J. M. Baker, A. P. Hall, R. F. Hoopes, Levi G. McCauley, Thomas W. Baldwin, Jesse Darlington, John E. Huey, H. P. Worth and Samuel R. Downing. The capital remains as at the beginning and the surplus is now $15,350.

The National Bank of Kennett Square was authorized to begin the business of banking by certificate dated May 16, 1881. The first board of directors was John Marshall, Thomas Marshall, George B. Sharpe, J. Mitchell Baker, Ellwood Michener, Thomas J. Webb, Ezra L. Baily and William Press. The first president was John Marshall, and the first cashier D. Duer Philips. On May 23, 1885, John Marshall died, and was succeeded by Edward B. Darlington, who is still president. The capital stock of the bank has been increased to $100,000, the deposits amount to from $210,-000 to $250,000, and the bank is in an unusually prosperous condition.

The National Bank of Coatesville was established March 9, 1889, and began business on the 25th of the same month with a capital of $100,000. On April 1, 1889, the erection of the present handsome brownstone structure occupied by this bank and the postoffice was begun, and by October 1 of the same year it was ready for occupancy. The first board of trustees of this bank was as follows: Samuel Greenwood, president, W. P. Worth, James B. Wright, J. S. Worth, J. W. Boyle, R. W. Schrack, Joseph

Beale, John Gilfillan, and O. A. Boyle. The cashier has been M. W. Pownall since the establishment of the institution.

The National Bank of Spring City was organized July 23, 1872, with directors as follows: Casper S. Francis, Charles Peters, Benjamin Prizer, Jacob Chrisman, John Stauffer, Benjamin Rambo, A. D. Hunsicker, John N. Miller, and Charles Tyson. The first president of this bank was Casper S. Francis, and the first cashier, John T. Eachus. The capital originally was $100,000, but in 1873 it was increased to $150,000. The second president of the bank was Daniel Latshaw, and the third and present one, A. P. Fritz. The second and present cashier was W. J. Wagoner. The directors of this bank at the present time are A. P. Fritz, Davis Knauer, Dr. W. Brower, Daniel B. Latshaw, Edward Brownback, Milton Latshaw, Franklin March and P. W. Brownback.

The Farmers' and Mechanics' National Bank of Phœnixville was incorporated February 5, 1872, with a capital of $50,000, which in 1874 was increased to $150,000. The first board of directors was composed of Elias Oberholtzer, Newton Evans, Matthias C. Pennypacker, Hyram H. Stover, Abraham Grater, Andrew Tyson, J. D. Wismer, and Jesse Gabel. The first president was Elias Oberholtzer, who died December 17, 1876. John Kennedy succeeded him and died September 4, 1877. Aaron H. Stover then became president and held the office until February, 1887; John Detwiler was president until 1889; J. Thomas F. Hunter until 1891, and the present president, I. J. Brower, was elected January 15, 1891.

The first cashier was J. Newton Evans, who was succeeded in the office July 1, 1875, by J. Theodore F. Hunter who held the office until 1887; George K. Roberts, until 1890; D. W. Brower, until 1892, and H. A. Jenks, the present cashier, was elected January 14, 1892. Harry W. Brower is now teller in the bank. This bank was re-organized in 1891, placed under new management and since then it has had a very successful career. The present board of directors is as follows: I. J. Brower, Mahlon Miller, Isaac Detwiler,

Hiram Buckwalter, J. G. Detwiler, E. L. Buckwalter, J. H. John-son, H. F. Ralston and Amos G. Gotwals.

The National Bank of Phœnixville. The first attempt to estab-lish a bank in Phœnixville was in 1852, when Messrs. Pennypacker, Sherwood, Kreamer, Bonner, Wheatley, Nicholas Bean and Joseph Whitaker organized themselves into such an institution; but the Legislature refused to grant a charter, and the attempt was aban-doned.

The next attempt was made in 1856, which resulted in the organization of the Bank of Phœnixville March 12, 1859, the first board of directors being Joseph J. Tustin, William M. Taylor, Nicholas Bean, Daniel Latshaw, Nathan T. MacVeagh, John Mor-gan, Levi B. Kaler, N. M. Ellis, Benjamin Prizer, William M. Stephens, Isaac Chrisman and Daniel Bucher. The first president was Samuel Buckwalter, and the first cashier, Jacob B. Morgan, who resigned in 1890, and was succeeded by Horace Lloyd, who has held the office ever since.

This bank on December 30, 1864, organized as the National Bank of Phœnixville, with the following directors: Samuel Buck-walter, John Morgan, Samuel Kreamer, Samuel Moses, Jacob B. Landis, Henry Fink, Casper S. Francis, Joel Fink, Levi Prizer, and C. B. Heebner. The first president of the bank, Samuel Buck-walter, held the position until his death, his successor, Henry Loucks, being elected March 18, 1869, and holding the office until January, 1890, and was succeeded by P. G. Carey who held the office until his death, in June, 1897, and then L. B. Kaler, the pres-ent official, succeeded him.

The capital of this bank was originally $100,000, but it was in-creased from time to time until it became $200,000. At first the business was conducted in a dwelling-house, but a commodious banking-house was afterward erected, which has all the modern appliances for convenience and safety. This bank has a surplus of $50,000, and for many years has paid its stockholders a semi-annual dividend of four per cent.

The Phœnix Mutual Fire Insurance Company was incorporated November 8, 1875, its first president being W. W. Waitneight and first secretary, George M. Bishop. The business of the company has always been conducted in a careful and conservative manner, and has in consequence been eminently successful. It has paid losses by fire aggregating $151,120, and has averaged only one assessment a year. The officers at the present time are as follows: George M. Bishop, president; P. Strode Brown, secretary, and G. C. Brownback, treasurer. The directors are as follows: George M. Bishop, Phœnixville; A. E. Eachus, Phœnixville; Daniel Rixstine, Phœnixville; L. R. Walters, Phœnixville; Abraham Detwiler, Phœnixville; H. Pratt, Coatesville; Gideon S. Moore, Milford Mills; John Rees, Aldham; Daniel Schlipp, St. Peters; John White, Honeybrook; John T. Comly Jenkintown; E. Krauser, Norristown; L. P. G. Fegley, Boyertown, Pa.

The Phœnix Mutual Storm Insurance Company of Phœnixville was chartered July 30, 1886, for the purpose of insuring property against losses by wind, hail and lightning; and also crops in the field, glass in houses and hothouses against loss by hail. Many people are protecting their property against losses of this nature by insuring in this company. Its officers and directors are as follows: Hon. D. F. Moore, president; P. Strode Brown secretary, and Abraham Detwiler, treasurer. The directors are: Hon. D. F. Moore, Phœnixville; Daniel Rixstine, Phœnixville; Abraham Detwiler, Phœnixville; P. Strode Brown, Phœnixville; Harry Pratt, Coatesville; Jacob Emery, Chester Springs; John White, East Earl; L. P. G. Fegley, Boyertown; Joseph Kelso, Douglassville; Henry Wamsher, Monocacy; Daniel Schlipp, Smedley; John Comly, Jenkintown; Jonathan Rees, Aldham.

The Penn Mutual Fire Insurance Company of Chester County was incorporated August 14, 1867, and its first policy was issued January 1, 1868. The first board of directors was as follows: William P. Townsend, William Darlington, Washington Townsend,

Elijah F. Pennypacker, Isaac Hayes, William Windle, Levi H. Crouse, John D. Worth, R. Haines Passmore, Jonathan Roberts, Pennock E. Marshall, and George C. M. Eicholtz. The first officers were William P. Townsend, president; Elijah F. Pennypacker, vice-president; and Enoch Harlan, secretary and treasurer. The succeeding presidents have been as follows: William Windle, January, 1870, to January, 1877; J. Smith Futhey, until February, 1879; Elijah F. Pennypacker, until 1887; Edwin James, until 1892; and Alfred P. Reid, from 1892 until the present time.

Enoch Harlan remained secretary and treasurer until his death in the summer of 1872, when he was succeeded by his son, Thomas W. Harlan, who resigned in July, 1873. He was succeeded by George M. Rupert, who held the office until 1884, and was then succeeded by Barclay Lear, the present secretary, the two offices being separated in 1884, William P. Sharpless becoming treasurer and serving until 1891, when Plummer E. Jefferis was elected and still holds the position.

The Mutual Fire Insurance Company of Chester County, located in Coatesville, was incorporated April 21, 1840, and was organized on May 16 following, at the public house of Hayes Clark in Doe Run village. Joseph M. Thompson was elected its first president; Amos Fredd, treasurer, and Enoch Harlan, secretary. On October 5, 1840, business was commenced with fire risks to the amount of $100,000, but the company was without a permanent office until 1860, the directors in the meantime meeting in various places throughout the county. During the summer of 1860 a building was erected in Coatesville, at which place the business of the company has since been conducted. This building was used until 1896, when the present commodious structure was erected.

Commencing with policies to the amount of $100,000 the company had policies out January 1, 1898, to the amount of $31,070,211, and the total amount of losses paid by the company up to the same date was $1,655,640.14, while the amount received for assessments was \$1,800,559.87. No extra assessment has ever been made.

The Storm Department of the company was organized in 1890, and on December, 1896, it had in force insurance to the amount of \$1,708,542.

The following officers have served the company since its organization:

PRESIDENTS.

Jos. M. Thompson,	from	1840	to	1844
Morris Cope,	"	1844	"	1848
Solomon Lukens,		1848	"	1850
Moses Whitson,		1850	"	1853
Charles Downing,	"	1853	"	1863

Smedley Darlington to fill unexpired term of Chas. Downing, dec'd.

Enoch Harlan,			to April,	1864
Jacob Edge,	from April, 1864	to	1868
Wm. W. Eachus,	" "	1868	"	1869
Archimides Robb,	" "	1869	"	1876
Levis Pennock, Jr.,	" "	1876	"	1880
Abraham Gibbons,	" "	1880	"	1894
John P. Edge,	" "	1894	"	date.

SECRETARIES.

Enoch Harlan,	from	1840	to	1863
Caleb H. Bradley,	"	1863	"	1880
Isaac Spackman		1880	"	1895
Brinton Cooper, Ass't,		1880	"	1895
B. P. Cooper, Sec'y,		1895	"	date.
Thos. Speckman, Ass't Sec'y,		1895	"	date

TREASURERS.

Amos Fredd,	from	1840	to	1841
Morris Cope,	"	1841	"	1844

Jos. M. Thompson,		1844 "	1854
Henry G. Thomas,		1854 "	1867
John A. Reynolds,		1867 "	1874
Dr. Charles Huston,		1874 "	1881
Levis Pennock, Jr.,		1881 "	1887
Alexander Mode,		1887 "	1894
Wm. H. Ridgway,	'	1894 "	date.

John M. Lindsay, of Bryn Mawr, appointed a receiver in 1857, and surveyor in 1862, still holds both positions, having served for a longer term than any other of the present officers.

Moses Rambo was elected manager in 1869, and still holds the office.

43

CHAPTER XVIII.

RELIGION.

CHAPTER XVIII.

IN writing the history of religion in Chester County it is not
deemed necessary to go further back into the history of the Province of Pennsylvania than about the time when William Penn
landed upon the Delaware, in 1682. Then there were churches at
Christina, New Castle, Wicaco and Tinicum. The church at Christina was built soon after the arrival of Minuit, the date of which
has already been given. Rev. Reorus Torkillus was the first minister to begin the performance of his duties, probably in 1640. A
handsome frame church building was erected on Tinicum Island
by Governor Printz, which was dedicated in September, 1646. The
first pastor here was the Rev. John Campanius. In what is now
Southwark, Philadelphia, there stood in 1682 a small block-house,
which appears to have been first used for religious purposes in
1677, the first sermon therein having been delivered on Trinity
Sunday, that year. In 1667 the people of Christina and New Castle
united in the building of a church at Cranehook, half way between
the two places. During or shortly after the close of the administration of Governor Printz, Rev. Lars Carlsson Loock, Rev. Israel
Holgh, and perhaps a few others, came from Sweden. Dominie
Loock had charge of two congregations, that at Christina and that
at Tinicum. Rev. Petrus Laurentii Hjort and Rev. Mathias Nico-
lai Nertimius came over with Governor Risingh in 1654, but left
with him the next year. Rev. Evardus Welius, a Dutch minister,

in 1657 came to New Castle and relieved Pietersen of his pastoral duties. Pietersen remained thereafter simply "fore-singer, zieken-trooster, and deacon."

For some years the necessity for religious instruction was greatly felt as those who had come over from Europe, as mentioned above, grew old and sick, unable to perform their usual duties, and for some time there was not one active Swedish clergyman in the province, none but lay readers. At Tinicum Church Anders Bengtson, an old man, sat and read postils, and at Christina, Charles Springer, a Swede who had been a slave in Virginia, read to the congregation. But at length under Charles XL, King of Sweden, missionaries and books were supplied at the expense of the government, and afterward, between 1696 and 1786, not less than twenty-four ministers were sent out by Sweden to the settlers on the Delaware.

Rev. John Campanius was pastor at Tinicum from 1642 to 1648, spent much time in missionary work among the Delaware Indians, and according to his own account converted many of them to Christianity. He studied Indian languages, and framed a vocabulary of the Delaware language, into which he translated for the benefit of that nation Luther's Shorter Catechism.

Dr. Smith in his History of Delaware County says: "This year" (1668) "a Swedish church was erected at Crane Hook, at which Mr. Loock officiated, as well as at the church at Tinicum." This has reference to the church built, as stated above, in 1667. On April 13, 1671, according to the same authority, a pass was granted "to the Magister Jacobus Fabritius, pastor of the Lutheran confession," to go to New Castle. Mr. Fabritius became the first pastor at Wicaco.

In 1675 Rev. William Edmundson, a minister of the Society of Friends, traveled through this new country and found Robert Wade settled at Upland, and at Mr. Wade's house, a few other Friends having been collected, Mr. Edmundson held a meeting, after which they went in a boat to Salem, where they met with John Fenwick and a few Friends, who that year had come from England with John Fenwick. These names are especially noteworthy, for Robert Wade and John Fenwick, who, together with other Friends who in 1675 came from England, were the first members of the Society of Friends that settled within the limits of ancient Chester County, or even within the limits of the Commonwealth of Pennsylvania, and this meeting at Robert Wade's house was the first meeting of Friends within the county or commonwealth. And, of course, the Rev. William Edmundson was the first minister of that Society to hold a meeting within the county. Robert Wade was a purchaser of land from John Fenwick. While there were doubtless several other meetings within the county earlier than 1681, yet there is no record of any such meeting in Pennsylvania before that year, the first minute being as follows:

"The 10th day of the 11th month, 1681. A monthly meeting of Friends belonging to Marcus-hook, alias Chester and Upland, held at the house of Robert Wade."

Meetings were held alternately at the places above mentioned and were but one monthly meeting; but later the meeting at Robert Wade's became Chester Monthly Meeting, and that at Marcus Hook, though at first calld the Chichester Monthly Meeting, became at length merged in the Concord Meeting.

According to Dr. Smith the only Friends or Quakers who were heads of families settled at Chester and Marcus Hook, at the time of the arrival of the first vessel sent out by William Penn, were as follows: Robert Wade, Roger Pedrick, Morgan Drewet, William Woodmanson, Michael Izzard, Thomas Revel, Henry Hastings, William Oxley, James Browne, Henry Reynolds and Thomas Nossiter.

But it would be scarcely proper to pass over the Rev. William Edmundson without further mention. He is spoken of as an "eminent minister of the Friends," and in 1675-77 made a missionary

tour along the Atlantic coast from Rhode Island to the Caro-
linas, stopping on the way at several places, holding meetings
with the Friends and taking part in several controversies upon
religious doctrines with ministers and others of other denominations, according as he was moved "by the Spirit of the Lord."

Inasmuch as the central idea, thought or principle of the
religion of the Friends has had a most powerful effect upon the
civilization of Pennsylvania, and other colonies and later States,
and so upon the entire country, in its educational, religious and
civil history, it is not only proper but actually necessary to present
in as clear light as possible that central thought or doctrine in this
connection. And it will doubtless be more entertainingly and in-
structively presented in the language of this eminent minister of
the Friends as he was holding an argument with a certain minister
of another religious society.

After describing his expulsion from a "Worship-House" and
his removal under guard to the "Guard Firelocks upon the Hill,"
in New Hertford, Connecticut, he says:

"So that the officer who had me in charge first complained of
the sharpness of the weather, and askt me, How I could endure the
Cold? For he was very cold. I told him It was the Entertain-
ment, that their great Professors of Religion in New England, afforded a stranger, and yet professed the Scriptures to be their
rule, which commanded to entertain strangers, and besides they
had drawn my blood, &c. * * * Then he took me to an Inn,
and presently the room was filled with Professors, much discourse
we had, and the Lord strengthened me, and by his Spirit brought
many passages of Scripture to my Remembrance; so that Truth's
Testimony was over them. As one company went away, another
came.

"When they were foiled a Preacher amongst the Baptists took
up the argument against Truth, charging Friends with holding a
great error, (which was) That every Man had a Measure of the

Spirit of Christ, and would know if I held the same Error? I told him, that was no Error, for the Scriptures witnessed to it plenti-fully: he said, he denied that the World had received a Measure of the Spirit, but Believers had received it. I told him, that the Apostle said, a Manifestation of the Spirit was given to every one, to profit with all; he said, that was meant to every one of the Be-lievers. I told him, Christ had enlightened every one that came into the World, with the Light of his Spirit; he said, that was every one of the Believers that came into the World: and as I brought him Scriptures, he still applied them to the Believers, saying, there was the Ground of our Error, in applying that to every Man, which properly belonged to Believers. Then the Lord by his good Spirit brought to my mind the Promise of our Saviour, (when he told his Disciples of his going away,) that he would send the Comforter, the Spirit of Truth, that should con-vince the World of Sin, and should guide his Disciples into all Truth; thus the same Spirit of Truth, that leads Believers into all Truth, convinces the World of Sin. So thou must grant, that all have received it, or else show from the Scriptures a SELECT Number of Believers, and besides them a WORLD of Believers, that hath the Spirit, also another WORLD of Unbelievers, that hath no Measure of the Spirit to convince them of Sin.

"Here the Lord's Testimony came over him, so that he was stopped, and many sober Professors, who staid to see the end, acquiesced therewith, and said, indeed Mr. Rogers, the Man is in the right; for you must find a SELECT Number of Believers, be-sides a WORLD that hath a Measure of the Spirit, that convinces them of Sin, and a WORLD that hath not the Spirit, so not con-vinced of Sin. This thou must do or grant the argument.

"He was silent and the people generally satisfied in that mat-ter, their Understandings being opened: so they took their Leave of me very lovingly, it being late in the Night."*

---

* The passage of Scripture on which the Friends rely to sustain this doctrine of the Light of the Spirit, or the Inner Light, is as follows: "That was the true light that lighteth every man that cometh into the world." John 1, 9.

This doctrine of the Inner Light is still entertained by and is still the fundamental doctrine of the Friends. In an address delivered in West Chester, February 1, 1898, John J. Cornell of Baltimore, a leading Friend, said that he had heard the silent monitor within address him on the "First day morning last, the command being 'Go to West Chester on Second day.'" And as he made it a rule to obey this voice he had come, and the passage of Scripture suggesting itself to him was "What shall I do to be saved?" In answer to this question he said that obedience to the inner voice to the highest expression of what is right, is that which will bring salvation. He said that a man needs not so much a pardon at the close of life for errors committed while he lived as he does guardianship during life that will keep him from error. To keep him from error is the mission of the inner light, and if a man be preserved from sin in the present life he will have no sin to atone for at the end of life. This is the substance of Mr. Cornell's remarks on the Inner Light. William Penn's idea as to religious liberty is clearly expressed in the following paragraph from his "Frame of Government":

"That all persons living in this Province, who confess and acknowledge the one almighty and eternal God to be the creator, upholder and ruler of the world, and that hold themselves obliged in conscience to live peaceably and justly in civil society, shall in no ways be molested or prejudiced for their religious persuasion or practice in matters of faith and worship, nor shall they he compelled at any time to frequent or maintain any religious worship, place or ministry whatever."

While this for the times in which it was promulgated was very broad and liberal, much more so than were the laws laid down for the government of religious matters in most of the other colonies, yet it is, as will be noticed, not without qualification. And it was the doctrine of the Friends regarding religious liberty and peace on earth and good-will toward men that drew so large a number of people from oppression in Europe, who entertained such a great variety of opinion on religious matters, to this province, and this great variety of opinion would have made religious toleration a necessity, even had there been any disposition on the part of the government or of any one denomination to interfere. The Friends, however, remained in the majority as to numbers up to the time of the Revolutionary War, yet there were many representatives of the German sects, as Mennonites, Dunkers, Amish, etc., and also Episcopalians, Lutherans, Presbyterians, Baptists, Catholics, etc.

It is with these various denominations that this history has now to treat. Among the Friends meetings were at first held in private houses; but at length, as soon as their numbers had sufficiently increased, they erected small, plain buildings, usually of logs, which plain buildings were used for religious or educational purposes, or both. Among the oldest of these buildings in what was once Chester County, but which is now Delaware County, were those at Springfield, Providence, Middletown, Radnor and Newtown, and the oldest in what is now Chester County were at Goshen, Uwchlan, Caln, Kennett, Birmingham, Nottingham, West Nottingham, New Garden, London Grove, Bradford and Valley.

"Meetings" among the Friends are of several kinds. The Preparative Meetings consist of one or more meetings for worship. The Monthly Meetings consist of one or more Preparative Meetings. The Quarterly Meetings consist of one or more Monthly Meetings. The Yearly Meetings consist of several Quarterly Meetings. The Monthly Meetings are the principal executive branch of the Society.

As nearly all of the Meetings within the limits of Chester County belong to the Philadelphia Yearly Meeting, the date of the organization of that meeting is here given, 1681. The Meetings in both Delaware and Chester Counties which belong to this Yearly

Meeting, are here presented, those in Delaware County having been in Chester County when established.

Philadelphia Quarterly Meeting, 1682; Haverford Monthly Meeting, 1684; Haverford Meeting, 1683; Radnor, 1686; Valley 1714.

Chester (Concord) Quarterly meeting, 1683; Chester Monthly Meeting, 1681; Chester Meeting, 1675; Springfield, 1686; Providence, 1696; Middletown, 1686.

'Darby Monthly Meeting, 1684; Darby Meeting, 1683 (?).

Concord Monthly Meeting, 1684; Chichester Meeting, 1683; Concord, 1685.

The dates of the organization of the several Meetings in the present Chester County are as follows:

Goshen Monthly Meeting, 1722; Goshen Meeting, 1702; Newtown (Delaware County), 1696; Willistown, 1784; Whiteland, 1816; Malvern, 1880.

Birmingham Monthly Meeting, 1815; Birmingham Meeting, 1690; West Chester, 1810.

Wester Quarterly Meeting, 1758; Newark (Kennett) Monthly Meeting, 1686; New Castle (Delaware) Meeting, 1684; Newark, 1686; Kennett, 1707; Wilmington, 1737; Marlborough, 1801; Kennett Square, 1812; Unionville, 1845 (Hicksite).

New Garden Monthly Meeting, 1718; New Garden Meeting, 1712; West Grove, 1787; London Britain, 1834; Mill Creek, 1838.

London Grove Monthly Meeting, 1792; London Grove Meeting, 1714; Fallowfield, 1792.

Fallowfield Monthly Meeting, 1811; Fallowfield Meeting, 1792; Doe Run, 1805.

Penn's Grove Monthly Meeting, 1842; Penn's Grove Meeting, 1820; Oxford Meeting, 1879; Homeville, 1839.

Centre Monthly Meeting, 1808; Centre Meeting, 1687; Hockessin, 1730.

Caln Quarterly Meeting, 1800; Bradford Monthly Meeting,

1737; Bradford Meeting, 1719; Caln, 1716; West Caln, 1756; Romansville, 1846.

Sadsbury Monthly Meeting, 1738; Sadsbury Meeting, 1723; East Sadsbury, 1810; Lampeter, 1732.

Uwchlan Monthly Meeting, 1763; Uwchlan Meeting, 1712; Nantmeal, 1739; Pikeland, 1758; Downingtown, 1784.

Baltimore Yearly Meeting includes the following meetings in Chester County: Nottingham Quarterly Meeting, 1819; Nottingham Monthly Meeting, 1730; East Nottingham Meeting, 1705; West Nottingham, 1719; Elk, 1825.

From the time of the first recorded meeting at the house of Robert Wade, already mentioned, meetings continued to be held there from time to time for some years. One was held on the 9th day of the 3d month, 1682, and another on the 3d day of the 6th month, 1682. At the first Quarterly Meeting held at Chester, 12th month, 4, 1683-4, it was ordered that the Chester Monthly Meeting be held on the first second day of every month, the time being changed in 1695 to one week earlier. The meeting having been held for some time at the house of Robert Wade, was in the 12th month, 1686, changed to the house of Walter Fosett, from that time on until 1700 being held at various places, private houses, and in this latter year it became settled at Providence.

In 1721 the number of meetings had increased to seven, viz.: Chester, Springfield, Providence, Middletown, Goshen, Newtown and Uwchlan, these meeting together for the last time, 12th month, 26, 1721, afterward Goshen, Newtown and Uwchlan holding a separate monthly meeting.

Newark Monthly Meeting was first held in 1686, and has been known as Kennett Monthly Meeting since 1760. The preliminary steps for holding this meeting were taken in 1685, but the meetings for a year or so were very irregular. It was held for the last time at Newark in 1707, and then for some time in Center Meeting-house. At length it settled at Kennett, when it dropped the old name, Newark.

Center Meeting met for some time at the house of George Harlan, who in 1689 lived probably in New Castle County, Delaware, but later he lived in what is now Pennsbury, Chester County. In 1702 the Friends belonging to this meeting were accustomed to meet at Newark, at Valentine Hollingsworth's house, one First day, and on the other side of the Brandywine on the other First day. In 1708 a meeting-house was directed to be erected; in 1710 Alphonsus Kirk was allowed 7s 6d per acre for such an amount of land as the meeting-house might need, not to exceed six acres, and in 1711 Mr. Kirk, George Harlan, Thomas Hollingsworth and Samuel Graves were appointed a committee to take the oversight of the erection of a meeting-house.

Birmingham meeting was held at the house of William Brinton for the first time 29th, 9th month, 1690, and in 1704 a meeting began to be held at the house of John Bennett. In 1718 permission was granted to the Friends of Birmingham to build a meeting-house, the place selected being upon Richard Webb's land near the "Great Road." Trustees were appointed and to them one acre of ground was conveyed by Elizabeth Webb for £3, and on this land the meeting-house was erected in 1722. This meeting-house is said to have been built of cedar logs. The western end of the present meeting-house was erected in 1763, and was used as a hospital during the Revolutionary War.

In 1701 some of the Friends dwelling at Goshen applied for permission to erect a meeting-house, applying again in 1702, their meetings being then held on every other First day at the house of Griffith Owen. In 1703 their meeting-house was built, and meetings were held therein every First day of the week, with the exception of the last First day in the 1st, 4th, 7th and 10th months, when they were held at the house of David Jones at Whiteland, in the Great Valley. These latter meetings in 1704 were transferred to the house of Robert Williams, and still later to the house of James Thomas. In 1707 they contemplated the erection of a meeting-house, which was later built, and was ready for occupancy in 1709. David Jones lived in what is now East Whiteland. In 1736 a new meeting-house was erected, which stood until about 1875, when it was superseded by the present meeting-house.

East Nottingham meeting, after being held in private houses for some years, began to be held in the new meeting-house in 1709. This meeting-house was replaced by one of brick in 1724, which was afterward partly destroyed by fire. A stone addition was made to what remained, and the entire structure was destroyed by fire in 1810. In 1811 the present building was erected, which, though one-half stone, is usually referred to as the "Brick Meeting-house." The land upon which it stands was granted by William Penn, but when the boundary line was finally located, the meeting fell into Maryland.

Kennett Meeting-house was erected in 1710, was enlarged in 1719, and again in 1731.

New Garden Meeting-house was erected in 1714 or 1715. In the latter year a preparative meeting was held therein, and in 1743 the south end of the present church was built, and the north end in 1790.

Uwchland Meeting was held for some time in the house of John Cadwallader, who allotted a piece of land for a burying-place and a meeting-house on the side of the King's Road. The building that stands there at present was erected in 1736, but was remodeled about 1875. The house erected in 1736 was used as a hospital during the Revolutionary War.

Valley Meeting was held for a time at the house of Lewis Walker, and in 1731 a meeting-house was erected at the graveyard near his house.

London Grove Meeting was held in 1714 at the house of John Smith in Marlborough. In 1724 the Friends here were granted permission to build a meeting-house where the corner of London

Grove Township joins Marlborough Township. The house erected in accordance with this permission was superseded by a larger one in 1743, which in turn gave way to the present one in 1818. A short distance to the southward the Orthodox Friends have erected their meeting-house.

Caln Meeting was first held in 1716, with Thomas Pierson and William Cloud as overseers, permission being given the same year to build a meeting-house. In 1720 this meeting proposed four Friends as trustees of their house and grounds, viz.: Thomas Parks, Aaron Mendenhall, Thomas Eldrech and Edward Tomson. In 1801 this house was enlarged to accommodate the new Quarterly Caln Meeting.

Bradford Meeting, composed of Friends in the forks of the Brandywine, was granted permission to assemble for worship in 1719, and in 1726 were allowed to hold a preparative meeting, their first meeting-house being on or near the corner of land owned by Abraham Marshall. The present site was purchased 10th month, 10th day, 1729, upon which site they erected a house which stood until 1765, in which year the present structure was erected. In 1788 the roof of this structure took fire and most of the building was burned, but by throwing snow in at the doors and windows the floor was saved. The building was soon afterward repaired by William Woodward at a cost of £115.

West Nottingham Meeting was first held in 1719 at the house of James King, and continued to be held there until 1726. Then permission was granted to erect a meeting-house, which was ready for occupancy in 1729. In 1730 this meeting was made a preparative one. The present church, which stands on the Maryland side of the line, was erected in 1811.

Goshen Monthly Meeting was set off from Chester Monthly Meeting in 1722, including at the time the meetings of Goshen, Newtown and Uwchlan. Afterward Nantmeal and Pikeland were added. For three years the meetings were held alternately at

Goshen and Newtown. In 1762 the Monthly Meeting was divided, leaving only the Goshen and Newtown meetings under the Goshen Monthly Meeting, to which were afterward added Willistown, Whiteland and West Chester, the latter remaining in this group only a short time. In 1801 the place of meeting was changed from Willistown to Goshen, and in 1827, when the division in the Society took place, the Orthodox Friends met at Goshen.

Sadsbury Meeting was granted permission in 1725 or soon afterward to erect a meeting-house. It stood on the edge of Lancaster County, but many of the members lived in Chester County.

Lampeter Meeting was established at the house of Hattill Varman in Leacock in 1732, and in 1749 was removed to Lampeter Township.

Sadsbury Monthly Meeting was formed upon the division of New Garden Monthly Meeting, and was comprised of the two preparative meetings of Sadsbury and Leacock. The first meeting was held 12th month, 6th day, 1737-8.

Nottingham Monthly Meeting was established in 1730, by the division of New Garden Monthly Meeting, and it comprises East and West Nottingham meetings and Elk.

Hockessin Meeting, named after an Indian town, which formerly stood near its location, was first held at the house of William Cox upon the Sixth day of the week, this day being changed to the First day of the week in 1737. In 1738 a meeting-house was built, which was enlarged in 1745. This house stands in Mill Creek Hundred, south of Kennett Square.

Bradford Monthly Meeting, established in 1737, had two branches, one at Bradford, the other at Caln, and alternated between the two meeting-houses.

Uwchlan Monthly Meeting was established in 1763 at the Uwchlan meeting-house. It was formed by the division of Goshen Monthly Meeting, and at the time included Uwchlan, Nantmeal and Pikeland. Later Downingtown Meeting was added.

44

Uwchlan Meeting has already been mentioned. Nantmeal Meeting was first considered in 1839 and first held in 1740, a meeting-house being immediately erected. In 1781 a preparative meeting was established, and in 1777 a new meeting-house was erected near the first one built. In 1795 the house was burned down, and since then affairs in this meeting have been quite unsatisfactory to the Friends.

Pikeland Meeting was first held in 1758, and for the reason that those who desired its establishment lived a long distance from any other meeting. In 1802 a new house was erected for the accommodation of the preparative meeting, then recently established.

Downingtown Meeting was permitted to be held first in the summer of 1784, in a school-house. This privilege was continued during the summer of 1785-89 by the Monthly Meeting. Meetings were also held in 1795 and 1798, and at length Downingtown Meeting was fully established by the Quarterly Meeting in 1806. At first after this it was held in a school-house which stood back of Clara Downing's, but in 1807 ground was purchased and a meeting-house built.

Willistown Meeting was first held in 1784, and was fully established by the Quarterly Meeting in 1788. In 1794 a preparative meeting was first held here, and in 1799 a new meeting-house was built to take the place of the old one.

West Grove Meeting was first held about 1787, in which year a house was built, and in 1788 the meeting was fully established by the Quarterly Meeting.

Fallowfield Meeting was held for some time prior to 1792 at the house of George Welsh by permission of New Garden Monthly Meeting, and later by the permission of London Grove Monthly Meeting. In 1794 a house was built and the meeting was fully established in 1795.

Doe Run Meeting was established in 1805, several Friends being permitted to hold meetings in a school-house. In 1808 a house was built and the meeting fully established as a branch of the Fallowfield Monthly Meeting.

London Grove Monthly Meeting was established by a division of New Garden Monthly Meeting, in 1792, containing at the time but one preparative meeting, that of London Grove.

Caln Quarterly Meeting, composed of Bradford, Sadsbury and Uwchlan Monthly Meetings, was established in 1800, and also of Robeson Monthly Meeting, which previously had belonged to Philadelphia, and which is outside the limits of Chester County.

Marlborough Meeting was established in 1801, when a meeting-house was built and the meeting established as a branch of Kennett Monthly Meeting. The members had previously been members of the Bradford and London Grove Meetings.

Center Monthly Meeting was formed in 1808, at which time Kennett Monthly Meeting was divided, Center Monthly being composed of Center and Hockessin, at which places the Monthly meeting was alternately held.

West Chester Meeting was established about 1810, the Friends there desiring at that time to erect a meeting-house; but their desires did not take tangible shape until 1812, they in the meantime holding meetings in a school-house. Their new meeting-house was first occupied in 1813. It stood on High Street, and in 1868 was considerably enlarged to accommodate the increasing attendance, and also the Quarterly Meeting.

The Orthodox Friends, when they separated from the other body, for a time held their meetings in the house of George G. Ashbridge; but in 1830 they erected a meeting-house at the northwest corner of Church and Chestnut streets, which was opened on the 26th of the 12th month, that year. In 1844 they built a neat stone meeting-house on the northeast corner of the same streets.

East Sadsbury Meeting, not now held, was established about 1810, and was located near Buck Run and the Lancaster Pike.

Londoñ Grove Monthly Meeting was divided in 1811, and Fallowfield Monthly Meeting established, with Fallowfield and Doe Run Meetings.   After 1828 the Orthodox Friends who had previously belonged to the Fallowfield Monthly Meeting returned to London Grove Monthly Meeting.

Kennett Square Meeting was held first in 1812, at the house of John Phillips, just west of Kennett Square.   In 1814 a meeting-house was erected and the meeting fully established.

Birmingham Monthly Meeting was formed with West Chester and Birmingham Meetings as branches, and was first held in 1815.   Previously these two branches had belonged to Concord Monthly Meeting.

Whiteland Meeting was first held in a meeting-house built in East Whiteland in 1816; but it was not until 1818 that the meeting was fully established.   A preparative meeting was established in 1822, and in 1878 the membership was transferred to Malvern Meeting and the former house closed.

Nottingham Quarterly Meeting was held at East Nottingham Meeting in 1819, and was composed of Nottingham, Little Britain and Deer Creek Monthly Meetings.   This is a branch of Baltimore Yearly Meeting.

Penn's Grove Meeting-house was erected in 1833.   A short time previous to 1828 New Garden Monthly Meeting granted permission to a few Friends to hold meetings at the house of Joseph Brown, which in 1828 were transferred to the house of Samuel Hadley, and in 1833 to the house erected as above mentioned.

Little Elk Meeting was established in 1825 and a house erected in 1826.   This meeting belongs to the Baltimore Yearly Meeting.

Homesville Meeting-house was erected in 1839, the Friends holding meetings here having previously held them in a school-house at Colerain, Lancaster County.

London Britain Meeting was first held in 1834, in the house

of Richard Chambers in White Clay Hundred, and in this year the Friends interested purchased a piece of land near Strickerville, upon which they erected a meeting-house.

Unionville Meeting was formed about 1845, in which year the Friends belonging thereto erected a meeting-house, they having belonged to Kennett and London Grove Monthly Meetings.

Romansville Meeting-house was built about 1846. When the division in the Society occurred in 1827, the Orthodox Friends retained the Bradford house, and the other Friends built a meeting-house on an adjoining lot. This house lasted them until 1846, when they built the present one, as mentioned above.

Oxford Meeting-house was erected in 1879, the Friends here having, by permission of Penn's Grove and Nottingham Monthly Meetings, previously held meetings at Oxford. The new house was opened for service on November 9, 1879.

Malvern Meeting-house was erected in 1879, of serpentine stone, and in the winter of 1879-80 the Whiteland Meeting was transferred thereto. The first meeting was held in this house February 15, 1880.

Longwood Meeting-house was erected in the later forties, upon a piece of land donated for the purpose by John Cox, in East Malborough. The purpose in the erection of this meeting-house was general, but most of those interested in the carrying out of this purpose were Friends. It seemed to them that more active efforts should be made in the cause of humanity and human rights, and they determined to hold meetings for the promulgation of their views, and in this they were aided by prominent philanthropists. They considered slavery and intemperance two of the greatest evils then afflicting the country. They styled themselves "Progressive Friends," and their central idea was that of progress in whatever might benefit humanity. From 1853 onward for many years a Yearly Meeting was held in this meeting-house, at which some of the most able and eloquent speakers delivered orations or made more commonplace addresses. Among the speakers were such persons as Lucretia Mott, William Lloyd Garrison, Theodore Parker, Frederick Douglas, Oliver Johnson, Charles C. Burleigh, Mary Grew and Abby Kelly Foster, besides a large number of people from Chester and adjoining counties.

In connection with the meeting there was laid out a cemetery.

That there are two divisions of the Society of Friends in Chester County cannot be overlooked. This fact is one for which the historian is not responsible, but he is responsible for a fair and truthful, even though brief, statement of the origin and results of the schism leading up to the division in the Society, which division is a matter of regret to many, even down to the present day.

From the fact that human nature is what it is it might be inferred that the division was not the work of a day. For many years the operation of the minds of the members of the Society of Friends, variously affected by various environments, led to different conclusions as to doctrinal teachings. The coming event cast its shadows before for many years, observers in England, Ireland and America perceiving the causes and pointing them out in clear language and with great concern. These causes were enumerated to some degree as follows: The fascinations of worldly life; the dread of sufferings to be inflicted by the enemies of the Truth; a state of lethargy within the Society itself; a sad ignorance of the fundamental truths or principles of the Society; their perversion on the part of a portion of the members; a relaxed and inefficient exercise of the discipline of the Society; its maintenance in a formal, legal and lifeless manner; a reckless spirit of "free inquiry;" a presumptuous determination not to believe what was not understood; the Deistical writings of Joseph Priestley; a worldly spirit and a lukewarm state of feeling as to the standard of truth; self-exaltation and spiritual pride on the

part of a portion of the ministers; and more than all else, perhaps, the influence of the institution of slavery.

A remarkable difference of opinion sprang up in Ireland in
the year 1797, which made the schism painfully manifest to those
who desired unity and harmony within the Society. In the answer
to the Queries from the several monthly meetings came in an
answer from Carlow, which differed from the others in the omission of the word "holy" from the phrase "Holy Scriptures." The
defense of this omission was that if the Scriptures were to be
denominated "holy," then all other writings proceeding from the
same Spirit must also be called "holy." Those who objected to the
epithet "holy" in this connection also believed that Christ was a
good man because he was wholly obedient to the Inner Light, or
the light which lighteth every man that cometh into the world. In
time this same party publicly declared their unbelief in the Divine authority of the Scriptures, discarded the doctrine of the
atonement of Christ and attempted to abolish the comely order of
the discipline long established among the Friends.

This brief narrative is here presented, in order to show that
although Elias Hicks, after whom the independent branch of the
Society of Friends has since been named may have been original in his thinking, was not in point of fact the originator of
the views that now for the most part distinguish those who are
looked upon as his followers. The views taken of several of the
orthodox doctrines by Elias Hicks have sometimes been denominated the Hicksian or Rationalistic system. The main differences
between the Orthodox and Hicksite Friends may be stated as
follows: The former affirm and the latter deny the following
propositions: The miraculous birth of Christ; the divine Sonship
and Mediatorship of Christ; His atoning sacrifice on the cross;
the existence of such places as Heaven and Hell; that the Scriptures were given by the special inspiration of the Deity; but the
latter do not insist upon uniformity of opinion on these points as
essential.

Both branches alike dispense with the sacraments and with a regular ordained ministry. Both believe in the doctrine of the inner light, and both practice the patient waiting upon God in silence.

During Elias Hicks' ministry and travels he was several times in Chester County and the counties adjoining, and it is not to be wondered at that several of those adhering to orthodox views should attempt to show to him the error of his ways, according to their way of thinking. Among those who thus labored with him was "an ancient and venerable Friend, William Jackson, a minister, of London Grove, in Pennsylvania." William Jackson was greatly astonished at the expression of such sentiments as those entertained by Elias Hicks, such as that Christ suffered as a martyr, that he was the son of Joseph and Mary, that Spirit could only beget spirit, and that the account we have of the creation is the account of Moses, only, and is allegorical. Upon this declaration it is reported that William Jackson left him with a heavy heart. William Jackson was of the third generation from Isaac Jackson, the original emigrant of this family from Ireland, in 1725.

But it was impossible to check the movement which resulted in the division of the Society into two bodies. In the winter of 1826-27 Elias Hicks made a visit to Philadelphia, and the apprehensions of many members of the Society were then fully confirmed, as his presence there tended to animate his adherents in the pursuit of those measures which resulted a few months later in the separation. Among those who labored zealously for the separation was John Comly, a minister of Byberry, near Philadelphia. It was at the Select Yearly Meeting, held on the 14th of the 4th month, 1827, that after careful consideration, William Jackson suggested that a committee be appointed to visit the Select Quarterly and Preparative meetings and endeavor to extend such advice and assistance as might conduce to the health of the body and the welfare of individuals. This suggestion was accepted, but on the 18th of the same month John Comly attempted to have the appointment rescinded, failing in which he bade the meeting an affectionate farewell.

In the Yearly Meeting there was great difficulty over the election of a clerk, which served to separate the two parties more than before, and at length, in the evening of the 20th of the month, those who had striven to elect John Comly clerk held a meeting, at which an address was adopted which recognized that a division existed in the Society, "developing in its progress views which appear incompatible with each other, and feelings averse to a reconciliation. Doctrines held by one part of society, and which we believe to be sound and edifying, are pronounced by the other part to be unsound and spurious. From this has resulted a state of things that has proved destructive of peace and tranquility, and in which the fruits of love and condescension have been blasted, and the comforts and enjoyments even of social intercourse greatly diminished." But the Yearly Meeting closed without a formal separation.

But those who had favored Mr. Comly for clerk of the Yearly Meeting were not satisfied to remain in religious communion with those they considered as having introduced and who seemed disposed to continue disorders, and they therefore proposed holding a Yearly Meeting for Friends in unity with them, and invited such Quarterly and Monthly Meetings as were prepared to do so to appoint representatives to meet in Philadelphia on the third second-day of the tenth month ensuing, that is, on October 10, 1827.

Those who thus separated from the Society rapidly increased their numbers and took possession of the meeting-houses to such an extent that, according to William Hodgson, in his "The Society of Friends in the Nineteenth Century," there were in Pennsylvania but very few meeting-houses left to the Society, except four or five in the city of Philadelphia. The same difficulty was felt all over the country where there were members of the Societies of Friends, for the next few years, and it was plain that nothing but an absolute separation could restore harmony, each division enjoying harmony within itself, but not when in meetings with each other.

As to the number of the respective members of the two branches at the time of the division, it may be stated that it is now estimated that in Chester County there were about 3,000 belonging to the orthodox branch and 13,000 belonging to the Hicksite branch. In the Philadelphia Yearly Meeting, to which both branches belonged in 1829, according to the account submitted by Halliday Jackson, on the part of the Hicksites, the whole number of members of both parties was 26,258, of whom 18,485 were Hicksites, 7,344 Orthodox, and 429 neutral.

With regard to the meeting-houses in Chester County, it cannot be definitely stated to which branch several of them belong. Some of them have ever been used, as it were, conjointly by both branches, and some are not used at all. Others are held by the Orthodox branch and still others by the Hicksite branch. Where it was impossible to agree to use the property conjointly the one branch which had to vacate the meeting-house has in some cases erected a separate meeting-house, as is the case in London Grove and in West Chester, the Hicksite branch in the latter place holding the meeting-house on the hill on North High Street, while the Orthodox branch erected for themselves a building on Chestnut and Church Streets. Throughout the county, besides the meeting-house in West Chester, the orthodox Friends have houses at Goshenville, which, however, is not now in use; at Malvern, built shortly before 1890; at Birmingham, Parkersville, Kennett Square, London Grove, New Garden, West Grove, Strickersville and Marshallton, and possibly one or two others. The Hicksite Friends, upon the division being made, were, as stated above, largely in the majority in Chester County, and retained most of the meeting-houses for that reason. They now have houses at West Chester, Goshenville, Willistown, Birmingham, Marlborough, Old Kennett, Kennett Square, Unionville, London Grove, New Garden, West Grove, Ercildoun, Doe Run, Penn's Grove, Homeville, Oxford, Lionville, Caln, Romansville, Schuylkill and Valley Meeting-house. There is also a house at Little Caln and Hickory Hill.

It appears altogether probable that Catholics came to Pennsylvania as early as 1708, and the fact that some of these religionists were located in the Province gave considerable annoyance to William Penn in the English court, but still he never made any attempt to suppress them; and it has been thought by some that it was on this account that he was looked upon in certain quarters as a Jesuit in disguise. The first Catholic Church in Pennsylvania was St. Joseph, mentioned about 1730, and in 1757 there were Catholics in most if not all of the counties in the eastern part of the State, including Chester Sounty, of course.

But the growth of the Catholic Church in Pennsylvania was quite slow during the eighteenth century, and also during the early part of the nineteenth century, because of the antagonism to it felt in the minds of the proprietors of the Province and by some of the people, as is shown in the instructions to the colonial governors in 1738, in 1763 and in 1766. The 6th article of those instructions is as follows:

"Whereas the said Province and counties were happily at first settled and afterward subsisted without any considerable mixture of Papists, it is with concern we now hear that of late times Papists have resorted thither. Now as their Political Principles (which they ever inculcate as Religious Principles) tend to the breach of public Faith, are destructive to morality and totally subvert every civil and Religious Right of a Free People, We recommend it to you to prevent as much as in you lies the coming in or settling of Papists within your government, and that you do not extend any Privileges to them nor admit any of them into any office, post or Employment whatsoever within your Government."

In 1757 there were in Chester County the following numbers of Catholics: Under the care of Robert Harding, 18 men and 22 women; under the care of Theodore Schneider (Germans), 13 men and 9 women; and of Irish, 9 men and 6 women; under the care of Ferdinand Farmer, Irish, 23 men and 17 women, and of Germans, 3 men. Owing to the antagonism above noted the Catholics in this county existed only in small groups in different parts of the country; but in later years the numbers of Catholics have so increased that now they are one of the strongest religious bodies in the county.

The first Catholic Church erected in West Chester was called "Christ's Church," a little chapel at the west end of Gay street, erected in 1793, in which mass was occasionally offered up. From that time on until about 1840 the priest holding services therein came out from Philadelphia, and on such occasions the Catholics of the surrounding country came in from miles around to attend services. In the meantime missionaries or priests were accustomed to travel through the county, holding services and saying mass at farm-houses and such other places as were convenient, wherever a group of members could be gathered together, but about the year last named Bishop Kendrick of Philadelphia sent out the Rev. D. D. Donahoe to West Chester as a permanent pastor. The name St. Agnes was adopted in the year 1853, the Rev. Father Donahoe remaining with the church until 1851, on the 20th of June of which year Rev. John Francis Prendergast entered this field of service and labored therein successfully for twenty years. At this time the following parishes were attached to the West Chester Church: Parkesburg, Downingtown, Doe Run, in Chester County; Ivy Mills, in Delaware County, and a parish in Lancaster County.

After remaining in West Chester a few months Rev. Father Prendergast began the erection of a church at Downingtown, which was named St. Joseph's, and which was dedicated in 1852.   In

August of that year the corner-stone of St. Agnes' Church was laid, the first mass was celebrated therein in May, 1853, and the church was dedicated in June following, the Rev. Dr. Moriarty, O. S. A., officiating. St. Mary's Sodarity was organized in 1857. Rev. Father Prendergast and Rev. John Wall both lie buried in the cemetery of this church, and the Rev. S. B. Spaulding came to the church in the year 1885, remaining here until the present time. William Barrett, in his history of the church, states that in the autumn of 1893, when the centenary of the church was celebrated, during a mission held by the Jesuit Fathers, Rev. F. A. Smith, Rev. M. O. Kane, and Rev. J. Goeding, and which lasted eight days, 1,457 confessions were made, and 1,310 communions, from which it may be estimated that now the members aggregate upward of 1,500 in number, many of them, as in the days of old, coming in from the country. The Sunday-school has about 250 members. The principal church societies are the following: The Temperance and Benevolent Society, organized in 1873, May 4, and having now a membership of 110; the Cadets' Temperance Society, organized in 1874, and having now a membership of 70; the Catholic Mutual Burial Society, organized in 1887, and now having a membership of 150; the League of the Sacred Heart, organized in 1892, and now having a membership of 800; the Independent Catholic Benevolent Union Society, organized in 1892, and now having a membership of 100, and the Angel Sodarity, for boys and girls, organized in 1893, and at the present time having a membership of 100. St. Mary's Sodarity has at present a membership of 275.

The property of the church is as follows: The church building, worth $25,000; the parochial school, worth $2,500; the Joseph J. Lewis mansion, worth $5,000, and the parochial residence, worth $8,000; total value of the property, $40,500. The parochial school is attended by about 250 scholars and has five teachers.

In Phoenixville the Catholics at first occupied the Tunnel Hill School-house, then recently abandoned by the Episcopalians,

their first pastor being Rev. P. D. Donahue. In 1841 they erected
their church building, and the church for many years was in charge
of Rev. Patrick O'Farrell, who died in 1868. He was succeeded
that year by Rev. Father Scanlan, who enlarged the church and
made it into the form of a cross. The next pastor was Rev. Father
Martin, who was succeeded by Rev. Father Lynch. The present
priest in Rev. Father John A. Wagner, and the congregation numbers about thirty-three hundred communicants.

. The Catholic Church at present in use at Coatesville, St.
Cecilia's, was erected in 1870-71, the corner-stone having been laid
December 11, 1870, during the pastorate of Rev. Charles McFadden, and it was dedicated November 22, 1874, by the Most Rev.
James F. Wood, archbishop of the diocese of Philadelphia.
Previous to this time services had been held in Midway, in Me-
chanics' Hall. The old parish, of which Coatesville was only a
mission, was named Our Lady of the Seven Dolors, Parkesburg,
the priest residing at the latter place, and from there as a center
attending the missions all around from Dry Wells and McCall's
Ferry, in Lancaster County, to Coatesville, Doe Run, West Grove,
Oxford and the country round down to the Maryland line. Rev.
L. V. McCabe succeeded Father McFadden, and was himself succeeded by Rev. James Brehony, by Rev. James Nash, by Rev. M. C.
Donovan, by Rev. Hugh Garvey and by the present pastor, Rev.
J. A. Calahan.

A little church building was erected at Doe Run in 1835, but it
was replaced by a larger one in 1865. It was attended from West
Chester until the church in Parkesburg was built, in 1855, from
which time on the church in Doe Run was attended from Parkesburg. Early in the seventies West Grove, Oxford and the lower
part of the county were cut away. The first resident priest at
Parkesburg was Rev, Father Doyle, who from the time of his
establishment here, in 1855, attended the church at Coatesville
once in three or four weeks; but as the number of Catholics in-

creased in and around Coatesville it became necessary to erect a church for their accommodation in 1870, and at that time the seat of the parish was located at Coatesville, Parkesburg becoming the mission. The new church at Coatesville was called St. Cecilia, and it was dedicated at the time above given under the pastorate of Rev. L. McCabe. The church at Doe Run, formerly known as the Church of St. Catherines, is now known as the Church of St. Malachi.

The corner-stone of St. Cecilia's Church was laid December 11, 1870, by the late Right Rev. Archbishop Wood, and the building itself was dedicated November 22, 1874. Rev. James A. Brehony succeeded Rev. Father McCabe, and remained two years. Rev. James Nash was pastor of this church ten years and was succeeded by Rev. M. C. Donovan, being himself succeeded by Rev. Hugh Garvey.

St. Patrick's Roman Catholic Church of Kennett Square was established as a mission in 1868, in which year a building was erected on South Side, and first opened for services December 25, 1868. Rev. Mr. McElroy was pastor for some time, and subsequently Rev. James F. Kelly of West Grove made visits to this congregation once in two weeks. The parish was organized in 1893 and the present pastor, Rev. John H. O'Donnell, placed in charge. One of the finest building sites in Kennett Square was purchased and upon it a modern and commodious parochial residence was built, and it is now in contemplation to erect a church building at an early date.

St. Joseph's Catholic Church at Downingtown was organized in August, 1869, when Rev. N. Bowden took charge. There had, however, been services there from 1850, and also at Gallagherville. Some time afterward Rev. John Prendergast organized a parish there and said mass for the people once a month. The first mass in Downingtown was said in a private house, still standing on Bradford Avenue, near the railway station. Later services were

held in a large room in the third story of Michael McFadden's
house, close to the railway station, and in this room Rev. Mr.
Prendergast said mass monthly until St. Joseph's parish was organized, as above stated. The church building was erected in
1852, being then, however, only half its present size. The cornerstone of this church was laid by very Rev. E. J. Sourin, V. G., and
Rev. Father O'Keefe of Philadelphia, stationed at St. Philip's
Church, officiated. Rev. Father Prendergast went to Europe in
1867, remaining a year, and during his absence the congregation
was attended monthly by Rev. Father Maroney, from West Chester. After the return of Father Prendergast he was assisted by
Father Mooney, who was afterward stationed at St. Malachi's
Church, Philadelphia, where he died.

In 1869, owing to the increase in the size of the congregation,
the Church was enlarged and otherwise improved. Still later
Father Prendergast was assisted by Father Maginn, who also occasionally attended in Downingtown, until Rev. Nicholas Bowden
was appointed resident pastor. A house just south of the church
was secured as a pastoral residence, and in this house Father
Bowden lived until his death, in 1871. The present fine residence
was erected on the site of that building by Rev. James Maginn.
In 1872 Father Maginn took charge of the parish, remaining until
1886, and about this time ground was secured for a cemetery. In
July, 1886, Rev. Thomas Toner was appointed to succeed Father
Maginn and remained until his death in 1892. Succeeding Father
Maginn came Rev. J. J. McAnany, who remained until 1894, when
Rev. James O'Reilly came to the church and still remains. He has
greatly improved the church, has remodeled the sanctuary, frescoed the entire interior, built a new sacristy on the north side of
the church and has added a handsome front porch. Three beautiful altars adorn the sanctuary, and on each of these altars is placed
a fine statue, imported from Europe and presented to the church
by Mrs. Margaret Murphy, a member of the congregation. A

BIRMINGHAM MEETING-HOUSE.

fine bell is in the tower of the church, which is much admired for its sweetness of tone. It is the gift of Michael Murphy of Milford Mills, Chester County.

There are two out missions attached to St. Joseph's parish— St. Mary's, at Glenloch, and St. Thomas', at Reilly's Banks. Father O'Reilly is assisted by the Rev. Father Martin Gorman.

The Church of St. Francis de Sales at Landenburg was established in 1893, the building being erected the same year, a frame on a stone foundation, which will seat 250 people, and which cost $3,300. The church was erected by Rev. James F. Kelly and it was dedicated October 21, 1893. Then Father Kelly was succeeded by Rev. John O'Donnell of Kennett Square, who has had charge of both parishes ever since. The membership consists of about twenty-five families.

West Grove Catholic Church building stands on Evergreen Street at the head of Prospect Street. It is 60x41 feet in size, in the clear, and two stories high, including the basement. It is of brick and cost $11,000. In 1897 a tower was erected at a cost of $750, and a bell was placed in this tower in July, 1898, and consecrated by Archbishop Ryan of Philadelphia on Sunday, July 3, 1898. The membership of this church is now 400.

Oxford Catholic Church is merely a mission from the West Grove Church. The building at Oxford is of brick, 70x28 feet in size, and cost $3,500. It was erected in 1877. The membership is now 150.

The Presbyterians of Chester County are in reality the descendants of the early Scotch-Irish settlers, who were animated by the same spirit which led to the American Revolution. Unable to bear the oppressions of their English King, they sought by a change of residence to find a field of greater liberty. Hence they sought Pennsylvania, where they were welcomed by the Friends, who were then the most liberal in their views upon religious subjects of any of those professing Christian sentiments.

45

The oldest Presbyterian Church in Chester County is the Great Valley Presbyterian Church, located in Tredyffrin Township, which was regularly organized in 1714. The membership was made up of Welsh and Scotch-Irish, and the first minister was Rev. Malachi Jones, who preached for this church until 1720, when he was succeeded by Rev. David Evans, who was pastor of the church for about twenty years. In 1720 a church building was erected which stood for more than seventy years. Succeeding Rev. Mr. Evans in the pulpit of this church came Rev. John Rowland, to whom there was strong opposition, which resulted in his being debarred from preaching in the church by the "Old Side" members, a majority of the membership being of the opinions known as "old side" by the religionists of that day. However, Rev. Mr. Rowland preached to the minority of the congregation in barns and such other places as could be utilized for the purpose, until a new church building could be erected for them. The foundations of this church were laid in 1743, on a lot given by Job Harvey, a Friend.

The next preacher of the Great Valley Presbyterian Church was Rev. Samuel Evans, a son of Rev. David Evans, who was installed in 1742, and who remained until 1747. Rev. John Kinkead was installed pastor in 1753, and Rev. John Simonton in 1761, he remaining until 1791.

The church established by Rev. John Rowland, called the Charlestown Presbyterian Church, in 1743, maintained a separate existence until 1791, having had as pastors Revs. John Campbell, John Griffith, Benjamin Chestnut, John Carmichael and Daniel McCalla, returned at this latter date to the Great Valley Church, the reunion being effected by Rev. John Gummel, who remained with the church until 1798. Where Rev. William Latta was pastor of the Great Valley, in 1799, a new church building was erected in 1793, and the Rev. Mr. Latta remained with this church until his death, which occurred in 1847. The next pastor was Rev.

William R. Bingham, from February 28, 1848, until January 3, 1859. Then came Rev. Robert M. Patterson, installed August 25, 1859, and remaining until 1867; Rev. Edward P. Heberton, from April 13, 1868 until October 14, 1871; Rev. Samuel Fulton, installed October 18, 1872, and remaining until 1881; Rev. Robert M. Patterson, D. D., LL. D., 1885 to the present time. The present membership of this church is 108.

The Charlestown again separated from the Great Valley upon the resignation of Rev. Mr. Bingham, and in 1859 united with the Phœnixville Presbyterian Church. Afterward it united with the East Whiteland Presbyterian Church during the pastorate of Rev. John Cylde, again uniting with the Phœnixville Church.

Upper Octorara Presbyterian Church, one mile north of Parkesburg, was organized in 1720, and for four years was served by Revs. David Evans and David Magill. The first regular pastor was Rev. Adam Boyd, who came to the church in 1724, being installed October 13. In 1741 this church, like others in this county, was divided into two branches by the "Old Side" and "New Side" controversy, a new church being organized by the New Siders, named the Second Congregation of Upper Octorara, of which latter church Rev. Andrew Sterling was pastor from 1747 to 1765. Rev. Mr. Boyd remained with the old church during the division, which was terminated in 1768, the two churches then becoming one again, and Rev. Mr. Boyd remained pastor of the reunited body until his death, November 23, 1768. A son of his, Col. Andrew Boyd, was a lieutenant of Chester County during the Revolutionary War.

Rev. William Foster became pastor of this church almost immediately after the death of Mr. Boyd, and remained until his death, September 30, 1780. Rev. Alexander Mitchell succeeded him, and remained until 1796, dying December 6, 1812. In 1810 Rev. James Latta was installed pastor and remained until 1850, the present church edifice being erected during his pastorate.

Since then the following have been pastors: Revs. James M. Crowell, Alexander Reed, John Jay Pomeroy, William B. Reed; James A. Marshall, May 29, 1897, to August 31, 1886; Matthew C. Woods, December 19, 1887, to January 20, 1889, and Thomas R. McDowell, May 22, 1889, to the present time.

On September 14, 1870, this church celebrated its sesqui-centennial anniversary, on which occasion J. Smith Futhey delivered an historical address, from which much of the matter here presented was taken. On September 4, 1895, the church celebrated its one hundred and seventy-fifth anniversary, at which there were present about 2,500 people. The membership of the church at the present time is 460, and of the Sunday-school 475, the church property being valued at $40,000.

Fagg's Manor Presbyterian Church, at first called New Londonderry Presbyterian Church, was established in 1730, the building standing on the northwest corner of what was known as Sir John Fagg's Manor. The first pastor was Rev. Samuel Blair, from 1740 to his death, June 5, 1751. He was succeeded by his brother, Rev. John Blair, who remained until 1767, after which time the church had no regular pastor until 1781, when Rev. John Evans Finley was installed. He remained until 1793, and was succeeded by Rev. Patrick Davidson. The next pastor was Rev. Robert White, who was installed in 1809, and remained until his death, September 20, 1835. Rev. Alfred Hamilton came next, remaining from March, 1836, until May, 1859, the present church edifice being erected during his incumbency. Since his removal to the West the pastors have been: Revs. J. T. Umsted, William B. Noble, John K. Andrews, 1881-83; Joseph L. Polk, Ph. D., 1885 to the present time. The present membership of this church is 389 and of the Sunday-school, including officers and teachers, 603.

Rock Presbyterian Church, first known as Elk River Presbyterian Church, was organized in 1720, its first house of worship being erected at what is known as the "Stone Graveyard," in

Lewisville, Elk Township. The second building was erected by the "New Side" people in 1741, at "Stump's Graveyard," at Fair Hill, Cecil County, Maryland. Its third church was erected at its present location in Cecil County, Maryland.

New London Presbyterian Church was organized March 20, 1728, it having separated from the Rock Church in 1726. The first pastor was Rev. Samuel Gelster, who preached for a short time after September, 1728. Next came Rev. Francis Alison, installed about 1736, and removed to Philadelphia about 1752. The second church edifice was erected about 1744, but from the time of the retirement of Rev. Mr. Alison, there was no regular pastor until October 15, 1771,.when Rev. James Wilson was installed, and served until October 27, 1778. Next came Rev. Robert Graham, installed December 13, 1809, and succeeded by Rev. Rovert Patterson Du Bois, who was installed November 20, 1836, and remained until November 1, 1876. Rev. B. F. Meyers became pastor April 24, 1877, and remained until April 8, 1879, being succeeded by Rev. Daniel R. Workman, October 23, 1879, who remained until 1883; Rev. James B. Clark, 1884-86; Rev. William Hayes Moore, 1889-90; Rev. Daniel E. Jenkins, 1891-96; Rev. Henry E. Jackson, 1897, and Rev Charles R. Williamson, 1898. The present church membership is 180, and of the Sunday-school, including officers and teachers, 124.

Doe Run Presbyterian Church was organized in 1740, and its building was erected the same year in East Fallowfield Township on the Strasburg Road. This organization belonged to the "New Side" Presbyterian branch. For the first seven years of its existence it had no regular pastor, the supplies being sent from the New Side Presbytery of New Castle, but in 1747 Rev. Andrew Sterling became pastor, and remained pastor of this and the Second Congregation of Upper Octoraro about eighteen years. In 1768 Rev. Mr. Foster became pastor of the two churches, giving Doe Run about one-fourth of his time. In 1785 Rev. Alexander Mitchell came to this church, dividing his time as his predecessors had done between the two, and remained until 1796 with the Octoraro Church and with Doe Run until 1809. Rev. Samuel Henderson became pastor in 1813, remaining about one year, and Rev. Elkanah Kelsey Dare was then pastor from May 13, 1817, until August 26, 1826. Since then the pastors have been Revs. Alexander G. Morrison, John Wynne Martin, D. D., John P. Clarke, Thomas Thompson, Robert E. Flickinger, Samuel Philips, and Van Derveer V. Nicholas, 1893-97. The membership of the church is 119 and of the Sunday-school 144.

Brandywine Manor Presbyterian Church was organized as a separate congregation in 1735, the first pastor being the Rev. Samuel Black, who was installed November 10, 1736, and remained until May, 1741. In this year the church became divided into an "Old Side" and a "New Side" branch, the latter branch erecting for themselves a new house of worship. Rev. Adam Boyd was pastor of the former branch until about 1743, when he was succeeded by Rev. William Dean, who remained until 1760, when the two branches reunited and Rev. John Carmichael became pastor, being installed April 21, 1761, and remaining until his death November 15, 1785. The church was incorporated September 1, 1786, and Rev. Nathan Grier became pastor August 22, 1787, and he remained until his death, March 30, 1814, being then succeeded by his son, Rev. John Nathan Caldwell Grier, who remained from 1814 until April 14, 1869. The pastorate of his father and himself extended over a period of eighty-two years. Since then the pastors have been Revs. W. W. Heberton, John McCall, and Hector A. McLean, the present pastor. The membership of this church is now 300, and of the Sunday-school, including officers and teachers, 329.

The church building erected in 1761 was burned down and rebuilt in 1786, and in 1839 the house was rebuilt and remodeled. In 1875 the old building was taken down, and in 1876 a new one erected, at the time being the most complete and convenient of any Presbyterian Church in Chester County. It was dedicated December 14, 1876, and stands on high ground, giving an excellent view of the surrounding country.

The Oxford Presbyterian Church was established at the time of the union of the Associate Reformed Church with the General Assembly of the Presbyterian Church in 1822, as is related in the sketch of the Oxford United Presbyterian Church. Rev. Ebenezer Dickey connected himself with General Assembly of the Presbyterian Church, and remained pastor of it until 1832. He was succeeded by his son, Rev. John Miller Dickey, in May of the latter year, who remained pastor until 1856. Rev. James R. Reardon came next as a supply, the next regular pastor being Rev. Casper W. Hodge, who remained until 1860, being succeeded then by Rev. William R. Bingham, who remained until the summer of 1862. Rev. F. B. Hodge was installed in the spring of 1863 and remained until the fall of 1868, and it was during his pastorate that a new church building was erected on the old site at a cost of $35,000. Rev. Orr Lawson became pastor in March, 1870, and was succeeded by Rev. M. W. Jacobus, and he by the Rev. Hugh L. Hodge. The membership of this church is about 600, and of the Sunday-school 300, and the church property is worth about $30,000.

Nottingham Presbyterian Church was organized with members formerly belonging to the Lower Nottingham Presbyterian Church in Cecil County, Maryland, these members withdrawing because of a change in the location of the church building in which they had been accustomed to worship. Upon withdrawing they formed the Upper West Nottingham Church, and erected a building in 1802, which was enlarged in 1810. Dr. Samuel Magraw was pastor of this church until 1821, after which time it was supplied until 1826, when it was connected with the Oxford Church, this connection remaining in force until the summer of 1862, when it became a separate church. The pastors since then have been Revs. William F. P. Noble, Robert Gamble, S. M. Pierce, Lindley C. Rutter, Jr., who was installed in 1872. In 1878-79 a new church building was erected at Nottingham Station, and the name of the church organization changed to the Nottingham Presbyterian Church about 1880. Since then the pastors have been as follows: Edward W. Russell, Kent M. Bull, and John M. Jenkins. The church membership is now 102, and that of the Sunday-school 100.

Oxford United Presbyterian Church was organized in 1735, though not as a unit of the present connection. A small house of worship had been erected in this part of Chester County as early as 1739, and this house was in use for many years before there was any organized body to occupy it. This church was organized in connection with the Associate Presbyterian Synod of Edinburgh, being one of the first of that branch of the Presbyterian Church in the colonies. This synod in 1753 sent out two ministers, Rev. Alexander Gellatley and Rev. Andrew Arnott, who left Scotland soon after receiving their appointment, the latter returning to Scotland in 1755, and the former remaining in this country. While both were in this country they organized, as they had been instructed to do, the Associate Presbytery of Pennsylvania, the principal settlements of its adherents being at Octoraro and at Oxford. From these two churches Rev. Mr. Gellatley received a call to become their pastor, and accepting the call he was pastor of both a short time, and of the Octoraro Church until his death in 1761. The next pastor of the Oxford Church, Rev. Matthew Henderson, came from Scotland, in 1758, and remained until 1775. The next regular pastor, Rev. Ebenezer Dickey, was installed in 1796, a union having in the meantime been effected between the Associate Presbyterian Church of Pennsylvania and the Reformed Presbyterian Church, the united bodies calling themselves the Associate Reformed Church, the union being effected June 13, 1782. The Oxford Church remained in this connection forty years.

Rev. Mr. Dickey continued to preach for this church until 1822, when at a small meeting of the General Synod of the Associate Reformed Church, a projected union with the General Assembly of the Presbyterian Church was declared consummated, and the Associate Reformed Synod dissolved. This was on May 21, 1822. Several of the members of the Oxford Church declined to enter this union thus effected, and uniting with a number of others who in 1782 had stood out against the union they were received with the congregation of Octoraro, into the Associate Presbytery of Philadelphia, and again taking the name of Associate, which they continued to bear until the union, May 26, 1858, of the Associate and Associate Reformed Churches, when entering that union they took the name of the United Presbyterian Church. Thus this church, while it has been known under several different names, has always maintained the same principles.

Succeeding Rev. Mr. Henderson the Rev. John Smith was pastor of this church from 1783 to 1794; Rev. Ebenezer Dickey from 1796 to 1822; Rev. William Easton, D. D., from 1827 to 1854; Rev. J. H. Andrew from 1855 to 1863; Rev. E. T. Jeffers, D. D., from 1865 to 1872; Rev. G. A. B. Robinson from 1873 to 1876; Rev. R. T. Wylie, from 1877 to 1880; Rev. A. H. Crosbie, from 1881 to 1887; Rev. W. M. Story, 1888 to 1891; Rev J. Leyda Vance, 1891 to 1892; Rev. A. P. Hutchson, 1892 to 1895; Rev. J. L. Hervey, 1896 to 1897, and Rev. McElwee Ross, June 4, 1898, to the present time.

The present brick church building was erected in Oxford in 1851, and in the spring of 1869 it was determined to build a parsonage, which together with a stable was erected for $3,900 and in 1889 the congregation became entirely free from debt. The church property now consists of one acre of land in a growing part of the town, a good brick church, 40x60 feet, and a two-story brick parsonage, 32x32 feet, the whole being worth $8,875. The membership of the church is now 95.

The First Presbyterian Church of West Chester was organized January 11, 1834, the field having been previously cultivated by the Rev. William A. Stevens, and a house of worship was erected on the corner of Miner and Darlington Streets, which was opened for worship in January, 1834. After the death of Rev. Mr. Stevens, which occurred October 3, 1834, Rev. James J. Graff became pastor, being installed April 29, 1836, and the succeeding pastors have been Rev. John Crowell, 1840 to 1850; Rev. William E. Moore, 1850 to 1872; Rev. Benjamin T. Jones, January 15, 1873, to April 11, 1883; Rev. John C. Caldwell, October 10, 1883, to August 15, 1891; and Rev. Washington R. Laird, November 17, 1892, to present time.

On the division of the Presbyterian Church into the Old and New Schools, this church became a part of the New School Presbyterian Church, and so remained until the reunion of the two branches in 1870. In 1860-61 the church building was enlarged by the addition of twenty-five feet to its length, and in 1874 the pipe organ was removed from the gallery over the entrance to an alcove in the rear of the pulpit. In 1880 a parsonage was purchased on Miner Street at a cost of $7,000. The membership of this church at the present time is 513, and of the Sunday-school, 500. A chapel in the form of an "L" on the east and south sides of the church building was erected in 1894-95, of brownstone, including auditorium, ladies' parlor and kitchen, the auditorium having a seating capacity of 1,000. The cost of this improvement was about $18,000.

Dilworthtown Presbyterian Church was organized in April, 1878, a building having been erected in 1877, at a cost of $4,417.15, the membership having been gathered together through the efforts of the Presbyterians of West Chester. Rev. Hector Alexander McLean was pastor from September 9, 1878, until February 24, 1881. Since then the pastors have been Revs. Joel S. Gilfillan, from April, 1881, to September 27, 1887; Josiah L. Estlin, June 6, 1888, to May, 1893, and Thomas W. Pearson, installed June 28, 1894, and still remains. In 1885 a parsonage was built of greenstone, at a cost of $2,642.49, not considering the work of members. A kitchen was added in 1889 at a cost of $229, exclusive of the value of the stone, which was given by Joseph Brinton. The principal contributor to building of the church erected in 1877, and to the maintenance of the organization since then was and has been Mrs. Henry I. Biddle. Church membership at the present time is about 75 and the Sunday-school has about 100 members.

Coatesville Presbyterian Church was organized in 1833, the first building being erected that year. This building was used by the Presbyterians, Baptist, Episcopalians, Methodists and Friends, but no minister was permitted to preach in it unless he could come well recommended as a member of one of the churches named above. The constitution also provided that no minister should receive a salary for preaching in that house, and that no collections should be taken up except for the incidental expenses of the congregation. This latter provision was, however, stricken out of the constitution by more than a two-thirds vote in 1838. In 1842 the trustees of the property were authorized to sell it to the Presbyterians, and it was conveyed to the Presbyterian Church at Coatesville, September 20, 1843. This building was taken down in 1849, and a new one, 43x55 feet in size, erected, which was used until 1866, and in this year and 1867 it was enlarged to its present size. In 1877 a neat stone chapel was erected at Rock Run for a Sunday-school and other religious purposes.

From April, 1823, to 1846, Rev. Alexander G. Morrison was the pastor of this church and of the Doe Run Church, at which time he became pastor of the Coatesville Church alone, and so continued until his death, October 20, 1870, although for the last three years of his life he took no active part in the ministry. He was followed by Rev. James Roberts, who was called January 15, 1868, and was installed May 28, 1868, remaining with the church until 1885, and being succeeded by Rev. Henry A. MacKubbin, who remained nine years, and was succeeded by the present pastor, Rev. S. Harry Leeper, who was installed in September, 1895. The membership of the church is about 519, and of the Sunday-school 618. The building stands at the corner of Main Street and Fourth Avenue, is a handsome stone structure, will seat 600 persons, and is valued at $45,000.

Honeybrook Presbyterian Church was organized November 28, 1835. It was the result of a great revival in Brandywine Presbyterian Church, some of the new converts living in the vicinity of Waynesburg, too far away from the Brandywine to attend. The first meeting was held January 10, 1835, and the first pastor was Rev. W. W. Latta, who was installed May 9, 1837, resigning in 1858. The church was incorporated April 16, 1840. The second pastor was Rev. John C. Thom, from May 19, 1859, to September, 1865, he resigning to go to St. Louis. Rev. J. H. Young became pastor in 1866, and remained until February 7, 1869. Rev. William A. Ferguson then came and remained until October 3, 1871; Rev. W. W. Totheroh was installed October 31, 1872, and remained until 1882; Rev. Thomas J. Sherrard became pastor in 1883, and remained six years; Rev. James B. Umberger came in 1890 and resigned in 1893, and Rev. Oswell Gifford McDowell, the present efficient pastor, was installed September 18, 1897.

The present large and commodious church edifice was erected in 1874 on a lot donated in 1852 by Rev. W. W. Latta and Abner Griffith. The property of the church is valued at $10,000, the membership is 287, and the Sunday-school in all a membership of 140.

Fairview Presbyterian Church, formerly West Nantmeal Presbyterian Church, was organized January 1, 1840, the first building being erected about that time. The first pastor was Rev. Alexander Porter, from 1840 to 1845. The second was Rev. William H. McCarer, until 1849; Rev. Beriah B. Hotchkiss, until 1858; Rev. David C. Meeker, until 1868; Rev. Ambrose N. Hollifield, until 1876; Rev. Adam Boyd, Jr., installed in June, 1876, and remained until 1883; Rev. William P. Breed, Jr., 1883-89; Rev. Albert F. Lott, 1893-96; Rev. Charles E. Gubler, 1897 to the present time. The church membership is now 200, and of the Sunday-school 180. The present church was erected in 1861.

ᵥ ' East Whiteland Presbyterian Church was organized in 1839, and was incorporated May 21, 1840. Its pastors have been Revs. D. H. Emerson, Mr. Barton, J. McKim Duncan, W. S. Drysdale, George Foote, Mr. Jones, John McLeod, A. M. Stewart, Thomas J. Aiken, John C. Clyde, William C. Stull, installed October 28, 1879, and remained until 1886; Rev. Villeroy D. Reed, D. D., 1887-89; Rev. Yates Dickey, 1890-92; Rev. Alford Kelly, 1894 to the present time. The present church edifice was erected in 1877, and the property of the church is now worth $5,000. The present membership is 105, and of the Sunday-school 55.

Phœnixville Presbyterian Church was organized April 16, 1848, in the Mennonite Meeting-house. A handsome church edifice was erected on Main Street, south of Washington Avenue, and dedicated September 30, 1850. The pastors of this church have been as follows: Revs. Jacob Bellisle, John Thomas, Joseph F. Jennison, Joseph W. Porter, George H. S. Campbell, 1876-80; Nathaniel P. Crause, 1881-96, and William Mudge, 1897-98. The church membership is 240, and that of the Sunday-school 239.

The Central Presbyterian Church, of Downington, was organized July 17, 1861, and had for its first preacher Rev. John L. Withrow, he being at that time a student at Princeton College. The first regular pastor was Rev. Matthew Newkirk, Jr., installed May 21, 1862, and remaining until 1868. Rev. John Rea was pastor until 1872, and was succeeded by Rev. Francis J. Collier, installed October 9, 1872, and remained until September 18, 1888; Rev. Charles E. Craven, from January 17, 1889, to December 12, 1894; the pulpit was then vacant about a year, and Rev. John S. Helm came and remained about a year, leaving in August, 1896, and was followed February 11, 1897, by the present pastor, Rev. William P. Patterson. The church membership is 165, and that of the Sunday-school 151. A parsonage was erected in 1889.

The Trinity Presbyterian Church, of Reeseville (Berwyn), was organized April 29, 1862, the church building being dedicated December 30, 1862. The pastors of this church have been Revs. John McLeod, A. M. Stewart, Thomas J. Aiken, William M. Rice, D. D., Dr. Hartman, Algernon Marcellus, installed October 17, 1879, and remained until 1885; Rev. Thomas J. Aiken, 1886 to the present time. The membership of this church is now 252, and of the Sunday-school 292.

Kennett Square Presbyterian Church was organized November 1, 1862, Rev. John S. Gilmor becoming its first pastor, he being installed May 15, 1863, and remaining until 1872. He was succeeded by Rev. James Frazer, installed May 22, 1872, and remained until 1883; Rev. D. W. Moore, 1883-86; supplies until 1890; Rev. R. A. Hunter, 1890-98. The present membership of the church is 139, and of the Sunday-school 160. In 1889 a Young People's Society of Christian Endeavor was organized, and in 1892 a junior society of the same order. In October of this year a Circle of the King's Daughters was formed, and there is also a Presbyterian Union which has aided the church largely in a financial way. There is also a Woman's Foreign Missionary Society and the Anemone Band.

The Presbyterian Church of Avondale was organized December 9, 1870, with Rev. John S. Gilmor as pastor. In May, 1872, Rev. James Frazer succeeded, remaining until April 9, 1873. Rev. William R. Bingham then became stated supply and remained in that relation until 1876, and since then the pastors have been Rev. Charles H. Whitaker, Rev. George B. Carr and Rev. J. Calvin Krause. The church membership is 74, and that of the Sunday-school 70.

The church building was erected in 1873 and dedicated January 17, 1874. There was a Presbyterian Chapel erected in Toughkenamon in 1877, and in 1878 the building which had belonged to the Episcopalians was purchased, repaired and fitted up as a Presbyterian Chapel. The pastors here since 1890 have been as follows: Rev. Malcolm J. McLeod, 1890-92; Rev. George B. Carr, 1895; Rev.

Charles C. Walker, 1896, and Rev. J. Marshall Rutherford, 1897-98. The mebership of this church is 39, and that of the Sunday-school 100.

There was a Presbyterian Church at Lincoln University, organized in 1867, and known as the Ashmun Church.

The Second Presbyterian Church of West Chester (colored), was organized May 2, 1887, with twenty members. A Sunday-school was organized some time previously. At the present time the church is without a pastor, but the membership is kept up to about fifty, and that of the Sunday-school to about the same number.

Westminster Presbyterian Church of West Chester was organized May 25, 1892, with 103 members, 100 of whom were from the First Presbyterian Church. The Suhday-school was organized May 29, 1892. A lot was purchased on the corner of Church and Barnard Streets, for $9,000, and a chapel erected thereon at a cost of $8,416.43. Rev. B. Canfield Jones was pastor from 1892 to 1895. Rev. Alexander Esler has been the pastor of this church since June 1, 1896, and the membership is 396. The Sunday-school has 516 members, that at Goshenville has 75 members and that at Copeland 65, total number of Sunday-school scholars, 510.

The Second Presbyterian Church of Oxford (colored) was established in 1881, and is the strongest church organization among the colored people at this place. First pastor was Rev. F. L. Logan, who remained until 1886; Rev. E. F. Eggleston from 1886 to 1887; Rev. W. A. H. Albony as a supply from 1891 to 1892, then Rev. Samuel W. Johnson from 1892 to the present. The church was erected in 1881, and is worth $1,700. The membership is 43, and of the Sunday-school 66.

The Presbyterian Church of Penningtonville (now Atglen), was regularly constituted by a committee of New Castle Presbytery, in 1851. In 1852 the present building was erected, and during the same year the church was dedicated. A unanimous call was extended to Rev. James Latta, who had been pastor of Upper Octoraro Presbyterian Church for a period of forty years, and in 1857, the village of Christiana, in Lancaster County, having no place of worship, erected a church in connection with that of Atglen. The pastors have been as follows: Rev. James Latta, 1852 to 1862; Rev. J. W. Edie, 1862 to 1868; Rev. W. F. P. Noble, 1869 to 1872; Rev. W. R. Halbert, 1872 to 1878; Rev. C. D. Wilson, 1880 to 1883; Rev. A. Marcellus, 1884 to 1887; Rev. J. D. Randolph, 1887 until near the time of his death, May 21, 1898, and Rev. J. B. Rendall, Jr., from October, 1897, to the present time. The membership of this church at the present time is 90, and of the Sunday-school, 50.

West Grove Presbyterian Church was the result of the establishment of a Sunday-school by Edward P. Capp, in August, 1866. In 1874 the Sunday-school moved to a hall, Dr. R. B. Ewing being then the superintendent. In 1876 Dr. W. R. Bingham became pastor, and services continued to be held in the hall until it became necessary to erect a church building. For this purpose money was raised in 1883, and in 1884 a building committee was appointed, consisting of S. K. Chambers, James Mendenhall, and Isaac Conard, who held the title to the property until the organization of the church. The cornerstone of the new building was laid October 3, 1884, Dr. Bingham, Rev. B. T. Jones and Prof. John B. Rendall officiating. The church was organized May 27, 1886, and Dr. Bingham continued as stated supply until 1890, when Rev. Charles H. Whitaker became pastor in connection with Avondale, remaining until October 17, 1893, when he resigned. On October 9, 1893, the relations existing between West Grove and Avondale Presbyterian Churches were severed, and West Grove and Unionville were united, at a congregational meeting held July 18, 1894. October 24, 1894, Rev. J. Calvin Krause was installed pastor of the two churches, and so remained until March 27, 1895, and he was called to West Grove exclusively April 23, 1895. At an adjourned meeting of the Presbytery held at Oxford September 19, 1895, a call was extended from the Avondale Church to the Rev. J. Calvin Krause, which call he accepted and he has since been pastor of the two churches. The church building in West Grove stands on Evergreen Street, and will seat 250 people The church membership is now 118, and that of the Sunday-school is 203.

The first Baptist Church in Pennsylvania was established at Cold Spring, in 1684, Rev. Thomas Dungan of Rhode Island being the pastor. This church was dissolved in 1702. About two years after the organization of this Cold Spring Church a young man by the name of Elias Keech arrived from England, dressed like a minister, and began to preach, but in his first sermon while he progressed fairly well for a time, he at length became confused and confessed that he was an impostor, becoming greatly distressed. Hearing of the church at Cold Spring he sought the pastor of it, sought his counsel and was by this pastor baptized and ordained. In 1688 he organized the Pennypack or Lower Dublin Baptist Church, which is now the oldest Baptist Church in the State. Four years later Rev. Mr. Keech returned to England.

In Chester County the Baptist Churches, classified according to the associations to which they belong are as follows:

Philadelphia Association.—Great Valley, organized in 1711; Brandywine, 1715; Bethesda, 1812.

Central Union Association.—Vincent, 1771; Beulah, 1823; Hephzibah, 1810; Goshen, 1827; Phœnixville, 1830; Glen Run, 1832; Windsor, 1833; West Chester, 1834; East Nantmeal, 1842; East Brandywine, 1843; Pughtown, 1856, and Coatesville, 1867; Lawrenceville, 1858; Oxford, 1881, and Green Valley, a branch of Hephzibah.

North Philadelphia Association.—Willistown, 1833; West Caln, 1842; Berean, 1878.

Other Churches.—London Tract, 1780.

The Great Valley Baptist Church was constituted April 22, 1711, Hugh Davis being chosen minister; Alexander Owen and

46

William Rees, elders. The former officiated until February, 1812, when Griffith Jones from Rydwilim, Wales, arrived in the county, and was appointed to the station. The meetings of this congregation were for the most part held at the house of Richard Miles in Radnor, until 1722, a log church building being erected in the meantime in Tredyffrin Township, 28 feet square. This little log church stood on high ground by the highway, near a small stream, called Nant yr Ewig. There was also a branch church at Yellow Springs and also a school-house, and in 1770 both churches had a membership of ninety-two families. Of these two churches Rev. Hugh Davis was the minister until his death, which occurred October 13, 1753. He was succeeded by Rev. John Davis, who had been for some time assistant to Rev. Hugh Davis, and who from 1753 until 1775 had sole charge of the church, and remained pastor until his death in 1778. In 1775 Rev. David Jones became assistant to Rev. John Davis, but during the Revolutionary War he was absent much of the time as chaplain in the American Army.

In 1805 a new meeting-house was erected and in 1816 a new parsonage. In 1820 the privilege of voting on all questions that might arise was conferred upon the women members of the congregation on equal terms with the men. In 1821 the pastor, Rev. Thomas Roberts, and Isaac Cleaver, John Farrier, Elizabeth Roberts, Elizabeth Jones and Rachel Cleaver, were dismissed for the purpose of forming a mission among the Indians in Tennessee, Evan Jones also accompanying them to the mission ground, where his son, Rev. John B. Jones, was born, and where he became a translator of the Bible into the Cherokee language.

This church also planted other churches in its own immediate vicinity, as the Seventh Day Baptist Church, at French Creek, in 1726; Vincent Baptist Church, 1771; Phœnixville Baptist Church, in 1830; Norristown Baptist Church, in 1832; West Chester Baptist Church, in 1834; Willistown Baptist Church, in 1833, and Radnor Baptist Church, in 1841.

Following is a list of the pastors of the Great Valley Baptist Church from the beginning of its history:

Hugh Davis, 1711-53; John Davis, 1732-78; David Jones, 1775-76, 1792-1820; Thomas Jones, 1776-83; Nicholas Cox, 1783; John Boggs, 1791-1801; Jenkin David, 1795-98; Thomas Roberts, 1814-21; Thomas J. Kitts, 1822; John S. Jenkins, 1823-27; Thomas Brown, 1828-31; Leonard Fletcher, 1832-40; Charles B. Keyes, 1841-45; James F. Brown, 1846-54; George Spratt, 1854-58; William M. Whitehead, 1858-61; James E. Wilson, 1863-65; B. C. Morse, 1867-70; James H. Hyatt, 1870 to 1874; George Pierce, 1874 to 1883; J. M. Guthrie, 1883 to 1886; H. B. Garner, 1887 to 1893; J. G. Booker, 1893 to 1896; E. M. Levy, D. D. (supply), January to September, 1897; and James Craighead, from November, 1897, to the present time. Isaac A. Cleaver has been clerk of this church since 1875.

In the latter part of the year 1886, a chapel was opened at Berwyn in Tredyffrin Township, for public worship. The cost of the ground and the building furnished was $7,000. July 26, 1895, the interior of this chapel was seriously damaged by fire. Having been repaired and improved it was reopened December 15, 1895, the cost of the repairs and other improvements having been $3,000. The parsonage farm of fifty acres was sold in 1892 for $10,000, and the proceeds invested in first mortgage on Chester County real estate. The present value of church and chapel properties is $15,000, and the investments of the church society amount to $10,800. The present membership is 130. There are two Sunday-schools, the superintendents being Isaac A. Cleaver and Dr. W. B. Farley, and the officers, teachers and scholars number 200.

During the latter part of the year 1896, fifty members of this church severed their membership therewith and formed the First Baptist Church of Berwyn.

Goshen Baptist Church is situated in West Goshen Township, at the junction of the old Philadelphia and Strasburg Roads. A few Baptists living in the vicinity of this place worshiped in an old frame school-house for some years before a church building was erected, which was in 1809, and in which any evangelical minister might preach, the understanding being that whenever the Baptists were strong enough to establish a church the property should be transferred to them. The building was opened for worship on Saturday and Sunday, December 16 and 17, 1826. Early in the year 1827, nine persons were dismissed from the Brandywine Church to form this church, and they were constituted a church on January 20, 1827. From that time until August they were without a pastor, and then Rev. Simeon Seigfried was called, remaining with them until February 20, 1830, when he resigned, and was dismissed to Bethesda Church. After a couple of years of supplies Rev. Robert Compton became pastor January 14, 1832, serving two years. Rev. Mr. Seigfried then returned and served from April, 1834, until July, 1835, when Rev. Mr. Compton again became pastor, remaining this time six months. Rev. Charles E Moore then became pastor July 16, 1836, and remained until September, 1838; Rev. Enos Barker served from September, 1838, until 1839, and then Rev. Mr. Moore returned and served six months. Rev. Mr. Compton then returned and served until January, 1841, and in 1842 Rev. Thomas Griffith was the pastor. Rev. George W. Mitchell became pastor in 1846, and preached two years. Rev. F. Jasinsky served from April 1, 1848, until January 20, 1851, when Rev. Mr. Compton returned once more and remained until 1856. Rev. John Reece served from 1857 until 1860, in which latter year Rev. J. W. Warwick became pastor and served until April 1, 1861. Joseph S. Evans was licensed to preach November 17, 1860, and was ordained pastor of this church November 4, 1861, serving the church from this time until the present.

In February, 1874, the church building was badly damaged by fire, and a new one was erected on the old site, the new one being dedicated November 25, 1874. In 1894 a two-story stone annex was added to the church for the uses of the Sunday-school. The total value of the church property is now $6,000, and the membership of the church is 245, that of the Sunday-school being 130.

The Brandywine Baptist Church was established June 14, 1715, at the house of John Powell of Providence, the first name given to it being the Baptized Church of Jesus Christ. It had fourteen original members, seven men and seven women. It was originally in Birmingham Township, Delaware County, and the meetings were held for a time at the house of John Powell in Upper Providence. In 1717 the meetings were removed to Birmingham. A division occurred in this church, but at what precise time does not appear, over the question of the Sabbath day, those preferring Sunday to Saturday forming the Brandywine Church. In 1741 a new meeting appeared to be necessary in Newlin Township, and a building was erected on land given for that purpose by Jeffrey Bentley.

In 1770 there were about twenty-six families in the two branches. Rev. William Butcher was the first pastor, remaining until 1721, and from that on until 1761 there was no regular pastor, Rev. Abel Griffiths coming in that year and remaining until 1767. The church at Birmingham was erected in 1718 on land given by Edmund Butcher, one of the original members of the church.

The Hephzibah Baptist Church, though not organized so early as 1710, was yet in a certain sense in existence then, and has since been a power for good. The people of religious instincts in the neighborhood of its location were ministered to until in the early day by Rev. Owen Thomas, who settled in Vincent in 1707, and was the first regular Baptist minister in Newlin Township. On January 7, 1747-48, Richard Buffington of Bradford in his will gave £5 to Rev. Owen Thomas, minister of the Anabaptist Society, which then held its meetings at John Bentley's house, in Newlin, and to the society itself he gave £20. After the death of John

Bentley, the meetings were held at the house of his son, Jef frey Bentley, who in 1752 gave a piece of land upon which with the assistance of others he erected a meeting-house. Rev. Owen Thomas, who first preached for this church, continued to do so until 1759, when he was succeeded by Rev. Abel Griffith, who remained until 1767, and who came again in 1775, remaining this second time until 1791, when he was succeeded by Rev. Joshua Vaughan, who remained until 1808. During his pastorate the meeting-house became too small and a new one was erected where the Hephzibah Church now stands. It was finished by May, 1793, and was dedicated on the 18th of that month by Rev. David Jones. At the death of Rev. Mr. Vaughan, August 2, 1808, the number of members of this church was 140. For a short time afterward Rev. Jethro Johnson supplied the pulpit, and in March, 1810, Brandywine Church granted a letter of dismissal to its members living in East Fallowfield in order that they might form a separate organization, the result of which was that on May 20, 1810, the Hephzibah was constituted, the first business meeting of this new church being held on Saturday, June 16, 1810. In 1823 about twenty members were dismissed to form Beulah Baptist Church, for which Rev. Jethro Johnson preached as well as at Hephzibah, until his death, July 15, 1838.

Rev. Silas C. James was ordained pastor December 3, 1838, remaining until April 1, 1840. Rev. John S. Jenkins became pastor in June, 1840, and remained until February, 1842, when twenty-six members were dismissed to form the West Caln Baptist Church. Rev. D. A. Nichols supplied the pulpit from April, 1844, until April, 1846, and Rev. George H. Mitchell from April 8, 1846, until September, 1852. During the latter pastorate the present church edifice was erected, being finished and ready for worship in January, 1848. Rev. Leonard Frescoln became pastor in January, 1855, and remained until April, 1857, when Rev. David W. Hunter began his pastorate in May, 1857, remaining until June, 1872.

Bethesda Baptist Church is situated in the northwest part of the county, about half a mile from the Berks County line. It was organized December 8, 1827, and the first pastor, Rev. Simeon Seigfried, served it from that time until about 1830. The other pastors of this church have been Rev. John Booth, Rev. Andrew Collins, Rev. Enoch M. Barker, Rev. Dieres A. Nichols, Rev. Leonard Freshcoln, Rev. William H. H. Marsh, Rev. John G. Perry, Rev. John Eberle, Rev. William Barrows.

Glen Run Baptist Church was established in 1832, being constituted December 8, that year. The name was derived from a small stream which has its rise in the immediate vicinity of the church building first erected. The original membership consisted of nine persons, from the Hephzibah Church, they being gathered together through the labors of Rev. Enos M. Philips, who was then performing missionary labors in the west part of Chester County. Almost immediately after the organization eleven more united with the nine, and the church building was dedicated December 9, 1832. Before the end of that month forty more joined, and when the Rev. Mr. Philips resigned his pastorate in 1840 the membership was 115. In January, 1841, Rev. Robert Compton accepted the call to the pastorate, and remained until 1842, when the Rev. Mr. Philips returned, and in 1843 sixteen members were dismissed to form the Coleraine Baptist Church in Lancaster County. In 1846 a church building was erected in Parkesburg, services being held in both houses for some time. Rev. Mr. Philips remained until 1849, when he resigned to go to Wisconsin as a missionary for the Home Missionary Society. Rev. Allen J. Hires, pastor of the Vincent Church, became pastor of this church in 1850, and in 1853 twenty-eight of the members were dismissed to form a new church organization at Parkesburg, Rev. Mr. Hires filling both pulpits until 1855, when he resigned. In this latter year Rev. Joseph Curran became pastor, and remained until 1856, about which time most of the members of the Parkesburg Church returned to the Glen Run Church.

The location of the church building having now become unsatisfactory, a new building was erected at Penningtonville, in 1858, the basement of which was ready for occupancy next year, in which year Rev. Leonard Fletcher became the pastor, serving from April 1 to August 16, when he died. Rev. William T. Bunker became pastor in November, 1860, and remained until 1862, the new church building being completed and dedicated in the meantime. In 1863 Rev. A. H. Bliss became pastor, resigned in August, 1864, to enter the Union Army as a private soldier, and was succeeded in the church by Rev. Joseph Sharp, who remained until 1869, when he was followed by Rev. W. W. Dalbey, who remained from 1870 until September, 1871. In 1872 he was followed by Rev. James Walden, who remained until 1877, and in September of that year Rev. T. S. Snow became and remained until 1885, when he was succeeded by Rev. Mr. Whitmarsh, who remained until 1887. Rev. J. B. Soule was pastor from 1887 to 1890; Rev. V. S. Marsh from 1890 to 1892; Rev. F. H. Buffum from 1892 to 1894; and Rev. R. J. Holmes from 1895 to 1898. The present membership of the church is 150, and of the Sunday-school, 90; the church property being valued at $10,000.

Vincent Baptist Church was organized in 1737 as a branch of the Great Valley Baptist Church, which built a church edifice within 200 yards of the present church building. The new organization was supplied for some years by the Rev. William Davis and the Rev. John Davis, the latter being pastor of the Great Valley Church. In 1748, Vincent Church was granted by the Great Valley Church independent action. Rev. Owen Thomas was minister here some time, and died November 12, 1760. For about ten years afterward Vincent Church was supplied more or less by the Great Valley Church pastors, but on October 12, 1771, the Vincent brethren were constituted a separate and independent church, forty-eight members of the Great Valley being dismissed to aid in forming the new organization. On April 6, 1791, it was incorporated by the Legislature. At this time Rev. John Blackwell was the minister, and was succeeded by the Rev. Abel Griffith, and he by Rev. Thomas Fleeson, these three ministers serving up to 1800. Since then the pastors have been Revs. Joshua Vaughan, H. G. Jones, Daniel James, Charles Moore, the latter resigning in 1842, having been pastor twenty-two years and eight months; J. V. Allison, A. J. Hires, J. N. Tucker, J. W. Griffith, A. J. Hay, George Sleeper, S. F. Forgues, J. S. L. Sagebeer, D. W. Shepperd, A. J. Grey, C. D. Parker, D. M. Lennox, and the present pastor, W. C. Leinback. The membership of this church is now 190, and the property is valued at $15,000.

The Sunday-school was opened in May, 1829, a tract society was formed in 1833, a missionary society was organized the same year, and in February of this year, thirty-nine members were dismissed to form Windsor Church. In May, 1833, the Vincent Church became a member of the Central Baptist Association. The property of the church contains 7.79 acres which was deeded to the society August 23, 1797. This is one of the endowed churches of the county, the Legislature about 1780 authorizing the sale of a farm which in 1775 had been so left in his will by Daniel Evans that two-thirds of its income should go toward the support of the pastor, and after sale two-thirds of the proceeds thereof were put at interest, the interest to go toward paying the annual salary of the pastor. The share of the church in the property amounted to $4,396.91. In May, 1862, Phebe Christman died, leaving a bequest of $300, the interest of which is to go to the same end.

Beulah Baptist Church was constituted June 3, 1823, with nineteen members. The meeting-house was built that year, and Rev. Jethro Johnson was the first pastor, remaining in this relation, and also of Hephzibah Church, until his death, July 15, 1838. The next pastor was Rev. Enos M. Philips, who was succeeded by Rev. Robert Compton. Rev. William Rudy became pastor April 23, 1842, remaining until March, 1845, when

Rev. Mr. Compton returned, remaining this time until 1849. Rev. William M. Whitehead was pastor eighteen months from October 17, 1850, and was succeeded By Rev. J. Perry Hall, who remained until 1859. The pastors subsequent to this have been: Revs. M. K. Williams, J. M. Perry, J. D. R. Strayer, J. M. Lyons, James P. Hunter, J. M. Lyons again, Samuel Godshall, W. R. McNeil.

Windsor Baptist Church was organized April 12, 1833, the first meetings for worship being held in the house of Rev. Josiah Philips. During that summer a church building was erected and in the fall Rev. Thomas C. Teasdale agreed to preach for them once each month during the year for $100. October 11, 1834, Rev. Enos M. Philips made a similar agreement. From this time on until 1835 there was preaching also by Rev. Josiah Philips, Rev. William Stedman and Rev. G. I. Miles. Rev. T. S. Griffith, who preached once each month from 1837 to 1840, began in this latter year to give his whole time to the church and remained until January 1, 1845, when he was succeeded by Rev. H. S. Haven, who died December 28, that year. Rev. J. M. Richards came next, remaining until October 1, 1850. The pastors who have since preached for this church have been as follows: Revs. J. S. Eisenbray, Uriah Coffman, J. W. Griffith, Jacob Lawrence, E. V. King, John Owen, during whose pastorate a union with East Nantmeal Church was effected and Rev. D. J. R. Strayor became pastor; then followed Rev. J. M. Guthrie, who remained pastor some years and resigned to become pastor of the Berean Baptist Church in West Chester, in 1879. Since then the pastors have been as follows: Revs. William Barrows, E. B. Waltz, R. R. Albin, and J. E. Keylor, the present pastor. Repairs have been recently made to the property which add much to its appearance. The church building is valued at $5,000 and the parsonage at $2,000. The membership of the church is now 124, and that of the Sunday-school 90.

The First Baptist Church of West Chester was organized in

1834, meetings having been held for some time previously at the house of Robert Ferguson to take into consideration the question of effecting such an organization. On January 23, 1834, this church was constituted with twenty-five members, Rev. Thomas C. Teasdale being the first pastor. A lot was purchased on Church Street, between Market and Miner Streets, for $400, and a new building erected thereon by Samuel Bart, at a cost of $1,065, the cupola costing $100. In 1842 the tower and steeple were added at a cost of $575, including the belfry. The church was chartered by the Legislature in 1844, and in 1855 the property was sold to George Fitzsimmons for $1,800, a lot having been purchased on South High Street upon which a new building was afterward erected, the corner-stone being laid July 4, 1854, the lecture room being occupied for the first time January 7, 1855, and the completed building dedicated August 28 and 29, 1857. This church, including the lot on which it stands, cost $10,811.67.

The pastors of this church, since the retirement of Rev. Mr. Teasdale, been as follows: Rev. George I. Miles, Lemuel Covell, H. R. Green, Silas W. Palmer, Emerson Andrews, Thomas S. Griffith, William A. Roy, Alfred S. Patton, Levi Parmley, Robert Lowrey, William E. Watkinson, James Trickett, Alfred Harris, William E. Cornwell, George H. Trapp, William E. Needham, J. H. Chambers, Joshua E. Wills. The church property is worth $12,000, seating capacity of church being 600.

The building was re-modeled in 1886, chairs taking the place of pews. A new pipe organ was put in in 1897, at a cost of $1,500, and was heard for the first time on Thursday evening, November 25, Thanksgiving evening. The church membership is now 413, and the Sunday-school has a membership of about 363. The present pastor, Rev. Joshua E. Wills, came to West Chester from Swarthmore, Delaware County. He is a literary gentleman as well as pastor, having published several books, among his most recent ones being a pamphlet entitled "Satan," in which he argues in favor of the doctrine of the personality of the arch adversary of man.

Phoenixville Baptist Church was organized May 28, 1830, with eight members, public services being held next day in the Methodist Church. A church edifice was erected in 1833, which was superseded in 1853 by a commodious structure at the corner of Church and Gay Streets, and was dedicated in July, 1834. The pastors here have been Revs. Jonathan G. Collon, William Smith, Thomas Larcombe, Dyer A. Nichols, Andrew Collins, William S. Hall, John P. Hall, Joseph Currin, William S. Hall, Joel E. Bradley, I. D. King, G. G. Craft, William H. Stenger, Jonathan Nichols, J. Madison Hare, and A. J. Hughes, the present pastor. The membership of this church is 512, and the church property is valued at $23,500.

East Nantmeal Baptist Church was organized November 5, 1841, with twenty-six members. Meetings were held for a couple of years in a school-house, but in 1843 a church building was dedicated, which cost $800. In 1880 a new church building was erected which cost $3,500. The pastors here have been Revs. A. Collins, D. A. Nichols, John Duer, William H. Ellis, F. Wilson, J. W. Plannett, C. H. Mellotte, and Walter Whitley, the present pastor. The membership of the church is 163, and the property is valued at $5,000.

East Brandywine Baptist Church was organized February 21, 1843, with fifty-three members, a church building having been erected the previous year. This building was burned down in 1856, and rebuilt the same year. The church was incorporated August 9, 1864, and the parsonage, which was purchased in 1870, is situated in Guthrieville. The pastors of this church have been Revs. Thomas S. Griffith, H. S. Haven, William J. Nice, John S. Christine, John M. Richards, George H. Mitchell, Jesse B. Williams, B. H. Fish, George H. Mitchell, S. Livermore, E. W. Ring, C. E. Young, T. G. Guessford, Maris Gibson, T. A. Lloyd, William Marlow, James

M. Guthrie, Morris Gibson, A. M. McCurdy, Walter Mayo, F. W. Randall and G. W. Renshaw, the present pastor. The membership of the church is twenty-five, and the property is valued at $4,500.

Pughtown Baptist Church was organized January 19, 1856, with twenty-five members. Two days previously it was resolved to abstain from the use of intoxicants for sacramental purposes. The pastors of this church have been as follows: Revs. Theophilus Jones, John Perry, John Entriken, J. G. Walker, E. P. Barker, S. Belsey, William Barrows, David Landis, J. H. Hyatt, W. O. Owen, and is now supplied by Rev. William T. Johnson. The membership of the church is now eighty-one, and the property is valued at $2,800.

The First Baptist Church of Coatesville was organized September 3, 1867, with forty-nine members, a building having been secured on April 3, previously, from the school board, and then fitted up for a place of worship. In 1869 most of this building was torn down and a new one erected in its place on the southwest corner of Third Avenue and Main Street, which was opened for worship January 1, 1870, and dedicated November 10, following. The pastors of this church have been as follows: Revs. A. C. Wheat, C. M. Deitz, E. Wildman, E. Edwards, from December 5, 1880, to July 9, 1882; E. E. Jones, November 1, 1882, to April 1, 1887; Joseph L. Sagebeer, September 1, 1887, until his death in 1890; Benjamin C. Needham, October 1, 1890, to 1896, when owing to failing health he was compelled to cease from labor and was succeeded by Rev. William E. Needham. The membership of the church is about 450, and the church property is valued at $25,000.

Willistown Baptist Church was organized in 1833, as a branch of the Great Valley Baptist Church. A church building was erected in 1875 at Malvern to take the place of the old building and the parsonage was erected in 1877. In 1881 the membership was 319, Rev. E. W. Bliss being pastor at that time. Since then there has been but one pastor, Rev. W. W. Dalbey, who came to the church June, 1893, the Rev. Mr. Bliss having closed his pastorate December 2, 1892. The church building is now valued at $15,000, and the parsonage at $4,000, total $19,000. The church society is entirely free from debt. The church membership is now 284, and that of the Sunday-school, 150. Since 1880 a fine double shed capable of holding 28 teams has been erected, and a bell has been put on the church weighing 700 pounds.

West Caln Baptist Church was organized as a branch of the Hephzibah Baptist Church in 1842 with twenty-six members, their petition for a separate church organization being granted upon condition that they pay all arrearages due the Hephzibah Church. Rev. Mr. Jenkins was permitted to devote one-fourth of his time to the new church. Subsequent to his pastorate the following have been the pastors of this church: Rev. David Jefferis, Rev. George H. Mitchell, Rev. A. G. Compton, Rev. W. H. H. Marsh, and Rev. George Coulter. At the present time no stated meetings are held by this church, which as an organization has ceased to exist, but preaching is supplied occasionally from Coatesville, as the pastors there may arrange.

Lawrenceville Baptist Church was organized April 14, 1858, and the church building erected that year was dedicated December 12, 1858, the cost of the building having been $1,700. The pastors of this church have been as follows: Revs. W. H. H. Marsh, John M. Perry, A. B. Still, Robert Dunlap, David Philips, A. H. Emmons, J. W. Griffith, C. W. O. Nyce, J. B. Soule, and the present pastor, Rev. W. T. Johnson. The membership of this church, now named Parkerford instead of Lawrenceville, is 186, and the property is valued at $5,000.

The Berean Baptist Church of West Chester was organized as the Mount Olive Baptist Church of West Chester, February 10, 1874. On April 2, the name was changed to the West Chester Baptist Church, and on the 16th of the same month the name was again changed to the Berean Baptist Church. The first sermon was preached by Rev. W. R. McNeil. November 2, 1874, the corner-stone of a church building was laid by the Rev. Edward McMinn, pastor, on a lot on the west side of Walnut Street, between Miner and Barnard Streets, the building being completed and dedicated in 1875. The pastors of this church have been as follows: Rev. Edward McMinn, William R. McNeil, T. A. Lloyd, James M. Guthrie, and David R. Landis, the last pastor. In 1889 this church property was purchased by H. J. Clouser, who lives adjoining it on the south, and in 1892 he sold it to the Second Presbyterian Church (colored), which has since occupied it. The building was erected in 1874.

The London Tract Baptist Church, so named because it was located on a tract of land purchased by the London Company, in Chester County, was made an independent church November 21, 1780. Previous to this date its history is involved in that of the Welsh Tract, which etends back to the beginning of the Eighteenth century. At the time of the organization of this church there were dismissed from the Welsh Tract church eighteen persons to aid in its formation. The Evans family were among the most prominent of the original members, and the church building stood upon their land. The first pastor appears to have been Rev. Thomas Fleeson, appointed November 22, 1780. In 1808 Rev. Jethro Johnson was pastor, preaching two Sundays each month, one at Brandywine and one at Hephzibah. Rev. Thomas Barton was pastor of this church for a period of fifty years, dying March 23, 1870. Rev. George W. Stator became pastor in March, 1873, and was succeeded by Rev. Joseph L. Stator in March, 1880.

Early in the history of this organization a new stone building was erected with the entrance on the south side; but in 1863, when this building was remodeled, the entrance was placed on the east side. The only pastor since the retirement of Rev. Joseph L. Stator, who died in 1892, has been Elder A. B. Francis. The membership of the church is now ten, and the property is worth $3,000. There is no Sunday-school connected with this church, as the members do not believe in them or in missions. This is an old-school Baptist Church, and they firmly believe in the doctrine that only the elect will be saved, hence Sunday-schools and missions are useless. In their view the Lord does all, and as a consequence of this belief their church seems doomed to continued decay and early extinction.

Green Valley Baptist Church was organized June 19, 1834, when a considerable number of members was dismissed from Hephzibah Church for that purpose. But it does not appear that a church building was erected for them until 1868, the question as to whether a building was needed in Newlin being investigated in 1866 by J. G. Powell, John Y. Woodward, and Job Keech from Hephzibah Church. In August, 1867, a "harvest home" was held in Daniel Pennock's woods, which brought in $320, and in June, 1868, a location was selected for the meeting-house, the corner-stone of which was laid July 30 that year. The basement of the building was opened for worship December 3, 1869, the sermon being preached by Rev. D. W. Hunter, and on October 9, 1870, the main audience room was opened for worship, the building being dedicated September 9 and 10, 1871. The sermon on this occasion was preached by the venerable Simeon Seigfried, and there was one preached also by the Rev. James Trickett.

The Oxford Baptist Church was constituted May 12, 1881, services having been held in that place then about two years by Rev. William R. McNeil.

Rev. William Barrows is pastor at the present time. At first Brinton's Hall was used as a place of worship, but in 1886 the society purchased the church building which had been formerly used by the Methodists and still own the building.

The Seventh Day Baptists of Pennsylvania first became known in the Province in 1697, when Abel Noble, who is claimed to have been the first Seventh Day Baptist to come to the Province (in 1684), baptized Thomas Martin, a friend, in Ridley Creek. Afterward Mr. Martin baptized other Quakers until nineteen had left their own society to become Baptists. On October 12, 1697, they were incorporated into a church with Thomas Martin as their minister. From that day no other Keithian Quakers were baptized. In 1700 a difference of opinion arose among them as to the Sabbath day, some claiming it to be Saturday, others, to be Sunday, and this difference of opinion broke up the church, those adhering to the Seventh day remaining together in Newtown.

This Newtown society held its meetings at the house of David Thomas, and after Thomas Martin had for ministers two named Buckingham and Budd. After the death of these two the society did not flourish to any great extent. The dead members of the church lie buried in the cemetery now owned by the Newtown Baptist Church.

Another society of Seventh Day Baptists was organized at Nottingham, Chester County, their meetings being held sometimes at the house of Abigail Price, but chiefly at the house of Samuel Bond of Cecil County, Maryland. They originated with the Keithians in Upper Providence, but, having no minister, they could not expect to grow.

There was still another society of this denomination at French Creek in East Nantmeal Township, which originated in 1726, a few members withdrawing from the Great Valley Baptist Church in Chester County. They had a meeting-house built in 1672 on a lot containing one acre of ground. There were six families belonging to this society, which had no regular minister. Their meeting-house, a frame one, was destroyed many years ago.

The German Baptists, or Dunkers, living in Coventry Township, organized themselves into a church in 1724, with the assistance of Bishop Peter Becker of Germantown. They celebrated a "love feast" and the Lord's Supper for the first time November 7, 1724, with eight communicants. Martin Urner was their first min-

47

ister, he being formally ordained in 1729 and serving the church until his death, in 1755. Mr. Urner's assistant, Casper Ingles, served also until Mr. Urner's death. The next regular minister was Martin Urner, a nephew of the first, who was ordained in 1756. Up to this time they had met in private houses, but under the supervision of Rev. John Price, familiarly known as "Johnny Price, the boy pastor," the present church building, known as "Price's Meeting-house," was erected. The Sunday-school was organized with about 110 members, some little time after the establishment of the church. Other noted ministers of the church, besides those already mentioned, have been Rev. George Price, the first bishop, and Rev. John Baugh. It has been found impracticable to secure later data in connection with this structure.

The Parkesburg Baptist Church was organized in 1888 with 48 members, after having been a branch of Glen Run Church for many years. In 1873 a lot was purchased on Rumford Street, near Gay, and a church building erected that year, which has a seating capacity of about 200, the cost of the building being $1,400. The pastors have been as follows: Revs. O. O. Owen, S. V. Marsh, F. H. Buffum, Harry S. Allen of Philadelphia, for about a year and a half; supplies then from Crozier; S. McGinnis about sixteen months; and at the present time William C. Stiver, who has been supplying the pulpit since December 1, 1897. The present membership of the church is 50, and of the Sunday-school 30. The church property is valued at about $1,200.

Olivet Baptist Church of West Chester was organized April 1, 1897, with 113 members, of whom 112 were regularly dismissed by letter from the First Baptist Church. Rev. J. H. Chambers, who had been for several years pastor of the First Baptist Church, became pastor of the new organization. The Sunday-school was organized April 4, 1897, with 144 members. For some time the congregation occupied the Opera House and later the Armory, but at length a lot was purchased on the corner of Union and New

Streets, on which a commodious chapel was erected early in 1898 at a cost of $8,000, the lot having cost $2,000. This chapel is constructed of blue stone, and contains 600 sittings. A church edifice is hereafter to be erected on Union Street front. The location of this church building is in a new and thriving part of West Chester, and it has made rapid strides in progress and prosperity. The pastor, Rev. J. H. Chambers, is an alumnus of Bucknell University and of Crozier Theological Seminary, and is an active, earnest man.

St. Paul's Baptist Church (colored) of West Chester, was organized in 1888, and a church building erected between Miner and Barnard Streets and between Penn and Adams Streets. Rev. Asbury Smallwood was the first pastor, remaining until 1893, when he was succeeded by the present pastor, Rev. J. C. King. The building belonging to this organization was destroyed by fire on Sunday, February 6, 1898, while church services were in progress in the other churches, St. Paul's congregation being driven out by the fire. They, however, immediately rented Sisters' Hall and continued their services therein while the old building was still burning. The building destroyed was worth about $500, on which there was no insurance, and the contents of the building, which were destroyed, were worth about $200.

A new building is now (July, 1898) in process of erection, the cornerstone to be laid August 7. When completed, the new building will be worth $3,000, and as the lots owned by the congregation cost $800, the entire property, including the furniture and organ, will be worth $4,000.

. The First Baptist Church of Kennett Square was organized December 20, 1882, at a council held for the purpose, seventeen churches being represented in the council. The first meeting held with this object in view was at the house of D. Duer Philips, and was under the direction of Rev. W. C. Naylor. Then came the evangelist, E. C. Romine, and after the organization of the church Rev. J. M. Lyons was sent as pastor, remaining from January 5,

1883, to January 24, 1884. Rev. Clarence Larkin became pastor October 12, 1884, and remained until June, 1898.

A lot at the corner of South Union and Cypress Streets was purchased October 22, 1883, and on May 12, 1885, ground was broken for the erection of a church. October 4, 1885, the building was opened for public services, Rev. W. H. Conard of Philadelphia preaching the sermon. Up to this time the services had been held in the second story of Taylor's Hall. The total cost of the new church was $5,649.25, and it was improved in 1892 at a cost of $280. On October 4, 1894, it was dedicated free from debt. The membership of the church is 160, and of the Sunday-school, 150. A mission of this church was organized at Unionville in March, 1897. Since the dedication of the church a lot has been purchased on the north for $1,100 and an annex built thereon at a cost of $1,300. There are several societies connected with the church, all of which are doing good work. The present pastor of this church, Rev. J. Ryland Murdoch, entered upon his duties on Sunday, July 3, 1898.

Methodism was introduced into Chester County, it is believed, by Rev. Isaac Rollins about 1772, he reaching the center of the county in 1773. Shortly afterward Francis Asbury came into the county, as, according to his journal, he reached Marlborough, where there was "a large congregation waiting," March 21, 1773. Isaac Rollins preached there that night and on the 23d Asbury was at Woodward's, on the Brandywine. In 1783, when not far from Yellow Springs, Isaac Rollins was thrown from his horse and killed on the spot. Between these dates, 1773 and 1783, there was preaching at several places in what is now Chester County. In 1774 Daniel Ruff and William Watters preached in this county, and it is thought that Rev Joseph Pilmore, one of the first Methodist missionaries to America, preached in the township of Uwchlan in 1772. In 1774 an appointment was made by several preachers in Uwchlan, near the Little Eagle Tavern, where Benson's Chapel was built in 1781, where Benjamin Abbott preached in 1780. From this meeting came Hopewell Methodist Church, and the lot on which it stood, still having on it a few graves, is still in possession of the Methodists.

Grove Methodist Church was founded in 1774, and is at the present time the oldest Methodist Church organization in the county, those formed previously having ceased to exist. The present church edifice was erected in 1844. The church was incorporated in 1868. In connection with this church there was what was called the "Smith Shop," which was located a short distance from Boot Tavern. It became a preaching place in 1834, being put in condition therefor by John S. Inskip. This was not a separate church, but was a kind of mission in connection with Grove Church. John S. Inskip was admitted on trial in 1836, and continued to preach for about fifty years.

The West Chester Methodist Episcopal Church was started in 1815, when the first class was formed in that place. Rev. William Hunted had preached there, however, in February, 1810, in the old court-house, he being presiding elder on the Schuylkill Circuit that year. The first church building was erected on Gay Street, east of Darlington, in 1816, and a new church was erected in 1840-42 on the corner of Market and Darlington. Under the pastorate of Rev. John B. McCullough in 1866-68 this building was remodeled and improved. The first preacher after West Chester was set apart from Chester Circuit was Whitefield Hughes, and since then the following have been pastors here: Revs. Daniel Parish, Jesse Thompson, Levi Scott, Thomas Sovereign, Josiah F. Canfield, James H. McFarland, Bartholomew Weed, John Lednum, Dallas D. Lore, William Urie, Matthew Sorin, John Nicholson, Thomas Muller, who filled the vacancy caused by the death of Rev. Mr. Nicholson; Elijah Muller, David E. Gardner, David Shields, James L. Houston, Alfred Cookman, Charles Karsner, Peter J. Cox, Michael D. Kurtz, James M. McCarter, James R. Anderson, Curtis F. Turner, John B. McCullough, William Major, Wesley C. Best, George Cummins, Sylvester N. Chew, Robert J. Carson, J. T Swindells, 1884-86; W. H. Schaffer, 1887-90; William J. Mills, 1891-92; T. M. Jackson, 1893-96; and D. M. Gordon, 1897 to the present time.

The church property is valued at about $20,000, and the parsonage at $3,000. The membership at the present time is about 480, and the number of probationers is somewhat more than fifty.

Phœnixville Methodist Church was formed in 1826, the first Methodist sermon being preached there by Rev. Samuel P. Levis. The first building used by this church congregation was a paint-shop, and their first church building was erected in 1828. The present building was erected in 1854, during the pastorate of Rev. C. J. Crouch. The regular pastors of the church have been as follows: Revs. David Shields, 1839-40; William W. McMichael, Thomas S. Johnson, Isaac R. Merrill, Joseph H. Wythes, Nicholas Ridgely, Henry R. Calloway, James Y. Ashton, Stearns Patterson; in 1853 Salem, Charlestown and Valley Forge were associated with Phœnixville and made a circuit, the preachers being C. J. Crouch and John F. Meredith; 1854, C. J. Crouch, and one to be supplied; 1855, Samuel R. Gillingham, Wesley Reynolds; 1856, S. R. Gillingham, Charles W. Ayars; 1857, John Shields, Horace A Cleveland; 1858, John Shields, George D. Miles; 1859-60, Phœnixville, a station, Allen John; William Major, Jeremiah Pastorfield, Allen John, James Flannery, George Heacock, Henry R. Calloway, John Dyson, Henry E. Gilroy, Goldsmith D. Carrow, T. C. Murphey, 1882-84; J. J. Timanus, 1885-87; H. Wheeler, 1888-92; H. T. Quigg, 1893-94; Theodore Stevens, 1895-97, and J. E. Diverty, 1898.

Anderson's Methodist Church, near Valley Forge, was organized soon after 1780, and was in existence until about 1825, about which time a class was organized at Daniel McCurdy's in the Valley. Anderson's Church was named after Isaac Anderson, a very prominent man in his day, at whose house the meetings of this class were held. Mr. Anderson had been a member of the Legislature of the State, and also a member of Congress. Francis Asbury preached at his house in 1812. Rev. Jacob Gruber was the preacher here in 1828. Isaac Anderson was for some time a local preacher among the Methodists. His grandson, Rev. James Rush Anderson, was a member of the Philadelphia Conference of the Methodist Church, and died November 8, 1863. This church belongs in Cochranville Circuit, Cochranville being in Lancaster County.

Laurel Methodist Church was established about 1800, meetings being held for several years at the house of William Ball, who moved to the neighborhood of Laurel in 1798. Rev. Richard Sneath was here as preacher about 1800, the church being then in Chester Circuit. He came again to this circuit about 1810. In 1812 a lot was purchased for a church building, for $1, the size of the lot being thirty-eight perches. The church building was erected on this lot in 1813. John McCarroll, father of Rev. Thomas McCarroll, was the first class at Laurel after the revival of the society. This church belongs to Thorndale Circuit, and is supplied from that place.

Romanville Methodist Church, in West Bradford Township, was established early in the present century. A cemetery was purchased here in 1811, upon which a church was to be erected. The land was conveyed by deed to Richard Webster, Isaac Rollins and John King, all of whom became famous in the ministry. One of the most noted Methodist divines that ever preached in Chester County was Rev. Thomas McCarroll, who was admitted on trial in 1829, and who died May 9, 1860. The church building was improved in 1868 by Rev. John C. Gregg, at a cost of $500, and an addition of twelve and three-fourths perches was made to the lot in 1871. The ministers of this church have been as follows: The same as in the Grove Methodist Church up to 1833; in this year Laurel became a part of a new circuit, called Soudersburg, on which were Revs. Thomas Miller and William Ryder; 1834, Revs.

John Lednum, Robert E. Morrison, Thomas Sumption; 1835, John Lednum, John Edwards; 1836, John Edwards, John A. Watson; 1837, Robert Anderson, Dallas D. Lore; 1838, Enos R. Williams, John A. Boyle; 1839, Enos R. Williams, Amos Griner; 1840, Brandywine Circuit formed, including Laurel, David E. Gardiner, Charles Wilson; 1841 to 1859, pastors same as in Marshallton Methodist Church; 1859, with Kennett Square; 1860, with Guthrieville Circuit, Thomas Newman; 1861, Thomas Newman, who left, and John A. Watson was appointed to take the place; 1862-63, Nehemiah W. Benham; then followed John C. Gregg, James Carroll and Alfred A. Fisher. In 1867 J. Pastorfield served this church and Marshallton; 1868, John C. Gregg; then followed William Coffman, J. W. Knapp, Frederick Illmau, Thomas Montgomery, John O'Neill, William W. Wisegarver, John T. Gray.

Springfield Methodist Church was formed in 1801, Elijah Bull being appointed to take charge of it. Regular services were held in various dwelling-houses until 1816, when the first church building was erected in Springfield, West Nantmeal Township, at a cost of $800. The present building was erected in 1868, just across the street from the old one, at a cost of $10,000, the parsonage being erected in 1879, at a cost of $1,450. The name of the circuit has been changed six times, and the following have been the pastors:

Strasburg and Chester Circuits.—1798, William P. Chandler, Daniel Higby; 1799, William Colbert, Edward Larkins, Robert Bonham (sup.); 1800, Stephen Timmons, Richard Sneath, Thomas Jones; 1801, William Hunter, Stephen Timmons, Robert McCoy; 1802, William Hunter, John Bethel; 1803, Anning Owen, William Brandon; 1804, William Hunter, Joseph Osborn, Joseph Stephens; 1805, William Hunter, David James, James Moore; 1806, John Walker, William Early; 1807, Daniel Ireland, Peter Beaver; 1808, Asa Smith, John Bethel, Thomas Miller; 1809 (Lancaster), James Smith, Thomas Burch; 1810 (Chester), Richard Sneath, John Fox; 1811, Richard Sneath, James Laws; 1812 (Lancaster), William Torbert, John Fernon; 1813, Richard Sneath, William Torbert, Joseph Samson; 1814, Asa Smith, James Mitchell, J. Samson; 1815, Thomas Miller, Phinehas Price; 1816, David Best, Thomas Miller; 1817, Robert Burch, John Woolson; 1818, Robert Burch, Phinehas Price; 1819, William Leonard, John Tally; 1820, John Woolson, William Ross; 1821, John Woolson, Henry G. King; 1822, H. Boehm, Wesley W. Wallace; 1824, Jacob Gruber, Thomas Miller, James Moore; 1825, Thomas Neal, George Wiltshire; 1826, Thomas Neal, Pharoah A. Ogden; 1827, Samuel Grace, George G. Cookman; 1828, Samuel Grace, David Best, John Lednum; 1829, (Reading), David Best, Manlove Hazel; 1830, (Waynesburg), John Lednum, Daniel Fidler; 1831-32, George Woolley, Jacob Gruber; 1833, David Best, Richard W. Thomas; 1834, Thomas Miller, John Spear; 1835, William Torbert, Allen John, John S. Inskip; 1836 (Springfield), William Torbert, Allen John; 1837, John Edwards, Henry Sutton; 1838, John Edwards, Henry Sutton; 1839-40, Jonas Bissey, Thomas Sumption; 1841, James Hand, William L. Gray; 1842, James B. Ayars, Arthur W. Milby; 1843, James B. Ayars, Peter J. Cox; 1844, James Hand, George D. Bowen; 1845, Richard M. Greenbank, Samuel Pancoast; 1846, Richard M. Greenbank, Henry B. Manger; 1847, John Edwards, John Walsh; 1848, John Edwards, Samuel R. Gillingham; 1849-50, Enos R. Williams, John Cummins; 1851, Eliphalet Reed, Peter Hallowell; 1852, Joseph Carlisle, Abraham Freed, John T. Gracey; 1853, Abraham Freed; 1854, Joshua H. Turner, Henry R. Bodine; 1855, Joshua H. Turner, Jerome Lindamuth; 1856, Lewis C. Pettit, William T. Magee; 1857, Lewis C. Pettit, William Smith; 1858, Elijah Miller; 1859, John Shields, E. Elliott; 1860-61, Valentine Gray, then follow: John A. Watson, William M. Ridgway, James F. McClelland, Charles J. Little, Joseph S. Lane, Thomas C. Pearson, John Dyson, John W. Knapp, Benjamin T. String, Adam L. Wilson, James I. Boswell, Samuel Howell, Maris Graves, J. O'Neill, 1882-84; R. A. McIlwaine, 1885-87; W. Powick, 1888-90; G. W.

North, 1891-93; A. L. Hood, 1894-95; T. A. Hess, 1896; John Priest. 1897-98.

Hopewell Methodist Church was known originally as Batten's Meeting-house. In this locality there there was a society as early at least as 1805. The second building occupied as a church was erected in 1823, the first one having been a log building. The name became Hopewell probably about 1828. The third church edifice erected was in 1872, during the pastorates of Revs. Allen John and George S. Quigley. The present edifice was erected in 1867. The pastors have been as follows: From 1805 to 1829, the same as those with Grove Church; 1829 to 1840, the same as those of the Waynesburg Church; 1840 to 1857, the same as those of the Coatesville Church; 1857 to 1880, the same as those of the Hibernia Church; in 1881 this was a separate charge, with Rev. John W. Geiger, pastor. Since then the pastors have been as follows: Revs. A. I. Collom, 1884-86; G. Alcorn, 1887-90; J. S. McKinlay, 1891-92; G. S. Kerr, 1893-97; R. C. Wood, 1898.

Coatesville Methodist Church was formed about 1824, though there had been preaching by Methodists in this vicinity as early as 1817. During the year 1827 Rev. William Cooper preached at Coatesville in a school-house. In 1830, as a result of a camp-meeting at Frendship in Highland Township, a number of persons were converted, and united with the church, and in the fall and succeeding winter a school-house was used for meetings, held every alternate Saturday night. As the society increased in numbers meetings were occasionally held in the Union Meeting-house, mentioned in connection with the Coatesville Presbyterian Church. During 1839 the Union Meeting-house became too small and a building which had been used as a blacksmith shop was secured. This building, popularly known as the "turtle-shell," was occupied as a church until May, 1845, when the first Methodist Church within the limits of Coatesville was erected, and dedicated by the Rev. William Urie. In

1856 a new church was built. From 1840 to the present time the preachers have been as follows:

Brandywine Circuit.—1840, David E. Gardiner, Charles Wilson; 1841, Henry Sutton, Wesley Henderson; 1842, Allen John, George S. Quigley; 1843, Allen John, Henry S. Atmore; 1844, James Harmer, George W. Lybrand; 1845, James Harmer, Stearns Patterson; 1846, John Bayne, William Robb; 1847, John Bayne, Jacob Dickerson; 1848, Joseph Carlisle; 1849, Joseph Carlisle, Joseph S. Cook; 1850, Henry Sanderson, Joseph S. Cook; 1851, Henry Sanderson, T. B. Miller; 1852, John Shields, Abel Howard; 1853, John Shields, James N. King; 1854, George W. Lybrand, E. S. Wells (six months), Edward T. Kenney (six months); 1855, George W. Lybrand, Edward T. Kenney; 1856, T. S. Thomas, A. M. Wiggins; 1857, Coatesville made a station and the pastors since then have been as follows: Revs. T. S. Thomas, William J. Paxon, William Rink, Isaac R. Merrill, Sylvester N. Chew, Wilmer Coffman, William S. Pugh, Wesley C. Johnson, John E. Kessler, Silas B. Best, Reuben Owen, Charles C. McLean, Samuel W. Gehrett, A. L. Wilson, E. C. Yerkes; 1891-96, H. Wheeler, D. D.; 1897-98, ———.

The church membership is about 475, and the church building, erected in 1883, standing on the corner of Chestnut Street and Third Avenue, cost $16,000, and will seat 900 persons.

Andrews' Methodist Church was established about 1828, meetings being at first held in the house of Henry Andrews. The meeting-house was built in 1831, on a lot of one acre given by Mr. Andrews on one corner of his farm. The building was sold in 1856 to James Smith, and by him converted into a dwelling. The pastors from 1831 to 1856 were as follows: 1831, Strasburg and Columbia circuit—Thomas Miller, Eliphalet Reed, R. W. Thomas; 1832, Thomas Miller, Eliphalet Reed, John Edwards, Robert E. Morrison; 1833 (Soudersburg circuit), Thomas Miller, W. Ryder; 1834, John Lednum, Robert E. Morrison, Thomas Sumption; 1835, John Lednum, John Edwards; 1836, John Edwards, John A. Watson; 1837,

Robert Anderson, Dallas D. Lore; 1838, Enos R. Williams, John A. Boyle; 1839, Enos R. W_{illi}a_{ms}, Amos Griner; 1840, Samuel Grace, Thomas S. Johnson; 1841, Samuel Grace, John D. Long; 1842, Gasway Oram, John C. Owens; 1843, Gasway Oram, G. D. Carrow; 1844, William K. Goentner, David Titus; 1845, William K. Goentner, Henry Sanderson; 1846, Allen John, John A. Whitaker; 1847, Allen John; 1848, James Harmer; 1849, John Bayne, George W. Brindle; 1850, John Bayne, John Thompson; 1851, William L. Gray, John J. Jones; 1852, Samuel G. Hare, Francis B. Harvey; 1853, Samuel G. Hare, John O'Neill; 1854, Thomas Newman, James L. Killgore; 1855, Thomas Newman, Abel Howard; 1856, John B. Dennison.

Elk Ridge Methodist Church, in East Nottingham Township, was organized about 1825, a class meeting being held that year in the house of Abraham Buckalew. The church building was completed in 1832, at a cost of $1,300. The pastors here have been as follows: 1830 (with Port Deposit Circuit), George Woolley, William Bloomer; 1831, Thomas McCarroll, Robert E. Kemp; 1832, Thomas McCarroll, J. B. Hagany; 1833, Jacob Gruber, John Spear; 1834, Levi Storks, Edward Kennard; 1835 (with Northeast Circuit), P. E. Coombe, C. J. Crouch; 1836 (with West Nottingham Circuit), Samuel Grace, John S. Inskip; 1839, W. Torbert, M. D. Kurtz; 1840, W. Torbert, Charles Schock; 1841, William C. Thomas, H. S. Atmore; 1842, Edward Kennard, James M. McCarter; 1843, George Barton, D. L. Patterson; 1844, George Barton, Abraham Freed; 1845, Eliphalet Reed, Henry B. Manger; 1846, Leeds K. Berridge, Thomas Miller; 1847, John D. Long, J. A. Whitaker; 1848, C. Schock, W. Robb; 1849, C. Schenck; 1850, Jonas Bissey; 1851 (Oxford Circuit), Jonas Bissey, John Thompson; 1852, John F. Boone, Reuben Owen; 1853, John Cummins, A. Howard; 1854, John Cummins, John Byson; 1855, John Edwards; 1856, T. B. Miller, E. T. Kenney; 1857, T. B. Miller, H. H. Bodine; 1858, John B. Dennison, John France; 1859, John B. Dennison, T. F. Plummer; 1860-61

(New London and Elk Ridge), John France; 1863, C. J. Crouch; 1864, G. L. Schaffer; 1865, H. H. Bodine; 1866-67, W. P. Howell; 1868, H. B. Manger, Levi B. Hoffman; 1869-70, John C. Gregg, J. C. Wood; 1871, John Shields, Robert C. Wood, F. B. Harvey; 1872, John Shields, F. B. Harvey, A. H. Maryott; 1873, John Shields; 1874-75, George W. Lybrand; 1876-77, Thomas Montgomery; 1878-79, Matthias Barnhill; 1880-81, Alden W. Quimby.

Flint Hill Methodist Church in Franklin Township was organized shortly prior to 1829, the first class meetings being held in Daughterty's paper mill. The first church building erected was destroyed by fire in 1850, and was rebuilt in 1861. For list of pastors the reader is referred to the sketch of the New London Methodist Episcopal Church.

Marshallton Methodist Church was organized about 1828, the first preaching place being a wheelwright shop, and there was also preaching by Rev. William Hodgson in the dwelling-house of Daniel Davis. The first church building was erected in 1829, and the appointments for this church appear in the West Chester list until 1841, since which time the pastors have been as follows: 1841, Henry Sutton, Wesley Henderson; 1842, Allen John, George S. Quimby; 1843, Allen John, H. S. Atmore; 1844, James Harmer, George W. Lybrand; 1845, James Harmer, Stearns Patterson; 1846, John Bayne, William Robb; 1847, John Jayne, Jacob Dickerson; 1848, Joseph Carlisle; 1849, Joseph S. Carlisle, Joseph C. Cook; 1850, Henry Sanderson, Joseph S. Cook; 1851, Henry Sanderson, T. B. Miller; 1852, John Shields, Abel Howard; 1853, John Shields, James N. King; 1854, George W. Lybrand, E. S. Wells, E. T. Kenney, the latter two six months each; 1855, George W. Lybrand, E. T. Kenney; 1856, T. S. Thomas, A. M. Wiggins; 1857, John Cummins, John France; 1858, John Edwards, J. O. Sypherd; 1859, made a station since when the pastors have been: 1859-60, Joseph Smith; 1861, Joseph S. Cook, then followed S. K. Kurtz, William H. Price, Alfred A. Fisher, John Edwards,

Jeremiah Pastorfield, Frederick Illmau, Thomas Montgomery, John O'Neil, William W. Wisegarver, John T. Gray, 1882-83; J. Dungan, 1884-86; J. H. Smith, 1887; L. B. Hughes, 1888-89; H. C. Boudwin, 1890-93; L. Eisenbeis, 1894; Edward Townsend, 1895-98.

Valley Forge Methodist Church was established about 1832, itinerant ministers having made their appearance here the year before, and the church building being begun in 1833. In the meantime Jacob Gruber and George Wooley preached in an old red frame school-house, known sometimes as the "synagogue." When the new church was nearly completed a fierce wind carried off the roof, and the congregation was compelled to worship in the basement for a time, and was unable to complete their building until 1837. This church has had a checkered history, sometimes being weak, at other times strong, but it has always held its ground in some way. About 1839 and 1840 Rev. David Shields and his brothers, John and Richard, were quite regular in their attendance, and among those who have since ministered to the spiritual necessities of this church have been Rev. George Haycock, Rev. C. I. Thompson, Rev. Robert A. McIlwain, Rev. L. Taylor Dugan, Rev. Joseph H. Boyd, Rev. William Powick, and Rev. John Bell. Since 1880 the preachers here have been as follows: T. K. Peterson, 1884; J. J. Timanus, 1885-86; John Flint, 1887-89; Samuel Gracey, 1890-94; J. M. Tomlinson, 1895-96, and D. C. Kauffman, 1897-98.

Good-Will Methodist Church was established about 1832, deriving its name, some say, from the Good-Will School-house, and as others say, from a dream of Thomas Millard, who had donated the land, and in his dream he heard the passage: "On earth peace, good-will toward men." The Church is on Good-Will Road, in West Nantmeal Township. The building was erected in 1832, at a cost of $1,600, was remodeled in 1877, and is valued now at about $3,000. The pastors from 1831 to the present time have been as follows: From 1831 to 1853, same as those of the Waynesburg Church; 1853 to 1871, with Springfield Circuit and same as those of the Springfield Church; 1871 to 1877, associated with Springton Circuit, ministers, William K. Macneal, Maris Graves, David M. Gordon, William W. Wisegarver; 1878, made a separate charge, ministers since then, George Mack, William Redheffer, C. Lee Gaul, George E. Kleinheim, J. S. McKinlay, E. Townsend, N. B. Masters, and Jethro B. Coleman, the present pastor. During the pastorate of Rev. Mr. Gaul 1884-87, a beautiful and substantial stone parsonage was erected, and while Rev. Mr. Masters was pastor, 1895-97, the church building was enlarged and improved at a cost of $2,000. The church property is worth $6,500; the church membership is 143, and the Sunday-school has 200 scholars.

Downingtown Methodist Church was established about 1825, preaching being had first at the house of William Wiggins, the first member. Meetings were held sometimes in a wheel-wright shop and sometimes in the house of Shepherd Ayres, who was the first class-leader. The church was built in 1833, on a lot purchased of Thomas Webster, the material being of stone, and the cost $648. The Sunday-school was established June 28, 1835. The old church having become too small for the congregation, in 1860 a lot was purchased across the street, on which a new church building was erected, and dedicated in 1868. This church has belonged to Chester Circuit, to Radnor, Brandywine, and Grove, becoming a separate charge in 1867. The pastors have been from 1824 as follows: From 1824 to 1840 same as those of Grove Church; 1840 to 1853, same as those of Coatesville Church; 1853 to 1867, same as those of Grove Church; since 1867 as follows: David W. Gordon, William W. McMichael, George T. Hurlock, George S. Broadbent, John Stringer, George G. Rakestraw, 1881 to 1884; George T. Hurlock, 1884 to 1887; Dr. Thomas Kelly, 1887 to 1889; A. L. Wilson, 1889 to 1894; George M. Brodher, 1894 to 1895; John Walker Jackson, D. D., 1895 to 1897, and William H. Pickop, 1897 to the present time. The present church building, located on Brandywine Avenue, at the head of Washington Avenue, was erected in 1889-90, and dedicated on the third Sunday in May, 1890. It is of stone, will seat, together with the Sunday-school room,700, and the church property is valued at $18,000. The membership is 282, and of the Sunday-school 240.

Sadsbury Methodist Church was established about 1833, in which year and the next the church edifice was erected. The pastors have been as follows: 1832, Thomas Miller, Eliphalet Reed, John Edwards; 1833 (Soudersburg Circuit), Thomas A. Miller, William Ryder; 1834, John Lednum, Robert E. Morrison; 1835, John Lednum, John Edwards; 1836, John Edwards, John A. Watson; 1837, Robert Anderson, Dallas D. Lore; 1838, Enos R. Williams; 1839, Enos R. Williams; 1840, Samuel Grace, Thomas S. Johnson; 1841, Samuel Grace, Thomas S. Johnson; 1842, Gasway Oram, John C. Owens; 1843, Gasway Oram, G. D. Carrow; 1844, William K. Goentner, David Titus; 1845, William K. Goentner, Henry Sanderson; 1846, Allen John, J. A. Whitaker; 1847, Allen John; 1848, James Harmer; 1849 (Cochranville Circuit), John Bayne; 1850, John Bayne, John Thompson; 1851, William L. Gray, John J. Jones; 1852, Samuel G. Hare, Francis B. Harvey; 1853 Samuel G. Hare, John O'Neill; 1854 (Brandywine Circuit), George W. Lybrand, E. S. Wells, E. T. Kenney, the latter two six months each; 1855, George W. Lybrand, E. T. Kenney; 1856, T. S. Thomas, A. M. Higgins; 1857 to 1880, same as those of Coatesville Church; 1881, with Hibernia and Thorndale, S. O. Garrison.

Unionville Methodist Church was organized about 1835, though there had been preaching in this vicinity from about 1774, at Thomas Preston's house, and from that time on up to the organization of the church. Rev. John Lednum preached in the summer time from 1835 to 1836 in Preston's woods, having quite a revival. An old log school-house was first used, then the academy building until the new church was erected in 1839-40, at a cost of about $500. The pastors here have been as follows: 1835 (Soudersburg Circuit), John Lednum, John Edwards; 1836, John Edwards, John A. Watson; 1837, Robert Anderson, Dallas D. Lore; 1838, Enos R. Williams, John A. Boyle; 1839, Enos R. Williams, Amos Griner; 1840 to 1858 (Brandywine Circuit), same as those of Marshallton Church; 1859 (Kennett Square), Lewis Chambers; 1861 (Marshallton and Unionville), Joseph Cook; 1862-63 (Marshallton and Kennett Square), S. W. Kurtz; 1864, William H. Fries; 1865, Alfred A. Fisher; 1866, John Edwards; 1867 (Kennett Square and Unionville), John Edwards; 1869-70 (Chatham and Kennett Square), Robert C. Wood; 1872, George Alcorn; 1873, A. L. Hood; and from that time on until 1881, the following: E. C. Yerkes, Edward L. McKeever, Elim Kirk, W. K. Galloway, W. F. Sheppard, and S. T. Horner. About this time, 1880, the society was disbanded and the church was closed.

Hibernia Methodist Church was established about 1840, a church building being erected that year or the next. The pastors here have been as follows: 1840 to 1857, the same as those at Coatesville Church; 1857 to 1860, part of Brandywine Circuit, John Cummins, John France, John Edwards, John B. Quigg; 1860-61 (Guthrieville Circuit), preachers since then: Thomas Newman, N. W. Bennum, John C. Gregg, James Carroll, Alfred A. Fisher, William Coffman, George A. Wolfe, Wesley C. Johnson, Edward Townsend, Henry F. Isett, Israel M. Gable, S. O. Garrison, W. Powick, 1882-83; A. I. Collom, 1884-86; G. Calloway, 1887-90; J. S. McKinlay, 1891-92; G. S. Kerr, 1893-97; R. C. Wood, 1898.

Charlestown Methodist Church was started about 1830, Methodism having been introduced into this neighborhood by Rev. David Best. The church was erected in 1840 at a cost of $1,200. From 1830 to 1852 the pastors were the same as those at Grove Church; 1853 to 1858, same as at Phœnixville; and since then as follows: Lewis C. Pettit, John O'Neill, James Hand, John Edwards, William Hammond, Thomas Sumption, Daniel L. Patterson, William T. Magee, George A. Wolfe, John D. Fox, Richard Kaines, Frederick M. Brady, 1881-82; A. W. Quimby, 1884-86; J. A.

48

Cooper, 1887; W. H. Zweizig, 1888; F. B. Harvey, 1889-91; A. A. Thompson, 1892-94; Frederick Illman, 1895-96; Allen Judd, 1897-98.

Temple Methodist Church, in North Coventry Township, was established about 1840, in which year a class was formed by Rev. James Harmer.   In 1843 a "slab shanty" was erected for a meeting-house on the site of the present church, and in 1844 a stone church building was erected, 30x40 feet, by Revs. Peter J. Cox and David R. Thomas, they calling it the Temple, hence the name of the church.   The pastors have been as follows: James Harmer, James Flannery, Henry B. Manger, D. Titus, Peter J. Cox, David R. Thomas, up to 1844.   From this year to 1859, same as with the Bethel Church.   Then followed John O'Neill, Silas B. Root, Jerome Lindemuth, Samuel T. Kemble, Valentine Gray, Samuel Lucas, Thomas Sumption, George S. Conoway, John T. Swindells, William M. Dalrymple, Thomas C. Pearson, John Shields, up to 1870, in which year this church became a separate charge, and since then: John A. Cooper, John Edwards, Joseph J. Sleeper, Hiram U. Sebring, George W. Lybrand, J. Ramford, H. H. Bodine, W. Bamford, and the following as supplies: Amos Crowell, R. Cooper, A. E. Piper, J. E. McVeigh and W. H. Stewart.

In 1874 the church building was rebuilt, the size being made 37x55 feet, with end gallery and two class-rooms, the cost being $2,300.   It was dedicated October 11, 1874.

Washington Methodist Church was formed in 1819, the membership springing up to seventy-five within eighteen months.   A school-house was used as a house of worship until the church was erected in 1841, at a cost of about $400.   It was repaired and improved in 1867 or 1868.   The pastors here have been as follows: 1821 to 1832, same as those with Grove Church; 1832, Thomas Miller, Eliphalet Reed, John Edwards, Robert E. Morrison, being then connected with Strasburg and Columbia Circuits; 1833 (Soudersburg Circuit), Thomas Miller, William Ryder; 1834, John Lednum,

Robert E. Morrison; 1835, John Lednum, John Edwards; 1836, John Edwards, John A. Watson; 1837, Robert Anderson, Dallas D. Lore; 1838, Enos R. Williams, John A. Boyle; 1839, Enos R. Williams, Amos Griner; 1840 (Brandywine Circuit), and ministers from that time to 1881, same as those with Laurel Church. Since then the ministers and supplies have been as follows: C. L. Gaul, W. C. Graff, W. E. Smith, G. J. Schall, H. R. Bozorth, J. E. McVeigh, J. P. Burdette, S. McWilliams and F. Mack, the latter in 1898.

Bethel Methodist Church, in South Coventry Township, was organized about 1844, the church building having been erected that year, although services according to Methodist forms had been held for several years. When the church was dedicated the membership was about twenty. In 1875 this church was associated with Temple and St. James' churches and made a separate charge. The following have been the pastors in connection with the Pottstown Circuit: 1844, Peter J. Cox, David R. Thomas; 1845, Peter J. Cox, John Shields; 1846, John W. Arthur; 1847, John W. Arthur; 1848, John C. Thomas; 1849, John C. Thomas, James E. Meredith; 1850, George R. Crooks; 1851, Allen John, Joshua H. Turner; 1852, James Hand, Levi B. Beckley; 1853, James Hand, William E. Manlove; 1854, Abraham Freed, John F. Meredith; 1855, Abraham Freed, Noble Frame; 1856, John Edwards; 1857, John Edwards, William T. Magee; 1858, Daniel L. Patterson, Lewis C. Pettit; 1859, Daniel L. Patterson, John Brandreth; 1860, John B. Dennison, Isaac Last; 1861, John B. Dennison, John A. Watson; 1862, Valentine Gray, Lorenzo D. McClintock; 1863, Joseph Aspril, D. W. Gordon; 1864, Samuel G. Hare, Samuel H. Reisner; 1865, Samuel G. Hare; 1866, John Allen, Adam L. Wilson; 1867, John Allen; 1868-69, J. P. Miller; 1870-71, Richard Turner; 1872-73, John H. Wood; 1874, John Raymond; 1875-77, Hiram U. Sebring; 1878-80, George W. Lybrand; 1881, J. Bamford; 1881-83, G. L. Schaffer; 1883, T. M. Mutchler; 1884, C. M. Simpson; 1885-86, W. Mullin; 1887, L. D. McClintock; 1888, A. M. Wiggins; 1890, E. W. Burke; 1891-92, N. H. Beyer; 1893-96, J. F. Kingsley; 1897-98.

Spring City Methodist Church, in East Vincent Township, was established about 1845, the first meetings being held in what was known as the Lyceum Building, on Main Street. The first church building, built as a union building in 1846, was purchased by the Methodists in 1848. Its cost was $1,120. The present edifice, which was begun in 1872 and completed in 1880, cost $8,000. The pastors here have been as follows: In connection with Pottstown Circuit, 1844, Peter J. Cox, David R. Thomas; 1845, Peter J. Cox and John Shields; 1846-47, J. W. Arthur; 1848, John C. Thomas; 1849, John C. Thomas, James E. Meredith; 1850, George R. Crook; 1851, Allen John, Joshua H. Turner; 1852, James Hand, Levi H. Beckley; 1853, James Hand, William E. Manlove; 1854, Abraham Freed, John F. Meredith; 1855, Abraham Freed, Noble Frame; 1856, John Edwards; connected with Evansburg mission in 1857, Joseph Dare; 1858 (with Perkiomen Circuit), William T. Magee; 1859-60, Jacob Slicher; 1861, William M. Ridgway; 1862, William M. Ridgway, D. W. Gordon; 1863, Reuben Owen; 1864, Reuben Owen, Henry F. Isett; 1865-66, James Hand; 1867, Edward Townsend, Thomas B. Neely; 1868-69 (Springville, associated with Bethel), Jacob P. Miller; and since then as follows: Richard Turner, John H. Wood, Eli Pickersgill, David H. Shields, Joseph P. Graff, N. D. McComas, 1882-84; J. O'Neil, 1884; H. B. Cassavant, 1885-87; J. Bawden, 1888-90; L. B. Brown, 1891-94; D. M. Gordon, 1895-96, and S. H. Evans, 1897-98.

Glen Moore Methodist Church, in Wallace Township, was established about 1832, a class being formed in 1831, near Glen Moore Station. In 1844 a church was built near Brandywine Creek, and named Springton Methodist Episcopal Church. The cost of the building was $1,100. In 1873 a new church was erected at a cost of $10,500. When organized this church was included in the Waynesburg Circuit, called, in 1836, Springfield. The pastors here from 1831 to 1871 were the same as those with Springfield Church; in 1871-72, William K. MacNeal, and since then, Maris

Graves, D. M. Gordon, William W. Wisegarver, Robert A. Mc-Ilwain, George Gaul, Edward Devine, William H. Pickop, William F. Shepard, Edward Townsend, Charles W. Green, C. M. Hadda-way, Francis B. Harvey, and Henry S. Beales, the present pastor, who came to this church in the spring of 1897. The value of the church property is $14,000, the church membership, 147, and that of the Sunday-school, 129.

Landenburg Methodist Church was established about 1848, a church building being erected that year at a cost of $800. From 1869 to 1881 the pastors were the same as those with Elk Ridge Church.

New London Methodist Church was established about 1850, the first class-leader being William Rudolph, and the first preach-ing in New London Academy. The church was erected in 1850, and leased by the Odd Fellows to the church society for ninety-nine years. On Sunday, August 17, 1851, Rev. Jonas Bissey was killed by lightning in the church. The pastors have been the same as those with Elk Ridge Church, but since 1880 they have been here as follows: A. W. Quimby, 1881-83; E. Potts, 1884-86; F. M. Brady, 1887; H. C. Boudwin, 1888-89; C. W. Langley, 1890-94; M. Barnhill, 1895-96; R. J. McBeth, 1897, and J. G. Cornwell, 1898.

Penningtonville Methodist Church was started about 1845, the first Methodist preaching being in the shop of Charles Reese. Afterward Independence Hall was rented, and services held therein once in two weeks. In 1853 a church edifice was begun, the basement of which was first used for worship in 1854, and the upper room was dedicated June 3 and 4, 1860, the cost of the building being $4,000. The pastors here have been as follows: 1845, William K. Goentner, Henry Sanderson; 1846, Allen John, J. A. Whitaker; 1847, Allen John; 1848, James Harmer; 1849 (Cochranville Circuit), John Bayne, George W. Brindle; 1850, John Bayne, John Thompson; 1851, William L. Gray, John J. Jones; 1852, Samuel G. Hare, Francis B. Harvey; 1853, Samuel G. Hare,

John O'Neill; 1854, Thomas Newman, James L. Killgore; 1855, Thomas Newman, Abel Howard; 1856, John B. Dennison, John Hersey; 1857, John B. Dennison, John E. Kessler; 1858, John Cummins; 1859, John Cummins, Nathan B. Durrell; 1860-61, William H. Burrell; 1862, Joseph Dare, Robert W. Jones; 1863, Henry B. Manger, Robert W. Jones; 1864, Henry B. Manger, Wilmer Coffman; 1865, Valentine Gray, Wesley C. Johnson; 1866, Valentine Gray, Levi B. Hoffman; 1867, Samuel Pancoast, John D. Rigg; 1868, Samuel Pancoast, Thomas Morris; 1869, Joseph Aspril, John W. Wright; 1870, Joseph Aspril, William Downey; since then, Joseph Aspril, William W. McMichael, Isaac R. Merrill, Ephraim Potts and Francis B. Harvey; Israel M. Gable and Francis B. Harvey; ,Israel M. Gable, William P. Howell David H. Shields, Hiram U. Sebring, David T. Smythe, Arthur Oakes, G. W. Beatty, Richard Bayliss, I. C. Kirkesleger, A. E. Piper, Thomas Price, Urban E. Sargent, Charles Burns, Francis B. Harvey, A. M. Strayhorn, Joseph L. Gensemer, and the present pastor, Rev. Bertram Shay. The church property is valued at about $5,000.

Salem Methodist Church was established in 1833, about which time a church was erected which lasted the congregation until 1874, when a new church was erected, which was dedicated May 1, 1875, and the cost of which was $6,000. The pastors of this church have been as follows: 1833 (Chester Circuit), James B. Ayars, Robert E. Morrison, John Edwards; 1834 (Radnor Circuit), David Best, Richard W. Thomas; 1835, Richard W. Thomas, John Perry; 1836, William Cooper, Jesse Ford; 1837, William Cooper, James Hand; 1838, James B. Ayars, Charles W. Jackson; 1839, James B. Ayars, Frederick Gram; 1840, Henry G. King, James Neill; 1841, Henry G. King, Levin M. Prettyman; 1842, George Lacey, C. J. Couch; 1843 (Grove Circuit), Thomas Sumption, Thomas C. Murphey; 1844, Thomas Sumption, James R. Anderson; 1845, David Dailey, John W. Mecaskey; 1846, David Dailey, George W.

Lybrand; 1848, H. S. Atmore and local preachers; 1849, James Harmer, Stearns Patterson; 1850, James Harmer, William C. Robinson; 1851, Joseph H. Wythes, John H. Boyd; 1852, John H. Wythes, John J. Jones; 1853 (Phœnixville Circuit), C. J. Crouch, John F. Meredith; 1854, C. J. Crouch; 1855, Samuel R. Gillingham, Wesley Reynolds; 1856, Samuel R. Gillingham, Charles W. Ayars; 1857, John Shields, Horace A. Cleveland; 1858, John Shields, George D. Mills; 1859 (Salem Circuit), Lewis C. Pettit; and since then, John O'Neill, James Hand, John Edwards, William Hammond, Thomas Sumption, Daniel L. Patterson, William T. Magee, Ravel Smith, Samuel W. Smith, whose unexpired term was filled by Andrew Cather; William H. Aspril, Ephraim Potts, Andrew L. Amthor, 1881; J. McQuoid, 1882-83; E. Townsend, 1884; Thomas Montgomery, 1885-87; J. W. Hudson, 1888-89; Richard Morelly, 1890; Lewis A. Pascells, 1891-96; T. N. Hyde, 1897-98.

The Berwyn Methodist Episcopal Church grew out of a Sunday-school organized in 1881, in the house of Peter W. Ziegler, living near Devon, who was its first superintendent. The movement was inaugurated by the Rev. Andrew Cather, and shortly afterward an inexpensive frame chapel was erected, in which Enoch S. Wells, William A. Fisher, G. Wilde Linn, M. D., and other local preachers officiated. This building collapsed in the winter of 1883, owing to an accumulation of snow on the roof, and then, as some of the members lived at Berwyn, the services were transferred to that place, but the charge was known in the minutes of the conference of that year as the Devon Church. In March, 1884, the society was connected with Salem charge, Rev. Edward Townsend, pastor, and a church lot was purchased. In March, 1885, Berwyn was made a separate charge, with Rev. Daniel Hartman, after whom Governor Hastings was named, as pastor. In March, 1886, Rev. Alexander M. Wiggins was appointed pastor, and in that year the erection of a tasteful stone church was begun. In March, 1888, Rev. Samuel C. Carter became pastor, and prosecuted the work of building the church, completing it, and dedicating it on December 30.   In March, 1889, Rev. Charles W. Straw became pastor, and remained until March, 1894, when Rev. Franklin F. Bond succeeded him, and remained until March, 1896, when the present pastor, Rev. Alden W. Quimby, became pastor.   The membership of the church is now seventy, and the value of the church property, including the parsonage, is $13,000.

The Pomeroy Methodist Church has had the following pastors: Rev. J. T. Gray, 1884-86; Rev. E. Devine, 1887-88; Rev. J. M. Wheeler, 1889-90; Rev. B. F Miller, 1891-92; Rev. Matthias Barnhill, 1893-94 Rev. Delaplain Gollie, 1895-96; Revs. J. W. Williams and Albert Clegg, 1897, and Rev. J. W. Miles, 1898.   Under the pastorate of Rev. B. F. Miller, the church building was remodeled and greatly improved, and the church itself is now a separate charge.

Oxford Methodist Church was established about 1828, services being conducted from that year to 1851 in Hopewill Mill.   In the latter year a church edifice was erected and dedicated by Revs. Francis Hodgson and Andrew Manship.   The delay in erecting a church building here was in the opposition to Methodism, which led everyone to refuse to sell ground upon which to erect a church. At length this difficulty was overcome by a stranger purchasing the land on which the present Baptist Church building stands.   The first parsonage was built in 1877 or 1878, and the present one in 1886.   The pastors here have been as follows: 1828 (Strasburg Circuit), George Woolley, John Nicholson; 1829, George Woolley, Thomas McCarroll; 1830 (Port Deposit Circuit), George Woolley, William Bloomer; 1831 (Cecil Circuit), William Torbert, James Nichols; 1832, William Torbert, William Spry; 1833, Eliphalet Reed, George M. Yard; 1834, Levi Stork, Edward Kennard, John A. Roach; 1835 (Northeast Circuit), Pennell Coombe, C. J. Crouch; 1836 (West Nottingham), William Ryder, C. J. Crouch; 1837-38 (Nottingham), Samuel Grace, John S. Inskip; 1839, William

Torbert, M. D. Kurtz; 1840, William Torbert, Charles Schock; 1841, William C. Thomas, H. S. Atmore; 1842, Edward Kennard, James McCarter; 1843, George Barton, D. L. Patterson; 1844, George Barton, A. Freed; 1845, Eliphalet Reed, H. B. Manger; 1846, Leeds K. Benidge, Thomas Miller; 1847, John D. Long, J. A. Whitaker; 1848, Charles Schock, William Robb; 1849, Charles Schock; 1850, Jonas Bissey; 1851 (Oxford Circuit), Jonas Bissey, John Thompson; 1852, John F. Boone, Reuben Owen; 1853, John Cummins, Abel Howard; 1854, John Cummins, John Dyson; 1855, John Edwards; 1856, T. B. Miller, E. T. Kenney; 1857, T. B. Miller, Henry H. Bodine; 1858, John B. Dennison, Nathan B. Durell; 1859, John B. Dennison, Thomas F. Plummer; 1860, Joseph Carlisle; 1861, James Hand; 1863-64, Thomas Sumption; 1865-66, Francis B. Harvey; 1867, H. B. Manger, W. M. Gilbert; 1868, made a separate station, and since then the ministers have been: John Stringer, A. M. Wiggins, Levi B. Hoffman, Samuel G. Hare, Benjamin T. Strong, George A. Wolfe, Matthew Sorin, James C. Wood, Richard Kaines, 1880-83; W. Bamford, 1884-87; A. G. Kynett, 1888; T. Kelly, 1889; J. P. Miller, 1890-91; W. W. Cookman, 1892-94; George Cummins, 1895; D. S. Sherry, 1896; W. J. Mills and A. D. Mink, 1897-98.

The membership of the church is 400; Sabbath-school, 250; value of property, $20,000.

Kennett Square Methodist Church appears first as a mission in 1853, and in 1854 there were eighteen members and forty-five probationers. The pastors have been as follows: 1854 (Mount Salem and Kennett Square Mission), Thomas W. Simpers, William M. Dalrymple; 1855-56 (Kennett Square Mission), Francis B. Harvey; 1857-58, John Dyson; 1859, L. Chambers; 1860, Joseph Cook; 1861 (with Marshallton and Unionville), Joseph Cook; 1862-63 (Marshallton and Kennett Square), Samuel W. Kurtz; 1864, William H. Fries; 1865, Alfred A. Fisher; 1866, John Edwards; 1867 (Kennett Square and Unionville), John Edwards; 1868 (Kennett Square), 1869-70 (Chatham and Kennett Square), Francis B. Harvey, William W. Barlow; and since then at Kennett Square, Robert C. Wood, George Alcorn, A. L. Hood, E. C. Yerkes, E. J. McKeever, Elim Kirk, W. F. Sheppard, S. T. Horner, H. R. Robinson, J. S. McKinlay, 1884; J. E. Grauley, 1885-86; H. C. Boudwin, 1887; A. F. Taylor, 1888-89; O. C. Burt, 1890-91; George Alcorn, 1892-94; T. N. Hyde, 1896, and J. H. Earp, 1897-98. In 1854 a frame church building was erected, which lasted until 1884, when it was superseded by a substantial brick edifice erected on the same site, which was dedicated in 1885, free of debt. Since then a neat parsonage has been erected. In 1891 an Epworth League was organized in connection with the church.

St. James' Methodist Church was organized first as a class at Cedarville in 1871. In 1872 John Edwards was pastor, and in 1873-74 Joseph J. Sleeper. During the pastorate of Rev. Mr. Sleeper George Wagner gave the organization a piece of ground on which to erect a church, which was 37x60 feet in size, and the basement of which was dedicated June 27, 1874, and the main audience room dedicated in 1877. The pastors here have been Revs. Thomas A. Fernley, Joseph J. Sleeper, H. W. Sebring, George W. Lybrand, J. Bamford, and Curtis T. Turner being the supply at the present time.

The Parkesburg Methodist Episcopal Church was organized in 1875, but there had previously been services there by Methodist ministers. A stone church building erected by the Baptists, but afterward owned by the Episcopalians, became their place of worship, they renting it until 1879, when they purchased it. This building was occupied until 1890, when it was sold to the Odd Fellows, and a fine new brick church building erected on Main Street, at a cost of $8,000. This new building involved the society in financial difficulties, but under the pastorate of Rev. J. W. Jackson the debt was reduced to $2,400; and during the pastorate of Rev. F. A. Gacks this indebtedness was paid, and the church is now free from debt. The church was connected with Atglen Circuit until 1882, when it became a separate charge. The present membership is 235, with a membership in the Sunday-school of 250.

The ministers have been as follows: Ephraim Polk, I. M. Gable, William P. Howell, David Shields, H. N. Sebring, John F. Gray, Edward Devine, John M. Wheeler, J. W. Jackson, J. E. Diverty and F. A. Gacks, the latter of whom came to the church in March, 1896, and is pastor at the present time.

Hamorton Methodist Church was started in 1872, when a lot was donated on which to erect a building, and on which a neat frame building was erected in 1873 at a cost of $3,000. The pastors have been the same as those at Kennett Square, up to 1881; since then they have been as follows: J. S. McKinlay, J. E. Grau ley, H. C. Boudwin, A. F. Taylor, O. C. Burt, George Alcorn, T. N. Hyde and J. P. Earp.

Thorndale Methodist Church was started in 1875, by Rev. George S. Broadbent, while he was pastor at Dowingtown. The services were continued through 1875 and 1877 by him, and by Rev. John Stringer through 1878-79-80, and during this latter year a neat chapel was erected and dedicated. In 1881 it was associated with Hibernia and Sadsbury Methodist Churches, Rev. S. O. Garrison being the pastor. Since then the pastors have been as follows: W. Powick, 1882-83; John Bell, 1884-86; I. C. Kirk, 1888; A. F. Greenig, 1890; L. B. McClintock, 1891-96; John Boehm, 1897, and J. W. Fryer, 1898.

Avondale Methodist Church had its origin during the summer of 1868, a meeting being held at the house of J. B. Steward, October 28, seven persons being present. The Sunday-school was organized May 23, 1869, and on June 7, 1869, the hall of Tiba Lamborn was used for the first time, the attendance having largely increased. In 1870 a two-story building was erected for church purposes at a cost of $1,400.90. This building was destoyed by fire in 1880, and in 1881 a new one was erected at a cost of $2,000 and dedicated in February that year. The pastors here have been as follows: Rev. J. B. Steward, May, 1866, to March, 1873; and since then John D. Fox, T. L. Nelson, W. B. Chalfant, S. H. Evans, William H. Aspril, L. T. Dugan, Reuben Johnson, James Sampson, John W. Rudolph, S. W. Smith, C. W. Langley, 1886-87; S. Pancoast, 1888-89; J. G. Wilson, 1890-91; J. W. Bradley, 1892-94; C. B. Johnston, 1895-97; R. E. Johnson, 1898.

The African Methodist Church at Oxford was established in 1884, in which year the present church building was erected. Rev. Robert Murray was pastor in 1894.

The Union American Methodist Episcopal Church at Coatesville was organized by Rev. William Hutchings, in 1864, Rev. Mr. Hutchings becoming its first pastor. During the same year a substantial brick church edifice was erected at the corner of Sixth Avenue and Merchant Street, which is still in use, though it has undergone extensive improvements within recent years. At the present time the church membership is about 100, and Rev. L. A. Purnell is the pastor. The church property is worth about $4,000.

St. Luke's African Methodist Episcopal Church was organized in 1860, by Rev. Luke Smith, assisted by Rev. John C. Ramsey, Rev. L. P. Hood, and Rev. William Dorsey. It is located on South Franklin Street, West Chester. The first place of worship was a small one-story frame building on East Union Street, which was used until 1864, when the present location on South Franklin Street was purchased. The first church on this site was a one-story brick, 30x40 feet in size, and together with the site valued at $1,500, and this church was used until 1881, when the present edifice was erected. The ministers in charge since the organization have been as follows: Revs. Luke Smith, William Hutchings, John Clements, B. T. Ruby, Perry Gibbs, Benjamin Jeffers, Isaac Williams, Lewis Roberts, Asbury Smith, Lewis Jones, William H. Eley, John L. Hood, L. A. Purnell, R. S. Accou, William H. Guy and Jacob F. Ramsey. The present membership of the church is about 200, and of the Sunday-school about 170. The church property is valued at $6,000.

Prior to 1882 the colored Methodists of Coatesville worshiped at the little church at "Buzzard's Glory," near Atglen, in accordance with the forms of the African Methodist Episcopal Church, but at this time they organized a church in Coatesville, erected a frame building, which was dedicated in 1883. Rev. William Grimes was the first minister, and the membership was about thirty. The building is on Seventh Avenue and Merchant Street, East Coatesville. The church is now in a prosperous condition, with about 70 members, and there is also a flourishing Sunday school.

The Union American Episcopal Church (colored) is located at Sixth Avenue and Merchant Street, Coatesville, the building having been dedicated in October, 1869. Rev. William Hutchings was the first pastor. The church has a membership of about 200.

Bethel African Methodist Episcopal Church was organized about 1833 at the residence of James Berry, who then lived at the lower end of West Market Street, West Chester. The corner-stone of a proposed church building was laid by Rev. Joseph Corr, of Philadelphia, but the building was never completed. Later the congregation erected a building, called Zion Church, in which they worshiped until 1861, when they removed to the school-house at the corner of Barnard and Adams Streets, but soon afterward they purchased the present site on East Miner Street, and in 1868 began the erection of a new building, which lasted until 1880, when it was enlarged to meet the necessities of a larger congregation, and thus enlarged it is still in use.

The pastors of this church since 1845 have been as follows: Revs. William H. Jones, John L. Armstrong, John Butler, Abram C. Crippen, Isaac B. Parker, Israel Scott, Richard Barney, George Greenly, Peter Gardiner, Henry Davis, James Hollon, Richard Barney, Stephen Smith, William R. Norris, J. P. Campbell, John

W. Stevenson, John R. V. Morgan, Jeremiah Young, Elisha Weaver, Edward Laws, Peter Gardiner, James V. Pierce, John C. Cornish, Henry J. Rhodes, Henry Davis, Isaiah S. Taylor, William R. Norris, Amor Wilson, Leonard Patterson, L. C. Chambers, Lewis Hood, L. C. Chambers, John C. Brock, John B. Stansbury, A. A. Cromartie, Theodore Gould, and M. C. Brooks, from 1894 to the present time.

In 1894 a parsonage was erected at a cost of $2,100. The membership of the church in 1897 was 193, and the membership of the Sunday-school 388. The church property is valued at about $10,-000.

St. Paul's African Methodist Episcopal Church, at Coatesville, located at the corner of Seventh Avenue and Merchant Street, was presented to the church society by Trinity Episcopal Church, and was moved in sections to its present site in 1883. The first minister here was Rev. William Grimes, and the present minister is Rev. W. B. Pearson. The church membership is twenty-two, and the Sunday-school scholars, about twenty-five. The property is valued at about $5,000.

Waynesburg Methodist Church was established about 1824, in which year the old church was erected, and a church building was erected about the same time at Cambridge. The present Waynesburg Church was erected in 1843, and was dedicated in a sermon by Rev. Matthew Sorin. Since 1830 the preachers have been as follows: 1831-32, George Woolley, Jacob Gruber; 1833, David Best, Richard W. Thomas; 1834, Thomas Miller, John Spear; 1835-36, William Torbert, Allen John; 1837, John Edwards, Henry Sutton; 1838, same and John A. Watson; 1839-40, Jonas Bissey, Thomas Sumption; 1841, James Hand, William L. Gray; 1842, James B. Ayars, Peter J. Cox; 1844, James Hand, George D. Bowen; 1845, Richard M. Greenbank, Samuel Pancoast; ⸱1846, Richard M. Greenbank, Henry B. Manger; 1847, John Edwards, John Walsh; 1848, John Edwards, Samuel R. Gillingham; 1849-50, Enos R. Williams, John Cummins; 1851, Eliphalet Reed, Peter

Hallowell; 1852, Joseph Carlisle, Abraham K. Freed, John T. Gracey; 1853, circuit divided, and a part called Waynesburg, Joseph Carlisle, A. Longacre; 1854, S. G. Hare; 1855, S. G. Hare, Nehemiah W. Bennum; 1856, William H. Burrell, Levi B. Hughes; 1857, William H. Burrell; 1858, John F. Meredith, Charles W. Ayars; 1859, John F. Meredith; 1860-61, John J. Jones; 1862-63, James Y. Ashton; then in regular order, E. I. D. Pepper, John Allen, George Cummins, S. W. Kurtz, John J. Pearce, Andrew Cather, Jacob M. Hinson, George Heacock, George W. F. Graff Henry R. Calloway, J. S. Lane, H. T. Quigg, William P. Howell, S. W. Smith, N. D. McComas, Josiah Bawden, John T. Gray, and William Quigley Bennett, the present pastor, who came to the church in 1898. The church building, erected in 1869, has been improved, will seat about 500, and is worth, together with the other property belonging to the church, $22,000. The membership is 380, and of the Sunday-school, including those of Cambridge, the White School and Poplar Grove School, about 250.

St. Peter's Episcopal Church is in the northeast corner of East Whiteland Township. The building was erected in 1744, and in 1752 the minister was Rev. William Currie, who had previously been a lay reader for the congregation. The church was incorporated in 1786, the Rev. Mr. Currie remaining rector until 1783, preaching, however, only by request, as he had not surrendered his original vows, which required him to pray for King George. Rev. Slaytor Clay became rector in 1788, remaining until his death, in 1821. From about 1824 for three years the Rev. Samuel C. Brinkle was rector, followed by the Revs. William H. Rees, Simon Wilmer, William Hilton, William Peck, William H. Woodward, William L. Suddalls, Thomas W. Winchester, who died in February, 1858: Samuel Hazlehurst, A. E. Tortat, W. R. Stockton, De Witt C. Loup, Thomas J. Taylor, and H. J. W. Allen, until the closing up of the church in 1894, since which time the vestry have preferred to expend the proceeds of the endowment fund for general repairs instead of for the employment of a rector. The property is worth about $12,000.

St. John's Episcopal Church in the township of New London was organized about 1744. The rectors have been as follows: Revs. John Gordon, Israel Acrelius, John Abram Lidenius, Elisha Riggs, George Handy, Jacob M. Douglass, George Kirk, from 1829 to 1869; J. H. MacElroy, J. L. Heysinger, George Vall, William A. White, who died June 1, 1898; G. L. Bishop, Thomas Burrows, J. J. Creigh and Frank P. Clark, present pastor. The church membership is now thirty-five as is also that of the Sunday-school, and the church property is valued at $6,000.

St. Paul's Episcopal Church, West Whiteland, was organized February 23, 1828, the church edifice being erected the same year and consecrated May 28, 1829. The rectors of this church have been as follows: Rev. Samuel C. Brinkle, through whose efforts the members were gathered together; Revs. R. N. Morgan, Cyrus H. Jacobs, William Hilton, William Henry Rees, William H. Woodward, William L. Suddards, H. Hastings Weld, Thomas W. Winchester, Thomas L. Green, Samuel Hazlehurst, Joseph W. Cook, A. E. Tortat, Robert F. Innes, G. Livingston Bishop, De Witt C. Loup, Thomas J. Taylor, and Henry J. W. Allen, who assumed charge of this church in 1882. The communicants number fifty, and the Sunday-school 25. The church property is valued at $12,000.

The Episcopalians have the following churches in Chester County as it is to-day: St. John's in West Caln, St. Peter's in East Whiteland, St. John's in Penn, St. Mary's in Warwick, St. Andrew's in West Vincent, St. Peter's in Phœnixville, St. Mark's in Honeybrook, St. Paul's in West Whiteland, St. James' in Downingtown, Trinity at Coatesville, The Church of the Good Samaritan in Paoli, and the Church of the Holy Trinity in West Chester.

There were, of course, Episcopal churches in what is now Delaware County before any of the above-named were established. It is claimed that St. Paul's at Chester and St. Martin's at Marcus

Hook were built in 1702. St. John's at Concord was built in 1722, and St. David's Episcopal Church, which is about one and a half miles southwest of Radnor Station on the Pennsylvania Railroad, at the junction of Newtown Township, Delaware County, and East-town Township, Chester County, was established by a colony of Welshmen about 1685. While but little is known as to the early his-tory of this church yet it appears clear that services were held from 1700 to 1704 at the house of William Davis, by Rev. Evan Evans, who preached in Welsh once a fort-night for four years. In 1714 John Chubb was formally appointed as missionary to this church at Oxford, and subscriptions had been raised for the building of a stone church. On May 9, 1715, the foundations of Radnor Episcopal Church were laid. After Mr. Chubb's death in December, 1715, Rev. Evan Evans was appointed missionary to Radnor and Oxford, remaining from the summer of 1716 to 1718. The next rector was Rev. John Humphrey, who supplied the pulpit until the appoint-ment of Rev. Robert Weyman, who began his duties here in De-cember, 1719, and remained until 1731. Rev. John Hughes was rec-tor from 1733 until 1737. Rev. William Currie, the last missionary to Radnor. During the Revolutionary War this church was closed to religious services, for the reason that Rev. Mr. Currie remained loyal to England. In 1783 Mr. Currie again took charge of the church and was succeeded in 1788 by Rev. Slaytor Clay, who was the first American minister of the church. The church was incor-porated in 1792. In 1818 Rev. Samuel C. Brinkle began preaching here once in each two weeks, continuing until Rev. Mr. Clay's death, when he became the regular pastor. Since then the pastors to this time have been as follows: Revs. Simon Wilmer, William Henry Rees, William Peck, William W. Spear, Breed Batchelor, Thomas G. Allen, John A. Childs, Henry G. Brown, Richardson Graham, Thomas G. Clemson, William F. Halsey, and Rev. George A. Keller, the present rector, who assumed charge in 1883.

49

Various repairs were made to the old church building, and in 1830 a new vestry room was built, and in 1871 the present church was erected on and beyond the site of the former house. The present parsonage was built in 1844. About 1895 the old church was restored and it is now as it was of old. In the cemetery belonging to this church lies the body of General Anthony Wayne.

St. John's Pequra Episcopal Church in the village of Compassville is one of the oldest churches of this denomination in Pennsylvania. The first building here was erected in 1720. Rev. Richard Backhouse conducted services here on the first Tuesday of each month for ten years, at the expiration of which time, in 1739, Rev. John Blackhall became rector. Rev. Mr. Backhouse returned to this church in a short time after leaving it and remained until his death in 1750. In 1751 Rev. George Craig began to officiate here, being with the church at least eight Sundays each year, and was succeeded in 1759 by Rev. Thomas Barton, who remained until 1776. During the Revolutionary War there was no regular rector, but in 1784 Rev. J. Fred Illing, of the Lutheran Church, became rector, remaining until 1788. Rev. Elisha Riggs was installed this year and remained until 1793, when came Rev. Levi Heath. Rev. Joseph Clarkson came in 1799 and remained until his death, in 1830. Rev. Richard Umstead Morgan became rector in 1831, remaining three years. Rev. Edward Young Buchanan was rector from 1835 to 1845; Rev. Henry Tullidge from 1846 to 1854; Rev. E. P. Wright from 1854 to 1856; Rev. George G. Hepburn from 1856 to 1860; Rev. Henry R. Smith from 1862 to 1872; Rev. Thomas Mee from 1874 to 1875; Rev. Henry R. Tullidge from 1875 to 188 , and since then the rectors have been as follows: Rev. J. W. Geiger about one year, and Rev. S. K. Boyer, who has been rector about thirteen years. A new rectory was built in 1891 the value of the property is $6,000, the church membership 284, and the Sunday-school has about 150 members.

The present church building was erected in 1830, a stone struc-ture 40x55 feet in size and a very imposing house.

The Church of the Good Samaritan was established about 1848, at Paoli, Chester County. From that time to 1877 services were held from time to time in the Paoli Inn, and for several years prior to 1877 the church and Sunday-school met in Masonic Hall. On October 31, 1876, the cornerstone of a church building, named the Church of the Good Samaritan, was laid by the Rt. Rev. William Bacon Stevens, bishop of the diocese, addresses being made by the bishop, by the Rev. Dr. Currie, of St. Luke's, Philadelphia; by the Rev. Dr. Frost, of Trinity Church, Wilmington, Delaware; by the Rev. Dr. Hay; by the Rev G. L. Bishop; by the Rev. Dr. Rumney, and the Rev. B. R. Phelps. The unfinished church edifice was oc-cupied for the first time for divine service on Sunday, July 15, 1877, the Rev. G. L. Bishop, rector of St. Paul's, West Whiteland, taking charge of the new enterprise at the request of the bishop and the desire of Edmund G. Dutille, by whom, with the assistance of a few friends, the church was built in memory of Mrs. E. S. Dutille.

The new building was presented to the bishop for consecration September 28, 1877, the sermon being preached by the bishop. Numerous notable ministers of the Protestant Episcopal Church were present, the Holy Communion being celebrated by the bishop, assisted by the Rev. G. L. Bishop. Since 1880 the rectors have been as follows: Rev. M. J. Meigs, Rev. James C. Craven, Rev. Thomas J. Taylor, Rev. H. P. Hay, Rev. George A. Keller, Rev. Charles A. Ricksecker, Rev. G. Livingston Bishop, and Rev. Edward T. Mab-ley, who by request furnished the data for this brief sketch of the church. Since 1880 there has been built a large rectory, the inte-rior of the church has been improved, and a beautiful memorial window of cathedral glass has been put in. The present value of the property is about $5,000, the membership of the church is twen-ty-nine families, and of the Sunday-school sixty-five scholars.

Holy Trinity Episcopal Church, of West Chester, was organized November 23, 1835, Rev. George W. Cole being chosen rector. The church was incorporated April 28, 1838, and the church edifice was erected on the north side of Gay Street. This Gay Street edifice was used for many years as a chapel and Sunday-school after it ceased to be used as a church, which was about 1868. The cornerstone of the present church building was laid July 3, 1868, by Rev. Henry J. Morton, the building standing at the northwest corner of South High and Union Streets. The property here is valued at $70,000, and consists of the church, parish house, rectory and Sunday-school. The rectors of this church have been Revs. Edward W. Willbank, Richard Newton, Rt. Rev. G. T. Bedell, John B. Clemson, Lewis P. Balch, William Newton, John Bolton, who came to West Chester in 1863, and remained rector until January 1, 1891, when he resigned, and was succeeded by the Rev. G. Heathcote Hills. Rev. Mr. Bolton secured the erection of the fine buildings referred to above, and died in Philadelphia May 18, 1898. He was rector emeritus from the time of his resignation until his death. Rev. Mr. Hills, on May 18, 1898, resigned as rector, the resignation to take effect October 1, 1898. The membership of this church at the present time is about 500, and of the Sunday-school, 275. The parochial societies are the Vested Choir, Brotherhood of St. Andrew, Woman's Auxiliary, Girls' Friendly Society, Mothers' Meeting, Sewing School, Working Guild, St. Ursula's Guild, Altar Society, and Junior Auxiliary.

St Peter's Episcopal Church, ot Phœnixville, was organized in 1838, the present church edifice being erected in 1840 on land given by Reeves, Buck & Co. The cornerstone was laid by Rt. Rev. Bishop Onderdonk, D. D., April 25, 1840, the building being completed in December, 1852, when it was dedicated by Rt. Rev. Bishop Alonzo Potter, D. D., LL. D. The rectors of this church have been as follows: Revs. Oliver C. Shaw, Marmaduke Hirst, I. P. Nash, Samuel Durburrow, Thomas W. Winchester, W. R. Stockton, who remained until 1894, and was succeeded by the present rector, Rev. Edgar Campbell. Improvements have recently been made to the property to the extent of $1,800, and the church property is worth about $20,000. The communicants number 130, and the member-ship of the Sunday-school is 125.

St. James' Episcopal Church, Downingtown, was organized in 1842 through the instrumentality of Rev. G. T. Bedell, services be-ing held for some time at the house of Dr. Andrew Wills. After-ward they were held in the Masonic Hall, which was later pur-chased and converted into a chapel. The cornerstone of the pres-ent church building was laid June 20, 1843, and the church was dedicated by Bishop Onderdonk, October 26, the same year. The name St. James' was given to it for the reason that St. James' Church in Philadelphia offered $400 per year for two years toward the support of a resident minister. Rev. William A. White, of Boston was the first rector, beginning here in November, 1843, re-maining until 1845. He has been followed by Revs. Samuel Hazle-hurst, H. Hastings Weld, William P. Ray T. Browne Morrison John B. Henry, Benjamin A. Rogers, Jesse Y. Burk. William White Montgomery, Robert F. Innes, W. G. Ware, H. Allen Grif-fith, John C. Fair, whose rectorship came to a close June 1, 1897. The church membership at present is 125, and of the Sunday-school, 140, and the value of the church property is now $15,000.

During the rectorship of Rev. Mr. Innes, which lasted from 1871 to 1880, a parish building was erected for Sunday-school and other purposes, and an addition was made to the rectory. The seating capacity of the church is 250.

The Church of the Trinity, at Coatesville, was organized in 1868, though Episcopal services had been held there as early as 1859. In 1871 a lot on Main Street was presented to the congre-gation by Benjamin Miller, and on it a spacious chapel was erected. Rev. George G. Field was the first rector, and has been followed by the following: Rev. Thomas T. Garland, in 1894; and Rev.

Arthur Wilson Wilde, in 1898; Rev. Mr. Field being made rector emeritus in 1894, and still being in that relation. A handsome stone church has recently been erected, the property is worth about $42,000; the membership is 145, and that of the Sunday-school about 100.

St. Mary's Episcopal Church, at Warwick, was founded about 1804, by Rev. Levi Bull, D. D., who remained rector thereof for about forty years. The house of worship was built in 1806, and rebuilt and enlarged in 1843. It was repaired in 1880 by using the sum of $1,000 left for that purpose by Rev. John Starrett in his will.

St. Mark's Episcopal Church, at Honeybrook, was organized in 1835. The rectors during recent years have been Rev. Francis E. Arnold, during whose rectorship three acres were added to the cemetery; Rev. Winfield S. Baer, lay reader for a year, 1889, during which time a rectory was built worth $2,800 and labor; Rev. L. R. F. Davis, Rev. Edward F. Mabley and Rev. John Henry Burton. In 1891 the church was greatly improved inside and stained windows put in. The property is now valued at $8,000, and the endowment fund is $203. The baptized members number 100, and the communicants 53. The Sunday-school has a membership of 50.

St. Mary's Episcopal Church, since 1880, has had the same rectors as St. Mark's. The property is now valued at $6,000, and the endowment fund is at present $2,450. The number of baptized members is 85, and the communicants number 25. The Sunday-school has a membership of 70. In 1880 extensive repairs were made to the church, both inside and outside; in 1888 a wall was built about the cemetery and a shed built; and in 1892 the old public school-house was repaired for use as a rectory.

The Church of the Advent was chartered during the winter of 1881-82, and the cornerstone of the church building was laid with impressive ceremonies May 17, 1885, by Rt. Rev. William Bacon Stevens, bishop of the diocese of Philadelphia. In 1880 Rev. John

Long began holding services here as a missionary, remaining two years, and was succeeded by Rev. J. H. McElroy, and he by the Rev. J. H. Heysinger. During the missionary services of these three clergymen funds were collected for the purchase of a lot on Broad Street, upon which the present neat Gothic church edifice was erected. Within one year after the laying of the cornerstone as above narrated, the building was completed, and it was consecrated according to the established form May 14, 1886, by the Rt. Rev. William Bacon Stevens. At that time the rector in charge was Rev. G. Livingston Bishop. In the address of Bishop Stevens he alluded to the beautiful memorial window of Bayard Taylor, the funds for which were collected by Mrs. William J. Baird, of New York City, and contributed to by such eminent men as the Very Rev. Dean Farrar, George W. Childs, J. G. Whittier, Bishop Brooks, George W. Curtis, James Russell Lowell, O. W. Holmes, Mrs. James Fields, Hon. G. H. Boker, Hon. S. L. Clemens, Will Carleton, Mrs. M. Mapes Dodge, and others, literary friends of Bayard Taylor. Following Rev. G. L. Bishop came Rev. Thomas Burrows, in 1888; Rev. Thomas Dickinson, Rev. Guy L. Wallis, in 1895; Rev. William Wirt Mills, 1896, and the present rector, Rev. Stanley F. W. Symonds, in 1897. In 1895 a new high altar was added. It is finished in white and gold, is of wood, and has all the proper appointments. The number of communicants is now 16, and the number of the baptized communicants 27.

The present Episcopal Mission, in Parkesburg, was established in 1890 as the successor of a similar mission started in 1870, under the name of Grace Mission, which was continued until the death of Rev. Henry E. Smith, about 1872. The present mission, named Ascension, was started by Rev. Mr. Boyer, present rector of St. John's Church, at Compassville. In 1892 it became a mission of Trinity Church, at Coatesville, and up to January 1, 1898, it was served by various ministers, and since then up to June 1, 1898, by Rev. Mr. Mabley, of the Church of the Good Samaritan. It is now in charge of the Rev. Mr. Bullitt. The membership is about 35, and of the Sunday-school 15. It is held in a rented building on Main Street, near Gay. A lot for the erection of a new church building was purchased in 1897 on Gay Street, near Highland Avenue.

The Church of the Sure Foundation, Rev. Sydney Neville Ussher, B. D., rector, is an old-fashioned Evangelical Episcopal Church. It is located on Union Street, between South High and South Church Streets, West Chester. As stated by the Assistant Bishop of Kentucky, Rev. George David Cummins, D. D., "It is the old and true Protestant Episcopal Church of the days immediately succeeding the American Revolution."

The founder of the present parish was the scholarly and distinguished divine and hymnologist, Rev. William Newton, D. D., a brother of the celebrated Rev. Richard Newton, D. D., and uncle of Rev. Heber Newton, of New York. The Rev. Dr. William Newton, D. D., was for many years rector of the Church of the Holy Trinity, of West Chester, and of the Church of the Nativity, Philadelphia.

The Church of the Sure Foundation was the gift of Miss Palmera C. Evans, and her sister, Mrs. Sarah E. Newton. It was organized April 15, 1884, with seventeen charter members, and was incorporated under the laws of Pennsylvania. The first service was held May 13, 1884. The Sunday-school was organized and held its first meeting June 10, 1884, with but four scholars. Dr. Newton labored long and faithfully in spite of failing health and eyesight. He was the author and publisher of "Lectures on the Book of Daniel," "The Morning Star," "Gleanings from a Busy Life," and a number of well-known hymns. Dr. Newton died February 16, 1893, and his devoted wife, Sarah Evans Newton, died February 17, 1897. A remarkable coincidence as to date, both being interred in Oakland Cemetery, February 20, 1893 and 1897, respectively.

The Church of the Sure Foundation has had but two rectors, the successor to the Rev. William Newton, D. D., being the Rev. Sydney Neville Ussher, B. D., under whose administration the church has greatly prospered. The present rector was called to this parish June 29, 1893, having at the time five calls from as many other parishes; but he decided to accept the Church of the Sure Foundation because, though the weakest of all, it was apparently the most spiritual.

The Rev. Mr. Ussher, in 1898, celebrated his fifth anniversary. Since his advent the parish, which is his first charge, has become for the first time self-sustaining. Its membership has increased from 30 to 123, and the membership of the Sunday-school from 20 to 175. The income has increased from $150 to $1,500 per annum. The church building, both the main auditorium and the Sunday-school room, have been remodeled and enlarged. The church building, property and grounds are valued at $10,000.

The present rector, Rev. Sydney Neville Ussher, B. D., is the eldest son of the Right Rev. B. B. Ussher, M. D., Bishop of the Reformed Episcopal Church in the Dominion of Canada and Island of Newfoundland, and was born in the city of Aurora, Illinois, November 27, 1868, where his father was licensed as a candidate for orders under Bishop Whitehouse. His parents early removed to Canada, residing in Toronto and Montreal. In the latter city Mr. Ussher received his education in the public schools, graduating with high honors one of the senior four of the Boys' High School. He became Associate in Arts at Magill University, after which he engaged for six years in mercantile pursuits, in which he rose step by step. Removing with his parents to Kansas City, success was his and he was finally made a traveling salesman for the largest wholesale dry goods house outside of Chicago, west of the Mississippi River, Messrs. Burnham, Hanna, Munger & Co., of Kansas City. A consecrated business life was his ideal, but he was divinely called to the ministry, without any previous love for the profession; and the way opening a four years' course of study was entered upon in the Divinity School, West Philadelphia. For three years from June to September, Mr. Ussher spent his vacations as summer clerk in the Central National Bank, Philadelphia.

From the seminary Mr. Ussher was called to the West Chester Church, and has resided there for the past five years, an honored and respected citizen, beloved by his parish. In addition to his parochial work he is pursuing his studies, a post-graduate in the University of Pennsylvania.

The Rev. Sydney Neville Ussher, B. D., is a direct descendant of a long line of distinguished ancestors on both his father's and mother's side, his ancestry being one of the few tracing their genealogy back without a break for six hundred years. The family name was originally Neville. The Nevilles (vide Burke's Extinct Peerage, and W. Ball Wright, M. A., "Genealogical Memoirs of the Ussher Families in Ireland," page E), were descended from Gilbert de Neville, Admiral of William the Conqueror's fleet, in 1066, and the Nevilles of Raby Castle, Yorkshire, marked this by a galley in their arms. The above works, to which the writer has had access, show that Rev. Mr. Ussher's family is descended from Richard Neville, the great Earl of Warwick, known in history as the "King Maker," one of whose descendants, for political reasons, took the name of the office which he bore, viz: Ussher of the Black Rod, thus retaining his influential and lucrative position when the name of Neville had become unpopular and the King Maker's influence had waned. To distinguish the family name from the office, the second letter, "S," was added many years ago.

The first recorded as bearing the name in Ireland was Arlantor or Arland Uscher, or Ussher, who appears to have been settled in Dublin as a leading merchant in and before 1439, and who was bailiff of that city in 1461, mayor in 1469, and died in 1479. A tradition as old as Archbishop James Ussher's time states that Arland Ussher was descended from a John Nevil of the Northern Nevils, who accompanied Prince John, in 1185, to Ireland as usher of the court, and adopted the surname of Usher or Ussher from his office.

Many of Mr. Ussher's ancestors have distinguished themselves in

Church, Law, and Court, as well as Army and Navy. His great-great-grandfather was Adam Ussher, archdeacon of Clonfert and rector of the parish of Clontarf near Dublin. This parish was held in the family from father to son for over 150 years.

Arland Ussher, founder of the Ussher family in Ireland, above mentioned, was the father of Thomas Ussher, whose eldest daughter was wife to John Garvey, Archbishop of Armagh, Thomas Ussher, his son, was father of Henry Ussher, Archdeacon of Dublin, who procured the charter and was made first Fellow of Trinity College, Dublin, by Queen Elizabeth. His youngest son, Robert Ussher, was provost of Trinity College and Bishop of Kildare.

Henry Ussher, on account of his connection with Trinity College, was made archbishop of Armagh, in 1613. James Ussher, a celebrated Roman Catholic priest in Kensington, died in 1771, author of "Clio, an Essay on Taste," was a famous schoolmaster and partner with John Walker, author of the Pronouncing Dictionary.

Arland Ussher, third of the name, was father of James Ussher, according to records in Trinity College, Dublin, Trinity's first student, Ireland's greatest scholar, antiquary, and divine, the most wonderful genius in the Episcopal Church since the Reformation, equally holy, humble, and innocent, as he was of commanding intellect and almost miraculous attainments. He was successively Professor of Divinity in Dublin University, Bishop of Meath, and Archbishop of Armagh. Appointed by Charles I. to hold the Bishopric of Carlisle, Author of Ussher's Chronology, the basis of all present chronologies, he lies buried in Henry VII. chapel in Westminster Abbey.

Christopher Ussher, son of the first Arland, who married into the great feudal family of Fitzwilliams, now represented by Earl Fitzwilliams and by the Earl of Pembroke, was father of John Ussher, alderman and collector of customs, Dublin. In his house, Bridgefoot, Dublin, was printed, at his expense, the first book in the Irish language. His son, Sir William Ussher, married the daughter of Archbishop Loftus and was clerk of Privy Council from 1593 to the fall of Charles I. In his house and at his expense was printed the first version of the Irish New Testament. His daughter, Mary Ussher, married Henry Colley of Castle Carbery, whose son, Richard Colley, assumed the name of Wesley, and was created Baron Mornington. His son, Garret, Earl of Mornington, married Anne, daughter of Arthur, Lord Dungannon, and was father of Richard, Marquis Wellesley; William, Baron Maryborough, the Earl of Mornington; Arthur Wellesley, the great Duke of Wellington, called the "Iron Duke;" and Very Rev. Gerald Valerian Wellesley, D. D., Dean of Windsor.

Mr. Ussher's great-great-grandfather, Archdeacon Ussher, rector of Clontarf, previously mentioned, was father of Rev. John Ussher, afterward first Astronomer Royal of Ireland, and the last of the family to hold the incumbency. Sir William Ussher, mentioned above, was father of Rev. Henry Ussher, D. D., Astronomer Royal of Ireland, and held the Andrews Professorship of Astronomy in Trinity College. His sons were Rear Admiral Sir Thomas Ussher, K. C. B., K. C. H., who entered the Royal Navy January 27, 1791, as midshipman. His naval career and exploits are detailed in O'Byrne's Naval Biographical Dictionary, 1849. On the evening of April 28, 1814, he embarked the first Napoleon on H. M. S. Undaunted, and landed him at 8 p. m., April 30, at Porto Ferajo, in Elba. King William the IV. was a warm friend of Sir Thomas Ussher, having served under him as a midshipman. He died naval commander-in-chief, at Cork, Ireland, 1862, and lies buried in one of the vaults of Monkstown Church, County Dublin.

Another interesting fact is that "three hundred years ago two brothers of name of Ussher were driven from Ireland during one of the troubles, and settled in the neighborhood of Melrose in Scotland, where they acquired considerable lands, and among them the property of Huntley-burn, one of the most celebrated spots on the borders." "The grandfather of the present Thomas

Ussher of Edinburgh, for seventeen years secretary of the Borders' County Association for the Advancement of Education, out of which arose the celebration of the Centenary of Sir Walter Scott, sold to Sir Walter Scott the chief part of the estate of Abbotsford (vide Lockhart's Life of Walter Scott)." By unbroken tradition this branch claims kinship with Archbishop Ussher, and the Rev. W. Neville Ussher, cousin of the above-named Thomas Ussher, is a canon of the Cathedral in Edinburgh.

On his mother's side the Rev. Sydney N. Ussher's family is even more interesting, leading back on the male side to the famous Thomas Carter, who took so active a part in the Irish Revolution, ending with the Battle of the Boyne, 1690. In the family tree appear the Countess of Roscommon, widow of Wentworth Dillon, the poet, who was publicly buried in Westminster Abbey; Dr. Philip Twysden, bishop of Raphoe and son of Sir William Twysden, baronet of Royden Hall, Kent; George Bussey, fourth Earl of Jersey, first cousin to Anna Maria Carter, Mr. Ussher's great-grandmother, whose eldest son was George, fifth Earl of Jersey, and whose daughters became Ladies William Russell, Ann Lambton, Sarah Bailey, Lady Ponsonby, Lady Henrietta, who married the Bishop of Oxford, and Lady Anglesea, wife of the Marquis Wellesley, the hero of Waterloo, and for her second husband the Duke of Argyle, which Duchess of Argyle was cousin germain to Mrs. Skiffington Thompson, Mrs. Ussher's paternal grandmother.

The Right Honorable Thomas Carter's second daughter, Susan, married Thomas Carter of Duleek Park and Castle, County Louth, and her granddaughter, Elizabeth, became Marchioness of Thomond by entering the family of William O'Bryen, decendant from Brien Boroimbe, King of Ireland, and whose line was continued by the King of Munster and of Thomond, to the reign of Henry VIII., King of England (vide Sharpe's Peerage). On the female side Mrs. Ussher's grandmother was Elizabeth Margaret, eldest daughter of the Rev. Joshua D'Arcy, Rector of Laca, County Kildare. The D'Arcy family came to Ireland, settling in Platten, County Meath, in the Fourteenth century. In a book written by the present Duke of Leinster, when Marquis of Kildare, called "Maynooth Castle," page 5, we read: "Sir John D'Arcy, Lord Justice of Ireland, married the Countess Johanna de Burgh, daughter to the Red Earl of Ulster, and sister to Ellen, wife of Robert Bruce, King of Scotland. They had a son, William, born at Maynooth, in 1330, from whom the present family of D'Arcy are lineally descended and are represented by George James Norman D'Arcy of Hyde Park, County Westmeath (vide Burke's London Gentry, also Walford's County Families)," the worthy head of both English and Irish families and representatives of twenty-eight peerages of Great Britain.

It is quite impossible in this sketch to give a full history of a family dating back to their ancient seat in Arques, in Normandy, when they came to England with William the Conqueror, into whose family they had previously married, then settled in Lincolnshire and given in extenso in Burke's Extinct Peerages.

The ancestry of Mr. Ussher's grandmother, on his father's side, Henrietta Boileau, can be traced back without a break for more than 600 years. The present Baron Boileau de Castleneau being the seventeenth in descent from Etienne Boileau, appointed by Louis IX., in the year 1255, Grand Provost of Paris, at that period the highest office of state. Another interesting fact is that "Richard Ussher of Cappagh, with Elizabeth Ussher, his mother, and his wife, Martha, and all his sisters, joined the Society of Friends, who carried on an intense religious movement in the South of Ireland, the church being then in a very dead state. Three editions of memoirs of Elizabeth Ussher the elder, and also letters of Elizabeth, Lucy, Judith, and Susanna Ussher of the Society of Friends, were published in 1812, 1815, in Dublin, and the third, 1845, in London, by J. Jones, South Great Georges

Street, Dublin. Richard Ussher, who was chief magistrate of County Waterford, though he did not conform to the Society of Friends, imbibed their conscientious objections to taking or administering oaths, and accordingly ceased to act as a magistrate." He died at Cappagh, M. 2, 25, 1854.

The Rev. Sydney N. Ussher is a facile and forceful writer, and has earned the reputation of being an eloquent speaker. His alma mater recently conferred upon him the degree of bachelor of divinity, in recognition of his scholarly attainments. Mr. Ussher has four brothers and one sister, his second brother, Rev. Clarence D. Ussher, M. D., having just been appointed professor in Euphrates College, Harpoot, Turkey, in Asia, under the A. B. C. F. M., whither he has gone as medical missionary.

Zion Lutheran Church was establshed about 1770, its church building being begun in 1771 and completed in 1774. It was used as a hospital while Washington's forces were at Chester Springs. The church was incorporated September 30, 1789, under the name of "The German Lutheran congregation, worshiping at the church called Zion, in Pikeland Township." While this church is in Pikeland Township, the line of the property joins the Vincent Township line. Previous to the erection of the church building the German Lutherans and the Reformed Calvinists jointly obtained about ten acres of ground, and each society had its own minister, the first Lutheran minister being Rev. Henry Muhlenberg, Sr., of Philadelphia. When the question arose as to the erection of a new house the members could not agree upon a location, some wanting it nearer French Creek, but those who would not agree to this satisfied the others for their share. Those who desired it nearer French Creek subsequently erected St. Peter's Church. The Reformed members also erected a new church. Their present building, which was then erected, fronting on the Schuylkill Road, composed of red sandstone, about two miles from the French Creek bridge and a half mile from the general pike. The site commands a view of a considerable portion of Berks and Montgomery Counties.

In 1787 this church and St. Peter's jointly purchased a place for the minister to reside at in their midst, a lot containing fifty acres, a mile above Zion Church. For some time before these two churches were erected the preacher was Ludwik Voigt, and after his death the Rev. Mr. Revenach preached a short time, and was followed by Rev. Frederick Jasinsky, who preached for both churches and was very much liked. During his life he occupied the parsonage, and a new stone house and barn were erected by the congregations. Next came Revs. Frederick Geisenheimer, father and son, and Jacob Wampole, and during the time of the Geisenheimers preaching in English in the afternoon in both churches was admitted. In 1836 Rev. Mr. Ruthrauff became the preacher, having possession of the parsonage; but in 1842 he was dismissed by the Vincent Consistory and ordered to leave the parsonage removing then near to Lionville and retaining the St. Peter's and Lionville congregations and also St. Matthew's on the Conestoga Pike, which was a new church a mile above that at what was formerly Ludwig's Tavern. Next came Rev. Joseph Miller, and still later Rev. Mr. Weldon, who became the regular preacher at Zion's and St. Paul's, using the German language in the morning and English in the afternoon. Rev. Mr. Weldon purchased the parsonage.

St. Peter's Church originated in the manner related in the sketch of Zion Lutheran Church. A lot was purchased containing about one and a half acres of ground for a church and cemetery, deeded to the church May 16, 1771. The church was completed and consecrated in November, 1772, Rev. Henry Muhlenberg, the pioneer of Lutheranism in this vicinity, being invited by the pastor, Ludwig, to preach on the occasion. Services began on Sunday, November 8, 1772, and continued until the evening of the following Tuesday. During this time Mr. Muhlenberg spoke in German, and Rev. Mr. Goeransson, the Swedish minister. in English. The first building, built of logs, was used by both congregations, Zion and St. Peter's, until 1811, when it was determined to build a new one, the cornerstone of which was laid August 13, and the completed edifice, which cost $2,836.45½, was dedicated under the name of St. Peter's Church, October 4, 1812. There was put into it a pipe organ, and the building was used on alternate Sundays by the Lutheran and Reformed congregations until January 20, 1835, when it was destroyed by fire. The cornerstone of a new edifice was laid April 24, 1835, and this building was dedicated April 12, 1836. By this time the demand for preaching in English had become so strong that it took the place of German altogether. When the East Pennsylvania Synod was formed, this church united therewith, and thereupon some of the members, dissatisfied because the English language prevailed, withdrew and formed a separate church, erecting a new church edifice at the opposite end of the cemetery. The Sunday-school was organized September 28, 1828.

The pastors here have been as follows: From 1811 to 1815, Ludwig Voigt, J. F. Weinland, Frederick Plitt, J. Rowenauch, Frederick W. Jasinsky; 1815-19, F. W. Geisenheimer, Sr., serving with his son of the same name, 1819-23; Jacob Wampole, 1827-36; Frederick Ruthrauff, 1836-43; John McCron, 1843-47; Daniel Miller, 1847-49; Peter Raby, 1849-58; Samuel Aughey, 1858-59; Cornelius Reimensnyder, 1859-63; N. H. Cornell, 1863-74; S. S. Palmer, 1874-75; J. F. Hartman, 1876-80; J. R. Dimm, 1880-82; J. A. Hackenberg, 1882-92; Rev. J. W. Henderson, 1892-98.

The cornerstone of the present church building was laid August 27, 1889, and the church was dedicated free from debt May 7, 1890, having cost about $7,000.

St. Peter's Evangelical Lutheran Church, located in Pikeland Township, was established by members of St. Peter's Church, the history of which is given briefly above. From twelve to fifteen

50

members of St. Peter's Church withdrew therefrom and erected
a new building for themselves, about the year 1840, on account
of the introduction of certain new measures into the old church. Of
this new church the cornerstone was laid May, 1843, the services
on the occasion being in both German and English. The reasons
given for the formation of this new church were substantially
that the members forming it had been deprived of their rights
and privileges of membership in the old church by the pastor
and vestry therof, because they adhered steadfastly to the doctrines of the Evangelical Church, as they had been taught them
by their fathers and former pastors. And they solemnly en-
joined and made it incumbent on their successors forever to maintain the doctrines and usages of the Evangelical Lutheran Church
as set forth in the Augsburg Confession of Faith, to preserve pure
doctrine and undefiled religion against all influences and changes
of the times and manners of the world; and that so long as the
Evangelical Lutheran Synod of Pennsylvania shall continue in its
adherence to the Augsburg Confession and remain an independent
body as then constituted, "that you and your pastors be and ever
remain in connection therewith."

The church edifice was dedicated October 4, 1843. The pas-
tors have been as follows: 1842-50, C. F. Weldon; 1850-54, J. C.
Miller; 1855-64, William Weaver; 1864-74, H. S. Miller; 1875, B.
C. Snyder.

The two Lutheran Churches constituting the Lionville charge
are St. Matthew's and St. Paul's, and the direct outgrowth of
Zion's and St. Peter's congregations. St. Matthew's Church, located in Upper Uwchlan Township, was organized in 1833, by
Rev. Jacob Wampole. A piece of ground was purchased on the
Conestoga Pike for $50, upon which a two-story stone church,
35x45 feet in size, with galleries on three sides, was erected at
a cost of $1,700. This church became a part of Zion's charge.
Rev. Mr. Wampole remained as pastor until 1836, when he was

succeeded by Rev. Frederick Ruthrauff, during whose pastorate Zion's Church withdrew, on account of what were known as "new measures" in church work.

At the time of this division Rev. Mr. Ruthrauff became pastor of three churches, St. Peter's, St. Matthew's and St. Paul's, which formed the Pikeland charge, and he remained in this field until 1843, and on December 17, following, he was succeeded by Rev. John McCron, D. D., who remained until 1847, when he and Rev. Daniel Miller exchanged pastorates, the latter being succeeded by Rev. Peter Raby, September 27, 1849. Rev. Mr. Raby remained until 1858, and was followed by Rev. Samuel Aughey, who remained until 1861, when he was succeeded by Rev. Christian D. Ulery, who soon afterward enlisted in the Union army, and died from pneumonia November 7, 1862. In 1863 Rev. S. Sentman became pastor, remaining until 1870, and Rev. J. R. Shoffner became pastor in 1871. In 1876 he was succeeded by Rev. H. S. Cook, who remained until 1882. In this year Rev. W. F. Rentz became pastor and remained until 1888, when he was succeeded by Rev. M. S. Cresman, who remained until December 31, 1894. The present pastor, Rev. Frederick Klinefelter, assumed charge of the church February 1, 1895. The membership of St. Paul's Church is now 112, and that of St. Matthew's 160. The value of the former is $9,000, and of the latter $8,000.

St. John's Evangelical Lutheran Church of Phœnixville, was organized in 1860, but there appears to be little definite knowledge as to the pastor or people. The first pastor who was called, that kept a record, was Rev. Henry Seiple Miller, he being called to Zion's and new St. Peter's in Chester County. The same year, while residing in Phœnixville, he gathered together about half a dozen Lutherans, and they worshipped in the Mennonite Meeting-house. Two years later he relinquished St. Peter's, September 29, he relinquished Zion's, and two years later, in November, he also relinquished St. Peter's, confining his labors to Phœnixville. The

first church edifice was erected on Church Street, between Jackson and Starr Streets, in 1872-73, the cornerstone being laid in
July, 1872, and the new building being consecrated July 20, 1873,
by Drs. Greenwald and Spaeth, and Rev. J. Neff.

The pastors of this church have been as follows: Rev. Henry
S. Miller, 1864-75; Rev. F. C. C. Kaehler, 1875-82; Rev. E. H. Ger-
hart, 1882-88; Rev. S. B. Stupp, 1888-89; Rev. K. L. Walters,
1889-93, and Rev. N. E. Miller, 1893-98.

In 1895 the congregation, feeling the need of a new building,
decided to erect a new edifice on a lot more pleasantly situated,
the site selected being on the corner of Jackson and Church
Streets. A spacious two-story edifice was erected, the cornerstone being laid June 4, 1896, and the church consecrated June
20, 1897. This building is of beautiful blue stone, with a seating
capacity of 400. This new edifice is one of the most imposing
and beautiful in the Schuylkill Valley, and the church property
is worth $40,000. The present membership is 200, and the Sunday-
school has 225 children enrolled. Luther League has 75 members,
the Mite Society 80 and the Ladies' Aid Society 60.

St. Paul's Lutheran Church of Lionville was organized February 9, 1838, the land on which the building was afterward erected
being donated by Peter Stitely, and being situated near the "White
School-house." The building erected here was of stone, one story
high, 38x45 feet in size, and cost $1,483. The building was dedi-
cated November 6 and 7, 1838. The original membership of this
church was sixteen, from St. Peter's and St. Matthew's Churches,
and the church became a part of Zion's charge. In 1880 the church
building was remodeled at a cost of $2,300, and it was re-dedicated
January 2, 1881. The Lionville pastorate has two churches, the
ministers having been the same in each.

The Centennial Lutheran Church of Kimberton was organized
in 1876 by Rev. J. F. Hartman. The church purchased a Quaker
meeting-house and fitted it up for a place of worship, dedicating it

in 1877, and during the summer of 1884 the building was frescoed and otherwise improved. Since its organization this church has been connected with St. Peter's, forming the Pikeland charge. Rev. J. A. Hackenberg resigned this charge April 1, 1897, and Rev. J. W. Henderson became pastor August 20, 1897.

The Central Lutheran Church of Phœnixville was organized December 5, 1875, by Rev. S. S. Palmer, with eleven members. Succeeding Rev. Mr. Palmer have been the following pastors: Rev. W. M. Baum, Jr., 1880 to 1883; Rev. Philip S. Hooper, 1883 to 1886; Rev. H. C. Crossman, 1886 to 1890; Rev. John Kling, 1891-94, and Rev. George E. Faber, 1894-98.

The following quotation is from a history of the church written in 1892 by Rev. John Kling:

"At a regularly called meeting held on December 25, 1875, the Mennonite congregation (being about to abandon their work in the town) unanimously agreed to convey their church property to the Lutherans upon the following conditions, viz.: That the latter should assume the indebtedness upon the property, and that they should hold the property for divine worship. These conditions were unanimously accepted by the Lutherans. In accordance with an act of the State Legislature passed in 1873, and by action of the courts of Chester County, on May 17, 1878, the church became an incorporate body. The circumstances which led to the organization were such as are common in nearly all growing towns, viz.: Lutherans were coming in from the surrounding country, locating in the town, and going into churches of other denominations."

The building, which is of stone, was erected by the Mennonites in 1789, and it was repaired by them in 1873, and again repaired, by the Lutherans, in 1890.

The following historical facts with reference to this church property were supplied at the request of the compiler of this work, by Col. Hamilton H. Gilkyson:

"One of the most valuable tracts of land in the borough of

Phœnixville is without a legal owner. This tract is situated on the southwest corner of Main and Church Streets in said borough, and originally belonged to the Society of Mennonites at Phœnixville, a corporation chartered by the court of common pleas of Chester County, on January 25, 1847, the charter being recorded in the Recorder's office of Chester County, in corporation book No. 1, page 33. It is now occupied by the Central Lutheran Church of Phœnixville.

"Jacob Buckwalter and wife, by their deed dated December 31, 1798, and recorded in the Recorder's office of Chester County, in Deed Book R, 2, page 206, granted and conveyed to Abraham Reiff and David Buckwalter the above tract of land, and upon the same date (December 31, 1798) David Buckwalter and Abraham Reiff executed a declaration of trust which will be found recorded in the Recorder's office, of Chester County, in Deed Book R, 2, page 208, by which deed of trust the tract of land is held for church purposes as therein set forth (see record).

"The Mennonite Society occupied the tract of land for many years for church purposes and used a portion of the ground as a place of burial, until the congregation became extinct.

"On October 23, 1873, a deed was executed by Israel Beidler and Henry A. Hunsicker, trustees, appointed by the court for that purpose, to Gates John for a portion of the premises above described, which deed is recorded in the Recorder's Office of Chester County in Deed Book K, 8, Vol. 182, page 322, and on July 31, 1877, a deed of confirmation was made by Henry A. Hunsicker, surviving trustee, to Gates John, which deed of confirmation is recorded in Miscellaneous Deed Book No. 17, page 168. Shortly after the year 1877 a new stone church was erected on the remaining portion of the grounds, mainly from the proceeds of the sale of that portion to Gates John.

"Mr. Beidler, one of the trustees, is long since dead, and Mr. Hunsicker is the only remaining trustee, and the Mennonite congregation has long since ceased to exist.

"By a verbal agreement made with a few of the surviving members of the Congregation of Mennonites the Lutheran Congregation organized a church and took possession of the building and grounds, and have continued to occupy them for the past twenty years.

"This congregation, known as the Central Lutheran Church, are neither the owners nor the lessees of the original owners, and therefore have no legal title, except that which possession gives to them.

"An examination of the deed of Jacob Buckwalter and wife in 1798 will, I think, disclose the fact that when the property ceased to be used by the Mennonite Society for church purposes it returns to the legal heirs of the original grantor. (This statement should be confirmed by examination of the deed.)"

It will be noticed that in the above sketch it is stated by Col. Gilkyson that the Lutherans took possession of the property by a verbal agreement. The present pastor of the church, however, Rev. George E. Faber, states in a communication to the writer that by a written agreement made March 25, 1876, between John H. Buckwalter, Amos Detwiler and M. C. Pennypacker, on the part of the Mennonite congregation, and the trustees of the English Lutheran congregation, the church property was, on almost nominal conditions, transferred to the Lutherans for church purposes, indefinitely.

The question as to the legal ownership of this property is one that may sometime be settled by the courts.

The Trinity Evangelical Lutheran Church of Coatesville was organized June 19, 1890. The organization was an outgrowth of Blessing Sunday-school, a union Sunday-school, which had been started some years previous with the special view of gathering in the children of some families who did not attend any other Sunday-school. The Blessing family and family of Mr. John S. Hope were the prime movers in this foundation work, which grew into the present Lutheran Church.   The organization numbered at first only seventeen communicant members.   Gradually, but surely and steadily, the number grew, until now, after nearly seven years of persistent, tireless effort, the congregation numbers about one hundred and fifty communicants.

The following figures and statistics, taken from the recent annual report of the treasurer, Mr. H. K. Kurtz, indicates in part the financial growth and success of the enterprise.   Cost of the church property to date, $13,730.96.   There has been paid of this amount before and since the dedication of the church building, Sunday, June 19, 1882, $9,730.23.   The pastor of this church from the time of its organization has been Rev. W. H. Steck, who has ever been faithful and efficient.   The membership of the church is about 200, and of the Sunday-school 150.

The First Reformed Church of Coventry had its origin many years ago, the earliest record bearing the date of 1743.   Fifty people of this faith on April 10, 1743, issued a call to the Rev. Jacob Lischey to become their pastor, they having then recently heard him preach a sermon, which he had done at their request, and they were satisfied with his earnestness and his doctrines. The church was organized in Philadelphia May 19, 1743, by the signing of the discipline, and this organization remained in force until June 11, 1837.   The first log church edifice was erected about 1750, it being of hewn logs, one and a half stories high, with twelve light windows in the lower story.   The Rev. Christopher Munz was the next preacher, and the third was Rev. J. Philip Leydick.   In 1784 the preacher was the Rev. Frederick Dallicker, who remained until 1799.   The present church building was erected in 1800, and from the time of its dedication which must have been soon afterward, Rev. Frederick Herman was the pastor, remaining until 1821.   Then came the Rev. John C. Guldin, and then followed several who remained each only a short time, as Revs. Hough, Andrew Young, J. S. Foulke, L. D. Leberman and David Heffelfinger. In 1855 Rev. William Sorber accepted a call, entering upon his duties June 22. He appears to have remained until his death, in 1878, when he was succeeded by his son, Rev. George S. Sorber, who remained until January 31, 1886, and was followed by Rev. J. W. Meminger, who began his labors June 1, 1886. Remaining but one year, he was succeeded by Rev. A. D. Wolfinger, who remained until May, 1890. On March 19, 1891, Rev. H. Hilbish became pastor and was succeeded by Rev. Frank N. Bleiler, who remained until 1898, when he was succeeded by Rev. Mr. Royer, the present pastor.

"The Reformed Congregation of Vincent Township beyond the Schuylkil," in East Vincent, was formed about 1758, Rev. John Philip Leydick being the first pastor, and the first church building, a log one, being dedicated in May of that year. From 1758 to 1833 there were baptized into this church 735 persons. In 1784 Rev. Frederick Dallicker became pastor, and since then the following have been pastors of this church: Revs. Frederick Herman, 1799 to 1821; John C. Guldin, 1821 to 1840; Mr. Honger, John R. Kooken and Mr. Hoffman each a short time; Alfred B. Shenkle, to October 4, 1868; Maxwell S. Roland, from 1869 to 1881; D. W. Ebbert, 1881 to 1887; Leighton G. Kremer, 1887 to 1890; I. Calvin Fisher, 1891 to 1892; Edward Weist, 1892 to 1896, and H. H. Hartman, 1897 to the present time.

St. Vincent Reformed Church, in East Vincent Township, was organized about 1848, by members that had withdrawn from the Reformed Congregation of Vincent Township, on account of certain doctrinal points of church discipline. The church edifice was erected in 1852, and was dedicated September 4, that year. The building is 42x60 feet, is two stories high, and cost $1,999.86. Following are the names of the pastors of this church: Rev. Samuel Seifert, a short time; 1853-54, Rev. E. W. Reincke; 1854-56, George D. Wolfe; 1857-58, Henry Weisler; 1859 to 1882, Jesse B. Knipe, who was born in 1805 and died in 1884. Since then the following have officiated here: Rev. S. P. Manger, 1882 to 1886; Rev. J. A. Mertz, 1887 to 1897, and Rev. Mr. Long, who was installed in June, 1898.

St. Peter's (Pikeland) Reformed Church was organized in 1811, and from that time up to 1830 was served by the following pastors: Revs. Frederick A. Herman, Jr., D. D., Jacob W. Dechant, and Casper Wach, and possibly by others. On September 30, 1830, Rev. Jesse B. Knipe was ordained pastor of the church, and continued to preach for it until January 1, 1881, when he resigned. Since that time the following have been the pastors: Rev. S. P. Manger, 1882 to 1888; Rev. James R. Lewis, supply, 1888 to 1889; Rev. F. C. Yost, 1889 to 1890; Rev. I. Calvin Fisher, 1891 to 1892; Rev. Edward Weist, 1892 to 1893; Rev. W. A. Korn, 1893 to the present time, assisted by Rev. J. L. Fluck.

St. Matthew's Reformed Church was organized in the summer of 1833, and they, in connection with the Lutheran congregation of the same township, West Vincent, during that summer erected a church edifice which was dedicated December 23, 1833, Rev. Jesse B. Knipe being the first pastor. Both congregations continued to use it for worship on alternate Sundays until the spring of 1879, when the Reformed Church purchased the interests of the Lutherans in the property. The Reformed congregation adopted a constitution March 18, 1834, and on May 25, 1834, thirty-two persons were present at the first communion service, the pastor being Rev. John C. Guldin, who remained until 1837. In 1838 Rev. Jacob Zeigler was pastor, and was followed by Revs. J. S. Wolf, 1839-40; Edward D. Smith, 1840-42; Jacob Hangen, 1842-43; Andrew S. Young, 1843-44; John C. Fulk, 1844-45; Jesse B. Knipe, 1850-69; Maxwell S. Roland, 1869-79; L. D. Stambaugh, 1879-83; E. D. Wettach, 1884-90; J. L. Fluck, 1891-95, and E. C. Sult, 1895 to the present time. In 1880 a new church building was erected which is 65x42 feet in size, and two stories high, is in the Gothic style and cost $7,000.

St. Paul's Reformed Church of Lionville was organized about 1838, a church building having been erected that year, with the assistance of the Lutheran Church, the two congregations using it for religious purposes on. alternate Sundays until 1851, the Reformed Church then purchasing the interests of the Lutherans. From the time of organization to January 16, 1881, Rev. Jesse B. Knipe was the pastor, he resigning on the latter date. Since then the pastors have been as follows: Rev. A. R. Thompson, 1881 to 1883; Rev. L. D. Stambaugh, 1883 to 1884; Rev. E. D. Wettach, supply, a short time, and was installed June 15, 1884 to 1889; Rev. J. Lewis Fluck, 1891 to 1895, and Rev. E. C. Sult to present time.

The Second Reformed Church of Coventry was organized about 1837, for in that year a church building was erected under the pastorate of Rev. John C. Gulden, who was then pastor of the First Reformed Church of Coventry, otherwise known as "Brownback's." It was for many years supplied by the ministers of the First Reformed Church. This church has been generally known as "Shenkle's," there having been for several years, before the church was erected, a cemetery there by that name.

The pastors of this church have been as follows: Revs. John C. Gulden, 1835-37; Jacob W. Hongen, Andrew S. Young, John C. Fulk, W. R. Work, and David Heffelfinger up to 1855; William Sorbin, 1855 to 1878; George S. Sorber, 1879-86; James W. Meminger, 1886-87; A. D. Wolfinger, 1887-91; W. H. Stubblebine, 1891-93; Frank N. Bleiler, 1893-98, and Rev. Mr. Royer, the present pastor.

The North Phœnixville German Reformed Church was established about 1860, but it was not long maintained.

The First Reformed Church of Spring City was organized April 25, 1882, with forty-seven members, Rev. D. W. Ebbert being the first pastor. Services were held in a hall until the lecture room of the neat stone church edifice was completed, and services were held in the lecture room for the first time December 25, 1884. The building itself was completed in March, 1885, and dedicated April 2, 1885. Rev. Mr. Ebbert remained pastor of this church until July, 1887, and was succeeded by Rev. L. G. Kremer, who began his pastoral duties January 1, 1888. Rev. Calvin Derr became pastor in January, 1891, remained until 1896, and was succeeded by the present pastor, Rev. S. H. Eisenberg, in 1896.

The Mennonite Church, it is believed, had missions or perhaps regular church organizations in Chester County at a very early day, as early as 1725, and from that time on up to 1785 there were three Mennonite Churches on the Schuylkill River, all of which are believed to have been in Chester County. There was a little church building in East Coventry Township on the Schuyl-kill road about three miles from Pottstown, which had in its wall the date, 1728, a one-story building. The first Mennonite Church in the vicinity of Phœnixville was located near the Heckel family residence. The Mennonite Meeting-house in Phœnixville was erected in 1772, on Main Street, near Nutt's Road, designed at first as a church and school building. The first preacher was Matthias Pennypacker, and upon his death he was followed by John Buckwalter, Daniel Showalter, George Hellerman, Jacob Halderman, Jesse Beitler, Joseph Halderman, John Showalter and Isaac Beitler. The members of this sect are gradually diminishing in numbers everywhere, and do not now maintain a church organization in Chester County.

The Disciples of Christ came into Chester County about 1839, in which year a minister of theirs by the name of George Austin began preaching in a barn. In 1841 the members of this society resolved to erect a meeting-house, building a small stone church at Chestnut Grove, in Penn Township, about half a mile from New London. In 1880 they began the erection of a large frame building which was completed in ———. Up to 1881 they had

had but two preachers, Edward Orvis and a Mr. Somers, each remaining only a few years, and otherwise services were conducted by the members of the church. At other times a preacher came up from Baltimore, preaching daily for a week or two.

The Christian Church was established in Chester County in 1845, in which year Elder Frederick Plummer began preaching in a grove near Kimbleville. Some time afterward the membership having sufficiently increased, a brick church edifice was erected in Franklin Township, which was named Mount Olivet, Elder Plummer remaining until 1850. His nephew, Charles H. Plummer, succeeded him, and there was also a preacher there by the name of William H. Pittman, and another named Parvin. Still later Rev. David Somers, of the Church of the Disciples, preached for them, and conducted a Sunday-school. Afterward the church was unoccupied, the membership being small, and at the present time it is ———.

CHAPTER XIX.

TOWNS AND TOWNSHIPS.

CHAPTER XIX.

FOLLOWING is a sketch of the formation of each township and a historical mention of each borough in Chester County. The number of the townships is fifty-six and the number of boroughs is ten. The borough sketches will be found in connection with the townships in which they are located.

Birmingham Township is in the southeastern part of the county, and is bordered by a township of the same name in Delaware County on the southeast, and by the Brandywine River on the southwest. It is believed to have been named by William Brinton, one of the first settlers therein, who came from the vicinity of Birmingham, England. It was surveyed about the year 1684, to various persons, on account of purchases they had made while yet in England, and was organized as a municipal district in 1686 by the appointment of John Bennett as constable. On Holmes' map of the early settlements of Pennsylvania the name is spelled Brummagen, and it was originally so pronounced, this pronunciation, according to Judge Futhey, having been brought from England by the early settlers. Judge Futhey also says that the name Brummagen is derived from Brumwycheham, the ancient name of Birmingham, and that it signifies the name of a Beorm, or Saxon chief.

The name Brinton was for many years pronounced Branton, and it is believed that all bearing the name Brinton are descended from William Brinton, who named the township. It is one of the most historic townships in the county, that part of the battle of Brandywine, fought in the vicinity of Birmingham Meeting-house, being fought within its limits, the site of operations near Chadd's Ford being in Delaware County, as the lines now run.

Bradford Township, now divided into East and West Bradford Townships, lies to the northwest of Birmingham Township. The division into two townships was made in 1731. In this, as in other townships, the first surveys were made for those who had made purchases of the land before leaving England, and it was also true that many of the first settlers had purchased the land of these first purchasers. An unbroken wilderness existed here in all its primeval beauty up to 1686, about which time surveys were made of most of the land south of the Strasburg Road Street Road, forming the southern limits of the township until about the year 1870.

The first settler of this township is believed to have been Richard Buffington, who was appointed constable in 1705, from which year the "organization" of the county dates. Richard Buffington had settled at Upland previous to the arrival of William Penn, and indeed before Penn had obtained his grant. Richard Buffington was the ancestor of the numerous Buffington family in Chester County. As constable he was succeeded in 1706 by Robert Jefferis, and he in 1707 by Abiah Taylor. It was in 1696 that Mr. Buffington, in connection with William Vestal, purchased 218 acres of land from the executors of John Loftus, and in 1701 they obtained the remaining 218 acres of the Loftus tract, which extended from the Brandywine, below the forks, nearly to Strode's Mill. In 1708 Mr. Buffington purchased from Thomas Martin of Middletown 210 acres, which extended northward from his first purchase to the east branch of the Creek.

Abiah Taylor, above mentioned, settled on the Brandywine in 1702, built a mill on a creek emptying into it, and in 1724 erected a brick house, the bricks having been imported from England. This statement is made on the authority of Futhey & Cope's short historical sketch of Chester County, published in Dr. Egle's "History of the Commonwealth of Pennsylvania," published in Philadelphia in 1883. But in the large "History of Chester County," written by the same gentleman, and published in 1881, the following statement is made: "It has been frequently said that the bricks were brought from England, but this is not correct. They were made on the farm, from clay procured a short distance south of the house." The statement that they were brought from England contains nothing improbable, for previous to the Revolution, at least, it was the firm policy of England that the mother country should supply the colonies with all their manufactured goods, of whatever kind.

Brandywine Township was formed in 1790, from the northern part of East Caln Township. It was named from the two branches of the Brandywine, which bounded it on the east and west sides. It was divided into East and West Brandywine Townships in 1844. In 1853 a small portion of the southern end of West Brandywine Township was taken in the formation of Valley Township, and in 1859 the line running between East and West Brandywine was so changed in its location as to take into West Brandywine a portion of East Brandywine. In 1860 an addition was made to West Brandywine from the southeast corner of Honeybrook and the western part of Wallace. In this addition was located the Brandywine Manor Presbyterian Church, which had previously been in Honeybrook Township, and which is situated on what was at one time Springton Manor, which embraced the larger part of the present Wallace Township. There never was any Brandywine Manor.

Charlestown Township is in the eastern part of the county next west of Schuylkill. It was named after Charles Pickering of Asmore, Chester County, England, as was also Pickering Creek. Charles Pickering crossed the ocean with William Penn, and when wandering up the Schuylkill River, in search of treasure, thought he discovered traces of silver on the banks of the stream which now bears his name, and afterward obtained from William Penn a grant of a large tract of land bordering on the stream. In 1863 he was tried for setting up a private mint for the "Quoining of Spanish bitts and Boston money," an account of the trial being presented on other pages of this work. According to Judge Futhey, Pickering was subsequently drowned while crossing the ocean, and his land in Chester County divided among sixteen of his friends, to whom he had devised it. In 1718 "Pickering Lotts," 4,640 acres, were included in the non-resident land of Whiteland assessment, and in 1722 the names of the actual settlers are obtained for the first time, in the "Charles Town Rates." Following are their names: Francis Buckholder and his sons; Samuel Richardson, John Humphreys, James Jones, Philip Jones, David Jones, Llewellyn David, Griffith Pritchard, Mathias Martin, Alexander Owen, John Rees, Manuel Jones, Thomas, John, Stephen David, James Anderson, Harry Griffith, and Lewis Martyn. The non-resident land owners were as follows: Cocks & Co., 20,000 acres; London Tract, John Moore, Joshua Carpenter, John Bud, Samuel Buckley, and there was a tract called Pike's Land. The aggregate value of land owned then by these non-residents was £2,397.

In 1722 the first constable in the township was appointed, in the person of Thomas John, and in 1724 there were the following settlers there, besides those whose names have been given: William Moore, John David, David Gilby, John Powell, David, James and Philip John, Thomas David, John, Joseph and Jacob Buckwalder, Benjamin Villauer, John Evan, Griffith and Azariah Thomas and John Jones.

Pickering Creek for many years ran many mills, of which the

most noted was that erected by Judge William Moore, above named.

The Manor of Bilton may be here appropriately mentioned. In 1681 William Penn conveyed to his sister, Margaret Lowther, 10,000 acres of land, in right of which a tract called the Manor of Bilton was laid out on the west side of the Schuylkill, and separated from the "Manor of Mount Joy," by the Valley Creek. When this Manor of Bilton was resurveyed in 1733 it was found to contain 2,850 acres, being the southeastern part of Charlestown Township. In 1737 William Allen of Philadelphia became the owner of the manor, selling it in 1739 to John Parry of Haverford. Afterward the land was divided up among the following persons: William John Adam, 500 acres; Widow Mathias, 263 acres; John Jones, 500 acres; William Griffith, 174 acres; Cadwalader Hugh, 176 acres; Griffith Thomas, 235 acres; Thomas James, George Rees and William Lloyd, 430 acres; Thomas Howell, 366 acres; Jenkin David, 200 acres, and Catharine Rees, 151 acres.

In 1826 the township was divided, the eastern division lying along the Schuylkill River, being named after that stream, and the name Charlestown being retained by the western portion. In 1827 the lines between the southwestern part of Charlestown and the townships of East and West Whiteland and Uwchlan were so altered as to correct defectiveness in former surveys.

Caln Township was originally very large, including within its limits what is now embraced in Caln, East and West Caln, East and West Brandywine, and a part of Valley Townships. It was named from a town named Calne, in Wiltshire, England, whence some of the early settlers came. In 1702 surveys were made from the west line of Whiteland to the west branch of the Brandywine, confined mostly to the valley; but which afterward extended to the northward and to the southward. It was first settled by the Baldwins, Moores, Parkeses, Mendenhalls Pims, Coateses, Millers and others. Downingtown now stands on land formerly owned by the Baldwins and Moores. On April 6, 1709, Joseph Cloud, Richard Cloud, and George Mendenhall, all of Caln, were indicted for an assault on Joseph Hickman in his house in Caln, and in 1714 Peter Taylor was constable for the township, but it does not appear to be now known whether or not he was the first officer of that kind.

On November 26, 1728, a petition, signed by thirty-one citizens, was presented to the court asking that, inasmuch as the township was so large, extending in length above fourteen miles and in breadth nearly fourteen miles, it might be divided into two townships, one of which should continue to be called Caln, and the other to be called Spefforth, or Spofforth, probably the latter, as it is often difficult to distinguish between an "e" and an "o" in the ancient manuscripts; but while the petition is indorsed "allowed," there is no evidence of the existence of a township by the name of Spefforth anywhere to be found. But West Caln was organized at that time, the Brandywine being the boundary line between the townships. On May 29, 1739, the boundaries of East Caln were definitely determined, and on May 29, 1744, the boundaries of West Caln were likewise determined. In 1790 the limits of East Caln were reduced and the township of Brandywine erected, taken from the northern part of East Caln. In 1853 it was again reduced in size by the creation of Valley Township, and in 1859 it was again reduced by the formation of the borough of Downingtown. In 1868 it was once more reduced, that portion lying east of the east branch of the Brandywine being made a separate township by the name of East Caln, and that part lying west of this east branch, together with a part of Valley Township, being erected into a township by the name of Caln. When Valley Township was created in 1853 West Caln was slightly reduced in size. The greater portion of Caln and East Caln lies within the Great Valley, and contains many beautiful farms, while West Caln is somewhat more hilly than the others.

Downingtown is on the east branch of the Brandywine, in the midst of the Great Valley. It was incorporated by a decree of the court May 12, 1859, and at an election held at the Swan Hotel on the 28th of the same month, James Lockhart was chosen burgess. This place was originally called Milltown, but more recently the name it now bears was given to it, in honor of the Downing family, that lived, and which still lives, in that neighborhood. One remarkable fact connected with the history of this cannot be omitted, and that is that during the early years of its existence it so strenuously resisted the attempt to make it the county-seat, that the county-seat had to be located elsewhere, and went to West Chester. It is probable that no similar instance can be found in the history of the country, and it is well known that in many cases, especially in western counties, there have been numerous "county-seat wars," rival towns making a most determined struggle to possess the county-seat, instead of driving it away. But in the case of Downingtown not a lot could be purchased upon which to erect the county buildings.

Downingtown is now an enterprising place, and a prominent station on the Pennsylvania Railroad. Its borough officers have been as follows:

Burgess—James Lockhart, 1859 and 1860; A. W. Wills, 1861; Charles Downing, 1862; Morgan L. Reece, 1863; J. Stuart Leech, 1864; David Shelmire, 1865; John S. Mullin, 1866; William Edge, 1867; Temple Jones, 1868; Eber Garrett, 1869; John S. Mullin, 1870; William B. Torbert, 1871; David M. Cox, 1872; G. C. M. Eicholtz, 1873-74; William B. Torbert, 1875; J. T. Carpenter, 1876; J. Stuart Leech, 1877-79; Thomas E. Parke, 1880-83; J. Stuart Leech, 1884; Thomas E. Parke, 1885; John McGraw, 1886; L. T. Bremerman, 1887-90; Joseph R. Downing, 1891-92; James R. Gordon, 1893-96, and A. P. Ringwalt, 1897-98.

Secretaries—J. Stuart Leech, 1859; Charles Downing, 1860; J. Stuart Leech, 1861; Isaac Webster, 1862; John S. Mullin, 1863;

John Webster, 1864; Charles Downing, 1865; John Webster, 1866-69; J. E. Parke, 1870; George E. Wills, 1871-73; John Webster, 1874; J. E. Parke, 1875; Harry L. Skeen, 1876; Samuel Lineinger, 1877-80; Eber Garrett, 1881; J. H. Roberts, 1882-84; Isaac Y. Ash, 1885-86; Thomas Holliday, 1887-96, and R. A. Swank, 1897-98.

Treasurers—William Edge, 1859-62; R. D. Wells, 1863-64; Eber Garrett, 1865; Temple Jones, 1866-67; Isaac Webster, 1868; G. C. M. Eicholtz, 1869-70; David M. Cox, 1871; William Edge, 1872; John S. Mullin, 1873; W. F. McCaughey, 1874; George A. Cobb, 1875-76; W. F. McCaughey, 1877; Francis O'Neal, 1878; Nathan Wilson, 1879-81; W. F. McCaughey, 1882; Jacob Shelmire, 1883; William McFarlan, 1884-86; F. Dunleavy Long, 1887; Nathan Wilson, 1888-90; F. Dunleavy Long, 1891-92; Downingtown National Bank, 1893-98.

The members of the council at the present time are as follows: S. Austin Bicking, James R. Gordon, Gayon Miller, W. I. Pollock, Frank McGraw and Mark Connell. The borough of Downingtown put in a gravity system of water works in 1895, bringing the water from springs three miles to the south, which furnish a pressure of 45 pounds, sufficient to throw the water over the tops of the highest buildings in the place. The water has been placed in most of the residences and business houses and manufactories, and the reservoir has a capacity of 2,500,000 gallons.

There is also an electric light, heat and power company, of which John T. Fox is president, Joseph R. Downing, treasurer, and Thomas E. Parke, secretary. The company was organized in the spring of 1898, and is composed of the citizens of Downington, the shares of stock being $10 each. The works are located on the "Y" branch of the Downingtown and Lancaster Railroad, and have two dynamos, two high speed engines, and two boilers, the latter being procured from the Coatesville Boiler Works. While it is the design to supply both arc and incandescent lights, yet up to the present writing (May 14, 1898) there is but one arc light, and that is over the bridge on Lancaster Avenue where this avenue crosses the Brandywine.

North, East and South Coventry lie in the extreme north of the county, extending from the Schuylkill River westward. The original township, it is believed, was named by Samuel Nutt, who came from Coventry, Warwickshire, England. The first list of settlers obtainable is from the assessment of 1718, and included the following names: Israel Robinson, John Sinclair, John Rumford, Thomas Miller, Richard Duncley, Marcus Overhult, John Oburne, Henry Castle, Hubert Castle, Henry Parker, Garrett Prompter, Simon Meredith, David Evans, James Pugh, William Philips, Owen Roberts, and John Blare.

In 1841 the township was divided into North and South Coventry, and in 1844 East Coventry was formed by dividing North Coventry. In this same year the line between South Coventry and East Vincent was established, as it was supposed to have been originally run.

Easttown Township lies in the southeast part of the county, and is bounded on the north by Tredyffrin, and on the east by Tredyffrin and Radnor, the latter township being in Delaware. Its territory was included in the original survey made for the Welsh and was settled by them. It was "organized" as early as 1704, as its constable, William Thomas, appeared at court December 27, 1704-05. In 1800 the town of Glassley was laid out by Robert McClenachan, near what is now Berwyn. This township is most noted as being the home of the Wayne family, the founder of which, Anthony Wayne, first appears in the assessment roll in 1724. It is also noted for containing the summer residence, which finally became the permanent residence of Julius F. A. Sachse, in 1877, formerly a merchant in Philadelphia and also a noted horticulturist. The name given to this place is "Sachsenstein," after the old family-seat near Erfurt in Germany, the ruins of which still exist.

Goshen Township, formerly a part of Westtown Township, was organized at least as early as 1704. It was included within the original survey for the Welsh, but owing to the delay of the Welsh to settle therein many surveys were made within its limits for other purchasers. The first settlers of Goshen Township in the eastern part were the Ashbridge family, which was for many years very prominent in county and State affairs, George Ashbridge serving in the General Assembly for twenty successive years. David Jones was also one of the early settlers. The first constable, appearing at court in 1704, was Cadwalader Ellis. There were two large tracts of land, each of a mile square, adjoining Gay Street, West Chester, one of which was owned by Richard Thomas, the owner of the other not having been ascertained. The southwest part of Goshen Township was taken up in the right of Thomas Lloyd, whose executors in 1706 sold two tracts of land, containing respectively 797 and 850 acres, to William Crouch of London. In 1702 they had sold to John Haines of New Jersey 965 acres, which now includes that part of the borough of West Chester south of Gay Street. North of this and west of High Street a tract of 630 acres was patented to Nathaniel Puckle, and later passed into the hands of the Hoopes family. Richard Thomas, mentioned above, lived in Whiteland, and sold his 1,100 acres of land which lay east of High Street, in allotments or divisions running from north to south, beginning at the west side, to different persons as follows: Edward Jones, 200 acres; Robert Eachus, 200; Joseph Collins, 125; Thomas Evans, 175; Mordecai Bane, 200, and Alexander Bane, 200.

East of the tract owned by Richard Thomas was one of 316 acres owned by Evan Jones & Co., and beyond this was one of about equal size owned by Ellis David. Then came a tract of 635 acres owned by Thomas Jones & Co. Perhaps the most interesting fact connected with the early settlement of Goshen Township is this: That John ap Thomas of Llaithgwm, Commott of

Pennllyn, Merioneth County, and Edward Jones of Bala, in the same county in Wales, chirurgeon, purchased from William Penn, by lease and release of September 16 and 17, 1681, 5,000 acres of land, as agents or trustees for themselves and others. They executed deeds to the other purchasers before coming to this country. One-half of each person's share was located in Goshen Township, by direction of a warrant for the subdivision of the Welsh Tract. John ap Thomas died in Wales in 1683, but his children, who arrived in Pennsylvania in November of the same year, and who bore the name of Jones, took up half his purchase in Goshen Township. Edward Jones, Edward Rees, William ap Edward and others arrived in 1682. Cadwalader Morgan and Hugh John sold what they owned in Goshen to John Roberts, who married Gainor Roberts, another purchaser, and thus came into possession of 262 acres in Goshen. In 1749 Robert Roberts, the only son of John Roberts, sold 230 acres of this 262 acres to Thomas Goodwin. The Goodwin homestead remained in the family for many years, having descended to Mary Goodwin, who married Samuel R. Downing. Griffith Owen had a house in Goshen at which Friends' meetings were held as early as 1702. In 1788 the size of the township was reduced by the erection of the borough of West Chester, and in 1817 the division into East and West Goshen was made.

West Chester, the county seat of Chester County, is situated in West Goshen Township, the southwest boundary line of the latter being the southwest boundary of the borough of West Chester. The latitude and longitude of the city were determined in 1843 by E. W. Bean and Walter Hibbard, the former being at the time principal of the public schools in West Chester, and the latter a surveyor and conveyancer of the same place. The latitude was then determined as being 39 57 31.3 and the longitude as being 1 24 51 east of Washington, District of Columbia. Its location is on the watershed between Brandywine Creek and Chester Creek, being about two miles from the Brandywine and quite near the head of one of the branches of the Chester Creek. It is five miles south of the great limestone valley, twenty-three miles west of the original city of Philadelphia and sixteen miles north of Wilmington, Delaware. Its elevation is about 460 feet above the level of the sea.

Until after the close of the Revolutionary War the county-seat remained at Chester, on the Delaware River, the county growing more populous in the meantime, even in the northern and western portions. About 1779 an effort was made to secure its removal to a more central location; yet, notwithstanding the admitted inconvenience to the great majority of the people in the location of the county-seat in the extreme southeastern corner of the county, there was, on the part of the inhabitants of the village of Chester, strenuous opposition made to its removal, as was quite natural to expect. The controversy was maintained several years, even after such removal was determined upon by law, with considerable bitterness and with varying success.

The result of the agitation thus persisted in was the passage by the Legislature of an act on March 20, 1780, authorizing William Clingan, Thomas Bull, John Kinkead, Roger Kirk, John Sellars, John Wilson and Joseph Davis, or any four or more of them, to build a new court-house and prison in the county of Chester, and to sell the old court-house and prison in the borough of Chester. No time was specified within which these commissioners should purchase land and erect the mentioned buildings, nor was there any restriction as to location, except what was expressed in the preamble against the inconvenience of the location then maintained.

But for some reason, either opposition to the removal itself, or mere negligence, the above-named gentlemen failed to act, except in so far as to purchase land for a site in the township of East Caln, which location seems to have been unsatisfactory to the most prominent gentlemen favoring the removal of the county-seat, and it was probably this dissatisfaction with the proposed location that led to the passage, on March 22, 1784, of an act supplementary to the original act, by which the names of John Hannum, Isaac Taylor and John Jacobs were substituted for those of of the original commissioners. The authority granted to the three gentlemen last named was similar to that granted to the original seven, but they were not authorized to erect the proposed new court-house and prison "at a greater distance than one mile and a half from the Turk's Head Tavern, in the township of Goshen, and to the west or southwest of said Turk's Head Tavern, and on or near a straight line from the ferry, called the Corporation Ferry, on the Schuylkill to the village of Strasburg."

Historians all appear to agree that this peculiar restriction was introduced into the supplementary act at the suggestion of Mr. Hannum, then a member of the Legislature, under the belief that it would permit the buildings to be erected on his lands on the left bank of the Brandywine; but actual measurement demonstrated the fact that his lands lay more than two miles from the Turk's Head Tavern, hence Mr. Hannum must have been grievously disappointed.

Being all active removalists, the committee at once contracted for the purchase of land near the Turk's Head Tavern, and in the summer of 1784 began the erection of the buildings, a court-house and a prison adjacent to each other. It is said that Col. John Hannum was the real founder of West Chester, and that in anticipation of its location he took care to become an extensive owner of lands and lots within the limits of the borough.

In an historical sketch of the borough of West Chester by "The oldest inhabitant," published in 1857, it is stated that:

"The colonel was a sort of County Autocrat, and, for a long time, managed matters pretty much in his own way. He built the old Washington Hotel, on High Street, with only a narrow alley between it and the court-house; and with a view to secure the patronage of the judges to the hotel, he projected a kind of gallery or passageway from the second story across the alley into the hall of justice, for the accommodation of their Honors; and even went so far toward effecting an opening as to remove some stones from the court-house wall, when the county commissioners mustered courage enough to forbid further operations. The gaps made in the wall testified to the liberty thus taken for many years, until the exterior of the old building was renovated by a rough coat of plastering and pebble-dashing.

"While these proceedings were in train at the Turk's Head the worthy burgers of ancient Upland were concocting a violent opposition to what they naturally regarded as an injurious if not ruinous project. The operations of the workmen at the new public buildings were suspended by the ensuing winter before the walls were quite completed; and the functions of the commissioners themselves were interrupted by an act of Assembly obtained on the 30th of March, 1785, to suspend the supplement," etc.

Now, turning to a History of Chester County, written by Joseph J. Lewis, and published in the Village Record in 1824, the following account of the high-handed proceedings taken by those citizens who preferred that the county-seat should still remain in Chester may be found: "The people generally in the neighborhood of Chester had been violently opposed from the beginning to the projected removal, and a number now resolved to demolish the walls already erected. Accordingly a company assembled, armed and accoutered, and having procured a field piece, appointed Major Harper commander, and proceeded to accomplish their design. A few days before this expedition left Chester notice of its object was communicated by some of the leaders to the neighborhood of the Turk's Head, and preparations were immediately made for its reception. In this business Col. Hannum was particularly active. He directly requested Col. Isaac Taylor and

Mr. Marshall to bring in what men they could collect, and began himself to prepare cartridges and to procure arms. Grog and rations were freely distributed, and a pretty respectable force was soon upon the ground. The windows of the court-house were boarded up on each side, and the space between filled with stones; loopholes were left for the musketry. Each man had his station assigned him. Marshall and Taylor commanded in the upper story—Underwood and Patton below, while Col. Hannum had the direction of the whole. All things were arranged for a stout resistance.

"The non-removalists, having passed the night at the Green Tree (hotel), made their appearance near the Turk's Head early in the morning, and took their ground about two hundred yards southeast of the Quaker Meeting-house. Here they planted their cannon and made preparations for the attack. They seemed, however, when everything was ready, still reluctant to proceed to extremities, and having remained several hours in a hostile position, an accommodation was effected between the parties, by the intervention of some pacific people, who used their endeavors to prevent the effusion of blood. To the non-removalists was conceded the liberty of inspecting the defenses of their opponents, on condition that they should do them no injury, and they on their part agreed to abandon their design and to return peaceably to their homes. The cannon which had been pointed against the walls was turned in another direction, and fired in celebration of the treaty. Col. Hannum then directed his men to leave the court-house, and having formed in line a short distance on the the right, to ground their arms and wait till the other party should have finished their visit to the building. Here an act of indiscretion had nearly brought on a renewal of hostilities. For one of Major Harper's men, having entered the fort, struck down the flag which their opponents had raised upon the walls. Highly incensed at this treatment of their standard the removalists snatched up their

arms and were with difficulty prevented from firing on the Major
and his companions.   Some exertion, however, on the part of the
leaders allayed the irritation of the men and the parties separated
at last, without loss of life or limb."

It is now pertinent to inquire as to why this attack was
made or threatened.   Why did the people in the lower end of Chester County attempt to prevent the completion of the public
buildings in West Chester?   For they must have had some ac-
tuating motive.   Probably the best answer to this question is that
given by Dr. Smith that the removalists, Col. Hannum and his
compatriots, had proceeded with the work on these buildings after
the suspension of the supplementary act, mentioned above, which
was suspended March 30, 1785; and if this is the case it of course
appeared to the Chester people that the West Chester people cared
nothing for the acts of the Assembly.   And if a promise to de-
sist from work on the public buildings was a portion of the treaty
of peace, as is also stated, this promise was kept only while
non-removalists were within hearing and sight of the place.   Then
again on the other hand it is said that the suspension act itself
was procured by some sort of underhand work, or misrepresenta-
tion as to the temper of the people of the county toward removal,
and if so, then the removalists were not so much to blame for
proceeding with the construction of the buildings.

The next step on the part of the Legislature of the State was
taken on March 18, 1786, when an act was passed repealing the
suspension act, and thus the work was permitted to go on.   By
this act the vexed question was finally put to rest, though not
until after a bitter fight had been made on both sides of the
question.   The removalists were naturally jubilant over their hard
won victory, and expressed themselves in sundry songs and dit-
ties, couched in language not the most complimentary of their
vanquished foes.   One of these, entitled, "Lament Over Chester's
Mother," was originally published in the West Chester Directory

LEVI G. McCAULEY.

for 1857, and is reproduced in Futhey and Cope's History of Chester County. Its length precludes its insertion in this history.

On the other hand the people of Chester were equally complimentary toward their friends in West Chester, their new town being thus described in an address to the Legislature: "That elegant and notorious place vulgarly called the Turk's Head (by some called West Chester), a place as unfit for the general convenience and much more so than any one spot that might be pointed out within ten miles square, of the above-described place (except toward the New Castle line)."

The new county building having been completed and made ready for occupancy, an act was passed by the Assembly September 25, 1786, authorizing the sheriff of the county, William Gibbons, to remove the prisoners from the old jail in Chester to the new jail in West Chester, or in Goshen Township, and to indemnify him for the removal. The old public buildings at Chester were finally sold to William Kerlin on March 18, 1788; but after the organization of Delaware County, which followed as a result of this removal of the county-seat, the same public buildings were repurchased by that new county from Mr. Kerlin.

The seat of justice having thus been secured, the people determined that Turk's Head should be dignified by a title becoming its newly acquired importance, and on March 3, 1788, the Legislature of the State converted a certain district of country into a county town. This town was about one and one-quarter miles square, and included six or eight small farms. The name West Chester was then given to it. The people of old Chester, down by the river Delaware, now themselves became dissatisfied because the county-seat by its removal had become so distant from them; and, as a consequence of this dissatisfaction, the Legislature, upon their petition, in which they stated their desire to be relieved of the great inconvenience of having to go so far to the county-seat, erected the borough of Chester and the southeastern

52

part of the county into a new county, the act which accomplished this purpose being passed September 26, 1789, this new county being called Delaware, and by its erection revenge had been fully wreaked on the people in the northern part of the county.

While the question as to whether it was wise to so divide the ancient county of Chester in this way, it may not be improper to state that after all there was but little gained in the way of saving distance in going to the county-seat on the part of the people of Delaware County, as a glance at the map will at once reveal; and as the county at that time had a population of only 9,483 the burdens of supporting the organization of the new county made it for a time at least somewhat of an expensive luxury, particularly as the people were then quite poor, not having recovered from the losses and destruction of the (then) late Revolutionary War.

The people of West Chester, having accomplished their design of securing the county-seat, began in greater earnest than ever to improve their town, and not long afterward began to aspire to corporate privileges. On March 28, 1789, the town was erected into a borough by an act of the Legislature. From this time on, however, the place seemed to grow very slowly, perhaps because of the slow development of the surrounding country, and during the succeeding twelve years of the town's history the population increased scarcely more than a hundred. In 1800 it was 374.

Following are the names of the burgesses of West Chester from the time of the first election in 1799 down to the present time: William Sharpless, elected in 1799; Jacob Ehrenzeller, in 1800; Philip Derrick, in 1801; Jacob Ehrenzeller, 1802; Richard M. Hannum, 1803; Joshua Weaver, 1804 and 1805; William Bennett, 1806; William Sharpless, 1807; Emmor Bradley, 1808; George Worth, 1809; Joshua Weaver, 1810; William Sharpless, 1811; Jacob Ehrenzeller, 1812 and 1813; Joseph McClellan, 1814; Daniel Hiester, 1815, 1816 and 1817; Jacob Ehrenzeller, 1818 to 1824; Ziba Pyle, 1825; Jacob Ehrenzeller, 1826; Ziba Pyle, 1827 to 1830; Thomas S. Bell, 1831 to 1833; William Williamson, 1834 and 1835; William Everhart, 1836 and 1837; Thomas S. Bell, 1838; Joseph J. Lewis, 1839 to 1843; William Williamson, 1844; Uriah V. Pennypacker, 1845 and 1846; William Darlington, 1847; Uriah V. Pennypacker, 1848 and 1849; Francis James, 1850; James H. Bull, 1851; Townsend Eachus, 1852 to 1854; Joseph P. Wilson, 1855 to 1858; William B. Waddell, 1859-60; Henry S. Evans, 1861; William Darlington, 1862-65; Wayne MacVeagh, 1866; Jefferson Shaner, 1867-77; S. G. Williams, 1878; Dr. J. B. Wood, 1879-86; Marshall S. Way, 1887-97; C. Wesley Talbot, 1897.

Clerks—Joshua Weaver, 1799-1801; Isaac Darlington, 1802; Nathan Sharpless, 1803-04; Emmor Bradley, 1805-07; Joshua Weaver, 1808-09; Reuben Eachus, 1810; David Townsend, Jr., 1811; John W. Townsend, 1812; John Wooley, 1813; David Townsend, 1814; Harper Pearson, 1815-16; Joshua Weaver, 1817-27; David Townsend, 1828-35; John Marshall, 1836-38; William Williamson, 1839-41; Walter Hibbard, 1842-44; E. D. Haines, 1845-51; J. B. Jeffries, 1852-54; William S. Kirk, 1855; John J. Pinkerton, 1856-61; William V. Husted, 1862-65; George M. Rupert, 1866-83; Frank P. Darlington, 1884; Charles B. Lear, 1885; Walter A. McDonald, 1886-87; William S. Underwood, 1888-98.

Treasurers—Down to 1840 the clerks and treasurers appear to have been the same person; John Marshall, 1840-43; John Rutter, 1844; W. Townsend, 1845-49; J. Smith Futhey, 1850-53; A. Marshall, 1854; James H. Bull, 1855; Clement Darlington, 1856; William S. Kirk, 1857-58; John J. Pinkerton, 1859-63; William V. Husted, 1864-66; George M. Rupert, 1867-84; Alfred P. Smith, 1884-87; W. D. Groff, 1887-88; William S. Underwood, 1888-98.

A system of waterworks was established by the borough of West Chester in 1841, a report of the entire matter being made to the borough council in January, 1842, which showed that lots had been purchased of Anthony Bolmar and Joshua Hoopes, the former receiving $2,344.28, and the latter $200. The entire cost of the water system was $25,019.50. The committee making this report consisted of John Marshall, Isaac Thomas and William Apple. In 1843 the water committee, composed of the first two of the above-named gentlemen and W. Townsend, expressed their gratification at the successful introduction of water into the borough, saying that it was generally admitted by the citizens and strangers that the water was as good and pure as could be anywhere found, and that the safety from fires was much greater than had been the case before.

This pumping station was in the southwest corner of Marshall Square, where the monument to the Ninety-seventh Regiment now stands. In 1854 a pumping station was erected at Fern Hill, on the Frazer branch of the railroad, a power pump, run by a stationary engine, being put in, and the water pumped into the reservoir in Marshall Square. In 1881-82 a distributing reservoir was constructed near Fern Hill Station, having a capacity of 2,000,-000 gallons, and at this time the reservoir in Marshall Square was abandoned, as was also the old pumping station in the square. A new Worthington 1,000,000 gallon Cross compound engine was put in at Fern Hill at this time. The reservoir at Fern Hill Station is 102 feet above the pumping station, the distance between the two points being 31,000 feet, and the main leading from the pumping station to the reservoir being ten inches in diameter. In 1891 an extra fifty horse power boiler was put in at Fern Hill, and in 1894 a new Barr tandem compound engine, capable of raising 1,500,000 gallons in twenty-four hours, was set up. The two reservoirs at Fern Hill are capable of holding 2,000,000 gallons of water.

About one mile above Fern Hill pumping station is a dam across Chester Creek, where the borough owns twenty-five acres of land, the lake caused by this dam holding about 7,000,000 gallons, and being for use in emergencies. It was formed in the spring of 1893.

The Milltown Pumping Station, on the West Chester and Philadelphia Road, is three miles east of West Chester. The settling dam here is fed from Chester Creek, by a race 600 feet long. The pumping station is of stone, 44x67½ feet in size, the double engine being a high duty Corliss Cross compound, capable of raising into the reservoir, which is 13,000 feet distant and elevated above the pumping station 175 feet, 2,000,000 gallons in twenty-four hours. This engine was put in in 1897 to take the place of the old station about three miles above this plant on Chester Creek. The settling pond at the Milltown Station holds 3,500,000 gallons. The cost of this station, together with its equipment, was $41,000, and the main connecting this station with the reservoir, which is about fifty feet above the average level of the city of West Chester, is twelve inches in diameter, and there is a main leading directly to West Chester from the Milltown Station, fourteen inches in diameter.

The original plan of the village of West Chester consisted of four squares, with two principal streets crossing in the center. Yet, strange as it may appear, these streets were not made to cross each other at right angles. That the streets should run at an angle with the meridian of longitude and parallel of latitude on which the town is located is not strange, since all the boundary lines within the original Chester County, including Delaware, run thus obliquely, the same remark applying to the boundary lines of farms and estates. This is probably to be accounted for by the fact that the Delaware River, along the front of William Penn's province of Pennsylvania, flows in a southwesterly direction, and the lines separating the several Indian purchases, so far as they were thus separated, run back into the interior generally at nearly right angles with the river. Still, it would seem more consonant with all ideas of taste and convenience in building fences and houses to have the main streets of the village run at right angles rather than at obtuse and acute angles.

At first the houses were built close to the street, and of course those so built in the central part of the village still remain; but in 1829 several additional streets were opened up and new squares formed, and it was then that those building houses began to set them back from the street, leaving room in front of them for front yards and lawns. This was a great improvement, not only to the appearance of the village itself, but also to the convenience and comfort of the inhabitants, for it gave opportunity to plant trees in such way as to shade pedestrians from the scorching rays of the summer sun, and it also furnishes opportunity to beautify the streets and lawns in front of residences, as could not be done before.

In 1838 a second enlargement of the town plat was made from the Matlock property on the northward side, the addition amounting to several streets and squares. Not long afterward a similar addition was made on the eastern side of the place, on the old Turk's Head or Patton estate; and still later a fourth addition was made on the northwest side by John Rutter.

In 1841 a most important improvement was made, though of a different kind. This improvement consisted in the introduction of good water, by means of steam power, through the streets of the village, from the fine old Bath Spring to the northward, and in order to secure a further supply of water, works were established on Chester Creek in 1854.

In the way of recapitulating early events in the history of West Chester it may be stated that the municipality, in 1802, established a small market-house in the rear of the public offices, but it was little used, owing to the market people preferring to call upon their respective customers rather than to wait for customers to call on them. In 1831 this small market-house was superseded by a larger building on Market Street, which was about 100 feet long, and which was enlarged from time to time during the next twenty or twenty-five years to meet the increasing demands of trade.

The first foot pavement in West Chester was put down in 1809, in front of the property of Dr. William Darlington, rough flagstones being used, bricks not having then made their appearance in the borough or its vicinity. Ephraim Buffington immediately followed the example thus set, and he in turn was followed by William Hemphill, who procured bricks for his pavement from abroad, and was thus the first to put down a brick foot pavement of any in the town. Mr. Hemphill's dwelling was on High Street, where afterward was erected the Bank of Chester County. Few followed these examples until the corporation, in 1823, began to build sidewalks, bricks being used generally, if not wholly. In 1829 and 1830 the two principal streets were macadamized, Gay and Church Streets, and good crossings provided. By 1857 almost all the sidewalks were well paved with brick, and the streets greatly improved.

Marshall Square.—A valuable improvement was begun in 1848, in the addition of a park to the city's attractions. This improvement was made in pursuance of the following ordinance passed by the borough authorities:

Whereas, It has been deemed expedient and proper to improve the public square, on which the upper reservoir connected with the waterworks of the borough is situated, by laying out the same in suitable walks, and introducing various ornamental trees and shrubbery; and, whereas, it will be convenient and necessary to designate the said square by some appropriate name: and, whereas, the late Humphrey Marshall, of Chester County, was one of the most distinguished horticulturists and botanists of our county, having established the second botanic garden in this Republic, and also prepared and published the first treatise on the forest trees and shrubs of the United States, and diffused a taste for botanical science, which entitles his memory to the lasting respect of his countrymen; therefore

"Resolved, By the Burgesses and Assistant Burgesses of the Borough of West Chester, in council assembled, That the Public

Square, aforesaid, shall forever hereafter be designated and known by the name of 'The Marshall Square,' in commemoration of the exemplary character and scientific labors of our distinguished fellow-citizen, the late Humphrey Marshall, of West Bradford Township, Chester County.

"Passed March 13, 1848."

Marshall Square contains about five and a half acres of ground, and is well filled with ornamental trees of many kinds, around and among which are fine gravel walks and drives. It was opened to the public in 1857, and at once became a popular pleasure resort for the people of the place, and a most interesting and attractive feature of the outskirts of the town.

In 1852 a company was formed for the purpose of introducing gas into the city, and from that time on to the present time this pleasant light has been in constant use.

On the northwest corner of Marshall Square stands a fine monument to the soldiers of the Ninety-seventh Pennsylvania Regiment, which was dedicated October 29, 1887. A large number of persons was present on this occasion, as was also a large number of military and other organizations from Chester and surrounding counties. The monument itself is fifty feet high from the bottom of the first base stone to the top of the soldier's head. It is of Ryegate granite, from South Ryegate, Vermont. Its construction is as follows:

Bases—1st. 12 feet square by 1 foot thick.
       2nd. 10 feet 4 inches square, by 1 foot thick.
       3rd. 8 feet 8 inches square, by 1 foot thick.
       4th. 7 feet 2 inches square, by 1 foot thick.
Plinths—1st. 6 feet square with molding on top, 2 feet thick.
        2nd. 5 feet 4 inches square, by 1 foot thick, cut
              with bases to relieve the columns.

The die is a polished stone 3 feet 4 inches square and 4 feet high, with columns at the four corners, and on the four sides of the die are appropriate inscriptions, the east side bearing the names of the field and staff officers at the time of the organization of the regiment, as follows:

Colonel, Henry R. Guss; Lieut.-Col., Augustus P. Duer; Major, Galusha Pennypacker; Surgeon, John R. Everhart, M. D.; Asst. Sur., George W. Miller, M. D.; Adjutant, Henry W. Carruthers; Quartermaster, David Jones; Chaplain, Rev. William E. Whitehead.

The following statistics of the regiment are interesting in this connection:

Total number of volunteers in 1861.................1,089
Total number of drafted men and substitutes......... 995

Total number of men that belonged to the regiment..2,084
Number killed in action............................ 69
Number that died of wounds....................... 71
Number that died of disease....................... 166

Total number of deaths......................... 306
Number that resigned 32
Number discharged during period of service........... 502
Number discharged at expiration of service.......... 267
Number transferred 98
Number that deserted............................. 151
Number not on muster roll......................... 15

Total 1,065
Number mustered 713

Total 2,084

The money with which this monument was erected was raised entirely within the members of the regiment, the fund being commenced while the men were yet in the service, and accrued from the percentage levied upon the sutler for the benefit of the regiment. On June 23, 1864, this fund amounted to $1,800, and a committee appointed to complete the fund, on April 7, 1867, continued their labors until 1886, when it amounted to $5,000, and it was then decided to erect the monument. In this year the borough council of West Chester gave the association the northwest corner of Marshall Square, upon which to erect the monument, and there it was erected, and dedicated as above narrated.

In 1852 a company was formed with the view of establishing a convenient and beautiful place for the repose of the dead. The location selected is about a mile and a half north of the village, and is known as Oaklands Cemetery. Drives and walks were laid out through the ground and graded, and other improvements were made by an engineer of taste and skill, and the cemetery was dedicated December 10, 1853. A considerable company was in attendance, and the services were both impressive and interesting, the principal address being made by the Honorable Samuel Rush. The dedication ode was written by George W. Pearce, and was as follows:

DEDICATION ODE.

"Solemn and slow, with measured tread,
We come to hallow for the dead,
    A calm and holy fame;
Where sweet and undisturbed repose
Shall o'er the weary pilgrim close,
    When Death shall round him reign.

"Those arching trees and shadowy dells,
Where nature's purest beauty dwells,
    A scene of tranquil bliss,
We consecrate by rite and prayer,
To human love, affection's tear,
    The last, the parting kiss.

"O sacred be this spot of earth!
From foot profane and idle mirth,
  We ask it to be pure;
For here shall molder into dust
The good, the brave, the meek, the just,
  The noble, the obscure.

"When death has beat his signal drum,
Hither the sable train shall come,
  To give the sleeper rest;
While out from yonder village towers
The knell shall float, like passing hours,
  And die amid the West.

"Here shall the living heart repair,
When the full tide of woe is there,
  To pour its note of wail;
And chasten'd and subdued by grief,
Shall drink those draughts of sweet relief,
  From streams that never fail.

"Amid the Winter's blighting breath, .
With Faith's uplifted eye, in Death,
  These sylvan shades we give,
And wait the summons that shall call
From forth its dark and gloomy pall
  The prisoned clay to live."

Like all wide-awake villages and towns, West Chester very early appreciated the fact that there was danger of loss by fire, and so, in 1797, organized the West Chester Fire Company, which had its engine house at No. 26 North Church Street, and held its meetings on the last Saturday of each month. This one company appeared to be sufficient until 1833, when the Good Will Fire Company was organized, and was incorporated in 1846. In 1857 it had its engine house at No. 44 North Church Street, and held its meetings on the last Saturday evening of January, March and May, each year.

In 1838 the Fame Fire Company was organized, and incorporated July 29, 1852, the date of organization being February 22, 1838. In 1857 the engine-house of this company was at No. 49 East Market Street, and its meetings were held on the second Saturday evening of each month. This company celebrated the sixtieth anniversary of its organization February 22, 1898, the committee on banquet being John C. Heed, Edward Brinton, O. F. Groff, Harry G. Johnson and William Cudlipp.

The West Chester Board of Trade was organized as a result of several meetings held in November, 1887, the first of these meetings being held on the 16th of the month. The president of these preliminary meetings was Marshall S. Way; the vice-presidents, Herbert P. Worth and George Achelis, and the secretary Robert G. Dock. The organization of the Board was effected November 30, with the following officers: Thomas Hoopes, president; Joseph W. Barnard and Marshall S. Way, vice-presidents; David E. Allen, secretary, and L. Cary Carver, treasurer. The directors were Frank P. Darlington, A. D. Sharpless, Plummer E. Jefferis, Abner Hoopes, D. M. McFarland, Herbert P. Worth, William P. Sharpless, Charles W. Roberts and Marshall B. Matlack.

For some time meetings were held in the council chamber, then in the Moore building on Market Street. In its earlier years the organization held its meetings regularly each month, that is, the directors of the board, but the entire body came together only on special occasions. In recent years the directors have held their meetings only on special occasions. During the existence of the board it has, in an indirect way, aided several industries to locate in West Chester, but its principal function has been to investigate the financial standing of such industries as might appear to desire to locate in this city, and to recommend to the business men and capitalists those that were, after such investigation, considered worthy of encouragement. It has published pamphlets, setting forth the advantages of West Chester as an industrial center, and as a place of residence, and on one occasion brought a large number of people from Philadelphia to make an investigation of these advantages. It originated the movement that led to the introduction of manual training in the public schools of the town, and raised a fund by subscription to aid in macadamizing a considerable portion of the road from West Chester to Paoli, called the Paoli Road. On several occasions it has carried advertisements of the city in such publications as the North American Review.

While of recent years it cannot be said to have been as active as when first organized, which is in part owing to the discouragements to all classes of business caused by the depression of 1893-97, yet it continues, whenever occasion presents itself, to aid in the establishment of such industries as possess merit, and to promote their prosperity, though not to the extent of advancing funds to any great extent.

The present officers of the Board of Trade are as follows: Marshall S. Way, president; Frank P. Darlington and Jerome B. Gray, vice-presidents; Herbert P. Worth, secretary, and I. Cary Carver, treasurer.

The West Chester Library Association was organized February 22, 1873, and was incorporated about the same time. During the first year there were 104 stockholders, representing $1,160, which sum was invested in books, and on February 22, 1898, when the twenty-fifth anniversary was held, there were 272 stockholders. At first the annual dues of stockholders were $3 per year, and of subscribers, $5 per annum; but there was only one small room used and no employe except the librarian, so that the expenses were light. Later the dues were reduced, of stockholders to $1 per annum, and of subscribers to $3 per year. When the room at first occupied was needed by its owner, the lot on which the present building stands was presented to the association by Mrs. Hannah M. Darlington, the deed being dated September 15, 1886. The building was almost immediately afterward erected, and cost $6,000.

As to the usefulness of the library, the following facts are indicative: In 1887, the first year of the occupancy of the present building, the number of books taken out was 5,970, while in 1895 the number had increased to 12,380. The number of readers in 1887 was 896, while in 1895 this number had increased to 6,044. There are now somewhat more than 3,000 volumes in the library, and the association subscribes for from fifteen to twenty periodicals. The expense of running the library is now about $1,200 per annum.

At the time of the celebration of the twenty-fifth anniversary of the organization of the association, a committee was appointed, consisting of Capt. R. T. Cornwell, Frank P. Darlington and John J. Pinkerton, whose special duty it was to consult with the board of managers as to the future of the association and the library.

A few weeks later the borough council of West Chester offered to appropriate $1,500 per annum toward the maintenance of the library, provided the library were made free to all residents of West Chester, and on June 6, 1898, at a meeting held to consider the matter the offer of the council was accepted in such a way as to preserve the identity of the management. At this meeting the following officers were elected: President, Mrs. Rachel L. Price; vice-president, Miss Margaret G. Townsend; secretary, Miss Hannah A. Marshall; treasurer, Mrs. William P. Darlington. Six directors were elected as follows: Mrs. Thomas Baird, Mrs. John R. Gilpin, Miss Sallie D. House, Mrs. William S. Kirk, Mrs. Richard G. Park, and Mrs. Joseph T. Rothrock.

The West Chester Philosophical Society was organized about 1878, through the active efforts of Dr. John R. McClure, Joseph J. Lewis and Charles H. Pennypacker. In its membership it has numbered nearly all the members of the bar, the judges of the courts, and the ministers of the various churches, and many eloquent and able lectures have been delivered before it, by various gentlemen from all parts of the country. Each lecture has been followed by a discussion, because it has a free platform, open for the discussion of every phase of every subject. Both men and women are admitted to membership, and its meetings are held on every Thursday evening, during nine months of the year.

Marshall S. Way, one of the most prominent and popular citizens of West Chester, is a lifelong resident of the borough, being born in the house in which he now resides. He is one of the citizens who has always been proud of his native town, and has striven for its welfare, always being identified with any step toward its progress and further development. He started business as a clerk in the hardware and grocery store of Wood & Fairlamb, in the old Townsend property, corner of Gay and High Streets, and in a few years, with T. Elwood Townsend, bought out the business. From the grocery business Mr. Way turned his attention to the coal and lumber business, and in 1867 was one of the partners in the purchase of the coal and lumber yard of Shoemaker & Robison, in which business he later became associated with his brother, Samuel E. Way, under the name of Way Brothers.

In 1877 Mr. Way started his real estate and loan business, which, together with insurance, he has followed to this time, and the success attained in these lines has made him well known throughout Chester County as one of its successful business men.

A Republican in politics, he was admitted to the borough council in 1885, and in the following year was elected Chief Burgess of West Chester, a position which he held by successive yearly elections until the spring of 1897, when an Act of Legislature went into effect electing the Chief Burgess for a term of three years and not allowing him to succeed himself. Mr. Way is justly recognized as having been one of the best and most progressive chief officials of West Chester, and perhaps there never was a more popular candidate to run for the office, and in his party no opposition was ever presented against him for the office of chief executive of the borough.

December 25, 1867, he married Miss Anna E. Smedley, and to them have been born two sons, viz., Marshall Warren and Channing.

Mr. Way is a busy man, for, in addition to the care and oversight of his large office business, he is vice-president of the First National Bank of West Chester, a director and member of the adjusting committee of the Mutual Fire Insurance Company of Chester County, a trustee of the State Normal School of West Chester, and one of the directors of the Assembly Association of West Chester.

The Jacobs family, of which Mr. Francis Jacobs is a member, and of whose father a portrait is herewith presented, is one of the most ancient and distinguished of Chester County. The founder of this family in America was John Jacobs of Perkiomen, who, together with his brother, Richard, came to America during the reign of Charles II and settled in the Province of Pennsylvania in the autumn of the same year in which William Penn obtained his grant, 1681. John and Richard Jacobs were young Quakers, and came from England near the border of Wales, and may have been in fact Welshmen. Upon arriving in the province they held patents for land from William Penn, which land they located in what is now Montgomery County. John settled on the Perkiomen, and Richard on the Schuylkill. John had six children, four sons and two daughters.

One of these four sons was named John. He married Mary Hayes, by whom he had ten children, as follows: John, Richard, Israel, Joseph, Benjamin, Elizabeth, Hannah, Mary, Isaac and Jesse. Of these, John, born in 1722, died in 1782, was in the direct line of descent to Francis Jacobs. He married Elizabeth

Havard. Hannah, the seventh of the above family, married David Rittenhouse, the famous mathematician of the early history of this country. Israel, the third of the family, was a member of Congress in 1778. Jesse, the youngest, was a soldier during the Revolutionary War, was at the battle of Cedars, the taking of Burgoyne, at the battle of Monmouth, at the battle of Brandywine, joined the Maryland brigade, was at the battle of Camden, at the battle of Guilford Court-house, at the battle of Cowpens, at the battle of Eutaw Springs, and would have been at the surrender of Cornwallis but for the fact that he was taken ill on the march. He held a captain's commission and died a bachelor. Isaac was a Quaker preacher.

The children of John and Elizabeth (Havard) Jacobs were four in number, viz., Benjamin, Hannah, John and Sarah. John and Elizabeth Jacobs lived on what was known as "Solitude Farm," in the Great Valley. John was a member of Council under the British Government for sixteen years in succession, and was the representative of his county. When the war of the Revolution broke out he became a violent Whig, and this drew upon him the vengeance of the Tories, his house becoming a target for British cannon under General Knyphausen, whose soldiers were encamped on South Valley Hill. The light-horse tried to capture him, but he fled to the woods, where they dared not follow for fear of ambush.

His son, John Jacobs, from whom these notes are taken, drew for General Washington a draft of the surrounding country, when encamped at Valley Forge. He procured commissions for several young men in the army, for his brother, Jesse Jacobs, for John McClellan, Benjamin Bartholomew, John Davis and Colonel Humphreys. He was speaker of the first General Assembly of the Commonwealth of Pennsylvania, which began its sittings in Philadelphia, November 28, 1776. While in the performance of his duties his health failed, and he was taken home by his son, John

53

Jacobs, and died in 1782. He had four children, two sons and two daughters, John, Benjamin, Hannah and Sarah.

John Jacobs, eldest son of the above, married Mary Brinton, daughter of Thomas Hill Brinton of Dilworthtown, Chester County. During the Revolutionary War he hauled wounded soldiers to Lancaster Hospital, and also Continental money. His brother Benjamin was one of the signers of the Continental money. He was born in 1757 and died in 1846, his wife, Mary Brinton, being born in 1767 and died in 1848. They were the parents of nine children, viz.: Phebe B., Elizabeth, Sarah, Thomas Hill Brinton, Christiana, George, John, Joseph Brinton and Brinton. Of these children Joseph Brinton Jacobs married Ann Bowen. He was born in 1798 and died in 1861, and she died in 1870.

Joseph Brinton Jacobs and Ann, his wife, had five children, viz.: Mary B.; Jane Bowen, Francis, Emily and Richard Brinton. Joseph Brinton Jacobs was a prominent citizen of his county, was a stanch Whig and was always identified with the old Whig and modern Republican party. He was highly honored by his fellow-citizens, took part in all public movements designed to benefit the community at large and was elected to several of the township offices. In 1835 he was elected county treasurer, and served two years. He lived in Chester Valley, and during his life was esteemed for his public spirit and high-toned moral charcter. When he died he was mourned by a large circle of relatives and friends.

Francis Jacobs, of West Chester, Pa., is the third child of Joseph Brinton and Ann (Bowen) Jacobs. Previous to his removal to West Chester he was engaged in the iron commission business in Philadelphia. He is one of the directors of the First National Bank of West Chester. During the Civil War he was actively engaged in filling the different drafts made by the military authorities for the Union army, on his township, East Whiteland, from which township numerous young men had volunteered, and which had the credit of being the first township in the county to fill its quotas. Mr. Jacobs is at present residing in the city of West Chester.

He married Jane Brinton Johnson, daughter of Edward and Ruth P. Johnson, of Philadelphia. Francis Jacobs and his wife have the following children: Carrol Brinton Jacobs, an attorney at law of West Chester; Florence Bowen Jacobs, living at home, and Francis Brinton Jacobs, a medical student.

The Chester County Hospital was incorporated in 1892 as the West Chester Hospital, under an act of Assembly, approved April 29, 1874, the name being changed to the Chester County Hospital, under a decree of the Court of Common Pleas, made August 7, 1893. The corporation has no capital stock, and its yearly income, other than from real estate, was limited to $100,000. The board of managers consists of fifteen members, those for the first year having been William P. Sharpless, Dr. J. T. Rothrock, Miss M. G. Townsend, William Scattergood, Dr. George M. Philips, George B. Thomas, Lydia W. House, R. T. Cornwell, Miss Mary H. Hartshorne and Thomas B. Taylor, all of West Chester; J. Preston Thomas, Whitford; Mrs. Richard Darlington, East Bradford; Mrs. C. W. Roberts, East Bradford; Richard G. Parke, West Goshen, and Dr. T. E. Parke, Downingtown. On June 2, 1893, an act was passed by the Assembly, making an appropriation of $5,000, or so much thereof as might be necessary, for the completion of the building, and of $2,000, or so much thereof as might be necessary, for the furnishing of the building. This hospital is open to all classes of patients without regard to pecuniary conditions, color or creed, so long as there is accommodation for the applicant. The corporation is composed of three classes of members:

First—Life members, or those who pay in cash to the treasurer $100 or more.

Second—Perpetual members, or such institutions or companies incorporated or organized under the laws of Pennsylvania, and unincorporated companies or firms, as pay to the treasurer $100; and

Third—Annual members, or such institutions or companies incorporated or unincorporated, firms and persons, as pay annually to the treasurer the sum of five dollars.

A contribution of $2,500 constitutes the endowment of a perpetual bed.

The property purchased upon which to erect the hospital buildings was located on the northwest side of Marshall Square, 375 feet front, and 175 feet deep. It had belonged to Mr. T. P. Apple, and the purchase price was $4,000, of which Mr. Apple donated $200. The erection of the building was commenced immediately after the purchase was made, the contract having been given to Mr. William Burns, and ground was broken October 1, 1892. On February 28, 1893, the board of managers held their first meeting in the building. On March 1, 1893, Miss Mary G. Marshall, head nurse and superintendent, took charge of the hospital, and on the same day the first patient was received. During the first three months there were received twenty-three patients. Numerous donations were made to the hospital during its first year, in money and necessary articles, the largest one being $6,000 in money by Mrs. Henry P. Norris, for the endowment in perpetuity of a private room as a memorial of her husband.

The main building was completed in December, 1893, and occupied during the month, and at the end of the year twenty beds in the wards and four private rooms were in readiness. Miss Mary G. Marshall resigned her position on March 1, 1893, as also did Miss Marian Pusey, assistant nurse. Mrs. Iola L. Carpenter, a graduate of the Philadelphia Hospital, succeeded to the position of head nurse and superintendent. During the first year there were endowed four beds, by Mrs. Sarah T. Bull, Miss Anne Bull, Mrs. Mary T. Jones, and Mrs. James C. Smith, respectively. The building fund was increased through the efforts of the Daily Local

News, which through an advertisement in its columns raised the sum of $1,400, in recognition of which assistance a bed received the name of the Daily Local News bed. The average expense of maintaining the hospital during its first year was $250 per month.

During the year ending June 1, 1895, there were received 273 patients, 122 operations were performed, and sixteen deaths occurred. St. Agnes' Catholic Church contributed $729.55, a single Sunday's offering, and the Fame Fire Company of West Chester provided an ambulance, which made its first trip in September, 1894, and during the remainder of the year ending June 1, 1895, conveyed sixty-four patients. In April, 1895, Mrs. Iola T. Carpenter resigned her position, and was succeeded by Miss Marion Forde, a graduate of Johns Hopkins Training School. During the year the Women's Auxiliary raised for the use of the hospital $1,950.72.

During the year ending June 1, 1896, Mrs. Sarah T. Johnson of Philadelphia endowed and furnished a private room in memory of her husband, and a legacy of $1,000 was left by Miss Sarah S. Scattergood. Many other donations were made, and the endowment fund then invested in the name of the hospital amounted to $23,000. In August, 1895, Miss Marion Forde resigned her position, and was succeeded by Miss Julie King. In July, 1895, Mrs. Sarah R. Bull and Rev. William L. Bull of Whitford, Chester County, offered to erect an annex ward to the hospital in memory of their daughter and sister, Miss Anne Bull, which offer was accepted, and in October of the same year Mr. and Mrs. Bull made the gift of a second annex, similar to the first, to be erected as a memorial to Mrs. Bull's sister, Miss Jane Thomas. By the gift of $12,000 the board of managers found themselves in a position to carry out the original plan of finishing the hospital, with a large central building, and a wing at each side. The average sum necessary to maintain the hospital had increased to between $600 and $700 per month, toward which the state granted $270 per month.

And the Women's Auxiliary continued to be of great assistance to the institution, particularly in the way of securing the means of support.

The increase in the usefulness of the hospital is seen by the statement that during the first year there were received 139 patients; the second year, 232; the third year, 292, and the fourth year, 445. In April, 1897, a clinical and bacteriological laboratory was established through the generosity of Dr. Thomas D. Dunn, who was in fact the originator of the hospital, and a small building was erected for the reception of such cases as required isolation.

During the year ending June 1, 1898, there were received into the hospital wards 557 cases, and besides these 60 occupied private rooms, making a total of 617 persons received in the hospital. In April, 1898, Rev. William L. Bull offered to present to the hospital a building for a nurses' home, and as a memorial to his mother, Mrs. Sarah R. Bull, deceased, who had intended to make the donation herself. This generous offer was accepted, and ground was purchased back of the property on which to erect the building. The Women's Auxiliary contributed to the treasury $3,624 during the year. Mrs. H. P. Norris offered to endow a bed in memory of Miss Virginia Norwood, which offer was gratefully accepted.

After the declaration of war with Spain the board of managers offered to the Governor of Pennsylvania the resources of the hospital for use in caring for such sick or wounded soldiers as might be in need of aid.

The treasurer's report for the year ending June 15, 1898, showed that the expenses of the institution had been $13,555.42.

The officers of the hospital have been from the first, Mr. R. T. Cornwell, president; Miss M. G. Townsend, secretary, and William P. Sharpless, treasurer.

This institution is one in which all the people of Chester County take great pride, as it is of increasing usefulness, and is well appointed in every respect, and most excellently managed. The one necessity remaining to be supplied is a comfortable annex or ward for those afflicted with' contagious diseases, who now have to be taken to the county almshouse.

During the year 1892-93 a Women's Hospital Auxiliary Society was formed, the membership of which extends over the county. Local branches were organized in different parts of the county, that at Kennett Square being the first of the county auxiliary. Mary Bacon Parke was the first president, and Martha G. Thomas, first secretary. In the year 1893-94 there were eight branches; in 1894-95, there were eleven; and in 1895-96, twelve.

In connection with the hospital is a training school for nurses, established in 1893. During the first year there were seven nurses in training, and during the second year ten, of whom two graduated in 1895, viz.: Miss Lily North and Miss Nellie Schwarder. In 1896 there were four graduates; in 1897, four, and in 1898, eight.

The first Masonic lodge originally chartered in Chester County was No. 50, which was permitted to hold meetings within five miles of the sign of the "White Horse." The petition to thus hold meetings was granted December 6, 1790, and there were twelve charter members. There had, however, been a lodge of this fraternity previously organized in Chester, but it was practically a branch of No. 11, Newtown, Bucks County, which was constituted August 17, 1768, and surrendered its charter December 24, 1781. A new warrant was issued to branch No. ——, and this branch held meetings at a place called "Halfway House," Londongrove Township, Chester County, February 16, 1782. This was surrendered and renewed March 7, 1791.

West Chester Lodge, No. 322, was the first chartered within the jurisdiction of lodge No. 50, after this lodge was dissolved, its charter being dated March 1, 1858. It had eight charter members, of whom four had been members of No. 50.

West Chester Lodge, No. 42, Independent Order of Odd Fellows, was chartered September 26, 1831. On the 28th of March, 1832, this lodge erected a building on a lot it had purchased on Church Street, but the enterprise was not prosperous, the property was sold by the sheriff, and the lodge soon afterward was dissolved.

Pocahontas Lodge, No. 316, was instituted June 19, 1848, and in 1871 this lodge purchased Cabinet Hall on Church Street, remodeled the building, and in the third story of this building holds its meetings weekly on Thursday evenings.

Canton Brandywine, No. 27, Patriarchs Militant, I. O. O. F., meets on the first and fourth Fridays of each month.

Florentina Lodge, No. 203, D. of R., I. O. O. F., meets every Friday evening in the postoffice building.

General Marion Encampment, No. 91, I. O. O. F., meets alternate Fridays at No. 26 West Gay Street.

Benjamin Bannaker Lodge, No. 14, Knights of Pythias, meets in Masonic Hall, on the second and fourth Thursdays of each month.

Brandywine Council, No. 758, Jr. O. U. A. M., meets every Monday evening at No. 111 North High Street.

Kenehha Council, No. 248, O. U. A. M., meets every Thursday evening at No. 20 East Market Street.

West Chester Council, No. 632, Jr. O. U. A. M., meets every Friday evening at No. 21 North Church Street.

Court No. 4, Heroines of Jericho, meets on the first Wednesday of each month at Masonic Hall.

Encampment No. 25, U. V. L., meets over the postoffice on the first Thursday of each month.

Junior O. U. A. M., Funeral Benefit Association of Chester County, meets at No. 28 West Market Street.

Orpheus Court of Calanthe, No. 5, A. C. C. K. of P., meets on the first and third Thursdays of each month in Masonic Hall.

Peace and Plenty Lodge, No. 2581, G. U. O. O. F., meets every first and third Mondays of each month in Masonic Hall.

Pilgrim Chapter, No. 11, R. A. M., meets on the last Saturday of each month in Masonic Hall.

Harmony Lodge, No. 21, F. & A. M., meets on the first Saturday in each month in Masonic Hall.

Howell Chapter, No. 202, F. & A. M., meets every Monday after the full moon in the Farmers' National Bank building.

Stella Lodge, No. 131, K. of P., meets every Monday evening at No. 21 North High Street.

Uppowac Tribe, No. 47, I. O. R. M., meets every Wednesday evening at No. 111 West Market Street.

Washington Camp, No. 673, P. O. S. of A., meets in Postoffice building every Monday.

West Chester Castle, No. 226, K. G. E., meets every Friday evening in the Assembly building.

West Chester Conclave, No. 61, I. O. H., meets at No. 21 North High Street.

West Chester Council, No. 1003, R. A., meets at No. 111 West Market Street every second and fourth Thursday of each month.

West Chester Lodge No. 322, F. & A. M., meets in the Farmers' National Bank building every Monday on or before the full moon.

West Chester Lodge, No. 42, I. O. O. F., meets every Tuesday evening at No. 24 West Gay Street.

General George A. McCall Post, No. 31, G. A. R., meets every Friday evening in the Postoffice building.

George F. Smith Post, No. 330, G. A. R., meets every Tuesday evening at No. 345 East Miner Street.

The J. C. Smith Memorial Home, at Oakbourne, Chester County, consists of property bequeathed by the late Mrs. Heloiese Drexel Smith to the Protestant Episcopal Mission as a retreat for white women twenty-one years of age and upward, who are ill and convalescent, "free and without charge." The funds for its maintenance were also bequeathed by Mrs. Smith. The house, which is a three-story stone building, is one and a half miles from West Chester, on the road to Media, and is surrounded by thirty-six acres of ground, twenty-four of which are woodland, and the remainder in a high state of cultivation. On these grounds, which are well laid out, is a lookout tower commanding a view of the surrounding country to a distance of fifteen miles.

The house is so arranged that it will accommodate twenty-one women, and another building has been fitted up to accommodate six women, so that there are now accommodations for twenty-seven. The convalescents are allowed to remain two weeks, and in special cases four weeks. Up to March 31, 1897, there had been admitted 148 patients, and to June 8, 1898, there had been admitted 290. The Home was opened with appropriate ceremonies May 9, 1896, and religious services held for the first time May 24, 1896. These services have since been held regularly every Sunday morning, according to the rites and forms of the Protestant Episcopal Church. The institution opened with Mrs. Matilda B. Stevenson, formerly of St. Stephen's Parish, Philadelphia, as matron, and Mrs. Martha Merchant as assistant matron, both of whom still retain their respective positions. The health of the patients is attended to by physicians from West Chester, Dr. P. C. Hoskins and Dr. Dunn being the physicians in charge until the death of the latter, and since Dr. Hoskins alone.

The Pennsylvania Epileptic Hospital and Colony Farm, located one mile from Oakbourne Station, on the Philadelphia, Media and West Chester Railway, sprang from the Hospital of St. Clement's Church, which was organized in 1886, and located on Cherry Street, Philadelphia, between Twentieth and Twenty-first Streets. In 1892 this hospital became devoted almost exclusively to the the treatment of epileptics, and its accommodations were soon taxed beyond their limits. The management therefore decided to found a colony of epileptics, and purchased the land near Oakbourne Station for a little more than $14,000, the amount necessary being contributed by Miss Rebecca Coxe and Eckley B. Coxe,

Jr. For the erection of the buildings Henry C. Lea donated $50,000 and money for other necessary work was contributed by James Dundas Lippincott, William Garrett and others.

Dr. Wharton Sinkler is president of this corporation, Charles M. Lea vice-president, J. Howard Climenson treasurer, and Dr. Samuel W. Morton secretary, and J. F. Edgerly, M. D., superintendent.

There are 110 acres in the farm, and there are now three buildings, an administration building with a cottage on each side. Besides these there is one tenement house and other buildings needed for the successful management of a model farm. The demand for accommodations such as supplied by this hospital are greatly in excess of its capacity, each cottage being capable of holding from twelve to eighteen patients, the number now being cared for being forty-three.

Fallowfield Township was originally a very large one. It lay in the middle west part of the county. It is believed to have been named after Lancelot Fallowfield, of Great Strickland, Westmoreland County, England, who was one of the first to purchase land from William Penn. John Salkeld, a noted preacher of the Society of Friends, came from the same part of England in which Fallowfield lived, bought the land from him, and took it up in 1714. In 1718 there were only three taxables in the township, viz.: Thomas Wooddell, George Lenard and Robert Holly. From this time on until 1728 Fallowfield and Sadsbury formed one assessment district, and then the boundaries were defined by order of the court, as follows: Northward with East Sadsbury, eastward with the settled limits of Bradford, southward with Marlborough, to the northeast corner of Penn's Manor, thence west 800 perches, and northwest to Octoraro Creek, and thence up the same to Sadsbury. In 1743 the township was divided by the north branch of Doe Run, since called Buck Run, and in 1841 the line between West Fallowfield and Upper Oxford Township was run by order of the court, in order to ascertain its exact location. As a result some farms which had previously been supposed to be in Upper Oxford were found to be in West Fallowfield.

In 1853 West Fallowfield was divided and the eastern division called Highland Township, the western division retaining the old name. Thus Highland Township comes in between East and West Fallowfield, which is not the case with any other townships in the county bearing the same general name.

Honeybrook Township was formed in 1789 from the western part of West Nantmeal Township, settlements having been made there as early as 1718 or 1720, when surveys were made at the head of the western branch of the Brandywine for Jeremy Piersol, James Gibbons, John Adams, William Cloud, Henry Batterton, William Buffington, Thomas Baldwin, Richard Parker, William and Jeremiah Dean, Matthew Wilson and Edward Harris.

The borough of Honeybrook was incorporated August 17, 1891, and the first council was as follows: Stephen Long, D. H. Buchanan, James Buyers, John E. Finger and W. W. McConnell. The burgesses have been as follows: John H. De Haven, 1891-94; John W. Morton, 1894-97; John E. Finger, 1897-1900.

Secretaries—A. M. Anderson, 1891-97; S. Marple Lemmon, 1897-1900.

Treasurers—John W. Morton, 1891-94; Stephen Long, 1895; John E. Finger, 1895-97; John W. Morton, 1897-1900.

The members of the council at the present time (1898) are as follows: John H. De Haven, L. R. Guiney, Thomas J. Hughes, Jacob Lemmon, William Lemmon, James McConnell and G. W. Piersol.

On May 11, 1896, the borough of Honeybrook accepted a proposition with regard to the establishment of a system of waterworks, the cost of which was to be $12,500, and purchased a small property on the side of Welsh Mountain, on which there was a spring having a flow of seventy-six gallons per minute. A reservoir was constructed capable of holding 1,200,000 gallons of water and from this reservoir the borough is bountifully supplied with the best of spring water, all of the inhabitants, except eight families, having put water in their houses. The pressure is thirty-seven pounds and gives force sufficient to throw the water over the tops of the highest buildings, so that now a fire department is not needed. The charge is five dollars per spigot and the payments on the bonds amount to $600 per annum.

A fire company was organized about 1887, which did good work until the introduction of the water into the village, as above recorded, but at present it is practically out of date.

The village of Hamorton is in the northeast part of Kennett Township. In the early days of the county it was known by the name of Logtown. Previous to 1830 it contained less than half a dozen houses, the name Hamorton having been given to the place when the post office was established in 1829. About 1844 a stock company built a hall which has since been used for various purposes, lectures by eminent men, concerts, etc. There are nearly fifty houses in Hamorton, and its people have always been noted for patriotism, morality and temperance. This village is undoubtedly one of the pleasantest spots in Chester County.

Kennett Township lies in the southern part of the county, bordering on the circular line and being between the townships of New Garden and Pennsbury. It originally included all of the latter township and a part of Pocopson. It is thought that the name was suggested by Francis Smith, who came from Devizes, Wiltshire, England, in which county there is a town by the name of Kennett. Francis Smith, in 1686, took up 200 acres of land within the original limits of the township at the mouth of Pocopson Creek. Smith's original purchase amounted to 500 acres, and 300 acres were surveyed to him afterward at a rate of one penny per acre per annum. The settlement of this territory appears to have proceeded slowly, for in 1703 the following amount of land

was returned by Isaac Taylor as having been surveyed: Francis
Smith, 440 acres; Henry Pierce, 190 acres; Robert Way, 425 acres;
Thomas Hope, 310 acres; George Harlan, Israel Helm, and the
Chandlers, 850 acres; total, 2,215 acres. Afterward Isaac Taylor, in
addition to the above resurveys, made new surveys for the follow-
ing persons: Peter Dicks, 554 acres; John Hope, 200; George Har-
lan, 500; total, 1,254 acres, in 1702; Isaac Few, 600, and William
Huntley, 200, in 1703, all of which was near the Brandywine.

An account of Letitia's Manor, which lay in part in this township, may be found on another page in this work.

Kennett Square was incorporated in 1855. It is on the line of
the Philadelphia and Baltimore Central Railroad in the midst of
an exceedingly fertile section of the country. The village which
had been known as Kennett Square from before the Revolutionary War, formed the nucleus of the borough, the name first appearing about 1769, when William Dixson conveyed a piece of land
to Joseph Musgrave, "near a place called Kennett Square." The
scene of Bayard Taylor's "Story of Kennett is laid in Kennett and
adjoining townships.

Kennett Lodge, No. 475, F. and A. M., holds its meetings each
Thursday evening on or before the full moon, in Chalfant Block.

Kennett Chapter, No. 275, R. A. M., meets in Chalfant Block,
on the first Wednesday after the full moon.

Kennett Castle, No. 243, K. G. E., meets every Tuesday night,
in Unicorn Hall.

Kennett Council, No. 182, U. O. A. M., meets in Unicorn Hall
every Thursday evening.

Kennett Conclave, No. 207, I. O. H., meets in Swayne Block,
on the second and fourth Monday evenings of each month.

Division No. 2, A. O. H., meets in Unicorn Hall on the second
Saturday evening of each month.

Kennett Grange, No. 19, Patrons of Husbandry, meets in Unicorn Hall, on Wednesday evening on or before the full moon.

Kennett Fire Company meets in the borough hall on the last Friday night of each month.

Kennett Square is well supplied with water, derived from springs about a mile north of the borough. A great deal of money has been spent in procuring water, changes in the source of supply having been made from time to time, the present springs, the east branch of Red Clay Creek, and of the west branch of Red Clay Creek, having been at different times the source. The pumping station is half a mile north of the borough, or half way between the borough and the springs which supply the water, and there are two standpipes on the borough lot, which cost almost $20,000. Nearly every inhabitant in the borough takes water from the system, and the revenue that is derived by the borough treasury is about $4,000 per annum.

The Kennett Electric Light, Heat and Power Company was incorporated in 1893, with W. W. Gawthrop president, John C. Yeatman treasurer, and N. P. Yeatman secretary. The capital at first was $25,000, but it was increased to $50,000 in 1896. The plant of this company is situated in the southwest part of the borough, and consists of a one-story brick building, 40x60 feet in size, with an equipment of two 100-horse power boilers, a 150-horse power engine, and two dynamos sufficient to maintain 800 incandescent lights each, each light of 16-candle power, and one dynamo of 300 incandescent lights of the same power. At present there are four arc lights on the streets, and about 70 incandescent lights, while in stores, churches and private houses there are about 2,000. From this plant goes out to Toughkennamon, Avondale and West Grove, electricity for lighting these villages, and other villages are constantly calling for the same kind of light, but as yet the company has not the means to wire these other towns.

The present council of Kennett Square is as follows: George R. Bowman, president; Dr. C. S. Reynolds, John Duncannon,

George W. Taft, F. T. MacDonald, H. D. Entriken, and H. Willis Taylor.

The Bayard Taylor Memorial Library was established February 10, 1894, several preliminary meetings having been previously held. On the date given a board of trustees was elected, consisting of the following persons: William W. Polk, Joseph S. Heald, William F. Wickersham, D. Duer Philips, Charles J. Pennock, and Edward Swayne. A lot was purchased on the corner of Broad Street and Apple Alley, upon which the building was erected, at a cost of $6,791.50, and it was dedicated September 12, 1896. Alice W. Swayne is the librarian, and 5,396 persons attend the reading department during the year 1897. The success of this library is assured.

London Britain Township lies in the southern part of the county, and contains the triangle which extends down between Maryland and Delaware. A considerable portion of this township was originally included in the survey of the lands for the London Company, an east and west line crossing the township about the latitude of Kimbleville, being the southern boundary of this tract. The township was at one time enlarged by taking a portion off from the west side of New Garden. The first settlers are believed to have been Welsh Baptists, who established a church. John Evans came from Radnorshire, in Wales, about 1700, and was one of the prominent men in his day. His son, John Evans, who died in 1738, held large tracts of land, and also fulling and grist mills on White Clay Creek, and there was formerly an Indian village on this creek, near Yeatman's Mill.

A petition for the organization of the township was presented to court in 1725, which was granted, Richard Whiting being the constable, John Devonald supervisor of highways, and John Evans and Thomas Morris overseers of the poor. And in 1775 the court appointed Thomas Woodward, Levis Pennock and Joseph Musgrove to make a survey and ascertain the line of London Britain and New Garden Townships.

Londonderry Township was set up in 1734, being separated from Nottingham, and then included the territory from London-grove to the Octoraro River. About one-third of the township, as it is at the present time, was included in Fagg's Manor, elsewhere described. In 1754 Oxford Township was taken from the west side of Londonderry, and in 1819 it was again reduced in size, by the organization of Penn Township, taken from its southern side. A small part was added to it in 1866, taken from Londongrove and West Marlborough. The settlers came originally and mainly from Ireland, which explains its name.

Londongrove Township lies west of New Garden and East Marlborough Townships, and was settled as early as 1714 by Francis Swain, John Smith, Joseph Pennock, William Pusey and a few others. On August 12, 1699, William Penn sold to Tobias Collet, Daniel Quare, Henry Godney and Michael Russell, all of London, England, a large tract of land and granted a warrant for the location thereof August 17, 1699. The above-named persons admitted others into partnership with them and formed the London Company, the number of shares reaching ultimately 8,800 and the shareholders numbering several hundred. This grant included a considerable portion of the present townships of New London, London Britain, East Nottingham, Penn and London-grove, the entire amount of land taken up by the company being 65,000 acres, 17,200 acres of which were in Chester County, the rest being in Lancaster, Delaware and Bucks Counties. The patent for the 17,218 acres in Chester County was granted June 25, 1718. As in the case of lands in other townships, much of this land was leased for a term of years to early settlers, with stipulations that a certain number of acres should be cultivated or cleared and plowed each year. According to Joseph J. Lewis the rents usually charged were 40s. per 100 acres, but there were a few tracts of land sold by the company itself to different purchasers, from 1718 to 1720. The rest remained in the possession

54

of the company until about 1762, by which time the heirs of those who originally constituted the company had become so scattered, many of them being entirely unknown, that an act of Parliament was procured authorizing the sale of the land, and Dr. Fothergill, Daniel Zachary, Thoas How, Devereaux Bowly, Luke Hinde, Richard Howe, Jacob Hagan, Sylvanus Grove and William Heron were the agents appointed to superintend the sale, their attorneys in this sale being Samuel Shoemaker, Jacob Cooper and Joshua Howell, and each settler purchased the land on which he was then living.

A large part of the settlers in Londongrove were members of the Society of Friends, among their names appearing the names of Allen, Chandler, Jackson, Lamborn, Lindley, Morton, Pusey, Scarlett, Starr and Underwood.

In 1866 the line separating Londongrove and West Marlborough was so altered that a small part of the northwest corner of Londongrove and the southwest corner of West Marlborough were attached to Londonderry Township, the territory thus annexed to the latter township including within its limits the famous old White Horse Tavern, in order that the inhabitants of the township might have a convenient place to hold elections.

West Grove was incorporated as a borough January 29, 1894, the following officers being elected: Chief Burgess, John P. Chevney; Councilmen, John H. Turner, president; T. C. Moore, Hickman W. Sparks, James A. Wilson, I. C. Jefferis and Isaac Martin. The secretary was John R. Strode, and treasurer, Walter W. Brown. Dr. C. F. Quimby was elected chief burgess in 1897 for three years, the secretary and treasurer being re-elected then for the same period. The council elected in 1897 was as follows: John H. Turner, T. C. Moore, I. C. Jefferis, Chester Reynolds, Eber Heston, John P. Cheyney and E. C. Austin.

The streets and business houses, as also many private residences, are lighted by means of the incandescent light, received from Kennett Square. On the streets there are forty lights and in business and private houses about 125. This light was introduced in 1894, the same year of the incorporation of the town.

West Grove is indebted to Joseph Pyle and his father-in-law, Milton Conard, for its water system, Mr. Pyle beginning this enterprise in 1862, when he constructed a reservoir holding 6,000 gallons of water. His second reservoir, built in 1875, had a capacity of 25,000 gallons. People gradually got into the habit of taking water from this system, and at length when new houses were erected they were so built that water was taken into them from the reservoir system. Mr. Pyle put in a hydraulic ram in 1878, and a second one in 1881. Later he put in two wind mills, and in 1881 he leased the water privilege on the farm adjoining that of his father-in-law on the north side of the town, bored a well 213 feet deep, from which there was a flow of twenty gallons per minute. In 1885 he put in a Dean steam pump, which was used until February, 1897, when he put in a gasoline engine, which pumps fifty gallons per minute. At the present time eighty-five families take water from this system and seventeen business houses.

The borough of Avondale was incoroprated in February, 1894, and the following officers elected: Chief Burgess, W. R. Shelmire; Councilmen, W. J. Pusey, president; Robert K. Mackey, Morris Watson, William Miller, John L. Hood and B. H. Chambers; Secretary, E. Pusey Passmore, and Treasurer, Edward Pusey. In 1897 the following officers were elected: Burgess, August Brosius; Councilmen, W. J. Pusey, president; Dr. J. L. Paiste, Robert K. Mackey, Joshua Thomas, Charles Y. Wilson, Morris Watson and Eber H. Greenfield; Secretary, Fred. Glenn, and Treasurer, E. Pusey Passmore.

Avondale, like West Grove, receives its electric light from Kennett Square. This light was introduced here in 1893, and now there are on the streets about forty lights, and in stores, churches, private residences, etc., there are about 500 others, making nearly 550 incandescent lights in all, ranging from 16 to 32 candle power.

In Avondale there are two societies, viz.: One of the Patriotic Order of Sons of America, and a social club, the latter organized in 1893, and which maintains a lecture course. Its work is highly appreciated and forms one of the most useful and delightful features of the social life of the place.

W. J. Pusey & Co., the "Co." being James C. Pusey, built their flouring mill in 1893. It stands on the railroad about 600 feet west of the railway station. The building is 76x56 feet in size and three stories high and contains machinery of the most modern pattern, the roller process being used, and the capacity of the mill being 150 barrels of flour in twenty-four hours.

Avondale Ice and Cold Storage Company was incorporated in 1894, its first officers being William F. Dowdall, president; Joel B. Pusey, vice-president; H. M. Carpenter, secretary, and E. Pusey Passmore, treasurer. The same persons have held these offices ever since. The plant is located on Pennsylvania, and consists of an ice plant capable of manufacturing fifteen tons per day, and of a storage house with a capacity of 500 tons. This company has its own electric light plant.

Marlborough Township lay in the southern part of the county, north of Kennett, New Garden and Londongrove. It was named from Marlborough, Wiltshire, England. It was laid out in part in 1700, in right of purchases made in England. It was organized as a township in 1704, Thomas Wickersham being the first constable. Among the first settlers were Joel Baily, Thomas Jackson, Caleb Pusey, Francis Swayne, John Smith and Henry Hayes. Joseph Pennock was one of the first in what is now West Marlborough, where he built Primitive Hall, which is still standing. In 1729 the township was divided into East and West Marlborough. In East Marlborough he obtained a patent for land which included the present Peirce's Park, or Evergreen Glade, and the famed home of Bayard Taylor, Cedar Croft, is in East Marlborough, less than a mile north of Kennett Square. A farm formerly owned by William Chalfont in East Marlborough Township, near Unionville, was named by him Clermont. In 1849 a part of this township was taken off in the formation of Pocopson, and in 1875 the line between West Marlborough on one side and Londonderry and Highland on the other was re-established by the court.

Nantmeal Township lay in the northern part of the county, northeast of Honeybrook and bordering on Berks County. The name is derived from Nantmel, Radnorshire, Wales, whence came some of the early settlers, and this is the proper spelling. The meaning of the Welsh word is sweet stream, or honey brook. Surveys were made in 1717-19 at the head of the north branch of the Brandywine for Thomas Callowhill, Howell Powell, Edward Thomas, William Iddings, Thomas Rees, John Broomall, David Thomas, Daniel Moor, William Trego, John Moore, and Richard and John Peirsol, and the first assessment was made in 1720. In 1722 the name Nantmeal first appears, when it contained eighteen taxables, among them being Samuel Nutt, noted as being one of the very first ironmakers in the country.

In 1740 the township was divided into East and West Nantmeal, in which year there were 83 taxables in East Nantmeal, and 123 in West Nantmeal. Originally the settlers were for the most part Welsh, but later the Scotch-Irish came up from the southern part of the county and settled in the western township.

In 1789 West Nantmeal Township was divided by the erection of Honeybrook Township, taken from the western part. In 1852 it was again divided by the erection of Wallace Township, and East Nantmeal was divided in 1842 by the erection of Warwick Township.

New London Township lies in the southern part of the county north of Elk, and like Londongrove and London Britain, is believed to have derived its name from the fact of its including a portion of the London Company's tract. In 1704 Abraham Emmitt purchased a square mile of land and had a mill on Elk Creek, one of the first in the neighborhood. Robert Assheton had 500 acres of land to the north of Emmit's land, and Michael Harlan, in 1714, had a tract of 900 acres surveyed. In 1720 several surveys were made in the northeastern part of this township—for Jeremiah Starr, for Francis, Alexander, James and Patrick Moore, for Susanna McCane, for William Reynolds, and for Gabriel Alexander. In 1721 there were surveys made for Thomas, John and Samuel Steel. In the northern part of the township were Samuel Campbell, James Shaw, Robert Mackey, Robert Finney, John Morrison and others. The land owned by Susanna McCane lay on the road leading from New London to Kimbleville, near the line of Franklin Township. She was the grandmother of Governor Thomas McKean, a brief sketch of whom appears elsewhere in this work.

In 1725 the township was divided and London Britain Township erected, and in 1852 the township of Franklin was taken from New London, since which time the latter township has contained none of the land belonging to the London Company.

New Garden Township lies in the southern part of Chester County and borders on Delaware and is west of Kennett Township. It was named from New Garden County Carlow, Ireland. It was included in the survey of 30,000 acres, made in 1700, to Henry Hollingsworth, of which 30,000 acres, 15,500 acres were patented to Letitia Penn, as has been elsewhere related. The remainder of 14,500 acres was patented to William Penn, Jr., May 24, 1706, by the commissioners of property, Edward Shippen, Griffith, Owen, and Thomas Story, and like the tract of Letitia Penn, received the name of Stenning. The boundaries of the manor have been elsewhere described, and it is only necessary to say here further that the township as it was before losing a corner to London Britain, embraced that part of the manor lying north of the circular line, or according to an early estimate, 8,913 acres. Before obtaining his patent William Penn, Jr., had appointed as his at-torneys, Griffith Owen, James Logan and Robert Ashton, and after a few years several families of Friends arrived from Ireland, and settled there, giving the name of New Garden to their new home in remembrance of their old home in Ireland. Among those who first settled in this township were John Lowdon, John Miller, Michael Lightfoot, James Starr, William Halliday, Joseph Hutton, Thomas Jackson, and Abraham Marshall, as early as 1712, and in 1714 Thomas Garnett and Joseph Sharp. The whole amount of land purchased by the above named settlers and a few others was 5,413 acres, at the price of £20 per hundred acres, or about $1 per acre. In 1715 William Penn, Jr., sold the remainder of his manor, except 500 acres, to Colonel John Evans, from which circumstance it was frequently referred to as Colonel Evans' Manor. It is said that John Lowdon or Lowden (the name is spelled both ways by local historians), who was a noted minister in the Society of Friends, suggested New Garden as the name of the township, he having been a member of the New Garden meeting, County Car-low, Ireland. He traveled much in the service of the ministry, and died in 1714. John Miller owned the land afterward owned by Mr. Ellicott, of Baltimore, and upon White Clay Creek, which passed through his farm, erected a mill, long known as the Old Mill, which did the grinding for the farmers for many miles around, even as far away as Lancaster. This was the second mill of the kind within the limits of the county, Townsend's Mill having been the first. The early inhabitants of this part of the county were in the habit of separating their farms by ditches to prevent the ravages of fire, to which they were exposed in the fall, that being the sea-son of the year when the Indians were accustomed to burn the woods in order to facilitate hunting.

Newlin Township lies south of West Bradford, and was named after Nathaniel Newlin, one of the most prominent citizens of the early day. On the 22d and 23d of March, 1681, William Penn granted 20,000 acres of land in Pennsylvania, and some lots in Philadelphia, to certain trustees for the Free Society of Traders, these trustees being Nicholas Moore, James Claypoole, Philip Ford, William Sharloe, Edward Pierce, John Simcock, Thomas Bracey, Thomas Barker and Edward Brooks. On September 20, 1688, there was surveyed unto Benjamin Chambers, president of the Free Society of Traders, for that society's use, 7,100 acres of land, in Chester County, a part of the said 20,000 acres, and on the 10th of June, 1724, the Free Society of Traders, by its trustees, Charles Read, Job Goodsonn, Evan Owen, George Fitzwater, and Joseph Pidgeon, conveyed this tract of 7,100 acres to Nathaniel Newlin, in consideration of £800, current money of Pennsylvania. Thus Nathaniel Newlin, who was an Irishman, became the owner of the tract of land which afterward became the township bearing his name. After its purchase by Mr. Newlin it was resurveyed and found to contain 7,700 acres, and Mr. Newlin made arrangements for the sale of portions of his purchase. Following are the names of some of the purchasers, and the amounts of their several purchases, together with the prices paid:

George Harlan, 169 acres, for £50 14s; Stephen Harlan, 20½ acres, £20 10s; Joseph English, 200 acres, £30; Mordecai Cloud, 326 acres, £97 16s; Abraham Marshall, 120 acres, £36; Joel Baily, 228 acres, £68 8s; William Dean, 124 acres, £37 4s; George Lashly, 75 acres, £22 10s; Ralph Thompson, 75 acres, £19 9s 9d, a total of 1,337 acres for £383, or very nearly 5s 9d per acre.

Nathaniel Newlin died in 1729, owning 7,843 acres of land, of which 533 acres were in Concord Township, Delaware County, and the rest in Chester County. It was in this township that a difficulty arose with the Indians, who had been allotted lands therein, but as this matter is treated of in another chapter in this work, it is merely referred to here. In the formation of Pocopson Township something more than 300 acres were taken from Newlin

Township and included therein. Up to 1738 the settlers here were
assessed as of Marlborough or Bradford, according as they were
on the north or south side of the Brandywine, but about this time
the inhabitants petitioned for the formation of a new township,
which petition was granted, and the township named Newlin. For
some time the name was frequently written Newlinton.

Nottingham Township was laid in the extreme southeastern
part of the county. At a meeting of the commissioners of property, at which all were present, held January 14, 1701, Cornelius
Empson, for himself and several others to the number of twenty
families, proposed to make a settlement on a tract of land about
half way between the Delaware and Susquehanna Rivers, or nearer
to the Susquehanna, on the Octoraro Creek, provided they could
have a grant of about 20,000 acres at a certain rental. To this
proposition the commissioners of property agreed, and issued a
warrant, in pursuance of which a tract of 18,000 acres of land
was laid out in May, 1702, commencing at a point about seven
and a half miles west of the northeast corner of Maryland, and
extending thence to the Octoraro, a distance of about ten miles.
The south line of this tract corresponded with or nearly with the
present southern boundary of the county, and was nearly straight,
but the northern line was crooked, in order to take in good lands
and leave out poorer tracts, and in width this tract was about
three miles. A road was laid out east and west through the middle of the tract, and dividing lines were run north and south at
sufficient distances from each other, so as to make thirty-seven
divisions, each division containing about 500 acres of land. This
large tract was called Nottingham when first laid out, probably
in remembrance of Nottingham County or shire in England. It
was supposed to be in Pennsylvania, but when the boundary line
was at last determined it was found to be largely in Maryland.
In the survey, although the lines were intended to be parallel to
the Maryland line, yet, owing probably to the variation of the

compass, not so well understood then as now, they run a little to
the south of west as they proceed to the west. The north line of
lots Nos. 5 to 10 crosses the State line between the fourteenth
and fifteenth milestones. Lots Nos. 11 to 16 were bounded on
the north by a straight line, which at its eastern end is a little
more than three-quarters of a mile, and at its western end less
than half a mile north of the State line.

Northward of these lots the territory was described as being
"back of Nottingham," but at length having been taken up by
settlers, was included in the township of Nottingham. In 1718
both East and West Nottingham appear, and in 1734-35 Londonderry was separated from Nottingham. Previous to the erection
of Lancaster County in May, 1729, this township extended beyond
Octoraro Creek. In 1833 a portion of East Nottingham was taken
off to form Oxford Borough, and in 1853 Hopewell Borough was
taken from it in part. In 1857 it was still further reduced by the
erection of Elk Township.

Oxford Township lies in the southwestern part of the county,
north of Nottingham. It was established in 1754, being taken
from the township of Londonderry. It is not now known whether
the name was given in honor of Oxford, England, or of Oxford
Township in Philadelphia County, which is now a part of Philadelphia. In 1797 it was divided into Upper and Lower Oxford.
In 1841 the line between Upper Oxford and West Fallowfield was
established. William Penn's Manor embraced all the eastern part
of Upper Oxford and a small part of Lower Oxford, and the settlers on these lands secured their titles after 1747.

Hopewell Borough was incorporated May 2, 1853, the territory being taken from Lower Oxford and East Nottingham Townships.

Oxford Borough was incorporated by an act of Assembly April
8, 1833, and was taken from Lower Oxford and East Nottingham,
principally from the latter. Still later its area was enlarged by a

decree of the court. It was not until about 1870 that the place began to assume the importance to which it has now attained. The first material improvement made by the borough was the establishment of water-works, one of the most difficult problems problems for solution in country towns. The Oxford Gas and Water Company was incorporated in 1868, for the purpose of erecting works to supply the borough with water. These works were built by the company in 1869, and were purchased by the borough in 1870 for $30,000. The supply was taken at first from Elk Creek, which had an available drainage area of three square miles; but later the source of supply was changed to artesian wells sunk to a great depth, the water thus procured being determined by chemical analysis to be the purest for drinking purposes, and also for manufacturing, causing but little rust in boilers. Inasmuch as the sources of supply are practically inexhaustible, fears of a water famine can never be felt in Oxford.

The water is pumped from two drilled wells into a reservoir, which is 80 feet square at the top, 25 feet square at the bottom, and is 18 feet deep, having a capacity of 500,000 gallons. The wells are each eight inches in diameter and have a depth respectively of 189 1-3 feet and 543 feet. The entire cost of the works up to 1894 was $50,808.96. The borough being the sole owner of the works, the result is that while a comfortable revenue is derived from them, yet citizens and industries are supplied at a fairly reasonable figure.

About the same time that the water-works were established an efficient fire company was also established, named the Union Fire Company, which has always deserved well of the community. It was chartered in 1872, erected a substantial frame building in 1874, which was remodeled in 1880. The building is two stories high, 27x55 feet in dimensions, and has a stable in the rear 16x27 feet in size. It has a Silsby steam fire engine, a hose wagon carrying 500 feet of cotton hose, one hand-hose carriage also carrying 500 feet of hose, and a hook and ladder truck. One of the most useful ordinances of the village, that establishing fire limits, was procured by the Union Fire Company.

Oxford is lighted by electricity, J. W. Bowman being the founder of the system, and the current being furnished by the Oxford Electric Light and Power Company. This company has a well-equipped plant, the streets, stores and churches being lighted, both arc and incandescent lights being used.

The Oxford Agricultural Society was established in 1870, its grounds are located in the northern part of the borough, and consist of twenty acres, well laid out. This has been since its establishment one of the greatest advertising features of the place.

The Oxford Board of Trade was incorporated December 19, 1892, for the purpose of promoting domestic commerce, and increasing commerce, manufactures and general industries. It has been largely instrumental in laying the foundations for a broad and liberal policy, which has awakened a spirit of progress, and has attracted the attention of railroads and manufacturers to the many advantages of the place.

At the election for borough officers in 1838, Thomas Alexander was chosen chief burgess, and L. K. Brown clerk and treasurer. The council was composed of the following gentlemen: Alexander Irwin, Levi K. Brown, John M. Dickey, Robert Murdagh, and Ebenezer Speer. The present officers and councilmen are as follows: Burgess, Thomas F. Green, elected in 1897; Councilmen, William T. Fulton, Joseph M. Showalter and Milton Walker, all elected in 1896 for three years; Samuel McDowell and David A. Caldwell, elected in 1897 for three years, and Samuel L. Martindale and Branson Slack, elected in 1898 for three years. The secretary, J. Cyrus Kerr, has held his office since 1877, and the treasurer, Jackson A. Watt, has been in his office since 1877, with the exception of the years of 1893-4-5.

Pocopson Township was formed in 1849, from parts of Pennsbury, East Marlborough, Newlin and West Bradford, and was named from the creek that flows through it. It is bounded on the east by the Brandywine. Benjamin Chambers of Philadelphia, in the early days of the Province, took a large quantity of land on the Brandywine, which he sold to settlers, Joseph Taylor purchasing several hundred acres of him in 1711, and afterward building a mill on Pocopson Creek. The Marshalls settled the northern part and were succeeded by the Bakers.

Penn Township was formed in 1817, by dividing up Londonderry Township. The settlers were largely from the north of Ireland, among them being John McKee, Daniel McClane, George Miller, Henry Charlton, Samuel Fleming, Hugh Luckey, Robert Brown, James Strawbridge, John McGrew, Matthew Harbeson, Richard Carson, Thomas Province, John Hayes, William Young, William Finney, and William Graham The southern line of this township, separating it from New London, was the southern line of Fagg's Manor.

In 1703 and 1704 surveys were made for William Bradford, Thomas Wickersham, Hannah Hammond, and Susanna Cadman, the surveys being made in right of old purchases, no one of these four persons settling on the land.

In 1857 the line between Penn and Londonderry was so altered as to include in the latter township a small portion of the former, this being done for the accommodation of school districts.

Jennerville, in this township, was so named by Dr. Josiah Ankrim in honor of Dr. Edward Jenner, the discoverer of vaccination.

Brook Haven is the name given by John D. Nelson to his fine farm, which is situated just east of Penn Station on the Philadelphia and Baltimore Central Railroad. The location is unusually pleasant and beautiful.

Pennsbury Township was created in 1770, from the eastern part of Kennett Township, and comprised the earliest settled part thereof. The first surveys were made about 1686, but there were

few settlements made before 1700. Among the names of those
who first took up land in this township, were those of Francis
Smith, Henry Peirce, Robert Way, Thomas Hope, George Harlan,
Isaac Few and William Huntley. Later came the Harveys, Tem-
ples, Mendenhalls, and Webbs. John Parker, who was located
therein during the time of the Revolution, was an eminent minister among the Friends, and it was after him that the village of
Parkersville was named. In 1849 Pocopson Township was taken
from the northern part of Pennsbury.

Pikeland Township lies northwest of Schuylkill and Charlestown Townships. In 1705 this township was granted by William
Penn to Joseph Pike, merchant of Cork, Ireland, the patent being
dated December 3. This was done in order to induce Mr. Pike to
emigrate to the Province of Pennsylvania. It embraced the territory now contained in the townships of East and West Pikeland,
equal to 10,116 acres. Joseph Pike died in 1727, seized of this
tract and also of about 1,400 acres in Caln Township, on the
southern part of which now stands Caln Friend's Meeting-house.
All his lands in America, Joseph Pike devised in fee to his wife
Elizabeth, who held them until her death, in 1733, devising them
likewise in fee to her son Richard Pike. Richard Pike died in 1752,
having devised in his will all his estates in Pennsylvania to his
kinsmen, Samuel Hoare and Nathaniel Newberry, merchants in
London, England, subject to the payment of certain legacies. In
1756 Samuel Hoare, having purchased the interest of Mr. Newberry, became sole owner. On December 3, 1773, Samuel Hoare,
by his attorney, Amos Strettle, sold and conveyed "the lands
known by the name of Pikeland," to Andrew Allen, taking from
him a mortgage thereon for £16,000, part of the purchase money.

Andrew Allen sold the lands in parcels to 115 persons, receiving from them the purchase money; but failed to pay off his indebtedness to Samuel Hoare, and hence the mortgage was sued
out against Allen and the 115 purchasers from him; and the en-

tire township was sold as one tract to Ezekiel Leonard, sheriff
of Chester County, and was repurchased by Samuel Hoare, holding the mortgage, and was reconveyed to him by deed dated
August 26, 1789. As those who had purchased from Allen
failed to procure from him releases from the mortgage, the
sheriff's sale to Samuel Hoare divested their titles, but they
generally compromised with Hoare, and by making additional
payments received deeds of confirmation from him; though some
were unable to make any agreements, and so lost not only their
lands, but also the improvements they had made thereon.
Samuel Hoare thus again becoming owner of Pikeland, appointed Benjamin Chew, Alexander Wilcoxe, and Benjamin
Chew, the younger, all of Philadelphia, his attorneys to make
sale of his lands, which they proceeded to do, and the titles to all
the lands in the two Pikelands are derived from him, either
through the agents named above, or through other agents subsequently appointed.

When the title to Pikeland was vested in Samuel Hoare it
was largely leased in small tracts to settlers, with the right to
purchase after twenty years' possession, at a valuation then to
be made. Among those who first settled in this township were
Samuel Lightfoot, Michael Lightfoot and Thomas Millhouse, the
first of whom built the first mill in the vicinity, and Michael Lightfoot was a tenant on the place afterward held by Mr. Pennypacker, living for some years in a cave.

The Yellow Springs, now known as Chester Springs, are located in West Pikeland Township, the mineral properties of the
waters having been discovered as early as 1722. For many years
these springs were a fashionable resort, but at length their popularity waned, owing in part, at least, to their distance from railroad facilities. They ceased to be kept up in 1868. Mr. Snyder
and his wife conveying the property in this latter year to Charles
W. Deans and others, who in 1869 conveyed it to the Chester

Springs Soldiers' Orphans' School and Literary Institute.   The old frame-house which stood on the hill-side in the rear of the former hotel buildings was erected by the direction of General Washington, during the Revolutionary War, and was used as a hospital for his sick and wounded soldiers.   For a long time it was known as Washington Hall.

In 1810 James Ross, a native of Chester County, wrote a Latin poem on the Yellow Springs.   The first stanza is as follows:

> "Quereret si quis, socios, amicos,
> Unde sanaret, vacuos salute,—
> Flavulor fontes adeant salubres
> Fontis ad undas."

In 1838 the township was divided into East and West Pikeland

Sadsbury Township, formerly written Sudbury, possibly after Sudbury, Suffolk County, England, lies in the middle western part of the county, bordering on Lancaster County.   The township was organized in 1717, though the name Sadsbury appears as early as 1708.   This township lies in the Great Valley and to the northward thereof, that part lying in the valley being taken up at an early day, in right of purchases made in England, and that north of it at a somewhat later period.   In 1718 the taxables were nine in number, William Grimson, James Hamer, Thomas ·Hayward, John Musgrave, William Smith, John Whitesides, and John Moore. The first township officer mentioned was William Marsh, November 26, 1717.   In 1728 a petition was presented to the court, asking for the definite location of the boundaries of the township, which on November 27 of that year was granted.   In 1813 the line between Sadsbury and West Caln Townships, was relocated and settled.   In 1852 Sadsbury was reduced in size by the formation of Valley Township, previous to which time it extended eastward to the Brandywine at Coatesville.   By an act of Assembly passed

March 1, 1872, the borough of Parkesburg was erected, thus reducing the township in size, and by a decree of the court of December, 20, 1875, the borough of Atglen was established, thus further reducing the size of Sadsbury. In 1878 the township was divided into East and West Sadsbury. The early settlers of this or these townships were Friends from England and Scotch-Irish Presbyterians

Among the noted citizens of this part of the county in the olden time was Colonel Andrew Boyd, son of Rev. Adam Boyd, who was lieutenant of Chester County during a part of the Revolutionary War. John Fleming, Sr., another prominent citizen of this part of the county, was a member of the convention that framed the State Constitution in 1776, and he was a member of the Assembly in 1778. Dr. Joseph Gardner was an active Revolutionary patriot, was three years a member of the Assembly, and was a member of the Continental Congress in 1784-85, and John Gardner, son of the former, was sheriff of Chester County from 1781 to 1783.

Atglen, formerly Penningtonville, was incorporated by a decree of the court, December 20, 1875. It is in the Great Valley, on the Pennsylvania, about one mile from Octoraro Creek, the western boundary of the county.

The borough officers of Atglen have been as follows:

Burgesses—Robert Futhey, 1876-77; Charles Reese, 1878; E. T. Good, 1879; Hibbert Chalfant, 1880; Andrew J. Irwin, 1881; Isaac Acker, 1882; Hibbert Chalfant, 1883-90; A. J. Hennis, 1891; Hibbert Chalfant, 1892-93; H. C. Yerkes, 1894-96; A. J. Hennis, 1897-1900.

Secretaries—Aaron Sill, Jr., 1876; Robert Holsin, 1877-78; William J. McKim, 1879; Jacob Airgood, 1880; William Wilde, 1881; P. Goodman, 1883; Frank Cowan, 1883; R. C. Cowan, Jr., 1896-98.

The council at the present time is composed of the following gentlemen: Robert Futhey, John Miller, John Hoover, Jacob

55

Heyberger, Samuel Whitson, and Samuel Rhoads, the terms of the first three expiring in 1899, and of the last three in 1900.

During the year 1898 the electric light was introduced into Atglen from Christiana, Lancaster County, only the incandescent lights being used. These vary in strength from sixteen to thirty-two candle power, the larger ones being in use to light the streets, the twenty-four candle power lights being used in churches and stores, and the sixteen candle power lights being in use in private houses. In all there are nearly 1,000 lights in the village.

Atglen prides herself on her public school building, erected in 1895. It stands on East Main Street and Newport Avenue. It is of brick, with green stone foundation, is one-story high, and contains two school-rooms, each room capable of accommodating eighty pupils. It cost $7,000, and is provided with the Smead system of heating and ventilating. The size of the building is 80x50 feet.

Parkesburg Borough was incorporated March 1, 1872. It is located on the Pennsylvania Railroad, and when the railroad was constructed from Philadelphia to Columbia the State shops were located here, remaining until 1861, when they were removed to Harrisburg, and the buildings thus vacated were afterward owned by Horace A. Beale, and used for a rolling-mill. The place received its name from an old and influential family by the name of Parke. Three generations of this family have occupied seats in the Legislature of the State, Joseph Parke, John G. Parke and Robert Parke, the latter having also been an associate judge of the county.

The first officers of this borough consisted of the following persons: Samuel R. Parke, burgess; J. M. Rawlins, secretary; J. W. Wright, treasurer. Since then the brugesses have been as follows: John Gilfillan, 1873; Amos Michener, 1874; J. Nevin Pomeroy, 1875; William B. Bassett, 1876; P. U. B. Stroud, 1877; Thomas Boyd, 1878; A. G. Wilson, 1882-83; Philip D. Handwork, 1884;

Amos Michener, 1885-86; Thomas C. Young, 1887; A. C. Ferree, 1888-89; S. Cromleigh, 1890; T. J. Kennedy, 1891; William C. Michener, 1892; T. J. Kennedy, 1893-95; S. Cromleigh, 1896; Amos Strickland, 1897-98.

Secretaries—J. M. Rawlins, 1873-74; John M. Dean, 1875-76; John D. Wilson, 1877-78; John D. Wilson, 1882; J. F. Matlack, 1883; M. F. Hamill, 1884-85; E. H. Brodhead, 1886; W. C. Michener, 1887-90; H. G. Book, 1891-93; M. F. Hamill, 1894-95; A. P. Reid, 1896; M. F. Hamill, 1897; Maris C. Mullin, 1898.

Treasurers—R. Agnew Futhey, 1873; Thomas Boyd, 1874-76; C. C. Owens, 1878; William B. Haslett, 1882; Samuel Jackson, 1883; A. J. Williams, 1884-85; J. V. Rice, 1886; A. G. Wilson, 1887; M. F. Hamill, 1888-93; A. P. Reid, 1894-95; M. F. Hamill, 1896-98.

The Parkesburg Water Company has its plant on the hills north of the town, and by means of wells and a wind engine pumps water into the mains, and thus supplies the inhabitants of the place with excellent water.

The Parkesburg Electric Light Company was established in 1893, and at the present time has eighteen arc lights for street lighting and numerous incandescent lights in stores, churches and private residences.

The borough erected a lock-up in 1885.

The borough of Coatesville was incorporated by a decree of the court, August 5, 1867, and it was ordered that the electors should meet on the second Friday of March, each year, to elect borough officers, except for the year 1867, the election being that year held October 8, resulting in the choice of Abram Gibbons, Craig Ridgway, Richard Strode, William T. Hunt and Joseph Suydam, councilmen, and William B. Morrison, burgess. Joseph L. Suydam was elected secretary and Abram Gibbons, treasurer. The burgesses since then have been as follows: George W. Price, Horace A. Beale, R. E. Smith, Joseph Doun, J. N. Woodward, J. T. Pierce, Moses Rambo, George G. Myer, N. H. Stone, T. H. Windle, John Speakman, and J. H. Dunlap, present burgess.

Secretaries—Joseph L. Suydam, William R. Ash, H. D. Harlan, Benjamin T. Lewis, H. C. Wilson, Caleb Brown, B. F. Wickersham, Isaac Spackman, W. S. Harlan, and J. W. Wingard.

Treasurers--Abram Gibbons, O. H. Branson, E. D. Baldwin, F. B. Speakman, W. S. Harlan, J. R. Van Ormer, and C. N. Speakman.

The council at the present time is as follows: C. P. Greenwood, president; J. W. Doan, Joseph Graham, Albert Pawling, Robert Yochum, Grier M. Hoskins and S. V. Hughes.

Not long after the incorporation of the borough it became evident that water-works were a necessity, and in 1871 the present system was introduced. The system is owned by the borough, and the capacity of the reservoir is 3,000,000 gallons. The original cost of the works was $80,000, and in 1897 money was borrowed to the amount of $23,000 for the purpose of increasing the supply of water. The reservoir was repaired, a new pump and engine installed, and the system otherwise improved and repaired.

The Coatesville Gas Company was organized June 28, 1871, with Dr. Charles Huston, president, and A. D. Harlan, secretary. On August 8, 1871, a permanent organization was effected by the election of Abram Gibbons, president; John L. Martin, secretary, and the following board of directors: Dr. Charles Huston, Richard Strode, S. B. Worth, W. B. Mendenhall, and Washington Miller. The capital stock originally was $20,000, but on November 28, 1871, it was increased to $30,000, and on December 30, following, the plant was completed, the first gas being manufactured that day. There was manufactured nearly 2,000,000 feet the first year, the price being $3.50 per 1,000 cubic feet. February 6, 1877, the price was reduced to $3, and on June 5, 1884, the price was reduced to $2.50, at which it remained until December 6, 1892. At this time the price was reduced to $1.70 per 1,000 feet for lighting purposes, and to $1 for heating purposes, and in 1893 a contract was made with the United Gas Improvement Company, of Philadelphia, to furnish a new plant complete, by which the "Lowe system" of water gas would be introduced. Under this arrange. ment each gas light was equal to 20-candle power, whereas before each light was only 18-candle power.

The Coatesville Board of Trade was organized about March 25, 1890, with C. W. Ash, president; M. W. Pownall, secretary, and John W. Thompson, treasurer. In a very short time nearly every business man of the place had become a member of the organiza- tion, and it was thought that a new era of prosperity had dawned upon the town. The influence of this board was soon felt in vari- ous ways. The Western Union telegraph poles were removed from Main Street, better train accommodations were secured from the Pennsylvania Railroad Company, and sanitary measures received proper attention. A board of health was soon established, an agita- tion was begun for a better water supply, and various committees were appointed to look after the various interests of the place.

Lewis B. Henson was elected president of the board January 12, 1891, and was later succeeded by William H. Gibbons, the lat- ter being succeeded by Hugh Kenworthy.

The Young Men's Christian Association of Coatesville was organized in the fall of 1891, with the following officers: Charles L. Huston, president; Lewis B. Henson and William H. Gibbons, vice-presidents; William H. Ridgway, secretary, and John W. Thompson, treasurer. A site on the south side of Main Street was purchased on which a building was erected, which cost nearly $30,- 000, is three stories high, the front being of Indiana limestone, and the building itself mainly of brick. To become a member of this association it is not necessary to be either a Christian or a church member, any man of good moral character being eligible to mem- bership.

The fact that Coatesville has a public library is due to the late Mrs. Isabella Huston, who fitted up a building at her own expense. for its use, and purchased many books for its shelves. The first officers of the Library Association were as follows: Dr. Charles Huston, president; Abram Gibbons, treasurer. and John S. Hope, secretary. The first board of directors was as follows: Rev. G. G. Field, Mrs. Isabella Huston, Clara Huston, S. B. Worth, Rev. Dr. Roberts, Benjamin Miller, and Mrs. Morris, and Col. Evart was the first librarian. People of wealth and liberality became interested in the cause, and the enterprise was a success from the first.

The Washington Fire Company of Coatesville was organized June 12, 1871, and it was incorporated August 17, 1871, the first meeting being held September 1 of that year. The borough council then purchased the old Kingsessing hose carriage, a hook and ladder truck, gum-buckets, and 500 feet of leather hose, and presented all to the new company. April 1, 1873, the company purchased the site of their present quarters at the corner of Chestnut Street and Third Avenue for $3,000, erected thereon a house worth $5,000, and moved into it November 15, 1873. In December, 1875, a Clapp & Jones steam fire engine, a hose carriage and 500 feet of rubber hose were purchased for $3,850 by the borough, and presented to the company, and the company is now one of the best equipped and most efficient of any in any inland town in the State.

The Coatesville Electric Light Company was chartered March 28, 1892, with a capital of $25,000, and the borough entered into a contract with the new company to light the town with arc lights at a cost per annum of $93.33 for each light, the contract to remain in force for five years. A substantial brick building was erected at the corner of Fourth Avenue and Railroad Street, and on January 2, 1893, the town was redeemed from darkness by the electric light, for the first time. The incandescent system is in general use by business and private houses.

The Coatesville Board of Health was organized in April, 1891, with Dr. E. V. Swing, president, and Dr. Ida Vriel, secretary, she being the first lady to serve on a board of health in the State. As a result of the labors of this board, Coatesville is one of the healthiest places in the State, as well as one of the most beautiful. The board holds meetings once each month, and is ever ready to take notice of any matter pertaining to the improvement of the sanitary condition of the corporation.

The population of Coatesville in 1870 was 2,025; in 1880, 2,766; in 1890, 3,680, and at the present time (1898) is estimated at 5,000.

The fraternal organizations of Coatesville are numerous and prosperous. Goddard Lodge, No. 383, F. & A. M., was chartered March 5, 1867, and at the present time has a membership of about 100. Its meetings are held in Goddard Hall, on the Tuesday evening which occurs on or first after the full moon.

Coatesville Lodge, No. 564, F. & A. M., was constituted October 22, 1886, and chartered with nineteen members. At present it has about 100 members and its career has been one of uninterrupted success.

Coatesville Royal Arch Chapter, No. 267, was constituted December 28, 1887, and its officers formally installed. The membership at the present time is about sixty.

Centennial Commandery, No. 55, Knights Templar, was constituted October 18, 1876, with nine charter members. The commandery has always been successful in its work, and is in a flourishing condition.

Lilly of the Valley Lodge, No. 59, F. & A. M. (colored), was constituted in 1875, and has a membership of about thirty. It meets on the second and fourth Wednesday evenings of each month in Masonic Hall Building, on Coates Street.

Star of Hope Lodge, No. 199, I. O. O. F., was established August 17, 1846, at Youngsburg. Being removed to Coatesville its place of meeting was for many years in West Coatesville, but in 1890 it sold its building and removed to the Opera House, where its meetings were held until April 1, 1892, when it moved into a new building, which had been erected for its use by its trustees, on the corner of Third Avenue and Main Street, and here it holds meetings each week, on Saturday evenings, and pays to those in need $4 per week.

Chosen Friends Encampment, No. 88, I. O. O. F., was instituted April 9, 1849, and meets on Wednesday evening of each week.

Huldah Lodge, No. 37, Daughters of Rebecca, was instituted September 27, 1892, with 76 charter members. It meets on the second and fourth Monday evenings of each month.

Sober Retreat Lodge, No. 2756, Grand United Order, was established in Coatesville about 1885, is distinct from the independent order, is composed of colored people, and holds meetings on the first Wednesday and third Saturday of each month, in Samaritan Hall, on Merchant Street.

The Household of Ruth Lodge, No. 514, was organized by the wives and daughters of the members of Sober Retreat Lodge, with twenty charter members, the organization being effected in 1888.

Coatesville Castle, No. 94, Knights of the Golden Eagle, was instituted April 26, 1886, with twenty-six charter members. This is a semi-military order, and pays $4. per week benefits for disability, $100 death benefit, and $75 benefit at the death of a member's wife.

Wayne Lodge, No. 266, K. P., was instituted September 20, 1870, with eighteen charter members. It has now about 60 members.

Charles Sumner Lodge, No. 18 (colored), was established June 14, 1890, with sixty-eight charter members. Uniformed Rank, No. 16, is a branch of this order, and the Court of Calanthe, No. 8 (ladies), is attached to Charles Sumner Lodge.

Onondago Tribe, No. 83, Improved Order of Red Men, was organized February 10, 1868, with fifteen charter members.

Onondago Haymakers' Association, No. 83½, was instituted June 21, 1886, and holds its meetings on the last Monday of each month.

Uncas Chieftan's League was organized 20th Sun, Sturgeon Moon, G. S. D., 398, and meets on the third Monday of each month.

Coatesville Council, No. 421, Junior Order United American Mechanics, was organized July 1, 1891, and was instituted on the 14th of the same month, with sixty-three charter members. The council pays $5 weekly for sickness or disability, $250 in case of death, and $30 on the death of the wife of a member.

White Star Council, No. 730, was instituted in November, 1891, with twenty charter members, and at the present time has about fifty members. This council pays $4 weekly benefits, and has the optional benefit fund of $250.

Coatesville Lodge, No. 16, Independent Order of Good Templars, was instituted July 27, 1889, and meets each Saturday evening in G. A. R. Hall, on Main Street.

Washington Camp, No. 549, Patriotic Order Sons of America, was instituted August 5, 1890, and has now a membership of about fifty. This camp pays $4 weekly benefits in case of sickness or accident.

St. Paul's Lodge, No. 19, Sons and Daughters of Samaria (colored), is a beneficial and charitable organization, and has been in existence since about 1880. It owns Samaritan Hall, on Merchant Street, in which several other organizations of colored people hold their meetings.

Brandywine Post, G. A. R., No. 54, was organized June 20, 1878, with thirteen charter members. This post meets every Friday evening.

Brandywine W. R. C., No. 149, is an auxiliary to the above, and was organized September 4, 1891, with thirty-six charter members.

Daniel C. Reed Post, No. 599, G. A. R., was organized October 20, 1890, with sixteen members. It is composed of colored members.

Schuylkill Township lies in the northeastern part of the county on the Schuylkill River, east of Charlestown, from which it was taken in 1826. Among the early settlers of this township were the families of Anderson, Buxzard, Boyer, Buckwalter, Bodley, Bartholomew, Coates, Coxe, Davis, Dehaven, Each, Fussell, Griffith, James, Kennedy, Longstreth, Maris, Miller, Moore, Roberts, Pennypacker, Rapp, Robinson, Rossiter, Starr, Steward, Schofield, Wagoner, and Wersler. Moore Hall in this township, more than a hundred years ago, one of the most aristocratic mansions in the county.

The borough of Phœnixville was taken from the east part of Schuylkill Township, and incorporated by a decree of the court March 6, 1849. The first election for borough officers was held April 13, following, it being a contest between those favorable to and those opposed to incorporation. The vote was as follows: For burgess, Isaac A. Pennypacker, 225; Samuel A. Whitaker, 156; for the councilmen that were elected: George Walters, 361; John Vanderslice, 271; Major MacVeagh, 256; William King, 248; Francis Bonner, 229, and John Mullen, 214.

Following are the names of the Burgesses of Phœnixville since its incorporation: Isaac A. Pennypacker, 1849, 1851 and 1853; Joseph B. McAllister, 1850; N. M. Ellis, 1852 and 1856; John Morgan, 1854; Isaac Z. Coffman, 1855; John Griffen, 1857; John R. Dobson, 1858; Isaac Phillips, 1859 and 1860, and Joseph Dobson to fill out the unexpired term of Isaac Phillips, deceased; Benjamin Hallman, 1861, 1865 and 1866; Levi Oberholtzer, 1862 and 1863; Harman Yerkes, 1864; Nathan Wagoner, 1867; Aaron B. Thomson, 1868; Jacob Baugh, 1869; Jacob B. Morgan, 1870, 1871, 1872 and 1873; Levi B. Kaler, 1874; J. B. Morgan, 1875; Benjamin G. Essick, 1876-77; N. B. Broomall, 1878-79; B. G. Essick, 1880; Frank L. Kreamer, 1881; Levi Oberholtzer, 1882; P. G. Carey, 1883; Z. S. Colehouer, 1884; N. M. Ellis, 1885; N. B. Broomall, 1886; N. C. Vanderslice, 1887; Daniel F. Moore, 1888; John Denithorne, 1889; S. Robert March, 1890-92; W. H. Mosteller, 1893; John Denithorne, 1894-96; William H. Bitting, 1897-98.

Clerks of the Council—Jacob B. Morgan, 1849-1851; O. E.

Strickland, part of 1852; J. B. Morgan, 1852-1854; P. G. Carey, 1855-56; David Bonner, 1857-58; P. G. Carey, 1859-62; Benjamin Hallman, 1863-64; P. G. Carey, 1865-72; Josiah P. Eachus, 1873-98.

Treasurers—Samuel Moses, 1849-77; Horace Lloyd, 1878-98.

The present council of Phœnixville is as follows: R. J. Henderson, J. R. Eyrich, E. L. Buckwalter, A. Y. Coffman, N. J. Waitneight, W. J. Hodge, E. J. McGettigan, M. J. O'Donnell, Noah Buck, S. R. Fitzgerald, C. G. Barth, William LaPorte.

The president of the council is E. L. Buckwalter, and the clerk, Josiah P. Eachus.

The Phœnixville Board of Health is as follows: M. G. Lippert, president; J. G. Shoemaker, M. D., vice-president; I. E. Miller, secretary; Joseph Moore, health officer; E. M. Massinger, V. S., milk inspector; Jesse Hall, Eugene McCabe, James O'Neill.

In 1859 an amendment to the charter of the borough was obtained from the Legislature, providing for a council of nine persons, three to be elected each year to serve three years, and authorizing the burgess and town council to borrow $10,000 for the erection of a town-hall and market-house. Previous to the securing of this amendment the burgess had not only presided over the meetings of the council, but he had also been an active participant in borough legislation, and the question then arose as to whether his authority had been superseded by the amendment, as was intended. This construction was put upon the amendment, and Isaac Phillips, who was burgess during 1859 and a part of 1860, quietly acquiesed in this construction; but Benjamin Hallman, elected in 1861, insisted on his right to preside, which was refused, and a motion to enter his objection to the proceedings of the council was voted down, by a vote of 4 to 5. The solicitor of the borough coincided in opinion with Burgess Hallman, and as soon as this was ascertained some of the active members of the council hastened to Harrisburg, and almost immediately returned with an act of Assembly so amending the charter that the burgess was deprived of all legislative power and made a mere executive officer. Since that time the burgess has not presided over the council.

In 1861 the council purchased a lot of ground on the east side of Main Street, below Bridge Street, upon which they erected a fine brick market-house, which has since been a great convenience to the people of the place. In 1872 arrangements were perfected to supply the town with water.

The construction of water-works in Phœnixville was commenced in 1872, and completed in 1873. Water is obtained from the Schuylkill River to the north of the borough and just above the tunnel bridge. It is pumped into a reservoir located about 500 feet from the pumping station, and elevated 185 feet above the level of the river. The reservoir has a capacity of 2,600,000 gallons, and from this reservoir it is piped through the town. The pressure is from 60 to 70 pounds, and almost every resident of the borough takes water from the system, those that do not paying a protection tax. The minimum water rate is $6 per year, and it may, according to circumstances, run up to $50 per year. There are two Worthington pumps, one having a capacity of 1,000,000 gallons, the other of 1,500,000 gallons per day, and the cost of the system as it stands today was $225,000. B. H. Willauer is water superintendent.

The Phœnix Military Band was organized June 5, 1847, in the home of W. W. Waitneigh, on Bridge Street, Phœnixville. There were at first seventeen members, all of whom are now dead except Philomen Richards, of Germantown, who is now over eighty years of age. The first leader of this band was Samuel T. Reeves, and the first set of instruments which were manufactured in New Hampshire cost $500. One of those instruments is still in existence, but is out of date. The band has had in all six sets of instruments, the aggregate cost has been $5,500.

Since Samuel T. Reeves, the leaders of this band have been Lawrence S. Fox, Robert B. Williamson, John G. Moses, from 1855 to 1878, and L. B. Vanderslice, nephew of Mr. Moses. Mr. Vander-slice having been elected April 29, 1876. The professional teach-ers of the band have been James P. Giffen, Philip Neuber, and John P. Rowbotham. This organization has had three band wagons, the present one having been purchased in 1868, costing $1,100, and being now as good as when new. The band has had three names—first the Military Brass Band of Phœnixville; sec-ond, the Phœnix Brass Band, and third, the Phœnix Military Band, being organized under this name July 27, 1867, and incorporated August 9, 1880. It has held the position since its organization of the best band in Chester County, and most of the time it has com-pared favorably with the leading bands in the State.

The Phœnixville Hospital was incorporated June 12, 1893, as the Stratford Castle Hospital, and re-chartered May 25, 1895, as the Phœnixville Hospital. The first year's work under its present name, showed 433 cases treated, 317 of which were sur-gical and 116 medical. The second year's work ending in June, 1897, showed 485 surgical cases and 245 medical, a total of 730, and a total for the two years of 1,163. The dispensary work of the hospital from the first grew rapidly, and was of great benefit to the sick and afflicted who were without the necessary means to purchase needed remedies or to employ a physician. The building occupied by this valuable institution stands near the Gay Street Viaduct and French Creek, but the work so rapidly increases that a new building is essential to its success, and a plot of ground on Nutts Avenue, in the southern part of the borough, was purchased about the beginning of 1897, on which the neces-sary buildings will be erected as soon as the funds can be secured. A building committee was appointed consisting of Samuel Wynne, Harry Sloyer, Paul S. Reeves, D. F. Moore, Clarence Keely, and L. B. Kaler, and this excellent committee will secure the erection of buildings as soon as practicable. The officers of the hospital are Levi B. Kaler, president; C. M. Vanderslice, vice-president;

Samuel Wynne, secretary, and Harry Sloyer, treasurer. Mrs. Alice Evans, matron; Miss Katherine N. Miller, chief nurse; Thomas Leidy Rhoads, chief surgeon; and Myron W. Snell, M. D., resident physician. The expense of conducting the hospital for the year ending June 1, 1898, was $3,209.25. For the year ending June 1, 1898, the number of patients treated was 942, making a total since the opening of the hospital, December 16, 1893, 2,203. The number of deaths occuring in the hospital has been 21. Plans for the new building reached Phœnixville in August, 1898. It is to be a three-story stone building above a basement, and is expected to cost $15,000.

The Phœnixville Park is one of the beauty spots of the county. It is situated on South Main Street, and occupies a full square of ground. It was donated to the city about 1874, and was opened to the public in July, 1878, with a grand demonstration of bonfires, music, and speeches. It will long remain an evidence of the generosity of its donor, David Reeves, of whom there is a fine bronze monument within its limits.

The secret societies of Phœnixville are as follows:

Phœnix Lodge, No. 75. F. & A. M., organized March 12, 1798, at Pughtown.

Phœnix Chapter, No. 198, R. A. M., organized September 13, 1861, and holds its meetings every Saturday next after the full moon.

Phœnix Lodge, No. 212, I. O. O. F., organized January 20, 1847, and meets every Wednesday at Temperance Hall.

Adelaide Lodge of Rebekahs, I. O. O. F., which meets in the postoffice building, on the third and fifth Tuesdays of the month.

Wayne Council No. 27, Sr., O. U. A. M., which meets every Wednesday evening at Temperance Hall.

Wayne Council, No. 46, Jr., O. U. A. M., which meets every Friday evening at Temperance Hall.

Lieut. Josiah White Post, No. 45, G. A. R., which meets every Friday evening in Caswell & Moore's building.

Andrew G. Curtin Camp, No. 100, Sons of Veterans, meets every Monday evening in Caswell & Moore's building.

Division No. 1, A. O. H., meets on the second Sunday of each month at Hibernia Hall.

The German Beneficial Society, No. 1, meets Thursday evenings after pay-day in the postoffice building.

Jerusalem Commandery, No. 15, K. T., meets at Masonic Hall on the Tuesday on or before the full moon.

Manarvon Council, No. 1,010, Royal Arcanum, meets in the postoffice building on the second and fourth Tuesday of each month.

Palestine Council, No. 8, R. & S. M., meets every Tuesday evening on or before the full moon, in Masonic Hall.

Phœnix Council, No. 164, P. of L., meets each Wednesday evening in the postoffice building.

Sanakac Lodge, No. 58, K. of P., meets every Monday evening at Temperance Hall.

Stratford Castle, No. 67, K. G. E., meets every Monday evening in the Whitaker building.

Washington Castle, No. 45, K. G. E., meets every Monday evening in the Postoffice building.

Spring City, formerly Springville, is on the Schuylkill River, and was taken from the east part of East Vincent Township, in 1867, being then incorporated by a decree of the court. The name became Spring City in 1872, in order that the name of the village and the postoffice might be the same. The village is located opposite Royer's Ford, on the Reading Railroad.

The Phœnixville Gas Light & Fuel Company was a corporation chartered by letters patent issued by the governor of Pennsylvania on the 18th day of November, A. D., 1873. Prof. S. C. Lowe, now of Los Angeles, California, was the principal incorporator of the company, and it was through his energy and largely by his capital that the first works were built in the borough of Phœnixville.

Prof. Lowe was the inventor of what is known as the water-gas process of making gas, and these works were built by him for the purpose of putting his invention into practice. Phœnixville, therefore, has the honor of having the first water-gas works erected in the United States.

The old works were built on Prospect Street, east of Main Street in the borough of Phœnixville, and were very small and crude.

Among the incorporators were J. P. Morgan, cashier of the National Bank of Phœnixville, Ellis Reeves, of the firm of Reeves & Starkey, and John Griffen, superintendent of the Phœnix Iron Company, all of whom are deceased.

The United Gas Improvement Company purchased all the patents of Prof. Lowe, and upon these patents and improvements thereon all the water-gas works were operated in the United States, as well as in foreign countries.

In 1887 the works were sold at the suit of the bondholders to the trustee named in a mortgage, and were purchased by a syndicate of bondholders, who reorganized the company and procured from the State a charter for the new company, under the name and title of the Phœnix Gas Light & Fuel Company.

This charter is dated March 15, A. D., 1888. The first president of the new company was George R. Griffen, and the first secretary was Henry R. Griffen. The new company continued to operate the old works until the year 1895, when they purchased a tract of ground along the Schuylkill River, abutting on the Philadelphia & Reading Railroad, where they erected new and improved works, at a cost of $30,000. The works were erected under contract with the Western Gas & Improvement Company of Fort Wayne, Indiana, and the company relaid a large number of the old mains, and have materially increased their business by the change. The annual output of gas from the present works is about seven million cubic feet.

W. P. Snyder.

The present officers of the company are as follows: President, H. H. Gilkyson; secretary, E. N. Pennypacker; treasurer, I. J. Brower. The board of directors are H. H. Gilkyson, N. H. Benjamin, Hon. L. B. Kaler, I. J. Brower, J. M. Reeves, Harry Sloyer and A. E. Eachus; the superintendent of the works is David Buck.

Thornbury Township lies in the southeastern part of the county, and was divided into two townships, each retaining the name, when Delaware County was created in 1789. It was named from Thornbury, Gloucestershire, England, being named in honor of the wife of George Peirce, she being a native of Thornbury, England. The township was organized in 1687 by the appointment of Hugh Durburrow as constable, when there were not more than five or six families within its limits. Thornbury, Birmingham and Westtown Townships are the only ones within the present limits of Chester County organized prior to 1704. That part of Thornbury which fell into Chester County was about one-fourth of the original township, and it is one of the smallest townships in Chester County.

Tredyffrin Township is situated in the eastern part of the county and mostly in the Great Valley. It is a portion of the famous Welsh Tract, and was settled largely by the Welsh. In Welsh the word or prefix Tro means town or township, and Dyffrin means valley, hence the meaning of Tredyffrin is the valley township. The township was organized as early as 1707, for in that year Thomas David was constable. Following are the names of the resident landowners in 1722, showing that the inhabitants were nearly all Welsh:

James Abraham, Morris David, Hugh David, James David, Sr., John David, Henry David, James Davies, William Davies, Timothy Davies, Stephen Evans, Lewis Evans, William Evans, Thomas Godfrey, John Howell, Mark Hubbert, Thomas Hubbert, Griffith Jones, Sr. and Jr., Thomas Jerman, Thomas James, Jenkin

Lewis, James Parry, John Robert, Owen Roblyn, Thomas Martin, Samuel Richard, John Richard, Daniel Walker, and Lewis Walker.

The population since then has gradually changed, so that at the present time other nationalities are largely represented in the township.

Uwchlan Township was settled principally by the Welsh, as its name implies, Uwchland meaning higher than or above the valley. These first settlers came in under the auspices of David Lloyd, who was more than ordinarily able and prominent among them. David Lloyd took up large tracts of land within this original township, selling it off in smaller divisions to settlers. The settlement was made about 1712. The first settlers are said to have been Samuel and Griffith John, brothers and sons of John Philips, taking their father's Christian name for their surname as was then customary among the Welsh. They were both ministers in the Society of Friends, and neither of them could ever speak English without a strong tincture of their native tongue. Other early settlers were Morris Reese, Cadwalader John, David Evans, Humphrey Lloyd, David Lloyd, a family of Philipses and other Welshmen. John Cadwalader purchased 250 acres of land from David Lloyd, June 2, 1715, and on January 16, 1716, sold it to Thomas Fell, with the exception of a small piece of ground by the side of the King's road, which he allotted for a burying-ground, and on which a meeting-house was to be built for the use of the Quakers. This piece of ground is now occupied by the Friends' Meeting-house at Lionville. Evan Evans, who came from Treeglws, in Montgomeryshire, Wales, in 1722, purchased a large tract of land in this township, and his descendants are among the prominent citizens of the Uwchlan Townships at the present time. His grandson, Evan Evans, was a member of the assembly from Chester County from 1780 to 1783.

Among the early settlers not mentioned above were the following: John Evans, James Pugh, Robert Benson, John David,

James Reese, Joseph Phipps, Noble Butler, Reese Jones, David Davies, Thomas John, and several others.

This original township was divided in 1858, and a new township formed by the name of Upper Uwchlan, the southern part being named Lower Uwchlan. From the northeastern part of Upper Uwchlan there is an extension into West Vincent Township, this extension originally forming a part of the lands of Sir Mathias Vincent, Dr. Daniel Cox, and others, and was known as Cox & Company's 30,000 acres. The taxes on this land remained unpaid from September 29, 1687, until September 29, 1715, a period of twenty-eight years, on which latter date suit was brought for their recovery by John Simcock, clerk of the county courts, in the name of William Penn, and a writ of execution was granted by the court August 30, 1717, under which 467 acres of the 30,000 acres were seized and sold by the sheriff, Nicholas Fairlamb, to David Lloyd of Chester, for £50, and confirmed to him by deed dated February 24, 1717-18. In 1728 David Lloyd sold a part of this land, 200 acres, to John Vaughan, and this 200 acres afterward became the property of his son, Jonathan Vaughan, who, together with his wife, Ann, conveyed the same, together with the brick house thereon, known as the "Red Lion," to Dennis Whelen.

Dennis Whelen also purchased other lands adjoining, and had in contemplation the selling of lots and the building up of a town upon his lands, "where the conveniences are so large that several Hundreds of Builders or Tenants may be served with dry and wholesome lots. Those of them now laid out are 60 feet wide and 250 feet deep, proposed to be lett at three dollars per annum yearly Rent, or the Value thereof, with a condition that the Tenants may purchase when they please upon paying 20 years' Rent. The said Town to be named .... after a place in Wales, from whence the late Judge David Lloyd came, who had been formerly owner of this place." But Mr. Whelen's hopes and plans failed of realization, and the little village of Lionville is now standing on the tract where it was fondly hoped that a large and flourishing town would grow up under the name of Welshpool.

Valley Township lies in the western part of the county between Caln and Sadsbury. It was formed in 1852 by decree of the court from parts of the townships of West Caln, West Brandywine, East Caln and Sadsbury, and it includes the village of Coatesville, which borough was established in 1867, reducing Valley Township in size, and its area was again reduced in 1868 by the erection of Caln Township. The township is now about one-half its original size.

Coatesville was incorporated by the Court of Quarter Sessions in 1867, and was named in honor of the Coates family. It embraces territory on both sides of the Brandywine. The Pennsylvania Railroad and the Wilmington Railroad both pass through this town, and contribute much to its prosperity, which, however, depends more upon the manufacturing establishments located there. A village known as Midway, situated on the Pennsylvania Railroad west of the Brandywine, was included in the limits of Coatesville at the time of its incorporation, and is frequently referred to as West Coatesville.

Vincent Township lies northwest of East and West Pikeland. On the earliest map of the Province the territory now embraced within the limits of East and West Vincent Townships is given in the names of Sir Mathias Vincent, Adrian Vrouzen, Benjohau Furloy and Dr. Daniel Cox. French Creek, which passes through the township, was at one time called Vincent River, and the tract of land was frequently Cox & Company's 20,000 acres.

The history of the early settlement of this township is unusually interesting. Benjohan Furloy, named above, as agent for William Penn, conveyed on March 7, 1682, 5,000 acres of land in the Province of Pennsylvania to Burgomaster Adrian Vrouzen, of Rotterdam, Holland, who, on June 10, 1704, conveyed the same lands to Benjohan Furloy, son of the first named Dr. Daniel Cox, or Coxe, the name being spelled both ways, was seized of a tract of land containing 10,000 acres, lying between the Schuylkill and Vincent Rivers, which in 1682 he ordered to be divided into two equal parts, on one of which several families were then already settled. Of the other part he granted on November 22, 1682, 1,000 acres to John Clapp of the Province of Carolina, 100 acres of which were to lie on the Schuylkill, and Clapp was to pay to Dr. Coxe a yearly rental of one grain of corn per year for the first six years, and afterward the yearly rent of £4 6s.

William Penn also sold to Major Robert Thompson of Newington Green, Middlesex County, England, 10,000 acres of land in Pennsylvania, April 20, 1686, which lands lay in this township, and which at length became the property of Joseph Reed, Thomas Willing and Robert Morris, all of Philadelphia, the price paid by them for the 10,000 acres being £5,500. Joseph Reed sold his interest to the other parties December 10, 1783, for £2,000, and a patent was granted to Morris and Willing June 28, 1787, for 10,098 acres in Vincent, called Westover. On December 1, 1789, Morris sold his interest to Willing for £12,000. This land covered the parts of East and West Vincent adjoining Coventry, and a patent was granted for the remainder of the land in Vincent to the West New Jersey Society, the number of acres being 10,098½ acres, December 5, 1791.

This Township was settled much in the same manner as Pikeland, leases being taken with the right to purchase reserved. And it was only when the tenants became the owners of their lands that marked and steady improvement became the order of the day. Among the early settlers were such men as the Ralstons, Jenkinses, Davises, John and Michael Paul, Gordon, Dennis Whelen and Garret Brombac. The latter gentleman established the first tavern north of the Lancaster route. It was in a little house of rude construction, but in it he performed the duties of host for many years, eventually becoming a rich man. The name Brombac has since his day been changed to Brownback.

Vincent Township was divided into East and West Vincent in 1832, and the borough of Springfield was taken from the eastern part of East Vincent in 1867, the name being changed to Spring City in 1872.

Wallace Township lies in the northwestern part of the county, and was formed in 1852 by the division of West Nantmeal. It includes very nearly the same territory as the ancient manor of Springton. The name of Springton was first given to this township, but the next year, upon application to the Legislature, the name was changed to Wallace, in honor of Robert Wallace, the settlers therein being mainly at that time of Scotch-Irish origin. According to some of the early settlers the land was promised to them at the rate of £45 per hundred acres. Among the early settlers in this township were the families of Mackelduff, McFeeterr, Alexander, Henderson, Starrett, Mackey and Kennedy. The elevation of this township above the level of the sea has always made it a remarkably healthy place, and up to 1880, according to Judge Futhey, only four physicians had resided within its limits, these four being Drs. Thomas Harris, Thomas Kennedy, Benjamin Griffith and Joseph T. Grier.

In 1853 a small portion of Wallace was added to Uwchlan, and in 1860 the line next to East and West Nantmeal was slightly changed.

Warwick Township lies in the northern part of the county, bordering on Berks County and between North Coventry and West Nantmeal. It was formed in 1842 from East Nantmeal, and derived its name from Warwick Furnace, within its limits. The casting of the Franklin stoves, an invention of Benjamin Franklin, was done at this furnace, the making of which was in charge of Robert Grace, who married the widow of Samuel Nutt, Jr., and according to Dr. Benjamin Franklin, "found the casting of the plates for these stoves a profitable thing, as they were growing in demand."

In 1860 the line between East and West Nantmeal was slightly changed, and East Nantmeal was altered at its western end, a portion of Warwick being added thereto. For many years were devoid of railroad facilities, but now the Wilmington and Northern and the East Brandywine Railroads supply this deficiency in an admirable manner. The French Creek Branch of the Wilmington and Northern Railroad, opened up about 1879, to the Warwick Furnace, is another valuable addition to the facilities of travel and transportation.

Westtown Township lies in the southeastern part of the county, and is a long and narrow rectangular parallelogram, five and a half miles long by about a mile and a half in width. The longer axis of this tract runs east-northeast. It is worthy of note in this connection that in most of the early surveys east of the Brandywine and south of the Great Valley, the lines were run east-northeast or north-northwest, to conform to the general course of the Delaware River; while those in the southwestern part of the county were run in the main to correspond with the cardinal points. In the northeastern part of the county the lines were run at right angles with or parallel to the general direction of the Schuylkill River. It is said that Westtown was so named because of its location relatively to Easttown, and was probably laid out as early as 1685, succeeding Thornbury as to date of survey.

Among those who owned land early in this township, some of whom were perhaps among the early settlers, were the following: Richard Collett, Richard Whitpaine, Barnabas Wilcox, Mathias Evans, John Eluny, John Bond, Thomas Coëburn, Thomas Rous, Benjamin Furlory, John Brazo, John Waite, Joshua Hastings, John Marsh, Mary Finch and Richard Sneed.

Others who came in about 1700 were Daniel Hoopes, who was the first constable in the township. Aaron James became a landowner in 1700, as also did Benjamin Hickman. John Bowater purchased land in this township in 1704, and was probably living

there for some time prior to his death in 1705.   The land owned by
Barnabas Wilcox, mentioned above as probably among the early
settlers, passed into the hands of the Gibbons family, and at length
was purchased by the Friends for the Westtown Boarding School.

Willistown Township, which lies between Easttown and East
Goshen, was organized as a township about 1704.   Thomas Garret was its first constable in 1705.   While a large part of this
township was within the limits of the Welsh Tract, yet numerous
surveys were made for other parties.   Among the earliest settlers,
according to Hon. Joseph J. Lewis, were Griffith Jones, Thomas
Brassey, Thomas Bowman, William Garrett, Samuel Lewis and
Joseph Barker & Co., the latter belonging to or being connected
in some way with the Free Trade Society.   Above them lay the
Welsh Tract, including the lands of James Stanfield, John Hort,
Anthony Sturdges, James Claypool, William Wood and William
Sharlow.   In addition to the above, according to Judge Futhey,
were the families of Hibberd, Massey, Smedley, Thomas, Garrett
and Yarnall, and many of their descendants inhabit the township
even down to the present day.

It was in this township that a tribe of Indians, known as the
Okehockings, held lands by special grant from the commissioner
of property, mentioned in the chapter on Indian occupation.

Whiteland Township was organized about 1704, its first settler being probably Richard Thomas, mentioned in the sketch of
Goshen Township, in right of Richard ap Thomas of Whitford
Garden, Flintshire, North Wales.   From this shire it is presumed
that the name Whiteland was derived.   The house of Richard
Thomas, built upon his allotment, was near the Valley Creek, and
in the immediate vicinity of some Indian huts, the reason for the
selection of this location being that the dogs in the Indian village
would be of service in keeping away wild beasts, which were then
numerous in the woods.   This little Indian village was named
in the Indian language, Katamoonchinck, which in English means
Hazel-nut grove.

Whiteland Township is in the northwest part of the original Welsh Tract of 40,000 acres, which were laid out to them in 1684, with the expectation, both on their part and on that of William Penn, that they should be a separate barony, managing their own municipal affairs in their own way. They also, of course, desired and expected to retain the use of their own language, but subsequent events rendered the entire scheme impracticable. The north- and west lines of this survey have, for the most part, been retained as township lines, but on the south other surveys so encroached that the original boundaries of this tract have become obliterated. The northern line of the original Welsh Tract is distinctly visible on the map of Chester County, running from the southeastern corner of Schuylkill Township toward the west until it reaches the northwestern corner of what is now West Whiteland Township, and from this point southward between West Whiteland and West Goshen Townships on the east, and East Caln and East Bradford on the west, until it reaches Westtown Township.

The constables of Whiteland Township, prior to 1726, were as follows: In 1710, Isaac Malin, then in succession, James Thoms, Edward Kinneson, Lewis Williams, David Meredith, Sr., Evan Lewis, Rees Pritchard, Thomas Owen, James Rowland, James David, Richard Anderson, Isaac Richardson, Thomas James, John Spruce, Owen Thomas and Evan Philips. The first supervisor was James Thomas, in 1714, and the first overseers of the poor were George Aston and John Spruce, in 1730. This township was divided into East and West Whiteland in 1765, and is situated wholly within the choicest part of the Great Valley.

Valley Forge, one of the most historic spots in the United States, lies partly in Chester County and partly in Montgomery County, Valley Creek being the county line. It is on the Philadelphia and Reading Railway, four miles from Phœnixville and twenty-two miles from Philadelphia, and on the west side of the classic Schuylkill. That portion lying in Chester County contains about 150 inhabitants, one general store kept by John Mulvaney, a hotel kept by James Hoy and a hall in which the lodge of P. S. O. A. hold their meetings. On the Montgomery side of the line Mrs. Sarah Shaw keeps the Washington Hotel, where travelers and tourists, of which there are in certain seasons of the year considerable numbers, mostly stop. The population of the place as a whole is not so large as formerly, for the reason that such industrial establishments as once existed there have now ceased to be.

In the early part of the present century there was a large cotton factory here, a grist-mill and numerous other buildings, which were operated by water power derived from Valley Creek, which at one time was said to be the finest in Pennsylvania, the stream passing between two abrupt hills distant more than a mile from the village. Near the base of these hills, named Mount Joy and Mount Misery, and their northern termination, there was constructed a large dam more than twenty feet in height, and in consequence even in the dryest season there was an abundance of water power to keep manufacturing business in full operation.

But it is of the burning of the Valley Forge, or rather of the buildings connected therewith, that it is desired here more particularly to mention. This was by a detachment of British soldiers under command of Colonel Grey. It was previous to the American army encamping at this place and while the possession of the city of Philadelphia during the ensuing winter was still a matter of uncertainty, that Valley Forge was selected as a place suitable for the depositing of military stores, arms and ammunition and provisions belonging to the Continental army, the selection being made because of its secluded situation and distance from the supposed route of the army under General Howe on its march from the Chesapeake to form a junction with General Burgoyne, who was on his way from Canada to take possession of Philadelphia. Among the inhabitants of the surrounding country were some who sympathized with British interests, and it was one of those who piloted the detachment of British soldiers to Valley Forge, who destroyed the buildings, the stores, arms, ammunition and provisions which had been deposited in fancied security near the banks of the Schuylkill.

Iron was then being manufactured at Valley Forge by a Mr. William Dewees, in connection with some of the members of the Potts family, and Mr. Dewees, in part because of his marriage into this family, founded a claim against the American Government for damages and losses sustained by the burning of the buildings at the Forge. This claim about nine years after his death was successfully prosecuted by his widow and heirs, and it is proper here to note that the main reason of the burning of the Forge was that Col. Dewees was well known to be a sympathizer with and strong supporter of the American cause.

Following is a most interesting statement of the headquarters of the several officers in General Washington's army during the famous winter of 1777-78, together with the then owners or lessees of the places and the names of the present owners:

Headquarters of General Officers at Valley Forge Encampment during 1777-78:

Officers' Names.	Owner or Lessee 1777-78.	Owner, 1898.
General Washington.	Issac Potts, Owner.	Valley Forge Cen. Ass'n.
General Knox.	Samuel Brown, Owner.	Matthews.
Count Pulaski and General Poor.	John Beaver's Estate.	Francis Wood.
Lord Sterling.	Rev. William Currie.	Henry S. Evans.
General Huntington.	Zachary Davis, Lessee of Maurice Stephens.	Heston Todd. *
General Mifflin.	William Godfrey, Tenant, Thomas Waters, Owner.	
{ General Woodford. } { Count Duportail. }	John Havard.	David Havard's Estate.
Marquis de Lafayette.	Samuel Havard, Owner.	Edward Wilson's Estate.
General Scott.	Samuel Jones, Owner.	Abram Latch.
General McIntosh.	Joseph Mann, (Colored).	
General Morgan.	Mordecai Moore, Owner.	J. W. Andrews.
General Muhlenberg.	John Moore, Owner.	Edwin Moore's Estate.
General Sullivan.	Thomas Waters, Owner.	Mordecai Davis.
General Green.	Isaac Walker, Tenant.	Matthew Walker.
General Potter.	Jacob Walker, Owner.	Havard Walker.
General Wayne.	Joseph Walker, Owner.	W. H. Walker.
{ General Weedon and } { Baron De Kalb. }	Abijah Stephens,	Abram Fisher.
General Varnum.	David Stephens.	William Stephens.
General Lee.	David Havard.	A. J. Cassatt. †

*Hut of Baron Steuben was located on this farm.
†Thomas Bradford, deputy commissary officer to the prisoners, was quartered here, General Lee remaining only a short time.

CHAPTER XX.

AGRICULTURE, &C.

CHAPTER XX.

IN connection with such remarks as may be made on the subject of agriculture in this work, it is proper at the outset to note the fact that on this, as on most other subjects, the men selected to represent the people in the Legislatures of the several States are better informed than are the people themselves, and have higher and more comprehensive views of the necessities and possibilities of the calling. This fact has a deep and wide mean- ing to those capable of appreciating it, it being a solemn and per- sistent tribute of the people to intelligence, and a sure guarantee of the perpetuity of the Republic so long as the people have sufficient intelligence to pay this tribute to intelligence.

That the value of agriculture to the community at large was early appreciated in Pennsylvania is evident from the fact that a message was laid before the Assembly by the President and Council of the Province on January 19, 1784, from which the fol- lowing is an extract:

"It is our most earnest wish that the General Assembly may always cherish and patronize in a very distinguished manner that basis of Pennsylvania's commerce, agriculture, by their assistance of the useful discoveries that have been or shall be made in coun- tries longer settled may soon be introduced and be generally communicated, that otherwise might remain little known here for ages to come. The ingenious and learned gentlemen that com-

957

pose the Philosophical Society, we are assured, would rejoice to execute the generous designs of the Legislature, and would faithfully apply and account for any sums of money that should be committed to their management for this purpose.

"Another great encouragement of agriculture would be afforded by rendering purchases of land more safe. This might, in a measure, be abolished by quieting possessions after a reasonable term of years, and by having the records in all the public offices kept in a manner easy to be prescribed, so that a title could be readily traced through them," etc.

That the early inhabitants of Chester County looked to agriculture mainly as a means of support is evident, from the fact that they, in 1683, adopted a seal, or, in other words, that a seal was adopted by the Council which met at Chester that year, on which the main device was a plow. In an early stage of civilization, and in the early settlement of a new country, agriculture gradually supplants hunting and fishing as a means of livelihood for the inhabitants. Commerce and manufactures, and a varied industry come in process of time, and mark the advance of civilization.

As has been elsewhere remarked in this history, the trees that covered the country when it was first visited by Europeans were very large, and stood at considerable distances from each other, for which reason the early settlers, instead of cutting down large quantities of timber, making log and brush heaps, and then burning it all to ashes, were in the habit of girdling the trees so as to kill them, and let them stand, burning the branches as they fell to the ground. The progress made in clearing up the land was necessarily slow, as it was well that it should be, for the clearing of a country has an appreciable effect upon its climate. In 1784, the year in which the action recommended above by the President and Council of the Province was made, the farms averaged in size from about 100 to 200 acres of land, and there was in cultivation from four to nine per cent.

.The land in Chester County is unusually fertile. Indian corn, of which there then were fewer varieties than now, was much cultivated in comparison with other cereal crops. Barley, oats, rye and wheat were all early cultivated, barley being used mainly in the manufacture of malt, and sold up to about 1822 to Philadelphia brewers. But about that time the farmers of Chester and Delaware Counties, laboring under the impression that the brewers were combined to keep the price of barley down as low as possible, formed the Farmers' Brewing Company, and themselves erected a brewery at Filbert and Tenth Streets, Philadelphia. This venture, however, was a failure, and the brewery was eventually sold at a considerable loss to the stockholders, and from that time the cultivation of barley gradually diminished until about 1840, when it practically ceased.

In the earlier days rye was much depended upon for a bread cereal, some of the patriots during the Revolutionary War saying they would rather eat rye bread during their entire lives than surrender their liberty and sell posterity. Buckwheat and flax were also generally raised during the eighteenth century, but neither is now raised to any considerable extent. With regard to clover seed it may be said that while it was early introduced into the county, probably from Lancaster County, yet its use did not keep pace with its value as a feed crop or as a fertilizing crop. Yet about 1840 there were numbers of clover hullers in Chester County, which have since then gradually gone out of use, and the clover seed now used comes in from the West.

The method of reaping grain is clearly indicated by the recital of the incident below, by a farmer of Chester County, published in the papers of the time, about 1818: "Being called upon to assist a neighbor near the close of harvest in reaping his grain, an ancient and respectable woman came out of the house to show us her dexterity at reaping. I, being on the leading land, of what are called double lands, she chose to be a partner for me.

57

We sat in—she reaped as fast as anyone, handled and laid her grain to admiration. She reaped a considerable distance with us. But what is most remarkable, she informed us she was one hundred years old, which we were well assured she was."

That men in those days were not satisfied with the slow processes then in vogue in cutting hay and grain by means of the sickle and scythe, is indicated by the fact that at least as early as 1824 a successful mowing-machine was invented by two of Chester County's citizens. A certain writer, presumably the editor of the Village Record, under date of July 10, 1824, relates an incident connected with such an invention, which took place a short time before. He says: "On Friday, the 2nd of this month, I went to view a new mowing-machine, formed by Messrs. Ezra Cope and Thomas Hoopes, Jr. It is in some respects like that of Mr. Baily, but whether considered as an improvement on his, or a new invention, I am not able to say. But of this I am satisfied, that it cannot fail to prove eminently useful to the farmer. It has cut this season two acres in two hours. And it can cut a field of eleven acres in nine hours, calculating the time the horses were hitched to it (not including the time of rest), so that it may be safely said that it will now mow neatly an acre of stout grass an hour." Mr. Baily's machine, referred to in this extract, was patented by him in 1822—Jeremiah Baily of East Marlborough. The machine invented by Cope & Hoopes, the working of which has just been described, was patented by them in 1825, and there were fifty or more of them made. It was in use for several years with tolerable success, but it was succeeded by what was known as the Allen machine, made by Caleb Pierce and his partners, Lee and Thompson, at Ercildoun, in East Fallowfield, in 1854, about which time the Pennock mowing-machine appeared. For some years E. T. Cope & Son were engaged in making mowing-machines, building a large number of what they called the "Buckeye Mowing-machine."

Mr. Baily's mowing-machine, mentioned above, was first exhibited in West Chester, August 17, 1821, being on that day put in operation in a field belonging to John Jefferis, in the presence of the Agricultural Society, the vice-president and several other members. This machine, was described as having a circular scythe, about five and a half feet in diameter, and was put in motion by horses, one or two, harnessed to it as to a cart. It cut grass at the rate of an acre in thirty-six minutes. The next Saturday, August 18, it cut the grass in the meadow of Joseph Taylor.

Attention was given early to the raking of hay in other ways than by hand, always laborious and slow. The first hay-rake in Chester County, of which any information could be obtained, was made by a farmer visited by Halliday Jackson, whose name Mr. Jackson, for some reason, failed to communicate with his description of the rake he saw at work. This rake was in operation in 1820, and the next year Mr. Jackson made one for his own use, which he described as consisting of a piece of white oak scantling, ten feet long and about three and a half by two inches in size. The holes for the teeth were bored with an inch auger, three and a half inches apart, the teeth being of dry, tough hickory, and eighteen inches long, the under sides dubbed off at the points, so as to prevent them sticking in the ground. For the handles two holes were made with the same auger, the handles slanting upward like the handles of a plow. A staple was fixed at a distance of two feet from each end, to which the horse was hitched by chains long enough to prevent his heels coming in contact with the teeth, and when the rake was full of hay it had to be lifted up and carried over the windrow. While this was an awkward pattern of a machine, yet Mr. Jackson said that, with a boy to ride the horse, he could gather as much hay as five common men could with the hand rake. Afterward Moses Pennock, aided by his neighbor, Samuel Pierce, added teeth to the other side of the head and found means to so make it that, when it was full of hay, or upon

coming to the windrow, it could be emptied by revolving it, so
that to stop and lift it over the windrow was no longer necessary.
Since that time great improvements have been made in hay rakes,
the steel toothed, wheel rake having long since superseded almost
every other kind.

Mention has already been made of the method of reaping wheat
with the sickle, which women handled with almost equal skill with
the men. While farmers were generally slow to give up the
sickle, yet the cradling scythe began as early as 1800 to take its
place, but this kind of a cradle the women could not rock, as it
cut so much more grain at a swing that only the strongest men
could handle it throughout the entire day, cutting from two to
four, or perhaps five acres in a day, under favorable conditions.
Cradles were manufactured by Joseph Smith of Newlin Township,
and also by James Embree of Marshallton, the latter of whom invented a machine for turning scythe poles, which was patented in
1844.

In the early days thrashing was mostly done by means of the
flail, though occasionally the Bible method of treading it out with
horses was employed. In 1770 mention is made of an "Act to
invest John Clayton with an exclusive privilege and benefit of
making and selling a machine for thrashing wheat on a model
invented by him." But this machine, while it indicates the fact
that the necessity of some other method of thrashing than by
the flail cannot have met with much success. The first thrashing
machine which attracted much attention in Chester County, so far
as could be ascertained by the writer of this chapter, was one manufactured by Thomas Fenn, and was called Ballou & McDonald's
thrashing machine. It was in operation at the barn of Richard
Strode early in the summer of 1826, and thrashed "forty dozen of
wheat an hour, large growth and bound with double bands." The
expense of erecting a durable machine complete was $15; the horse
power cost $25, and for varying the construction of the boxes, $5;

total cost, $45. The thrashing machine proper was in this case designed to be stationary, and each farmer was expected to have one of his own.

On January 15, 1830, Warren's thrashing-machine was patented, and in the following July Joseph P. Sharpless advertised that he had purchased the right to sell this machine in East and West Bradford Townships, East and West Goshen Townships, and in Brandywine Township. He also offered patent rights for sale in those townships, single patents, $10. The machines, ready-made, sold for the following prices: Two-horse power machines, $40; one-horse power machines, $30, and those operated by hand, $25. The two-horse power machine would thrash, with the assistance of two men and a boy, 120 bushels of wheat per day.

Since that time great progress has been made in the nature and style of thrashing machines, as well as in the motive power, horses having given way to steam, and the portable steam-engine in part to the powerful and somewhat cumbrous traction-engine.

So far as can be ascertained, the better class of mowing-machines, such as the Ketchum, made in Baltimore, the McCormick, made in Chicago, the Manny, and the Buckeye, made in Akron, Ohio, were brought into Chester County from 1850 to 1865. The precise date when each or any of them first appeared here would be difficult to determine. The self-binder reaping-machine was introduced about 1883, and the steam thrashing machine came in about 1888, the steam traction-engine coming in about the same time.

As showing what was thought at an early day of the possible value of the Chester County Agricultural Society to the farming community, it may be stated that a certain devout writer, in a communication to the daily press, in 1821, made use of the following language:

"Had it not been for the original transgression (of Adam and Eve in the Garden of Eden), all knowledge necessary would have been intuitive.   Distinct professorships of physic, law, divinity, etc., would have been unknown.   Knowledge now attainable by the few would then have been accessible to all, nor would the Agricultural Society, gentlemen, have been of any utility, had not this among many other lamentable denunciations been issued against our first parents:

"Cursed is the ground for their sake," etc.

It was in 1821 that John Cox, on the French Creek farm, raised a hog which was very large and which he sold for $50.   He was eight and a half feet long, seven and a half feet girth, and was estimated to weigh 800 pounds.

It is believed that the first agricultural exhibition held in Chester County was that of the State Agricultural Society, at Paoli, October 22, 23, and 24, 1823, which was the first held by that society.

In 1838 an agricultural society for Chester and Delaware Counties was organized, which held exhibitions for several years, one of them being held at West Chester in 1845.

About this time Chester County Horticultural Society was organized, and, after holding a few exhibitions, erected a hall, called horticultural hall, in 1848, for an annual display of fruits, flowers and vegetables, and this was continued for several years, the building being afterward used for the accommodation of teachers' institutes, lectures and other entertainments.

For the purpose of showing the size of sheep raised in the early days in Chester County, the following facts are taken from the "Register of Pennsylvania," for March 12, 1831:   John Bradley of Willistown had twelve sheep in market for the 22d of February of the following weights: 105, $108\frac{1}{2}$, $123\frac{1}{2}$, $105\frac{1}{2}$, $125\frac{1}{2}$, 121, 121, 110, 123, 115, 128 and 124.   Joseph Gheen of Goshen had four weighing as follows: 125, $113\frac{1}{2}$, 112 and 103.   These were the weights of the carcasses dressed.   John James of East Bradford sent to the Philadelphia market ten sheep of the following weights: 153, 142,

141½, 135½, 121, 117, 108, 125½, 113½ and 125; total, 1282, or a trifle over 128 pounds each, dressed.

Jesse McCall sent to market a fine fat ox, weighing 1,125½ pounds, and T. S. Woodward of East Bradford had two slaughtered, weighing respectively 1,389 and 1,221 pounds. Samuel Worth of East Bradford slaughtered one that weighed 1,488 pounds, and T. Hickman, two, weighing 1,289 and 1,154 pounds.

The Chester County Agricultural Society was organized in Horticultural Hall April 25, 1853, John J. Parker being president of the meeting, Jacob Massey and John Baldwin, vice-presidents, and James Pierce and Alexander Marshall' secretaries. A committee consisting of Dr. J. R. Walker and John S. Bowen prepared a constitution for the society, which provided for a president, four vice-presidents, a corresponding secretary, two recording secretaries and one treasurer, and also a committee of ten on agricultural matters, all to be elected annually. Semi-annual meetings were provided for, to be held on the last Mondays in April and October, and there were to be annual meetings to provide for such exhibitions as the society might determine to give.

At a meeting held June 18, 1853, the following officers were chosen:

President, Isaac W. Van Leer; vice-presidents, Paschall Worth, John D. Evans, Dr. Ebenezer V. Dickey and Lewis Brinton; corresponding secretary, J. Lacey Darlington; recording secretaries, Alexander Marshall and James H. Bull, and treasurer, Dr. George Thomas. The executive committee elected was composd of the following gentlemen: Abraham R. McIlvaine, Dr. Isaac R. Walker, Joseph Dowdall, Gen. George Hartman, Nathan Walton, Jacob Massey, William E. Dripps, John Parker, Abner Garrett and John J. Monaghan.

Committees were appointed to report on the prevalence and injurious effects of the fly in wheat; on the subject of deep plowing; on the potato plant and the best varieties and modes of culture; on the culture of barley, and on the utility of guano as a fertilizer.

An exhibition was held September 16 and 17, 1853, which was highly successful and gave great satisfaction to the agricultural community especially, the committee of arrangements being James Powell, Emmor Elton, Oliver T. Jefferis, George D. Ashbridge and Henry D. Sharp.

At a meeting held at the court-house in West Chester January 21, 1854, J. Lacey Darlington, M. B. Hickman and Benjamin J. Passmore were appointed a committee to confer with gentlemen who purposed buying a lot, with a view of leasing it to the society for the purpose of holding annual fairs, and a committee was also appointed to procure a charter for the society.

Emmor Brinton was awarded a special prize or premium of $5 for having raised 170 bushels of wheat on four and three-fourths acres of land.

The officers for 1854 were as follows: Isaac Van Leer, president; corresponding secretary and treasurer, J. Lacey Darlington; recording secretaries, J. H. Bull and William Torbet Ingram. They were the same for 1855, 1856, and 1857, except that William D. Suger was one of the recording secretaries.

During the year 1856, the society purchased ten acres of land in the borough of West Chester, with a view to the erection of permanent fixtures thereon, in which to hold the future exhibitions of the society, and a trotting course of one-fourth of a mile in circumference was laid out and graded, and included by a strong post and one-rail fence. The cost of the ground was $4,000 and the expense of fitting it up was $2,150.

The officers remained the same as last given for 1858 and 1859. In 1860 D. B. Hinman was elected president; J. Lacey Darlington, corresponding secretary and treasurer, and William D. Suger and E. H. Townsend, recording secretaries. In 1861 and 1862 the officers remained the same. In 1863 Charles E. Heister was elected president; J. Lacey Darlington, corresponding secretary, and E. H. Townsend and William Sharpless, recording secretaries. The same officers served in 1864 and 1865, and in 1866, except that C. H. Kinnard became one of the recording secretaries, in place of E. H. Townsend.

In 1867 the president elected was J. Lacey Darlington; treasurer, E. H. Townsend; William Sharpless, corresponding secretary, and C. H. Kinnard and Charles Fairlamb, recording secretaries. During 1868 and 1869 the officers were the same as in 1867. In 1868 the "Model and Experimental Farm for the Eastern District of Pennsylvania" was located in Londongrove Township, Chester County, the farm of Thomas Harvey being purchased for this purpose for about $3,000.

In 1870 Evans Rogers was elected president; George M. Rupert, corresponding secretary; Fred D. Reid and John F. Ingram, recording secretaries, and Thomas U. Marshall, treasurer. In 1871 Evans Rogers was again elected president; Joseph T. Murtagh, corresponding secretary; John F. Ingram and William H. Morgan, recording secretaries, and Fred D. Reid, treasurer. In 1872 and 1873 the officers remained the same. In 1874 the only changes made were that Josiah Hoopes became corresponding secretary and W. H. Morgan, treasurer. In 1875, 1876, 1877 they remained the same and also in 1878, except that A. M. Eachus became treasurer, and A. M. Eachus and John F. Ingram recording secretaries. In 1879, 1880 and 1881 the officers remained the same, and in 1882 also, with the exception that Jefferson Shaner was elected president. There was no change then in officers until 1888, when they were as follows: Fred D. Reid, treasurer; Joseph Kilt, Jr., corresponding secretary, and A. M. Eachus and Thomas J. Edge, recording secretaries. In 1889 they remained as in 1888.

In 1890 Henry Durnall became recording secretary in place of A. M. Sharpless, and J. Preston Thomas became treasurer. In 1891 Barclay Lear became recording secretary in place of Henry Durnall. In 1892 R. E. Monaghan became president, the other officers remaining the same. In 1893 the officers remained as in

1892. This was the case also in 1894, except that Marshall H. Matlack became treasurer. In 1895 the changes made were in the recording secretaries, Fred D. Reid and Thomas J. Edge taking these offices. In 1896 Jesse J. Hickman became president, succeeding R. E. Monaghan, who died about July 1, 1895. In 1897 the officers were Jesse J. Hickman, president; Fred D. Reid, corresponding secretary; Barclay Lear, recording secretary, and Marshall H. Matlack, treasurer.

These were the last officers elected, for the society then became extinct. In the fall of 1895 the last annual fair was held, for in September of that year under foreclosure of mortage the property passed into the hands of the West Chester State Normal School. In 1897 the officers of the society would have held a fair, but for the fact that the State Normal School asked $500 for the use of the old grounds, the society offering $150, and, as no agreement could be reached, no fair was held.

The first grange of Patrons of Husbandry was Pioneer Grange, No. 9, at West Grove, July 30, 1873, with nineteen charter members. Since then there have been somewhat more than twenty granges organized, among them the following:

Kennett Grange, No. 19, September 11, 1873, with nineteen charter members; Schuylkill Grange, No. 23, September 15, 1873, with twenty-five charter members; Upper Uwchlan Grange, No. 53, December 20, 1873, with eighteen charter members; Brandywine Grange, No. 60, December 30, 1873, with twenty charter members; Londongrove Grange, No. 63, January 1, 1874, with thirty charter members; Oxford Grange, No. 67, January 2, 1874, with twenty-seven charter members; Chester Valley Grange, No. 77, January 14, 1874, with twenty charter members; Russellville Grange, No. 91, January 31, 1874, with twenty-five charter members; Willistown Grange, No. 114, February 17, 1874, with eighteen charter members; Goshen Grange, No. 121, February 21, 1874, with charter members not known; New London Grange, No. 123,

February 23, 1874, with thirty-six charter members; Lincoln Grange, No. 130, February 24, 1874, with twenty-two charter members; Franklin Grange, No. 141, March 2, 1874, with thirty charter members; Lewisville Grange, No. 180, March 28, 1874, with twenty-eight charter members; East Lynn Grange, No. 271, May 27, 1874, with thirty charter members; Pomona District Grange, No. 2, June 3, 1875, with nineteen charter members.

The granges have been and are of great benefit to Chester County, for they serve to bring farmers together, for the purpose of exchanging ideas about their calling, and increasing their sociability. There is a county committee, a State committee, and a national committee, each of which has its peculiar function to perform. Supplies for the farm are purchased much cheaper than formerly, wholesale prices being now obtained where formerly retail prices had to be paid. The secrecy attending the workings of the granges in their meetings, are no more objectionable than is secrecy in Masonic lodges, or in Grand Army posts, it being used only for the protection of the members of the grange.

The dairy interests of Chester County are large and important. Previous to the war of the Rebellion, and perhaps for some years thereafter, the business of dairying was carried on in a far more primitive style and manner than since that period. In the earlier days each farmer carried on his own dairying in his own way, milking his cows, making butter and cheese at home, and feeding the refuse to his pigs, all with the assistance of the female members of his family, or with the aid of hired men and women. The farmers were accustomed to do all their own marketing in Philadelphia, going to that city often in droves, there selling their products and making their purchases, often, if not generally, receiving a smaller price for what they had to sell and paying more for what they had to buy than now. Butter then sold for what was called a "levy" per pound, while now it seldom or perhaps never gets so low in the market, except, possibly, the very poorest qualities of home-made butter, which cannot compete with that made by the most improved methods now in vogue. Much of the hard labor connected with early butter-making devolved on the women, and it was in part for this reason that farmers gladly drove into Philadelphia when living sufficiently near, and sold their milk to the city dealers. This change, which, though for some years seen to be coming, was for some time opposed by the farmer, because he did not favor selling his products off the farm any more than seemed to him absolutely necessary; but when it was once begun, and especially when it was realized that milk thus sold brought seven cents per quart, farmers made a great effort to secure profits from their dairies that could be secured in no other way; and by thus rushing to the front soon caused the price of milk to fall in proportion, or nearly so, with the quantity shipped.

Among those who first sold milk in Philadelphia in the manner just described were the following: Edward Seale of Birmingham Township, Samuel Bailey and Mitchell Baker of the same township, John C. Huey and George B. Temple of Pennsbury. As intimated above many others followed their example, until another change had to be made in the manner of disposing of dairy products. But while milk was being thus shipped from the different parts of the county to Philadelphia, it was necessary for the railway companies not only to put on extra cars but also to run special milk trains, so extensive did the business become, though as the distance into Philadelphia is so short, it was never found necessary to use refrigerator cars..

The change which next occurred in the dairy business was the establishment of creameries in which the cream was converted into butter by means of water or other power, thus effecting a great saving of labor. One of the first to establish a creamery was Isaac Morgan of Parkerville in 1870. He was a farmer who had a fine private trade in butter, shipping to Philadelphia and New York mainly. His milk was set in large flat Dewitt pans, the skimming being done by hand and the churning by water power, because that power was easily obtained and inexpensive. He made a remarkably fine article of butter, and obtained very high prices, from 35 to 45 cents per pound in the summer season, and as high as 65 cents in the winter season. But it should be borne in mind that then it required nearly, if not quite, one-third more milk to make a pound of butter than is now required. Others to go into the creamery business early were as follows: John I. Carter, Chatham; Milton Darlington, Doe Run; Joseph Brosius, Oxford; Pennock Sharpless, Edward Brinton in the vicinity of West Chester; William Sharpless, George Faucett & Sons; John Gray of Unionville; Henry Taylor, and many others. One of the features of the creamery business, now almost extinct, was the coöperative creamery, in which each farmer selling milk to the creamery had to become a stockholder in the concern, and depend upon his profits on the success of the business, which was managed by a board made up of a few of themselves. Among the creameries thus established and conducted were the Pikeland Creamery, the Fairmount Creamery, and there was one at Whitford, besides about three others, only about half a dozen of them ever having been established, and all of them having now been abandoned, except the two first named. One of the alleged reasons for the failure of the co-operative creamery, as furnished the writer by men who have been engaged in the creamery business, was that, inasmuch as the farmer's profit depended altogether on the quality of milk delivered to the creamery, some of the farmers were tempted to pour water in their milk in order to derive an unfair advantage over their more honest neighbors. These coöperatives started up from about 1876 to 1880, and gradually went out of existence for the reason named.

Two methods of setting the milk were in vogue in the earlier days of butter making, and down to the introduction of the cream separator, which has, in recent years, so completely revolutionized

the making of butter.   One of these methods was called the shal-
low setting and the other the deep setting process.   Both depended
on the greater specific gravity of the milk than of the cream, by
reason of which the milk settled to the bottom of the pan, the
cream thus being forced to the top.   In the deep setting method
there was usually a means of drawing off the milk from the bottom
of the can, thus leaving the cream in the can alone.   When the
West Chester Dairy was established it was a deep setting establishment.   This dairy at the present time receives the milk from
about 1,300 cows, about 22,000 pounds per day.

At the present time much of the milk delivered at the creamery is tested as to its quality, and the price paid is governed thereby.
The cream separator was introduced about 1880 or perhaps a few
years later.   One of the first to thus introduce this revolutionary
method of making butter was Mr. Edward Brinton, who established
his creamery in 1882, and set up his separator in 1885.   This was
the Danish Weston Separator, manufactured in Philadelphia.
Afterward came in the De Laval Separator, and still later the P.
M. Sharpless Separator, many thousands of which are sold in all
parts of the civilized world.   John I. Carter was also among the
first to appreciate the value of this new method, by which very
nearly all the cream is obtained from the milk, by which means it
is possible to sell butter cheaper, but yet, on account of the superior quality, and still more by the more uniform quality the price
is, the price does not fall so much as might otherwise be the case.
All the creameries in the county at the present time are in the
hands of individuals but two, the Pikeland and the Fairmount, and
all use the separator, and besides this many individual farmers
find it profitable to own a separator, and thus remain independent
of the creamery, selling their butter instead of their milk.

An industry that was once extensive and profitable to those
engaged therein and of use to all the inhabitants, but which has
of recent years gone largely to decay, is the milling business.   In

preceding pages of this chapter mention has been made of several grist or flouring mills, owned and operated by individuals, but it would be impracticable and unnecessary to mention and locate them all. According to the best opinion, there were, when this industry was at its height, from two to three of these mills in each township of the county, in which the flour was manufactured by means of buhrs, propelled by water power mainly, though occasionally a mill was fitted up with steam power. By means of these millstones flour was not ground so fine as it has been since the introduction of the roller process, and when this process was introduced extensively throughout the Western States, where wheat has long been raised in comparatively large quantities, and, as a consequence, at much less cost than has so far been found practicable in the Eastern States, Western flour began to take the place of Eastern flour, even in the Eastern States, and thus the milling industry in Chester County, as well as in other counties in this and in other states in the East, began to decline, and the mills in Chester County, many of them, gave up the grinding of wheat and contented themselves with running merely as feed mills. Other mills in Chester County determined to do what they could to keep up with the progress of events, introduced the roller process, and still continue to manufacture flour. It is now estimated that there are in existence about one-half as many mills as before Western competition began to be felt, which was about 1880. In some townships there are not more than one-third as many mills as formerly. In some cases the mill buildings have been converted into barns, and in other cases the buildings have gone to decay or have been taken down.

In the early day there were perhaps half a dozen linseed oil mills, which have also gone out of use because farmers have ceased to raise flax.

The general destruction of the timber of the county caused the saw-mill industry to decline even to a larger extent than the milling industry, for now there is but little timber to spare. Clover hulling has also gone to decay, for the reason that clover seed can be shipped into the county cheaper than it can be raised.

One of the noted industries of Chester County is the growing of carnations for the markets of the large Eastern cities. This industry is carried on in what is known, from the nature of the flowers raised therein, as the Carnation Belt, which extends from Concord on the Philadelphia and Baltimore Central Railway to the Chester County line bordering on Maryland, a distance of about twenty miles, its average width being about five miles.

The carnation is a member of the pink family, which is not indigenous to Chester County, but which is indigenous to the southern part of Europe. It has been cultivated there for many centuries, even from ancient times, for its fragrance and its beauty. In its wild state it is of a lilac purple tint, but under cultivation it has assumed a wide variety of colors, and numberless combinations of these colors. Florists group these varieties into three classes, viz.: bizarres, flukes and picotees.

The name carnation is the common name of the Pink Dianthus Caryophyllus, there being seven different varieties of the Dianthus.

The business carried on within the limits of the belt above outlined is the growing of carnations, and other plants, and was first begun by Charles T. Starr, about one mile below Avondale, in 1865 or 1866. Mr. Starr began in a small way, having but one greenhouse, which was only forty feet long. He continued the business until his death in 1888, at which time it had assumed very large proportions, not only in his own hands but also in the number of others therein engaged. It is now an important industry, and furnishes a large amount of business to express companies.

Mr. Starr was followed in the raising of carnations by Mr. William Swayne at Kennett Square, and by Joseph T. Philips at

West Grove, Warren Shelmire at Avondale, and Thomas F. Seale of Unionville. From that time on others established themselves in the business, and there now are several hundreds of different establishments thus engaged. The entire output of the belt is very large, being shipped to New York, Philadelphia and Washington mainly. Besides carnations there are grown within this belt tomatoes and mushrooms, the latter under the benches on which the carnations and tomatoes are grown. The growing of tomatoes and mushrooms has also become a large and important industry. The wholesale prices of carnations vary from one cent to five cents each, according to the season and the size and beauty of the flowers. Florists are continually increasing the variegation of color by the use of seedlings.

Among those engaged in this pleasant and profitable business are the following:

At Oxford, Mrs. Dickey and Mrs. McCowan; at West Grove, Benjamin Connell, Dingee & Conard, the Conard & Jones Company, and Joseph T. Philips; at Avondale, Warren Shelmire and Search; at Toughkennamon, Chambers Bros. and Isaac Larkin; at Kennett Square, Edward Swayne, William Swayne, Theodore Pennock, William Davis, Thompson Richards and Joshua Ladley & Sons; at Longwood, Wesley Flowers; at Unionville, Thomas F. Seale and G. Love; at Willow Dale, Rakestraw & Pyle; at Concord, Pennock Sharpless and Styer Bros.

As to the general farm crops, such as the cereals, potatoes, it can be scarcely said that any one part of the county is better adapted to their growth than another. The entire county is excellently adapted to the raising of grain and to dairying. The same remark applies to the raising of potatoes, both Irish and sweet, and also to the cultivation of fruit and berries. The raising of tobacco, however, was in years gone by largely carried on in the southern part of the county, but of late years, on account of the reduction of the price, this crop has been to a considerable

58

extent abandoned.   The sheep industry has also declined to a considerable extent, which can hardly be said of the raising of cattle.
The agricultural report of 1896 states that the raising of horses
was then entirely abandoned; but this remark cannot now truthfully be made, for farmers say that the spring of 1898 saw more
colts in Chester County than had been seen for many a year.   The
farmers of Chester County prefer the fast trotting horses as a
general thing to the heavy draft horse, the latter being preferred
more generally by the sturdy German farmer of Lancaster County.
The raising of flowers appears to be confined more to the southern
part of the county, notably to the famous carnation belt, though
this industry also flourishes in and around West Chester to a large
extent.

John A. M. Passmore, a native of Chester County, and a man of
State as well as local reputation, was born June 30, 1836, in West
Nottingham, a son of John W. and Deborah (Brown) Passmore.   He
was reared in the moral and refining influence of the Friends' Society, as a farmer's boy, and at the youthful age of sixteen years,
began teaching public school.   His proficiency in this line of endeavor was so encouraging as to induce him to take a four-years
course in the State Normal School, at Millersville, from which
he was graduated in 1860.   He subsequently taught school at Pottsville for a number of years and became widely known as an able
and successful educator.   Since 1886, Mr. Passmore has resided in
Philadelphia, having been connected with D. Appleton & Company, and is at present the representative of the American Book
Company.   An ardent Republican in politics, he was twice nominated for Auditor-General of the State, but was defeated in election through no fault of his.   At various other times he has been
nominated and served in public positions of honor and trust, in all
of which he has displayed signal fidelity and ability.   He is a member of the State Historical Society, State Teachers' Association,
National Teachers' Educational Association, is a Knights Templar

of the Masonic Fraternity, an Odd Fellow, a Knight of Pythias, a member of the Grand Army of the Republic, a member of the Union League Club, of Philadelphia, and various other organizations. In 1884 he was a delegate to the National Republican Convention, at Chicago. Reared as a Friend, his religious convictions are in sympathy with the tenets of the Society of Friends. Mr. Passmore was married March 23, 1854, to Harriet, daughter of James and Ann (Taylor) Woodrow, by whom he is the father of one daughter, Harriet H.

An attempt was made by the writer of this work to obtain from the State Agricultural Department statistics regarding dairying and farming interests for some year later than 1890, but without avail, as the following letter will show:

"Harrisburg, Pa., July 19, 1898.

Dear Sir:—In reply to your favor of the 18th I would state that, realizing their utter unreliability, we have not for several years past collected and statistics in relation to crops; the latest that I can direct you to are those of the last census.

"Respectfully yours,

"THOMAS J. EDGE."

Josiah Hoopes, in October, 1853, first conceived the idea of a nursery and green-house business, and began with one small green-house and one acre of ground. This land and green-house were located where now stands the residence of Mr. Montgomery, adjoining the present nursery. In 1857 Abner Hoopes, brother of Josiah, became a partner, and the firm took the name of Hoopes & Bro., and it thus remained until the close of the war of the Rebellion, when George B. Thomas was taken into the firm, the name of which was then changed to Hoopes, Bro. & Thomas, as it still remains. From the commencement down to the present time, the object of this firm has been to keep on hand a full assortment of stock, both in the fruit department and the ornamental. Formerly the business took a wide range, a large mail business being carried on, both in this country and abroad, and it gradually drifted into a wholesale trade, with traveling salesmen in all parts of the country. At the present time this firm is carrying on an extensive Southern business, having an office in Nashville, Tenn., which is in charge of a superintendent. From one acre at the beginning the firm has now in cultivation 600 acres, and special attention is given to growing fruit trees, of all kinds and qualities; but still more particular attention is given to the ornamental department, such as trees for shade and especially for lawns, and to shrubbery, to which many acres are devoted. Roses are also cultivated for the wholesale trade, and in the packing seasons, spring and fall, about 100 hands, men and boys, are employed.

The Conrad & Jones Company, owning the West Grove Floral Nursery, was organized July 1, 1897, with Alfred F. Conrad, president; S. Morris Jones, secretary and treasurer, and Antoine Wintzer, vice-president and general superintendent. Mr. Wintzer has had many years' experience in the floral business, and is thoroughly competent. Here are thirty-six acres of land, but little of which is under glass, the number of feet of glass being 25,000. The most improved facilities for growing roses are here enjoyed, the company being growers of roses and the originators of a species of American pedigree cannas.

John Bartram opened the first botanical garden on the Schuylkill River within the present limits of the city of Philadelphia, about 1834, the next being that of Humphrey Marshall, at Marshallton. The third was that of John Evans of Radnor, Delaware County, and the fourth and last was that founded by George Pierce, in the corner of East Marlborough, just south of Red Lion Tavern. This was about seventy-five years ago, or probably in 1823. Since the death of Mr. Pierce it has passed into the hands of his sister, the widow of Dr. Sumner Stebbins, and his children. Some thirty or forty years ago it began to be called Pierce's Park, as it is still known; but the condition of the park itself has greatly changed, the park being much less beautiful than it formerly was, which is the case with all the others. Enthusiasm and a love for nature are required to keep up a place of this kind, and in all probability public parks are the only ones that will retain their beauty and freshness.

The Botanic Garden at Marshallton, the first in Chester County, was established by Humphrey Marshall in 1773. Humphrey Marshall was the eighth child of Abraham and Mary (Hunt) Marshall, both natives of England, and was born in West Bradford, Chester County, October 10, 1722. After his marriage to Sarah Pennock, daughter of Joseph Pennock, of West Marlborough, he began to turn his attention to the acquisition of knowledge, preferring astronomy and natural history to all other branches. He also then began the collection and culture of the more curious and interesting indigenous plants. In 1764 he enlarged the dwelling in which he lived, and added thereto a green-house, which is thought to have been the first ever seen or thought of in Chester County. In 1774 he removed to a dwelling newly erected by him near the Bradford Meeting-house, and adjoining the present village of Marshallton, having commenced the garden the year before.

This botanical garden soon began to receive some of the most interesting trees and shrubs of the county, together with many curious exotics, as well as a numerous collection of native herbaceous plants. In this garden Mr. Marshall planted a large number of oaks, pines and magnolias, which remain standing and which are of majestic size, though the garden itself, from neglect, has become a wilderness.

"For several years prior to the establishment of the Marshallton Garden Humphrey had been much engaged in collecting native plants and seeds and shipping them to Europe; but after that event, being aided by his nephew, Dr. Moses Marshall, he greatly extended his operations, and directed his attention with enhanced zeal and energy to the business of exploring and making known abroad the vegetable treasures of the United States. The present generation of botanists has but an imperfect idea of the services rendered to science by the skill and laborious industry of these faithful pioneers."*

In 1780 Humphrey Marshall began to prepare an account of the forest trees and shrubs of this country, which was completed and printed in 1785, under the title of "Arbustum Americanum and the American Grove, with an Alphabetical Catalogue of Forest Trees and Shrubs, Natives of the American United States." This is believed to have been the first truly indigenous botanical essay published in the Western Hemisphere.

Humphrey Marshall died August 6, 1823, at the age of eighty-two, and was buried in the cemetery at Bradford Meeting-house; but as no stone marks the precise spot where his remains lie, it is difficult to be ascertained, and in process of time, if no more care shall be taken of it than has been heretofore, it will become impossible.

The excellent products of the farm, the dairy, the orchard and the garden in the immediate vicinity of every borough and village and hamlet in Chester County render those places most desirable for residences to wealthy business men of Philadelphia, as well as delightful places of retirement for the older and more success-ful class of farmers and others belonging to the county itself. The numerous suburban sites of West Chester, Phœnixville, Berwyn, Malvern, Downingtown and Coatesville are most attractive and are fit for the mansions of any of the wealthier citizens of the country, and for all that like the quiet and retirement of a country home. Every wayside and field are ornamented with tree, shrub, and in the summer time flower, all supported by a luxurious and fertile soil. In Chester County there is no low, swampy, marshy

---

* From a biographical sketch of Humphrey Marshall by William Darlington.

land, but on the contrary, the surface of the county is unusually undulating, giving perfect drainage, and extensive, unrestricted and picturesque views from almost every home for miles around.

But notwithstanding the county has all these advantages for suburban life within its limits, yet it would appear that so far but little determined effort has been made to utilize these advantages to the greatest possible extent. This might be done, to the benefit of all farmers, tradesmen and merchants. Even in the largest towns in the county prices of real estate are remarkably low and the conveniences connected with country homes are numerous and great. Every town has excellent water, fire hydrants, and a fire department, and many of them have electric lights, gas and telephone exchange. No town of any size in the county, except Oxford, is more than an hour's ride from Philadelphia, and hence the time spent in traveling to and from business, by those doing business in the city, is not great.

Schools in the suburban towns are nearly, if not quite, as good as those in the city, and the superior healthfuless of the country is well known. Building is cheaper and rents are lower than in Philadelphia, and the streets are wider and houses further apart. Taxes are lower and water rates are lower, and the borough authorities are constantly giving more and more attention to sanitary measures, thus increasing, as the years go by, the desirability of living in the country town. Market facilities are both numerous and excellent, much of what is consumed being produced at the very doors of the people, and hence the supplies are both fresh and good. So well supplied are many of the stores that numerous families derive from them their daily supplies. Creameries are scattered throughout the county, and butter is as good as can anywhere be found. Vegetables and fruit of all kinds are produced in great abundance, and taken all in all, there is scarcely a better county in the entire United States for everything that constitutes desirability of a place to live.

The following statistics, taken from the United States Census of 1890, show the condition of the agricultural industry for that year:

The total number of farms was 6,119, of which 4,466 were cultivated by their owners; 1,094 were rented for a fixed money value and 559 were rented on shares.

The number of acres in farms was 5,863,800. The value of farm products for 1889 was $30,683,210; of improvements and machinery, $1,706,380, and of live stock, $3,894,500.

The number of sheep in the county was 11,157; the number of fleeces clipped, 6,862, and the number of pounds of wool, 38,363.

The number of neat cattle was 61,311, of which there were of pure bred record, 1,502; of one-half blood, 6,948, and less than half blood, 52,801.

The number of gallons of milk produced on farms was 19,945,366; pounds of butter, 1,628,235; of cheese, 6,127.

There were 19,264 horses, 1,104 mules, 7 asses, 35,577 swine.

The number of dozens of eggs produced was 1,601,308; the pounds of honey, 15,567; bushels of barley, 190 from five acres; of buckwheat, 837 from 56 acres; of Indian corn, 1,958,962 from 45,206 acres; oats, 868,304 from 34,070 acres; rye, 19,415 from 1,158 acres; wheat, 882,383 from 42,639 acres; hay, 161,823 tons from 109,507 acres; tobacco, 679,265 pounds from 718 acres; pulse, 30 bushels; broom corn, 2,100 pounds from two acres; potatoes—Irish, 452,460 bushels from 5,545 acres; sweet, 2,587 bushels, from 31 acres. Apples, 124,919 bushels; peaches, 4,449 bushels; pears, 2,667 bushels, and of market garden products, $25,092 worth.

The assessed valuation of real estate was $61,378,178, and the true valuation, $67,620,336.

CPSIA information can be obtained
at www.ICGtesting.com
Printed in the USA
BVHW04*0956160818
524721BV00008B/93/P